A DICTIONARY OF MARY

Other Works by DONALD ATTWATER

A Catholic Dictionary
A Dictionary of the Popes
St. John Chrysostom
Eric Gill: Workman
Eastern Catholic Worship
Christian Churches of the East (2 vols.)
Saints Westward
Butler's Lives of the Saints (co–editor)

A
DICTIONARY
of
MARY

Compiled by
DONALD ATTWATER

P. J. KENEDY & SONS

New York

R
203
A8 86

Nihil obstat:

J. A. O'DRISCOLL, S.M., D.D., PH.D.
Censor deputatus

Imprimatur:

CYRIL MAHONEY
Vicar Capitular

Plymouth
9 March 1955

Library of Congress Catalog Card Number: 56-10460
Copyright © 1956 by P. J. Kenedy & Sons, New York
Printed in the United States of America

ALMAE · DEIPARAE

SEMPER · MARIAE · VIRGINI

PREFACE

THE OBJECT OF this book is to provide the reader, whether a member of the Catholic Church or not, with a work of quick reference to matters connected with the many aspects of the life, significance, and veneration of the Blessed Virgin Mary. It is a dictionary rather than an encyclopedia: that is, the author's chief aim has been to produce a work which the user can turn up on a given question, phrase, term, name, etc., and find out "what it is about"; to give general ideas or concrete facts, and in debatable matters to state what is more or less common ground to everybody: and to express these things so far as possible in ordinary, non-technical language. The book is not meant to be apologetic or justificatory, but mainly descriptive and informative; some matters of importance and discussion are dealt with only briefly, because to survey the whole "state of the question," even broadly, is outside the scope of a work of this kind; so, too, are a number of theological questions and considerations which have been omitted entirely.

For those who want to go into these matters more in detail, there are excellent general works available. In English, I may refer to Father Juniper Carol, O.F.M.'s *Mariology*, three volumes in course of publication by the Bruce Publishing Company, Milwaukee; to Father R. Garrigou-Lagrange, O.P.'s *The Mother of the Saviour* (Herder, St. Louis and Golden Eagle Books, Dublin); and in French, to *Maria: Études sur la Sainte Vièrge*, edited by Father Hubert du Manoir, S.J., which will be complete in five volumes (Beauchesne, Paris). There are innumerable books dealing with particular topics, such as (among the more recent ones) *Mary in Our Life*, by Father William G. Most, PH.D., and *Mary's Part in Our Redemption*, by Canon George D. Smith, D.D. (both published by Kenedy, New York).

It can hardly be necessary to add that a summary work such as the present provides only a skeleton, so to speak, of Mary's place and meaning in traditional Christianity: for the particulars to become a unity and to have body, life, and proportion, our Lady must be seen and studied in her widest setting, in relation to Jesus Christ, to the Church, and to the whole mystery of man's salvation.

Grateful thanks are due to my publishers, Messrs. P. J. Kenedy & Sons, for continual help and encouragement; and to the following, who have responded generously to my importunities for information, the loan of books, and other assistance: Mr. Peter F. Anson, Mr. Zsolt Aradi, Father Bernard Basset, S.J.,

Father Paul Bezdiguian, the Reverend John Brady, Commander Roger Brien, s.g.g., the Reverend Edwin Bruggmann, Miss Maryvonne Butcher, Father Juniper Carol, o.f.m., Father J. Cassidy, w.f., the Abbé L. Châles, Miss Annie Christitch, the Reverend Henry L. Clarke, Father Gerard Corr, o.s.m., Father J. B. Darblade, w.f., the Reverend J. Barrett Davies, Dom Godfrey Diekmann, o.s.b., Father Dominic, o.f.m.cap., Father F. L. Dubois, s.m., Mr. T. Charles Edwards, the Reverend Patrick K. Egan, Msgr. C. Flandrop, Miss Joan Ford, the Reverend R. M. French, Father F. M. Galdau, Dom Hildebrand Garza, o.s.b., the Reverend G. Gorissen, Mr. Brian Green, Colonel C. H. Green, the Reverend David L. Greenstock, Father Paul Grosjean, s.j., the Reverend James E. Hathway, Father Philip C. Hoelle, s.m., Dom Edmund Jones, o.s.b., Kyr George Kalavassy, Bishop of Theodorium, Father Jacob Kalayil, the Reverend Antony Kaslaukas, the Reverend David Keith, Father Denis R. Kiwicz, o.f.m., the Reverend A. S. MacWilliam, Dr. K. F. McMurtrie, Father J. E. Maguire, o.carm., Father Allan Maloof, the Marian Library of the University of Dayton, Ohio, Mr. Theodore N. Marier and the McLaughlin & Reilly Company, the Mariological Society of America, Father C. C. Martindale, s.j., the Maryknoll Information Bureau, Father Joseph P. Merrick, s.j., Mr. Austin Mohrbacher, Mr. Clement Naoumov, Miss Maureen Nigro, the Reverend John M. Oesterreicher, the Reverend W. O'Malley, the Paris Foreign Missions, Mr. L. R. N. Percey, Dom Eugene Perez, o.s.b., the Prioress of Princethorpe, Prinknash Abbey Library, the Reverend A. J. Proudman, Mr. Ion Ratiu, Father M. Ratushynsky, Mrs. Teresa Reid, the Reverend H. A. Reinhold, Professor D. Talbot Rice, Dom Theodore Richardson, o.s.b., Brother Cyril Roberts, f.m.s., the Reverend J. K. Robertson, Mr. C. F. L. St. George, the Dean of Salisbury, the Reverend J. Savickis, the Scheut Missionaries, Sister Pientia Selhorst, m.m., Father Brocard Sewell, o.carm., Mr. and Mrs. L. C. Sheppard, the Reverend Mr. John Sheridan, Father David M. Stanley, s.j., St. Dominic's Convent, Stone, Storrington Priory, the Nuns of Syon, Father J. Trémorin, c.m., Mr. George D. Walton, the Earl of Wicklow, Dom J. Cuthbert Wilson, o.s.b., the Reverend Alfonso de Zulueta.

Among the numerous books consulted, special mention must be made of the Reverend F. B. Thornton's *Catholic Shrines of the United States and Canada* (New York, 1954) and H. M. Gillet's *Famous Shrines of Our Lady* (2 vols., Westminster, Md., 1952). Father C. C. Martindale's translation of *Memento rerum Conditor* is printed by kind permission of the Catholic Truth Society of England; and acknowledgment is made for sundry quotations from the *Westminster Hymnal* by courtesy of the editor.

A

ABBESS, PERPETUAL. There was formerly widespread in France a bad custom of appointing a lay person abbot or abbess of a monastery in order that he or she might enjoy some of its revenues. In order to avoid such a misfortune, the Benedictine nuns of Montargis (established there in 1630 from the royal abbey of Montmartre) in 1658 formally elected the Blessed Virgin Mary, under the title "of Peace," perpetual abbess of their convent, reserving their right to elect their own prioress. At the French Revolution these nuns came to England and the community (now English) still flourishes, at Princethorpe Priory, near Rugby. The Montargis tradition is maintained, and in the stall of the abbess there stands a statue of our Lady. At the Greek Orthodox monastery of St. Andrew on Mount Athos there is a modern icon of our Lady, Abbess of Athonite Monks; she is depicted wearing the abbatial mantle.

ABERDEEN, OUR LADY OF. A feast of our Lady under the title "of Help" is the only local feast of Mary observed in the British Isles, in the Scottish diocese of Aberdeen on July 9 (with the common Mass "Salve"). It seems that a statue set up in St. Machar's cathedral in that city in 1436 was later removed to a chapel near or on the bridge over the river Dee, whence it was known as our

Lady of the Brig o' Dee. At the Reformation this image was hidden for safety, and in 1626 it was smuggled abroad to Flanders, where it was set up in the Austin canons' church at Brussels and venerated as the Mother of Good Success. The Augustinians were driven out at the Revolution, and one John Morris took charge of the statue for a dozen years. Eventually it came to rest in the parish church of Notre-Dame-de-Finistère in Brussels, where it still is. The diocese of Aberdeen was revived in 1878, and in accordance with the wishes of his people the fourth bishop, Aeneas Chisholm, chose the Mother of Good Success as patroness of the diocese. But the title was disallowed at Rome, on the ground that it was not for our Lady to command success but to give help: so our Lady of Help it is. Meanwhile the diocese remains deprived of its tutelary image; but devotion to our Lady of Aberdeen has been kept alive in St. Peter's church there, where there is a replica of the Brussels statue. She is also commemorated in a chapel of St. Mary's cathedral, where in due course a copy of the original statue is to be set up. The Success (*de Successu*) of Brussels is still the Help (*de Succursu*) of Aberdeen.

ABSAM, OUR LADY OF. Absam is a village in Austrian Tyrol, where there is treasured a small image of

1

Mary's face on a pane of glass, measuring about 7 inches by 5. This was first seen in 1797, by a young woman, among the panes of a window in her parents' home. Its apparently inexplicable presence naturally aroused much interest, and eventually it was enshrined in a small chapel near to the Buchers' cottage. It has been an object of devotion ever since.

ABYSSINIA, SHRINES OF. See ETHIOPIA.

AD CAELI REGINAM. An encyclical letter of Pope Pius XII in 1954, inaugurating the feast of Mary the Queen. See QUEEN, MARY AS.

AD DIEM ILLUM. An encyclical letter of Pope St. Pius X, written to commemorate the fiftieth anniversary of the definition of the Immaculate Conception. This important document is referred to and quoted several times in these pages.

AFRICA, OUR LADY OF. The statue of our Lady of Africa venerated at Algiers is a bronze image, very dark in color but with European features. It was brought from France in 1840 and was for long entrusted to the Cistercian monks of Stauéli; then Cardinal Lavigerie, founder of the White Fathers, enshrined it in the new basilica at Algiers, where in 1876 the image was crowned. At this and other North African shrines the veneration given to Mary by Mohammedans is very marked (cf., Islam, The Virgin Mary in). The full name of Cardinal Lavigerie's congregation of White Sisters is Missionary Sisters of our Lady of Africa; and there is an indulgenced prayer to Mary under that title for the conversion of the Africans. There is a proper feast commemorating the crowning of the Algiers statue, on April 30.

AFRICA, SHRINES OF. There is evidence that the Gospel was first preached in Alexandria in apostolic times by the evangelist St. Mark; but today the once great Church of Egypt is reduced to a minority, mostly dissident Copts, in a Mohammedan state. The Church of Ethiopia began in the middle of the fourth century and still exists, but has for long been separated from Catholic unity. Christianity in North Africa, west of Egypt—the Church of SS. Perpetua and Felicity, of St. Cyprian, and many other martyrs, of Tertullian and St. Augustine—was utterly destroyed after the Arab invasions of the seventh century. Here the organized Church of today, called into being by the presence of French colonists, began with the setting up of the see of Algiers in 1838. Before long the shrine of our Lady of Africa (q.v.) was established at Algiers, followed by those of our Lady of Carthage and of Oran.

Other shrines are scattered about the missionary territory of the African continent, often at great distances from one another and of simply local importance. There are, for instance, the shrines of our Lady of Divine Providence at Dakar in Senegal, and of our Lady of the Redemption, built on a headland in Senegambia in 1888.

The Blessed Virgin was proclaimed protectress of the Congo in 1891, and in 1954 a statue of our Lady of the Congo was enshrined in a great new church at Leopoldville. In the same year a pilgrimage of some importance was instituted in the Congolese vicariate of Kabinda, at Ngombe Nyama. As in other missionary lands, local shrines of our Lady of Lourdes are very popular. In some sections of Central Africa, little shrines to Mary are to be found at cross-roads, on hill-tops, and at mission out-stations; and the people of Buddu, in Uganda, have built a shrine in thanksgiving for deliverance from plague. Another new shrine in Uganda is at Koboko (*q.v.*) and the center of the White Fathers near Masaka is appropriately called Villa Maria. In South Africa the chief sanctuaries are our Lady of Shongweni and a new one at Ramabanta (*qq.v.*), and the well-known mission of Mariannhill is a great center of Marian devotion. Zululand has its Fatima shrine, and there is one of our Lady of Einsiedeln near Richmond in Natal. A pilgrimage sanctuary is projected on The Bluff cape near Durban, in honor of our Lady of the Assumption, to whom South Africa was dedicated in 1932.

There are several shrines in insular Africa. Mention may be made of those of the Immaculate Conception in Antananarivo, Madagascar, and at Port Louis, Mauritius; our Lady of Refuge at Mahebourg in the same island; and our Lady of Tenerife (*q.v.*). In the Madeiras there is a shrine to our Lady of the Hill, near Funchal, commemorating a vision seen there by a young herdsman. Torchlight processions appear to be a special feature of African shrines; and, as a missionary has said, the shrines may be of only local significance, but the religion behind them is very real. See also EGYPT; ETHIOPIA.

AID, OUR LADY OF. A variant form of our Lady of Help (*q.v.*), etc. The cathedral of the Scottish diocese of Motherwell is dedicated in honor of our Lady of Good Aid.

AKATHISTOS HYMN, The. The most famous Marian devotion of the Eastern Church. It is not really a hymn but an office, sung in churches of the Byzantine rite in part on the first four Saturdays of Lent and in its entirety on the fifth, "Akathistos Saturday"; it is also in use, whole or in part, at all times of the year for private devotion. It consists of twelve sections: each consists of two stanzas, of which the first always ends in "Alleluia" and the second is followed by thirteen (in the first one, fourteen) apostrophes of Mary, some of which are reminiscent of the Litany of Loreto, e.g., "Gate of hallowed mystery," "Mirror of angelic life," "Key of Christ's kingdom." Every apostrophe begins with "Hail!", and the last of each section is always "Hail, Maiden Bride!" The whole is preceded by a verse referring to the incarnation of the Son at the angel's announcement to Mary. The Akathistos Hymn has several times been published in English: the following is an example of one section (no. ix):

"All the angelic spirits marvelled when Thou didst take flesh; they saw the unreachable God draw nigh to us as a man, living amongst us and hearing from all, Alleluia!

"The most eloquent are dumb as fish before you, O Forth-bringer, for they cannot tell how you, a maiden, were able to bear a Son. But we, also wondering at the mystery, cry out in faith:

"Hail! container of God's wisdom.

Hail! store-house of His providence.

Hail! bewilderer of the wise.

Hail! confounder of the eloquent.

Hail! for the deep thinkers are made foolish.

Hail! for the myth-mongers are useless.

Hail! thou who dost tear webs spun of words.

Hail! thou who dost fill fishermen's nets.

Hail! raiser from the depths of ignorance.

Hail! enlightener with knowledge.

Hail! ship of salvation.

Hail! harbour of the tempest-tossed.

Hail! Maiden Bride!"

When the Akathistos is sung entire it is divided into four parts, between which psalms and hymns are sung, and then alone the faithful may sit. This is one of the reasons suggested for the name of the office, which means the "Not-sitting Hymn." The historical lesson in the Byzantine office for the fifth Sunday of Lent assigns this observance to the people's vigil of thanksgiving after the fleet of the Persians and Avars besieging Constantinople had been scattered by a mighty wind, and cast away on the shore near the church of the Theotokos at Blakhernae, on the eve of that Sunday in the year 626. "From that time therefore the Church wished this day to be a festival in honor of the Mother of God in memory of so great and divine a miracle." Many of the praises seem to be borrowed from the Marian hymns of St. Ephraem and others, but the authorship of the hymn is uncertain. The recitation of the Akathistos has been indulgenced by Popes Benedict XIV and Pius XII.

ALBANIA, SHRINES OF. The majority of Albanians are Mohammedans, but there is a sizeable minority of Eastern Orthodox and a smaller one of Catholics. Their principal Marian shrine is at Skodra (Shkoder, Skutari). According to local tradition, the image called our Lady of Good Counsel (*q.v.*) was long venerated at Skodra, until it "took flight" to Genazzano in Italy before the advancing Turks. The image now venerated is a copy of the old one, made by order of Pope Pius IX in 1856. The chief pilgrimage day is the third Monday in October. There is another sanctuary of our Lady at Troshani, in charge of the Franciscans. The chief Orthodox shrine is at Ardenica, not far from Tirana. The Albanians in Yugoslavia go on pilgrimage to our Lady of the Black Mountain at Létnica (not to be confused with the former state of Montenegro); this is also frequented by Orthodox and by Mohammedans. The people of Albanian descent in Sicily have shrines, of Byzantine rite, at Piana dei Greci and Contessa Entellina, of our Lady Hodegetria (*q.v.*) and *della Favara*, respectively. Veneration of the last named was carried by immigrants to New Orleans in the United States.

ALMA REDEMPTORIS MATER. The opening words and title of the first of the anthems of our Lady (see ANTIPHONS), said or sung from the first Vespers of Advent Sunday to the Purification inclusive. Father Edward Caswall's translation, "Mother of Christ! Hear thou thy people's cry," is well known: it is in the Baltimore *Manual of Prayers* and the *Westminster Hymnal*, no. 261a. The following translation is from the *Primer* of 1706:

Bright parent of our Lord, whose prayers display
The heavenly gates; whose light directs our way;
Bright ocean's star, with sacred influence guide
Our straggling course in spite of nature's tide.
Thou in whom nature stood amazed to see
Both God and man; thy Maker born of thee,
In whom alone the maid and mother meet;
Remember sinners at thy Infant's feet.

The versicle, response, and prayer that follow vary according to whether it is sung before or after the first Vespers of Christmas. This hymn was almost certainly written by Bl. Hermann the Cripple (d. 1054), a monk of Reichenau, who was so deformed as to be almost helpless physically. The author of the *Ancren Riwle* (c. 1200) recommends it to the women solitaries for whom he wrote; and Chaucer in his Prioress's Tale refers to the "litel child" who

. . . as he came to and fro,
Full merrily would he sing and cry
O Alma Redemptoris evermo.
The sweetness hath his hearte pierced so
Of Christ's mother, that to her to pray
He can not stint of singing by the way.

ALTÖTTING, OUR LADY OF. Altötting (Oettingen) in Upper Bavaria, sixty miles east of Munich, was the site of a ducal palace during the Carolingian age; and here in 877 Duke Karlman founded a monastery, with the Holy Chapel adjoining, which became a sort of mausoleum for the hearts of the Bavarian sovereigns. The chapel may already have been a shrine of Mary in these early days; but its later history begins in 1228, when the Benedictines left and a college of canons took charge. The present image, of a most archaic appearance, dates from about that time: it stands in the Liebfrauen-Kapelle in an alcove plated with silver, and, except on Ash Wednesday and Good Friday, cannot be properly seen as it is vested in jewel-studded robes. Jesuits, Franciscans, Redemptorists, and Mary Ward's Institute of Mary (Englische Fräulein) have had a part in the history of Altötting; today the collegiate church again has its chapter, and the Capuchin friars are in charge of the pilgrimage, to which their lay-brother St. Conrad of Parzham (d. 1894) was so devoted. There used to be 300,000 pilgrims a year before 1939; there are now said to be more, and the sanctuary of our Lady of Grace of Altötting is a meeting place for the Pax Christi movement.

At Altötting is found the famous Golden Horse, so called, a work in gold and jewels made in the fourteenth century by a French goldsmith. It is really a group of the donor or former owner worshiping the Child Jesus, who sits on Mary's lap, with adoring cherubs. The horse is a subsidiary part, beneath the group: it is held by a groom, waiting for his master above.

AMERICA, CENTRAL, AND THE WEST INDIES, SHRINES OF. The Marian shrines of the Central American republics and West Indian islands are rather overshadowed by Mexico's Guadalupe. The principal ones are as follows. *Costa Rica:* Mary, Queen of Angels, Cartago; Our Lady of Refuge, Ujarraz. *Cuba:* O.L. of Charity (*q.v.*). *Dominican Republic:* O.L. of Ransom of the Holy Hill; O.L. of Great Grace, Higuey. *Guatemala:* O.L. of Bethlehem, Santiago de Guatemala. *Honduras:* O.L. of Suyapa; O.L. of Iuticalpa. *Martinique:* Notre Dame de la Délivrande (*q.v.*). *Mexico:* the Queen of Angels, Puebla de los Angeles; O.L. of Belem, Lower California; O.L. of Campeche; O.L. of Guadalupe (*q.v.*); O.L. of Guanajuato; O.L. of Hope, Tajon, the first of Mary's statues in Mexico to be crowned, in 1895, nine months before O.L. of Guadalupe; O.L. of the Lakes, Guadalajara; O.L., Mother of Light (*q.v.*); O.L. of Ocotlan, Tlascala, a sixteenth-century image; O.L. of the Pueblito, Queretaro; O.L., Refuge of Sinners (*q.v.*); Nuestra Señora de los Remedios (*q.v.*); N.S. de la Soledad in Mexico City and at Oaxaca. *Nicaragua:* O.L. of Viejo (the image was brought from Spain by a relative of St. Teresa of Avila). *Puerto Rico:* O.L. of Montserrat, Hormingueros; the Mother of Providence in San Juan cathedral. *Salvador:* O.L. of Peace, San Miguel. Many of these sanctuaries have a proper local feast.

AMERICA, SOUTH, SHRINES OF. There is a considerable number of Marian shrines scattered over South America, many of them unknown outside their immediate neighborhood. Some of them go back over 300 years, to the earlier days of European colonization and evangelization. The following is a selection from among them. *Argentine Republic:* Our Lady of Aránzazu (*q.v.*); O.L. of Catamarca (*q.v.*); O.L. of Consolation, Sumampa, dating from 1630; O.L. of Córdoba; O.L. of Cuyo (*q.v.*); O.L. of Itatì; O.L. of Lujan (*q.v.*). *Bolivia:* O.L. of Copacabana (*q.v.*); O.L. of Peace, La Paz. *Brazil:* Nossa Senhora Aparecida (*q.v.*); O.L. of the Rock (Penha), Olinda; O.L. of Nazareth, Belèm do Pará; the Joys (Pazeres) of our Lady,

Olinda; O.L. of the Purification (*Candelaria*), Rio de Janeiro; O.L. of the Rock, Pernambuco; O.L. of Safe Travel, Rio de Janeiro. *Chile:* O.L. of Aranco (*q.v.*); O.L. of Andacolo, La Serena; O.L. of Ransom, Santiago. *Colombia:* O.L. of Chiquinquirà (*q.v.*); O.L. of Help, Socorro; O.L. of the Rocks, Ipiales; O.L. of Topo, Bogotá; O.L. of Torcaroma. *Ecuador:* O.L. of Quito (*q.v.*); O.L. of Quinche (*q.v.*); O.L. of the Swan, Cisne (image dates from 1594); O.L. of Guálapo. *Paraguay:* O.L. of Caacupé. *Peru:* O.L. of Chapi; O.L. of Characato; O.L. of Potosi; O.L. of the Rosary, Lima; the church ("of Triumph") at Cuzco, where Mary is said to have appeared in 1664. *Uruguay:* O.L. del Pintado. *Venezuela:* O.L. of Great Grace, of Ransom, and of Sorrows at Caracas. Many of these sanctuaries have a proper local feast.

ANGELICAL SALUTATION, The. The proper name of the prayer colloquially and generally called the Hail Mary, the first part of which consists of the words addressed to Mary by the angel at the Annunciation. See HAIL MARY.

ANGELS, ST. MARY OF THE. This dedication derives from the tiny chapel, Santa Maria degli Angeli (see PORTIUNCULA), near which St Francis of Assisi died, now enclosed within the great basilica of the same name in the plain of Assisi: a famous shrine both of the Queen of Angels and the Seraphic Father. The feast of its dedication is solemnly observed by the three branches of the Order of Friars Minor on August 2. On the same day a feast of St. Mary of the Angels is kept in several other places, including Costa Rica and Mexico, where the cathedral of Puebla de los Angeles has a well-known image of our Lady of this name; elsewhere she is commemorated on other dates, e.g., in Ecuador on September 1. Cardinal Newman connects this title with Mary's motherhood, with the coming upon her of the Holy Ghost at Nazareth when the Angel Gabriel delivered his message, and the consequent birth of our Lord at Bethlehem. As the Mother of Jesus, he says, Mary comes nearer to Him than any angel, nearer even than the seraphim who surround Him and ever cry, "Holy, holy, holy!"

ANGELUS, The. A prayer in honor of the Incarnation in the form of a commemoration of the Annunciation. It is said in the morning, at midday, and in the evening, and in very many places an angelus-bell (see below) is rung at the appropriate time. The prayer is as follows:

℣. The angel [*angelus*] of the Lord declared unto Mary,

℟. And she conceived of the Holy Ghost.

Hail Mary, etc.

℣. Behold the handmaid of the Lord,

℟. Be it done unto me according to thy word.

Hail Mary, etc.

℣. And the Word was made flesh,

℟. And dwelt among us.

Hail Mary, etc.

Then follows this prayer (which, however, is not of strict obligation for gaining the indulgences): "Pour forth, we beseech thee, Lord, thy grace into our hearts; that we, to whom the incarnation of Christ thy Son was made known by the message of an angel, may by His passion and cross be brought to the glory of His resurrection. Through the same Christ our Lord. Amen."

The Angelus is said standing on Saturdays and Sundays, but kneeling at other times; during paschal-time *Regina caeli* (*q.v.*) is said instead of it, always standing. The history of its development is rather complex and uncertain. A form of the Angelus seems to have been known in places in the thirteenth century, for the evening only, much encouraged by the Franciscan friars. The morning Angelus came later, and the midday one later still. The observance was popularized by St. Peter Canisius (d. 1597), in whose time the prayer took its final form, and its practice was regularized by Pope Leo XIII. In several countries the Angelus was, and is, particularly associated with the idea of peace, arising from the tradition that the Annunciation took place in the peace of the evening.

ANGELUS-BELL. From the first the saying of the Angelus (see above) seems to have been associated with the ringing of a bell, and this is still done generally in many countries, individual places and churches, as well as in religious houses and institutions. From early times this ringing consisted of nine strokes in groups of three with a pause between; nowadays this is followed by a series of even strokes, usually nine in number. The times are generally about 6 A.M., noon, and 6 P.M., or after Compline. In the middle ages the bell on which the Angelus was rung often had a special inscription, such as the two words *Ave Maria,* or longer; in England it often referred to the angel Gabriel. In the same country the bell was called the Ave or Ave Mary bell ("Ave" to rhyme with "Davey").

ANN, SAINT. See PARENTS OF OUR LADY.

ANNONCIADE. An old French word for Annunciation. It still distinguishes certain orders of women, such as the Annonciades of Bourges and the Sky-Blue Annonciades. The first named, founded by St. Joan of Valois in 1501, have a house in England, at St. Margaret's-at-Cliffe, near Dover; there is here a shrine of the Child Mary.

ANNUNCIATION, Feast of the. This is one of the earliest of Mary's feasts (*q.v.*), perhaps the first, for before the year 400 a church was built at Nazareth in commemoration of the event and that may well imply some liturgical celebration; it was certainly celebrated in Palestine before 500. In some senses, too, it is the most important of those feasts, because of the significance of the event commemorated (see ANNUNCIATION, below). In old calendars the feast bears several names referring to these things, such as the Incarnation, the Beginning of the

Redemption, the Conception of Jesus Christ, the Announcing of the Lord. The christological aspect is strongly marked in all liturgies, notably in the Byzantine with its repetition of "To-day is the beginning of our salvation and the manifestation of the mystery from the ages." The first solemniza-tion of the feast in Rome was *c.* 700, but it, or an analogous observance, was known in certain parts of western Europe before then, especially in Spain.—However the date, March 25, may have been arrived at, there is some reason to suppose that it was the starting point for the whole "Christ-mas cycle" of feasts: December 25 for our Lord's birth, January 1 for His circumcision, and February 2 for Mary's purification would all follow naturally.

The great pilgrim-shrine of this mystery is of course the church of the Annunciation at Nazareth, for which a great new building was begun in 1954. The previous church, which was small, stood across the site of the origi-nal basilica and of the crusaders' church that followed it. Steps went down under the high altar to what is believed to be the site of Mary's house, and there beneath the altar of the Annunciation are engraved the words: *Verbum caro hic factum est,* "Here the Word was made flesh." In a town that is so full of memories and monu-ments of Jesus, Mary, and Joseph, not a few visitors return by predilection again and again to the fountain of water, Mary's Well, which must have been so well known to the Holy Fam-ily; it still flows to typify "the foun-tain of the waters of life" to which the

Lamb shall lead us (Apoc. 7:17; 21:6), here where He was made man among men.

On this and on other days lessons are read at Matins from the works of St. Ambrose, who spoke on the An-nunciation perhaps as movingly as any of the Fathers. "Neither compan-ion nor witness was there," he says, "so that what passed might not be de-based by gossip." Mary "was in her room; she was alone; she said nothing until she heard that she was to be the mother of the Lord. Then she spoke: not to call the angel's word in question, but simply to learn in what manner the marvel should come to pass." And then, "Look at her humble-ness, look at her religious spirit. She whom the Lord has chosen for His mother is not forthwith puffed up on this account: she calls herself His servant."

ANNUNCIATION TO OUR LADY, The. Except for the narratives of the actual birth of Jesus, and the events connected therewith, and of the last hours of His earthly life, there is no passage of the New Testament more familiar than St. Luke's account (1:26-38) of Mary's receiving the tidings of her destiny, brought to her by the an-gel Gabriel. It is a fundamental part of the Christian gospel; time and again that passage of St. Luke is read at Mass; and the Annunciation has been depicted by artists perhaps more frequently than any other event in the life of the Mother of God.

The angel Gabriel, we are told, came to Mary in Nazareth and greeted her with the words, "Hail, full of grace, the Lord is with thee. Blessed art thou among women." Mary was troubled at these words, wondering what to make of such a greeting, and the angel went on: "Do not be afraid, Mary, for thou hast found grace with God. And behold, thou shalt conceive in thy womb and shalt bring forth a son; and thou shalt call his name Jesus. He shall be great, and shall be called the Son of the Most High; and the Lord God will give him the throne of David his father, and he shall be king over the house of Jacob forever; and of his kingdom there shall be no end." Not for a moment did Mary doubt what was told her; but she was a virgin and intended so to remain, and she asked, "How shall this happen, since I do not know man?" And the angel replied: "The Holy Spirit shall come upon thee and the power of the Most High shall overshadow thee; and therefore the Holy One to be born shall be called the Son of God. And behold, Elizabeth thy kinswoman also has conceived a son in her old age, and she who was called barren is now in her sixth month: for nothing shall be impossible with God." Mary asked no more questions. She said, "Behold the handmaid of the Lord; be it done to me according to thy word."

At the moment of this assent to the angel's words the Son of God, the Second Person of the Holy Trinity, took flesh in Mary's womb for the salvation of mankind. The way of salvation was opened to all men, and she was the first to walk in it, following her Son to the end; but her assent was not simply given in her own name, or even in the name of all, but mysteriously the whole people of God spoke through her. Mary's acceptance of God's will, "Behold the handmaid of the Lord; be it done to me according to thy word," is the condition of all her honor, all her privileges, all her glory: in that moment she consented to be, and became, the Mother of God. That it was at this moment that the Incarnation took place has always been the tradition of the Church, and the mystery of God made man and Mary's divine motherhood is thus summed up by the Catechism of the Council of Trent: "As soon as the Blessed Virgin Mary expressed her assent to what the angel had said . . . then at once, that is, in the very first instant, the most holy body of Christ was by the power of the Holy Spirit formed in the pure womb of the Blessed Virgin, a human soul created out of nothing was joined to that body, and the Godhead was joined to that body and soul. So it came to pass that in the same instant of time there existed perfect God and perfect man, so that the Blessed Virgin could be truly and rightly called Mother of God and of man, for in that same moment she conceived a man who was God."

In a lesson read at Matins on the feast of the Annunciation Pope St. Leo the Great says: "When therefore the fullness of the time appointed for man's redemption was come, our Lord Jesus Christ came into this lower world. He came down from His throne in Heaven, without withdrawing from the equal glory which He has with the Father, and was born by a new order, a new birth. A new order, because He who is invisible in His own nature became visible in ours; He whom the mind of man cannot comprehend willed to be comprehensible; He who was before all time began to live in time; the Lord of the universe veiled the dignity of His majesty and took on the form of a servant; God, who cannot suffer, stooped to become a man capable of suffering; God, who cannot die, put Himself under the laws of death." St. Leo was speaking particularly of the birth of Jesus; but all these things began at the moment of the Annunciation, and through the willing instrumentality of a daughter of men, Mary of Nazareth. *Cf.,* Knowledge, Our Lady's.

ANNUNZIATA, The, Florence. In 1252 the newly founded Servite friars commissioned a painter to paint them an Annunciation for their little house in Florence. According to the tradition, the painter set himself to work, but could not get on with it; tired out, he fell asleep at his easel, and when he awoke, behold, there was the picture finished. It was before this image that St. Aloysius Gonzaga made his youthful vow of chastity in 1579. The first modest dwelling and chapel of the Servites is now a beautiful fifteenth-century building, which Andrea del Sarto helped to decorate, and for the cloister of which the Medici family paid: one of the most famous Marian monuments in Italy.

ANTHEM OF LE PUY, The. It appears that this name was formerly sometimes given to the *Salve Regina* (*q.v.*), because its authorship was by some attributed to Adhémar, Bishop of Le Puy (d. 1098). It has been suggested, apparently quite arbitrarily, that this crusading prelate wrote the anthem to be sung by crusaders while on the march: as a soldier's marching-song its melody obviously leaves much to be desired.

ANTIPHONS, or ANTHEMS, OF OUR LADY. An antiphon is properly a short scriptural text said or sung before and after a psalm or psalms or other composition. But the antiphons of our Lady are four hymns, each with a versicle, response, and prayer, sung according to the season of the Church's year. They are *Alma Redemptoris Mater, Ave, Regina caelorum, Regina caeli,* and *Salve Regina* (*qq.v.*). In the Divine Office the antiphon B.V.M. is said or sung after Compline, kneeling; but standing on Saturday and Sunday and throughout paschal-time. The antiphons B.V.M. also figure in the Little Office B.V.M. (*q.v.*), and are sometimes used for parochial services and private devotion. These hymns may be distinguished from real antiphons by calling them "anthems," another English form of the same word. The use of these anthems seems to have had its origin in the daily singing of the *Salve Regina* by Cistercians, Dominicans, and other religious in the thirteenth century, and the Franciscans were soon using all four. These were first adopted in the Roman Office in 1350, and were made obligatory for all the Western Church in 1568; their frequency in the Office was reduced from 1955.

ANTIPOLO, OUR LADY OF. The national Marian shrine of the Filipinos. The image that bears this name, a statue carved of very dark wood, was brought from Mexico to Manila, now capital of the Philippine Islands, in 1626. At different times the statue has been located at Santa Cruz and Antipolo on Palawan, at Manila and Cavite on Luzon, and back to Antipolo, surviving wars and insurrections and sea-voyages. Five times between 1648 and 1748 it was taken on the dangerous round trip to Mexico, without mishap, and was accordingly given the name of the Virgin of Peace and Safe Travel. In 1926 it was taken to Manila to be solemnly crowned. When the Japanese occupied Antipolo in 1944, the statue was smuggled away, again to Manila, to be returned safely in the fall of the following year. It is reckoned that 20,000 people visit the shrine of our Lady of Antipolo in May alone of every year, and huge crowds assemble at the annual commemoration of the crowning of the image, which is enshrined above the altar of the Antipolo church.

APARECIDA, NOSSA SENHORA. In 1719 some fishermen found a headless wooden statue in the river Parahyba in Brazil, and it was dubbed accordingly Nossa Senhora Aparecida, the Madonna that Appeared. It was given a head and became very celebrated, and in the middle of the nineteeth century it was enshrined in a fine new church near Guaratinguetá, close to São Paulo; in 1895 the Redemptorists were given charge of this much-frequented sanctuary. Nossa Senhora Aparecida was declared patroness of Brazil in 1929; devotion to her is found also in Uruguay. Feast: May 11.

APOCRYPHAL WRITINGS. The expression "apocryphal writings" has several meanings: here it refers to certain early books written in imitation of the books of the New Testament, in the form of gospels, epistles, etc., falsely claiming to be the work of one of the apostles or of some contemporary of theirs. They do not form part of the sacred writings of the Church, even in a general sense; indeed, parts of some of them seem to have been written in the interests of heresy. As literary works they are very inferior: even the unlearned reader can detect the difference in style and spirit between them and the genuine New Testament books. But this does not mean that they are entirely worthless: they reflect beliefs popular among some Christians at the time they were written, and the events that they narrate as facts are not necessarily all false. Whether in a given case the information they give is true, false, or uncertain has to be decided by the same study and tests that are applied in the examination of other ancient writings; and in their conclusions scholars may, and do, disagree. Pope St. Leo I in 447 wrote strongly against these pseudo-apostolic works, and Pope Benedict XIV criticized them as sources of tradition apropos certain Marian feasts.

Some of the apocryphal writings are of importance here because some of the events and particulars commonly associated with the life of our Lady depend on them, wholly or in part. From what has been said above, it follows that these events and particulars are not necessarily true and not necessarily false; it has to be decided by the ordinary criteria of literary, historical, and religious study and judgment: in practice, certainty either way is often impossible. People then are free to make up their own minds: but the fact that something is believed or rejected unquestioningly by large numbers of pious people does not make it factually true or false. The apocryphal writings wherein our Lady has a large part are the *Protevangelium of James,* the *Gospel of Pseudo-Matthew,* the *Nativity of Mary,* and the *Passing of Mary (qq.v.).* These and similar works were regarded with more respect in the East than in the West, where a sixth-century official document, formerly attributed to Pope St. Gelasius I, condemned some of them because of their doctrinal eccentricities. It was Bl. James of Voragine (d. *c.* 1298) who in Europe popularized much of their matter about Mary, through his *Golden Legend.* See MARY: HER LEGEND.

APPARITIONS. See VISIONS.

APPEARING OF THE IMMACU-LATE VIRGIN MARY, The. The name of the feast commonly called the feast of our Lady of Lourdes (*q.v.*).

ARA CAELI, SANTA MARIA IN. The name given to an ancient church on the Capitoline hill at Rome. It derives from a legend that Octavian Augustus, who was Roman emperor when Christ was born, here saw a vision of our Lady upon an altar in Heaven (*ara caeli*). The growth of the legend apparently owes something to Virgil's fourth eclogue, which was often interpreted as a prophecy of the coming of the Savior:

Come are those last days that the
  Sybil sang:
The ages' mighty march beings anew.
Now comes the Virgin; Saturn reigns
  again:
Now from high heaven comes down
  a wondrous race.
Thou on the new-born babe—who
  first shall end
That age of iron, bid a golden dawn
Upon the broad world—chaste Lu-
  cina, smile . . .

This church has a famous image of the Child Jesus, and is the scene of children's festivals at Christmas and the Epiphany.

ARANCO, OUR LADY OF. A shrine at Concepción in Chile. Its origin was the discovery, by a child in the eighteenth century, of an image of the Virgin and Child drawn or engraved on a rock-face. The attention of the Jesuit missionaries was drawn to it, and it became a place of pilgrimage. It is sometimes called our Lady of Chile.

ARÁNZAZU, OUR LADY OF. This Spanish shrine is at the Franciscan church near Oñate in the Basque province of Guipúzcoa. The statue is said to have been hidden during the Moorish invasions, and was found on a rough mountainside in 1469, in a thicket of brambles (Aránzazu is said to mean "among the thorns"). Feast: September 9. The *cultus* has spread to South America, where a copy of the image is venerated in the church at Victoria in the Argentine.

ARCACHON, OUR LADY OF. A sailors' shrine on the shore of southern Biscay, which has had to contend both with the sea and with the French Revolution. Its white marble statue of Mother and Child, crowned in 1877, dates perhaps from the fifteenth century. The pilgrimage, in charge of the Oblates of Mary Immaculate, is very popular on account of its sea processions.

ARK OF THE COVENANT. In a figure of the Litany of Loreto our Lady is addressed as Ark of the Covenant (*Foederis arca*), that is to say, of the new covenant between God and man, as distinct from the Old Covenant between God and Israel, whose representative Ark of wood is so often referred to in the Old Testament. Mary was referred to as *Arca* by St. Ambrose, St. Ephraem, and others; *Foederis arca* was apparently first used by Richard of Saint-Victor (d. 1173). In the apostolic constitution *Munificentissimus Deus* (*q.v.*), Pope Pius XII points out that, "In the Ark of the Covenant, built of incorruptible wood and placed in the Temple of God [theologians and preachers] perceive an image of the most pure body of the Virgin Mary, preserved free from all corruption of the tomb and exalted to such great glory in Heaven." The

pope refers to and quotes a sermon of St. Anthony of Padua on the Assumption: "Just as Jesus Christ, so he remarks, rose triumphant from death and ascended to the right hand of His Father, so in like manner 'arose the Ark which He had sanctified, when on this day the Virgin Mother was taken up to her heavenly bridal-chamber.' "

Our Lady as Ark is particularly stressed in the Chaldean and Ethiopic liturgies. On December 26 (*cf.,* Synaxis) the Chaldeans sing of the Ark in another sense:

Mary is the ark of flesh
which sheltered that true Noah
who was to free our nature
from slavery to Satan.

The next verse refers to her as the Burning Bush (*q.v.*).

ARMENIA, SHRINES OF. The Armenians are one of the oldest Christian peoples, and for long they have been one of the most scattered. (There were Armenians in New York when it was still New Amsterdam.) Their homeland now forms part of the U.S.S.R. and of Turkey. Among the shrines of the Mother of God in Armenia proper in the past were those of Abarank, Alexandropol, Amagha, Ani, Erivan, Hokiats-Vank, Khakh (whose miraculous image was afterward moved to the monastery of Kelata), Kinte, Paknaïr, Pitchny, and Talina. Relics said to be of a garment (*q.v.*) of our Lady were venerated at Ankegh and the monastery of Khatun

Diramaïr, and at the Hok monastery was an image supposed to have been brought to Armenia by St. Bartholomew, the apostle (*cf.*, Likenesses). In the district of Vaspuragan alone there were thirty-eight monasteries dedicated in honor of the Mother of God, and wherever Armenians go they have churches bearing her name. Catholics of the Armenian rite are now a small minority: their principal Marian shrines are at Bzommar (*q.v.*) and our Lady "of the Swoon" (*q.v.*) at Jerusalem.

ART, Our Lady in. To the Romans of pagan antiquity, any thing (*res profana*) that a person put privately under the protection of a god became a religious thing (*res religiosa*); but if he made the thing over to the god by a public act, it became, not simply a religious thing, but a sacred thing (*res sacra*). There are analogous categories among Christian works of art. A statue, a poem, a book-illustration, or anything else whose subject is religious, is religious art; but if in addition it be intended for use in, or to be ancillary to, Christian worship, then it is also sacred art. And such sacred things will have, or should have, certain qualities or characteristics not necessarily required of religious art in general: religious and theological significance, a certain stillness and dignity, a kind of "unearthliness," speaking of that Heaven where Mary and the saints rejoice, objectivity that befits an image that is to be publicly venerated. The biblical pictures of Doré or Tissot are religious, but they are not sacred,

either in quality or use; the picture called our Lady of Perpetual Help is sacred, both in quality and use. The lovely address to Mary that Chaucer puts into the mouth of his Prioress is religious; it is not sacred. Dante's address to her, "Vergine Madre," in canto xxxiii of the *Paradiso,* is religious; it is not sacred: but, appropriately translated into English (as in the *Westminster Hymnal,* no. 114) and sung at worship, it is put to sacred use.

Confining our attention to painting, mosaic, carving, etc., in earlier days, and for centuries, all religious art, whatever its use, was sacred in quality. That is still true of the most venerated images of the East (*cf.*, Icons). As Professor D. Talbot Rice writes: "The spiritual quality is endemic, not superimposed, and it is perhaps this character above any other that distinguishes the outlook of the Russian icon painter, or for that matter, the Romanesque painter in the west, from that of the painters of the Italian Renaissance" (*Byzantine Art,* chap. xvi). But Western religious art gradually lost much of its sacred quality and became "humanized" (even sometimes in later Renaissance times in a sense "dechristianized"). And so it has come about that many famous paintings and statues, and most of those now found in ordinary churches, while put to sacred uses, are lacking in intrinsic sacred quality. Of many pictures and statues of the Mother of God, some of them great works of art, it can be truly said that there is nothing in their presentation that distinguishes them from representations of any other mother and child.

The distinction between "religious" and "sacred," which was obscured for so long, has been put this way: sacred art is a movement from God to man, it is concerned with His word to us; religious art is from man to God, our human ideas, aspirations, and affections. Abbot Vonier writes in *The Divine Motherhood*, "Between Mary and the Child there is more than the sweet affection between a beautiful mother and her first-born"; and he adds that any artistic presentment of her falls short of its Christian message if it fails to contain and express the Mother's faith in her Son's destiny. The image must somehow show that she is the Mother of God, just as every crucifix in itself should remind the beholder that this man is God. In view of the discussions that arise on "church art" in general, and images of our Lady in particular, and having regard to her very "ordinary" background and "extraordinary" experiences, St. Bernadette's comments on a bookfull of pictures of our Lady are of special interest. The Renaissance pictures revolted her; Fra Angelico's she liked, with reservations; the only one that seemed to her to have something in it "like" the Mother of God was a Byzantine icon—that is, a picture that made no attempt at realism. On the other hand, she also found "not quite unlike" a simple, homely statue she knew at Nevers, called our Lady of the Waters.

The multitudinous existing images of Mary, even if confined to those set up in churches, or intended so to be, make up an immense field in the world's graphic and plastic arts; some aspects of them are mentioned herein under ICON; ICONOGRAPHY; IMAGES; LIKENESSES.

ASSUMPTION, Feast of the. This chief of the five universal feasts (*q.v.*) of Mary has had several names in the course of its history: *Koimesis, Dormitio* = Falling Asleep; *Transitus* = Passing Over; *Pausatio* = Repose; and others, including in England, Marymass and our Lady in Harvest (*q.v.*). The precise occasion of the feast only gradually became clear, the name Assumption generalized, and the date fixed for August 15 (in some Eastern rites the date differs somewhat). It is, and has been for centuries, our Lady's day *par excellence,* and is the patronal festival of all churches dedicated in honor of the Blessed Virgin Mary without any other qualification. The feast originated in Palestine or Syria, and when at the end of the sixth century the Emperor Maurice ordered it to be kept throughout the Empire it was doubtless already widespread. About the year 690 St. Aldhelm in England speaks clearly of our Lady's "birthday" (to Heaven) being kept in the middle of August. It was during Aldhelm's lifetime that Pope St. Sergius I ordered its solemn observance with a procession in Rome, and in 847 Pope St. Leo IV added the vigil.

After the definition of the dogma of the Assumption in 1950 a new Mass and Office were provided for the feast. In the Mass, wherein there was previously no unequivocal reference to bodily assumption, a lovely passage from the book of Judith (13:22-25; 15:10) is chosen for the lesson, and the gospel is Elizabeth's greeting to Mary and the first part of the Magnificat (Luke 1:41-50), which has always been the Assumption gospel at Matins in the Byzantine rite. In the Divine Office new hymns are provided: for first Vespers, *O prima, Virgo, prodita;* for Matins, *Surge! jam terris fera bruma cessit;* and for Lauds, *Solis, O Virgo, radiis amicta;* second Vespers retains the traditional *Ave maris stella.* The lessons of the third nocturn are taken from the writings of St. Peter Canisius. In the second nocturn St. John Damascene says with lofty rhetoric: "On this day the sacred and life-filled Ark of the living God, she who conceived her Creator in her womb, rests in the Temple of the Lord that is not made with hands. David her ancestor leaps, and with him the angels lead the dance; the archangels make celebration, the virtues glorify, the principalities exult, the powers rejoice, the dominations are glad, the thrones keep holiday, the cherubim sing praises, the seraphim proclaim her glory. This day the Eden of the new Adam receives the living Paradise wherein the condemnation was made void, the tree of life planted, and our nakedness covered. . . . The Mother of the living God was taken up to Him, as was befitting."

ASSUMPTION, PLACE OF THE. The place where Mary died (*cf.,* Death of Mary) and from whence her body was taken to Heaven has been the subject of considerable discussion from time to time, and the matter is not decided with certainty. Two places claim the honor: Ephesus and Jerusalem. The residence and death at Ephesus of St. John, to whose care Jesus entrusted His Mother, are not mentioned in the New Testament, but there is early evidence for them. On the other hand, the evidence that our Lady died there is neither early nor clear. There seems to be no doubt at all that the Jerusalem tradition is the better supported: it can be traced back in apocryphal and other writings perhaps to the fourth or earlier century (*cf.,* Passing of Mary).—There are two relevant shrines at Jerusalem. The handsome modern Benedictine church of the Dormition on Mount Zion stands on the site of an ancient basilica, which at least since the early seventh century was believed to cover the site of the house wherein our Lady died. In the valley of the Cedron (of Josaphat), close to Gethsemane, there stands another church where, according to the tradition, her body was buried and after three days was assumed into Heaven. Early in the fifth century at least her tomb was shown here, soon enclosed within a church. The present church, shared by several Christian bodies, is partly twelfth-century and partly earlier; therein Mary's rock-hewn tomb is venerated.

ASSUMPTION OF OUR LADY, The. The doctrine of the Assumption is that the Blessed Virgin Mary, when the course of her earthly life was finished, was taken up body and soul into the glory of Heaven. It is generally held that she died before being so taken up, but this is not included in the dogma as defined in 1950 (*cf.,* Death of Mary). That this historical event is true is deduced not at all from historical evidence. The New Testament, which is both history and revelation, says nothing about it. It is referred to, and even described, in certain early documents, such as the *Passing of Mary (q.v.)*; but these documents are not of the kind that inspire confidence, and the Church does not rely on them. As an Anglican scholar has well said of the above writing: "The belief was never founded on that story. The story was founded on the belief, and testifies to the fact of that belief: the belief, which was universal, required a defined shape, and that shape at length it found" (J. B. Mozley, *Reminiscences of Oriel*, 1882). The Church teaches this truth as revealed by God and contained in her tradition from the beginning, believed for a long time implicitly and afterward explicitly; it is usually difficult to decide whether early references to Mary's death envisage her bodily Assumption or not. St. Gregory of Tours (d. 594) affirms unambiguously that, "The Lord took [Mary's] holy body and conveyed it on a cloud to Paradise; there it was again united with her soul and, glorified with the elect, it enjoys the eternal blessings that shall have no end" (*Glories of the Martyrs*, i, 4). But the great doctor of the Assumption is St. John Damascene (d. 749), whose "Praise at the Falling-asleep of the Mother of God" is quoted in every writing on the subject: "Just as the holy and unsullied Body that had been born of her . . . rose from the tomb on the third day, so she too had to be snatched from the grave, the Mother restored to her Son; as He came down to her, so she

too had to be taken up . . . to Heaven. . . . She who had kept her maidenhood inviolate in childbirth had to maintain the integrity of her body even after death. She who had carried the Creator as a babe in her arms had lovingly to dwell in the house of her God. The bride whom the Father had betrothed to Himself had to live in the bridal-chamber of Heaven. She who had beheld her own Son on the cross, who then felt in her heart the sword of sorrow she had been spared at His birth, had to behold Him seated with His Father. . . ."

As well as the testimony of the Fathers and those teachers who came after them, the Church adduces the common belief of the faithful and the evidence of the liturgy of public worship (though in this not all the references, whether Eastern or Western, are free from ambiguity). Moreover, although the Bible cannot be appealed to historically in this matter, all the "arguments and considerations of the Fathers and theologians rest on Sacred Scripture for their ultimate foundation. The Scriptures present the beloved Mother of God as most intimately united with her divine Son and as ever sharing His lot. Hence it seems all but impossible to see her who conceived Christ . . . as separated from Him, if not in soul, yet in body, after her life on earth was over. . . . Seeing that by preserving her from the corruption of the tomb He could give her such great honor, we must believe that He actually did so." As the New Eve (*q.v.*) the Blessed Virgin, subject as she was to Him, was closely associated with the New Adam in the struggle with the powers of Hell. "Hence, as Christ's glorious resurrection was an essential part and the final sign of [the victory over sin and death], in like manner the struggle which the Blessed Virgin endured in common with her Son was to end in the 'glorification' of her virginal body" (Pope Pius XII).

From the thirteenth century any reserves about acceptance of the doctrine of the Assumption practically disappear. Pope Benedict XIV (d. 1758) declared it to be a probable opinion, the denial of which would be impious and blasphemous; and after the definition of the Immaculate Conception in 1854 the question of the definability of this other doctrine was raised more and more often, and petitions to the Holy See for a definition became frequent from all parts of the world. In 1946 Pope Pius XII wrote to the bishops of the whole Church asking them whether they thought that the bodily assumption of Mary "can be proposed and defined as a dogma of faith, and do you, together with your clergy and people, so desire?" Of this inquiry the result was that " 'the bishops, whom the Holy Ghost has appointed to rule the Church of God' (Acts 20:28) replied in the affirmative to both questions, with almost unanimous voice. . . . This showed us what was the common doctrine of the ordinary teaching authority [magisterium] of the Church, as well as the common faith of the Christian people, which faith the same authority upholds and directs. This common consent is of itself an absolutely certain proof, which admits of no error, that the privilege in question is a truth revealed by God, and one contained in that divine deposit which Christ entrusted to His Bride to be faithfully guarded and infallibly proclaimed" (Pope Pius XII). Accordingly, after four more years of study, consideration, and prayer, the Pope on All Saints' day, 1950, solemnly defined the dogma of the Assumption of the Blessed Virgin Mary, by the constitution Munificentissimus Deus (q.v.; the above quotations from Pius XII are from this utterance). Cf., Assumption, Feast of; Assumption, Place of. For the Assumption in the Eastern Orthodox Church, see EASTERN CHURCHES.

The Church's solemn definitions are not made, as is sometimes too easily supposed, simply to enhance the glory of divine or sacred persons, or simply to satisfy the loving devotion of the faithful, though these results also are intended and follow. Every definition has a number of far-reaching significances, some of them relating to the particular needs or errors of the time at which the definition is made. What these significances are where the Assumption is concerned has been the subject of much writing and preaching since 1950; it is here possible to refer only to one aspect, but that a very important one. It is suggested by the last sentence in the following words of Pope Pius: "We also hope that, while materialistic theories and the moral corruption arising from them are threatening to extinguish the light of virtue, and by stirring up strife to destroy the lives of men, the exalted destiny of both our soul and body may [by this definition] be brought clearly to the notice of all men." Following her divine-human Son, Mary has returned wholly to her eternal source, to God; she has anticipated that final resurrection which is to be the lot of every child of Adam, whether for bliss or bane. (Some reputable theologians hold that others had preceded her: cf., Matthew 27:52-53.) Here at once is a most striking manifestation and exemplification of the truth affirmed in the baptismal creed: "I believe in the resurrection of the body and the life everlasting." As it has been put, "The doctrine of the Assumption 'concretizes' and particularizes the universal abstract ideas of the reintegration of matter, the rehabilitation of nature, the taking up of the feminine principle into the divine Principle, the redemption of our body" (Father Victor White). For centuries there has been going on a progressive profanation and secularization of matter, and it has not left Christians untouched: religion tends to become a thing apart, everything else being accounted secular and profane, "unspiritual," even, where body is concerned, "nasty." The disintegration and opposing of matter and spirit have reached an alarming pitch. The definition of Mary's bodily Assumption recalls all men and women to their wholeness: body, matter, is destined to life in "a new heaven and a new earth" when the old heaven and the old earth are no more (Apoc. 21:1). Mary has attained her—and our —destiny.

AUSTRALIA AND NEW ZEALAND, SHRINES OF. The principal patroness both of Australia and New Zealand is our Lady, Help of Christians, and there are many small local shrines of Lourdes, Fatima, etc. throughout these lands. But they are "young" countries, and they have not yet any old-established Marian sanctuaries of wide importance to which people go on pilgrimage. Rather may it be said that "Mary goes on pilgrimage to them," and the itinerant statue of our Lady of Fatima was received with great manifestations of devotion and love wherever it was taken. There is a project to build a pilgrimage chapel of Mary under this title in the Dandenong mountains of Australia. At the Benedictine abbey *nullius* of New Norcia in Western Australia is a domestic shrine of our Lady of Good Counsel. The image is a copy of the Genazzano picture, and it was given to the founders of the abbey by Bl. Vincent Palotti (d. 1850). The saving of their first crops from destruction by fire in 1847 was attributed to Mary's intercession when this image was brought near the flames. As "our Lady of the Southern Star," New Zealand has given a new title to the Blessed Virgin. A big statue of her was set up by the Marists on Cape Meketepun in 1887.

AUSTRIA, SHRINES OF. There are numerous sanctuaries of the Blessed Virgin in Austria, many of them small shrines in remote places, little known outside their own district. Among those recommended to pilgrims in the Marian year were the following. In Burgenland, Maria-Loreto (Eisenstadt); in Carinthia, Maria-Luggau (Kötschach), Maria-Rain, Maria-Saal, and Maria-Wörth (Klagenfurt); in Lower Austria, Mariahilferberg (Gutenstein), Maria-Laach, (Melk), Maria-Taferl (*q.v.*), Maria-Brunn (Hutteldorf), and Maria-Schutz (Semmering); in the Salzburg district, Dürrnberg (Hallein), Kirchenthal (*q.v.*), and Maria-Plain (*q.v.*); in Steiermark, Maria-Strassengel, Maria-Trost (Graz), and Mariazell (*q.v.*); in Tyrol, Absam (*q.v.*), Maria-Schnee, Maria-Stein (*q.v.*), and Maria-Waldrast; in Upper Austria, Lauffen (Bad Ischl), Freystadt, and Pöstlingberg (Linz); in Vorarlberg, Rankweil and Tschagguns. In Vienna there are among others the Faithful Virgin in the Piarist church (a copy of the picture in St. Pantaleon's at Rome); Mary our Protector, an icon in the church of the Armenian Mekhitarist monks; our Lady of Victory; and our Lady of the Domestic Servants in the cathedral. In Austria, as in Germany, special local feasts are unusual: a shrine generally celebrates its day on one of the greater Marian feasts. The shrine of Maria-Luschari (*q.v.*) is no longer in Austrian territory; see also MONTE SANTO.

AVE MARIA. The first words of the Hail Mary (*q.v.*) in Latin, which runs:

"Ave Maria, gratia plena; Dominus tecum: benedicta tu in mulieribus, et benedictus fructus ventris tui Jesus. Sancta Maria, mater Dei, ora pro nobis peccatoribus, nunc et in hora mortis nostrae. Amen."

In Rome and elsewhere "at the Ave Maria" means at the time of the evening Angelus (*q.v.*).

AVE-MARIA NUNS, The. St. Colette (d. 1447) founded the branch of the Order of Poor Clares that is known by her name, Colettines. Such was her devotion to the Angelus (*q.v.*) that her religious were called Ave-Maria Nuns and their convents bore the same name. The Colettine house in Paris is still known as the Monastère de l'Ave Maria.

AVE, MARIS STELLA. First line and name of the Vespers hymn, of seven verses, on most feasts of the Blessed Virgin, and in her Saturday and Little (*q.v.*) offices; it is also in common use on other occasions, whether in Latin or another tongue. The custom of singing the first verse kneeling began locally and gradually spread. Its authorship is unknown. It has been attributed to, among others, St. Bernard (d. 1153), which is much too late, and to St. Venantius Fortunatus (d. *c.* 600), which is probably too early: it is found first in a manuscript of the ninth century. The best-known English version is Father Caswall's, beginning:

Hail, thou star of ocean,
   Portal of the sky;
Ever-virgin Mother
   Of the Lord most high.
Oh! by Gabriel's Ave,
   Utter'd long ago,

Eva's name reversing,
'Stablish peace below.

This may be compared with the following, of which the first, found in a prayer-book of 1555 at Downside abbey in England, is perhaps rather older than that:

Hayle steere of the sea most bryghte
  O Mother of God immaculat.
A pure virgin in Godde's own syght,
  The gate of Heaven most fortunate.
Saluted thou wast, with great humil-
  itie
When Gabriel sayed, Ave Maria.
Establishe us in peace and tranquil-
  litie
  And chaunge the name of sinfull
  Eva.

From a prayer-book of 1706:

Bright Mother of our Maker, hail,
  Thou Virgin ever blest,
The ocean's star by which we sail
  And gain the port of rest.

Whilst we this Ave thus to thee
  From Gabriel's mouth rehearse,
Prevail that peace our lot may be,
  And Eva's name reverse.

By Monsignor R. A. Knox (contemporary):

  Star of ocean, lead us:
  God for mother claims thee,
  Ever-virgin names thee;
  Gate of Heaven, speed us.

  Ave to thee crying
  Gabriel went before us;
  Peace do thou restore us,
  Eva's knot untying.

And in the meter of the original, by T. I. Ball (contemporary):

  Star of ocean fairest,
  Mother, God who barest,
  Virgin thou immortal,
  Heaven's blissful portal.

  Ave thou receivest,
  Gabriel's word believest;
  Change to peace and gladness
  Eva's name of sadness.

AVE, REGINA CAELORUM. The first line and title of an anthem of our Lady (see ANTIPHONS), said or sung from the feast of the Purification until Maundy Thursday, exclusive. It was probably written in the twelfth century and it has been attributed to St. Bernard, but the author is unknown. Like *Alma Redemptoris Mater* (*q.v.*) it was recommended in the *Ancren Riwle*. The following translation is from the *Primer* of 1706:

Hail, shining Queen of the celestial
  train,
O'er angel-powers extend thy brighter
  reign.
Hail, fruitful root of life; hail, orient
  gate
From whom earth's better light derives its date.

O glorious Maid, rejoice; alone possess
The highest seat of creature's happiness,
And, crowned with beauty, thence
  implore thy Son
To grant our prayers from his indul-
  gent throne.

Father Edward Caswall's version, "Hail, O Queen of Heav'n en-thron'd," may be found in the *Pius X Hymnal* (McLaughlin and Reilly Co.), no. 108, and in *Westminster Hymnal,* no. 262a. A number of medieval Marian hymns began with the same line, "Ave, Regina caelorum"; some of them are still in use.

AVIOTH, OUR LADY OF. This pilgrimage goes back perhaps to the eleventh century. The ancient statue of the Blessed Virgin in the great medieval church at Avioth, in the diocese of Verdun in France, is of wood and is vested on special occasions. It was specially visited by ex-prisoners and by the mentally afflicted. A proper office of our Lady of Avioth was granted in 1934. Feast: July 16.

AYLESFORD. The friary at Aylesford in Kent was a principal house of the Carmelite Order in England from its foundation in 1241-42 till its dissolution by King Henry VIII in 1538. Part of the buildings were subsequently altered and added to, and used as a private residence; and in 1949 they were acquired and occupied again by Carmelite friars of the Old Observance ("Calced"). In 1951 relics of St. Simon Stock (see SCAPULAR, BROWN) were translated from Bordeaux in France to Aylesford, and the friary rapidly became one of the most popular places of pilgrimage in England. The medieval and later buildings are of the greatest interest, beautifully situated by the river Medway, and they have been restored and adapted with much care and skill. The sanctuary is notable for its paintings and carvings, old and new, outstanding among which is the statue of our Lady as Guardian of The Friars, by Michael Clark. The old church, dedicated in honor of the Assumption, was pulled down at the dissolution; it is being rebuilt on the original foundations.

concerned, this national devotion is recognized in the Jesuit church at Ghent, where a feast is observed on May 9 in honor of the Virgin Mary, Gracious Lady of Flanders; this church has the first statue of our Lady to be crowned in Belgium, in 1860. Other shrines are: our Lady of Aerschot; O.L. of Assebroek; O.L. of the City ("of the Stump"), Antwerp; Banneux (*q.v.*); O.L. of Basse-Wavre, where the original object of honor (still there) was an ancient *châsse* or box-reliquary; Beauraing (*q.v.*); O.L. of the Pottery, Bruges; O.L. of Chevremont (*q.v.*); O.L. of Reconciliation, Esquermes; O.L. of Foy, near Dinant; O.L. of Hanswijk (*q.v.*); O.L. of Hal (*q.v.*); O.L. of Louvain; O.L. of Montaigu (*q.v.*); O.L. of Oostacker (*q.v.*); O.L. of La Sarte (*q.v.*); O.L. of Good Help, Péruwelz; O.L., Consoler of the Afflicted, Vilvorde; O.L. of Walcourt (possibly the oldest image of Mary in Belgium, now completely plated with silver); O.L. of the Hedges, Ypres.

BELL DEDICATIONS. Church bells are dedicated to the service of God by a rite of such length, complexity, and meaningfulness that it is colloquially referred to as a "baptism," and it is part of the observance that each bell should be given a name. As in the case of church dedications (*q.v.*), Mary is the favorite name for this purpose. Of 2,584 medieval bells recorded in England, 900 were dedicated in her honor, St. John the Baptist being second, with about 250, and St. Catherine of Alexandria third, with 170. The reasons for Catherine's popularity in this connection seem to be that she was the patroness of London bell-founders, and bells are rung with a rope and wheel, which figure in the legend of St. Catherine's martyrdom. The double reference is found in the inscription on one English bell (spelling modernized): "I, Catherine, God's darling, to thee, Mary, shall I sing." Many of these ancient inscriptions are still extant, e.g.:

Virginis egregie vocor campana Marie.
"I am called the bell of Mary, the excellent maiden."

O Mater Dei, memento mei.
"Mother of God, remember me."

Hac non vade via, nisi dicas Ave Maria.
"Hail Mary say when you pass this way."

Serva campanam Sancta Maria sanam.
"Holy Mary, keep this bell well."

Protege pura via quos convoco Virgo Maria.
"Those whom I call together, keep, Virgin Mary, in the right path."

Ora mente pia pro nobis Virgo Maria.
"Virgin Mary, pray for us with loving heart."

Maria vocor. O rex gloriae veni cum pace.
"I am called Mary. Come with peace, O King of glory."

The third inscription, given above, was also put over doors. The last, popular on German bells, seems certainly to refer to the Incarnation; it was indeed sometimes followed by the words, *Et homo factus est:* there was, and is, a close association in people's minds between bells and the Annunciation. *Cf.*, Angelus.

BENADA, OUR LADY OF. The greatly venerated statue of our Lady Immaculate known by this name is enshrined above the altar in the chapel of the Irish Sisters of Charity at Benada Abbey, County Sligo. It was given by Pope Pius IX to Father Daniel Jones, s.j., and in consequence of certain particular graces granted to his own family in connection therewith, Father Jones presented it to the nuns. The previous history of this wooden image is not known: Pius IX described it as miraculous, and it may have belonged to a traveling missionary, as it can be taken apart and screwed together again.

BENEDICTA ET VENERABILIS ES. The first words of the gradual in the common and many other Masses of our Lady: "Blessed art thou and to be revered, Virgin Mary, who without loss of maidenhood was found to be mother of the Savior. Virgin mother of God, He whom the world cannot hold enclosed Himself within thy womb, and was made man. Alleluia, alleluia! Thou didst bear a child, yet didst keep thy maidenhood unspoiled. Alleluia!" This is an excellent example of the beautiful prayers and praises, available for the use of the faithful, that are to be found throughout the Roman liturgy: short, concise, dignified, meeting the needs of men and women of all times, and living up to "the grace and dignity of the Catholic mind."

BENEDICTION. It may be surprising that a work expressly concerned with the Blessed Virgin should include an entry about Benediction of the Blessed Sacrament; but it appears to be definitely established that this service is of Marian origin. In the later middle ages a custom grew up for the devout to meet in church in the evening to sing our Lady's praises, especially the *Salve Regina* (*q.v.*); it became customary on Saturdays to add solemnity to this observance by exposing the Blessed Sacrament, and thence our Benediction eventually developed. This no doubt accounts for the common association of certain Marian devotions, notably the singing of the Litany of Loreto, with Benediction. It is significant that the French name for the old *Salve* service was *Salut,* which is the word now commonly used in French for the service that in English we call Benediction.

BENOÎTE-VAUX, OUR LADY OF. The original statue of the Blessed Virgin at Benoîte-Vaux (holy valley), in the diocese of Verdun, is said to have been found by foresters working in a wood; it was destroyed at the French Revolution. Its successor, also very old, is said to resemble it, and was crowned in 1875. It is the center of a pilgrimage, especially on the second Sunday in July. There is another shrine of the same name in the diocese of Lyons.

BERNARD, ST., PRAYER OF. See MEMORARE, THE.

BÉTHARRAM, OUR LADY OF.
This shrine in the French Pyrenees has existed at least since the fifteenth century, but claims a very much older origin. The statue of the Blessed Virgin is supposed to have been found by shepherd boys; when its chapel was destroyed by Huguenots in 1569, it was taken into the Basque country of Spain for safety. Bétharram is the headquarters of the society of Priests of the Sacred Heart, founded by St. Michael Garicoïts in 1833, and pilgrims also visit his shrine and a famous calvary.

BETHLEHEM. The little town where Jesus Christ was born of the Virgin Mary lies on a ridge five miles south of Jerusalem; the stable-cave, venerated from very early times as the scene of the divine birth and the events that followed, is under the eastern end of the great church of the Nativity: this is substantially the Emperor Constantine's fourth-century basilica, as restored by Justinian *c.* 545—one of the oldest church buildings in the world. On the floor of the cave is a vermilion star, surrounded by an inscription: *Hic de Virgine Maria Jesus Christus natus est,* "Here Jesus Christ was born of the Virgin Mary." There are two specifically Marian shrines. One, Mary's Spring, on the way from Jerusalem, was probably a resting place for travelers, and therefore of Mary and Joseph. The other is a cave close to the church of the Nativity, called Lady Mary's Cave, or colloquially, the Milk Grotto. This last name is due to the color of the limestone, to account for which the story grew up, among people who knew nothing of geology, that its whiteness was caused by some falling drops of the Mother's milk when suckling the Child here. Pieces of the stone were carried away by pilgrims, and this in turn accounts for the chalky stones still kept in some European churches under the name of "the Virgin's milk"; there was one of these "relics" at Salisbury cathedral. The Milk Grotto has for centuries been frequented by both Christian and Mohammedan nursing mothers who lack milk.—A *feast* of our Lady of Bethlehem, in honor of the Incarnation, is kept at Nevers in France and by the Marists (February 28), and in Mexico and other Spanish-speaking lands on other dates. This last is due to the activities in those regions of a religious order called Bethlehemites, now extinct. There is an image and shrine of our Lady of Bethlehem at Ferrières in France, at Barcelona in Spain and at Belem, Lower California, in Mexico; and in Ireland there is an ancient wooden statue venerated as our Lady of Bethlehem at the Poor Clare convent in Galway. *Cf.,* Manger.

BETROTHAL OF OUR LADY.
Mary was "betrothed to a man named Joseph" (Luke 1:27). Among the Jews, as for long among Christians, marriage was preceded some time before by a solemn betrothal or engagement; but this Jewish betrothal was much more than simply a promise of marriage. A feast of this name is first heard of in certain French churches during the fifteenth century, and the

first papal approval was in 1537, when it was granted to the Franciscans; it became popular in Spanish-speaking countries. Today a feast of the Betrothal of our Lady (*Desponsatio*, "Espousals") is celebrated by the Latin Catholics of Palestine and in some other places, on January 23 and other dates.—"The divine mysteries," says St. Ambrose in one of his sermons, "are in truth hidden from us, nor, as the prophet says, can anyone easily understand the designs of God. . . . For some good reason, she who was chosen to bring forth the Lord was betrothed to a man. Why did she not become with child without being betrothed?" The same question is still sometimes put, and St. Ambrose suggests the answer is that it was to protect Mary's good name—it would appear to men's eyes that she had a husband in the same way as other women. She would, too, need a husband's love and care, and in their life together all families would find a pattern of love, devotion, and godliness. *Cf.*, Joseph, Saint.

BIBLE, MARY IN THE. Apart from the Church's teaching about our Lady's prerogatives (*q.v.*) and significance, the only indubitably authentic information about her is to be found in the Bible; it is nearly all in the four gospels, and especially those of St. John and St. Luke, our Lady's evangelist (*q.v.*). What the four tell us is summarized herein under MARY: HER LIFE. No doubt Christian love and devotion would like to know a good deal more; but the evangelists relate all that they deemed necessary for their purpose, and, if it seems but little in amount, it is not less than tremendous in content and meaning. They present Mary, not for her own sake, but in her deepest significance, in relation to Jesus Christ: above all, as the mother of that divine Savior— St. John does not even call her by name, but always "the Mother of Jesus." Like all Catholic teaching about Mary, what the evangelists say of her has to be read in the whole context of the gospels and the mystery of salvation. The Bible's testimony about Mary is not confined to what it states in so many words; as Pope Pius XII declared when defining the Assumption, "All these arguments and considerations of the Fathers and divines rest on Holy Writ for their ultimate foundation."

Outside the gospels, our Lady is referred to, in the New Testament, at the beginning of the Acts of the Apostles and in St. Paul's letter to the Galatians (4:4). But in the Apocalypse also there is a passage (12:1-6) very commonly associated with her: the passage beginning "And a great sign appeared in heaven: a woman clothed with the sun, and the moon was under her feet, and upon her head a crown of twelve stars. . . ." In its literal sense, this woman is probably a figure of Israel bringing forth Christ and merging into His Church. But parts of the passage may have a secondary reference to our Lady; and many teachers, from popes downward, have at least applied them in this way, especially the first verse quoted above: in any case, Mary is a type (*q.v.*) of the Church. So, too, the liturgy, in the office for the Immaculate Conception feast, the lesson for our Lady of Lourdes, and the introit for the Assumption; and the idea has been widely popularized by pictures and statues.

It is generally agreed that, in the Old Testament, there are two passages that are in a literal sense directly prophetic of Mary. These are Isaias 7:14, the familiar "Behold a virgin shall conceive, and bear a son, and his name shall be called Emmanuel," and Micheas (Micah) 5:2-3, where the words "until the time when she who is with child hath brought forth" are surely an echo of the words of Isaias. But there is a third classic Old Testament passage, about which there is not such complete agreement, Genesis 3:15: "I will put enmity between you [the serpent] and the woman, between your seed and her seed: He [or she] shall crush your head, and you shall lie in wait for His [or her] heel." A long and weighty tradition identifies the woman here with Mary, and this interpretation has grown in favor during the past hundred years; but according to another view the woman was Eve, though, Mary being the New Eve (q.v.), the words can be referred to her also. Here again iconography has popularized the Marian interpretation among the faithful. The verse of Genesis is read and referred to in the office for the Immaculate Conception; and there are important uses of it in *Munificentissimus Deus* and *Fulgens corona* (qq.v.).

In the Church's liturgies and the works of religious writers, passages are freely taken from the Old Testament and used in a sense and with a reference not intended by the writers of the Sacred Scriptures. For instance, psalm verses are applied to our Lord in the communion-verse of the Mass of Christ the King, and words about the patriarch Joseph are applied to Mary's husband in the Mass *Adjutor* of St. Joseph. This process (which of course cannot be used for purposes of argument from Scripture) is technically called "accommodation," and it is very common with reference to our Lady. (Such usage of course does not really come under the heading "Mary in the Bible," but it is convenient to refer to it here; there are other references under LITURGY: WESTERN.) For this purpose much use is made of the sapiential books (Proverbs, Ecclesiastes, Song of Songs, Wisdom, and Ecclesiasticus), as chapter 8 of Proverbs, whose description of Wisdom is applied to Mary in the Roman liturgy. Another characteristic example of accommodation or appropriation is from the Song of Songs, 6:9, found, e.g., as a *capitulum* in the Little Office B.V.M. and in the gradual of the Mass of our Lady's Purity: "Who is she that cometh forth like the dawn, fair as the moon, bright as the sun, terrible as an army set in array?", where "terrible" may be referred to Mary warning impenitent sinners. Like some others, this passage is also applied to the Church. But some exegetes hold that the Song of Songs, for example, calls for a Mariological interpretation stronger than simply in an accommodated sense, namely, in the typical sense (sometimes called spiritual or mystical).

In varying measures, great women of the Bible are taken as figures or types of our Lady: Mary (Miriam), the sister of Moses, in Exodus 15:20-21; Judith, especially in Judith 15:10-11, though the choice of this national heroine is perhaps not altogether happy; Deborah, in Judges, chapters 4-5; Esther, who pleaded for her people. Titles for Mary, too, are taken from the Old Testament; such as the Burning Bush, Ark of the Covenant, a Garden Enclosed, Tower of Ivory (*qq.v.*); Jacob's Ladder (Gen. 28:12), joining earth and Heaven; the Closed Door (Ezech. 44:2), with reference to her virginity; and even Noah's Ark, as bearing within herself the Head and fount of a saved people.

BIRNAU, OUR LADY OF.   A sanctuary beautifully situated on Lake Constance, at a Cistercian monastery. The church, built in 1745, is one of the most notable rococo churches in Germany, and here the image called the Lovely Mother is venerated. The church is also well known for its wall-paintings and for the *Honigschlecker,* a statue of a little boy licking honey off his fingers.

BIRTHDAY OF OUR LADY, Feast of the. This is one of the five universal feasts (*q.v.*) of Mary, and is kept on September 8. It was first observed in the East perhaps in the sixth century, but in Rome not till *c.* 700; however, there is evidence for its having been celebrated in some other parts of the West before that.

In France it used to be called the day of Notre-Dame-l'Angevine, because of a story, long ago discredited, that St. Maurilius (d. 453) established the feast in his diocese of Angers; he did this, it was said, because on the night before September 8 a man had heard angelic voices singing and been told it was in celebration of Mary's birthday on the morrow. The real reason for the choice of date is not known. —The antiphon of the Magnificat at second Vespers of the feast is the same as a hymn sung at the same office in the Byzantine rite: "Your birthday, maiden mother of God, has proclaimed joy to all the world: for from you arose the Sun of justice, Christ our God, who took off the curse and bestowed blessing, overcame death and gave us life for evermore."

BIRTHPLACE OF OUR LADY.   It is not known with certainty where Mary was born. According to the apocryphal *Nativity of Mary* (*q.v.*) she was conceived and born in the same house where later the power of the Most High overshadowed her and she too conceived: and that, of course, was in Nazareth. There is an equally unreliable association of her parents with Sepphoris, once the capital of Galilee, three miles north from Nazareth. But there is an early and enduring—though far from certain—tradition that her birthplace was in Jerusalem, and from the sixth century there are references to a church built over the site of the house, near the Sheep Pool. A new church was built here by the crusaders in the twelfth century, and called St. Ann's, whose ruins were in 1856 given to France by the sultan of Turkey. The French government had it rebuilt, and confided it to the White Fathers, of whose seminary for Melkite students it now forms a part. In the Byzantine crypt beneath this church is the little sanctuary which for so many centuries has been venerated as the place where Joachim and Ann lived and their daughter Mary came into the world. The near-by gate in the city wall is called *Bab Sitti Maryam*, Gate of the Lady Mary, by the Mohammedans of Jerusalem, but not, strangely enough, by the Christians; they call it St. Stephen's Gate. It represents the Sheep Gate of some translations of John 5:2.

BISKUPEĆ, OUR LADY OF. The oldest statue of Mary in Croatia, dating from the eleventh century. Its shrine in a new church was completed in 1939, decorated by the sculptor Ivan Mestrović and the painter Jozo Kljaković; but it suffered destruction during the subsequent war.

BISTRICA, OUR LADY OF. When the Turks annexed Bosnia in 1463, some refugees from Vinski Vrh came to Bistrica, bringing with them a statue of the Blessed Virgin. It was almost forgotten till 1684, when the church in which it stood became a pilgrim shrine, and eventually the Croatian national sanctuary. In 1935 the statue was solemnly crowned as Queen of the Croats, a witness, as Cardinal Stepinać has said, to the faith and trust of the Croatian peo-

ple in the intercession of the Mother of God.

BLACK VIRGIN or MADONNA. A statue (less often a picture) of our Lady which is black in color, either because of the material of which it is made, or the way in which it is painted, or on account of age. Among the most famous black virgins are our Lady of the Pillar at Chartres and the images at Einsiedeln, Montserrat, and Oropa (*qq.v.*). There are many others, and, though there is no special significance attaching to a Black Virgin as such, they seem to attract popular devotion particularly strongly. This can hardly be because of the antiphon in the Common Office of our Lady, from the Song of Songs (1:3-4): "I am black but beautiful, O ye daughters of Jerusalem; therefore the King hath loved me and hath brought me into his chamber."

BLAKHERNAE. A quarter of Constantinople where formerly was the most famous sanctuary of the Mother of God among her sixty-four churches in the city. It was at the church of the imperial palace, built in the fifth century. Here was enshrined the relic called the garment (*q.v.*) of our Lady, which was regarded as a palladium of the city, and also the icon of our Lady of Blakhernae (see NOVGOROD, OUR LADY OF). Christian Constantinople, the "New Rome," came to an end, after a history of over a thousand years, when it was captured by the Turks in 1453; for most of that time it had been in secular prestige the first city of Christendom and ecclesiastically the second see of the Church.

BLANDYKE, OUR LADY OF. At the Cistercian monastery of Blandecques, near Saint-Omer (now in France), there was formerly a wonderworking statue; medals of our Lady of Blandecques were struck so late as the eighteenth century. In the days of the famous English college conducted by the Jesuits at Saint-Omer, the boys went once a month to "Blandyke" for a day in the country. This name has been perpetuated at Jesuit schools in England (Stonyhurst is the successor of St. Omer's) as that of their monthly holiday.

BLESSINGS. Among the many forms of blessing used by the Church, invoking the graces and mercies of Almighty God upon His children, directly or through the devout use of things, a considerable number have reference to the Blessed Virgin, such as the blessings for various rosaries, scapulars, and the like. But there are others, not so well known as these. For instance, there is one for grain and fields, whose prayers do not refer to our Lady, but its special date is her birthday (September 8); and a long one for the Assumption, upon grass crops for animals and other harvests for humans and "the wine that delights man's heart": here it is asked that, through Mary's merits on her festival, these things of earth may be used for heavenly ends. A blessing that is perhaps now little used is of water for the sick, in honor of our Lady and St. Torello (an Italian hermit who died in 1282): the prayer refers to the angel moving the healing waters (John 5:4). In the blessing of candles for members of the Rosary Confraternity the Church prays that, as the light from candles dispels the darkness of night, so may the unseen light of the Holy Spirit keep the blindness of sin from our hearts. A few blessings are proper to certain places; among them, in the diocese of Turin in Italy, a blessing of persons in honor and with the invocation of our Lady, Help of Christians.

BLIESKASTEL, OUR LADY OF. According to the local story this picture of Mary belonged to a hermit, and once when robbers shot arrows at it it bled; it was accordingly called the Sorrowful Mother with the Arrows, or the Compassionate Mother of Gräfintal, from the German monastery where it was venerated. The monastery was closed in 1802, and the picture was lost sight of for over a century. In 1911 it was found and again enshrined, in a chapel on the Marienberg at Blieskastel.

BLUE. See COLORS.

BOLZANETO, OUR LADY OF. The shrine of our Lady of the Lookout (*della Guardia*), on Monte Figogna outside Genoa in Italy, attracts 200,000 pilgrims a year. It began in 1490, when a peasant said that the Blessed Virgin had appeared to him and asked for a chapel to be built in that place. The present big church was finished in 1890, and the modern wooden statue of Mary is surrounded by *ex-voto* tablets said to number 40,-000. The original statue and a seventeenth-century successor are kept in neighboring chapels. The present one includes a figure of the shepherd, Benedict Pareto, kneeling at the feet of the Mother and Child. There are several other shrines in Italy commemorating this appearing, and a few in other parts of the world. Feast: August 29.

BOULOGNE, OUR LADY OF. So far as is known, and putting aside some rather extravagant legends, the shrine of our Lady of Boulogne-sur-Mer has been popular since the twelfth century, especially among sailors, both French and English. The latter showed their enthusiasm by pillaging the shrine in 1544 and carrying off the statue, but it was eventually returned. Boulogne was one of the most important sanctuaries of medieval France, and later: among English pilgrims have been Henry III, Edward II, and other kings, the Black Prince and John of Gaunt. The shrine also had Scottish associations; and there was a chapel of our Lady of Boulogne at Leith, where the burgh arms still bear her image. At the Revolution the statue of Mary was burnt to ashes and her church pulled down. A new statue was made in 1803 and pilgrimages began again; the new church of the Immaculate Conception, on the old site, was consecrated in 1866, and yet another statue made, which was crowned in 1885. The image represents the Mother, with the Child on her arm, standing in a boat, with an angel on either side. Before the Marian congress at Boulogne in 1938 a custom was inaugurated of taking replicas of the statue of our Lady of Boulogne "on tour" in France, and even abroad to England, for whose reconciliation with the Church a branch of the Confraternity of our Lady of Compassion (*q.v.*) is established at Boulogne. The English visit was on the occasion of the "cross-bearing" pilgrimage to Walsingham (*q.v.*) in 1948. The sanctuary church at Boulogne was badly damaged in World War II and the image smashed; but the enthusiasm of the "great return" of one of the copies, which began in 1943, will be long remembered in France. It had been sheltered at Lourdes. Feast: October 22. There is an ancient offshoot of this shrine at Boulogne-sur-Seine.

BRIDE OF THE HOLY SPIRIT. Every faithful soul open to the action of the Spirit of God may be called a bride of the Holy Spirit. But the Virgin Mary became so in an altogether unique way when, over-shadowed by that same Spirit, the Word became flesh in her womb. Religious writers and the public worship of the Church delight to apply to her passages in the Song of Songs relating to the Bride: such as the antiphon, "His left hand is under my head, and his right hand shall embrace me"; and the responsory, "Arise, my love, my beautiful one, my dove, and come. . . ."

BRIDGE (BRIG) O' DEE, OUR LADY OF THE. See ABERDEEN, OUR LADY OF.

BRIDGET, ST., REVELATIONS OF.

St. Bridget was a Swedish noblewoman, born about the year 1303; after the death of her husband in 1344 she founded the Order of the Most Holy Savior for men and women, which still exists as an order of nuns; she ended her remarkable life at Rome in 1373, and was buried in her monastery at Vadstena. St. Bridget was raised to high mystical states, and was the recipient of numerous visions and revelations. Accounts of these she dictated to secretaries in Swedish; they were then translated into Latin by Prior Peter of Alvastra, and edited in eight books and an appendix by Bishop Alphonsus of Vadaterra. The celebrated hagiographer Alban Butler wrote that if instead we had these accounts directly as narrated by St. Bridget, they "would have been compiled with more simplicity and with greater life and spirit, and would have received a higher degree of certainty." The lively discussions and differences of opinion to which the book of the Revelations of St. Bridget have given rise from time to time, and even at general councils of the Church (Constance, Basle), need not be gone into here. It was with reference to these revelations (among others) that Pope Benedict XIV declared that even though many private revelations have been approved, we cannot and we ought not to give them the assent of divine faith, but only that of human faith.

By her rapturous descriptions of the beauties of our Lord and His Mother, St. Bridget aimed at rekindling love for them, but where our Lady is concerned perhaps her most attractive writing is the *Sermo angelicus,* "Angelic Discourse," so called for this reason: St. Bridget was wondering from what books the religious of her order should take their readings at Matins, and we are told that, in accordance with a promise made to her by Christ, an angel several times appeared and dictated to her three lessons for every day of the week. The subjects of these lessons are: Sunday: God's love for Mary from all eternity; Monday: the angels and Mary; Tuesday: Adam, the patriarchs, and prophets and Mary; Wednesday: Mary's conception and birth; Thursday: her virtues and qualities; Friday: her joys and sorrows; Saturday: her life after her Son's ascension, her death and going up into Heaven, body and soul. These readings form the Matins lessons in the Bridgettine office (*q.v.*) to this day, but they are suitable for anyone's spiritual reading: under the title *Revelations and Prayers of St. Bridget* they were translated into English by Dom Ernest Graf, monk of Buckfast, in 1928. Father Graf points out that the *Sermo angelicus* does not profess to tell us anything new, but simply presents in a moving way beliefs common to Christians. The value of all private revelations, he writes, lies in their ability to strengthen faith in and love for the truths of religion.

The following passage is from the second lesson on Fridays: "Wherefore even as she was of all mothers the most blessed when she beheld the

Son of God born of her, whom she verily knew to be true God and man, mortal in His manhood but eternally immortal in His godhead, so also was she of all mothers the most afflicted, by reason of her foreknowledge of His most bitter passion. For in such wise was her keenest joy always mixed with bitterest grief, as if someone were to speak thus to a woman in child-birth: 'You have brought forth a son alive and whole, but the pain you have endured in his birth shall last till your death.' The mother then would indeed joy in the life and health of her offspring, but she would sorrow in her own suffering and death. Assuredly the sadness of such a mother could not be more grievous than the sorrow of the Virgin Mary whenever her mind dwelt upon the future death of her dearly loved Son."

BULGARIA, SHRINES OF. The people of Bulgaria belong almost entirely to the Eastern Orthodox Church, and share the devotion to the Mother of God that distinguishes the Orthodox. Many parish churches and sixteen monasteries are dedicated in her honor, notably those at Bachkovo and Pazardzhik in the eparchy of Sofia. But the veneration of icons seems to be less used in Bulgaria than in other Orthodox countries, and there does not appear to be any outstanding shrine of our Lady. Catholics are a very small minority, of whom a quarter are of Byzantine rite. They have no Marian sanctuary of special note, but the people's devotion is none the less fervent, especially at

this time of oppression behind the iron curtain.

BURMA, SHRINES OF. A shrine of our Lady of Lourdes was inaugurated in the Karenni district of this mission territory in 1902; there is another Marian sanctuary at Nyaunglebin.

BURNING BUSH, The. The bush, burning but unconsumed, from which God spoke to Moses (Exod. 3:1-4), is used by the Fathers as a figure of our Lady; an antiphon at Lauds of the Circumcision (*q.v.*) and in the Little Office B.V.M. says: "The bush which Moses saw unburnt we recognize as your glorious virginity: Mother of God, intercede for us." Some Greek calendars have a commemoration of her under this title, on September 4; and *cf.,* Thorn-Bush, Our Lady of the. St. Bridget writes in the *Sermo angelicus:* "Wherefore this chosen Mother is appropriately likened to the bush which Moses saw all on fire, which yet remained unconsumed: for He who abode so long in the bush until He made Moses believe and carry out what He told him, to whom also when he asked His name He said, '*I am who am,* this is my name for ever,' the same abode in His mother's womb for as long a time as other children must remain there before birth. And as the Son of God took entire possession of the Virgin's body in His conception, so did He come forth from her in His nativity as the perfume yielded by the rose, in all the glory of His godhead and manhood, the virginal glory of the Mother remaining untouched." Or, more briefly, in the *Mirror of Our Lady* (*c.* 1440): "Moses being in the desert saw a bush all on fire, and yet it burnt not. . . . By this bush is understood our Lady that was afire and burnt not, for she was mother without loss of maidenhood." But the classical reference in English literature is in Chaucer's *Canterbury Tales,* when the Prioress invokes our Lady's help in the telling of her story:

O mother maid, O maid and mother free,
O bush unburnt, burning in Moses' sight . . .

BYZANTINE RITE. There are numerous references herein to the Byzantine rite. This is the system and forms of worship, Mass, sacraments, and the rest, used in various languages by the largest body of Catholics of Eastern rites, notably the Melkites, Ukrainians, Ruthenians, and Rumanians. It is also used by the whole of the great Eastern Orthodox Church, which is not in communion with Rome. The very large part accorded to the Mother of God in the Byzantine rite is frequently referred to in these pages. The word Byzantine is derived from Byzantium, the old name for Constantinople, where this liturgy received its final form.

BZOMMAR, OUR LADY OF. Since 1749 Bzommar, near Beirut in the Lebanon, has been an important center of Armenian Catholics: their principal seminary and a residence of the patriarch-katholikos of Cilicia. A few years earlier Pope Benedict XIV had given to the Patriarch Abraham Artzivian a picture of the Mother of Sorrows, painted by Raphael or one of his pupils. This was enshrined at the seminary, and our Lady of Bzommar today is an important pilgrimage shrine of the Near East.

C

CANADA, SHRINES OF. French Canada shares with the sections of Spanish influence farther south the privilege and responsibility of being the first home of Catholic Christianity in North America, and therefore the first part of the continent where the Mother of the Redeemer was honored with the rites of the Church and the devotion of the faithful. The cathedral of Quebec, the first church of that dignity in North America (1674), was dedicated under her name and protection. The Montreal company was named the Compagnie de Notre-Dame-de-Montréal, and the original name of that city was Ville-Marie. To-day the leading Marian sanctuaries of Canada are St. Mary-among-the-Hurons and our Lady of the Cape (*qq.v.*). Others are Notre-Dame de Bon Secours, founded by Bl. Margaret Bourgeoys, N.-D. de Grâce and N.-D. de Liesse (*q.v.*) at Montreal, our Lady of Sorrows at Pointe Navarre, N.-D. de la Paix at Joinville, N.-D. de Toute Grâce (*q.v.*) at Nicolet, and our Lady of Victories (*q.v.*) at Quebec, all in the province of Quebec; our Lady of Grace at Marylake, King City, Ontario, and another Augustinian shrine, our Lady of Consolation, at Monastery, Nova Scotia. There are Lourdes shrines (*q.v.*) at Lac Bouchette, Lachute and Rigaud, P.Q., at St. Louis de Kent, N.B., at St. Boniface, Man., at St. Peter's Colony, near Kronau,

Sask., and at Cormac and Ottawa in Ontario; the last was established by the Montfort fathers in 1883. The shrine of our Lady of Guadalupe at Halifax, N.S., had its origin in the Marian year 1954. At a convention of the Maritime provinces held at Memramcook, N.B., in 1889, it was declared that the chief Acadian holiday was Assumption day and *Ave, maris stella* the provincial hymn. At Nicolet (Quebec) there is the important Centre Marial Canadien, with its museum, library and numerous publications, including the monthly *Marie*. La Société Canadienne d'Etudes Mariales has its headquarters at the University of Ottawa.

CANDLEMAS. The colloquial name for the feast of the Purification (*q.v.*), because of the blessing of and procession with candles that takes place on February 2. It is a very old observance, whose origin has been much discussed; although it may have begun in the East, it is unknown there today except among the Catholic Melkites (at Vespers). The Song of Simeon, "Now thou dost dismiss thy servant, O Lord" (Luke 2:29-32), is solemnly sung, but the observance has no necessary connection with the Purification; it is penitential in character, and the emphasis of the prayers is on Christ as the light of the world. *Cf.,* Processions.

CANONIZATION. The question is sometimes asked, "When was the Blessed Virgin canonized?" If by that is meant, "When was she canonized by a formal act of the Church?" the answer is "Never." But canonization properly includes any recognition by the whole Church of a person's outstanding holiness. Our Lady, the Apostles, and others of those days were recognized as saints (in our modern sense) by the spontaneous and universal judgment of all members of the Church; and for a long time holy persons, including very many of the greatest saints, were canonized in similar informal ways, recognition of their holiness by the faithful at large being (as indeed it still is) a very important element in it. The first recorded solemn canonization (of St. Ulric of Augsburg) by a pope was not till the year 993; and our present long and complex process has been in full operation only since the time of Pope Urban VIII (d. 1644).

CANTICLE OF MARY, The. See MAGNIFICAT, THE.

CAPE, OUR LADY OF THE. This one of Canada's two principal pilgrim-shrines of the Mother of God is at Cap-de-la-Madeleine, which juts into the St. Lawrence River just east of Trois-Rivières and takes its name from a chapel of St. Mary Magdalen built there in 1659 by Jesuit missionaries. It was here in 1694 that Canada's earliest Rosary Confraternity was established. A new chapel was finished in 1720, in which an image of our Lady was set up in 1854. Ten years later a new pastor, Father Desilet, found a pig in the chapel, chewing up a rosary, and he took it as a symbol of his unsatisfactory flock—"they drop their rosary and a hog picks it up." But he recalled them to better ways, built a new church, rededicated the shrine-chapel in honor of our Lady of the Rosary, and put her statue above the altar. The building of the church was accompanied by marvels, notably when the river unexpectedly iced over in March, 1879, and enabled the last loads of stone to be brought across by sleigh.

The old chapel with its statue became a place of pilgrimage, and now tens of thousands of people come there, especially on August 15 and September 8, to accommodate whom a larger church has been built. But our Lady of the Cape is still in her old chapel, crowned in 1904, surrounded with flowers and votive hearts, beneath a canopy festooned with a great rosary. Around her the national Marian congress met in 1954, and Indians came in special pilgrimage to dedicate their tribes to the Mother of God. This shrine and its annexes is now in the care of the Oblates of Mary Immaculate; more than one and a half million pilgrims visited it in 1954.

CARAFA, OUR LADY OF. A well-known Maltese shrine in St. John's cathedral at Valletta. The image of Mary is a picture, with a silver covering in the Byzantine manner; it was crowned in 1954. On the neighboring island of Gozo is the sanctuary of our Lady *ta Pinu*.

CARAVAGGIO, OUR LADY OF.
An Italian shrine near Milan. It had
its origin in 1432, when the Mother
of God is said to have appeared in
vision to a sick peasant woman and
pointed out a healing stream. The
present church is due to the initiative
of St. Charles Borromeo: it is approached through an arch on which
stand statues of Mary and the woman
she helped. There are three main pilgrimages a year. Feast: May 26.

CARFIN. A parish in the Lanark-
shire coalfield of Scotland, largely peopled by the descendants of Irish immigrants. During the industrial depression and disturbances after World
War I the parish priest, Canon
Thomas N. Taylor, gave unemployed
men "something to live for" by organ-
izing them to build a Lourdes grotto.
It was finished in 1922, and within a
year thousands of people were coming to the place. Subsequently the
original one acre of ground was increased to fifty, where there had been
one shrine there were now twenty-
four, and all the work involved was
done by volunteer labor. Carfin has
also become a center of devotion to
St. Teresa of Lisieux, but the Lourdes
grotto is still its heart; among other
Marian shrines there are a replica of
the Holy House (q.v.) of Loreto and,
in an artificial lake, the statue of our
Lady of Carfin, Star of the Sea. Carfin
is perhaps the most striking sanctuary
in Great Britain. A frequent pilgrim
has said of it: "It is so utterly genuine
and spontaneous, not in the least
'precious' like X . . . ; a sort of spiritualized Butlin's Holiday Camp,

dumped down in a sordid mining village. It is thrilling to watch the people praying there—just the same atmosphere as Lourdes."

CAROLS. A carol is a religious song
of a special type, not easy to define in
words: among its characteristics are
that it is simple, "artless," popular,
loving but not sentimental, and generally cheerful. But the distinction between carol and hymn is best appreciated in singing: "As I sat on a sunny
bank" and "The holly and the ivy"
are carols; "Good King Wenceslas"
and "Silent Night" are not. As often
as not a carol is a folk-song, and therefore anonymous. Few, if any, surviving English carols are older than the
year 1400, and they were produced in
good number down to about 1650;
after that, their production was fugi-
tive, but continued to our own day: a
Christmas carol was written by G. K.
Chesterton (d. 1936), "The Christ-
child lay on Mary's lap," and set to a
traditional tune from America; another, by Father Edward Caswall (d.
1878), "See amid the winter's snow";
another, by an American Episcopalian
clergyman, Dr. J. H. Hopkins (d.
1891), "We three kings of Orient are";
and, by another American, Louise
Imogen Guiney (d. 1920), there is
"Tryste Noel." Carols are commonly
associated with Christmas; but there
are also carols for Easter and Whitsun,
for the natural seasons of the year,
even for Lent and Passiontide, and
others of a general kind.

Christmas and Epiphany carols obviously are concerned with the Mother
and Child, and some of them draw

attention to Mary in particular, either because of their content or the name by which they are known. "A virgin most pure," "Sweet was the song the virgin sang," and "The other night I saw a sight" are well-known examples. There are, too, specifically Salutation or Annunciation carols, such as this (first verse):

The angel Gabriel from God
　Was sent to Galilee,
Unto a maiden fair and free,
　Whose name was called Mary.
And when the angel thither came,
　He fell down on his knee,
And looking up in the maiden's face,
　He said, "All hail, Marý."

(Chorus)
Then sing we all, both great and
　small,
　Nowell, Nowell, Nowell;
We may rejoice to hear the voice
　Of the angel Gabriel.

Or this (last verse):

Then bespake the maid again
　And answered womanly,
"Whate'er my Lord commandeth me
　I will obey trulý."
With *"Ecce sum humillima*
　Ancilla Domini;
Secundum verbum tuum."
　She said, *"Fiat mihi."*

This mixture of two languages, called "macaronic" verse, is not unusual in carols. There are many versions of a carol about Mary's joys (five, seven, ten, or twelve), which was still remembered traditionally in England fifty

years ago. For Passiontide there is the lovely "Seven Virgins," beginning:

All under the leaves, the leaves of life,
　I met with virgins seven,
And one of them was Mary mild,
　Our Lord's mother from Heaven.

Mary and Joseph together are the subject of several carols, such as "When righteous Joseph wedded was" and the "Cherry-Tree Carol." This last, which seems to derive ultimately from an anecdote in *Pseudo-Matthew* (*q.v.*), is nowadays found offensive by some people, as presenting St. Joseph in too "human" a light; but our medieval ancestors were very "realist": the same legend occurs in the Coventry cycle of miracle-plays. Rather different is the one whose first and last verses are as follows:

O Joseph being an old man truly,
He married a virgin fair and free;
A purer maiden could no man see
Than he chose for his wife and his
　dearest dear.

The king of all power was in Bethle-
　hem born,
Who wore for our sakes a crown of
　thorn.
Then God preserve us both even and
　morn
For Jesu's sake, our dearest dear!

One short Marian carol may be quoted in full, if only because it is still sung traditionally in a west of England parish not far from the place where these lines are being written, the "Saint-Day Carol";

Now the holly bears a berry as white
as the milk,
And Mary bore Jesus, who was
wrapped up in silk.

(Chorus)
And Mary bore Jesus Christ our saviour for to be,
And the first tree in the greenwood, it
was the holly! holly! holly!
And the first tree in the greenwood it
was the holly.

Now the holly bears a berry as green
as the grass,
And Mary bore Jesus, who died on the
cross.

Now the holly bears a berry as black
as the coal,
And Mary bore Jesus, who died for us
all.

Now the holly bears a berry, as blood
is it red,
Then trust we our Saviour, who rose
from the dead.

All the carols that have been mentioned still have their traditional airs,
which perfectly match the words in
simple beauty, and whose melodic
basis is quite independent of harmony. Carols are best sung unaccom-
panied, or to some simple instrument
such as a fiddle or whistle-pipe. One
other may be mentioned, of the fifteenth century, "I sing of a maiden,
that is matchless," whose gentle loveliness has been given a fitting tune by
an organist of Westminster Cathedral,
Sir Richard Terry.

There has been a considerable revival of carol-singing during the past
half-century, and several good collections, arranged for singing in church,
street, and home, have been published: such are the *Oxford Book of
Carols,* the *Cowley Carol Book,* and a
smaller selection by R. R. Terry, *Old
Christmas Carols.* But it is still possible to take part in a "carol-service" at
which not a single genuine carol is
sung: the difference between carol and
hymn may be elusive, but it is real.—In
North America carols have of course
been brought from other countries besides England; these are a study in
themselves, and there is much work to
be done in collecting and translating
them. One of interest here has been
translated from Ukrainian as "A virgin today." Some of the best German
and French carols and tunes are included in the books mentioned above.
Cf., Hymns.

CASIMIR'S HYMN, ST. A name
sometimes given to the hymn which
is familiar in English, in Father H.
Bittleston's translation, as "Daily,
daily, sing to Mary." St. Casimir of
Poland (d. 1483) used often to recite
it, and he asked that a copy of it be
buried with him. But he did not write
it: it forms part of a long Latin rhyming lyric composed three centuries before his time, probably by Bernard of
Cluny (author of the well-loved *Urbs
Sion aurea,* translated by J. M. Neale
as "Jerusalem the golden"). Another
English version of *Omni die dic
Mariae* was made by Cardinal Wiseman (d. 1865); it is rather jingly:

Sing, sing, each day,
A tuneful lay,

My soul, to Mary's glory:
  Her feasts employ
  With pious joy,
To con her wondrous story.

CATAMARCA, OUR LADY OF.
The statue of Mary at this Argentinian shrine, called our Lady of the Valley of Catamarca, was found in a cave by a Spanish colonist. He set it up in his home, and before long miracles were reported. In 1688 our Lady under this title was chosen as the patroness of the Tucuman colony, and in 1891 the image was crowned. This crowning is commemorated locally in an annual feast on the second Saturday after Easter.

CAUSE OF OUR JOY. Latin, *Causa nostrae laetitiae,* an invocation of our Lady in the Litany of Loreto. Fundamentally, Mary is the cause of our joy because she brought into the world the Son of God made man for our salvation. And she who experienced such unexampled joys on earth is ever interceding with Him in Heaven that our joy, too, may be full, now and hereafter. A feast of our Lady under this name is observed in some churches in France and in Canada; *cf.,* Liesse, Our Lady of.

CAVERSHAM, OUR LADY OF.
Caversham is on the river Thames in Oxfordshire. Already in the twelfth century there was a separate chapel of the Blessed Virgin there, which was transferred to the bridge over the river, and became an important place of pilgrimage. It was looted and destroyed by King Henry VIII. The Catholic faith was brought back to Caversham by the Sisters of Mercy of Séez in 1896, and a church was built and consecrated. To it a benefactress gave an eighteenth-century statue of our Lady from Italy, which has gradually become an object of pilgrimage. Another statue, a medieval image of Mary suckling her Child, was acquired in 1955, and this will eventually grace a new shrine of our Lady of Caversham.

CEIGNAC, OUR LADY OF. The image of Mary at this shrine near Rodez in France has been venerated from remote times. The sanctuary was destroyed at the Revolution, but it was restored by Benedictine monks in 1825 and the statue was crowned in 1876. The great pilgrimage (*pardon*) of Ceignac takes place on the Sunday after the Assumption, and there is a lesser one on Ascension day. A commemoration of the crowning of the statue, with proper Mass and Office, is observed on July 9.

CENACLE, OUR LADY OF THE.
In some churches (e.g., in the dioceses of Charleston and Savannah, U.S.A.) a feast of our Lady under this title is kept on the Saturday after Ascension day. It is in effect the same feast as that of our Lady, Queen of Apostles (*q.v.*), and has reference to the time between our Lord's return to His Father in Heaven and the day of Pentecost, during which the Apostles "continued steadfastly in prayer with the women and Mary, the mother of Jesus, and with His brethren" (Acts 1:14). The title has been popularized by the

nuns of the Congregation of our Lady of the Retreat in the Cenacle, founded by Bl. Teresa Couderc in 1826. The word *cénacle* is the French form of Latin *coenaculum,* literally a "dining-room": the traditional English rendering is "upper room."

There is a very popular pilgrimage to the shrine of our Lady of Mercy in St. Similien's church at Nantes in Brittany, between Ascension and Pentecost, whose object is to keep watch with Mary and the Apostles in the upper room in preparation for the promised gift of the Paraclete. The institution of this observance is ascribed to an exiled Irish bishop about 1650: probably Patrick Comerford of Waterford, who was active in the work of redeeming captives in the name of our Lady of Ransom or Mercy.

CEYLON, SHRINES OF. The chief shrine of the Blessed Virgin in Ceylon is our Lady of Madhu (*q.v.*). In thanksgiving for preservation during World War II, the archbishop of Colombo, Msgr. J. M. Masson, o.m.i., proclaimed our Lady of Lanka as Queen of Ceylon; the building of a special sanctuary under this title at Tewatte was begun at the same time. Other shrines are our Lady of Lourdes at Kimbulapitiya, of Fatima at Padiewatte in the diocese of Kandy, and at Nattandiya in the diocese of Chilaw.

CHAOKIALING, OUR LADY OF. In 1870 a young Chinese priest, Father An, was struck by the beauty of the hill of Chaokialing in the province of Shensi, and determined to build a church in honor of Mary there. A serious difficulty to be overcome was lack of water at the spot, but the sinking of a well struck an unexpected supply, which Father An took to be a sign from Heaven. He persevered with his undertaking, and the church he built became the pilgrim-shrine for all Shensi, until communists destroyed it in 1943.

CHAPEL, OUR LADY OF THE, Würzburg. This German shrine is situated on a low hill near Würzburg, on which a chapel was built in honor of St. Nicholas in the seventeenth century. The image of the Blessed Virgin therein has been long famed for miracles, and it attracts many pilgrims to the chapel, which is attached to a Carmelite friary.

CHAPLET. A general name for the rosary and other devotions which are said with the help of beads. The Old French word *chapelet* meant the garland of flowers which in the middle ages was often worn on the head by clergy and others taking part in such special observances as a Corpus Christi procession; roses, violets, and sweet marjoram were commonly used for this purpose. Similar chaplets were offered to statues of our Lady, and eventually the word came to be applied to such circlets of beads as that of the rosary (*q.v.*). A medieval legend tells of our Lady taking rosebuds from the mouth of a young monk who was saying Hail Marys, plaiting them into a garland, and putting it on his head. This tale spread all over Europe and beyond, even to Ethiopia.

CHARITY, OUR LADY OF. It is interesting to find a church dedicated under this name in Brooklyn, N.Y., for it is very rare. In medieval England there was one such church, at the small inland port of Faversham in Kent, and there is one among the Catholic churches there today, at Daventry. The title is rather more common as a name for images (e.g., in Spain), and Malta keeps a feast of Mary under the title. There is a shrine of our Lady of Charity in the archdiocese of Santiago de Cuba. The image is said to have been brought there by a Spanish soldier in the seventeenth century. Our Lady of Charity is patroness of Cuba (Feast: October 27), and of such religious congregations as the Sisters of our Lady of Charity of the Refuge and the Good Shepherd nuns.

CHARTRES. Of all the ancient pilgrimage centers of France, Chartres is the greatest. The cathedral of Notre-Dame is probably the most beautiful gothic church in the world; in its crypt is the shrine of our Lady Underground (*q.v.*) and in the choir the statue of our Lady of the Pillar (*q.v.*); a reputed garment (*q.v.*) of hers is preserved in the treasury. Kings and princes, popes and prelates, saints and sinners, thousand after thousand of ordinary people have come here on pilgrimage for seven hundred years. The patronal feast of Chartres cathedral is Mary's birthday, September 8; the feast of its dedication is kept as a commemoration of our Lady, on October 17.

CHEVREMONT, OUR LADY OF. The shrine of the Mother of God on the hill called Chevremont, near Liége in Belgium, is of special interest to English people because it owes its existence to the English Jesuits who opened a college in Liége in 1616. They had a country house near by, and in 1688 restored a ruined chapel on the hill: the date may still be read on the building, with the inscription: *Sancta Maria, ora pro Anglia,* "Holy Mary, pray for England." The statue of the Mother of Mercy and her Child that they put there is only eight inches high, carved in sandstone, and now all dressed up. So numerous did pilgrims eventually become that in 1878 the Barefooted Carmelites were put in charge, and a church and friary were built close by. This church was very seriously damaged in World War II; at its restoration in 1948 the Belgian government issued a series of picture postage-stamps of the sanctuary to help pay the cost. Feast: July 9.

CHILDREN OF MARY. This is a general term used of members of various associations which promote fidelity to religion, virtue of life, and apostolic activity by fostering devotion to the Blessed Virgin. Such associations are, declared Pope Pius XII, "schools of godliness and active Christian life," and they form part of Catholic Action, provided they are organized in accordance with the points laid down in his constitution *Bis saeculari* (1948). For, said the pope, their "warm zeal for the life of the spirit comes as it were naturally to flower in new apostolic activities, answering to new circumstances and needs. We say without any hesitation that the Catholic formed to perfection as the Marian society has formed him, from its beginnings, is no less suited to the requirements of to-day than to those of days gone by."

At the beginning of the twelfth century a canon regular, Peter de Hones-tis, founded at Ravenna in Italy a confraternity of Sons and Daughters of Mary; the members wore a medal and a blue sash, and were associated with an icon called the Greek Madonna. Somewhere about 1600 another canon regular, St. Peter Fourier, established at Mattaincourt in France a similar society, of the Immaculate Conception, for girls. The early efforts of these canons eventually came to fruition through the work of Abbot Orestes Passeri, of the Canons Regular of the Lateran, at their church of St. Agnes-outside-the-Walls of Rome. He organized a sodality called Children of Mary under the protection of the Immaculate Virgin and St. Agnes, for girls and unmarried women: its aim was to foster personal goodness and fulfilment of duty towards God, neighbor, and self under our Lady's care. It was canonically established in 1864; two years later it received its first indulgences, and was made an archsodality, with power to affiliate and impart its own privileges to other similar sodalities in any part of the world.

The badge of the members is a medal, whose design includes our Lady welcoming children presented to her by St. Agnes, and the full name of the archsodality. The dress worn on special occasions, processions and the like, is a white gown and veil, with a blue sash. Only the unmarried may be admitted to membership; members who marry may continue as "honorary members." Affiliation to the archsodality rests with the abbot general of the Canons Regular of the Lateran, in Rome.—For other Children of Mary organizations, see the next two entries and under SODALITY OF THE BLESSED VIRGIN.

CHILDREN OF MARY IMMACU-LATE. Early in the nineteenth century Sisters of Charity of St. Vincent de Paul organized the girls under their care into a religious confraternity, and the visions of St. Catherine Labouré in 1830 gave great impetus to the movement. In 1847 Pope Pius IX granted the same indulgences as those of the Sodality B.V.M. (*q.v.*) of the Society of Jesus, and authorized the establishment of the association of Children of Mary Immaculate in any house of the Sisters of Charity; in 1931 this was extended to parochial churches anywhere. The badge of membership is the Miraculous Medal (*q.v.*), and the element of apostleship is emphasized, as Pope Pius XII declared to a pilgrimage of the members in 1947. The director general of this society is the superior general of the Priests of the Mission (Vincentians), in Paris.

CHILDREN OF MARY OF THE SACRED HEART. About 1818 St. Madeleine Sophie Barat established a Marian sodality for the pupils of her school in Paris; Father Joseph Varin, s.j., drew up the rules, and its motto was suggested by one of the members: *Cor meum jungatur vobis,* "May my heart be joined to you." Some years later the association was extended to include former pupils of the schools of the Society of the Sacred Heart; new rules were provided, and canonical recognition was given at Rome to the Children of Mary of the Sacred Heart. The sodality is now found all over the world in association with convents of the Sacred Heart, and its members have a fine record of apostolic works.

CHINA, SHRINES OF. The *cultus* (*q.v.*) of our Lady in China has been strongly conditioned by the religious and cultural temperament of the Chinese people: the emphasis is on reverence for Mary as Queen of Heaven and as the heavenly Mother of the individual, the family, the parish, the whole people. Her sanctuaries have not generally grown up around some wonderworking image or miraculous happening, but simply as particular centers of veneration. It has been said that Chinese devotion to Mary is "based on faith rather than sight, on gratitude more than on the unusual." The following old Chinese poem of natural relations is extended by the Christians to spiritual relations:

Father begot me,
Mother conceived me.
Together they gave me life,
fed me,
helped me to grow up,
wholly looked after me,
caressed me,
protected me in their arms,
and never left me.

How I long to love them in return, with a love that is as big as the sky!

Many Chinese parishes have separate little chapels of our Lady which are ordinarily hardly used, but on her special feast-days they are crowded with pilgrims come from over the neighborhood. The Chinese attach notable importance to the natural surroundings of their shrines; they should be in beautiful places, by preference on a hill, and these surroundings are an integral part of the shrine itself. The existence of a particular shrine of Mary in a particular spot may well be wholly due to the beauty of that spot, which is seen as an expression of their religious feelings.

China is of course a land of vast distances, and most of its shrines are known only locally. Three that deserve special mention are Zoseh, Tonglu, and Chaokialing (*qq.v.*), of which the second and third are at present in ruins owing to destruction by communists, a fate which has befallen so many other Chinese shrines and churches. Among the others, there is a sanctuary of our Lady of Sorrows at Tungerhkow, and of our Lady of the Angels at Hungkowtse, and of our Lady of Liesse (*q.v.*) near Kweiyang; the Marian processions at Chengtu in Szechwan are well known, and the shrine at Muozechan, in the diocese of Tsining, north of the Great Wall, attracts pilgrims from considerable distances. Two of Mary's churches in Peking (Peiping) are specially notable on account of their age: Nant'ang (of the Immaculate Conception) and Sit'-ang (of Mount Carmel) built in 1650 and 1723, respectively. In Manchuria, there is an old-established pilgrimage of our Lady of the Snows, whose sanctuary dominates the town of Siaohaichan.

CHIQUINQUIRÀ, OUR LADY OF. A shrine near Medellin in Colombia. A statue of our Lady of the Rosary was set up in a chapel here, in or before 1586, for at Christmas of that year attention was called to it by certain unexplained phenomena of light. From that day on it was much frequented by the faithful, and many graces and cures were reported. The *cultus* is found also in Venezuela and Ecuador. Feasts: November 18, July 9.

CHURCHES of Our Lady. See DEDICATIONS OF CHURCHES.

"CHURCHING." The blessing of a woman after childbirth and her act of thanksgiving. See PURIFICATION, FEAST OF THE.

CINCTURE. See GIRDLE.

CIRCUMCISION, Feast of our Lord's. Whoever examines the proper of the Mass for this feast cannot fail to notice the strong elements referring to Christmas (of which it is the octave-day) and to Mary, of whom the collect and post-communion make mention while ignoring the mystery celebrated. The same is true of the Divine Office. The explanation appears to be that we have here a relic of the time when the Roman Church observed January 1 as the octave of Christmas with special reference to our Lady—per-haps the first Marian feast in the West. There is also mention of a January feast of our Lady in Gaul and elsewhere. *Cf.,* Synaxis.

CLIENT. In classical Latin *cliens* meant a plebeian who was under the protection of a patrician, his *patronus;* etymologically the word perhaps meant one who was at the call of another. Hence among Catholics the word has come to be used of one who puts himself under the care of, and has a corresponding reverence for, our Blessed Lady or some other saint. The usage is perhaps not an altogether fortunate one in these days, since in English "client" now ordinarily suggests a business relationship between a man and his lawyer, or other professional person. *Cf.,* Patron.

CLONFERT, OUR LADY OF. Mary is venerated under this title in the church at Clonfert in County Galway, Ireland. The image is a statue of Mother and Child, standing, carved during the late thirteenth or early fourteenth century. It is somewhat damaged, but there is no good evidence that this was done deliberately by Cromwellian soldiers, as is sometimes stated. The history of the statue is unknown (it is said to have been found in a tree); it was enshrined at Clonfert about a generation ago. *Cf.,* Györ, Our Lady of.

COLORS. The custom in the Western Church of dressing the altar and wearing vestments according to colors associated with categories of feast and seasons was not finally regulated till the time of Pope St. Pius V (d. 1572). The color for feasts of the Blessed Virgin was then fixed as white (which includes cloth of gold and silver). Before that, throughout the later middle ages, the variety in choice and allocation of liturgical colors was endless; this was in part due to ingenious excursions into color symbolism and allusion. An early color-sequence, that of the Latin-rite canons at Jerusalem in the twelfth century, gave black to our Lady, by which no doubt was meant any dark neutral shade. (This may have had reference to the Song of Songs 1:4: "I am black but beautiful.") But at the same era in Rome her color was white, and in many places there seems to have been little variation from this: Mary's feasts were white nearly always in all parts of medieval England. But everywhere there was a tendency to use the best vestments, of whatever color, on great feasts.

In the middle ages blue was treated as a variant of violet or purple, and it was worn for at least some of our Lady's feasts in some European churches till recent times. In 1839 the Congregation of Sacred Rites referred to this as an abuse to be got rid of. But later in the century the use of blue was conceded to Spain and Spanish America for the feast of the Immaculate Conception and its octave. (This has also been allowed to a few particular churches, e.g., Downside abbey in England.) The idea that blue is peculiarly our Lady's color is quite modern and confined to the West. It has been popularized by pictures and statues, and perhaps especially by St. Bernadette's statement that Mary appeared to her wearing a blue sash. Certainly in England, where blue has been a token of fidelity at least since the sixteenth century ("true blue"), this color seems not inappropriate, though liable to be spoiled by the choice of "baby" shades.

There is an expression in French, *Vouer au blanc et au bleu,* literally, "To dedicate to the White and Blue." It signifies the dedication of a child to our Lady. It seems originally to have been *Vouer au blanc* only, and it appears that, when the child was brought to be consecrated, its white clothes were given to some other child who needed them.

COMMEMORATION. When a feast of our Lady (or other saint) falls upon a day of higher rank than itself it is sometimes ignored for that year, sometimes deferred, and sometimes commemorated. This last means that, at Mass, the collect, secret, and post-communion of the lower feast are added after those prayers in the proper of the feast kept. Thus, for example, when the Holy Name of Mary falls on a Sunday (as in 1954), the day's Mass is of the Sunday, with a commemoration, as above, of our Lady.—But for a few feasts the word "commemoration" is part of the title, as the Commemoration of our Lady of Mount Carmel.

COMMUNION OF SAINTS, The. (Lat. *communio,* sharing in common, fellowship). The communion of saints affirmed in the baptismal creed of the Church is the unity under and in Christ of the faithful on earth, the souls in Purgatory, and the blessed in Heaven, among whom there is communication of and sharing in spiritual goods of all kinds. Among these goods are the superabundant merits of Mary in which we all share; the Christian is able fruitfully to pray to her, and to benefit from her intercession in Heaven, by virtue of the communion of saints; and our love for her and hers for us is all part of that fellowship of prayer, faith, and love which unites the potential saints on earth, the suffering saints in Purgatory, and the blessed saints in Heaven under Christ Jesus, who is her Head and ours. "Each of us has one body, with many different parts, and not all these parts have the same function; just so we, though many in number, form one body in Christ, and each acts as the counterpart of another" (Rom. 12:4-5).

COMPASSION OF OUR LADY. Devotion to Mary's sorrows (*q.v.*) had its origin in meditation on our Lady and St. John standing at the foot of the cross on Calvary, her "compassion" in the deepest meaning of the word, "suffering with." It is first found in the writings of St. Anselm of Canterbury (d. 1109) and other monks of his age, then in an office attributed to St. Bonaventure (d. 1274), and was later developed by such mystics as Bl. Henry Suso, Tauler, Gerson, and St. Bridget. Many hymns were devoted to the theme, of which few are now remembered except *Stabat Mater dolorosa* (*q.v.*), and it inspired many pictures and statues, especially in the form of the *pietà* (*q.v.*). The old feast of the Compassion of our Lady (or her Piercing or Lamenting and other names), observed in various parts of Europe, is now represented by the general Lenten feast of the Seven Sorrows (*q.v.*); this feast is still called our Lady of Pity or of Compassion by the Dominicans and Carthusians, in the dioceses of Hildesheim in Germany and of Goa in India, in Mexico, and elsewhere. It is due to the origin referred to above that the gospel at Mass on both feasts of the Seven Sorrows is St. John 19:25-27 and not the passage from St. Luke containing Simeon's prophecy of the sword; the epistle is a particularly fitting passage from the book of Judith (13:22-25), accommodated to Mary.

Pope Leo XIII, who had a special devotion for Mary's sorrows and issued an encyclical letter on the subject (*Jucunda semper,* 1894), founded at the church of St. Sulpice in Paris a Confraternity of our Lady of Compassion whose members should pray for the return of Great Britain to the Catholic faith; St. Pius X extended its object to all English-speaking peoples. Churches dedicated in honor of our Lady of Compassion are not unknown in England today. See also SUFFERINGS.

CONCEPTION, Feast of Mary's. See IMMACULATE CONCEPTION.

CONFITEOR, Our Lady in the. In its earliest known forms (ninth century) the Confiteor was addressed to Almighty God alone; but the names of our Lady and then other saints were later introduced. For example, in 1184 the Cistercian monks adopted a form beginning "I confess to God, and to blessed Mary and all the saints. . . ." In those orders that have retained medieval forms, e.g., the Dominicans, Mary is the only saint named besides the founder of the order. All the several forms of the Confiteor now in use in the Latin rite invoke the Mother of God as a witness to the self-accusation and usually add a petition for her prayers.

CONFRATERNITIES, MARIAN.

Confraternity is the word generally used in English to designate all societies of lay people, canonically set up under ecclesiastical direction, for the promotion of the spiritual welfare of their members; with this is often associated general or particular works of apostleship. When such a confraternity has been accorded the right to aggregate other similar societies to itself, with participation in its own indulgences and other privileges, it is called an archconfraternity. A confraternity usually has its origin in, and associates itself with, devotion to some particular mystery of religion, some holy person, or some special religious observance. Not infrequently a confraternity is associated with and directed by a religious order or congregation; however, "third orders" are not confraternities, but an integral part of the religious order concerned. Many confraternities are world-wide, others are purely local.

A Confraternity of the Mother of God existed at Naupaktos in Greece in the middle of the eleventh century, and many religious and charitable societies were organized under her name during the later middle ages; it was at this time that the older existing confraternities came into being. But most of the present Marian confraternities date from the Catholic revival after the Protestant Reformation, or subsequently, the Jesuit sodalities being the example on which many others were based. Confraternities of our Lady of one sort or another are very numerous; the following is a list of the chief of them, and nearly all are archconfraternities.

The Confraternity of the Assumption for prayer for the dead; the Children of Mary (q.v.); Confraternity of our Lady of Compassion (q.v.); C. of O.L. of Consolation (q.v.); the same, "of the Girdle" (q.v.); C. of O.L. of Good Counsel (q.v.); C. of O.L., Health of the Sick (q.v.); C. of O.L., Help of Christians (founded by St. John Bosco); C. of the Immaculate Conception (founded at Lourdes, 1872); the same, of the Theatine Order (cf., Scapular of Mary Immaculate); C. of the Immaculate Heart (q.v.) for the conversion of sinners (this was established by Bishop B. J. Flaget at Louisville, Ky., so early as 1843); C. of O.L. of Reconciliation of La Salette; the Legion of Mary (q.v.); C. of O.L. of Loreto; C. of the Miraculous Medal (q.v.); the Militia of Mary Immaculate, under the direction of the Conventual Friars Minor; C. of O.L., Mother of Mercy (cf., Pellevoisin); C. of the Heart of the Wonderful Mother (founded by St. John Eudes); C. of the Name of Mary; C. of O.L. of Perpetual Help (q.v.); C. of O.L. of Prompt Succor (q.v.), of American origin; C. of O.L., Mother of Divine Providence (founded by the

Barnabite fathers in 1744); C. of O.L., Queen of our Hearts (*cf.*, Slavery to Mary); C. of O.L. of Ransom (*q.v.*); the Rosary Confraternity (*q.v.*); C. of O.L. of the Sacred Heart, founded in 1864 at Issoudun in France; the Scapular Confraternity (*q.v.*) of O.L. of Mount Carmel; the Sodality (*q.v.*) of the Blessed Virgin; C. of the Seven Sorrows (*q.v.*); C. of O.L. of Sorrows for Christian Mothers (several associations); C. of the Three "Hail Marys" (*q.v.*). Some of these confraternities have their own special rosaries and scapulars (*qq.v.*).

In his *Glories of Mary*, St. Alphonsus Liguori writes: "Confraternities, especially those of our Blessed Lady, are so many Noah's arks, in which those who live 'in the world' find a refuge from the flood of temptations and sins that deluge it. From our own experience in giving missions we know how much good these confraternities do. As a rule, a man who does not belong to and go to the meetings of a confraternity commits more sins than twenty who do. A confraternity may well be called a tower of David. . . . Each member should be careful about two things: First, the object he has in view, which is to serve God and God's mother Mary and to save his soul alive. Then, not to let worldly affairs prevent his attendance at meetings, for there he has to attend to the most important business of all, his eternal salvation."

CONGRESS, MARIAN. A Marian congress is analogous to a Eucharistic congress, being an assembly of clergy and laity for the study of matters connected with our Lady, by the reading and discussion of papers, and for religious services in her honor. Such congresses range in scope from international to specific groups, as when, in the Marian year 1954, the Catholics of Eastern rites in the whole United States held a Marian congress at Philadelphia, at which, of course, many Western Catholics attended. In France, a national Marian congress has been held every four years (except during World War II), beginning in 1927; and in 1950 and 1954 congresses were organized on an international scale at Rome. In the same year a national congress was held in Canada. Other international Marian gatherings have been held at Fribourg (1902), Einsiedeln (1906), Saragossa (1908), Salzburg (1911), Trier (1912), and of sodalities of Mary at Barcelona in 1947.

CONQUISTADORA, LA, Santa Fe. After Diego de Vargas reoccupied Santa Fe, N.M., for Spain in 1692, he brought a small statue of the Blessed Virgin from Mexico and made a vow annually to commemorate her in thanksgiving. That statue, called *La Conquistadora,* our Lady of Victory, is now in the cathedral at Santa Fe, and every year, on the Sunday after Corpus Christi, De Vargas' vow is still honored. The statue is taken in procession to the Rosary chapel, two miles away (where the vow is said to have been made), and left there till the following Sunday; it is then returned in procession to its home in the cathedral. Special services are held during the week, and many pilgrims assemble.

CONSECRATION TO MARY.

The consecration of oneself to our Lady is commonly understood in a general sense of dedication to her service and example, and its practical significance depends on the devotion of the person making it: a daily act of consecration may be no more than one more pious formula, or it may be a daily inspiration.—The most common example of consecration of someone else is the usage in many places of the priest, on behalf of the parents, offering a newly baptized child before the Lady altar or statue. Some diocesan rituals contain prayers for this purpose, e.g.: "Lady of ours, who on Calvary heard your dying Son entrust to you the apostle John, and in that moment became also our Mother, be pleased to accept as your son (daughter) this child of God N . . . , who has just been hallowed by baptism in the blood of Jesus your Son . . ." (Cambrai; medieval).—Of consecrations *en masse* by their religious head, an outstanding example is the consecration of the human race to the Immaculate Heart (*q.v.*) of Mary by Pope Pius XII in 1942.

Personal consecration to Mary is particularly associated with the name of St. Louis Grignion de Montfort, who in his *True Devotion* (*q.v.*) gives a form for this consecration: "As your slave, I give up and consecrate to you my body and my soul, all my goods, interior and exterior, and the worth of my good deeds, past, present and to come. I give you the full and com-plete right to dispose of me and of everything whatever that belongs to me according to your good pleasure, for the greater glory of God, now and for ever." The outward practices recommended by the saint in support of this consecration include the frequent saying of the Magnificat (*q.v.*). The inward dispositions are that all things should be done through Mary, with Mary, in Mary, and for Mary. This consecration is of course linked with Cardinal de Bérulle's "slavery to Mary" (*q.v.*), and like him Montfort sees it as a binding to Jesus in or through His Mother: "As the principal mystery celebrated and honored in this devotion is the Incarnation, wherein Jesus Christ is seen only in Mary, incarnate in her womb, it is better to speak of servitude to Jesus in Mary, Jesus dwelling and reigning in her. . . . This way of speaking better expresses the close unity between them. . . ."—Among those who have preached this consecration were Father Henry Ramière, s.j., promoter of the Apostleship of Prayer, and the revered Cardinal Mercier. Bl. Theophane Vénard consecrated himself to Mary by St. Louis' formula the day before he was martyred at Tongking in 1861.

CONSOLATA, The, Turin.

This is the most important Marian sanctuary in Piedmont and one of the best known in Italy. The people of Turin are said to have had a special devotion to Mary under her aspect of consoler or comforter from very early times, but the first certain reference to the venerated image seems to be

in the eleventh century. It is a Byzantine icon of the Hodegetria (*q.v.*)
type, not unlike the one in St. Mary
Major (*q.v.*) at Rome. Among the numerous pilgrims who have visited it
were St. Charles Borromeo, St. Francis de Sales, and Pope Pius VII. In
recognition of delivery from plague,
the Confraternity of the Consolata
was established in the sixteenth century. The city's victory over the besieging French in 1706 was attributed
to our Lady's intercession, and the
event has been commemorated yearly
ever since, on September 7. The picture, crowned in 1829, is kept in an
imposing chapel in the church built
for it in 1682 by the Savoyard duke,
Victor Amadeus II. The Consolata
gives its name to a society of foreign-
missionary priests. Feast: June 20. *Cf.*,
West Grinstead, Our Lady of.

CONSOLATION, OUR LADY OF.
A feast of our Lady of Consolation
(or "of Comfort") is kept in a number of places on June 20 and other
dates, and it is the title of the pilgrimage images at Turin, at the
Capuchin church of Reggio in Cala-
bria, at Épinal in France, Carey in
Ohio, and elsewhere. It is the patronal
festival of St. Mary's abbey at Stanbrook in England, a house of Benedictine nuns founded at Cambrai in
France in 1625.—The invocation
(which sometimes appears in America
as "of Solace") is of course the same
as that in the Litany of Loreto, *Con-
solatrix afflictorum,* "Comforter of
the Afflicted"; the feast is kept under
that name in some places, e.g., Luxemburg, by the Marists, and by the

Russians (October 24). The friars of
St. Augustine have a special devotion
to our Lady of Consolation and direct the confraternity of that name,
with its girdle and rosary (*qq.v.*). See
also CONSOLATA; WEST GRINSTEAD.

In 1875 Father Joseph P. Gloden
set up a replica of the statue of our
Lady of Luxemburg (*q.v.*) in his
church at Carey, Ohio, and zealously
fostered devotion to Mary under the
invocation "of Consolation." Then
the Conventual Franciscan friars took
charge of the parish, and the devotion became so popular that a larger
church had to be built, which was
dedicated in 1925. It is a building of
severe and dignified lines, in the Italian romanesque style, and the sanctuary attracts so many pilgrims that
a hostel has had to be opened for
their convenience. The robes of the
statue of Mother and Child are varied
according to the season of the
Church's year. Father Gloden established a Confraternity of our Lady of
Consolation, to which Pope Leo XIII
granted indulgences in 1878.

The collect of the proper Mass of
our Lady of Consolation runs: "Lord
Jesus Christ, Father of mercies and
God of all consolation, grant in thy
mercy that we, who gird up our loins
that on earth we may joyfully venerate thy all-pure Mother Mary as
our Lady of Comfort, may be found
worthy to enjoy fellowship with her
in Heaven for ever." Cardinal Newman writes: "This is the secret of true
consolation: those are able to comfort others who in their own case
have been much tried, and have felt
the need of consolation, and have re-

ceived it. . . . And this too is why the Blessed Virgin is the comforter of the afflicted. We all know how special a mother's consolation is, and we are allowed to call Mary our Mother from the time that our Lord from the cross established the relation of mother and son between her and St. John. And she especially can console us because she suffered more than mothers in general."

CONSTANTINOPLE, OUR LADY OF.

Several of the many Byzantine icons in southern Italy and Sicily are venerated under this title. The most celebrated, a Hodegetria (*q.v.*), is in the cathedral at Bari. It was crowned in 1772, and the feast of our Lady of Constantinople as patroness of Apulia is observed on the first Tuesday in March. Another such icon is at Monte Vergine (*q.v.*), and there is one in the church of St. Matthias at Trier in Germany.

COPACABANA, OUR LADY OF.

One of the oldest sanctuaries of Mary in the Americas, at an Indian village by Lake Titicaca in northern Bolivia. Here, in a chapel called the Camarin, a statue of the Blessed Virgin was enshrined in 1583; it had been made, of plaster and wood, by an Indian named Yupanqui, and was a fishermen's thank-offering for deliverance from a tempest on the lake. The shrine became so popular that eventually a large church was built by order of a Spanish viceroy. The intense devotion aroused by this image is not only local: pilgrims flock to the shrine from distant places in Bolivia and Peru. Copacabana was a place of religious importance before the coming of Christianity; and, at least till recently, pilgrimages were often accompanied by disorders of heathen origin that the clergy had tried in vain to get rid of. A curious piece of local folk-lore is that the image must never be taken from its shrine, as "she does not want to be outside." The statue of our Lady of Copacabana was crowned in 1925.

CO-REDEMPTRESS or CO-REDEMPTRIX.

See REDEMPTION, MARY AND THE.

CORONATION OF OUR LADY, The.

The idea of a coronation of Mary in Heaven after her Assumption took its rise in an accommodation of the words in the Song of Songs (4:8), "Come, my bride, from Lebanon . . . thou shalt be crowned . . . ," and was chiefly developed and popularized by iconography (*q.v.*). The earliest existing example is probably the mosaic in Santa Maria in Trastevere at Rome, where our Lady is depicted already crowned, sitting at the right hand of her Son; this dates from about 1140. A century later there appears what became the usual design, Christ putting a crown upon His Mother's head. The theme was popular in English medieval carving, and it was everywhere highly embroidered and developed at the Renaissance. Among more recent artists the subject has aroused little interest, and Catholics today are familiar with it chiefly from the last glorious mystery of the rosary. But even there the Coronation is a comparatively recent version of a wider theme (*cf.*, Mystery). Its meaning clearly is symbolically to suggest the final "moment," as it were, of the Assumption, and the reference of the Apocalypse to "a crown of twelve stars" (12:1) has had its influence. St. Bernard and St. Albert the Great, among others, interpret these stars by reference to Mary's life and virtues. *Cf.*, Queen, Mary as.

A *feast* of our Lady's Coronation in Heaven used to be kept in a few places, but it is now disused. Other local so-called Coronation feasts, of which there are a few, are commemorations of the crowning (*q.v.*) of an image. The feast, kept in the Bridgettine Order on August 29, called the *Glorificatio B.M.V.*, is called in a calendar of 1748, and still by the nuns in English, the Coronation. Whatever its exact origin, it seems to be a second feast of the Assumption, emphasizing the bodily aspect of that mystery: the Mass is as on August 15 (*Et te in glorificatione beatae Mariae* in the preface). —The Catholic church at Glossop in England is dedicated under the name of St. Mary the Crowned, recalling the verse of a medieval carol:

After to Heaven He took His flight,
And there He sits with His Father of
    might,
With Him is crowned that Lady
    bright,
        Redemptoris Mater.

And this fifteenth-century stanza:

Filia Sion, thou art the flower;
Full sweetly shalt thou sit by me

And bear a crown with me in tower;
And all my saints to thine honór
Shall honor thee, Mother, in my bliss,
That blessed body that bear me in
    bower—
Veni, coronaberis.

COVADONGA, OUR LADY OF. About the year 718 the Visigothic hero Pelayo gained a victory over the Moors at Covadonga in the Cantabrian mountains. It is with this battle that the reconquest of Spain is traditionally said to have begun, and our Lady of Covadonga is a national sanctuary. It is in Asturias, near Oviedo. The image of Mother and Child is enshrined in a cave, reminiscent in shape of that at Lourdes, but much less accessibly situated, at the source of a river that dashes down beneath the shrine. The figures are vested in stiff robes, but the Virgin's face is notably impressive.—The first long poem of the American writer and actress Anna Cora Mowatt (d. 1870) was called "Pelayo, or The Cavern of Cavadonga."

CRAG, OUR LADY OF THE. See KNARESBURGH, OUR LADY OF.

CROWN. The name given to some devotions in which beads are used; it has the sense of wreath or garland (see CHAPLET). In Latin, *corona*, it is used of rosary beads of all kinds: for example, in the Roman Ritual there are forms for Blessing the Crown of the holy Rosary of the Blessed Virgin Mary, Blessing of the Crown of the Seven Sorrows B.V.M., and so on. Other "crowns" are mentioned below.

CROWN, FRANCISCAN or SE-RAPHIC. See ROSARY OF THE SEVEN JOYS.

CROWN OF OUR LADY, LITTLE. This devotion is recommended by St. Louis Mary de Montfort in his *True Devotion* (*q.v.*). Essentially it consists of the Lord's Prayer thrice and Hail Mary twelve times in honor of the Blessed Virgin's twelve privileges, but in detail it takes several forms. The indulgenced version has three prayers, invoking Mary by twelve privileges, from her immaculate conception to her power of intercession; the Lord's Prayer is said once and the Hail Mary four times after each of these prayers, and there is a final collect. *Cf.* the entry below.

CROWN OF TWELVE STARS. The name and idea of this devotion are derived from the twelve stars of Apocalypse 12:1, which are interpreted by St. Bernard, St. Albert, Thomas à Kempis, and other writers in varying ways. The indulgenced version of the prayer consists principally of three groups of four praises of the Persons of the Holy Trinity, in this form: "Praised be God the Father, who predestined her [Mary] to be the mother of His Son," followed by the Hail Mary. The other "stars" enumerated are: the Immaculate Conception, Mary's birth, her marriage, the Incarnation, Christ's birth, His upbringing by Mary, His revelation to her of the mystery of the Redemption, the revelation to her of the Holy Spirit's name at the Annunciation, Mary as virgin yet mother, Mary as the living temple of the Godhead, and her exaltation in Heaven. Each group is preceded by a praise of the pertinent divine Person, followed by the Lord's Prayer. *Cf.* the entry above.

CROWNING OF IMAGES. The crowning of a statue or picture of the Blessed Virgin (or other saint) is not simply the making of an image with a crowned figure or the adding of a crown or diadem to an image: it is an honorific rite, that may be carried out only with authoritative permission. A prerogative of granting such permission is vested in the chapter of canons of St. Peter's basilica at Rome; it is accorded, at the ordinary's request, in respect of images of notable antiquity or dignity, to which the faithful are wont to resort in considerable numbers. The symbolic crowning of an image is a custom of great antiquity, going back to before the Christian era. Its present popularity among Catholics dates from 1597, when Pope Clement VIII crowned the icon of Mother and Child in St. Mary Major (*q.v.*). Soon after this, Count Alexander Sforza-Pallavicini (d. 1640) bequeathed a sum of money to the chapter of the Vatican basilica for the provision of crowns for images of our Lady. Already during his lifetime he had enabled the canons to crown one of her statues in St. Peter's, and ever since then the matter has been largely in their hands. But not infrequently the pope grants authorization directly.

The rite used on the occasion of a crowning, which is done by the bishop of the place, or a canon of St. Peter's or other prelate (occasionally by the pope himself), is found in the Roman Pontifical. It begins with the antiphon *Sub tuum praesidium* (*q.v.*). Then the crowns are blessed, with the following prayer: "Almighty and ever-living God, who in thy mercy didst ordain that all things should be created out of nothing, we humbly beseech thy majesty that thou wouldst be pleased to bless and hallow these crowns, made to adorn the sacred image of thine only-begotten Son, Jesus Christ, our Lord, and of his Mother, the most blessed Virgin Mary. Through the same Christ our Lord. Amen." *Regina caeli* (*q.v.*) is then sung. Afterward the celebrant puts the crowns on the image, saying these words, for the Holy Child: "May we who crown thee on earth deserve to be crowned by thee one day in Heaven." And for the Mother: "May we who crown thee on earth deserve through thee to be crowned one day in Heaven by Christ Jesus thy Son." Then follows a prayer for those who visit the shrine, the singing of *Te Deum laudamus,* and a final prayer.

When the image is a picture, the crowns are fixed to the canvas or board, or suspended immediately above the figures. The addition of crowns not only gives honor to the Divine Child and His Mother, they sometimes enhance the dignity and beauty of the material image. More often, it is to be feared, they detract from that dignity, through lack of proportion and unity of treatment between figure and crown: the visual effect of the crown on certain statues is not less than grotesque. In the United States and Canada the best-known crowned images are our Lady of Prompt Succor and our Lady of the Cape (*qq.v.*), and there is a number of them in Latin America. In Ireland our Lady of Knock and our Lady of Limerick (*qq.v.*) were crowned in 1954. In Great Britain five images have been crowned, viz., our Lady of West Grinstead, of Walsingham, of Willesden, of St. George's cathedral, Southwark, and of the Miraculous Medal in the church of the Assumption, Warwick Street, London. In addition, it has recently been discovered that, by brief of Pope Pius IX, two statues at the Convent of the Faithful Virgin, Upper Norwood, were crowned in 1878—the first in England.

The crowning of Mary's statue with a wreath of flowers or the like is a common custom of May devotions (*cf.,* Chaplet; Month of Mary). It is an old custom in churches of the Servite Order that, after Compline on Holy Saturday, flowers are blessed and distributed to the faithful, that "there may be in them goodness, virtue, tranquillity, peace, victory, plenteousness of good things, fullness of blessing, thanksgiving to God the Father and the Son and the Holy Ghost, and a most pleasing commemoration of the glorious Mother of God." Then, while *Regina caeli* is sung, the statue of our Lady is crowned. *Cf.,* Queen, Mary as.

CSIKSOMLYO, OUR LADY OF. The Seklers are an element among the Hungarian minority that lives side by side with the Rumanians in Transylvania. At Csiksomlyo (Sumuleu) they have a shrine of Mary that is venerated among all Catholics of those parts, especially those of Latin rite. It is in the church of the Franciscan friars, where there is a wooden statue of Mother and Child that has been esteemed miraculous since at least the sixteenth century. The provenance of this image has been much discussed, but it seems to be of local workmanship. Mary's face is strong and composed, but, as on so many statues, the crown is badly designed.

CULTUS, CULT (Latin, worship; the word is derived from *colere,* to till). In current usage the English word "cult" tends to degenerate into a colloquial expression for widespread popularity, e.g., "the cult of T-V"; but the religious meaning of *cultus* in Christianity is primarily the giving to God of all that worship and manifold service which is due to Him as God. In a secondary and very common sense, it is the veneration accorded to our Lady, the angels, and the other saints, and the various ways in which that veneration may be expressed. The nature and conditions of the *cultus* of the Blessed Virgin are referred to in various places in this book (see, e.g., HYPERDULIA); but a special case arises when she is reported to have appeared, or otherwise manifested herself at some particular place or some particular occasion, say, at "Notown." Unless and until the ecclesiastical authority rejects the alleged happening, any person is at liberty prudently to give a *private cultus* to our Lady with reference to the alleged events at Notown. But the corresponding *public cultus* is strictly forbidden until the competent ecclesiastical authority, in the person of the local bishop, expressly sanctions it. Public *cultus* includes such things as the organization of public prayers or pilgrimages in such a way as to appear to commit the Church, the setting-up of an image of "our Lady of Notown" above an altar, the putting of *ex-voto* tablets or vigil lights at the place concerned, and so forth. But contrary customs sometimes grow up and are tacitly allowed in respect of some of these provisions.—*Relative cultus* is that given indirectly to a person through a thing, e.g., the veneration of a picture or relic of a saint. *Cf.,* Devotion; Veneration.

CURSUS MARIANUS. See OFFICE OF OUR LADY, LITTLE.

CUYO, OUR LADY OF. A sanctuary at Mendoza in the Argentine Republic. The statue goes back to the earliest Spanish days, and appears to have been in the Jesuit church which was handed over to the Franciscans when King Charles III drove out the Jesuits in 1767. This statue was an object of special devotion to General José de San Martín, leader in the war for independence against the Spaniards; in 1812 he sent his military baton to the shrine as an *ex-voto* (*q.v.*). The image of our Lady of Cuyo was crowned in 1911.

CZECHOSLOVAKIA, SHRINES OF. Sanctuaries of Mary are very numerous in Czechoslovakia, and the people's devotion to her is very marked. Among them may be mentioned the following, grouped in regions. *Bohe-*

mia: our Lady of Sorrows in the Franciscan church at Bechyne; O.L. of Loreto at Hajek, near Prague; the Franciscan church at Heinice (now a communist prison for clergy); O.L. of Tyn, and others, at Prague; O.L. of Pribram; at Stara Boleslav, a crowned icon in the Redemptorist church, called the Protection of Bohemia; Svata Hora, at Pribram, a crowned statue. *Moravia:* O.L. of Hostyn, an icon in the Jesuit church; O.L. of Sloup; Velehrad (*q.v.*); Svata Hora, in the Norbertine church at Olomuc. *Slovakia:* shrines at Levoč, Klokočov, Šašov, O.L. of the Valley, near Bratislava, and many others.

The *Subcarpathian* region (Podkarpatska Rus) has now been incorporated in the U.S.S.R., but may be mentioned here. A large majority of the people are Ruthenian Catholics of the Slav-Byzantine rite. In 1946 the chief shrines of our Lady were at Bukova Hirka, Čirč, Krasny Brod, Mikhalovce, Mukačevo (*q.v.*), and Sabinov. Two of these, Mikhalovce and Sabinov, were at houses of Byzantine Redemptorists.

CZESTOCHOWA, OUR LADY OF. This most famous of Polish sanctuaries has grown up around an icon of the Mother of God attributed to St. Luke (*cf.,* Likenesses). It is a popular belief that it was brought from Constantinople by Princess Anna when she married St. Vladimir, grand-prince of Kiev, about the year 988; or that it was sent later, by one of the Com-

nenian emperors, to a royal abbess at Polotsk. Certainly in the fourteenth century it was at Belz in western Ukraine, whence in 1382 it was taken and entrusted to the monks of St. Paul the Hermit, newly arrived from Hungary, at Czestochowa, some 140 miles southwest of Warsaw. The image has ever since been the occasion of very great devotion and of numerous miracles. The great sanctuary is the heart of an amazing complex of churches, hostels, ancient fortifications, arcades, and shops; it dominates the rocky hill below which modern industrial Czestochowa sprawls. The icon itself (which inspired a well-known ballad by Hilaire Belloc) is of uncertain age: it has been attributed to the ninth and to the thirteenth century. It seems to be Greek, possibly Italo-Greek, in origin. It is of the Hodegetria (*q.v.*) type, our Lady's face scarred by blows of a weapon; but it cannot ordinarily be seen properly because of its ornaments. It was crowned in 1726 and again in 1910.

At the restoration of Poland after World War I, Czestochowa was made a bishopric; the pilgrimage became more popular than ever, and the place (which as a fortress has played a most notable part in Polish military history) was confirmed as the national shrine. In 1948 it was visited by two million pilgrims. Feast: the last Wednesday in August. Several churches in the United States are dedicated in Mary's honor under this title, which is often written Czenstochowa.

D

DAVID, HOUSE OF. See GENEAL-OGY OF MARY.

DE BEATA [Virgine Maria]. A Mass or Office *de Beata* is a Mass or Office of our Lady. At one time it was the custom in many monasteries and other big churches to celebrate a community Mass *de Beata* or *de Domina* every day (as well as the Mass of the day), called in England the Mary-Mass. This has now mostly been abolished, but is still observed in, e.g., the larger houses of canons regular of Prémontré (Norbertines); and in some monasteries (e.g., Carthusian) a private Mass is offered in Mary's honor daily. As well, each Carthusian priest recites privately every day in his cell the prayers of a Mass of our Lady, omitting those of the offertory, canon, and communion (a "dry Mass"). See also OFFICE, BRIDGETTINE.

DEATH OF MARY. It is probably true to say that, unless the matter be brought to his notice, it never occurs to any ordinary Catholic that it is possible to question that our Lady died before she was taken up, body and soul, into Heaven. The Redemption did not restore immunity from death and the other pains of this life to human nature; even the Savior willed Himself to be subject to them. In his *Catholic Catechism* (Eng. trans., 1934), Cardinal Gasparri stated plainly: "The Church holds that the body of the Blessed Virgin Mary was separated from her soul (for that is the meaning of death), but that her soul was reunited to her incorrupt body and that she was taken up into Heaven. . . ." Nevertheless, a few theologians have maintained, and still maintain, that Mary did not die; and when Pope Pius XII defined the Assumption (*q.v.*) in 1950, his constitution *Munificentissimus Deus* (*q.v.*) did not define that she died. But he does say therein that the faithful "had no difficulty in accepting the fact that even the great Mother of God departed this life, as her only Son had done"; and he quotes many Fathers who take it for granted that our Lady did die; and this, coupled with the long and almost unanimous tradition among Christians to the same effect, makes it difficult to sustain any other view. It certainly seems significant in this connection that the second nocturn lessons at Matins in the old office of the Assumption have been retained in the new office; they are from a discourse of St. John Damascene and affirm Mary's death periphrastically but unequivocally: "This day the unsullied Virgin . . . took her place in the courts of Heaven, for true life had flowed from her to all mankind, and how should she taste of death? But she yielded to the law laid down by Him whom she had brought forth;

and as a daughter of the old Adam she underwent the old sentence, which even her Son, who is life itself, had not refused . . ." (Lesson 5). Mary's complete conformity to her Son and her unique part in the Redemption (*q.v.*) would seem to require that she should follow Him in this too.

Mary, writes St. Francis de Sales (d. 1622), died of love; on Calvary love had made her experience the deepest sorrows of death, and her own death gave her the highest happiness of love. "The Virgin Mary's memory ever garnered in her mind all the loveworthy mysteries of her Son's life and death, finding in them the burning inspirations which the Sun of Justice cast upon the world at the high noon of His charity, making of them a constant act of contemplation. And at last the sacred fire of divine love wholly consumed her as a burnt-offering of joyousness, so that she died of it, her soul being rapt and carried away into the arms of her Son's love."

DECADE (Gr. *deka,* ten). A fifth, or one mystery (*q.v.*), of the rosary, consisting of the Lord's Prayer, Hail Mary ten times, and Glory be to the Father once, with meditation on one or other of the mysteries; also the corresponding beads on a rosary (*q.v.*).

DEDICATION, FEASTS OF. A number of festivals in the Church's calendars originated in the commemoration of the dedication of a church, for instance, St. Peter *ad Vincula* on August 1, Michael the Archangel on September 29. Where churches of our Lady are concerned the outstanding example is the feast familiarly called our Lady of the Snow (August 5), really the commemoration of the dedication of the basilica of St. Mary Major (*q.v.*) at Rome. Another well-known Roman example is our Lady of the Martyrs (*q.v.*) on May 13, and a feast of the same name on the same date is kept in the archdiocese of Lisbon, in respect of a church dedicated in that city in 1147. The Franciscan feast of our Lady of the Angels on August 2 marks the dedication of the church of that name at Assisi. There are other local examples. In the East, the Syrians observe the dedication of the church of the Mother of God at Caesarea Philippi, and the Copts have three such feasts or memorials: of Mary's churches at Caesarea, Atrib, near Old Cairo, and Matariah (Heliopolis, On). The church at Caesarea was quite erroneously supposed to be the first church ever dedicated in Mary's honor, by St. Peter himself. *Cf.,* Dedications.

DEDICATIONS OF CHURCHES. A church is commonly and conveniently said to be dedicated *to* Saint So-and-so, but in fact no church is dedicated to any saint. A church is dedicated to God, and to God only: but to do honor to the saints, and to distinguish one church from another, the custom arose of dedicating churches *to* God *in honor of,* or in memory or under the name of, a saint. At first no primary emphasis was put on our Lady in this matter: the first particular recorded church bearing her name seems to be one at Ephesus in the year 431; the church of St.

Mary Major (*q.v.*) in Rome was consecrated soon after. Writing about 730, the English St. Bede mentions only six Marian churches in his country. A century later, however, an incomplete but fairly representative list of English churches shows 19 dedications in honor of St. Mary, out of 82 (St. Peter was first, with 28). That development was carried on in subsequent church building. Of some 11,700 old parish churches in England, 450 bore no saint's name (the majority of these are called Holy Trinity). Of the remainder, our Lady comes first, with 2,335 dedications (All Saints is second, with 1,255; St. Peter third, 1,140; St. Michael the Archangel fourth, 687).

The custom of calling a church, not by the name of a person, but of a religious mystery, is late. Of the 2,335 parish churches just mentioned, some 38 were said to be named for the Assumption, a few for the Annunciation, and apparently one for the Purification, one for the Conception, and one for the Sorrows. All the rest were simply St. Mary's, St. Mary the Virgin's, and the like. A few were distinguished by epithets: e.g., St. Mary of Pity (two), of Charity (*q.v.;* one). Where there was more than one Marian church in a place we find St. Mary the More, St. Mary the Less, etc. (*cf.,* St. Mary Major). The titular or patronal feast-day of a church dedicated in honor of our Lady was ordinarily August 15, the Assumption, because, like any other saint's day, this was the festival of her "birthday to the better life." Sometimes other feast-days of Mary were chosen, especially the An-

nunciation, which was so "popular" a mystery in medieval England; but the Assumption had an additional "pull," in that it was in full summer, for the day's holiday from work.

The dedication of Catholic churches in England and Wales today show an even greater proportionate predominance of our Lady. Of about 2,000 churches, 668 are dedicated in her honor. Just on 200 of these are simply "St Mary's church," as in the past. Of the remainder, a number are called "our Lady's," without qualification; 58 are "of the Immaculate Conception," closely followed by our Lady of Lourdes. There are, too, local dedications, such as our Lady of Furness, of Gillingham, of Lincoln, of Walsingham, of the Garioch (in Scotland), and others. Dedications in the United States present a similar picture, with our Lady's churches easily the most numerous; here, too, many are still simply "St. Mary's," and "of the Immaculate Conception" is a very frequent qualification. Some American churches perpetuate local European titles: our Lady of Czestochowa, of Gostyn (Polish), of Vilna (Lithuanian and Polish), of Pompeii (Italian), and the like.

Of the 130 cathedral churches in the United States, 42 are dedicated in honor of our Lady (12 are St. Mary's, 17 are our Lady of the Immaculate Conception, 5 of the Assumption, 2 of her Birthday, and one each of Lourdes, Peace, Perpetual Help, the Rosary, Sorrows, and Help of Christians); in Canada, there are 19 Marian dedications out of 57. These are about the same proportions as in England before the Reformation, when 6 out of 21 cathedrals were St. Mary's or double dedications; the English proportion is hardly altered today, 6 out of 18. It is the same all over the world: almost any representative list of churches shows a relative predominance of Notre-Dame, Nuestra Señora, Santa Maria, Frauenkirche, etc. The most notable partial exception is in Celtic countries, where for historical reasons Marian dedications did not become common till much later than elsewhere. *Cf.,* Patron Saint; Place Names; Shrines; Titles.

DEESIS. Parallel to the Calvary group of Christ crucified, flanked by His Mother and St. John the Apostle, the East has an iconographical group of Christ enthroned, with His Mother and St. John the Baptist on either side: they are turned to Him with hands outstretched in an attitude of supplication. This is accordingly called a *Deesis,* "Supplication," and represents the last of the prophets of the Old Covenant joined with the first of the saints of the New to intercede for mankind with the redeeming Messiah. In a Byzantine church a full picture-screen (*eikonostasis*) includes a Deesis. There is such a group over the monastery gateway at Grottaferrata (*q.v.*), and it is occasionally found represented above the chancel arch in some Western churches as part of the Doom, or Last Judgement. A Deesis in the Donskoy monastery at Moscow is an extraordinary combination of some of the conventions of icon-painting with Western baroque technique; it was painted in the eighteenth century.

A Deesis is figured on the fillet with which, in Russia, the head of a dead person is bound.

DEFINITIONS OF MARIAN DOGMA. The following truths about Mary have been formally defined or declared by the Church: that she is the Mother of God, in consequence of Jesus Christ being truly God (by the Council of Ephesus in 431); that she "brought forth Jesus without loss of integrity, and after His birth preserved her virginity inviolate" (at the Council of the Lateran in 649 and at Constantinople in 681); that she was conceived free from original sin (by Pope Pius IX in 1854); and that at the end of her earthly life she was taken up body and soul into Heaven (by Pope Pius XII in 1950). Mary's sinlessness was expressed by the Council of Trent in 1547 (Canon 23 on Justification), and the same council formally confirmed as "good and useful" the Church's tradition of invoking and venerating the saints and honoring their images and relics.—A definition by the Church is a solemn declaration that the doctrine in question has always been a part of the deposit of faith (which may have been hitherto held only implicitly): it is not the statement of a new belief. "For," as the Vatican Council declared in 1870, "the Holy Spirit has not promised to Peter's successors that by His revelation they might make known new doctrine, but that by His assistance they might inviolably keep and faithfully expound the revelation or deposit of faith transmitted through the Apostles."

DEIPARA (Lat. *parere,* to bring forth). The Forth-Bringer, or Mother, of God, equivalent to the Greek Theotokos (*q.v.*).

DELIVERY, OUR LADY OF HAPPY. SEE LECHE, OUR LADY OF LA.

DÉLIVRANDE, NOTRE-DAME DE. Devotion to our Lady of Deliverance is very old, and has spread from its chief shrine, at Bayeux in France. On their appointment the bishops of Bayeux visit her church even before they take possession of their cathedral. The feast is kept on the Thursday within the octave of the Assumption, the anniversary day of the crowning of the statue in 1872. A shrine under the same invocation was established in the island of Martinique a century ago (feast: August 30).

DENMARK, SHRINES OF. In medieval Denmark, 130 out of 2,000 churches were dedicated in honor of the Blessed Virgin; outstanding among them were those at Aalborg, Aarhus, Flensborg, Haderslev, Copenhagen, Odense, Ribe, and Roskilde. In 300 churches frescoes depicting her life still survive today. The principal pilgrim-shrine, with a Lady well, was at Karup, in Jutland. The small minority of Catholics who now constitute the diocese of Copenhagen have a sanctuary to which pilgrimages have been made since 1949. It is at the chapel of the Benedictine nunnery at Aasebakken; the image of our Lady is a late-medieval statue, carved at Lübeck.

DESOLATION OF MARY, The. This Good Friday service is particularly associated with the Servants of Mary, but its use is not confined to Servite churches. It consists essentially of three sermons, on our Lady desolate at her Son's tomb, her passing by Calvary on her return to the city, and her sorrow at home—the Lord has been slain by those to whom He came. *Stabat Mater,* or other appropriate hymns, are sung and Hail Mary said seven times after each address. When used privately, meditations take the place of the sermons. The devotion was first indulgenced by Pope Pius VII (d. 1823).

DESTROYER OF HERESIES. "Be joyful, Mary, virgin, for all alone hast thou brought the heresies of the whole world to nought." These words occur on several occasions in the Roman liturgy. Originally they seem to have recalled particularly Mary's divine motherhood, belief in which is incompatible with the false beliefs about her Son condemned by the Council of Ephesus (*q.v.*) in 431; by consenting to be the human instrument of the Incarnation, Mary witnessed to the error in all heathen or alien faiths. The Venerable Bede says of the woman who exclaimed "Blessed is the womb that bore thee" (Luke 11:27): "It is obvious that she was a woman of great faith and devotion, for while the Scribes and Pharisees were tempting and blaspheming the Lord, she alone above all the rest so truly understood His incarnation, and so fearlessly confessed it, that she confounded both the falsehoods of the important men there present and the faithlessness of the heretics who were yet to come . . . those of a later day who denied that by the power and operation of the Holy Spirit the ever-virgin Mary did verily give of her own flesh and blood to bring forth the human body of the Only-begotten of God. . . ." Through her power as queen and mediatress (*qq.v.*) of all graces, Mary has an active part in bringing heresies to naught.

DETTELBACH, OUR LADY OF. The origin of this German shrine near Würzburg was toward the end of the fifteenth century, when a vinegrower set up a small *pietà* (*q.v.*) as a wayside-shrine. In 1504 attention was drawn to it in connection with the sudden cure of a man who had been hurt in a quarrel. A small wooden chapel was built, then a stone one, and in 1613 this was enlarged. The shrine was first called our Lady in the Sandy Place, but is now known locally as our Lady of the Vineyards, and Dettelbach is a lovely example of a quiet, lesser-known German sanctuary. For four hundred years the Friars Minor have cared for it, and the seal of St. Francis is stamped on the place. The *pietà* is a very small image, only about 18 inches high; it stands on a pedestal, beneath a marble canopy that towers up to the vault of the church.

DEVOTION to Mary. Devotion to the Blessed Virgin is here understood as the religious attachment of individual persons to Mary, in herself and her various aspects. What may perhaps be regarded as the first known example of its expression is found in St. Luke's gospel (11:27), when a woman exclaimed to our Lord, "Blessed is the womb that bore thee, and the breasts that nursed thee." It is known that in the early Church Mary was particularly revered as the pattern of virginity, especially by the ascetics; and the development of such ideas as that of the New Eve (*q.v.*) and the recognition that Mary was Mother of God greatly increased the devotion of the faithful toward her. Early in the fifth century a writer declared rhetorically that she was "reverenced throughout the whole universe"; and already before that St. Epiphanius (d. 403) had had to rebuke certain heretical excesses. But it was during the middle ages that public veneration (*q.v.*) of our Lady by the Church and the personal devotion of the faithful, acting and reacting on one another, together produced and spread Marian devotion of an enthusiasm and extent not known before. In some of its more popular manifestations it was not always free from exaggeration and even superstition (*cf.*, Legends of our Lady); but its best aspects had a lasting effect. Its confidence and childlike trust was summed up by St. Bernard (d. 1153) who said in a sermon: "Are you in danger, in trouble, in doubt? Think of Mary, call upon Mary. . . . If you follow her guidance, you will not go astray; if you appeal to her, you will not lose hope; if she supports you, you will not stumble; if she protects you, you will not be afraid; if she leads you, you will not grow weary; under her kindness, you will reach your goal."

Those words are happily echoed by numberless devotees of Mary eight hundred years later. But they represent only one expression of it, for it must be recognized that the individual's devotion to our Lady is a personal thing, which displays the variety of such. Subject to the Church's dogmatic teaching, with fullest respect for all that the Church recommends and approves, Marian devotion may, and does, vary from person to person in its degree of intensity, in its scope, in the way that it is expressed. Every serious Catholic loves and honors the Mother of God: the part that love and honor have in his personal religion, the form and expression, inward or outward, of his devotion, these are matters for himself, in liberty of spirit. It is improper that, as sometimes happens, any Catholic should use his own estimate of devotion to Mary as a yard-stick for measuring his neighbor's religion. Mary is our spiritual mother, and it has been well said that her way with each one is personal, as a mother's way must be (see also DEVOTIONS, below). But, says Pope Pius XII in *Ad caeli Reginam,* "Let no one consider himself exempt from this tribute [reverence for the Queen of Heaven and earth] of a grateful and loving soul."

Like every other good thing, devotion to our Lady can be spoiled and get out of touch with the mind of the Church (*cf.,* Errors and Excesses). It is possible more or less to lose sight of the fact that its origin and fundamental justification is in the incarnation of the Word of God; devotion to Mary has a solid dogmatic basis in her God-given position as the inseparable associate of His divine Son in all His mysteries. Mary is indeed men's loving mother, but praise of her may be swallowed up in requests for this or that, things that may have little relation to everlasting life; the Mother of God may appear to be thought of rather as the kind mamma who will "make everything all right" for us. The Holy See has pointed out the remedy for such deviations: "Who can number what precious gifts this mighty love for Mary . . . would bring upon the Church, on each member and on the whole body, were that love guided and developed in accord with the spirit of liturgical worship. Then, so far from frittering itself away in superficial sentimentalism, or in a restless and self-centered seeking for favors, it would acquire those characteristics of maturity and depth that are the guarantee of solid and fruitful religious life" (*Osservatore Romano,* July 12-13, 1954). True devotion to Mary may be summed up in terms of the three fundamental Christian virtues. Through faith in her motherhood of God, she is to be honored and venerated above all other creatures: through hope, she is to be relied on with complete trustfulness; through charity, she is to be loved with all one's heart. *Cf.,* Hyperdulia; Mariology.

DEVOTIONS, MARIAN. "Devotions" is the name commonly given to certain forms of prayer and other observances expressive of the devotion of the faithful towards a mystery of the faith or a particular holy person or some historical event connected therewith. Devotions to and in honor of the Blessed Virgin are numerous, and accounts of some of them may be found herein under AKATHISTOS HYMN, CONSECRATION, CROWN OF OUR LADY, CROWN OF TWELVE STARS, DESOLATION, ENTREATY, FIVE PSALMS, LITTLE OFFICE OF THE IMMACULATE CONCEPTION, JOYS, LITANY OF LORETO, MIRACULOUS MEDAL, MONTH OF MARY, NOVENA, ROSARY (several titles), SCAPULAR (several titles), SORROWS, THREE HAIL MARYS, and others.

Particular private ways of honoring Mary, particular expressions of devotion toward her, allowed and even recommended by the authorities of the Church, are nevertheless optional. Whether or not a person uses them is a matter of personal choice. In commending the use of approved devotions, among which he expressly mentions the rosary and the month of Mary, Pope Pius XII in his encyclical letter *Mediator Dei* requires—as would be expected—that all devotions shall be such as to promote the spiritual progress of the faithful. As has been pointed out with reference to personal devotion (above) an element of subjectivity enters here: amid the great variety of Marian devotions, there are necessarily some that do not appeal equally to all the faithful. As there are different types of character and temperament, so persons differ in the temper of their devotion and its preferred mode of expression: reserved or demonstrative, talkative or sparing of words, emotional or phlegmatic, and so on. Edmund Bishop characterized the public worship of the Roman rite by its soberness and good sense; and perhaps it is principally a certain "floweriness" and artificiality of expression that make some Marian devotions unacceptable to some people. Cardinal Newman wrote of devotional feelings: "Burning thoughts and words are as open to criticism as they are beyond it. What is abstractedly extravagant, may in particular persons be becoming and beautiful, and only fall under blame when it is found in others who imitate them. When it is formalized into meditations and exercises, it is as repulsive as love-letters in a police report." Those who feel this way, and are repelled by certain devotions to Mary which others cherish, may find encouragement in Pope Pius XII's words about spiritual exercises of another kind: "There is only one Spirit, but He 'breathes where He will,' and the souls that He enlightens He leads to holiness with various gifts and by various paths. Their freedom, and the supernatural action of the Holy Spirit in them, are a thing sacrosanct, which no man may hinder or violate under any pretext" (*Mediator Dei*, iv, 1).

DIVINE GRACE, MOTHER OF. A title accorded to our Lady in the Litany of Loreto (*q.v.*), which follows from the preceding one, "Mother of Christ"; for He is the source of grace to all men and in Him grace is absolute. The title may be extended to refer to Mary's own fullness of grace (*q.v.*) and to her mediation (*q.v.*) of grace to the faithful. *Cf.*, Grace, Our Lady of.

DIVINE PROVIDENCE, MOTHER OF. A feast of our Lady under this name is celebrated in some places, especially in Italy and Sicily, on various dates. The offertory verse of the proper Mass is from the book of Wisdom (14:3), "Father, thy providence governs all: thou hast opened a passage across the sea, a firm path amid the waves"; and the post-communion prayer asks: "May those who seek thy kingdom and thy righteousness above all things never be without thy help in this world, O God, through the intercession of the Mother of divine providence."

DIVINE SHEPHERD, MOTHER OF THE. This feast is celebrated in a number of places and by certain religious congregations, Capuchins, Marists, and others, on widely differing dates. On the first Sunday in May it is a special festival of the shrine of our Lady of Brebières, a very old sanctuary near Albert in France, formerly much resorted to by shepherds. This pilgrimage was revived after 1870, the statue was crowned in 1901, and, devastated in both world wars, the basilica has again been rebuilt. The collect of the Mass prays that, by following the Good Shepherd on earth, we may reach the pastures of eternal life in Heaven.

DOCTOR OF MARY, The. *Doctor Marianus* is a name given to St. Anselm, archbishop of Canterbury and doctor of the Church (d. 1109). As well as his great writings on Christ's atonement, he wrote some prayers in Mary's honor that were so fine that others as

well were wrongly attributed to him. Although he was not convinced of the Immaculate Conception (he lived 750 years before its definition), Anselm laid down the principle that: "It was fitting that the Blessed Virgin should shine with a purity than which none greater can be imagined below God: she the maiden to whom God the Father had determined to give His Son, that Son whom He had begotten as His equal, whom He loved like Himself; and the Father gave Him in such wise that He should be Son both of God the Father and of the Virgin." —John Duns Scotus (d. 1308), defender of the doctrine of the Immaculate Conception, also is sometimes called *Doctor Marianus,* but more usually the Subtle (i.e., acute) Doctor. St. Bernard, too, is at times accorded the title.

DOGMAS, MARIAN. The use of the word "dogma" is not uniform; but in the sense of a truth defined or otherwise explicitly laid down by the Church for the belief of Christians, dogmas touching our Lady are her divine motherhood, that she was full of grace, conceived free from original sin (Immaculate Conception) and thereafter actually sinless, her perpetual virginity, her going up body and soul into Heaven (Assumption), and that it is lawful and praiseworthy to venerate and invoke her and to honor her in her images (*qq.v.*). See DEFINITIONS.

DOLORS, DOLOURS. See SORROWS.

DON, OUR LADY OF THE. A famous icon painted in the latter part of the fourteenth century by a Greek, Theophanes of Novgorod, who had assimilated Russian iconographical traditions: it is double-sided, having the Assumption on the back. It is now in the Tretiakov Gallery in Moscow. Formerly it was in the cathedral of the Annunciation there, and a feast of our Lady of the Don was observed on August 19, in thanksgiving for victory over the Tartars at Kulikovo Pole in 1380 and the capture from them of Kazan in 1552.

DONCASTER, OUR LADY OF. A very celebrated medieval shrine in the north of England, in the Carmelite church of that place. This "right goodly house of Whitefriars" was dissolved by King Henry VIII in 1538, and the wonderworking statue disappeared without leaving a trace. In the modern church of St. Peter's Chains, devotion to our Lady Mary Virgin of Doncaster has now been revived: the almost life-size stone statue in the shrine chapel is a copy of a characteristic medieval image of the Mother and Child. A prayer invoking the help of our Lady of Doncaster has been indulgenced by the Bishop of Leeds.

DORMITION (Lat. *dormitio*, falling asleep). An old name for the feast of the Assumption. The Dormition church at Jerusalem is on the reputed site of the house in which our Lady died. The site was bought by Emperor William II in 1898 and given to the Catholics of Germany, whose Palestine Society built the present church and entrusted it to the Benedictine monks of Beuron in 1906.

DOWRY, OUR LADY'S. A complimentary name given to the realm of England. According to Thomas Arundel, Archbishop of Canterbury, the name was well known in 1399: "The contemplation of the great mystery of the Incarnation has drawn all Christian peoples to revere [Mary], from whom came the first beginnings of our redemption. But we [the English], being the servants of her own inheritance and liegemen of her especial dowry, as we are commonly called, ought to surpass others in the warmth of our praise and devotion." To what extent the phrase was current and popular during the later middle ages is not clear; it occurs again from time to time in books written during the penal times after the Reformation, and it was frequently used in writings and sermons during the nineteenth century, and since. Today every English Catholic is familiar with it through the opening of the Prayer to our Lady for England: "O blessed Virgin Mary, Mother of God, and our most gentle queen and mother, look down in mercy upon England, thy dowry. . . ." But the expression can hardly be said to be on the people's lips otherwise, perhaps because of its rather archaic and rhetorical flavor. "Dowry" is the property brought by a wife to her husband; "dower," also used, is a widow's estate: either word can be used simply to mean an endowment or gift, and this figurative use of the word was already known in the middle ages. Bl. Claud La Colombière, preaching before the court of Charles II's Catholic queen, spoke of *le dot et le partage de Marie,* "Mary's dowry and portion." Some pictures have been interpreted as showing a king kneeling before our Lady and making an offering of England to her; but the actual doing of this by certain sovereigns, e.g., Edward III, Richard II, is not clear.

Rather than quote the well-known prayer referred to above, there may be given a translation of a Latin prayer of early penal times: "Holy Mary, Mother of God, who dost not cease with all the saints to pray to the Lord our God for all the needs of the whole Catholic Church in general: we humbly beseech thee that, as it hath pleased thee to undertake the special protection of this kingdom of England, thou wilt care for the same continually and prevail with thy Son, Jesus Christ our Lord, that it be turned to the unity of the Catholic faith; so that all English people, above other nations, may henceforth call thee blessed, and honor thy name for ever, saying 'Dos tua Virgo pia, per te est conversa, Maria,' Thy dowry, blest Virgin Mary, has been brought back by thee." *Cf.,* Te Deum Mariale.

DUBLIN, OUR LADY OF. When the Cistercian abbey of St. Mary at Dublin was dissolved in 1541, the image of Mary in the church was thrown into a fire. It was rescued before more than the back had been damaged, and kept concealed in an inn yard; eventually it was set up in old St. Michan's chapel in Mary's Lane, where it remained throughout the eighteenth century. In 1824 it was restored, and enshrined in the Carmelite church in Whitefriars Street, where it is still greatly venerated.

DUSENBACH, OUR LADY OF. A celebrated pilgrimage shrine near Ribeauvillé in Alsace, founded in 1221 by the lord of the place on returning from the crusades. Our Lady of Compassion of Dusenbach was patroness of the fiddlers and gleemen of the region, and all members of their guild wore a silver medal of Mary when performing in public. The sanctuary was entirely destroyed by the Swedes in 1632 and again at the French Revolution; it was restored in part in 1894, and is now looked after by the Capuchins. The present statue dates from the fifteenth century.

E

EASTERN CHURCHES and the Mother of God. The Christians of the East are divided into a small minority in communion with the Holy See (Catholics of Eastern rites) and a large majority not in communion with the Holy See (dissidents). The various Churches, Catholic and dissident, derive from common religious traditions and share the same rites of worship (Byzantine, Armenian, Syrian, etc.). Particulars given in various places of this book of the Byzantine rite (*q.v.*), and the conclusions concerning the Mother of God that can be drawn from them, hold good, not only for Catholics of that rite, but also for the Orthodox Church, which is by far the most important of the dissident Eastern Churches. Those liturgical particulars in themselves are sufficient to justify the words of Dr. Adrian Fortescue: "Most of all saints, of course, [is] the All-holy Mother of God the object of [Orthodox] devotion. Of all the generations that have called her blessed, none have done so with such eloquence as the Eastern Christians. And devotion to our Lady is still a special mark of these churches. It seems useless to bring quotations to prove what no one will deny." All the earlier developments of the theology and *cultus* of our Lady were brought to the West from the East, and so far as she is concerned (as in so many other things) Christians of the Orthodox Church are at one with Catholics: with one very notable exception, the Immaculate Conception.

The Orthodox Church teaches clearly and firmly that the Blessed Virgin was entirely sinless, in the sense that she was free from every spot of personal, actual, fault and sin. In the past, at a time when the matter was still under discussion in the West, some Orthodox theologians appear to have held, more or less explicitly, the doctrine of the Immaculate Conception (*q.v.*). But today, with very few exceptions, they agree in rejecting it. It must be recognized with regret that this change is in part due to polemical opposition to the Catholic definition in 1854. But it is in no way due to any desire to diminish the glories of the All-holy Mother of God. Orthodox spokesmen think that entire freedom from original sin would have separated her from the rest of the human race; and they generally agree in holding that she was sanctified at the Annunciation, the moment of the Incarnation. But the Orthodox Church as such has never formally denied the Immaculate Conception, and it is probably true to say that the rank and file of Orthodox faithful believe it implicitly; some individuals certainly hold it explicitly. The definition of the Assumption (*q.v.*) in 1950 aroused much interest and dis-

72

cussion among Orthodox theologians, partly in relation to the Immaculate Conception. Explicit belief in the Assumption originated in the East; and that, after Mary's falling asleep, her body was taken into Heaven is clearly expressed in the liturgical books and elsewhere.

Other dissident Eastern Churches, while also not teaching the Immaculate Conception, are no less enthusiastic in their veneration for the Mother of God and devoted to traditional Christian doctrine in her regard. In his encyclical letter *Fulgens corona* (*q.v.*), Pope Pius XII appealed to all separated Eastern Christians, "whom we love with a father's heart," to join with him in the prayers and supplications of the Marian year of 1954. "May the Blessed Virgin Mary," he said, "see the eyes and hearts of all who are proud to be Christians raised to her in the union of charity, at least—see them pleading for enlightenment from above and for that full union in which there shall finally be one fold and one Shepherd." *Cf.*, Liturgy, Our Lady in the: Eastern.

EGYPT, SHRINES OF. As would be expected, the shrines of the Blessed Virgin in Egypt mostly have a traditional connection with the flight of the Holy Family. The one best known to Europeans is at Matariah, the site of ancient Heliopolis on the outskirts of Cairo, with its Virgin's Spring and Virgin's Tree. The Copts commemorate the dedication of the first church there on June 2. In Old Cairo there is another traditional site in the church of Abu Sarga; the ancient

shrine of the Ezbekiah grew up round an icon of our Lady. In Upper Egypt, across the Nile from Smallut, there is the sanctuary of the rocky Mount Tera, to which pilgrims come from all over Egypt to honor the Mother of God, Mohammedans as well as Christians.

EIKON. See ICON.

EINSIEDELN. The most famous shrine in Switzerland, and one of the great Marian sanctuaries of the world. It is situated at a place in the canton of Schwyz where in the year 861 a hermit, St. Meinrad, was murdered by robbers (the name Einsiedeln means "hermitage"). A monastery for Benedictines was founded there some fifty years later. The black statue of our Lady of the Hermits is traditionally said to have been set up by St. Meinrad himself. This wonderworking image is now enshrined in a small chapel, the Chapel of Grace, that stands in the middle of the nave of the magnificent rococo abbey-church. The pilgrimage still flourishes as it has done for centuries past; the chief feast-day is July 16. The abbey of St. Meinrad in Indiana was founded from Einsiedeln in 1854, and the Swiss-American Benedictine congregation observes the feast of our Lady of Einsiedeln.

EMBLEMS AND SYMBOLS. In religious usage an emblem is a badge associated with a person in pictorial or other representation; a symbol (in this sense) is a device which represents something else, a "sign." Thus a palm-branch is the emblem of a martyr; a bee-hive, of St. Bernard; while a dove, by itself, is a symbol of the Holy Spirit. Some designs may be used in either way, e.g., St. Peter's keys. The official book called the *Ceremonial of Bishops* directs that sacred symbols and monograms, representations of saints, and so on should not be woven into carpets and rugs for use in church, for it is unseemly that such things should be trodden on. The same would seem to hold good of cushions and other things that are knelt or sat upon.

In early centuries representations of the Blessed Virgin in the East were often labelled Ἡ ἁγία Μαρία, "The holy Mary." Later, Μήτηρ Θεοῦ, "Mother of God," became customary, of which the abbreviation $\overline{MP}$ $\overline{\Theta Y}$ is still found on icons. Another common Eastern emblem of Mary is three stars on her veil, one on the head and one on either shoulder, interpreted as referring to her maidenhood before, during, and after childbirth. In the West, the use of emblems has been less regular and consistent, except perhaps for the lily at the Annunciation: whiteness for the "fair maid that was flower of all maidens, for right as the lily is white and fair among briers and other flowers, right so was our Lady among other maidens." But nowadays the rosary is very common, together with the crescent moon, and the serpent beneath the Virgin's feet, and twelve stars on her halo (*cf.*, Gen. 3:15; Apoc. 12:1). The seven swords (*q.v.*) also are emblematic of a particular aspect of Mary, her sorrows; and the scapular is emblematic of our Lady of Mount Carmel.

The Queen of Heaven and earth shares a crown as an occasional emblem with several royal saints, but it is used as a symbol for her, surmounting the letter M. This is the only Marian symbol in very frequent use; but the Miraculous Medal (*q.v.*) has now introduced the initial M surmounted by a cross above a bar, and also the heart pierced by a sword (*cf.*, Luke 2:35).

Besides the letter M, other abbreviations or monograms commonly met with are: B.M.V., for Beata Maria Virgo; B.V.M., for Blessed Virgin Mary; D.N., for Domina nostra; N.D., for Notre-Dame; N.S., for Nossa Senhora, Nuestra Señora; S.M., for Santa Maria.

EMMERICH, ANN C., REVELATIONS OF. Ann Catherine Emmerich was born at Flamske in Westphalia in 1774, and became an Augustinian nun; when Jerome Bonaparte suppressed the convent in 1811 she went to live at Dülmen, and remained there till her death in 1824. As well as being a holy woman and a stigmatic, she was from her childhood extremely sensitive to spiritual realities and predisposed to supernatural experiences, of which some took the form of visions of events in sacred history. From 1818 she had the services as "secretary" of Clement Brentano, a German poet of the "romantic" school, and he made notes of her visions. Nine years after her death he published *The Dolorous Passion of Our Lord Jesus Christ,* "according to the meditations of Ann Catherine Emmerich." Brentano died in 1840, and in 1852 his brother, Christian, published another work (begun by Clement), *The Life of the Blessed Virgin Mary*, "according to the meditations of Ann Catherine Emmerich." A third similar book appeared subsequently, *The Life of Our Lord*. These books, full of telling detail, are written very vividly and graphically, and enjoyed a considerable success down to our own day. They at first provoked no controversy, though certain inconsistencies and clear mistakes were noticed in them and questions were raised about the nature of the visions, and also about how much of the books were "Emmerich" and how much "Brentano." But eventually in 1923, in the course of the process for the beatification of Sister Emmerich, Father Winfried Huempfner, o.s.a., examined the works critically and came to the conclusion that Brentano had "misled the Catholic public by falsifying what the religious woman had told him." Brentano, it seems, took down only quick desultory notes from Sister Emmerich, and then worked them up with the aid of much material drawn from widespread sources, and the result included not a few contradictions, puerilities, and errors. Whatever the merits, then, of the *Life of the Blessed Virgin* mentioned above, it would be very rash to attribute any special weight to it on the strength of the holiness and experiences of Sister Emmerich; nor can she be held responsible for its defects: she had no opportunity to check what the Brentanos had written, having died years before. *Cf.,* Revelations and Communications.

ENGLAND, OUR LADY OF. The only church having this title is that at the priory of Premonstratensian (Norbertine) canons regular at Storrington in Sussex; their house was dedicated under this name at its foundation in 1882. A statue of St. Mary of England, made by a Tyrolese carver, stands above the high altar, and there has been a steady flow of pilgrims since conventual life was reestablished in the monastery in 1952. In the Marian year of 1954 there was formally inaugurated an open-air shrine opposite the church. Within the monastery there is a fine copy of an icon of our Lady of Vladimir (*q.v.*), presented to the community by Pope Leo XIII. The original was painted by Prokop Chirin, one of the best Russian icon-painters of the seventeenth century.

ENGLAND, SHRINES OF. What are perhaps the earliest lines in praise of the Blessed Virgin in any Western vernacular tongue were written in England, attributed to the poet Cynewulf, in the later part of the eighth century. They begin, as rendered into modern English by Margaret Williams:

Lo, thou the glory of the great earth,
purest of women over all the world
of all who have been since time began,
how right it is that all voices,
all heroes on earth, hail thee, and say
with blithe mood that thou art the bride
of the Noblest One, the sky's King.

Since then, many English poets have sung of Mary, and their praises have taken material form in a long succession of pilgrim-shrines. Among those of the middle ages were those at Bisney, Bradstow (Broadstairs), St. Mary Undercroft at Canterbury, Coventry, Dover, Durham, Ely, Fountains Abbey, Gloucester, Ipswich, Islington, Jesmond, Liskeard, at All Hallows Barking by the Tower of London, Northampton, Norwich, our Lady of Mount Grace at Osmotherly, Pershore, Salisbury, Scarborough, Tewkesbury, Thetford, our Lady of the Pew at Westminster, Warwick, Worcester, Yarmouth. These no longer exist; but other medieval sanctuaries have been commemorated or revived in modern times, in degrees varying from a church dedication to an actual pilgrimage shrine. Among them are: our Lady of Abingdon (revived, with a restored medieval statue, 1954); O.L. of Axholme (at Crowle); Aylesford (q.v.); O.L. of Beauchief (Woodseats); O.L. of Buckfast; O.L. of Caversham (q.v.); O.L. of Doncaster (q.v.); O.L. of Dunmow; O.L. of Evesham (q.v.); O.L. of Fernyhalgh (q.v.); O.L. of Furness (Ulverston); O.L. of Gillingham (Kent); O.L. of Glastonbury (q.v.); O.L. of Grace (q.v.); O.L. of Guisborough (revived 1945); O.L. of the Crag, Knaresborough (q.v.); O.L. of Lincoln; O.L. of (King's) Lynn (q.v.); O.L. of Muswell; O.L. of Sudbury (revived 1937); O.L. of Walsingham (q.v.); O.L. of Willesden (q.v.); O.L. of Winton (q.v.); O.L. of York (q.v.).

English shrines of later or modern origin include our Lady of Warwick Street (q.v.); O.L. of Canvey; O.L. of England (q.v.) at Storrington; O.L. of Farnborough (Hampshire); O.L. of Hartley (q.v.); Lanherne (q.v.); O.L. of Lourdes, Harrow Road, London; O.L. of Marnhull; O.L. of Prinknash; O.L. of Perpetual Help (q.v.), Bishop Eton; O.L. of St. George's (q.v.); O.L. of Salmestone (q.v.); O.L. of Stone (q.v.); O.L. of West Grinstead (q.v.). See also IMAGES.

ENTERING INTO THE TEMPLE, Feast of the. The name given in the East to the feast of our Lady's Presentation (q.v.).

ENTREATY OF THE MOTHER OF GOD. A service of the Byzantine rite, called in Greek *Paraklesis* and in Slavonic *Moleben*. It consists principally of Psalm 142; twenty petitions and greetings in groups of four, e.g., "Mother of the Doer of good in whom is all good, pour out your compassion upon us; this you are able to do, blessed one of God, for the almighty Christ is your child"; three short litanies and several chants; a gospel reading (Luke 1:39-55); further greetings and petitions; the Magnifical Hymn (q.v.) and other praises; the Thrice-holy Hymn and the Lord's Prayer; ending with "Lord Jesus Christ, have mercy on us through the prayers of thy holy ones. Amen." This is sung every evening on the fourteen days of fasting before the feast of the Assumption. The Catholic Ukrainians use a shortened form of this long *Moleben* during the month of May.

EPHESUS. One of the twelve Ionic cities of Asia Minor, near the mouth of the river Kayster in Lydia; its site is now occupied by several poor villages, of which the chief is Ayasaluk. Early Christianity in Ephesus is particularly associated with the name of St. Paul; and St. Justin (d. *c.* 165), St. Irenaeus (d. *c.* 202), and others record that St. John the Evangelist lived for a time and died there. Since Christ on the cross had committed His Mother to St. John, the idea naturally grew up that Mary too lived and died there, but the evidence for this view is not very weighty (*cf.,* Assumption, Place of the). The discovery some miles away, at Panaghia Kapouli, of the remains of a house in which Mary is supposed to have dwelt, is mixed up with the dubious business of the revelations attributed to Ann Catherine Emmerich (*q.v.*).

But in another connection the association of our Lady with Ephesus is certain and very important. It was at Ephesus in the year 431 that the third oecumenical council assembled. This council condemned the heresy called Nestorianism, which asserted that God the Son and the man Jesus were two distinct persons joined together in Jesus Christ, that Jesus was only the dwelling-place of the Word, and He alone was born of Mary and died on the cross. Consequently Mary was *Christotokos,* "Mother of Christ," but not *Theotokos,* "Mother of God." The Catholic teaching is, of course, that Jesus Christ is one person but of two natures, human and divine, and Mary was the mother of that person: Christotokos, therefore Theotokos

(*q.v.*). In the course of its proceedings the council approved a letter written by St. Cyril of Alexandria, vindicating the use of the expression God-bearer with reference to Mary. The Council of Ephesus was a critical point in the history of Christianity, and of the highest significance in the development of Mariology: when she conceived and gave birth to the God-man, and thus became Mother of God, Mary was taken from the ordinary plane of holiness and given a place that no other created being could share; Mary's divine motherhood is the whole mystery of Mary.—It is appropriate that the church of St. Mary at Ephesus in which the council was held was perhaps the first to bear that name, and it was perhaps the first place outside of Palestine to celebrate the feast of the Annunciation (about 500). Pope Pius XI issued an encyclical letter, *Lux veritatis,* at the fifteenth centenary of the Council of Ephesus in 1931, and gave the feast of the Motherhood of our Lady to the whole Western Church. See MOTHER OF GOD.

ERRORS AND EXCESSES concerning Mary. From time to time ideas about the Blessed Virgin and practices relating to her become current which call forth the intervention of ecclesiastical authority. For example, the Church has had more than once to condemn the idea that Mary's flesh and blood are really present in the Blessed Sacrament; and a related idea, that consecrated hosts can be regarded as "relics of Mary," has been condemned as false and scandalous. At different times specific forms of Marian image and some particular titles have been forbidden by authority (e.g., "Queen of the Heart of Jesus"; and *cf.*, Pellevoisin). Certain Marian confraternities were dissolved by Pope Benedict XIV in 1758 (*cf.*, Slavery to Mary); and at the end of the following century there was the unhappy business of the Mariavites in Poland. The excesses of these last people were such that they were condemned by the Holy Office and ordered to disband their associations: instead, many of them left the Church. More lately still, the Holy Office had to intervene to discourage devotion to Mary's priesthood (*q.v.*) and to forbid images of the "Virgin Priestess." These examples are sufficient to show the Church's unfailing watchfulness lest people's enthusiastic devotion or the speculations of the learned lead them to exceed the bounds of true religion and sound theology. Ideas and practices sometimes have to be forbidden or warned against as wrong or objectionable in themselves, sometimes as exaggerations of what is true and good, sometimes simply as inopportune or conducive to misunderstanding, according to the differing circumstances. *Cf.*, Heresies involving Mary; Mariolatry; Swoon of our Lady.

ESPOUSALS. See BETROTHAL.

ETHIOPIA, SHRINES OF. Catholics are a very small minority in Ethiopia (often improperly called Abyssinia); but through the centuries the Christians of the dissident Ethi-

opian Church have been very faithful to the Mother of God. Indeed, veneration for Mary has among them perhaps a bigger place than in any other Christian body, though it sometimes takes forms that are impossible to defend. An unexceptionable custom is the giving of baptismal names thus: Gabra Maryam, "Mary's servant"; Khidana Maryam, "Mary's promise"; Walda Maryam, "Mary's blossom"; Haila Maryam, "Mary's power"; Tasfa Mariam, "Mary's pillar." The first of these is exactly equivalent to the Gaelic name Gilmary. The Ethiopians have a number of Marian pilgrimage shrines. One popular one is Amba Maryam, between Gondar and Dabra Tabor; another, further south, is that of her Falling Asleep, Mahdara Maryam.

ETTAL, OUR LADY OF. Ettal lies amid the mountains about three miles south of Ober Ammergau in Upper Bavaria. A Benedictine monastery was founded there in 1330 by the Emperor Ludwig IV, who also established a community of twelve knights with their families to guard the place. He gave a small stone statue of the Mother of God, carved in Italy, and Ettal was soon famous both for its shrine of Mary and the learning of its monks. In 1744 the medieval church was burnt down, its successor being built and decorated in the German baroque manner. The other buildings had already mostly been remodelled as they appear today. A century later the abbey was suppressed, with other Bavarian religious houses; but it was restored in 1904, and our Lady of Ettal is still a resort of pilgrims. This great sanctuary has a truly magnificent mountain setting.

EUROPE, OUR LADY OF. Mary is venerated under this title at one of the extreme points of the continent, namely, Point Europa at Gibraltar. The image is enshrined in the church there, and a feast under this title is celebrated throughout the tiny diocese of Gibraltar on May 30.

EVANGELIST, OUR LADY'S. It is with good reason that St. Luke is often called our Lady's evangelist, for it is in his gospel alone, written as he says "after following up all things carefully from the very first," that certain most important matters connected with her are related: the Annunciation, her visit to St. Elizabeth, the shepherds worshiping at her Son's birth, His presentation in the Temple and Simeon's words to Mary on that occasion, and the loss and finding of the Boy there in later years. Some of the things that Luke relates he could hardly have known unless Mary herself had told him; and that he should be chosen for her confidence bears out the impression given by his writings that he, "the beloved physician," was a man of most tender and sympathetic disposition, especially, it would seem, where women were concerned (Acts 9:36-41; 16:14-15; and elsewhere). A number of pictures of our Lady have been popularly attributed to St. Luke (which is why he is a patron saint of painters). These attributions cannot be sustained (*cf.*, Likenesses); but as an artist in writ-

ing he tells his readers more about Mary than any painting could do.

EVE, SECOND, The. See NEW EVE, THE.

EVESHAM, OUR LADY OF. The first monastery at Evesham in Worcestershire was founded by St. Egwin, Bishop of Worcester, about the year 709. It was established, and dedicated in honor of the Blessed Virgin, at a place where she was said to have appeared, first to a herdsman and then to St. Egwin himself. The name Evesham means "Eof's meadow," and it is said that Eof or Eoves was the herdsman's name. Devotion to our Lady of Evesham has been restored at the church of the Immaculate Conception and St. Egwin there; in recent years organized pilgrimages have taken place, and a regular shrine is in process of establishment.

EX VOTO. To do something *ex voto* is to do it in fulfilment of a promise; by extension, it is to do something out of gratitude, irrespective of any promise. The expression has come also to be used as a noun to designate a promised gift or thank-offering, especially one deposited at a shrine of our Lady or other saint. Such an *ex-voto* often takes the form of an inscribed tablet, a silver heart, or similar thing hung up near a statue; or it may be a piece of jewelry, a precious rosary, a ring, or the like. The crutches and surgical appliances seen at the Lourdes grotto of Holy Cross monastery at Cincinnati, Ohio, at Lourdes itself, and at many other places, are given *ex voto* by those who have experienced relief or cure after praying there. A candle or a vigil light put up before an image is an *ex-voto,* either of gratitude, in hope, or simply offered up; so we speak of votive candles.

EXPECTATION OF OUR LADY, Feast of the. In the days when no feast, however important, was supposed to be celebrated in Lent, a feast corresponding to the Annunciation was kept in Spain on December 18. When the Annunciation was adopted for March 25 this other feast was retained, and eventually was given the name of the Expectation. It is still kept in Spain and a few religious orders, on that date. Apart from the words "this festival of the Expectation of blessed Mary" in the preface, the Mass makes no more explicit reference to our Lady's expectation of childbirth than is involved in the Saturday Mass in Advent. The mystery of the divine motherhood is beautifully expressed in the office: "Virgin of virgins, how will this thing be, for no one was ever like you before nor will be in time to come?—Daughters of Jerusalem, why do you wonder at me? What you see is a mystery of God."—The day is known in Spain as our Lady of the O. The explanation often given of this is that formerly its Vespers ended in a long drawn-out "O," to express mankind's longing for the Savior who was expected; but the name really refers to the first of the O antiphons, *O Sapientia,* sung at first Vespers of the feast. Father F. W. Faber wrote a hymn on our Lady's expectation, "Like the dawning of the morning on the mountain's golden heights"; it can still be found in some hymnbooks.

F

FAIR LOVE, MOTHER OF. "I am the mother of fair love and reverence and wisdom and holy hope" (Little chapter at Compline in the Little Office B.V.M.). A feast of our Lady, Queen of All Saints and Mother of Fair Love, is observed in some places, on various dates. In the church of St. Christopher at Lucca in Italy there is a fourteenth-century image of our Lady of Fair Love, the occasion of a special local feast.—The lesson of the proper Mass is from Ecclesiasticus (24:22-31) and includes the words: "It is I that gave birth to all noble living, all reverence, all true knowledge and the holy gift of hope"; and the collect prays that we may love God "in all things and above all things on earth, and in Heaven enjoy the happy fellowship of the saints." There is a church dedicated under this title (N.-D. de Bel Amour) in Montreal.

FALLING ASLEEP OF OUR LADY (Gr. *koimesis;* Lat. *dormitio*). A common name for the Assumption in liturgical books. It is also often used for a well-known apocryphal writing on the subject: see PASSING OF MARY.

FASTS. The only fast in the Roman calendar associated with Mary is that on the vigil of the Assumption. The Saturday (*q.v.*) fast or abstinence that used to be general in the West (it is now abolished) was simply a continua-tion of that of Friday: in spite of what is sometimes stated, it had nothing to do with our Lady in origin. All Eastern rites have a period of fasting, strict or mitigated, before the Assumption; the periods laid down are: Byzantine rite, 14 days; Armenian and Chaldean, 5 days; Coptic and Ethiopic, 15 days; Syrian, 7 days; Maronite, 8 days.

FATHERS, THE. The Fathers of the Church, referred to in various places in this book, are all those teachers, preachers and writers of the earlier Christian centuries whose teaching is considered to be specially weighty and specially worthy of respect. As well as by great learning, they were distinguished by notable holiness of life, and most of them are numbered among the saints. Those who are entitled to be esteemed Fathers of the Church do not form an exact category, and the era of the Fathers is not exactly delimited; most of them lived before the year 750, but there are a few names after that to which the epithet Father is sometimes given. Among the Fathers who are of special significance where the Blessed Virgin is concerned are St. Justin (Palestinian; d. *c.* 165); St. Irenaeus (Greek; d. *c.* 202); St. Ephraem (Syrian; d. *c.* 373); St. Basil (Cappadocian; d. 379); St. Ambrose (Roman; d. 397); St. Epiphanius (Palestinian; d. 403);

St. John Chrysostom (Antiochene; d. 407); St. Jerome (Dalmatian; d. 420); St. Augustine (African; d. 430); St. Cyril of Alexandria (Alexandrian; d. 444); St. Vincent of Lérins (Gallo-Roman; d. c. 445); St. Proclus (Greek; d. 447); St. Peter Chrysologus (Ravennese; d. c. 450); Pope St. Leo I (Roman; d. 461); St. Fulgentius (African; d. 533); Pope St. Gregory I (Roman; d. 604); St. Ildephonsus (Spaniard; d. 667); St. Germanus of Constantinople (Greek; d. 732); St. Andrew of Crete (Damascene; d. 740); St. John of Damascus (Damascene; d. c. 749).

Names of important spiritual writers and theologians after the patristic age particularly associated with our Lady include St. Anselm (Savoyard; d. 1109), Eadmer (English; d. c. 1124), St. Bernard (Burgundian; d. 1153), and Rupert of Deutz (German; d. 1175); and later on, St. Peter Canisius (German; d. 1597), St. Lawrence of Brindisi (Italian; d. 1619), St. John Eudes (French; d. 1680), St. Louis Mary Grignion de Montfort (French; d. 1716), and St. Alphonsus Liguori (Italian; d. 1787). *Cf.,* Lessons at Matins.

FATIMA. Fatima is a scattered parish in high, hard country, roughly in the middle of Portugal. Here, as in so many other places, the appearings of our Lady were seen by children. They were natives of the village of Aljustrel: Lucia dos Santos, aged ten, Francisco Marto, aged nine, and his sister Jacinta, two years younger. (The boy saw the Lady but never heard her speak.) On May 13, 1917, these children were in an open hollow, the Cova da Iria, and were surprised by two flashes of light out of a clear sky; they then saw a "young lady," a girl dressed in white, apparently standing above a small tree. She said she came from Heaven, and asked the children to return to the same place at the same hour of the same day for six months running. There was further conversation, and the Lady told them to accept sufferings on behalf of sinners and to pray for peace. On June 13 she repeated the instructions and said that Francisco and Jacinta would be taken to Heaven before long. On July 13, in the presence of a large crowd, Lucia asked the Lady for a miracle, and was told to say the rosary daily for peace, adding a prayer for sinners after each decade. A secret also was imparted. The visit of August 13 did not take place, because a secularist legal official threatened the children and had them locked up. (And up till now Lucia's mother had kept on thrashing her for "telling lies".) But on August 19 the Lady appeared to them in another place, and promised that a miracle would be wrought on October 13. Some members of the crowd on September 13 saw an unexplained luminous globe moving in the sky, and other phenomena of light ("white petals"). The Lady repeated her instructions about the rosary and promised to return in October with the Holy Child and St. Joseph.

Fifty thousand or more people were present on October 13, a wet day, and the crowd stood under upraised umbrellas. The Lady appeared to the children and said, "I want you to tell them to build a chapel here in my honor. I am the Lady of the Rosary. They must say the rosary daily." She said that the war [that of 1914-18] was going to end, and that some people's requests would be granted and not others: "They must amend, ask forgiveness for their sins, and offend against our Lord no more." Lucia then saw in succession Mary as our Lady of Sorrows, and as of Mount Carmel, St. Joseph with the Child, and our Lord as a man. At this moment the rain stopped, and the sun was suddenly seen through a rift in the clouds. It then seemed to rotate, throwing out rays of brightly colored light, and then appeared to fall toward the earth, giving off heat. The crowd was seized with panic, fearing the end of the world; fear was changed to wonder as things returned to normal. This extraordinary occurrence (which a few people saw miles away: it lasted about ten minutes) has not been thoroughly explained, either in itself or in its significance.

Francisco Marto died happily in 1919 and Jacinta a year later, and soon after Lucia dos Santos became a nun. What has been narrated above is summarized from evidence given at the time of the occurrences. What follows is due to memorials written by Lucia in her maturity, in 1936-1937 and 1941-42, documents which have not been published verbatim and in their entirety. They both amplify what she had said before and add new matter. It is learned from these that already in 1916 the children had had unusual experiences, and that the first part of the secret (July 13, 1917) was a vision

of Hell. And it is in the second memorial that our Lady is reported as saying (in 1917) that "The Lord wishes to establish devotion to my Immaculate Heart in the world. If what I say is done, many souls will be saved and there will be peace." But if men do not mend their ways there will be war again. "To prevent this, I shall come and ask for the consecration of Russia to my Immaculate Heart and communions of reparation on the first Saturdays. If my requests are heeded Russia will be converted," and if not, worse will befall. "But in the end my Immaculate Heart will triumph." For many years before Lucia's evidence was known, petitions had reached the Holy See for the consecration of *the world* to the Immaculate Heart of Mary (*q.v.*); in 1942 this was done by Pope Pius XII, with special reference to Russia (though this country was not named). In his letter to the peoples of Russia in 1952 the Pope said that he dedicated them to that Heart in a very special way as a testimony of his particular good will toward them.

There was much doubt about Fatima in many minds, not excluding Portuguese bishops and other clergy; but after full inquiry the local ordinary, the Bishop of Leiria, in 1930 formally declared that the visions were worthy of belief and that he authorized the *cultus* (*q.v.*) of our Lady of Fatima. A great sanctuary has developed at the Cova da Iria, whither thousands of pilgrims come in quest of spiritual and bodily health, and do not come in vain: many cures are wrought at the spring found when a reservoir was being dug. The statue of our Lady at Fatima, according with Lucia's simple description, was crowned by a papal legate in 1946. As time went by, Lucia more and more described the Lady's appearance in terms of light, and the underlying message of Fatima seems to be the darkness of sin over against the light of goodness, the passage from one to the other being along the path of prayer and reparation. The rosary in particular was much emphasized: perhaps because, as Father Cyril Martindale has suggested, it is, in Lucia's own words, "a very good way of drawing nearer to God for those who do not know how to pray." In other words, every one without exception can pray the rosary. Among the Fatima shrines in America is one at the pilgrimage-center of our Lady of the Rosary at the Dominican sisters' monastery at Summit, N.J. The best statue of our Lady of Fatima has been made by an American Dominican, Father T. Mc-Glynn; his modelling of it was supervised by Lucia dos Santos in the smallest detail. It is intended to stand above the main door of the church. *Cf.,* Revelations and Communications; Visions.

FEASTS OF OUR LADY. A feast is a day upon which the public worship of Almighty God has special reference to an event or mystery in the life of our Lord Jesus Christ, the Blessed Virgin Mary, the angels, or the saints, or to some other event or matter of religious significance. Feasts normally last one day, from the evening before till the evening of the day itself. In the earliest days of the Church there were no feasts as we understand them. But every Sunday, the Lord's Day, was a sort of feast of Christ's rising from the dead, and there was an annual celebration of man's redemption by the Cross and Resurrection, the Pascha (now Good Friday—Easter), and fifty days later of the coming of the Holy Spirit at Pentecost. Later on, the Epiphany, the manifestation of God to the world in Jesus Christ, was inaugurated, and then Christmas as a separate observance, and later still came other feasts of our Lord. The first saints to be commemorated were all martyrs, which is understandable in days when persecution, if intermittent, was acute and their annual feasts began locally, at the place of the martyr's burial: the first such observance of which there is record is of St. Polycarp, at Smyrna, from about the year 156 or 178. One of the earliest non-martyred saints ("confessors") to have a feast-day was St. Martin of Tours (d. 397), for centuries one of the most widely venerated men of western Europe. In those days the liturgical veneration of saints depended not so much on a high degree of popular devotion as we understand it, but in origin on more local considerations, such as the possession of a saint's tomb, or of a relic of some sort, or of a church dedicated in his honor; and from that center the *cultus* often spread. And so we find that feasts of the twelve Apostles, for example, came in rather late, from the fifth century on, later than that of St. John the Baptist or of St. Stephen, though of course the feast of SS. Peter and Paul was celebrated in Rome from early times.

After what has just been said it comes as less of a surprise to learn that feasts of our Lady were also late in making their appearance; and two of the most important of them were at first not clearly differentiated from feasts of our Lord—the Annunciation and the Purification. We hear of Marian feasts sporadically in the East from the fifth century, or perhaps the late fourth; but in Rome itself—always slow and careful in adopting new things—there were apparently none till about the year 700; though before this the octave-day of Christmas had special reference to the Mother of God (cf., Circumcision), and there were certain Marian solemnities in other parts of western Europe. St. Sergius I, a Syrian who was pope from 687 to 701, ordered the solemn observance of four feasts that were already kept every year at Constantinople, namely, Mary's Birthday, the Annunciation, the Purification, and her Falling Asleep (Assumption). On these days the pope used to walk in procession barefooted (that is, in sandals) to celebrate Mass in St. Mary Major (q.v.). From then on, feasts of our Lady have continually increased in number and extension, especially in the Western Church. There are at the present time five *universal* Marian feasts, in the sense that they are observed everywhere in both East and West: the Immaculate Conception, Birthday, Presentation, Annunciation, and Assumption (qq.v.). Then there are thirteen feasts that are observed *everywhere where the general calendar of the Western Church is in force,* namely: the Immaculate Heart of Mary, our Lady of Lourdes, the Motherhood of Mary, our Lady of Mount Carmel, the Holy Name of Mary, our Lady of Ransom, our Lady of the Rosary, her Seven Sorrows (two feasts), Mary the Queen, the Visitation, the Purification, and the Dedication of St. Mary Major (qq.v.). Finally, there is a very large number of feasts of limited observance, some of wide extension, others confined even to one place or church. Many of these last are mentioned herein under their own names; others are noted in F. G. Holweck's *Calendarium liturgicum festorum Dei et Dei Matris Mariae* (St. Louis, 1925): that painstaking American scholar traced more than 2,000 Marian feasts and memorials, including variant names and dates, in the ecclesiastical records of churches throughout the world and in various ages. See also SHRINES, IMAGES, and under specific names.

In addition to the five universal feasts named above, Catholics of *Eastern rites* keep the following throughout their respective churches (for further particulars see herein under their names). *Byzantine rite:* the Garment of our Lady, her Girdle, her Protecting Veil, the Miracle of Miasena, Praises of Mary, Synaxis of Mary, the Visitation (Melkites only). In this rite, no feast of our Lady or other saint ever displaces the Sunday Resurrection office: the respective texts are, when necessary, combined. *Armenian rite:* our Lady's Garment, her Girdle. *Chaldean rite:* Praises of Mary, our Lady of Sheaves, the Visitation. *Coptic rite:* Graces received at Mary's intercession, three dedication feasts (*q.v.*). *Ethiopian rite:* St. Mary of Zion, the Manifestation of our Lady. (Normally the Copts have one and the Ethiopians two commemorations of our Lady each month.) *Syrian rite:* Dedication of St. Mary's church at Caesarea, our Lady in Seed-time and of Sheaves, Praises of Mary. *Maronite rite:* our Lady of Sheaves, Praises of Mary, the Visitation, Name of Mary, Rosary Sunday, and a commemoration on August 31. *Malabar rite:* the Western calendar is followed.

The feasts of the Assumption and the Immaculate Conception are holydays of obligation throughout the Church, but there is an exception for the second in some places (e.g., England and Wales). In some Eastern rites other feasts of Mary are of obligation as well. It was a project of Pope Benedict XIV (d. 1758) to remove our Lady of Mount Carmel, of Ransom, and other lesser Marian feasts (and many other feasts as well) from the overcrowded general calendar; he died before he was able to carry out his reforms, but the liturgical legislation of Pope St. Pius X led to the dropping of many minor feasts of our Lady from local calendars.

FERNYHALGH, OUR LADY OF. The first shrine chapel at Fernyhalgh, near Preston in Lancashire, was built in association with a holy well in 1348, in thanksgiving, it is said, for escape from shipwreck. The medieval building was destroyed at the Reformation, but Catholics continued to frequent the place throughout penal times, and

even built a chapel there in 1685, which was very extensively used. This building is now part of the convent of the Holy Child, whose nuns have care of the shrine; a statue of the Mother and Child has been set up over the well. Our Lady of Fernyhalgh in the north, our Lady of West Grinstead (*q.v.*) in the south, and Lanherne (*q.v.*) in the west, with their record of Catholic worship unbroken through the centuries, have a very special place among English Marian shrines. Fernyhalgh, moreover, is the place where Dame Alice Harrison kept her famous school in the eighteenth century.

FINLAND, OUR LADY OF. Finland is a Lutheran country, with a minority of Orthodox and a few Catholics. At the Orthodox monastery of Konovo (Konevits), in Lake Ladoga, there is a historic icon of our Lady of Finland or of the Dove: the Child is playing with a white bird on a string, and the formalized face of the Mother is very powerful. There is a copy of this striking icon at the Anglican shrine of our Lady at Walsingham (*q.v.*) in England.

FIVE PSALMS, The. The saying of a canticle and four psalms whose first letters in Latin spell out the name Maria, namely:

Magnificat (Luke 1:46-55)
Ad Dominum cum tribularer (Ps. 119)
Retribue servo tuo (Ps. 118:17-176)
In convertendo (Ps. 125)
Ad te levavi (Ps. 122)

This devotion was popularized by Bl. Jordan of Saxony (d. 1237) and others in the middle ages, and has taken various forms. In England, the psalms were said in honor of Mary's five greatest joys, and were interspersed with other prayers. This devotion is still known and used, and it has been indulgenced.

FLOS CARMELI. The first line and title of the sequence (*q.v.*) sung at Mass in the Carmelite rite on the feast of our Lady of Mount Carmel.

Flos Carmeli
   Vitis florigera
Splendor caeli
Virgo puerpera
Singularis.

Mater mitis
   Sed viri nescia
Carmelitis
Da privilegia
Stella maris. Alleluia!

"Flower of Carmel, blossoming vine, radiance of Heaven, sole maiden who bore child. A gentle mother, yet knowing not man; be good to your Carmelites, Star of the sea. Alleluia!" The medieval church of York had two somewhat similar hymns; the authorship of this one is attributed to St. Simon Stock (*cf.,* Scapular, Brown). In Carmelite communities *Flos Carmeli* is sung every night before retiring to bed.

FLOWER NAMES, MARIAN. A large number of English flower names, especially of wild flowers, are compounded with such words as Lady, Maiden, Mary, Virgin, suggesting association with the Mother of God. It is not certain that such is always the case; some of the Lady names, for instance, may well have been given with a more general allusion: but the *Oxford English Dictionary* on the whole favors Marian origin. In a few examples it is proved by the survival of a more definite form: e.g., our Lady's bedstraw (*Galium verum*), our Lady's cushion (thrift; mossy saxifrage), our Lady's hair (two grasses).

The principal of these names are: Lady-bracken, Lady-fern, Lady-smock (cuckoo-flower), Lady's or Virgin's bower (a clematis), Lady's comb (shepherd's needle), Lady's delight (violet), Lady's fingers (kidney vetch), Lady's fringes (*Gentiana ciliata*), Lady's glove (foxglove), Lady's laces or fringes (*Phalaris arundinacea*), Lady's looking-glass, Lady's mantle (*Alchemilla*), Lady's seal, Lady's slipper (bird's-foot trefoil, etc.), Lady's thimble (harebell; foxglove), Lady's thistle (milk thistle), Lady's thumb (spotted knotweed), Lady's tresses (*Spiranthes*), Mariet (Canterbury bell), Marigold, Mary-lily (now generally called Madonna-lily). Maidenhair (a fern) and Maiden pink (*Dianthus deltoides*) are only very doubtfully Marian, and Rosemary has nothing to do with her. Hawthorn is called "may" from the month in which it blossoms.

The association of Mary with flowers requires no explanation. "As a lily among thorns, so is my beloved among daughters," the Church sings. "Mystical Rose" (*q.v.*), the Litany of Loreto calls her, and the rose even more than the lily is the poet's choice: "There is no rose of such virtue, As is the rose that bare Jesu"; "This rose of flowers she is flower; She would not fade in any shower"; "For now is risen the bright day-star, From the rose Mary, flower of flowers"—so they sang in the fifteenth century. And as well as blossom, Mary is stem, bearing a yet lovelier flower: "Jesse's rod has blossomed; a maiden has born the incarnate God" are words the Church puts into our mouths. It is all summed up in one of the loveliest of Latin carols: "Flos de radice Jesse est natus hodie . . . Flos ille Jesus est: Maria virgo radix De qua flos ortus est": "A flower is born today from the root of Jesse . . . Jesus is that flower: the maiden Mary is the stem from which it has grown."

FOLGOËT, OUR LADY OF LE. Brittany is a land noted for its pilgrimages, and this is one of the chief of them. In 1419 a church took the place of a small chapel of our Lady in the forest of Lesneven, and it became the center of a big ecclesiastical establishment, with a pilgrim-shrine. After a chequered history it fell into decay before the Revolution and suffered from fire. In 1808 local people restored the ruined church and brought back the venerated image; it was crowned in 1888, and the pilgrimage has grown in popularity ever since. The principal day is September 8, but the shrine is also specially frequented on Sundays in May.

FORSAKEN, MOTHER OF THE (Sp. *Madre de los Desamparados*). About the year 1400 a confraternity was organized at Valencia in Spain to look after children who had been abandoned by their parents. A statue was made of our Lady as patroness of this work, and in 1667 she was chosen patroness of all Valencia under the title Mother of the Forsaken. Her feast is kept here, on the second Sunday of May, and in other places in Spain and Latin America on other dates.

FOUNTAIN SEALED, A. See GARDEN ENCLOSED, A.

FOURVIÈRE, OUR LADY OF. This famous French shrine of our Lady of Good Counsel stands upon a Roman site at Lyons; but old as the sanctuary is, the building is recent, its predecessors having been much damaged by Calvinists and again at the Revolution. During the Franco-Prussian War the people of Lyons pledged themselves to build a new church for the shrine should their city be spared: accordingly, the present basilica was begun in 1873 and consecrated in 1896. The older building, dedicated in honor of St. Thomas of Canterbury, still stands. The new church, overtopping the town of Fourvière, is a great pilgrimage center, especially on our Lady's birthday, September 8, when the Lyonnais fulfil their 300-year old promise of an annual pilgrimage in Mary's honor. Feast: 2nd Saturday after Easter.

FRANCE, SHRINES OF. There is a very large number of shrines of Mary of varying degrees of interest and importance in France: in an exhibition held at Dunquerque in 1928, there were pictures of over 500 in that country alone. The following are some of the more outstanding: Our Lady of Alet, Gascony; O.L. of Arcachon (*q.v.*); Notre-Dame des Ardents, Arras; O.L. of Ardilliers, Saumur, whose sanctuary was destroyed by war in 1940; O.L. of Aubervilliers, near Paris; O.L. of Avioth (*q.v.*); O.L. of Benoîte-Vaux (*q.v.*); O.L. of Bétharram (*q.v.*); O.L. of Boulogne (*q.v.*); O.L. of Brebières, Albert (*cf., Divine Shepherd, O.L. of the*); O.L. of Buglose, in the Landes (also the birthplace of St. Vincent de Paul); O.L. of Ceignac (*q.v.*); O.L. of Celles-sur-Belle, Poitou; Chartres (*q.v.*); O.L. of the Fountain, Chiévres; N.-D. de la Délivrande (*q.v.*); O.L. of Déols, Berry; O.L. of Dormans, Marne; O.L. of the Dunes, Dunquerque; O.L. of Dusenbach (*q.v.*); O.L. of the Thorn, Evron, in Mayenne; O.L. of Folgoët (*q.v.*), Brittany; O.L. of Fourvière (*q.v.*); N.-D. de la Garde (*q.v.*); O.L. of Good Help at Compiègne, Blosseville, and several other places; O.L. of Grace, Cambrai; La Salette (*q.v.*); of Le Laus, in Dauphiné; O.L. of Le Puy (*q.v.*); O.L. of Liesse (*q.v.*); O.L. of the Railings, Lille; Lourdes (*q.v.*); O.L. of Locmaria, Brittany; Mariental, Alsace; O.L. of Mézières; O.L. of Mercy, Nantes (see CENACLE); O.L. of Mighty Power, Périgueux; O.L. of Miracles at St.-Maur, Paris, and at St.-Omer; O.L. of the Miraculous Medal (*q.v.*), Paris; O.L. of Mantaigu, near Montpellier; O.L. of Myans (*q.v.*); O.L. of Piétat, Béarn; Pontmain (*q.v.*); N.-D. du Port (*q.v.*), Clermont-Ferrand; Rocamadour (*q.v.*);

O.L. of the Rock, Servières, in Limousin; O.L. of Rumengol, Brittany; O.L. of the Sacred Heart, Issoudun; the "Three Hail Marys" (*q.v.*), Blois; N.-D. des Tables (*q.v.*), Montpellier; O.L. of the Thorn-Bush (*q.v.*), Châlons-sur-Marne; O.L. of Vassivière, Puy-de-Dôme; O.L. of Victories (*q.v.*), Paris; O.L. of the Water-Willow, Vinay, near Grenoble; O.L. of Zion, Nancy.

FULGENS CORONA. The opening words and title, "The radiant crown," of an encyclical letter of Pope Pius XII proclaiming a Marian year to be observed in 1954, the first centenary of the dogmatic definition of the Immaculate Conception. After briefly tracing the history of the doctrine and bringing it into relation with the Assumption, the Pope turned to the special needs of the present day. "It is not enough," he wrote, "that this centenary celebration should rekindle Catholic faith and an ardent devotion to the Virgin Mother of God in the hearts of all. It must also lead Christians to conform their lives as closely as possible to her example." Her words, "Whatsoever he shall say to you, do ye" (John 2:5), she repeats today, when "the root cause of all the bitterness and violence which afflict individual men and whole peoples and nations is to be sought in this, that so many have forsaken Him who is 'the fountain of living water. . . .' " We have to look higher than earthly remedies for our ills; to our personal efforts to follow Christ more closely— for "faith without works is dead" (James 2:20,26)—must be added unwearying prayer: prayer for all men and women, for those afflicted in mind, body, or estate, especially the victims of injustice or of spiritual blindness; prayer for the Church and for those separated from her; and particularly those bishops who, "after being forced into silence and made the victims of every kind of intrigue, have to look on while their Christian flocks are harassed and thrown into confusion with no man to help them." "May they," says the Pope, "be inspired by the words of St. Bernard, 'We shall stand and fight unto death, if need be, for our mother [the Church], with those weapons that are allowed to us: that is, with prayer and lamentation to God, not with shields and swords.'" Finally, if we are to attain peace "we must all be instant in prayer to the Blessed Virgin Mary that she, who brought forth the Prince of Peace, will be our advocate and protectress in promoting a covenant of friendship among men."

The Pope's appeal for prayer has been actualized in the following summary of his words: "Mary, Mother of God and Mother of men, look graciously upon your children who bring their petitions to you. Obtain bread for the hungry, justice for the oppressed, a speedy return for all exiles and refugees, homes for those who have none. To the prisoners, to bishops, priests and people who are unjustly kept captive, bring courage and release. Give sight to the blind, whether in body or spirit. For all who are divided by hatred, ill-will or discord obtain the gift of charity from your own divine Son, who so loved men as to give His life for them. Amen."

FULL OF GRACE. These words were spoken of and to our Lady by the angel at the Annunciation; and in the prayer called the Hail Mary they have been repeated daily on the lips of numberless Christians for many centuries. The words mean simply that Mary had the grace necessary to fulfil that to which she was called, to be the mother of God made man: but that in itself was sufficient to give her grace far above all other creatures, angelic or human. The Fathers expatiate on this. Mary was, says St. Epiphanius, "full of grace in every respect"; she was, says St. Anthanasius, "full of grace because, filled with the Holy Spirit, she overflowed with all graces and was overshadowed by the power of the Most High"; and in a famous passage St. Augustine, contemplating her virginal divine motherhood, asks the angel "Whence has Mary this?" and puts in the angel's mouth the reply, "I already said when I greeted her —'Hail, full of grace.'" Pope Pius IX declares in *Ineffabilis Deus* (*q.v.*) that God endowed Mary, "more than all the angels and saints, with such an abundance of heavenly gifts that she was always wholly free from sin; so that, perfect and all beautiful, she shone in such complete innocence and holiness that no greater holiness can be imagined except that of God himself, no mind but God's can measure it."

Father R. Garrigou-Lagrange, o.p., writes in his *Mother of the Saviour*

(Dublin edn., pp. 49-50): "When speaking of fullness of grace it is well to note that it exists in three different degrees, in our Lord, in Mary and in the just. . . . There is, first of all, the absolute fullness of grace which is peculiar to Jesus, the Saviour of mankind. Taking into consideration only the ordinary power of God, there can be no greater grace than this. It is the eminent and inexhaustible source of all the grace which men have received since the Fall, or will receive till the end of time. It is the source also of the beatitude of the elect, for Jesus has merited all the effects of our predestination. There is, in the second place, the fullness of superabundance which is Mary's special privilege, and which is so named since it is like a spiritual river which has poured of its abundance upon the souls of men for almost two thousand years. There is finally the fullness of sufficiency which is common to all the just and which makes them capable of performing those meritorious acts . . . which lead them to eternal life. . . . Mary's fullness of grace did not cease to increase up to the time of her death. For that reason theologians usually speak of (1) her initial fullness or plenitude; (2) her second sanctification at the instant of the conception of the Saviour; (3) the final fullness (at the instant of her entry into glory), its extent and its superabundance."

In the hymns of the Eastern Church the phrase "Full of grace" is sometimes used as a title of address to Mary, without her name, which is just how the angel addressed her at the Annunciation; many commentators stress the importance of this last fact. Already in the third century Origen remarked that the angel's form of salutation is unique in the Scriptures and reserved exclusively to the Blessed Virgin. *Cf.*, Holiness; Immaculate Conception; Sinlessness.

G

GARDE, NOTRE-DAME DE LA.
This shrine is familiar to whoever has approached Marseilles from the sea, the statue of the Mother and Child dominating the city from the top of the western tower of the church, which in its turn is perched on the top of a high hill. It is well named "of the Look-out." The pilgrimage is said to date from the thirteenth century, but the statue of our Lady is relatively modern, having been made to take the place of the one lost during the Revolution. Feast: Saturday after the Assumption.

GARDEN ENCLOSED, A. An expression from the Song of Songs (4:12), accommodated to the Blessed Virgin: "My bride, my true love, is a garden enclosed, a fountain sealed up." St. Jerome uses it in a passage read at Matins in the Saturday office (*q.v.*) of our Lady during February: "Christ was a virgin, and the Mother of our virgin Lord was always a virgin, maiden and mother. Jesus came through closed doors. . . . A garden enclosed and a fountain sealed up. . . ." By a garden is meant mystically, Cardinal Newman says, "a place of spiritual repose, stillness, peace, refreshment and delight. Thus our first parents were placed in 'a garden of pleasure' shaded by trees, 'fair to behold and pleasant to eat of,' with the Tree of Life in the midst, and a river to water the ground. Thus our Lord, speaking from the cross to the penitent robber, calls the blessed place, the Heaven to which He was taking him, 'paradise,' or a garden of pleasure. Therefore St. John, in the Apocalypse, speaks of Heaven, the palace of God, as a garden or paradise, in which was the Tree of Life giving forth its fruits every month." Such is the far-reaching allusiveness and significance of these symbolical figures of speech.

GARMENT OF OUR LADY, Feast of the. On July 2 in the Byzantine rite there is commemorated the enshrining, about the year 473 at Blakhernae (*q.v.*), of what was believed to be a garment of the Mother of God (referred to indifferently as robe, gown, tunic, veil, shift). A similar feast is observed in the Armenian rite. To the exposition on the walls of this and other relics and icons was attributed the successful defense of Constantinople against the Persians in 625, and this gave rise to similar stories about besieged cities elsewhere, e.g., in Russia. The hymn of the day says: "Ever-virgin Birth-giver, refuge of mankind, you have bestowed upon your city [Constantinople] the robe and girdle of your pure body as a sheltering mantle. Through your seedless birth-giving they have been kept undecayed, for by you nature and time are regenerated. Wherefore do we implore you to give safety to your city

and the great mercy to our souls."
See also GIRDLE; PROTECTING VEIL.

Similar relics have been claimed for the West, the best known being that which is still preserved in Chartres cathedral: a piece of plain silken material about two yards long by eight inches wide. According to a twelfth-century tradition it was sent to Charlemagne by the Byzantine emperor, Constantine V, and was given to the cathedral by Charles the Bald in 876. Nothing is known of its earlier history. A famous relic known as our Lady's cloak is venerated in the cathedral at Aachen in Germany.—About 1750, when repairs were being done to the spire (404 ft. high) of St. Mary's cathedral at Salisbury in England, a reliquary was found containing a piece of bluish material. It was surmised, probably correctly, that this was a reputed piece of a garment of our Lady, built into the top of the spire when it was finished c. 1330, perhaps to preserve it against lightning. So far as is known the relic is still there, though subsequent repairs did not bring it to light. *Cf.,* Relics.

GATE OF HEAVEN. Latin, *Janua caeli,* a title given to our Lady in the Litany of Loreto; she was the gate through whom Christ came to open Heaven to man, and at her prayers the gates of Heaven are opened to the souls in Purgatory. The first recorded use of the expression is by a doctor of the Church, St. Peter Damian (d. 1072), and the same idea occurs in the *Alma Redemptoris Mater* and *Ave, Regina caelorum* (*qq.v*). "Mary is called the Gate of Heaven, because it was through her that our Lord passed from Heaven to earth. The prophet Ezechiel, prophesying of Mary, says, 'The gate shall be closed, it shall not be opened, and no man shall pass through it, since the Lord God of Israel has entered through it—and it shall be closed for the Prince, the Prince himself shall sit in it.' Now this is fulfilled, not only in our Lord having taken flesh from her, and being her Son, but moreover in that she had a place in the economy of Redemption; it is fulfilled in her spirit and will, as well as in her body. . . . With the full consent of a full heart, full of God's love to her and her own lowliness, she said, 'Behold the handmaid of the Lord, be it done unto me according to thy word.' It was by this consent that she became the Gate of Heaven" (John Henry Newman, *Meditations and Devotions*).

GENAZZANO. See GOOD COUNSEL, OUR LADY OF.

GENEALOGY OF MARY. The genealogy of the Blessed Virgin is not recorded in the New Testament, but it is the Church's tradition that she was descended from David, the second and greatest of the kings of Israel. That the man Jesus was descended from David was recognized by His contemporaries: "Jesus, son of David, have mercy on me," was the cry of blind Bartimeus (Mark 10:47-48), and the awaited Messiah was to be a descendant of David (*cf.,* Matt. 22:41-46). But it was not simply *natural* ancestry that was in question, and St. Matthew (1:1-17) and St. Luke (3:23-38) both give genealogies of the *legal* descent of Christ from David through

His foster-father, St. Joseph. The discrepancies between these lists and the problems to which they give rise do not concern us here. But they are of importance as concerns our Lady because they have been used in attempts to throw doubt on the virginity of her marriage with Joseph, in spite of St. Matthew's statement (1:18) and St. Luke's evidence (1:30-35) about the circumstances of Christ's birth. Such misunderstandings arise in part from failure to realize the importance given by the ancients to legal recognition by a father, as distinct from physical parentage. The Christian tradition of physical descent from David through Mary can already be inferred from St. Paul's letters (Rom. 1:3; II Tim. 2:8), and indeed from the words of the angel of the Annunciation: "the Lord God will give him the throne of David his father" (Luke 1:32).

In the middle ages Christ's Davidic descent through Mary was sometimes represented in a series of figures, in stained-glass or carved. This is called a Jesse-window or Jesse-tree, from David's father, Jesse the Bethlehemite, the first figure in the series. The various persons forming the line are depicted on branches or sprays of foliage. The same idea was occasionally used for a branched candlestick. In hymnody, both Latin and vernacular, there are frequent references to the root of Jesse or the house or family of David in relation to Mary, and in the liturgy, too; e.g., the first antiphon at Lauds on her birthday: "This is the birthday of the glorious Virgin Mary, of the seed of Abraham, born of the tribe of Judah, of the noble race of David." Some liturgies have the following responsory: "The root of Jesse put forth a shoot, and the shoot put forth a blossom, and the fruitful Spirit rests upon this flower"; cf. the antiphon (first Vespers, Circumcision and Purification), "The root of Jesse has budded, the star has risen out of Jacob, the Virgin has given birth to the Savior."

GERMANY, SHRINES OF. The Protestant Reformation played havoc with Mary's shrines in many parts of what is now called Germany, but there is still today a good number of no little importance, as well as others less well known. Only a few of these German shrines have a proper feast attached to them, the local festival being generally celebrated on one of the great feasts of our Lady. In the dioceses of the former kingdom of Bavaria a feast is kept on May 14 of the Blessed Virgin, Patroness of Bavaria, and this is a special pilgrimage day at Munich. Among the chief sanctuaries are Aachen (cf., Garment); Our Lady of Altenberg, patroness of youth; O.L. of Altötting (q.v.); O.L. of Bamberg; O.L. of Birnau (q.v.); O.L. of Blieskastel (q.v.); O.L. of Bornhofen in the Rhineland; O.L. of the Chapel (q.v.), near Würzburg; O.L. of the Crescent Moon, at the Benedictine abbey of Andechs; O.L. of Peace at Cologne; O.L of. Dettelbach (q.v.); O.L. of Ettal (q.v.); O.L. of Freystadt (Neumark); O.L. of Help at Passau and Regensburg; O.L. of Kevelaer (q.v.); O.L. of Lorch (a shrine that perhaps goes back a thousand years); Maria-Birnbaum; Maria-Eich (q.v.); Maria-Siebeneich, near Augsburg; O.L. of the Pardon, Cologne; O.L. of the Pine

Tree, Triberg in Baden; Sankt März-gen, near Freiburg in Breisgau; O.L. of Sossau, near Straubing in Bavaria; the Sorrowful Mother at the Duke's Hospital in Munich, at the convent of Marienstatt in Westerwald, at Telgte in Westphalia, and elsewhere; O.L. of Schönstatt (*q.v.*); O.L. of Werl (*q.v.*); O.L. of Zell, in Baden. O.L. of Alben-dorf, "the Jerusalem of the Plains," and O.L. of Wartha are now in Po-land.

GIRDLE OF OUR LADY, Confra-ternity of the. According to the tra-dition of the Augustinian Order our Lady appeared to St. Monica, mother of St. Augustine, and gave her a leather girdle or belt, saying, "Take this; it is a thankworthy sign of my love. . . ." In due course a leather belt was adopted by the hermit friars of St. Augustine as a part of their habit, and the Archconfraternity of the Blessed Virgin, the holy father Augustine, and St. Monica was estab-lished. Members of the confraternity wear a black leather belt (*cinctura*), fastened through a bone ring, which is blessed with prayers asking Al-mighty God for the grace of conti-nence for the wearer; at the same time he or she receives the rosary of our Lady of Consolation (*q.v.*), whose day, the Saturday after St. Augustine's feast (August 28), is the feast-day of the confraternity. An alternative ex-planation of the origin of the girdle is that, in 1315, a paralytic woman of Palermo in Sicily was cured by being girt with a cincture by our Lady in vision in the Augustinian church.

GIRDLE OF OUR LADY, Feast of the. On August 31 in the Byzantine rite is commemorated the enshrining, about the year 940, in the church of Khalkoprateia at Constantinople, of what was venerated as Mary's girdle. This festival is observed also in the Armenian rite. One story says this relic was brought from Jerusalem about the year 400; another says it came from Zileh in Pontus about 550; but it seems to have come from there in the tenth century.—In 1953 a ves-sel was found beneath the altar of a dissident Jacobite church at Homs in Syria, containing a piece of silken material. The Jacobite patriarch claims to have ancient evidence that this also was a girdle or sash of the Blessed Virgin. The cathedral of Tor-tosa in Spain also claims a girdle relic, of which it is related that it was found miraculously deposited on the altar on the eve of the Annunciation in 1178. A similar relic is preserved at Prato cathedral in Italy; it was brought there from Jerusalem in 1141. *Cf.,* Garment; Relics.

GLASTONBURY, OUR LADY OF. Glastonbury, situated below a hill amid the marshes of Somerset, was a religious settlement of great antiquity, first peopled by monks of the British Celtic church. Later ages surrounded it with picturesque but untrue stories, of which one of the best known, first recorded only in the thirteenth cen-tury, relates to St. Joseph of Ari-mathea. He, we are told, came to the Isle of Britain and at Glastonbury built a church of wattles in honor of the Blessed Virgin, fifteen years after her taking up into Heaven. The Lady chapel of the medieval Benedictine abbey was believed to stand on the site of this legendary first church. Devotion to Mary came to an end at Glastonbury after 1539, when the monastery was destroyed. (The abbot, Bl. Richard Whiting, and two other monks were hanged.) The present Catholic church of our Lady stands opposite the abbey ruins and was consecrated in 1941; in 1954 the revived shrine of our Lady of Glastonbury was formally inaugurated in this church.

GLORIA, FARCED. "Farcing" is filling up (Lat. *farcire*), or more exactly interpolating, between the phrases of a psalm, hymn, etc. with other words. It was a common medieval custom, especially in the *Kyrie* at Mass. In some places the *Gloria in excelsis Deo* was farced on feasts of our Lady, in the following form: "Glory be to God on high. . . . Lord Jesus Christ, only-begotten Son. Courage and bountiful comforter of orphans. Lord God, Lamb of God, Son of the Father, first-born of the maiden-mother Mary, who takest away . . . receive our prayer, to Mary's glory. Thou who sittest . . . For thou alone art the Holy One, hallowing Mary. Thou alone art the Lord, ruling Mary. Thou alone, Jesus Christ, art the Most High, crowning Mary, with the Holy Ghost in the glory of God the Father. Amen." The Gloria so treated was called *Gloria de Domina,* "Gloria of the Lady." All such farcings were abolished by Pope St. Pius V in 1570. But the above continued to be allowed in the diocese of Braga in Portugal until 1924. *Cf.,* Te Deum Mariale.

GLORIES OF MARY, THE. A book written by St. Alphonsus Liguori (d. 1787), doctor of the Church, published in 1750: one of the most famous and influential of all works on our Lady. It is very long (624 pages in the English translation of 1852), and in three parts: the first consists of a detailed commentary on the *Salve Regina;* the second, of discourses on the chief feasts of Mary, with special sections on her sorrows and virtues and on several devotions; while the third includes sermons, meditations, and prayers, and some answers to objections. The general method of the book is a doctrinal exposition of each point, followed by an example or anecdote, and a prayer. At the time it was written many orthodox writers were intimidated by the Jansenists, and minimized Marian theology for fear of being accused of going too far. St. Alphonsus was not intimidated, but he admits himself that he did not issue his book without some apprehension; and criticism indeed there was. For example, of his teaching that "every grace that comes to us from God comes through the mediation of Mary." In those days the doctrine of her universal mediation was far from holding the position it does today; and St. Alphonsus deduced from it that a certain "zeal for Mary and trust in her intercession" is normally necessary for salvation, which was very unfavorably received by some. But Liguori's learning, combined with an infectious piety, succeeded in firmly establishing his book, which had a very great influence.

A century later *The Glories of Mary* became a sort of symbol or representative work in the difference of opinion among English Catholics about "continental influences." The hereditary Catholics hoped for "a revival of English piety, on the lines, not of the *Glories of Mary,* or what Faber called 'hot prayers,' but of Challoner's *Meditations.*" But many others followed Father Faber, who "drew his inspiration less from directly medieval sources than from such collections of their modern counterparts as St. Alfonso's *Glories of Mary*" (W. Ward, *Life of Cardinal Wiseman,* II, 218-221). To some readers this famous book still seems in parts exaggerated in expression; but it has to be borne in mind that it is the work of a writer of expansive religious temperament, written at a time when some people were trying to "regulate" devotion to our Lady in such a way as to do away with it altogether. For St. Alphonsus, no less than for Cardinal Newman and all other Catholics, "the glories of Mary are for the sake of her Son."

GOLDEN LITANY, The. A long English late-medieval litany of the redeeming work of the incarnate Son of God. The following passages refer to our Lady St. Mary:

"By that ineffable love whereby thou chosest Mary most pure virgin unto thy mother—Have mercy on us.

By that most holy name Mary, that descended and flowed from the high throne of the glorious Trinity—Have mercy on us.

By the conception of thy blessed Mother and virgin which was sanctified in her mother's womb—Have mercy on us.

By her most holy nativity—Have mercy on us.

By her virginity and great meekness —Have mercy on us.

By that meek affection and love that drew thee from the bosom of the Father into the womb of the Virgin —Have mercy on us.

For that unspeakable delectation and gladness that thy blessed Mother had in thy nativity—Have mercy on us.

For the sword of sorrow that went through the soul of thy blessed Mother, and her great compassion and tears that standing by the cross lamentably she shed—Have mercy on us."

It will be noticed that the reference to our Lady's conception is a little ambiguous: the doctrine of the Immaculate Conception had not yet been clarified and defined.

GOLDEN MASS (Missa aurea). In Poland, Bohemia, parts of Germany, and elsewhere on many days in Advent there is celebrated the Mass of our Lady, *Rorate caeli,* instead of the Mass of the day. It is not clear why this is called the Golden Mass. The same name was given to the votive Mass of Mary sung in some German churches on the three Saturdays after September 29, and to the votive Mass of the Annunciation sung in many Belgian churches on the ember Wednesday in Advent.

GOOD COUNSEL, OUR LADY OF. This image of the Mother and Child, at first called St. Mary of Paradise, is in the Augustinian church at Genazzano, some thirty miles southeast of Rome. It is painted upon an extremely thin sheet of plaster, which rests upon a narrow ledge, without being supported by the wall behind. A bomb exploded close by in the church during World War II, doing much damage, but the picture was hardly scratched. This image is first heard of in 1467, when it is supposed to have appeared miraculously in Genazzano; according to the story, it had formerly been venerated at Skodra, in Albania, in similar circumstances. It soon became an object of pilgrimage, miracles were claimed, and in 1630 Pope Urban VIII visited it; the image was crowned in 1682. Our Lady of Good Counsel is probably the most venerated picture of Mary in the West, after our Lady of Perpetual Help (*q.v.*). It has often been reproduced: there are good copies in the Oratory church in London, at St. Augustine's, Hammersmith, and at St. Mary of the Angels, Stoke-on-Trent, in England, and at Villanova College, Pa., and elsewhere in the United States. There is a pilgrimage shrine of our Lady under this title at the Kentucky mountain mission-center at Hazard, Ky.

The Genazzano church has always been in charge of the hermit-friars of St. Augustine, and in 1779 a *feast* of our Lady of Good Counsel was granted to that order, with proper Mass and Office, and it is observed also in a number of other churches, on April 26. There is a confraternity and scapular (*q.v.*) under this invocation, which was added to the Litany of Loreto by Pope Leo XIII. The name "of our Lady of Good Counsel" is given to an English Catholic society that gives free legal advice and assistance to the poor, and to an organization, Filiae Matris Boni Consilii, for the encouragement of religious vocations among women.—The gradual of the proper Mass of the feast is from the book of Proverbs: "I am the wisdom that dwells in the council, I have my place among the thoughts of the learned. Blessed are they who listen to me, keep vigil, day by day, at my threshold, watching till I open my doors. Alleluia, alleluia! He who finds me will find life, he will draw from the Lord salvation. Alleluia."

GOOD STUDIES, OUR LADY OF. The Holy See has indulgenced a prayer for students addressed to the Blessed Virgin under this title. The house of studies of the School Sisters of Notre Dame at Washington, D.C., is named in honor of our Lady of Good Studies.

GOSPEL OF THE INFANCY. See PROTEVANGELIUM OF JAMES; PSEUDO-MATTHEW.

GOSTYN, OUR LADY OF. The Oratorian church at Gostyn is an important pilgrimage place in the Polish region of Poznan, on account of an icon of Mary enshrined there. Devotion to our Lady of Gostyn has been transplanted to the United States, where there is a church dedicated under this name at Downers Grove, Ill.

GRACE, OUR LADY OF. A large number of churches observe, on very various dates, a feast of our Lady of

Grace or of the Mother of Graces, accordingly as she is considered as herself "full of grace" or as the mother who brings down graces and benefits on us. But indeed the two aspects go together, as is shown by the proper collect of the feast kept on June 9 by the Redemptorist Congregation and elsewhere: "God conferred the grace of regeneration on mankind through Mary's fruitful virginity, may we then share her happiness in Heaven." In medieval times there was a celebrated shrine of our Lady of Grace at Ipswich in England, and a Cistercian abbey, St. Mary Graces, stood near the Tower of London; today a Catholic church stands near the site and perpetuates the memory in a shrine of our Lady of Graces. There are similar shrines at Altötting (*q.v.*) in Germany, Cambrai in France, Cork in Ireland, and elsewhere, including Colebrook, N.H., near the Canadian border. This was established by the Oblates of Mary Immaculate in 1949, in thanksgiving for the twenty-fifth anniversary of their junior seminary at Colebrook. The statue of the Mother of All Graces stands in the open air. There is a shrine of our Lady of Grace in the Jesuit church in Montreal, and another, conducted by Augustinian friars, at Marylake, King City, Ont.; church dedications in her honor are fairly common in North America.

In the Coptic rite a commemoration recalling benefits conferred at the intercession of our Lady is supposed to be made on the 30th of every month.—The "Praise of our Lady of Grace" is a short office said by the Augustinian friars after Compline. It consists of three psalms and three short lessons, with responsories, taken from a sermon in praise of Mary attributed (though apparently wrongly) to St. Augustine of Hippo. *Cf.,* Liesse; Youghal, Our Lady of.

GRAZIE, SANTA MARIA DELLE, Milan. Of the several shrines of our Lady of Graces in Italy, this is probably the best known, partly because of the presence of Leonardo da Vinci's painting of the Last Supper in the refectory of the priory. In 1465 Ludovico "the Black" commissioned Bramante to build a church over a small chapel on the wall of which an image of Mary had been painted by Leonardo il Civerchio. This church has been one of the most frequented Lombard places of pilgrimage since the plagues of the sixteenth and seventeenth centuries in Milan. Feast: June 9.

GREECE, SHRINES OF. The small minority of Catholics in Greece is mainly composed of people of hellenized foreign descent and of the Latin rite, many of them living in the islands. They have three principal sanctuaries of the Mother of God: our Lady Manifest (festival day on September 24), on the island of Siros; O.L. of Vryssi, on Tinos (August 15); and O.L. of Cassiope, on Corfu (May 8), where the image is reputed wonderworking. The three most important shrines of the Orthodox Church of Greece are our Lady of the Annunciation on Tinos (here again the icon is said to be miraculous), O.L. of the Hundred Gates on Paros, and O.L.'s Purification at Messinia in the

Peloponnese. Others are the Annunciation at Nauplia, the Healing Virgin near Loutraki, the Virgin of the Sweet Kiss on Mitylene and of the Beautiful Voice near Pharsala, the Fountain of Life at Kalavrita, the Virgin of the Myrtles on Kithira, and sanctuaries of the Falling Asleep of Mary on Samothrace and elsewhere. On the Holy Mountain (Athos), there are such well-known images as the Consoling Virgin at Vatopedi, the Three-handed Virgin at Khilandari, and our Lady of Iviron (q.v.).—Among Greek shrines outside of Greece are the Virgin All-blessed and the Life-giving Fountain (q.v.) at Constantinople; and our Lady of Kykko and others on Cyprus.

GREEN VALLEY, OUR LADY OF THE. This Sicilian shrine is said to have originated about the year 1040, when a bandit, who operated around Mount Etna, was converted by a vision of our Lady, who appeared to him in an earthquake (Etna is a volcano). The robber turned hermit, and built a chapel at a spot in a green valley to which he was directed by a flight of cranes; it was provided, miraculously, the story goes, with a picture of our Lady in the form of a Byzantine icon, which is still venerated. A feast of St. Mary of the Green Valley is kept throughout three dioceses of Sicily in August.

GROTTAFERRATA. This Italian sanctuary is of special interest as being in a church of Eastern rite. It is at the Byzantine monastery of Grottaferrata in the Alban Hills near Rome, founded for his Greek monks by St. Neilos in 1004, the spot having been pointed out by our Lady in a vision. The local tradition explaining the name of the place is that there was once a shrine of the Mother of God here behind an iron grating (ferrata) in a cave (grotta). The icon of our Lady now venerated in the church of the Italo-Greek monks at Grottaferrata is a Hodegetria (q.v.); it is the center of a local pilgrimage.

GUADALUPE, OUR LADY OF. There are two sanctuaries of this name, in Spain and in Mexico, the second taking its name from the first, but not otherwise connected with one another. According to a Spanish tradition, Pope St. Gregory the Great gave an image of the Mother of God to St. Leander of Seville (d. 596); when the Moors invaded Spain it was hidden in a cave in the Guadalupe mountains of Estremadura. Here it was found in 1326, and enshrined in a Franciscan monastery which became one of the great pilgrimage-centers of the country. The feast of our Lady of Guadalupe is kept throughout the province of Estremadura on September 6.

The Mexican image of our Lady of Guadalupe is a painting on a piece of very coarse woven material. Mary is represented almost life-size, Indian in appearance, with hands together, completely surrounded by an aureole of golden rays; she is standing on a crescent moon, supported by a cherub. The story as it has come down to us is that in December, 1531, our Lady appeared at Tepeyac hill, outside Mexico City, to an Indian neophyte, a man baptized Juan Diego; she asked him to tell the bishop to build a church there. He did so, and the bishop asked for a sign. Diego saw the vision twice more, and was told as a sign to gather some roses that had miraculously sprung up. When he opened his cloak to show the bishop the flowers, the painting described above was found upon it: it had not been there before. Other people were present at the time, and depositions of the whole occurrence were taken by various commissions. A chapel to enshrine the picture was soon built at the site of the first vision. An English visitor in 1568, Miles Philips, left an interesting account of the sanctuary in his day, including the spring of water that was suddenly discovered where Mary was said to have appeared for the third time.

The shrine was soon given the name of Guadalupe after the one in Spain, and rapidly became famous. In 1709 the image was translated to the present great church, where it was crowned in 1895. In 1756 our Lady of Guadalupe was declared patroness of New Spain, and in 1910 of all Latin America, where her feast is observed on December 12, with proper Mass and Office. The feast is also kept in the states of Arizona, California, Nevada, and New Mexico, and there are Guadalupe shrines at Mesilla Park, N.M., and Halifax in Canada. There is a large number of churches dedicated in honor of our Lady of Guadalupe even outside Mexico, and nearly all of them take their name from the Mexican shrine, to which tens of thousands of pilgrims flock every year.

Pope Pius XI named our Lady of Guadalupe patroness of all the Americas. Copies of the image are numerous: there is a well-known one in the church of St. Nicholas-in-the-Jail at Rome.

GUARD OF HONOR, OUR LADY'S. See Association of the Perpetual Rosary under ROSARY CONFRATERNITY.

GUIDE OF THE WAY, OUR LADY. See HODEGETRIA.

GYÖR, OUR LADY OF. Györ is one of the best-known sanctuaries of Hungary, owing to the presence over the altar of the cathedral there of a picture known as the Irish Madonna. An exiled bishop of Clonfert in Galway, Walter Lynch, came in 1655 from Vienna to Györ, bringing this picture with him; he died there and was buried in the crypt of the cathedral, after bequeathing the picture to the local bishop. It is sometimes said that Bishop Lynch had brought away the picture from his own cathedral at Clonfert, but this is not certain; nor is its origin known—it has been ascribed to Italian, Flemish, and Spanish painters. It shows our Lady kneeling beside her Child, asleep in bed with a crown on His head. The great popularity of the Irish Madonna in Györ dates from St. Patrick's day, 1697; on that day, at a time when new penal laws were afflicting the Catholics of Ireland, many people testified that the picture exuded blood and tears.

H

HAIL, HOLY QUEEN. See SALVE REGINA.

HAIL MARY, The. The colloquial and usual name of the prayer properly known as the Angelical Salutation, the most common and familiar of all prayers addressed to the Blessed Virgin. It consists of three parts, of which the first and second are scriptural (Luke 1:28, 42), and the third is added by the Church, thus:

"[1] Hail, Mary, full of grace, the Lord is with thee, blessed art thou among women [2] and blessed is the fruit of thy womb, Jesus. [3] Holy Mary, mother of God, pray for us sinners now and at the hour of our death. Amen."

The Hail Mary occurs in numberless forms of devotion, sometimes frequently repeated, and in private prayer has a place only second to the Lord's Prayer itself. But it is not used as a prayer in the liturgy, wherein all prayers are addressed directly to the Triune God or one of the Persons of that Blessed Trinity. The first and second parts, however, are used as offertory and alleluia verses in certain Masses and as an antiphon in offices of our Lady, and in the Little Office (*q.v.*). The Hail Mary in entirety is said (with the Lord's Prayer) at the end of the preparatory prayers at Mass in the Carthusian rite, and among those prayers in several local uses.

In the West the scriptural portion of the Hail Mary was set down as the offertory on the fourth Sunday of Advent in the Gregorian Antiphoner, but there is no sign of its use in popular devotion before the eleventh century. It is in the following century that short forms of the Hail Mary, deriving from the Little Office B.V.M., seem to have come into common use among the faithful; but the full form we have now developed only gradually. An English manuscript Primer (prayer-book) of the fifteenth century gives the prayer thus (spelling modernized): "Hail, Mary, full of grace, the Lord is with thee. Thou art blessed among women: and blessed the fruit of thy womb, Jesus. So be it." This can be taken as representative of the common form in the later middle ages. The short form is by no means obsolete: for example, it is still said at the beginning and the end of the hours of the Little Office B.V.M. in the Carmelite, Cistercian, Dominican, and Premonstratensian rites and in the Bridgettine office, and the Servite friars say it thus at the beginning of Mass and at each hour of the office. Until quite lately two forms of the prayer were still well known in Ireland, one ending at "Jesus," the other complete. Our present version was known by the end of the fifteenth century, and something very like it was translated from French into English in 1503; but Lawrence

102

Vaux in his English catechism (1st ed., 1567) still gives the short version. But in the previous year the Roman Catechism had said: "The Church of God has very rightly added petition and an invocation of the most holy Mother of God to this thanksgiving, thereby showing that we ought to turn to her humbly and religiously, in order that through her intercession she may reconcile us sinners with God and obtain for us the blessings we need both for this present life and the life which shall have no end"; and in 1568 Pope St. Pius V fixed the form we have now. It appears that in England throughout the middle ages the Hail Mary (and the Creed and Our Father) was always taught in Latin, even to the illiterate, and seems generally to have been thus used even in private prayer. This is the opinion expressed in Father H. Thurston's *Familiar Prayers* (1953). (For the Latin text, see AVE MARIA.)

In the East the scriptural part of the Hail Mary already occurs in liturgical use from about the fifth century, but among the Orthodox and others not in communion with Rome it does not figure in private devotion. Catholics of Eastern rites, however, now use the prayer, often in the same form as in the West. But the authentic Eastern version, recognized by the Holy See by the granting of indulgences for its recitation, is as follows:

"Hail, Mary, full of grace, maiden Mother of God, the Lord is with thee: blessed art thou among women and blessed is the fruit of thy womb, be-cause thou hast brought forth Christ, the savior of our souls. Amen."

In the three most-used liturgical languages of the Byzantine rite, this runs:

Greek: "Theotoke parthene, khaire, kekharitomene Maria, ho Kurios meta sou: eulogemene su en gunaixi, kaieu-logemenos ho karpos tes koilias sou, hoti sotera etekes ton psukhon hemon. Amin."

Slavonic: "Bogoroditse dievo, ra-dujsya, blagodatnaya Marije, Gospod's toboyu: blagoslovenna ty v zhenakh i blagosloven plod chreva tvojego, yako spasa rodila jesi dush nashikh. Amin."

Rumanian: "Născătoare de Dum-nezeu, fecioară, bucură-te ceea-ce eşti plină de dar, Marie, Domnul este cu tine: binecuvântată eşti tu între muieri, şi binecuvântat este rodul pântecelui tău, că ai născut pe Hristos mântuitoral sufletelor noastre. Amin."

There is record of almost precisely the same version as above as known in Egypt thirteen hundred years ago. The Ethiopian rite, used in Ethiopia (Abyssinia), is unique in that it in-cludes a form of the Hail Mary in the ordinary text of the Mass, just before the gospel. It runs, "Hail Mary . . . thy womb. Pray and inter-cede with thy beloved Son that He will forgive us our sins"; and it is said in alternate clauses by priest and people. See also ROSARY.

HAL, OUR LADY OF. The na-tional Marian sanctuary of Belgium, near Brussels. At the east end of a lovely fourteenth-century church is enshrined the image given to the town in 1267, the seated Mother suckling her Child; like other statues elsewhere, it has a regular wardrobe of clothes, and it was crowned in 1874. Among the benefactors of the church was Henry VIII of England, who gave it a monstrance that is still there. Around the town are numerous chapels and shrines, which pilgrims visit one by one in a sort of "grand tour." The Belgian church at Camden Town in London is dedicated in honor of our Lady of Hal. Feast: September 1.

HANSWIJK, OUR LADY OF. Hanswijk is a hamlet near to Mechlin (Malines) in Belgium, where there was a popular shrine of our Lady during the later middle ages. During the troubles of the sixteenth century the seated walnut-wood figure of Mother and Child was taken into Mechlin for safety, and in 1678 it was transferred to a great new church by the Louvain gate of the city. The statue was crowned in 1876, our Lady of Hanswijk being acclaimed as patroness of the ecclesiastical province of Belgium. Feast: May 30.

HARISSA. On a mountain at Harissa, northeast of Beirut, there stands a great statue of our Lady of the Lebanon, looking out over the sea. During the year 1954 a Marian congress was held at Beirut, in the course of which another statue, specially made for the occasion, was crowned by a papal legate, in the presence of a huge gathering of Catholics of half-a-dozen rites,

with many other Christians and also non-Christians. This statue had previously been carried from village to village in the Lebanon, where Mohammedans and Druzes vied with Christians in doing it honor. The image is carved in cedar wood and represents our Lady at the moment of the Annunciation: Mary, the Handmaid of the Lord. It is now enshrined at Harissa at the Melkite monastery of the Missionaries of St. Paul.

HARTLEY, OUR LADY OF. This shrine in Kent is housed in a church made from a thatched barn of great age. The shrine itself was established in 1913, the image being an eighteenth-century statue from Belgium; many are the graces connected with it, to which a number of *ex-voto* (*q.v.*) hearts give testimony. The sanctuary has received papal indulgences.

HARVEST, OUR LADY IN. The Roman Ritual provides for August 15 a long blessing that is in effect a miniature harvest-thanksgiving; it is directed to take place immediately before Mass. It begins with Psalm 64, "O God, thou shalt yet have praise in Zion," followed by versicles and responses, referring to rain, grass and vegetables, wheat, wine and oil. Then follow three prayers. The first asks God's blessing on the fruits of the harvest, samples of which the people are holding in their hands. The second is a thanksgiving, asking, too, for bodily health for man and beast, and protection against the wiles of the Devil: it ends, "May we, carrying the sheaves of good works, deserve to be taken up to Heaven, through the merits of blessed Mary the Virgin, the feast of whose Assumption we are celebrating." The third prayer is: "O God, who on this day didst raise to highest Heaven the branch of Jesse, the Mother of Jesus Christ, thy Son, our Lord, that through her prayers and aid thou mightest communicate the fruit of her womb, that same Son, to our mortal nature: we pray thee that we may use these fruits of the earth for our welfare in time and in eternity, helped by the power of thy Son and the renowned support of His Mother." Then the grain and other fruits are again blessed, sprinkled with holy water, and incensed.—In times past in England, "our Lady in Harvest" was a familiar name for her Assumption feast. A sixteenth-century verse says:

The Blessed Virgin Mary's feast hath
    here his place and time,
Wherein, departing from the earth,
    she did the heavens climb;
Great bundles then of herbs to church
    the people fast do bear,
The which against all hurtful things
    the priest doth hallow there.

The Syrian, Maronite, and Chaldean rites celebrate a feast of our Lady in Harvest, "of Sheaves," but earlier in the year.

HEALING WATER, Shrine of the. An Italian shrine near Voltri in Liguria. It has its name (*Acquasanta*) from a spring of warm medicinal water, whose properties are said to have been revealed by a vision of our Lady in 1360. A wooden statue was put up soon after, but the church was not built till 1680. It is a great center of local pilgrimages and processions. There is another shrine with the same name at Montalto, in the same province; and in the Spanish diocese of Valencia there is a shrine of our Lady of the Living Waters.

HEALTH OF THE SICK. Latin, *Salus infirmorum*, an invocation in the Litany of Loreto. A feast of our Lady under this title is kept in a few places, notably by the Ministers of the Sick (on November 16), founded by St. Camillus of Lellis. *Salus* means salvation as well as bodily health, so the invocation has a double significance. Accordingly, the introit of the proper Mass is from Psalm 33: "I am the salvation of the people: call they upon me in whatsoever affliction, I will hear them"; and the collect asks for "lasting health of mind and body," deliverance from the sorrows of this life, and endless happiness hereafter. —A picture of our Lady, Health or Help of the Sick (attributed to Fra Angelico), in St. Mary Magdalen's church at Rome, suggested to a Camillan brother the establishment of a confraternity, with a special scapular (*q.v.*), under this name to help the sick poor: this was done in 1860.

HEART OF MARY, THE IMMACULATE. "Come, let us worship Jesus reigning in Mary's heart, He who is our life and our love." In those words St. John Eudes (d. 1680), who did so much to forward devotion to the Heart of Mary, expressed its final aspect. Whereas devotion to the Heart of Jesus is specially directed to that heart as overflowing with love for mankind, and answers love with love, the Heart of Mary, as Father John Bainvel has pointed out, attracts us in the first place by her love for Jesus and for God: men's minds go easily beyond her heart of flesh to the love and virtues that it symbolizes, and they seek to follow her example. Like all devotions, this one has several aspects, and different people at different times have developed and emphasized now this, now that: to try to imitate the Heart of Mary, to praise it, to associate oneself with it, to make reparation for men's indifference to its love for them, but none of these things to the exclusion of the others. More and more has the Heart of Mary been seen as a pattern of goodness—"most pure," "most holy," "immaculate"—especially in its aspect of merciful concern for "poor sinners" and of love for all mankind. There are two passages in the Holy Scriptures that are specially relevant for this devotion: when Mary stood at the foot of the cross and her heart suffered a mother's anguish at the sufferings of her Son (cf., Luke 2:35); and when we are told that "Mary kept all these words, pondering them in her heart" (Luke 2:19; cf., 2:51)—a precious reminder of that quietness and thoughtfulness that is so necessary if religion is to grow and bear fruit in human hearts.—Every good thing has its dangers, and a danger in this devotion is to allow it to weaken into sentimentality. To quote the words of Father William G. Most: "That is a real danger. Sentimentality is only a caricature of real warmth. But we do insist that this devotion to the Hearts of Jesus and Mary should be marked by a genuine, a solid warmth, not necessarily emotional" (*Mary in Our Life*, 1954).

Adumbrations of this devotion can be found in some early commentaries on the Song of Songs, and it was adopted privately by St. Mechtildis (d. 1298) and St. Gertrude (d. 1302); but its "father, teacher and apostle" was, as St. Pius X declared, St. John Eudes during the seventeenth century in France. It was only natural that it should be encouraged by the spread of devotion to the Heart of Jesus, after the death of St. Margaret Mary (1690), and eventually an image of Mary's heart was incorporated in the Miraculous Medal (*q.v.*). A Confraternity of the Heart of Mary for the Conversion of Sinners was founded at the church of our Lady of Victories in Paris in 1836, devotion increased after the definition of the Immaculate Conception in 1854, and in 1877 its scapular (*q.v.*) was instituted. When the events at Fatima (*q.v.*) were made widely public, devotion received further impetus, and, following many petitions, including one from Canada, in 1942 Pope Pius XII consecrated the whole world to the Immaculate Heart of Mary. On that occasion the Pope referred to the analogy with the consecration of mankind to the Sacred Heart of Jesus by Leo XIII in 1899. The analogy between the two devotions is obvious, and they have latterly grown side by side; but their fundamental difference must not be overlooked: Christ is true God and true man, wholly to be worshiped with divine worship; but Mary is wholly human, and the devotion to her heart is metaphorical. "However, in each case the 'heart' is meant to express the very selfhood, so to say, of Him, or her, whom we are contemplating and with whom we seek so far as possible to unite ourselves" (Father C. C. Martindale).

HEART OF MARY, Feast of the Immaculate. A feast of the Heart of Mary was first celebrated privately, by St. John Eudes, in 1648, but it failed to get the formal approval of the Holy See till 1805. Fifty years later a feast of the Most Pure Heart of Mary was authorized, with proper Mass and Office based on that which Eudes had composed. This or other similar feasts were afterward approved for various places, including the whole of Spain (1862). Pope Pius XII in 1944 gave the feast of the Immaculate Heart to the whole Western Church, for August 22, octave-day of the Assumption. The introit of the Mass on this day puts into the mouths of the faithful St. Paul's words (Heb. 4:16), "Let us come boldly before the throne of grace, to meet with mercy and win that grace which will help us in our needs"; and the collect asks Almighty God that this grace may be given so that, in keeping the feast of Mary's heart devoutly, we may have the strength to live according to His heart's desire.

HEILOO, OUR LADY OF. The name Heiloo is a contraction of *Heilige Loo,* Holy Wood, and designates a shrine near Alkmaar in North Holland. It was a medieval center of devotion, destroyed at the Reformation; but the ruined chapel continued to be resorted to, often in secret, for the next three hundred years, in spite of the efforts of the civil authorities to put down what they regarded as "godless impiety." In 1905 the Bishop of Haarlem gave permission for the shrine to be restored, the ground having come into Catholic ownership. The chapel was rebuilt on its old foundations, the holy well cleared, and a statue of our Lady of the Needy set up, following the pattern provided by a seventeenth-century medal. Renewed enthusiasm followed and other buildings became necessary; the sanctuary has been given into the charge of St. Louis Grignion de Montfort's Company of Mary.

HELP, OUR LADY OF, or of Good Help. This title is of course similar to Help of Christians and of Perpetual Help (*qq.v.*): in Latin several words are used, *auxilium, remedium, subsidium, succursus.* A feast under this name, on various dates, is found especially in Italy, parts of Latin America, and among the Augustinian friars. The last named keep it on May 13, the origin of the observance being appearings of Mary in their church of our Lady of Help at Palermo in Sicily in 1306 and 1315. There are shrines of our Lady of Help, with crowned images, at Guincamp in Brittany and San Cassiano, near Lucca in Italy: this last is said to have originated in 1480, when an angry farmer said to his little son, "The Devil take you!" Whereupon the Devil appeared, but was driven off by our Lady in response to the cries of the child's mother—a story that presents certain difficulties. Besides Guincamp, there are a dozen other pilgrim-shrines of Notre-Dame de Bon Secours in France. See also ABERDEEN, OUR LADY OF; REMEDIOS, NUESTRA SEÑORA DE LOS.

At New Franken, Wis., there is a shrine of our Lady of Good Help which has for long been a place of local pilgrimage and is now beginning to be known further afield. It had its origin about 1861, when a young Belgian, Adèle Brisse, had a spiritual experience which many believe to have been a vision of our Lady. The school that Adèle founded became a home for crippled children in 1933, run by the Sisters of St. Francis of Bay Settlement; the new chapel of our Lady of Good Help is the center of the pilgrimage, and cures have been reported there.

HELP OF CHRISTIANS, Feast of our Lady. This invocation figured in the Litany of Loreto (*q.v.*) in the middle of the sixteenth century; it may be older than that, or a variation of Pleader (*advocata*) for Christians. There was no feast of this name until 1815, when Pope Pius VII instituted it for the States of the Church in Italy, as an act of thanksgiving for his deliverance from captivity under Napoleon Bonaparte and the subsequent removal of further threats to the Roman see. This is referred to in the fourth stanza of the special hymn at Vespers:

O happy day, which knows at last
The five sad years of exile past,
When Rome receives back Peter's heir,
Who sits again in Peter's chair.

Reference is made at Matins to other previous victories, spiritual over the Albigensians, military over the Turks, which are connected with the history of our Lady's rosary. The feast of Mary, Help of Christians, on May 24, was taken up in other places, and the invocation was specially popularized by the Salesians after their founder, St. John Bosco, chose it for the name of their mother-church at Turin. This feast is now kept in many places, including the whole of Australia and New Zealand, the diocese of Shrewsbury in England, and the diocese of Menevia in Wales. *Cf.*, Holy Hill, Our Lady of the.

HELP OF THE DYING, OUR LADY. A feast of this name is found in some places, notably in Italy. Its collect at Mass recalls Mary at the foot of the cross: "O God, who didst will that His mother the Virgin Mary should be there when thine only-begotten Son was hanging on the cross to save the souls of men, grant that through her intercession we may be helped not to waver in the last dread moments of life."

HERESIES involving Mary. Apart from direct denial of anything formally taught by the Church concerning her, the following classical heresies involve the Blessed Virgin. *Adoptianism* taught that Christ as man is only the adopted son of God; it was a forerunner (third century) and a follower (eighth century) of Nestorianism (see EPHESUS). *Apollinarianism* (Apollinaris, d. *c.* 390) denied that Christ had a human soul. It implies that Mary was not the mother of a real man. *Arianism* (Arius, d. 335) taught that the Son was inferior to the Father and of a different substance. It implies that Mary is not mother of God. *Docetism* (Gr. *dokein,* to seem) taught that Christ only seemed to have a body and to lead a human life. His birth of Mary was therefore not real but an illusion, and she was not really His mother. *Gnosticism* (Gr. *gnosis,* knowledge). One form of this heresy was docetic; another said that Jesus at His birth was the son of Joseph and Mary. *Marcionism* and *Manicheism* (Marcion, d. *c.* 160; Mani, d. *c.* 276) taught that all matter is evil. Christ's body was therefore not a real one (*cf.,* Docetism, above). *Monophysism* (Gr. *mone phusis,* one nature) taught that there is only one nature, and that divine, in Jesus Christ, and His body was not of one substance with ours. Mary was therefore not the mother of a real man. *Nestorianism:* see EPHESUS. *Cf.,* Mariolatry.

HERMITS, OUR LADY OF THE. See EINSEIDELN.

's HERTOGENBOSCH, OUR LADY OF. The image called The Kind Mother at 's Hertogenbosch, in the North Brabant province of the Netherlands, was an object of derision when it is first heard of, in 1380. It had been found, dirty and damaged, in a builder's junk-yard. But it soon became celebrated for the wonders associated with it, and it was enshrined. At the Reformation it was taken to Brussels for safety. In 1856 it was returned to the Bishop of 's Hertogenbosch, and it soon again became an object of popular devotion in the cathedral. The statue, of oak, is of an unusual pattern: our Lady's forearms are extended at right angles to her body; the Child is balanced on her left hand and in her right she holds an apple. It was crowned in 1878. Feast: July 7, with proper Mass and Office.

HODEGETRIA. This Greek word means Guide of the Way, and distinguishes a large class of icons (*q.v.*) of Mary of a primitive type, in which the Child is held in the Mother's left arm: why they should have been given this name has not been decided, but its general symbolic significance is clear enough. The first-known Hodegetria is said to have been sent from Jerusalem to the Empress St. Pulcheria (d. 1453): she enshrined it at Constantinople, where it became a palladium of the city and was associated with many events in its history. At the conquest by the Turks in 1453, the icon was hacked to pieces, but copies of it, real or alleged, were in existence; one reputed copy is the Our Lady of Smolensk, carried with the Russian army at the battle of Borodino in 1812; and the famous our Lady of Czestochowa (*q.v.*) is of Hodegetria type. The church of Santa Maria d'Itria (or "of Constantinople") in Rome is really Santa Maria Odigetria, and under the same corrupt form of the name our Lady is venerated in several places of southern Italy and Sicily (formerly Magna Graecia), and even in Sardinia. There are images of this type, or called by some form of this name, at Messina (several), Catania, Mazzara, and Piazza in Sicily, and at Bari and Naples. Mary our Guide is the patroness of icon-painters, and she is commemorated liturgically on various dates, e.g., July 28 in Russia ("of Smolensk"), 1st Tuesday in March at Bari ("of Constantinople").

HOLINESS OF OUR LADY. The Blessed Virgin was preserved from the taint of original sin, she was confirmed in grace at her immaculate conception, and she lived guiltless of all actual sin, even venial; she was full of grace, with that overflowing fullness that was required to fit her for the unique destiny to which she was called. In the bull *Ineffabilis Deus* (*q.v.*) Pope Pius IX declares that God endowed Mary, "more than all the angels and saints, with such an abundance of heavenly gifts that she was always wholly free from sin; so that, perfect and all-beautiful, she shone in such complete innocence and holiness that no greater holiness can be imagined except that of God himself, no mind but God's mind can measure it."

Mary's was a twofold blessedness: she was the mother of God made man, and hers was the holiness befitting so unutterable a destiny. Cardinal Newman says in a famous discourse: "A Redeemer was at hand; God was about to do a great work, and He purposed to do it suitably; 'where sin abounded, grace was to abound more'. . . . It was fitting, for His honor and glory, that she, who was the instrument of His bodily presence, should first be a miracle of His grace; it was fitting that she should triumph where Eve had failed, and should 'bruise the serpent's head' by the spotlessness of her sanctity. . . . She was from the first clothed in sanctity, destined for perseverence, luminous and glorious in God's sight, and incessantly employed in meritorious acts, which continued till her last breath. Hers was emphatically 'the path of the just, which as the shining light, goeth forward and increaseth even to the perfect day'. . . . Such is her prerogative of sinless perfection, and it is, as her maternity, for the sake of Emmanuel; hence she answered the angel's salutation, 'Full of grace," with the humble acknowledgement, 'Behold the handmaid of the Lord'" (*Discourses to Mixed Congregations*, no. xvii). *Cf.*, Full of grace; Immaculate Conception; Sinlessness.

HOLLAND, SHRINES OF. Among the "popular superstitions" about Europe is the idea that Holland (more properly called The Netherlands) is a solidly Protestant country. In fact, some 38 per cent of its people are Catholic, and they have some old and important shrines of our Lady, notably those of Heiloo, s' Hertogenbosch, Maastricht, and Roermond (*qq.v.*).

HOLY HILL, OUR LADY OF THE. One of the best-known pilgrimage shrines of the United States, at Hubertus, in the beautiful Wisconsin countryside. It is said that Father James Marquette, discoverer of the Mississippi, was the first to plant a cross on Holy Hill, but the present sanctuary began in a log-cabin in 1863; it has grown rapidly since 1906, when the Barefooted Carmelites took charge. Its center is the statue of our Lady, Help of Christians, made in Munich (Hubertus was a German settlement) and brought hither in 1878: the Mother shows her Child, who stands at her feet, His hand raised in blessing.

HOLYROOD, OUR LADY OF. A wooden statue of our Lady with her Child, formerly belonging to the ancient Scottish abbey of Holyrood, was for long in the possession of the family of the earls of Aberdeen, by whom it was eventually sold in 1860. Five years later it was seen at Peterborough, adorning the door of an antique shop. It was at once purchased by Edmund Waterton, author of the book *Pietas Mariana Britannica,* who gave it to the Jesuit church of the Sacred Heart in Edinburgh. In that church it has been enshrined for the veneration of the faithful ever since.

HOPE, OUR LADY OF GOOD. A feast under this or a similar name is observed in a few places on various dates, e.g., at Dijon in France and Saint-Brieuc in Brittany. The monastery of Benedictine nuns known as St. Mary's Abbey at Colwich in England, founded in Paris in 1652, has as titular our Lady of Good Hope.

HOŠIV, OUR LADY OF. A wonder-working icon at the Basilian monastery of the Transfiguration at Hošiv in western Ukraine. Early in the eighteenth century it was left by war-refugees in the house of the Hoshovsky family at Dunay; and in consequence of marvels connected with it they gave it to the monks of Hošiv in 1737. Many miracles of healing were reported at this shrine down to contemporary times.

HOURS OF OUR LADY. Another name for the Little Office (*q.v.*). A Book of Hours was a medieval prayer-book, of which the Little Office was the principal content; these books were highly valued and were often beautifully written and illuminated. In England the Book of Hours developed into the prayer-book called a Primer.

HOUSE OF GOLD. Latin, *Domus aurea,* an invocation of our Lady in the Litany of Loreto. Mary, writes Cardinal Newman, "is the house and palace of the Great King, of God himself. Our Lord, the co-equal Son of God, once dwelt in her. . . . [He] was actually *born in* this holy house. He took His flesh and His blood from this house, from the flesh, from the veins of Mary. Rightly then was she made to be of pure gold, because she was to give of that gold to form the body of the Son of God. She was golden in her conception, golden in her birth. She went through the fire of her suffering like gold in the furnace, and when she ascended on high, she was, in the words of our hymn, 'Above all the angels in glory untold, Standing next to the King in a vesture of gold.' "

HUMILITY OF OUR LADY, Feast of the. A feast in honor of Mary's humility is kept in some churches on July 17 and other dates. The collect of the Mass connects humility with purity of heart and recalls that it was in humility that our Lady conceived the Son of God; and accordingly the gospel read is that of the Annunciation: "Behold the handmaid of the Lord. . . ."—At Pistoia in Italy there is a celebrated miraculous image of our Lady of Humbleness; it was crowned in 1716.

HUNGARY, SHRINES OF. The devotion of Hungarians, or Magyars, to our Lady is specially marked by an annual feast of her as Great Queen of the Hungarians, observed on October 8. Among the principal shrines are: Györ (*q.v.*); our Lady of the Snow (*q.v.*) at Szeged; Máriabesnyö (*q.v.*); Andocs, in the county of Somogy; Máriapócs (*q.v.*); Máriagyüd, near Pécs; Máriaremete (*q.v.*); Mátraverebély-Szentkút, with its wonderworking holy well (*szentkút*); Márianosztra (*q.v.*); Celldömölk, an offshoot of Mariazell (*q.v.*) in Austria; O.L. of Passau at Bodajk, in the county of Fejér; O.L. of Sorrows at Eger; O.L. of Help at Csobánka and Tétszentkút; O.L. of Lourdes at Buzgó; and, among more local sanctuaries, Osly, in the county of Sopron, and Hétkápolna ("Seven Chapels," of the Seven Joys), near Vác. The primatial basilica at Esztergom and the Coronation ("Fortress") church at Budapest, both dedicated in Mary's honor, are also great pilgrimage centers; other shrines in Budapest are at the Krisztinaváros and Sziklatemplom churches. In spite of the communist regime, all these and other shrines seem still to exist in one form or another, though the religious of various orders who were formerly the custodians of some of them have been driven out. Outside the political frontiers, there are important Hungarian shrines at Csiksomlyó (*q.v.*), Máriáradna, and Kolozsvár in Transylvania, and at Máriavölgy in Slovakia.

HURONS, ST. MARY AMONG THE. The oldest shrine of our Lady in Canada; it was founded in honor of Notre-Dame de la Conception by Father Jerome Lalemant, s.j., in 1639, as a place of pilgrimage for the Huron Indians. It was destroyed by the Iroquois in 1649, at the time of the martyrdom of St. John de Brébeuf and St. Gabriel Lalemant, and remained a heap of ruins in the forest till 1925. The shrine was then revived and, largely through the efforts of Father Thomas J. Lally, s.j. (d. 1953), it is now known throughout North America; a quarter million pilgrims visit it every year. It is situated at Martyrs' Shrine, near Midland, Ont. Archeological research has uncovered evidence of the Indians' devotion to Mary: e.g., each of the Indians buried near the shrine had a rosary round his neck. The Jesuit Collège Sainte-Marie at Montreal possesses a document of Pope Urban VIII, dated February 18, 1644, granting for seven years a plenary indulgence to all who, on the feast of St. Joseph, should visit St. Mary's chapel in the Huron country.

HYMNS. As ordinarily understood, a hymn is a metrical composition sung to the praise and glory of God, which praise may be direct, or indirect by singing in honor of one of His saints. The history of hymns in Christian worship is very long and complex; but at the present day in the Western Church hymns may be divided into three classes: those sung in Latin in the Divine Office; other Latin hymns; and those sung in the people's mother-tongue, or "vernacular." Some of the better-known Marian Office hymns are referred to in various places in this book; cf., for example, Rosary Hymns, and under Office of our Lady, Common. Other Latin hymns of the Blessed Virgin are numerous, and some of them were used in the Divine Office in former times. Among those that are popular with some congregations (for their music if not their words) are: *Concordi laetitia* (known in America in Cecilia Caddell's adaptation, "Maiden Mother, meek and mild"); *Inviolata* (*q.v.*); *Languentibus in purgatorio,* asking Mary's help for the holy souls; *O quam glorifica; O vos aetherei,* for the Assumption; *Rosa vernans; Stabat Mater speciosa* (*q.v.*); *Salve Mater misericordiae,* of which the English have an ingenious translation in their *Westminster Hymnal* (no. 259a), and see the *Pius X Hymnal* (McLaughlin & Reilly Co.), no. 85; and in the Westminster book (no. 260a) there is also a translation of the so-called Sicilian hymn (*q.v.*), *O Sanctissima, O piissima.*

Vernacular hymns. It is a mistake to suppose (as some do) that the singing of hymns in the mother-tongue is an innovation first introduced by Protestantism: indeed, some Protestants long opposed the singing of hymns (as distinct from psalms) as "popish." Hymn-singing as we understand it goes back at least to the fourth century, when first St. Ephraem in Syria, and then St. Gregory Nazianzen in Cappadocia and St. John Chrysostom in Constantinople, popularized hymns, especially as a means of inculcating sound doctrine against the teachers of error. St. Ephraem, indeed, was Mary's first poet and hymnodist; and the following version, by Father J. W. Atkinson, s.j., shows how his hymns can be adapted to another age and another people:

Virgin, wholly marvellous,
Who didst bear God's Son for us,
Worthless is my tongue, and weak,
Of thy purity to speak.

Who can praise thee as he ought?
Gifts, with every blessing fraught,
Gifts that bring the gifted life,
Thou didst grant us, Maiden-
    Wife. . . .

Cherubim with fourfold face
Are no peers of thine in grace;
And the six-wing'd seraphim
Shine, amid thy splendor, dim.

Purer art thou than are all
Heav'nly hosts angelical,
Who delight with pomp and state
On thy beauteous Child to wait.

At just the same time St. Hilary of Poitiers (d. *c.* 368) and St. Ambrose

(d. 397) at Milan were encouraging hymn-singing in the West. Hilary and Ambrose wrote their hymns in Latin, because in those days Latin was "vernacular" among their people; the hymns of the East were in Syriac and Greek. To come nearer home and somewhat nearer our own times, the French *cantique,* the German *Leisen* (from which the "choral" developed), and the English carol were firmly in favor long before the Reformation; St. Aldhelm was teaching English hymns to the people of Wessex at the end of the seventh century. That is to name only three peoples, and of them the German Catholics particularly have maintained their love for vernacular singing in church; but the same can be said of others, the Lithuanians, for instance, or the Poles. Among English-speaking Catholics, however, hymn-singing has now somewhat fallen into decay, of which a very limited repertory is both a cause and an effect. There are hardly a dozen Marian hymns in English that can be said to be well known and popular, and they are mostly not of the best.

In the United States many hymns have been brought by immigrants from other countries and have maintained their popularity. Apart from a few translations of Latin office-hymns mentioned in other parts of this book, such as *Stabat Mater dolorosa* (*q.v.*), the following seem to represent the English repertory of an average congregation: "Ave Maria, thou Virgin and Mother" (by Sister M.); "Daily, daily, sing to Mary" (see CASIMIR'S HYMN, ST.); "Hail, Queen of Heav'n, the ocean star" (John Lingard, d. 1851); "I'll sing a hymn to Mary" (J. Wyse, 1898); the Lourdes Hymn (*q.v.*); "Maiden Mother, meek and mild" (trans. Cecilia M. Caddell); "Mother of Christ, what shall I ask"; "Mother dear, O pray for me"; "Mother dearest, Mother fairest"; "On this day, O beautiful Mother." A corresponding list for Great Britain would include the first five of the above, adding thereto: "Look down, O Mother Mary" (E. Vaughan, C.SS.R., 1908); "O Mother blest" (trans. by the same); "Mary Immaculate, star of the morning" (F. W. Weatherell); "Mother of mercy, day by day" (F. W. Faber, 1863); "O purest of creatures" (ditto); and "This is the image of the queen" (E. Caswall, 1878).

It is a pity that choice should be so restricted, when there is a considerable body of other Marian hymns in English to draw upon. They fall into two categories. There are the simple, easily sung verses which have survived from, or been written in the spirit of, earlier times; something has been said of some of these under Carols (*q.v.*). And there are the more "literary" compositions and translations, some of which, on one hand, tend to be difficult in form or thought or, on the other, to allow simplicity to degenerate into banality and sentimentality. Of the following among other dignified hymns it may safely be said that they are rarely sung nowadays in the Catholic churches where they belong: "Who is she ascends so high" (by John Beaumont, d. 1627); "O Lady Mary, thy bright crown" (Francis Thompson, 1907);

"Maiden, yet a mother" (Dante; trans. R. A. Knox); "Daily let us sing in varied tune" (St. Cucuimne; trans. Shane Leslie); "All spotless heart" (Josephine Errington, 1902); "Of one that is so fair and bright" (a carol); "Ave Maria, gratia plena: So greets thee" and "Rejoice, all ye that sorrowed sore" (trans. John O'Connor, 1952); "Sing we Ave, word endearing" (trans. M. J. Blacker); "O what light and glory deck thee" (*O quam glorifica;* trans. T. I. Ball). The singing of hymns has very considerable instructional and religious value. If it has fallen out of use or favor among many Catholics, it is because it has been neglected and even despised. For it to be fruitful, as much care and attention must be given to hymn-singing as to other adjuncts of communal worship.

HYPAPANTE (Gr. meeting). The name of the feast of the Purification (*q.v.*) in the Byzantine rite, the Meeting of Jesus with Simeon (Luke 2:22-33). It formerly sometimes had the same name in the Latin rite, *Occursus Domini.*

HYPERDULIA. In the technical language of theologians that supreme homage and religious worship that is given to God alone is called *latria;* the veneration and honor given to angels, saints, and all the blessed in Heaven is called *dulia;* and the special reverence accorded to the Virgin Mary is called *hyperdulia,* that is "more lofty *dulia." Latria* differs from *dulia* and *hyperdulia* in kind, with a difference as vast and essential as that between the Creator and the created. Many theologians hold that *hyperdulia* differs from *dulia* not only in its greater degree, but in kind as well; they argue that a specific veneration is due to our Lady in accordance with her unique position as Mother of God. See VENERATION.

I

ICON, IKON. The Greek word *eikon* simply means an image, but the word has come to be used to designate those religious pictures painted on wooden panels that are the characteristic sacred images of the Christian East, especially in churches of the Byzantine rite. An icon is often covered with a sheet of metal (*riza*), on which the garments etc. of the picture are embossed, being cut away to show the painted face and hands; except on cheap "commercial" icons the whole of the picture is painted underneath and the metal is removable. These metal coverings are a late and undesirable innovation, and there is now a tendency to get rid of them. The characteristics of nearly all icon-painting, Greek, Cretan, Russian, Ukrainian, Serbian, Rumanian, etc., derive ultimately from the post-Iconoclasm Byzantine painters and in some places have been perpetuated to this day; they had a long and strong influence on religious imagery in the West, especially through Italy. But icon-painting is much more than just an artistic "style": its aim is to express the spiritual significance of the person or scene depicted, and it is not concerned to arouse emotion or to represent physical beauty in human terms. It is perhaps not possible to imagine more really religious sacred images than our Lady of Vladimir or, in another medium, the mosaic Deesis

(*q.v.*) in the Hagia Sophia at Constantinople. The sacred art of the Christian East "does not attempt to represent human reality, but seeks to lead the worshiper into a realm of spiritual tranquillity—into that peace of soul which our troubled existence here can neither give nor take away" (Baron Meyendorff).

Icons are essentially hieratic, idealized, looking toward Heaven rather than to the beauty of this world. It is perhaps significant that, while later Western images are grouped according to the man who made them—the Madonnas of Jan van Eyck, of Botticelli, of Raphael, of Murillo, of Bouguereau—those of the East belong to persisting types governed by ideas: Hodegetria (*q.v.*), Tenderness (see VLADIMIR), of the Sign (see NOVGOROD), Protectress (see PROTECTING VEIL), of the Passion (see PERPETUAL HELP), and others. The icon-painter is not concerned with "self-expression": his business is to conform to religious truth and the tradition of its pictorial representation, and there are definite iconographical rules to be observed. Generally speaking, the Mother of God is not represented alone, without the Holy Child; but she sometimes stands thus in the apse of a church, as in the famous eleventh-century mosaic in the Holy Wisdom cathedral at Kiev. Of the mysteries of Mary's life, the most often represented are the birth of her Son and her own Falling Asleep. In the latter she is shown lying on a bed, with the Apostles grouped at its head and foot, St. Peter holding a thurible, St. John weeping at her shoulder; behind stands our Lord, holding His Mother's soul in the form of a swaddled baby. Her bodily going up to Heaven is less often represented directly, and then generally as part of a whole death-assumption composition.

Nothing could be stranger than a true icon to the contemporary popular taste in sacred images of Western peoples. It is, then, the more remarkable that icons provide some of the images of Mary most widely venerated in the Western Church. Outstandingly, there are our Lady of Perpetual Help and (iconic in type) of Good Counsel (qq.v.); then there are our Lady of St. Luke at Bologna, of St. Mary Major at Rome, of Consolation at Turin, of Czestochowa in Poland (qq.v.), and others; and in Italy and elsewhere there are many little-known icons of Byzantine origin that have locally been objects of popular reverence for centuries. It may be recalled that an ancient icon was almost the only representation of our Lady that St. Bernadette of Lourdes found even tolerable. Cf., Art; Iconography; Images.

The following is a prayer from the Byzantine liturgy that may be said when the icon of the Theotokos is kissed:

"Mother of God, well-spring of sympathy, make me worthy of compassion and clemency. Look upon all who sin. Show forth your wonted power so that we, like Gabriel, captain of the bodiless hosts, of old, may bid you Hail."

ICONOGRAPHY of our Lady. Iconography (Gr. *eikon,* image; *graphein,* to write) is the branch of knowledge and practice which deals with representative art and its visual symbols in general; it is not confined to what are technically called icons (q.v.). From the fifth century, Christian art gave increasing prominence to the Mother of God, and for very long (as still in the East) it was rare for her to be represented alone, without the Child, and she was always shown in a hierarchic, frontal attitude. The apse behind the altar became her special place in church; she appears enthroned with her Child in this position in a mosaic in the cathedral of Parenzo in Dalmatia, made about the year 530; and five centuries or so later, standing, in the superb apse mosaics at Torcello, near Venice, and at Kiev (without the Child). In St. Mark's at Venice there is a lovely marble relief, showing Mary standing, with arms upraised in the attitude of prayer. The addition of the Child to this early *orans* position led to the "Sign" type of image, as at Santa Maria Antiqua in Rome (*cf.,* Novgorod, Our Lady of). One form of this is sometimes called Blakherniotissa, a name also given to the Deesis (q.v.), for there were several famous images at Blakhernae (q.v.). Another early pattern is the Hodegetria (q.v.), and also the Galaktotrophousa or Galaktissa, the Mother suckling her Child; this is already found in the sixth century in Egypt, in a carving at Saqqara. Other familiar iconic types, such as our Lady of Vladimir, came in later times.

Christian iconography of the earlier ages, whether mosaic, wall- or panel-painting, or carving, was in general but little concerned with naturalistic realism; its aim was rather to direct attention to heavenly things. Anatomy and perspective were of little importance, even color was used symbolically rather than "naturally." For centuries the influence of Byzantine art was very marked in Europe: it extended even so far as England and Ireland. The Madonnas and other Western painting followed Eastern types, and until the thirteenth century there was nothing "humanistic" about them: even at the end of that century Cimabue of Florence, Duccio of Siena, and others were still thoroughly Byzantine in their painting. It is commonly said that Giotto (d. 1337) was, as Vasari chose to put it, "the first to put more kindness into his figures." Actually, a new tenderness and feeling had begun to come into iconography a hundred and fifty years before that, in Macedonia and in such images as our Lady of Vladimir (q.v.). But from Giotto onward the images of our Lady in central and western Europe became consistently less hieratic, they spoke less of the all-holy Virgin Mother of God as Queen of Heaven, more and more they showed her as a mother in this world. She came to be no longer represented conventionally by sign and symbol, but as an ideal figure of womanly grace. In the later middle ages Western art, with superb skill and unsparing detail, represented subjects that had before been avoided, presumably through awe and delicacy —the sorrows of Mary, the physical sufferings of her Son. North of the Alps the same thing happened in a somewhat different way. With romanesque and gothic building came in a golden age of stone- and wood-carving; and, though the themes were the same, these materials lent themselves less readily than paint to excessively naturalistic and emotional treatment. But when sculptors modelled in clay before cutting in stone, the way was open to the excesses of later statuary. In the meantime there were wonderful examples of biblical and theological iconography; and our Lady with her divine Child presided over the main doors of the great churches, in the form of a crowned and seated image that is repeatedly found in the northern countries.

Medieval Marian iconography enlarged its scope by frequent representations of the mysteries of her life (especially the Annunciation and the Nativity at Bethlehem), often using particulars taken from apocryphal writings (q.v.), and by reference to the books of "Legends of our Lady" (q.v.). Inessentials were no longer excluded, the previous conventions of sacred art were discarded, and the time came when every painter and carver "did what was right in his own eyes" (or what is now called "self-expression"). The result is that, while Marian iconography in the East has been petrified into a relatively small number of more or less fixed types, in the West it eventually dissolves into what may fairly be called anarchy. Some still regard the Madonnas of Raphael (d. 1520) as the high point of Christian painting; to others they are magnificent examples of religious pictures that are not also sacred (cf., Art); in any case the primrose path is clear from him, through Bernini (d. 1680), to what has been called "the whirling, ecstatic 'Assumptions' and 'Coronations'" of later baroque, until Tiepolo (d. 1769) at length "gives us a foretaste of the film-star's appeal" (Father William Purdy).

Any extended consideration of the iconography of the Blessed Virgin would have to give special attention to the effects of Iconoclasm in the eighth and ninth centuries, of the Protestant Reformation, and of modern methods of mass reproduction. At what is called the Counter-Reformation, primary emphasis was put on the value of images as providing salutary examples and lessons for the building-up of the faithful, rather than as sacred symbols of those persons whom we worship or revere. But this coincided with the serious beginnings of mechanical reproduction; and works designed for a popular devotional and moral appeal are, in the words of Dr. T. S. R. Boase, "dangerously susceptible to the debasement of cheap materials and mass production." On the other hand, mechanical reproduction, taken with other factors, has favored a certain emergence of new general "types" of Marian image. In the Prado at Madrid there is a famous painting by Murillo (d. 1682) called an Immaculate Conception; it might just as well be called an Assumption. But today our Lady Immaculate is at once recognizable; so is our Lady of Lourdes, our Lady of Fatima, the Immaculate Heart. Whether the iconography of these and other images is altogether satisfactory, and worthy of their high themes, is another matter.

Church art, like any other art, has always been inescapably dependent on the culture that surrounds it; the twentieth century is characterized by very acute cultural confusion, and this is faithfully reflected in the adornment of churches. Much religious iconography is still imbued with nineteenth-century romantic naturalism, weakened and sentimentalized; at the other extreme is an esoteric and inhuman abstractionism. An image of our Lady must be of such a kind as in itself to honor her; it must also be suitable for its particular purpose (for example, to be set up in a church). But such is our state of confusion that it is extremely difficult to reach generally satisfactory conclusions on these matters in a given instance: the sensitivity that produces bigger and better automobiles is not the sensitivity necessary for the making and judging of sacred objects. For the growth of a better iconography of the Mother of God both those who are artists and those who are not can well make their own that prayer used by a bishop when he puts on his ring: "Adorn my fingers and my heart with virtue, Lord; and surround me with the seven sanctifying gifts of thy Holy Spirit." See ART; ICON; IMAGES.

There is one aspect of Christian iconography that has so far been little studied. During the past half-century, under various influences, including notable encouragement from the Holy See, the faithful in missionary countries have shown increasing interest in making religious images for themselves and in their own way. The outcome seems to be mixed. Much of the work is disappointing, since it consists simply in reproducing iconographical conventions of European origin dressed up in a local style, Chinese, Indian, or whatever it may be. Such a purely external approach gets nowhere. But it is now possible also to see statues and pictures that are really indigenous. Where our Lady is in question, there are Indian statues that adapt the contemplative Buddha pattern (e.g., Avorio's "Our Lady of India"), and such pictures as Masoji's "Annunciation"; the Chinese pictures of Luke Ch'en and Lu Hung-nien; the "Wonderful Mother" of the Japanese Hasegawa, and the "Maria-Kwannon" images; and some truly regal carvings in Java. These, and many others, are essays in presenting universal truth through indigenous, instead of foreign, religious and iconographical terms. Nor is this confined to countries of ancient civilization; Africans of various peoples, for instance, are producing images that owe little or nothing to European models.—It must not be overlooked that there is, somewhat analagous to the above, an indigenous iconography in America: the *santos* and *bultos* of the Southwest and Mexico.

IMAGES OF OUR LADY. A Christian religious image is any direct representation, by means of a picture, a carved statue, a mosaic, or otherwise, of our Lord, the Blessed Virgin, or other of the saints. Such images, usually painted on walls, as in the Roman catacombs, were familiar to Christians from very early times, when their purpose was for decoration (secular as well as sacred subjects were used, often no doubt symbolically) and for instruction: veneration of images was a gradual development and had not taken definite shape before the middle of the fifth century or later. The earliest known representation of our Lady is generally said to be a fresco in the Catacomb of Priscilla, painted probably during the first half of the second century: it is a decorative wall-painting, and it shows her sitting, with the child Jesus on her knee. On one side stands a figure that is conjectured to represent Isaias, the prophet of the Messiah; and above the figures are the blossoming branches of a tree. The whole thing is beautifully springlike.

After the Peace of the Church in 313 decorative and instructive representations were multiplied in the newly built churches, and the honorific element was introduced and spread. One of the earliest of existing Madonnas is a painting on a panel in Santa Maria Nuova at Rome, which perhaps goes back to the fifth century. But the development of the veneration of images was interrupted and affected in the East by the opposition of the iconoclasts during the eighth and ninth centuries: it is said to be an effect of Iconoclasm that there are no statues in Eastern churches today. But there are many pictures (icons), and these receive perhaps even more veneration than do the images in Western churches. Moreover, in the Byzantine rite icons have a definite place in public worship: for example, our Lord and our Lady are always represented on either side of the door of the sanctuary screen, and these images are referred to, by incensing and in other ways, during Mass. The Council of Trent (session 25) lays it down that images should be kept and venerated in churches, but no particular image is of obligation except the altar crucifix at Mass; but in practice, of course, every Western church contains at least a picture or statue of the Blessed Virgin. It was in the gothic churches of the later middle ages that carved statues reached the height of their glory, particularly on the outside walls, where they perpetuated their primitive purpose of decoration and instruction. Inside, the place of a statue was normally at its appropriate altar: our Lady stood above the Lady altar, and so on. But the development of shrines and pilgrimages thereto, and of particular devotions, led to other arrangements, and the putting up of isolated statues, without any relation to an altar or to its architectural setting; this is commoner than ever today.

Images are set up in church in the first place to do honor to our Lord and His saints and to contribute to the religious atmosphere of the building; secondly, they are focal points for the devotion which the faithful wish to express toward those whom they represent. The principles governing the paying of respect to images of Mary are the same as those for all images: "Due honor and veneration should be paid to sacred images, since the honor shown to them is offered to the persons they represent, so that by our reverence we worship Christ himself and venerate the saints whose images they are" (Gasparri's Catechism). Prayer is not made to images, "for they can neither see nor hear nor help us." At the same time church images are something more than mere reminders of what they portray. The second Council of Nicaea in 787 regarded them as "venerable and holy," sacred things which must be treated with reverence, and St. John Damascene (d. 749) regarded holy images as "channels of divine grace." These ideas were developed by St. Theodore Studites (d. 826), among others, and they help to explain what is distinctive in Eastern thought and practice on the subject today. After it has been blessed, an icon is esteemed to have as it were a "presence," quite independently of its artistic merit, or lack of it.

When it is set up in a church an image must be blessed, and if the blessing is to be public and solemn it must be given by the bishop or his delegate. The following is the prayer of blessing in the Roman Ritual for an image of our Lady: "Almighty and ever-living God, who dost not forbid images of thy saints to be carved or painted, so that, whenever we see them with our bodily eyes, we may inwardly determine to emulate their deeds and holiness: be pleased, we beseech thee, to bless and hallow this image in honor and memory of the most blessed Virgin Mary, mother of our Lord Jesus Christ. And grant that whoever shall seek in front of it humbly to revere and honor the most blessed Virgin, may by her merits receive grace from thee here and endless glory hereafter. Through Christ our Lord. Amen."

Numerous particular images of our Lady are listed herein under the names of countries, and many of them are referred to separately under their own names. See also ART; BLACK VIRGIN; ICONOGRAPHY; ICONS; LIKENESSES; WONDERWORKING IMAGES.

Older images of our Lady venerated in American churches are generally of Spanish or American-Spanish origin, of the sixteenth and seventeenth centuries. The oldest is said to be one of our Lady of Victories at Albuquerque, N.M. In English Catholic churches there are a few statues dating back to before the Reformation, such as those at Buckfast abbey (found built into a wall there), at Prinknash abbey (an image once belonging to St. Thomas More), at the house of the Austin canonesses in Cromwell Road, London (fifteenth century), and the delightful Annunciation in St. Joan's church. Farnham. Other images of Mary of special interest are: at Aylesford (*q.v.*); at the Franciscan convent at Goodings, near Newbury, brought to England by the nuns in 1794; our Lady of Stone (*q.v.*) and of Brewood in Staffordshire; O.L. of York (*q.v.*); the seventeenth-century painting treasured by the Bridgettine nuns at Syon abbey in Devon; and the group by Jacob Epstein at the Holy Child convent, Cavendish Square, London.

IMMACULATE CONCEPTION, Feast of the. One of the five feasts (*q.v.*) of Mary that are universal in the Catholic Church, kept on December 8 in the Western Church and on the following day in the East. A feast commemorating our Lady's conception by the power of her father in the womb of her mother Ann (without reference to Mary's sinlessness) was probably general in the East by the year 1000, and before that had spread to the Byzantines in southern Italy and Sicily. The first known observance of the feast in the West, on December 8, was at Winchester and elsewhere in England just before the Norman Conquest. The controversy about the doctrine of the Immaculate Conception naturally entailed considerable fluctuation in the spread of the Conception feast in Europe. It was adopted by the whole Franciscan Order in 1263, but it was not extended to the whole Western Church till 1476; it became a holyday of obligation in 1708.

The feast continued to be called officially simply the Conception of the Blessed Virgin until the definition of the dogma in 1854. One of the earliest examples of the use of the present name is in the calendar of the Carmelite Missal of 1733 (the Carmelites supported the Franciscans in their upholding of the dogma). In 1863 the feast was given a proper Mass and Office, including a new hymn at Matins, *Praeclara custos virginum*, and in 1879 Pope Leo XIII accorded it a vigil. There is a confraternity, rosary, and scapular (*qq.v.*) of Mary Immaculate. In the Byzantine rite the feast is officially called the Childbegetting of the Holy Ann, Mother of the Mother of God, and is kept on December 9.

In a sermon read at Matins on this feast St. Jerome says: "The blessing of Mary took away wholly whatever curse was put upon Eve; and Solomon in the Song of Songs says, as if in praise of her, 'Come, my dove, my spotless one . . . Come from Lebanon, come, thou shalt be crowned.' Not unfittingly is she bidden to come from Lebanon, for Lebanon means a radiant whiteness, and dazzlingly white was she in all her virtues and merits, cleansed whiter than snow by the gifts of the Holy Spirit. She had a dove's simplicity in all things, everything about her was purity and unassumingness, truth and grace; all was mercy and righteousness from Heaven. No sin was found in her, therefore was she without spot."

IMMACULATE CONCEPTION, NATIONAL SHRINE OF THE, Washington, D.C. The heavenly patroness of the United States of America is the Blessed Virgin Mary as conceived free from original sin, and toward the beginning of this century the idea was mooted of building a national shrine in her honor at the nation's capital. A piece of land for the purpose was set aside on the campus of the Catholic University, and the enterprise received the blessing of Pope St. Pius X in 1914, some three months before he died. The cornerstone was laid and building began in 1920, but such is the vast scale on which the church is planned that progress can be but slow. By the middle of the century the north and south crypt, with a great vestibule between them, and two large sacristies were built, but only the north crypt was completely finished. This, with its beautifully plain and dignified central altar, dedicated in honor of our Lady—the gift of the Marys of America—and fifteen others ranged around in the arms of the square cross, gives a suggestion of what may be looked for in the completed building: constructional materials have been brought from all parts of the world for this great sanctuary. In one of the sacristies is a mosaic of a Murillo painting of the Immaculate Conception, treasured as being the gift of Popes St. Pius X and Benedict XV; but the technique of mosaic is not well adapted for reproducing such work as that of Murillo. A statue of our Lady, Mother of Mankind, stands in the south crypt. Already, far from finished as it is, this American national shrine of Mary is a great place of pilgrimage; when completed it will be one of the great churches of the world.

IMMACULATE CONCEPTION OF OUR LADY, The. The doctrine of the Immaculate Conception is that the Blessed Virgin Mary, by a unique grace and privilege of Almighty God, in virtue of the merits of Jesus Christ the Savior of mankind, was in the first instant of her conception kept free from all stain of original sin. This means that Mary's soul, at the very moment of its creation and infusion into her body, was clothed in sanctifying grace: the stain of original sin was not removed (as at Christian baptism) but altogether excluded from her soul. It does not mean that Mary stood outside, as in no need of, the universal Redemption of man achieved by her Son; for her to obtain exemption from original sin, the redeeming Savior was absolutely necessary: she was redeemed by anticipation. "It was completely becoming that as the Only-begotten Son had a Father in Heaven whom the seraphim acclaim as thrice-holy, so He should have a mother on earth who should never be without the splendor of holiness" (Pope Pius IX).

The truth of the Immaculate Conception does not depend on any direct explicit statement of the Bible, though testimony to it can be brought forward from both the Old Testament (e.g., Gen. 3:15) and the New (e.g., Luke 1:28). It rests ultimately on God's revelation contained in the tradition of the Church; it was there from the beginning, but for a long time believed only implicitly—"concealed," so to say. In all this the doctrine of the Immaculate Conception resembles that of the Assumption; but it differs from it in something else, viz., that during the middle ages the Immaculate Conception was for some time the subject of lively, even fierce, controversy. It arose from the observance in some places of a feast of the Conception of our Lady, which was strongly criticized by none other than that great devotee of Mary, St. Bernard; and he was followed by, among others, St. Albert the Great, St. Bonaventure, and St. Thomas Aquinas. It would seem that their objections were due in part to formulations of the doctrine different from that in which it was defined six hundred years later. But the dispute became embittered by party-spirit, e.g., the Dominicans followed St. Thomas contra, and the Franciscans followed Duns Scotus pro; and Pope Sixtus IV (d. 1484), while approving the feast of the Conception and extending it to the whole Western Church, had to warn the disputants not to call one another "heretics," since "the matter has not yet been decided by the Roman Church and Apostolic See." The truth of the doctrine became more and more widely recognized, by both the simple and the learned; and in 1546 the bishops at the Council of Trent expressly excluded the Mother of God from their decree concerning original sin. But there continued to be opposition up till the time of Pope Alexander VII; in 1661 his bull Sollicitudo set forth "the ancient piety of the Christian faithful" concerning Mary's freedom from original sin, in practically the words of the ultimate solemn definition. That definition took place on December 8, 1854, by the bull Ineffabilis Deus, after Pope Pius IX had taken counsel with all the other bishops of the Church. Already, eight years before, the bishops at the sixth Provincial Council of Baltimore had chosen our Lady under the title of the Immaculate Conception as patroness of the United States. For the feast of the Immaculate Conception, see above. Cf. also, Death; Full of Grace; Sinlessness. For the Eastern Orthodox and this doctrine, see EASTERN CHURCHES.

In his letter to the Reverend E. B. Pusey, printed in the second volume of Certain Difficulties Felt by Anglicans, Cardinal Newman brilliantly and lovingly vindicates the doctrine of the Immaculate Conception. In the course of it he writes: "Is it any violent inference that she, who was to co-operate in the redemption of the world, at least was not less endowed with power from on high than she who, given as a helpmate to her husband, did in the event but co-operate with him for its ruin? If Eve was raised above human nature by that indwelling moral gift which we call grace, is it rash to say that Mary had even a greater grace? . . . And if Eve had this supernatural inward gift given her from the first moment of her personal existence, is it possible to deny that Mary too had this gift from the very first moment of her personal existence? . . . This is simply and literally the doctrine of the Immaculate Conception. . . . What is there difficult in this doctrine? What is there unnatural?" And as Mary's assumption into Heaven is a foretaste of our resurrection, so her perfection from her first moment is the pattern and pledge of the final perfection promised to all who follow Christ faithfully.

It may be noted that the words "immaculate conception" have not been a cause of misunderstanding to the men of the middle ages alone. They involve a distinction between active conception (*by* Ann) and passive conception (*of* Mary), a distinction that is not formulated in everybody's mind. Hence it is sometimes found that people not informed about the matter confuse the Immaculate Conception (of Mary; passive) with her virginal conception of Christ (active); or even (less often) with the false notion that Ann's active conception of Mary was virginal. The two uses of the word "conception" can

be illustrated from liturgical terms: in some calendars the feast of the Annunciation was called the "Conception of Christ" (passive), while the official term for the Immaculate Conception feast in Byzantine usage is still the "Conception by St. Ann" (active). In any case, the doctrine is concerned with the moment of infusion of Mary's soul, which might or might not coincide with the moment of her bodily conception.

INDESTRUCTIBLE WALL. In the Song of Songs, from which the Church adapts so much to our Lady, the bride sings, "I am a wall, and my breasts are as a tower . . ." (8:10). No doubt this was in mind at the composition of the Saturday *theotokion* (*q.v.*) which begins, "Rejoice, thou unpassed gate! Rejoice, thou wall and protection of those who haste to thee!" And in the tenth section of the Akathistos Hymn (*q.v.*) is found, "Thou, maiden Forth-bringer, art a wall to all maidens and to all who haste to thee. . . ." This idea was applied to a material monument in the cathedral of the Holy Wisdom at Kiev, "the God-protected mother of Russian cities." In the eleventh century a grand, 15-feet high, single figure of the Mother of God was made in mosaic in the semi-dome of the east wall, which accordingly came to be known as the Indestructible Wall (*Nerushimaya Stena*).

INDIA, SHRINES OF. India is in a special sense a land of pilgrims, for pilgrimage is a familiar and important act of religion to Hindus, Buddhists, and Mohammedans: the crowds that resort to Benares, the Hindu holy city, are especially famous. That the Blessed Virgin has been venerated in certain parts of India from very early times is shown by the existence of large numbers of Catholics of Syrian rite and other Christians in Malabar, who claim that their forefathers received the Gospel from St. Thomas the Apostle. The cathedrals of the Syro-Malabar bishops are all dedicated in honor of our Lady, that of Ernakulam being under the title Mary, Lady of the Haven; in the same archdiocese the Marian churches of Nagapuzha, Muttom, and Vhechur were founded in the years 900, 1023, and 1463, respectively. In the diocese of Changanacherry the very ancient shrine at Kudamallore is visited by people of all religions and castes on the feast of the Presentation; there is a popular shrine at Changanacherry itself and another at Parel. The diocese of Kottayam has a sanctuary at Kaduthuruthy (q.v.), and the diocese of Palai one at Kuravilangad which is the oldest in India. In the episcopal city of Trichur the churches of our Lady of Lourdes and of Sorrows are great centers of devotion to Mary; the latter is the biggest church in all India. The dissident Christians of Malabar have an important pilgrimage of our Lady in Manarkad. Thanks to the activity of the Indian Carmelites, the use of the brown scapular is widespread among the Malabarese, and the family rosary was established long ago.

After the coming of the Portuguese to the west coast of India in 1498, the first recorded Latin-rite shrine of Mary is that at Bandel (q.v.); other sanctuaries with a history of some centuries are those at Bandra (q.v.), our Lady of Health at Vailankanni (founded 1600) in the diocese of Tanjore, our Lady of Ransom at Vallarpadam (1676) in the archdiocese of Verapoly, and at Yella Consitchy (1697). There are locally noted Lourdes shrines at Chetpet on the Satan Maley mountain, at Pallapalayam in the Madras province, and at Vellenur in the same, which attracts great crowds during Easter week. Other shrines are at Mokameh (q.v.), at Tranquebar, and Kilpauk in Madras, our Lady of Miracles at Milagres in the diocese of Mangalore, at St. Mary's convent at Palluruthy in the diocese of Cochin, and at Baroda and Karjat in the archdiocese of Bombay. A national Marian congress was held at Bombay in 1954, to mark Mary's year.

INDO-CHINA, SHRINES OF. The history of the Church in Indo-China (which is largely made up of the territory now known as Vietnam) goes back to the sixteenth-seventeeth century and has been made glorious by the blood of many martyrs. Two of the chief shrines in Vietnam are our Lady of La-vang (q.v.) and our Lady of Thai-ha-ap; the latter, near Hanoi, is in charge of the Redemptorists and is a great place of pilgrimage. The principal Lourdes shrine is the chapel first built by Father Gernot, of the Paris Foreign Missions, in 1902; others in Vietnam are at Baonham and at Kongkhe-thuang. At Saigon in Cochin-China there is a Lourdes shine at the seminary of the Paris missions, and another in Cambodia, at Phnom-penh.

There is a fine church of our Lady of the Rosary at Phat-diem, built in the Tongkingese style. The most outstanding public event in the history of Marian devotion in Indo-China was in 1950, when the pilgrim statue of our Lady of Fatima was welcomed at the ancient Dominican mission center of Haiphong; it was enthusiastically received throughout the country.

INEFFABILIS DEUS. The opening words and title, "The unutterable God," of the bull wherein, on December 8, 1854, Pope Pius IX defined the Immaculate Conception (*q.v.*) as a dogma of faith. The doctrine, in the words of the Pope, is "in the judgment of the Fathers vouched for by the Sacred Scriptures, transmitted in many weighty statements of the same Fathers, expressly proclaimed in many famous records of venerable antiquity, and proposed and confirmed by the highest and gravest decision of the Church." The Pope dilates at some length on these matters, pointing out some of the relevant patristic declarations and interpretations, referring to the evidence of the liturgy of public worship and the belief of the faithful, and emphasizing the agreement of the bishops of the Church about the doctrine. A particular stress is laid on Mary as the New Eve (*q.v.*): "To vindicate the original innocence and righteousness of the Mother of God, [the Fathers] not only compare her with Eve while Eve was still virgin, innocent and inviolate, not yet deceived by the death-dealing snares of the treacherous Serpent; they also give her precedence over Eve, using expressions of praise in wonderful variety.

For it was Eve's unhappiness to obey the Serpent, to fall from her state of original innocence and become his slave. But the most Blessed Virgin constantly added to the gift that was originally given her; not only did she never give ear to the Serpent: by a power from above she completely destroyed his strength and might." The doctrine is solemnly defined in the following terms: "By the authority of Christ Jesus our Lord, and of the blessed Apostles Peter and Paul, and by our own, We declare, pronounce and define that God has revealed, and that all the faithful must therefore firmly and unswervingly believe, the doctrine which maintains that, by a unique grace and privilege of Almighty God, in virtue of the merits of Jesus Christ the Savior of mankind, the Blessed Virgin Mary was in the first instant of her conception kept free from all stain of original sin."

"Let all the very dear children of the Catholic Church hear our words," concludes the Pope, "and with yet warmer zeal for devotion, religion and love go on cherishing, invoking and beseeching the Blessed Virgin Mary, Mother of God, conceived free from original sin; let them with complete confidence turn to this most kind Mother of grace and mercy in all dangers, difficulties, necessities, doubts and fears. . . ."

INN SIGNS. See SALUTATION.

INNER LIFE OF MARY. Human life is one and indivisible: the same man is leading the same life, but in different aspects, when he prays and when he plays; no part of the life of a Christian is separate from the rest, least of all its religious activity. But for convenience of speech and thought different aspects can be considered separately, though so far as possible not in isolation; and so it is very common to speak of a person's inner or interior life. By that is meant, religiously speaking, the whole of his inward, personal relations with God and holy persons and things that minister to God; in particular, his personal religious dispositions and private activities, prayer and meditation, which in turn carry over into the dispositions with which he joins with his fellow Christians in public worship. In a word, inner life is what is often called spiritual life, and it may cover anything from the highest states of mystical contemplation to the first fumbling prayers of a convert from heathenism.

It is clear at once that nothing is known of Mary's inner life, in the sense that we have no record of her own spiritual strivings, aspirations, gifts, graces, watchings, and consolations: if she spoke of these things to any of her contemporaries, St. John the Evangelist or St. Luke, for instance, they respected her confidence and kept it to themselves. Unless he speaks of it himself, every man's really inner life is hidden from all but God; and it is perhaps not fanciful to think that Mary particularly valued this element of hiddenness and privacy. There are two indications: St. Luke tells us that, after the shepherds had worshiped the new-born Babe at Bethlehem, "Mary kept in mind all these words, pondering them in her heart." And again, after the Boy Jesus had been found in the Temple, in almost the same words, "His mother kept all these things carefully in her heart." It may be supposed that St. Luke learned this from our Lady herself.

But it is also clear that something may be known of Mary's inner life in general terms, in the sense of what may be safely inferred from what is known of herself and her circumstances, and from such hints as the above. Nowadays the word "meditation" has acquired a somewhat narrow, almost technical, religious meaning. But the implication of "pondering," of "keeping carefully in her heart," is obvious: she meditated on, she thought about, the things of God. And since she had been chosen out of all humankind herself to have so crucial a part in the things of God, to bear His divine Son and to co-operate in the redemption of the world, it is not possible to suppose other than that she fed her soul upon the things of God ceaselessly, day and night. Nor surely is it going too far to say that she must have enjoyed what is now called the gift of contemplation to a degree far beyond what has ever been vouchsafed to any other human being; surely the fact that she was in a special sense full of grace involves that. Like any other loving mother she was "wrapped up" in her Son and His life, but her Son was God and her very love for Him was divine contemplation. There is, too, the evidence of the Magnificat (*q.v.*) "My soul doth magnify the Lord . . . holy is His name." Praise of and thanksgiving to Almighty God were the very stuff of Mary's life, a pattern of what they are meant to be in all Christianity—the heart of the matter. (The Mass is a eucharist, that is, a thanksgiving; it is also, in its own words, a "sacrifice of praise.")

There was much speculation about our Lady's inner life among French spiritual writers of the seventeenth century. It was emphasized that the Holy Spirit was the principle and author of her perfect dispositions, and M. Olier, founder of the seminary of Sant-Sulpice, had this illustrated by an engraving. Mary, her hands crossed on her breast, is represented among clouds, wherein the Holy Spirit in the form of a dove is conferring His graces. The Blessed Virgin's eyes are fixed on the monogram of the words "Jesus, Savior of mankind," to show that while the Holy Spirit is the principle of all her actions, love for Jesus and the salvation of souls was their end and object. It was at Saint-Sulpice that there was first kept a feast of the Inner Life of Mary, whose special object was expressed in the antiphon, "This [woman] is the most perfect image of Christ, livingly portrayed by the Holy Spirit." The feast is also observed by the Marists, on April 27.

INTERCESSION, Our Lady's. Intercession is the praying by one person for another. The Council of Trent reaffirmed, "in accordance with the practice dating from the earliest ages of the Christian faith, and in harmony with the consentient teaching of the Fathers and the decrees of councils," that "the saints reigning with Christ offer prayers to God for us men," and that accordingly it is a good thing to ask their intercession on our behalf. That the angels and the martyrs, and

then all the blessed, have power to intercede with God was recognized very early; indeed, it was known in part to the Jews (cf., Tob. 12:12; Zach. 1:12-13; II Mach. 15:12-16). Already in the earlier part of the third century St. Hippolytus, Origen, and St. Cyprian take it for granted. And it came to be realized that man's most powerful advocate among the saints must be Mary, the Mother of the Savior: the example of her power narrated by St. Gregory of Nyssa (see VISIONS), long after it had happened, was doubtless but one among many that impressed the minds of the faithful.

Mary's intercession is universal, she intercedes with God for the Church as a whole, for each individual Christian in particular, and for every grace for everyone; and her voice, as Mother of the Divine Word, is all-powerful with God. Her prayer is never unheard: God will not refuse whatever Mary prays—but she will not pray except as God wills. When her intercession is invoked, it is the supreme mediatorship of her Son that is sought; when the prayers of other saints are asked, Mary is involved, for she is the queen of all saints. Prayer is at the heart of Christianity, and Mary's prayers as our mother are inseparably bound up with the love and veneration of Christians for her. "Pray for us sinners, now and at the hour of our death" is the conclusion of the prayer so ceaselessly addressed to her. "Holy Mother of God, pray for us," the Church cries again and again; and puts into our mouth that for which she is asked to pray: "that we may be made worthy of the promises of Christ."

Mary's power is indirect; her work

is one of intercession. "It is her prayers that avail, and her prayers are effectual by the will of Him who is our all in all. Nor need she hear us by any innate power, or any personal gift; but by His manifestation to her of the prayers which we make to her. When Moses was on the mount, the Almighty told him of the idolatry of his people at the foot of it, in order that he might intercede for them; and thus it is the Divine Presence which is the intermediating Power by which we reach her and she reaches us" (Cardinal Newman). Our Lady and the other saints do not, in the objectionable sense, "come between" the faithful on earth and their one mediator and advocate, Jesus Christ. See MEDIATION; PRAYER TO MARY.

INVIOLATA. The first word and title of a rhythmical prose, *Inviolata, integra et casta es, Maria;* developed from the last two words of the responsory *Gaude, Maria virgo.* It was widely used liturgically in the later middle ages, and was popularized by the "Legends of our Lady" (*q.v.*). The story told was that a blind man composed it to defend Mary's virginity against slander, and she in recognition restored his sight. *Inviolata* is still sung, especially in Dominican churches after the Litany of Loreto. The phrase "Mary's inviolate, whole and chaste womb" occurs in one of St. Bernard's sermons.

INVOCATION. Invocation is a call or appeal to somebody, generally for help. Where our Lady is concerned, the word is also sometimes used to designate a particular title under which she is invoked, e.g., "calling on

her under the invocation of Health of the Sick." See PRAYER TO MARY.

IRAQ, SHRINES OF. The great majority of the people of Iraq are Mohammedans; the most numerous among a varied Christian minority are the Catholics of Chaldean rite. They have an ancient sanctuary at the Antonian monastery of the Lady Mary, Protectress of the Harvest (Mart Mariam, Natrath Zara'e), at Dair es-Saida, near Alqosh. Another Chaldean shrine, at Mosul, was established in thanksgiving for the repulse of a Persian attack under Nadir Shah in 1733; both Christians and Mohammedans attributed their victory to the prayers of Mary the Virgin, and the Catholics of West Syrian rite also have a commemorative shrine at Mosul. Other important shrines are at Tell Qaif (Chaldean) and Qaraqosh (Syrian). Among the Western religious orders working in Iraq are the Carmelites and Dominicans, who have popularized devotion to our Lady of Mount Carmel and the use of the rosary among the Eastern Catholics there.

IRELAND, SHRINES OF. In 1647 the assembly of the Confederation of Kilkenny declared the Blessed Virgin to be patroness of Ireland; her statue was set up in the assembly, and presided over its deliberations. Three years later, at Loughrea, it was decreed that "the Virgin Mother of God, under the title of her Immaculate Conception, should be solemnly and publicly proclaimed patroness of the kingdom of Ireland. . . ." In blessing the people of Ireland by radio during the international eucharistic congress of Dublin in 1932, Pope Pius XI referred to this sovereignty of our Lady: "the Blessed Virgin Mary, Queen of Ireland." These three striking tributes to Irish love for our Lady are reinforced by the number of her shrines in that country. Among the more important, both past and present, are: our Lady of Benada, O.L. of Clonfert, O.L. of Dublin, O.L. of Kilcorban, Knock, Lady's Island, O.L. of Limerick, O.L. of Muckross, O.L. of Trim, O.L. of Waterford, O.L. of Youghal (qq.v.), and O.L. of Navan, destroyed at the dissolution of the Augustinian monastery there.

ISLAM, THE VIRGIN MARY IN. Islam, the religion of which Mohammed is the prophet, accords a special place to the Virgin Mary, both in its sacred book, the Koran (Qur'an), and in popular belief. The Koran relates Mary's birth, her upbringing in the Temple (no mention is made of St. Joseph), the Annunciation (twice), and the birth of Jesus, "under a palm tree" (surahs iii, xix). Certain particulars and legends recounted in connection with these events clearly derive from what is found in Christian apocryphal writings (q.v.). The angel of the Annunciation, understood as the Spirit of God, is represented as telling Mary that "God has chosen you and sanctified you, choosing you over all other women" (surah iii, verse 37); and elsewhere Mary is joined with her Son as "a sign to the worlds" (xxi, 91). More popularly, Mary has to share this preeminence with other heroines of Islam; but all Muslims regard her as the great pattern of chastity, "The Virgin." There is a saying attributed to Mohammed, "Every child is stung by Satan, except Mary and her Son," which, with similar sayings, has been taken by some as an assertion of what Catholics call her freedom from original sin; but Islamic theologians understand it as a reference to personal sinlessness only.

Islam then recognizes, as well as Mary's virginal motherhood, her resplendent holiness throughout her life and her complete submission to God's will, which for the Koran raise her above other women: "We have made the Son of Mary and his mother to be a sign . . ." (xxiii, 52). In some countries where Muslims and Christians live side by side, the followers of Mohammed resort freely to shrines of the Blessed Virgin: e.g., to our Lady of Africa at Algiers, our Lady of Mount Carmel in Palestine, our Lady of Saidnaia in Syria, and in India. A later element in the Koran (v, 116) accuses Christians of worshiping Mary as a "third god"; and of her divine motherhood it says, "It is not for God to take to Himself any offspring . . ." (xix, 36). Prayer to her is rejected by inference (xxxix, 3-4).

ITALY, SHRINES OF. There are probably more shrines of Mary in Italy than in any other country of the world. Piedmont and Lombardy alone have over seventy each, while in Apulia and Sicily there is scarcely a town or village that has not its own venerated image, generally reputed miraculous and often with its special liturgical feast. The following are some of the more important of these sanctuaries, going from north to south: our Lady of Tirano, near Como; O.L. of Cornabusa, Bergamo;

The Consolata (*q.v.*), Turin; St. John Bosco's St. Mary, Help of Christians, Turin; O.L. of Oropa (*q.v.*); Mary, Queen of Mondovì (*q.v.*) Santa Maria delle Grazie (*q.v.*), Milan; O.L. of Miracles, Milan; S.M. del Sacro Monte (*q.v.*) di Varese; O.L. of Caravaggio (*q.v.*); St. Mary the Crowned, Lodi; S.M. della Croce, Crema; O.L. of Miracles (*q.v.*), Brescia; O.L. of Help and O.L. of Graces, Mantua; S.M. della Salute (*q.v.*), Venice; O.L. of Monte Berico, Vicenza; O.L. of the Crown, Monte Baldo, in the Val d'Adige; Monte Santo (*q.v.*), Camporosso and Gorizia; O.L. of Bolzaneto, Genoa (*q.v.*); O.L. of the Healing Water (*q.v.*); O.L. of Mercy (*q.v.*), near Savona; O.L. of Bonaria, Sardinia; O.L. of Montallegro (*q.v.*); O.L. in the Country, Piacenza; S.M. della Ghiara, Reggio Emilia; the Madonna of St. Luke (*q.v.*), Bologna; the Greek Madonna, Porto Ravenna; O.L. of the Fire, Forlì; S.M. delle Grazie, Faenza; the Madonne del Monte and del Popolo, Cesena; Queen of All Saints, Ancona; Loreto (*q.v.*); O.L. of Light, San Severino; O.L. of Macereto; the Annunziata, Florence (*q.v.*); Monte Senario (*q.v.*); O.L. of the Jail, Prato; O.L. of Miracles, Lucca; Monte Oliveto Maggiore (*q.v.*); O.L. of the Promise, Siena; O.L. of Montenero (*q.v.*); O.L. of the Angels (*q.v.*), Assisi; for Rome, see ROMAN CHURCHES; Grottaferrata (*q.v.*); O.L. of the Oak, Viterbo (*q.v.*); O.L. of Good Counsel (*q.v.*), Genazzano; O.L. of the Rocks (*q.v.*), Castel Sant' Elia; O.L. of Foggia (of Seven Veils, or the Old Picture); O.L. of the Carmelites and O.L. of the Cave, Naples; O.L. of Pompeii (*q.v.*); Monte Vergine (*q.v.*); O.L. of Constantinople (*q.v.*), Bari; O.L. of the Chain, Palermo; O.L. of Consolation, Termini; O.L. of the Sacred Letter (*q.v.*), Messina; O.L. of the Green Valley (*q.v.*), Sicily; and, also in Sicily, Byzantine-rite shrines at Piana dei Greci and Contessa Entellina.

IVIRON, OUR LADY OF. According to the legend this icon was thrown into the sea by iconoclasts at Constantinople and years later washed up on the shores of Mount Athos. It was taken to the monastery of Iviron (of the Iberians or Georgians) and enshrined; there it is still venerated under the name of the "Portaïtissa." In 1648, at the request of the ailing Tsar Alexis, a copy was made with solemn ceremony and taken to Russia, where it became as famous as the original: the chapel in which it was kept at Moscow was perhaps the most frequented shrine of the city, and the icon was often taken to "preside" at some public occasion, or at a wedding, sick-bed, and so on. This chapel was destroyed by the bolsheviks at the revolution; but the icon was saved and it is now again enshrined in a Moscow church. The Russians commemorate our Lady of Iviron on October 13.

J

JAPAN, SHRINES OF. St. Francis Xavier tells us that when his Japanese convert Paul Anjiro showed a picture of our Lady and her divine Child to the *daimyo* of Satsuma, that Buddhist potentate "prostrated before it and venerated it most reverently, and bade his courtiers do the same." That was in 1549, and the *daimyo* was probably only being polite. Four hundred years later there is a number of shrines of Mary in Japan, resorted to by the Catholic successors of the Japanese to whom Xavier preached. Notable among them are those of Ura and Otome Toge (*qq.v.*). As in some other missionary countries, there is particular devotion to our Lady of Lourdes, which was introduced by Bishop Joseph Laucaigne in 1863. Among the shrines under this designation are those at Tamanura (*q.v.*), Fukuyama, Nagoya, and at Sekiguchi and the Marist Brothers' School in Tokyo. A recent discovery in a library at Madrid shows that at the end of the sixteenth century the missionary authorities appointed the feast of our Lady of Protection ("Patronage") to be specially observed annually by the Christians of Japan.

JERUSALEM. The earthly Holy City by excellence, the Holy of Holies of all Christian sanctuaries, visits to which were the origin of all Christian pilgrimages (*q.v.*). The sacred places associated with the final acts of man's redemption by the God-man, the Upper Room, Calvary, the tomb of Resurrection, and the rest, are of course associated with Mary too; and in addition there are shrines specifically connected with her, notably her supposed birthplace (*q.v.*) and the place of the Assumption (*q.v.*). Our Lady's meeting with her Son on His way to death is marked by a church, of Armenian rite, our Lady of the Swoon (*q.v.*). In the church of the Holy Sepulchre there are commemorative altars of her receiving her Son's dead body and, in the Franciscan choir, of His appearing to her when He had risen again. The church of the Dormition (*q.v.*) is at the place of her death, according to the Jerusalem tradition. Other spots connected with her name commemorate events that belong to the domain of pious supposition, or even folk-lore, rather than religious tradition. The Spring of the Lady Mary, between Gethsemane and the pool of Siloam (Siloë) in the Cedron valley, is so called because of its proximity to the church of the Assumption; it is the Ain Rogel of II Kings 17:17 and III Kings 1:9.—A *feast* called our Lady of Jerusalem is kept in a few places.

JOACHIM, SAINT. See PARENTS OF OUR LADY.

JOSEPH, SAINT. The husband of the Virgin Mary and the foster-father of Jesus Christ. Joseph was of royal descent, of the house of David, and his genealogy (*q.v.*) is set out in the gospels of St. Matthew and St. Luke; but he was a poor man, as is proved by the offering of only a brace of turtle-doves at Mary's purification in the Temple. English versions of the Bible call him a carpenter, though the Greek word in the gospels, *tekton,* means no more than an artisan or handicrafts-man. If the evidence of the *Protevangelium of James* may here be trusted, he may have been a carpenter on buildings. The *Protevangelium,* the *Gospel of Pseudo-Matthew* (*qq.v.*), and the *History of Joseph the Carpenter* (fifth century) profess to give a certain amount of information about Joseph, especially concerning his betrothal to Mary, the discovery of her pregnancy, and his own death (also a fine passage in the *Protevangelium,* chap. xviii, where Joseph describes how all things stood still at our Lord's birth), but no credence can reasonably be given to most of it. We may assume that he was betrothed to Mary his bride with the formalities prescribed by Jewish ritual, but the nature of this ceremonial is not clearly known, especially in the case of the poor; Joseph's age and the circumstances of his death are quite unknown. The *Protevangelium* states that he was an old man, a widower with children, when he married Mary; but St. Jerome maintained his perpetual viriginity and declared that "it is nowhere written that he had another wife," and that view has gained acceptance. It is much more probable that he was a young man at his marriage with Mary, but clearly he was dead before the Crucifixion. We have to be content with the simple facts given in the gospels: that when he was grieved by Mary's state his fears were set at rest by an angelic vision; that he was again warned by angels, first to seek refuge from Herod in Egypt, and afterward to return to Palestine; that he was present at Bethlehem when our Lord was laid in the manger and the shepherds came to worship; that he was present also when the Child was placed in the arms of holy Simeon; that he shared his wife's sorrow at the loss of her Son and her joy when they found Him discussing with the elders in the Temple. It has been pointed out that Mary herself seemed to invest Joseph with full parental rights when she said without qualification, "Thy father and I have sought thee sorrowing"; and St. Luke adopted her phrase and tells us, with reference to Simeon's words when Jesus was presented in the Temple, that "His father and mother were wondering at those things which were spoken concerning Him." St. Joseph's merit is summed up in the words "he was a just man," that is to say, a godly man: and those are the words of the written word of God itself.

In his encyclical letter *Quamquam pluries* (1889) Pope Leo XIII wrote: "That St. Joseph . . . was the husband of Mary and the father—as was thought—of Jesus Christ was the source of all his dignity, grace, holiness and glory. The dignity of the Mother of God is such as nothing could surpass; yet since between Joseph and the

Blessed Virgin there was the bond of marriage, it seems evident that he approached more nearly than anybody else to that overwhelming dignity which raises the Mother of God above all other created beings. . . . God, then, surely gave Joseph to Mary as her husband not simply to be her companion for life, the witness of her maidenhood, the guardian of her good name, but also, by reason of the bond of marriage, to be a sharer in her lofty dignity. So he is preeminent above all men in that through the divine wisdom he was the guardian of the Son of God, and in men's eyes His father."

So far as the evidence goes, Egypt was the home of the earliest *cultus* (*q.v.*) of St. Joseph; in the West his veneration was as late in beginning as it is now intense and diffused. A Frankish martyrology of the eighth century commemorated him, on March 20, and devotion to him was spreading in the later middle ages, e.g., at Evesham abbey in England; but it was not till 1482 that his name was found in the Roman calendar. He now has two feasts, on March 19 and on May 1. In the same way, that aspect of St. Joseph's *cultus* that connects him with a happy death was known in the East centuries before it became widespread in the West.—St. Bernard draws parallels between St. Joseph and that other Joseph, the patriarch in Israel: "If the first Joseph, sold by the envy of his brothers into Egypt, foreshadowed the selling of Christ, the later Joseph, fleeing from Herod's envy, carried Christ into Egypt. The first, keeping faith with his lord, would not lie with his lord's lady;

the second, recognizing his Lady, the mother of his Lord, to be a virgin, guarded her faithfully, himself being chaste. To the first was given understanding of the mysteries of dreams; to the second it was given to know and to share in the mysteries of Heaven."

JOYS OF MARY, SEVEN. Although devotion nowadays seems more given to the sorrows (*q.v.*) of Mary than to her joys, it apparently was not always so; indeed, writers and preachers seem first to have spoken of her (five) sorrows to match and complement (five) joys already venerated. So early as the middle of the eleventh century devotion to the joys appears in a poem written at Canterbury, and a considerable literature grew up on the subject. The biggest factor in its popularizaton was the enthusiasm of the Franciscans, especially the efforts of St. Bernardine of Siena (d. 1444) in Italy, of St. John of Capistrano (d. 1456) in Germany, and of Bl. Gabriel Mary (d. 1532) in France, though it was already widespread before their time. It was long before the number seven was settled on—five, twelve, and fifteen were often found—and there was a similar variety in the subjects. An old English carol enumerates them as Mary suckling her Son, Jesus curing the lame, giving sight to the blind, reading the Bible, raising the dead, His own resurrection, and His going up into Heaven. It will be noticed that these differ very considerably from what is now the accepted enumeration; the above seem to be the choice of the common people who made the song, while the following are the choice of theologians: the Annunciation, the Visitation, the birth of Jesus, the visit of the Wise Men, the finding of Jesus in the Temple, His rising from the dead, and the Assumption.

The Franciscans celebrate the *feast* of the Seven Joys on August 27 with a proper office and sequence (*q.v.*); another feast of the Joys of Mary, having her happiness at the Resurrection particularly in view, is kept on the second Monday after Easter in Portugal, and elsewhere. Devotion to our Lady of the Seven Joys is notably strong in the diocese of Trois-Rivières, Canada. There is a rosary of the Seven Joys (*q.v.*), also known as the Franciscan Crown or Seraphic Rosary.

JUDAISM AND MARY. The Church is the Israel of Newness, the Israel of God (Gal. 6:16), Christians are, as Pope Pius XI reminded them, spiritually Jews, spiritual descendants of Abraham; Mary, a Jewess of Nazareth, of the house of David, is for them "the glory of Jerusalem, the joy of Israel, the honor of her people." Yet of Judaism as such and Mary there is little that can be said, for she figures hardly at all in Jewish consciousness: there is no "official" Jewish opinion about her, as there is none about her Son. It can hardly be denied that for long the general feeling of most Jews toward both was one of deep hostility. There was a time when certain Jewish writers, for controversial purposes, made light of Mary's virginity: it was perhaps to something of this sort that Mohammed referred as "a mighty slander" (Koran, iv, 155). But it has to be recognized that, side by side with the circulation in the middle ages, and later, of such shocking writings as the *Toledot Yeshu,* were words and deeds of many Christians that were no less horrifying to Jews—accusations of ritual-murder, for example, and accompanying persecutions. One wickedness does not cancel out the other: they aggravated one another.

Modern times have shown a notable change in attitude toward Jesus among such Jews as Joseph Klausner, Germain Levy, C. G. Montefiore, Stephen Wise, H. G. Enelow, and Martin Buber. This as it grows in influence must modify ignorance about and indifference to Mary. Of such an opening of the heart there is evidence at the popular level, in such books as Franz Werfel's *Song of Bernadette* and the *Mary* of Sholem Asch—different from one another as those books are. "The root of Jesse has budded, the star has risen out of Jacob, a maiden has brought forth the Savior: we praise thee, O thou our God" (fourth antiphon at Lauds on the Circumcision).

JULIAN, REVELATIONS OF DAME. Dame Julian, who lived from about 1350 to about 1423, was an ankress, or solitary, living in a cell adjoining St. Julian's church at Norwich in England. The book of her *Revelations of Divine Love* (which she called "shewings") has been called "perhaps the profoundest work that has ever come from an English pen." The short passages from her shewings concerning our Lady are reproduced here for two reasons: first, for their intrinsic worth and beauty; second, as examples of the differences of "temper" and atmosphere to be found in writings of this kind, and of a literary simplicity and spiritual sobriety not found in some similar works that are far more widely known. The spelling and a few words have been modernized. Julian says that our Lord shewed her His Mother three times: "The first was as she was with child; the second was as she was in her sorrows under the Cross; the third as she is now in pleasing, worship and joy."

"(1) In this God brought our Lady to mine understanding. I saw her spiritually, in bodily likeness a simple maiden and a meek, young of age, in the stature that she was when she conceived. Also God showed me in part the wisdom and the truth of her soul: wherein I understood the reverent beholding in which she beheld her God that is her maker, marvelling with great reverence that He would be born of her that was a simple creature of His making. And this wisdom of truth, knowing the greatness of her Maker and the littleness of herself that is made, made her for to say meekly to the angel Gabriel, 'Lo, me here, God's handmaiden!' In this sight I saw truly that she is more than all that God made beneath her in worthiness and in fullness. For above her is nothing that is made but the blessed manhood of Christ.
"(2) Here [in the pains of the Passion] I saw a part of the compassion of our Lady St. Mary: for Christ and she were so oned in love that the greatness of her loving was the cause of the greatness of her pain. . . . Love, continued by grace, that creatures have to Him . . . was most fully showed in His sweet Mother, and overpassing; for so much as she loved Him more than all others, her pain passed all others'. For ever the higher, the mightier, the sweeter that the love be, the more sorrow it is to the lover to see that body that is loved in pain.
"(3) And with this same cheer of mirth and joy our good Lord looked down on the right side and brought to my mind where our Lady stood in the time of His passion, and said, 'Wilt thou see her?' And in this sweet word it was as if He had said: 'I know well that thou wouldst see my blessed Mother; for after myself she is the highest joy that I might show thee, and the most dear and honorable to me; and most she is desired to be seen by my blessed creatures.' And for the high, marvellous, singular love that He hath to this sweet Maiden, His blessed Mother, our Lady St. Mary, He showed her highly rejoicing as by the meaning of these sweet words, as if He said: 'Wilt thou see how I love her, that thou mightest joy with me in the love that I have in her and she in me?' And also (to more understanding this sweet word) our Lord God speaketh to all mankind that shall be saved . . . 'Wilt thou see in her how thou art loved? For thy love I made her so high, so noble and so worthy; and this liketh me, and so will I that it doth thee.' . . . When our good Lord had said this word, 'Wilt thou see her?'

I answered and said, 'Yea, good Lord, gramercy, if it be thy will.' Oftentimes I prayed this, and I weened to have seen her in bodily presence, but I saw her not so. Jesus in that word showed me spiritual sight of her, not as before, little and simple, but high and noble and glorious, and pleasing to Him above all creatures. And He willeth that it be known, so that all those that like in Him should liken them in her, and in the liking that He hath in her and she in Him."

So much of Dame Julian on the Maiden that is Christ's dearworthy Mother. *Cf.*, Revelations and Communications; Visions.

K

KADUTHURUTHY, OUR LADY OF. A shrine of the Catholics of Syro-Malabar rite in their diocese of Kottayam in India. It is said to have been founded in the sixth century. On the name-day of the church the pilgrims celebrate a temporal as well as a religious feast, holding their *agape* (love-meal) in the open air. Formerly food was taken home to those who could not join in the pilgrimage, that thereby they might share in it from afar.

KAZAN, OUR LADY OF. This miraculous icon was found in the ruins of a burnt-out house at Kazan on the river Volga in 1579. Before the revolution, perhaps still sometimes, a Russian mother would give a copy of this picture to her daughter at her wedding, as a blessing on her and her new home. There is a Russian feast of Mary under this title on October 22 and a commemoration of its finding on July 8. There are many replicas of the picture, of which the best known was in the church of the same name at Moscow. The Byzantine chapel of the Oriental Institute at Rome is dedicated in honor of our Lady of Kazan.

KEVELAER, OUR LADY OF. This sanctuary, in the fertile plain of the lower Rhine between Krefeld and Kleve, is in a sense a daughter-shrine of Luxemburg (*q.v.*). In 1642 a tradesman of Kevelaer, Hendrik Busmann, heard a voice telling him to make a shrine at a certain spot by the wayside. This he did, putting in it a print of the Luxemburg statue of Mary, Consoler of the Afflicted. Very shortly pilgrims began to visit it, and within a century annual pilgrimages were being made from over a hundred parishes, both in the Rhineland and Holland; and the custom has grown ever since. The first church was built in 1645 and is now called the Candle chapel, where the pilgrimages set up their great candles and *ex-votos* (*q.v.*). Adjoining it is the little Chapel of Grace that protects the original brick pillar-shrine and its copperplate engraving. It was crowned in 1892. Kevelaer suffered rather seriously in World War II; but the shrine was saved, largely through the courage of a Bavarian officer, and it continues to draw very large numbers of pilgrims.

KILCORBAN, OUR LADY OF. This image of the Blessed Virgin enthroned with the Child is a work of an Irish school of woodcarving that flourished in the Shannon basin from the twelfth century; the statue may be of that date. But it is first heard of at the Dominican church of Kilcorban in Galway, in the later fifteenth century. It was long regarded as miraculous, and during penal times it was looked after by the family of Burke of Pallas, near Kilcorban. More recently it was in the parochial house of Tynagh. Devotion to our Lady of Kilcorban continued into modern times; but the statue is now on loan in the National Museum at Dublin. It is the oldest and finest of surviving Irish medieval wooden images.

KIRCHENTHAL. A very popular shrine of our Lady in the Salzburg country of Austria. It is situated close to Sankt-Martinus, near Lofer on the Saalach River, and dates from 1688.

KNARESBOROUGH, OUR LADY OF. The tiny chapel of our Lady of the Crag at Knaresborough in Yorkshire was cut in the rock at the foot of a limestone cliff about 1408. It was the thank-offering of a mason, John Lovell, for the preservation of his little son from falling stone, and its altar etc. are all carved from the rock. The chapel has been restored to Catholic hands, and a replica of the old statue—the Child standing on His Mother's left knee—again stands in its niche. St. Robert's Cave at Knaresborough was the dwelling-place of the holy hermit Robert Flower (d. 1218).

KNOCK (Cnoc Mhuire). A village of County Mayo in the west of Ireland. Here, from about 8 P.M. on August 21, 1879, a wet windy evening, over a dozen people, aged from six to seventy-five years, declared that they saw certain figures about two feet above the ground against a gable-wall of the church. The wall appeared to be illuminated, and the figures were identified as our Lady, crowned, St. Joseph, and (more doubtfully) St. John the Evangelist, and beside him a lamb standing on an altar. About other details (e.g., a cross, stars, angels) testimony differed, and some said the figures moved, while to others they appeared motionless. Nobody professed to hear any message, whether inwardly or with the ears; a woman who tried to kiss the Lady's feet felt only the wall. The phenomena lasted ninety minutes or more.

A commission of inquiry appointed soon after by the Archbishop of Tuam reported that the evidence of the fourteen witnesses examined was, taken as a whole, "trustworthy and satisfactory"; and for some years cures were reported. But for about thirty years after 1891 little was heard of Knock, doubtless in part due to the apostasy from the Church of a woman who had been an enthusiastic supporter of the shrine. Another episcopal commission in 1936 examined the only two surviving witnesses, and some of those who claimed to have been physically healed at Knock. Its findings were sent to the Congregation of Sacred Rites at Rome, but no approval or rejection has so far been issued. Nevertheless, a chapel has been built at the spot, which, with episcopal permission, is visited by many pilgrims. Cures have been and are reported (some from North America) in sufficient numbers to justify the opening of a medical bureau in 1935. The statue of our Lady at Knock was crowned in 1954.

KNOWLEDGE, OUR LADY'S. The Blessed Virgin was endowed with all the knowledge that was necessary for the fulfilment of her destiny; there is no evidence that she was given supernatural light or powers which were not necessary or useful for that purpose. It would appear certain that there was a progressive development of her understanding of the mysteries in which she had so great a part, that God only gradually unfolded to her all that was involved in her unconditional "Yes" to Gabriel, from Bethlehem to Pentecost, and the ways in which Jesus would become ruler in the house of Jacob forever. "Nothing compels us to believe that Christ's external career was manifested to her at once, at an early stage; it unfolded itself to her eyes gradually; she wondered and suffered . . ." (Abbot Vonier, *The Divine Motherhood*). That some things were for a time hidden from Mary is shown in several places in the gospels, for example, when she found her young Son in the Temple, and she and her husband "did not understand the word He spoke to them" (Luke 2:49-50). A few recent theologians have suggested that at the time of the Annunciation Mary did not know that the Child to be born of her would be divine; but St. Augustine long ago expressed the traditional belief when he said that "she had already conceived Him in her mind before conceiving Him in her womb." It would indeed seem evident that such knowledge was necessary to enable her to give full and understanding assent to the divine message delivered by the angel. The extent of her knowledge of what she was doing and what was involved are surely indicated by her own words in the Magnificat (*q.v.*), "All generations shall call me blessed."

Our Lady's knowledge was the knowledge of faith: she was blessed because she believed that the things promised her by the Lord would be accomplished (Luke 1:45). This faith, her familiarity with the promises about the coming Messiah in Jewish scripture and tradition, her contemplative spirit, that vision of divine things which is promised to the clean of heart (Matt. 5:8), the conversation of her Son—all these things combined to give Mary supernatural knowledge above that of men and angels. And not a few theologians would add to them the gift of infused knowledge, that is, knowledge imparted directly by God. But for mundane affairs, there is no reason whatever for supposing that Mary's knowledge exceeded what would be expected of a woman of her humble background and station in life. *Cf.*, Seat of Wisdom; Sufferings, Our Lady's.

KOBOKO, OUR LADY OF. Koboko is near Ladonga in Uganda, a mission in the care of the Verona missionaries. The church there has a shrine of Mary, Queen of Africa, whose statue was crowned in 1954. The crown is surmounted by a cross and a crescent, the latter emblem being of double significance in a place where Mohammedan opposition to Christianity has been so strong.

KOREA, SHRINES OF. An important Marian sanctuary in this unhappy land is our Lady of Mokpo; there are Fatima shrines at Sok-cho-ri and Kwanju, and the seminary at Pyong-yang had a shrine of our Lady of Lourdes. The churches of the vicars apostolic at Seoul and Taiku are dedicated in honor of the Immaculate Conception. An image of Mary painted in the Korean manner is illustrated in Zsolt Aradi's *Shrines of Our Lady* (New York, 1954, p. 131).

KURSK, OUR LADY OF, New York. This icon is of the Novgorod (*q.v.*) type, but it portrays only the upper part of our Lady's figure, which is surrounded by small representations of other saints. For centuries it was at Kursk in Russia, but after the revolution it was taken to Sremski Karlovci in the care of the group of exiled Russian Orthodox bishops that had headquarters there. During World War II it was secretly conveyed to Munich, and later was taken from thence to New York, N.Y. Here its home is in the chapel of the Russian metropolitan of the former Karlovci obedience, but it is continually taken from place to place for the veneration of Russian congregations—a veritable traveling shrine for Russians in the New World.

L

LA SALETTE. The famous vision of La Salette consisted of one appearance, on September 19 in 1846, in two children, Mélanie Calvat (Mathieu) and Maximin Giraud, aged fifteen and eleven. They were minding cattle on a high mountain, some miles from La Salette-Fallavaux, near Corps in the French diocese of Grenoble. Here, in bright sunlight, they said they saw a tall "beautiful lady," curiously dressed and giving off light. Speaking partly in French and partly in the local dialect, she complained with tears of the people's irreligion, mentioning in particular working on Sunday and using bad language, and threatened famine if they did not mend their ways. Then she told each of the children a secret which the other did not hear, and asked them if they said their prayers properly. "Hardly at all," was the reply. The Lady told them that at least they must say Our Father and Hail Mary night and morning. She reverted to the impiety of the people, and reminded Maximin of the diseased wheat his father had once shown him. Finally, before disappearing, she impressed on them that they must "make all this known to my people."

The children did so, and there resulted long drawn-out controversies that were not confined to France. Many people went on pilgrimage to the mountain, where miracles were soon reported; others, especially among the clergy, denied the authenticity of the whole business. On both sides were those who were bitter and fanatical, as well as those who were reasonable and moderate. An attempt was even made in 1850 to use the happening for political ends (as seems to have been done at Beauraing too), which precipitated "The Ars Affair" and brought St. John Vianney into the controversy. In July, 1851, Mélanie and Maximin were induced to write down their respective secrets for Pope Pius IX, to whom they were conveyed. Four months later the Bishop of Grenoble officially declared that the vision bore the marks of truth, that the faithful were justified in believing it, and that the *cultus* (*q.v.*) of our Lady of La Salette was approved. In the following year the Holy See allowed a feast of Mary's patronage to the Grenoble diocese for September 19.

But the strife continued, encouraged by the subsequent career of Mélanie. She made several abortive attempts to become a nun, including some years with the Carmelites at Darlington in England (a country that she found barbarous). In 1879 she published what she averred to be the secret (*q.v.*) imparted to her by our Lady, and her ideas became more and more deranged and fantastic. She died in Italy in 1904. Maximin's life too was unsettled and unhappy, but in more normal ways; he died at Corps in 1875, affirming that he had never lied about the vision at La Salette. The pitiable subsequent lives of the two people concerned has no necessary bearing whatever on what took place on that September afternoon in 1846. Some years after he had seen what the children wrote to him, Pius IX declared, "The secrets of La Salette are this—unless you repent you will all perish."

The sanctuary of La Salette, high up among sweeping bare mountains, is one of the most impressively situated of Marian shrines. It includes a church and other buildings, and a statue which was crowned by a papal legate as our Lady of Reconciliation. To look after the sanctuary and minister to the pilgrims a society of priests was organized that grew into the congregation of Missionaries of La Salette, now found in several parts of the world. When these priests first came to the United States in 1892 they found that devotion to our Lady of La Salette had reached North America before them. In 1948 they initiated a shrine in her honor among the woods of Shaker Hills at Enfield, N.H., where twenty years before the Shakers had sold them a property for a house of studies at a generously low price. Suggested by what she had said on the subject, one of the works undertaken in France in the name of Mary, Reconciler of Sinners, was for the better observance of Sunday. This had such good effect that its founder, Count Louis de Cissey, declared in 1878: "A few years ago Le Mans was like any other French town [in disregard of Sunday]. Now you would think you were in England."

Among the very varied people who in one way or another came under the influence of La Salette were Msgr. Dupanloup, Bishop of Orleans, Msgr. Ullathorne, Bishop of Birmingham in England, J. K. Huysmans, Léon Bloy, Léon Harmel, Ernest Psichari, Bl. Julian Eymard, and St. John Vianney: the last named underwent years of uncertainty, due to his belief that Maximin had denied to him the story of the vision ("The Ars Affair"). *Cf.*, Secret of La Salette; Revelations and Communications; Visions.

LA SARTE, OUR LADY OF. La Sarte, above the town of Huy in the Meuse valley, is a very popular shrine among the Walloons of Belgium. Nothing is known of the earlier history of the statue venerated there: a seated Virgin and Child, the whole carved out of a single block of oak. Early in the seventeenth century it was standing neglected in a roofless chapel; attention was drawn to it by reports of strange happenings, and in 1621 the chapel was repaired. Pilgrims multiplied, great processions were organized, and the shrine prospered. Today it is in charge of the Dominicans, who have enshrined the image on a beam behind the high altar of their church, surrounded by a golden aureole; it was crowned in 1896.

LA-VANG, OUR LADY OF. The oldest and best-known Marian shrine in Vietnam. It was established in the year 1800, in consequence of a vision of Mary to a group of the faithful at prayer. The sanctuary is at Hue, the capital, just below the communist frontier, and it attracts large numbers of pilgrims, both Catholics and others. Cardinal Spellman, Archbishop of New York, paid tribute to this shrine when he visited Vietnam in 1954.

LADY ALTAR. An altar dedicated in honor of the Mother of God, surmounted generally by a statue or other image of her; it is usually in a conspicuous place on the gospel (north) side of the church, often in a side chapel. There is usually a special Lady altar even though the whole church, and consequently the high altar, be dedicated in her name.

LADY CHAPEL. A side chapel in a church, containing the Lady altar. In many large gothic churches it is situated at the extreme east end, behind the high altar, and is of conspicuous size.

LADY DAY. In England, the feast of the Annunciation (March 25). In that country national accounts were formerly made up to that date; when in 1752 the adoption of the Gregorian calendar involved the suppression of eleven days the date was altered to April 5, "old Lady day," so that the Englishman's income-tax return still has an uncovenanted association with the Blessed Virgin. In England and Wales the Annunciation is a quarter-day, when rent etc. becomes due; in Scotland Candlemas is a quarter-day. The Assumption was sometimes called "Lady day in harvest."

LADY'S ISLAND, Wexford. Lady's Island (really an isthmus) is in Lake Togher, some ten miles from the city of Wexford in Ireland. It was made a sanctuary of our Lady by the Augustinian canons regular in the thirteenth century, and has been frequented by pilgrims practically without a break ever since then. From 1760 there was a pilgrimage church on the adjacent mainland, first a small thatched chapel, now a stone church; and there is today an altar and a statue of Mary of the Assumption on the island itself, to which large crowds resort on August 15. Many miracles of healing have been reported from time to time at this shrine.

LANHERNE. The faith was kept alive at Lanherne in Cornwall throughout the penal times by the family of Arundell. When the English Carmelites fled from Antwerp at the French Revolution, the eighth Lord Arundell gave them his mansion at Lanherne, and they have been there ever since. The nuns brought with them a statue of the Blessed Virgin known as our Lady of the Oak of Sichem, it being made from the oak of our Lady of Montaigu (q.v.). In 1954 the Bishop of Plymouth granted an indulgence to pilgrims who visit this shrine. The Lanherne convent is the oldest community of English Carmelite nuns, having been founded at Antwerp in 1619.

LATVIA, SHRINES OF. Of the three small northern Baltic states, Finland and Estonia are practically solidly Lutheran, but about one quarter of the inhabitants of Latvia are Catholics. In 1215 their land was dedicated to our Lady, and churches bearing her name were very numerous; after the Reformation devotion to Mary was maintained among Latvian Protestants for a considerable time. At the time the U.S.S.R. reannexed the country in 1944 there were shrine churches of our Lady of Sorrows at Riga and at Alsunga; but the best-known sanctuaries, to which people came in large numbers from all over the country, were Skaistkalne, near the Lithuanian border, and Aglona. The image of our Lady of Aglona is a fourteenth-century crowned icon, reputed miraculous; the Child's eyes are fixed on a flower held in His Mother's left hand. The great pilgrimage days were Whitsunday and the Assumption.

LE PUY, OUR LADY OF. Le Puy-en-Velay in France claims to be the scene of the earliest vision of the Blessed Virgin, to a sick woman in the first (third?) century A.D., but the claim would be very difficult to substantiate. In 1254 St. Louis IX gave an ebony image of Mary to the cathedral, and it has been a place of pilgrimage ever since, though the original statue was burnt at the Revolution: the list of holy and other great men who have been pilgrims here is as impressive as the numbers of ordinary people. Already Pope St. Leo IX (d. 1054) had declared that the Mother of God "is nowhere given a more special and filial veneration"; much later, Le Puy is found observ-

ing a privileged jubilee or holy year whenever Good Friday falls on the feast of the Annunciation: this does not happen often—the last time was in 1932, and the next will not be this side of the year 2000. In 1860 a huge statue, our Lady of France, was blessed at Le Puy: it is made of the metal of over two hundred pieces of artillery, captured by the French at Sevastopol in the Crimean War. Before the rise of Lourdes, Le Puy, Chartres, and Liesse (*qq.v.*) were the greatest Marian centers of France. Feast: December 1.

LEBANON, SHRINES OF. See under SYRIA.

LECHE, OUR LADY OF LA, St. Augustine. It is in the fitness of things that St. Augustine in Florida, the home of the first permanent Catholic community in what is now the United States, should also be the home of a very notable sanctuary of Mary. The mission of Nombre de Dios (Name of God) was founded in 1565, and about 1620 there was enshrined in its chapel a small statue of Nuestra Señora de la Leche y Buen Parto, our Nursing Lady of Happy Delivery. The first part of the title is immediately explained by the image (a replica of the original): the Mother, whose expression is of a striking calm and lovingness, is seated, suckling her Child. The second part is derived from a devotion said to have had its rise in Madrid some time earlier, in these circumstances: a woman was safely delivered at a difficult labor after her husband had prayed before a statue of the Nursing Mother, which statue he had recovered from a looting soldier. The title may now also be referred to the many young brides and expectant mothers who ask our Lady's intercession at this shrine, which stands on or near the site of the old Nombre de Dios chapel. The chief pilgrimage day is September 8, Mary's birthday, on which day in 1565 Mass was first offered at St. Augustine.

LEGENDS OF OUR LADY. This title does not refer to legends ("things to be read") about our Lady in general, but to medieval collections of stories, mainly concerning miracles, about her brought together into books for the edification of the faithful: they are often referred to by their German name, *Marienlegenden*. These collections were immensely popular during the later middle ages, and they had a very important effect on Marian devotion: for example, they helped to spread use of the Little Office and of the *Salve Regina*, with its idea of Mary as Mother of Mercy, and popularized such devotions as her Joys and Saturday as her day. They also spread stories of certain miracles and graces all over western Europe, and further, such as that of Mary's gift of a chasuble to St. Ildephonsus of Toledo (d. 667).

Examples of these stories can be found in a book translated into English in two volumes in 1929: *The Dialogue on Miracles,* by a Cistercian monk of Heisterbach in Germany, named Caesarius (d. *c.* 1245). Book vii, at the end of the first volume, is devoted to the Blessed Virgin, and

an idea of the nature of the stories can be gained from their headings: Of a canon who was converted by Mary's intercession; Of two beggars whom she urged to confession; Of the sacristan at Locheim who one night saw Mary come down upon the altar; Of the monk Adam whom Mary cured of eczema; Of a beheaded knight who by her help avoided Hell; Of a robber whom she caused to be buried in a church after his execution; Of a recluse who escaped the Devil's wiles by saying the Ave Maria; and so on. A fuller collection available in English is the *Miracles of the Blessed Virgin Mary,* by John Hérolt (d. 1468). The famous *Golden Legend* of Bl. James of Voragine (d. *c.* 1298) is concerned with the saints at large, and is important from the Marian aspect chiefly because it did so much to diffuse knowledge in the West of the stories about Mary related in the early apocryphal writings (*q.v.*). The first English printed edition was made by Caxton at Westminster in 1483; it has been several times modernized and reprinted. A new translation, in two volumes, was published in New York in 1941.

The *Marienlegenden* were works adapted to the needs, temper, and mind of their time and place, hence their popularity. Readers in other times and places find them too credulous, and their atmosphere sometimes antipathetic, at the least. As, for instance, when our Lady is represented as causing punishments to fall upon wrongdoers in a way that is more suggestive of human retaliation than of divine justice; when a man steals and robs in defiance of Almighty God on every day of the week, except Saturday in honor of Mary; when an almost magical efficacy is attributed to certain prayers, and so forth. Of these and similar things can hardly be said what Father Hippolyte Delehaye, Bollandist, said of the *Golden Legend* in general: ". . . when reading it, it is somewhat difficult at times to refrain from a smile. But it is a sympathetic and tolerant smile. . . ." Some of these tales have done not a little to bring the word "legend" into disrepute; *cf.,* Tradition and Legend.

LEGION OF MARY, The. The Legion of Mary, founded by a layman, Frank Duff, came into being in Dublin, where the first enrollment of members took place on September 7, 1921. Since 1928 it has spread to many other parts of the world. The object of the Legion, in the words of its handbook, is "the sanctification of its members by prayer and active cooperation, under ecclesiastical guidance, in Mary's and the Church's work of crushing the head of the serpent and advancing the reign of Christ." It is at the disposal of bishops and parish clergy for any form of social service and Catholic Action, but it does not undertake the collecting of money or the giving of material relief. The Legion is highly organized and disciplined, and has shown a remarkable degree of effectiveness. This is particularly notable in China, where it is the object of special uneasiness to and attack from the communist government. Every year, on or about March 25, there is a special consecration (*q.v.*) of legionaries to our Lady, which comprises both an individual and a collective consecration: this is known as the *Acies.* "The essential idea of the Legion, upon which all else is built, is that of working in union with and in dependence on Mary, its Queen. The 'Acies' is the solemn declaration of that union and dependence, the renewal—individual and collective—of the legionary promise of fealty."

LENT, OUR LADY IN. An old English familiar name for the feast of the Annunciation. In the year 366 the Council of Laodicea forbade the celebration of feasts during Lent, and this rule was for long in force, which in part accounts for the earlier observance of the Annunciation on various dates. The Church still has a certain reserve about feasts in Lent; and the Ambrosian rite of Milan has the old rule in almost all its rigor: it has admitted only the Annunciation and St. Joseph during that season.

LESSONS AT MATINS. In the Roman Divine Office, when there are three nocturns ("nine-lesson feasts"), the first three lessons are scriptural, the second generally historical or quasi-historical, and the third three from the Fathers and some later writers. At those feasts of our Lady that are observed throughout the Western Church the sources of the lessons for the first and third nocturns are as follows. *Biblical:* Genesis, Exodus, Leviticus, Song of Songs, Proverbs, Ecclesiasticus, Isaias, Jeremias, and the first Epistle to the Corinthians. *Patristic:* St. Irenaeus, St. Basil, St. Ambrose, St. Epiphanius,

St. John Chrysostom, St. Jerome, St. Augustine, St. Peter Chrysologus, Pope St. Leo I, Pope St. Gregory I, St. Sophronius (Damascene; d. *c*. 638), St. Germanus of Constantinople, St. Bede the Venerable (English; d. 735), St. John of Damascus, St. Tharasius (Greek; d. 806), St. Peter Damian (Italian; d. 1072), St. Bonaventure (Italian; d. 1274), St. Bernard, St. Bernardine of Siena (Italian; d. 1444), St. Peter Canisius, St. Robert Bellarmine (Italian; d. 1621). Passages from Pope Pius IX and Pope Pius XII occur in the second nocturn of the Immaculate Conception, the Assumption, and the Queenship. For the nationalities and dates of the other writers, see FATHERS, THE.

LETTER, OUR LADY OF THE SACRED. The title of the principal Marian celebration, at Messina in Sicily on June 3, of a city and island outstanding for warmth and variety of devotion to the Blessed Virgin. The name of the festival, *de Sacris Literis,* is commonly referred to a reputed relic of a surprising kind, no less than a letter said to have been dictated by Mary to neophytes of St. Paul at Messina. There is no mention of any such letter in the proper Office of the day; and the name in fact seems originally to have referred to a greatly venerated icon, of which there are copies in some other Sicilian and Italian churches, all called "of the Letter." See RELICS.

LIBERIAN BASILICA. See MARY MAJOR, ST.

LIESSE, OUR LADY OF. According to the story, three French knights were captured at Askalon during the Crusades and the Saracen emir made every effort to convert them to Islam, even going so far as to send his daughter to undermine the loyalty of the young men. But instead she herself was converted to Christianity, being especially moved by the prisoners' devotion to our Lady, of whom they had an image. They than managed to escape—girl, image, and all—and arrived back in France about 1134. At their home at Liesse in Picardy the knights built a church in thanksgiving, and enshrined their image under the title Cause of our Joy. Many wonders were reported and the place became an important pilgrimage center, especially around Whitsuntide. The image was crowned and a special feast granted in 1857, under the name Mary, Cause of our Joy, Mother of Grace. Our Lady of Liesse was a very popular French shrine and its feast spread to Canada (June 1), where there are several churches dedicated under this name; a copy of the statue is in the church of the Holy Name at Montreal.

LIFE-GIVING FOUNTAIN, OUR LADY OF THE. In Some churches of Byzantine rite a commemoration is made on the Friday after Easter of the dedication of the church of the God-bearer at the Seven Towers at Constantinople. The story goes that the Emperor Leo I (d. 474) had a vision of the Blessed Virgin who pointed out a certain spring; he took a blind man to wash in its waters and the man was healed. Later on, the Emperor Justinian built a church at the spot. This church was destroyed after the Turks took Constantinople, but in 1834 it was rebuilt and brought back to use by the Orthodox Greeks. The icon called our Lady, Fountain of Life, refers to her bearing the Word of God who brings the waters of life to mankind.

LIGHT, OUR LADY OF. Mary is venerated by this name at several places in Europe, as at San Severino in Italy, where she has a shrine, and South America. One center of the *cultus* is in Mexico, where the cathedral of León has a wonderworking image. It was brought to Mexico in 1732 from Sicily, where it had been painted in accordance with a vision seen by Father John Genovesi, s.j. It is a rather complicated design, of a sort not calculated to appeal to all beholders: it includes the Mother pulling a naked man out of a dragon's mouth, and the Child taking men's souls out of a basket proffered by an angel. This seems a somewhat extravagant commentary on the idea of Mary as the Morning Star through whom the Light of the world, Sun of justice, and Day-spring from on high came to us.—There are two churches of our Lady of Light in England, at Clacton in Essex and Sclerder in Cornwall, where the title is joined with Bride of the Holy Ghost.

LIKENESSES OF MARY. Nothing whatever is known about the physical appearance of the Blessed Virgin Mary. St. Augustine, who was in close touch with Palestine, wrote even in his time (354-430) that they did not know what she looked like. About a century after his death it was recorded that the Empress Eudocia had sent from Jerusalem to St. Pulcheria (d. 453) in Constantinople a certain picture of Mary which, it was averred, had been painted by St. Luke. This picture is no longer in existence, nor are any authentic copies of it known. But certain icons have been claimed as copies, and others have been reputed to be independent works of St. Luke: indeed, for a time it was almost common form for any greatly venerated ancient icon of our Lady to be attributed to him. Among the pictures thus credited to St. Luke are the icons at St. Mary Major (*q.v.*), San Sisto Vecchio, Sant' Agostino, and elsewhere in Rome; the Madonna of St. Luke (*q.v.*) at Bologna, of Constantinople (*q.v.*) at Bari, in St. Mark's at Venice, and elsewhere in Italy; our Lady of Czestochowa (*q.v.*); O.L. of Saidnaia (*q.v.*); O.L. of Kykko, Cyprus; O.L. of Korsun, Tikhvin, and Smolensk and others in Russia. There is no evidence that any of these, or other similar pictures, were painted until hundreds of years after the Blessed Virgin had been taken from this world; they can all be dated by iconographers. *Cf.*, Hodegetria.

LIMERICK, OUR LADY OF. About 1622 Patrick Sarsfield had a statue of Mary and her Child made in Flanders, and presented it to the Rosary Confraternity of Limerick in reparation for his father's part in the judicial murder of Sir John Burke of Brittas. At the "general exile" in 1698 it was concealed in the ground, where it lay till 1733, when it was set up in the Fish Lane chapel. In 1816 it was enshrined in the new Dominican church, and there our Lady of Limerick is still venerated. The citizens of Limerick have always been among the most devoted in Ireland to the Mother of God, and she is believed to have manifested herself there during the siege of 1651. The statue, in the base of which a chalice was hidden during penal times, was crowned in 1954.

LITANY OF OUR LADY. See LORETO, LITANY OF.

LITHUANIA, SHRINES OF. Lithuania, now incorporated in the U.S.S.R., is—or was—a land of wayside calvaries and shrines, which are now being exhaustively studied by Dr. Vaišnora. Among the best-known pilgrimage sanctuaries before 1939 were Vilnius Aušros Vartai (see VILNA, OUR LADY OF), Žemaičiu Kalvarija, Pažaislis, and Šiluva, each of which had its miraculous picture. The first was a crowned Madonna (without the Child) in a golden mantle; the third a fairly modern picture surrounded with wreaths of flowers; and the last a crowned Mother and Child of a later icon type.

LITTLE OFFICE. See OFFICE OF OUR LADY, LITTLE.

LITURGY, OUR LADY IN THE: EASTERN. The All-holy Mother of God has a very striking place in all liturgies of the East, and this veneration is sometimes expressed in ways and terms that the Westerner may at first find disconcerting; they are not characterized by the restraint and sobriety of the Roman rite, and so are liable to surprise those whose traditions and temperament are different. On the other hand, in spite of a sometimes remarkable audacity of language, a proper balance is maintained, and devotional exaggeration and subjectivism are averted, by the firmness of the theological foundation and setting. To appreciate the full extent of the Marian element in Eastern public worship it would be necessary to examine the relevant texts at length; but the following examples may be noticed in the "ordinary" parts of the Byzantine (q.v.) Mass.

When the celebrant approaches the sanctuary to make ready the bread and wine before Mass begins, the curtain of the screen is drawn aside and he says, "Open the door of mercy to us, blessed Mother of God. . . ." He kisses and prays before the icon (q.v.) of Christ on the screen, and then turns to that of Mary: "Mother of God, look down upon a sinful people and show thy power as of old. . . ." (These icons are again kissed later on, after the entrance with the gospel book.) Then, during the preparation, an altar-bread is set forth in honor and memory of our Lady, as of other saints. Four times during the Mass litanies and invocations are concluded with a commemoration, in these words: "Remembering our all-holy, stainless, most blessed and glorious Lady, the mother of God and ever-virgin Mary, and all the saints, we commend ourselves and one another and our whole life unto Christ our God"; and several times during the Mass the celebrant or singers refer to the prayers of the Mother of God. The principal reference to our Lady, however, comes at once after the invocation of the Holy Spirit at the consecration: "Moreover we offer thee this worship in spirit on behalf of our forefathers . . . and [the priest sings aloud] especially our all-holy, stainless, most blessed and glorious lady, mother of God and ever-virgin, Mary"; and the Magnifical Hymn (*q.v.*) is then sung to her.

But it is in the rhythmical chants of the Office "propers" that Byzantine liturgical celebration of our Lady reaches its height. It has been remarked that this theological poetry is not simply versified dogma, but rather meditation on the mystery concerned, contemplation breaking into song. Nor, where the Mother of God is concerned, are these hymns confined to her festivals; every office, except on feasts of our Lord, includes a *theotokion* (*q.v.*) and other references. And the other Eastern rites do not fall behind the Byzantine in the richness of their Marian content. The following short quotations must suffice as examples.

"Bride whom earth offers to Heaven, we raise our hearts to thee. Pray that, as thou didst hear the message of the Annunciation, so we may hear the voice of thine only Son saying, Come, ye blessed of my Father. Bless, men of earth, the Fruit of the Maiden in whom you are blessed" (*Armenian:* Wednesday Matins).

"May we who have taken refuge in the prayers of her who is blessed, the holy Virgin Mary, mother of Jesus our Savior, be kept by them from the Evil One and all his wiles. And in the great day of searching of hearts, when the dead rise from the grave and the good are separated from the wicked, may we be found worthy to have joy with her in the bride-chamber of the Kingdom on high, there to sing threefold praise to the Father, the Son and the Holy Spirit" (*Chaldean:* Wednesday office).

"Hail, Mary, fair dove who didst bear God the Word for us! We greet thee with the angel Gabriel, and say: Hail, full of grace, the Lord is with thee! Hail, ever virgin and very queen; hail, glory of the race of men, who has borne Emmanuel for us! Be mindful of us, we beseech thee; be our faithful advocate with Jesus Christ, that He may forgive us our sins" (*Coptic:* when incense is offered to the icon of Mary at Mass).

"Hail to thy conception, thy spiritual conception in which was no stain, no disorder. I, a husbandman, work hard for thy praise, Mary: may thy holiness rain upon the field of my heart, may thy loving kindness ripen my tongue's harvest!" (*Ethiopian* hymn of praise).

"Hail, Mary, ever-virgin, mother of the Almighty who fills Heaven and earth.

"Hail . . . , mother of the Ancient of days whose name was before the sun was created.

"Hail . . . , Mother of Him who made Adam from the dust of the earth.

"Hail . . . , mother of Him who formed Eve and gave her to Adam.

"Blessed art thou, Mary, the mother of Him who gave righteousness and power to the sons of Levi.

"Blessed . . . , for within thee dwelt the Only-begotten, the Splendor of the Father, the Son of God.

"Blessed . . . , for thou didst feed

Him who giveth to all creatures to eat.

"Blessed . . . , whose arms carried the Son of the Most High whom the heavenly hosts acclaim" (*Maronite* and *Syro-Malabar:* prayer from the Mass in honor of our Lady).

"Particularly do we commemorate the holy Mother of God, Mary, in whose honor this sacrifice is offered, that she may intercede with thee, Lord, on behalf of whoever asks her prayers. Through those well-pleasing and acceptable prayers, God good and merciful, give ear to the plea of him who praises her: turn aside from him all temptation, adversity and thine own chastisements; mercifully wash away his sins and transgressions. Through the prayers of thy Mother and of all thy saints" (*Syrian:* from the Mass in honor of our Lady).

Throughout the Eastern liturgies, with all their imagery and allusiveness, Mary is always the All-holy Mother of God. For all their spontaneity of expression and lyricism of language they keep a feeling for her mystery, as one aspect of the mystery of the Incarnation. "Of a truth, neither grave nor death could hold the God-bearer, who ever intercedes for us and is ever heard. She was the mother of Life, and He who dwelt in the Virgin's womb has translated her to life" (Byzantine *kontakion*, feast of the Assumption). See AKATHISTOS HYMN; ENTREATY; FEASTS; etc.

LITURGY, OUR LADY IN THE: WESTERN. In the "ordinary" parts of the Roman Mass references to the Blessed Virgin are few in comparison with the usage of some Eastern rites (see above). She is named in the confession of the preparatory prayers, and of course in the Nicene creed when it is said; apart from these, her name occurs three times. First, at the offertory, in the prayer *Suscipe, sancta Trinitas;* then, at the beginning of the canon, in the first commemoration of the saints (*Communicantes*); lastly, in the prayer *Libera nos* which follows the Lord's Prayer. The first of these declares that the sacrifice is offered to the Holy Trinity "in memory of the passion, resurrection and ascension of our Lord Jesus Christ; and to the honor of blessed Mary, ever-virgin, of blessed John the Baptist . . . and of all the saints. . . . May they whom we remember here on earth be pleased to plead for us in Heaven." The second is a solemn commemoration of "the glorious ever-virgin Mary, Mother of our God and Lord Jesus Christ, of thy blessed apostles and martyrs Peter and Paul . . . and of all thy saints," asking for God's protection through their merits and prayers. The third asks for peace, "at the intercession of the blessed and glorious Mary, ever-virgin Mother of God, of thy blessed apostles Peter and Paul, and Andrew, and of all the saints." Of these three references to the Blessed-Virgin in the supreme act of divine worship, the second is the oldest, dating back perhaps to the end of the fifth century.

To appreciate to the full the praise and veneration accorded to Mary in the public worship of the Western Church, it is necessary to study the propers (*q.v.*) of the Mass and Divine Office on her feasts, both general and local. Whoever does this will at once notice the extensive use made of the words of the Psalms, of such books as Ecclesiasticus and Proverbs, of the prophets of Israel and other writers of the Old Testament. These writers were very rarely looking forward to the Maiden-Mother to come—often they were writing about divine Wisdom—but the Church takes their words and applies them to her whom God has chosen from all eternity.

On the feast of the Immaculate Conception, for example, the introit at Mass is from Isaias (61:10): "[God] hath clothed me with the garments of salvation and with the robe of justice He hath covered me . . . ." The lesson is from Proverbs (8:22-35): "The Lord possessed me in the beginning of His ways . . ."; and the gradual is adapted from Judith (13:23). The offertory is Gabriel's greeting; and the communion-verse is a combination of words from a psalm (86:3) and from the Magnificat (Luke 1:49). In the same way the proper for the Office of this feast is largely made up of apt quotations from the Old and New Testaments. This scriptural element is particularly noticeable in the Common Office (q.v.) of our Lady, with its antiphons from the Song of Songs, little chapters from Ecclesiasticus, lessons from Proverbs, and so on.

The doctrinal content of a liturgical celebration is generally summarized in the antiphons at Lauds, and often referred to again in those of Vespers. There is a specially striking example on the feast of the Circumcision (q.v.). Here the antiphons are the same at Lauds and both Vespers, and they are repeated a month later, at first Vespers of the Purification. They are:

"Wonderful transaction! The Creator of mankind takes body and soul, and stoops to be born of the Virgin; coming forth as a man, yet not begotten by a man, He imparted His Godhead to us."

"When thou wast born unutterably of the Virgin, the Scriptures were fulfilled: like dew upon the fleece [cf., Judg. 6:36-38] thou didst come down to save mankind. We praise thee, our God!"

"The bush which Moses saw unburnt [Exod. 3:1-4] we recognize as your glorious virginity: Mother of God, intercede for us!"

"The root of Jesse has budded, the star has risen out of Jacob, the Virgin has given birth to the Savior. We praise thee, our God!"

"Behold, Mary has brought forth our Redeemer; and seeing Him, John cried out: Behold the Lamb of God, behold Him who takes away the world's sins, alleluia!"

In these ancient and beautiful verses there is clearly set forth, in respect of Mary, the truths that she is really Mother of God and that her child-bearing was virginal; and the figure of the burning bush (q.v.) emphasizes her motherhood as the crown of her virginity. These antiphons underline her unique human part in the work of Redemption; and show that men, who have nothing except what God gives them, nevertheless can bring something positive to His purposes, for something of His divinity has been imparted to them by Him who took on their manhood in Mary's womb—

"Wonderful transaction!" These antiphons examplify how the liturgy of public worship combines praise of God with the teaching of religious truth and the drawing of the faithful ever nearer to their Savior and Head.

Regular Marian elements in the Western liturgy are the daily singing at Vespers of the Magnificat (*q.v.*), which in the mouth of the faithful honors her as well as praises Almighty God, and the singing of the appropriate Antiphon B.V.M. (*q.v.*). Among numerous hymns and other non-scriptural pieces of various kinds, *Ave, maris stella* and *Stabat Mater dolorosa* (*qq.v.*) have a special place, as has the introit of Sedulius (*q.v.*). As well as certain feasts, proper offices, and other observances, some religious orders have special Marian customs with relation to the Mass: see HAIL MARY and SALVE REGINA. In the liturgy all formal prayers of the celebrant or president of the assembly are addressed directly to the Triune God or one of the divine Persons. Often He is asked that we may be upheld by the prayers of our Lady or other saint whose feast it is; e.g., the collect for the Annunciation: "O God, who didst will that thy Word should take flesh in the womb of the blessed virgin Mary at the message of an angel, grant to us thy suppliants who believe her to be truly the Mother of God that we may be helped by her intercession with thee."

The principal feasts of the Blessed Virgin celebrate the outstanding events of her life, and her part in those of her Son's life on earth: her Immaculate Conception, Birthday, and Presentation; the Annunciation and her visit to Elizabeth; the Circumcision may be regarded as Mary's special Christmas commemoration, followed by the Purification; her Compassion or Sorrows in Passion week; and finally her Assumption into Heaven. Other feasts celebrate special aspects of Mary, as mother, as queen, and the rest. For these festivals, see under their titles and the general article FEASTS.

On the occasion of a liturgical congress at Vicenza in 1954, the mind of Pope Pius XII was thus expressed by Msgr. G. B. Montini: "The liturgy not only teaches doctrinal truth; it is also and principally a school of holiness and the best of all ways of incorporating souls in Christ. The work of this congress is, then, anticipated to be specially directed toward this particular aspect of Marian liturgy, so that devotion to the Blessed Virgin, recalled where necessary to its proper ends, will fulfil its true purpose of leading us to Jesus, through a sincere, full and loving change of the old self into the new man of righteousness and Christian holiness. Any form of Marian devotion that neglects this aspect is necessarily deficient, and less acceptable to the heavenly Mother, who wants nothing so much as our renewal in the life of her divine Son" (*Osservatore Romano*, July 12-13, 1954.

LOMARY, OUR LADY OF. A shrine on the Fijian island of Viti Levu. The place was established as a mission station by Marist missionaries, who gave it the name "Lo Mary" in the hope it would become also a local Marian center. This it did beyond expectation, and the sanctuary is visited as well by Fijians and Europeans from Suva and other places on the island.

LORETO, HOLY HOUSE OF, The.
Loreto is situated on the eastern sea-board of Italy, south of Ancona, and is the site of what, until the rise of Lourdes, was no doubt the most famous Marian sanctuary of the world outside of Palestine. Its center is what purports to be the little building in which the Blessed Virgin was born and the Word was made flesh at the Annunciation, the Holy House or *Santa Casa*. There was a church of our Lady at Loreto at least by the year 1193; and during the following centuries indulgences were granted to pilgrims to it, references being made in the grants to an image of the Mother of God which was said to have been transported thither by angelic hands, but with no mention of the Holy House. The earliest existing authentic reference to the Holy House dates from about 1472, and a fuller account was written in 1531. According to these, in the year 1291 the former dwelling-place of our Lady was conveyed by angels from Nazareth to Tersato, near Fiume in Dalmatia; in 1294 it was again removed by the ministry of angels, across the Adriatic sea to Italy, and eventually came to rest on the Recanati road at Loreto, where it still is.

This remarkable story has been accepted as worthy of credence by a long line of popes, beginning with the somewhat guarded reference of Julius II in 1507. The translation of the Holy House of Nazareth was noted in the Roman Martyrology in 1669, a local feast having been allowed in 1632, for which a proper Mass and Office were provided in 1699. The shrine became very famous; it was richly indulgenced and endowed, and the popes took it under their special protection. Among the earlier of the saints who visited it were Francis Xavier, Francis Borgia, Charles Borromeo, and Francis de Sales.

In expressing their judgment on this matter of history, which has no doctrinal significance whatever, the popes were necessarily subject to the state of knowledge and opinion at the times in which they lived. From early in the eighteenth century serious doubts began to be expressed, and during the past sixty years the work of Catholic scholars has shown that the story of the Holy House is beset with very grave historical difficulties. These cannot be gone into here. But it may be remarked that pilgrims and other writers about Nazareth before 1291 (the date of the reputed first translation) associate the Annunciation, not with any cottage, but with a cave-dwelling hollowed out of the rock. And it is extremely curious that, if the event really happened, there is no sign of any Eastern reference or local tradition about the sudden disappearance of a most sacred shrine from Nazareth; when the Loreto story reached the East in the late fifteenth century, its truth was denied there. It is no less curious that such an astounding thing should have happened without leaving any trace in existing European records for almost two hundred years after. These considerations and every other aspect of the problem were gone into in detail by Canon Ulysse Chevalier in his *Notre-Dame de Lorette,* and most Catholic scholars of weight support his unfavorable conclusions; since the publication of that book in 1906 the question of the authenticity of the Loreto building has been on a quite new footing. The detailed *Guide to the Holy Land* (1923) of Father Barnabas Meistermann does not even mention Loreto when dealing with Nazareth. Those who uphold the authenticity of the Holy House lay stress on the approval given by the popes, on the numerous miracles reported at the shrine, on the lack of foundations beneath the walls, and on the allegation that the materials of which it is built are foreign to Loreto but familiar in Galilee.

The objections raised do not affect the fact that for centuries Loreto has been a very great center of religious devotion. The little Holy House stands inside the domed basilica which has been built around it. It is a rectangular structure of rough stone and brick, measuring about 30 by 13 feet within. Outside, the walls have been encased in white marble; inside, behind an altar, stands the statue of our Lady of Loreto. The original was destroyed in a fire at the shrine in 1921; the present statue was set up three years later, after being crowned in Rome by Pope Pius XI. It is swathed in a stiff formal robe, from which the heads of Mother and Child protrude.—It is of interest to English-speaking people that the poet Richard Crashaw was presented to a benefice in the collegiate church of Loreto a month before he died there in 1649. For the Loreto *feast,* see below; and *cf.,* Miracles.

LORETO, LITANY OF. This is the common name for the Litany of the Blessed Virgin Mary, from the sanctuary where it originated. It begins in the usual way of litanies, with *Kyrie eleison* and invocations of the Persons of the Holy Trinity. Then follow 49 invocations of our Lady, with the prayer "Pray for us." Nineteen of these are addressed to her as Mother or as Virgin, each with an epithet; the next thirteen are less usual terms, expressive of her powers and qualities; then come four common titles and twelve addressed to her as Queen. After "Lamb of God . . ." (thrice), and sometimes the anthem *Sub tuum praesidium* (*q.v.*), the litany ends with the collect from the common Mass of our Lady. This litany is often sung at Benediction (*q.v.*) and on other extra-liturgical occasions, and is used for private prayer. Parts of it have been sometimes objected to as extravagant and innovational; but in fact most of the titles can be found or paralleled in the writings of the Fathers of the first six centuries. The principal titles are referred to separately herein.— There were a number of Marian litanies in both private and public use during the late middle ages, but the reforming activities of Pope St. Pius V (d. 1572) drove them all out of use, with the exception of that sung at Loreto (see above); this was authorized for general use in 1587. Ten years later it was introduced at Rome, in St. Mary Major's; and in 1613 Pope Paul V directed it to be sung there every Saturday and on Mary's feasts. From then on use of the Litany of Loreto spread and gained very wide popularity. From time to time the Holy See has ordered invocations to be added to it, the latest being "Queen taken up into Heaven," after the definition of the Assumption in 1950.

LORETO, OUR LADY OF, Feast. A feast in commemoration of the Translation of the Blessed Virgin's Home, first granted to the Italian province of Piceno in 1632, is now observed, on December 10, in Italy and some places and religious congregations elsewhere (including the English diocese of Middlesbrough). The proper Mass and Office include elements from the proper of the dedication of a church; the gospel is that of the Annunciation. The sixth lesson at Matins relates briefly the story of the miraculous translation, and the collect refers to Mary's house being "wondrously placed in the heart of the Church."—In 1920 Pope Benedict XV declared our Lady of Loreto to be patroness and protectress of airmen, in view of the belief that her house was carried through the air (see LORETO, HOLY HOUSE OF).

LOURDES. Lourdes lies between Tarbes and Pau, in the French *département* of Hautes-Pyrénées: a century ago it was a quiet, remote country-town; today it is a pilgrim shrine more famous and more frequented than any other in Christian history, except the holy places of Palestine and the tombs of the Apostles in Rome. The fourteen-year-old girl Bernadette Soubirous belonged to a very poor and rather disreputable family; from February 11 to July 16, 1858, our Lady appeared to her eighteen times. The first occasion was when she went gathering firewood with two younger children. She bacame separated from them on the bank of the river Gave, and her attention was attracted by a rustling of bushes at the mouth of a shallow cave or grotto in a rocky cliff called Massabielle. Then she saw "a girl in white, no taller than I, who greeted me with a little bow of the head." The figure was very beautiful, with a blue sash round her white dress, a yellow rosette on each shoe, and a long rosary hung over her arm. She seemed to Bernadette to invite her to pray; the child knelt, took her rosary from her pocket, and began to say it; the figure also passed the beads of her rosary through her fingers, though her lips did not move. No words passed, and at the end of five decades the figure smiled and disappeared. That was on a Thursday. On the following Sunday Bernadette saw the vision again, and four days later again: this time the Lady spoke (in the Lourdes dialect) and said, "Will you please come here every day for a fortnight. I do not promise to make you happy in this world but in the next." During that fortnight Bernadette saw the Lady (who appeared to her to be of her own age) almost every day, and increasing numbers of people accompanied her to the grotto, which was the scene of all her visions; the child fell into trances or ecstasies sometimes lasting an hour.

On February 25 the spring of water (which had always existed underground) was pointed out. Bernadette relates that the Lady said to her, " 'Go and drink at the spring, and wash yourself in it.' . . . She pointed with her finger, showing me the spring. I went there. I saw only a little dirty water; I put my hand in, but could not get enough to drink. I scratched and the water came—but muddy. I threw it away three times, but the fourth time I could drink it." Later in the day the water was running into the river Gave, and within a week there was the strong head of water that there is today. On the following three days the vision enjoined sorrow and penance for sin; on one of them a cure took place, though this was not known till later; and on March 2 Bernadette was bidden to ask that a chapel should be built and a procession held. The parish priest was unsympathetic; but the people brought a crucifix and pictures of the Blessed Virgin, lit candles, and drank of the water. Bernadette did not visit the grotto from the end of the fortnight, March 4, till March 25, the feast of the Annunciation. On that day the Lady again appeared, and Bernadette said to her, "Madam, will you please tell me who you are?" The Lady smiled, but said nothing. Bernadette repeated her question, twice. Then came the answer that has echoed round the world: *Qué soy era Immaculado Conceptiou,* "I am the Immaculate Conception."

Mary appeared again to Bernadette on April 7 and July 16, feast of our Lady of Mount Carmel. On this last occasion the cave was now boarded up by the civil authorities, alarmed by people's confidence in the visions and the remarkable cures that were reported. Bernadette, with an aunt and two other women, went to a field across the river from the grotto. It was toward night. They knelt, and Bernadette passed into ecstasy for a quarter of an hour. "How could you see the Virgin from La Ribière?" she was asked afterward, "The river is so wide there and the barrier so high." She replied: "I did not see the river or the wooden barrier. I saw only the Blessed Virgin . . . I had never seen her look so lovely." Thereafter, never again did she see her. At no time during those visions did any person but Bernadette profess to see or hear what she saw and heard: for what passed on those occasions we are dependent on what bystanders saw of her behavior and what she herself told various people. Neither in Bernadette nor in the onlookers was there any emotional extravagance, and the girl's accounts of her experiences were as simple and candid as her own character—all this in marked contrast with the repellent features which characterized the epidemic of false visionaries that broke out at Lourdes after Bernadette's visions had ceased.

The first of the great national pilgrimages to Lourdes, from France, took place in 1873; since then the number of pilgrims has continually increased: in 1953 there were 2,207,-110. Only a very small proportion of them are afflicted in body (26,325 in 1953): Lourdes always has been, and continues to be, primarily a sanctuary of spiritual health—it does not appear that our Lady ever promised bodily cures there. The examination of people who claim to have been healed, during the procession of the Blessed Sacrament, in the baths (the water of which has no natural therapeutic property) or elsewhere, is carried out by the Bureau des Constatations Médicales, set up in 1882: this is conducted by unpaid and independent doctors, and any visiting medical man may take part. This bureau is concerned solely with medical questions, and many of the cures claimed are never brought to its notice: but of the large number examined since 1882 a conservative estimate by Dr. Leuret (d. 1954), president of the B.C.M., gives about 1,200 as beyond the explanation of medical science. The decision that a given cure is miraculous is a matter only for the ecclesiastical authorities; the bishop of the person cured has officially decided in favor of a miracle in some 50 cases.

The message of Lourdes seems to be threefold. The healings of the sick again show forth the God-man's power and sympathy for all human suffering (He "went about doing good": Acts 10:38). The call to penitence emphasizes once more the Christian's obligation to live in accordance with his lofty profession as follower of Christ. The vision of March 25 testifies to the truth of an article of faith concerning our Lady. It is this last aspect that gave rise to a charge against Lourdes: some unfriendly critics declared that the whole thing was worked up by the ecclesiastical authorities in order to confirm and popularize the dogma of the Immaculate Conception, which had been defined less than four years before. In that case it would have been curious to choose so obscure a place as Lourdes. In fact, the local clergy were sceptical, aloof, and discouraging; and it took the intervention of a neighboring bishop to induce the Bishop of Tarbes to institute a commission of inquiry. It was not till 1862 that he decided that the faithful were justified in believing in the reality of what was said to have happened.—In place of the chapel asked for there are now three churches at Massabielle: the lower church (1856), the upper

church of the Immaculate Conception (1876), and the Rosary church (1889). Most of the cures seem to happen during the processions of the Blessed Sacrament; at night there are massed processions in which every pilgrim carries a candle, and the Holy Mysteries are celebrated in the Rosary Square with sometimes 50,000 and more people taking part. The statue of our Lady of Lourdes was crowned in 1876. This image, with its joined hands and raised eyes, is now famous all over the world; but it does not do even relative justice to its subject. St. Bernadette (she was canonized in 1933) was very dissatisfied with all attempts to portray what she had seen, calling them "dreadful things"; the furthest she would go in praise of them was, "Not too bad."—For the Lourdes *feast,* see below. *Cf.,* Revelations and Communications; Visions. The best-known Lourdes shrines in the British Isles are Carfin (*q.v.*) and at the church of our Lady of Lourdes in the Harrow Road, London. For North America, see below.

LOURDES, Feast of our Lady of. The feast of our Lady of Lourdes was given to the whole Western Church by Pope St. Pius X in 1907, for February II, the day of St. Bernadette's first vision in 1858. The official name of the feast is the Appearing of the Immaculate Virgin Mary, and it is in effect a festival of the Immaculate Conception. The events at Lourdes (see above) and their aftermath are narrated in the lessons at Matins and referred to in the Vespers hymn; but otherwise the references thereto in the proper of the Mass and Office are incidental, e.g., in the collect and communion-verse at Mass. There are proper hymns for Vespers (*Omnis expertem maculae*), Matins (*Te dicimus praeconio*), and Lauds (*Aurora soli praevia*), of which there are translations in the Stanbrook *Roman Breviary* in English (1936). The fifth lesson at Matins records how "almost innumerable crowds of the faithful come here every year from France, Belgium, Italy, Spain, from all corners of Europe and the most remote parts of America. The name of the Immaculate at Lourdes is famous in every land. Water from the spring has been taken all over the world and restored health to the sick." It is perhaps a little surprising to find no reference to "a great multitude of the sick, blind, lame, and those with shrivelled limbs, waiting for the moving of the water" (John 5:3).

In the lessons of the third nocturn for this feast St. Bernard addresses Adam: "What were you saying? 'The woman, whom thou gavest me, gave me of the tree and I did eat.' Those are spiteful words, and more likely to aggravate your misdoing than to obliterate it. But Wisdom overcame malice, when she found in the treasure-house of her never-failing tenderness an opportunity for forgiveness which God, by His question, tried to get from you, and could not. A woman is given for a woman, a wise woman for a foolish, one humble for one proud. This woman does not offer you the fruit of death but the food of life; instead of bitter poison she gives you the sweetness of an everlasting fruit. So change the words of your wicked excuse into thanksgiving. . . . It was

for this that the angel was sent to the Virgin, that wondrous Virgin, so worthy of every honor, to repair the sins of the fathers and give life to their children."

LOURDES HYMN, The. A hymn sung by pilgrims in various languages during the night processions at the shrine of Lourdes, and on other occasions, of which the first verse runs in English:

> Immaculate Mary,
>   Our hearts are afire;
> That title so wondrous
>   Fills all our desire.

(Refrain)
>   Ave, ave, ave Maria!
>   Ave, ave, ave Maria!

It is a long hymn, of a dozen or more verses, varying somewhat in different hymnbooks; it has no very clear pattern of content, and gives an impression of jerkiness. The English version was found so unsatisfactory that it was omitted from the new edition of the *Westminster Hymnal* in 1940; and there was substituted for it a new hymn to the same tune, with the same refrain of Aves. This was written by Monsignor R. A. Knox, based on a hymn of the Venerable Bede, *Adesto Christe vocibus*. It is in seventeen verses, touching on the events of Mary's life in relation to her Son from the Annunciation to Pentecost, the general effect being to transfer the theme of the hymn from man's needs to the glories of Christ and His Mother.

LOURDES SHRINES IN NORTH AMERICA.

Shrines of our Lady of Lourdes, great and small, well known and little known, are too numerous in the United States and Canada to enumerate. An outstanding American shrine is that at Providence Heights, Euclid, Ohio, in association with a natural spring of water, at which unusual cures have been reported. This shrine was begun by Sisters of the Good Shepherd in 1926, and is now tended by Sisters of the Most Holy Trinity.—In 1905 the Society of Fathers of Mercy formed a sanctuary in their church at Brooklyn, N.Y. Behind the high altar is a replica of the Lourdes cave, and the whole of the wall above is filled with a painting of Lourdes as it is today; pilgrims flock to the special services here, which are modelled on those of the original shrine.—In the city of New York there is a popular Lourdes shrine in the church of Notre Dame on 114th Street, and in the east of the same state another at New Lebanon.—Across the continent, a mile from Seboyeta, N.M., at a rock-hewn altar adjoining a spring, is a very interesting shrine. It was set up in Spanish colonial days in honor of our Lady of Mercy, when the colonists had been decimated by Navaho Indians; and our Lady of Lourdes is venerated here today.—The Lourdes grotto on Mount Adams at the Passionist monastery of the Holy Cross in Cincinnati is resorted to by large numbers of pilgrims all the year round. The grotto was built in 1898, and became well known through a Good Friday pilgrimage during which the faithful were blessed with a relic of the True Cross at the grotto. There are many testimonies to the cures claimed to be effected here.—Among other Lourdes shrines in the United States are those at the church of the Annunciation at Aurora, Ill., at Notre Dame University, Ind., at the church of St. Aloysius at Covington, Ky., at San Juan Pueblo, Chamita, N.M., and cf., Our Lady of the Sioux.

Two among the Canadian Lourdes sanctuaries may be mentioned. That near Rigaud is on a hillside between Montreal and Ottawa. It originated in 1874, when a lay-brother from the neighboring college of the Clerics of St. Viator set up a statuette of Mary on a pinnacle of rock. A dozen years later it was replaced by a Lourdes group, and the pilgrimage continues to grow in popularity.—On the north shore of Lac Bouchette in the province of Quebec there stand the buildings of a friary and the sanctuary of our Lady of the Saguenay. Thirty-five years ago it was a lonely spot, called l'Ermitage-de-S.-Antoine, where a seminary professor lived in retirement, Father Elzear de Lamarre. Finding a cave in the rock there, he set up in it an altar and a statue of our Lady of Lourdes, and so began the pilgrim-shrine that has since grown steadily in popularity. After Father de Lamarre's death in 1925, the Capuchin Franciscans took over the property, built their house and church there, and minister to the thousands of pilgrims who seek out the sanctuary.

LUJAN, OUR LADY OF.

This statue is a small terra-cotta figure, with blue eyes, dressed in jewel-studded robes, and it has been venerated at Lujan in the Argentine for over three hundred years; it was crowned in 1886. The image was originally brought from Brazil and was intended for Córdoba; but in mysterious circumstances it came to rest where is now Lujan, and its first home was a ranch-house, where it was looked after by an African slave. In 1685 it was transferred to a newly built church, where it attracted so many pilgrims that a town grew up; the present very large church is the third that has enshrined it. The sanctuary is in charge of the Vincentians, and a special feast is observed on the fourth Sunday after Easter. Lujan is the national Argentinian shrine, and our Lady of Lujan is patroness also of Paraguay and Uruguay.

LUKE, SAINT. See EVANGELIST, OUR LADY'S; LIKENESSES.

LUX VERITATIS. The opening words and name of an encyclical letter addressed to the Church by Pope Pius XI in 1931, on the occasion of the fifteen-hundredth anniversary of the Council of Ephesus (*q.v.*). In it there is set forth an account of the epoch-making council, and the divine motherhood of the Blessed Virgin is fully expounded; Mary and the family of Nazareth are put before the faithful as the greatest pattern and example of the dignity and sacredness of wedlock and the bringing-up of children; and the feast of the Motherhood of our Lady (*q.v.*) is instituted.

LUXEMBURG, OUR LADY OF. The city of Luxemburg, capital of the grand-duchy of that name, has a Marian shrine of considerable importance. In 1607 the Jesuits opened a college there, and soon after built a chapel wherein was enshrined a statue of our Lady, Consoler of the Afflicted. The statue, baroque in expression, the Mother and Child clothed and crowned, is made of wood from the oak-tree of Montaigu (*q.v.*) in Belgium, and resembles the statue there. The chapel is now part of a bigger building, the cathedral of the diocese, and the feast of our Lady of Luxemburg on the fourth Sunday after Easter is a national festival; during fifteen days corporate pilgrimages come from all over the duchy to venerate Mary at her wonderworking image. A proper Mass and Office were granted in 1854. A copy of the Luxemburg statue is the center of the shrine of our Lady of Consolation (*q.v.*) at Carey, Ohio.

LYNN, OUR LADY OF. King's Lynn was privileged to be the place where the *cultus* of our Lady of Walsingham (*q.v.*) was first formally revived. Pope Leo XIII blessed the statue, a copy of that in Santa Maria in Cosmedin at Rome, and authorized the restoration of the devotion; the statue was enshrined at the King's Lynn church in 1897, in a chapel modeled on the Holy House of Loreto (*q.v.*). Fifty years later the main seat of the Walsingham devotion was officially recognized as being at the Slipper Chapel at Walsingham itself. There was a medieval shrine of our Lady of Lynn on the Red Mount, at a chapel which still stands there. The present shrine has received papal indulgences.

M

MAASTRICHT, OUR LADY OF. Maastricht is an inland town in Dutch Limburg, yet the official title of its shrine is our Lady, Star of the Sea: the explanation is presumably the town's situation on a busy waterway, the river Maas (Meuse). The statue is a fourteenth-century wooden carving of great beauty, the Mother leaning away in that graceful attitude so beloved of later medieval carvers, the naked Child reaching toward a lily in her other hand. The Maastricht sanctuary suffered many vicissitudes after the Reformation and at the Revolution, but it was finally restored in 1807. There is a "walking" over a certain route observed at Maastricht, as at several other shrines in northwestern Europe.

MADHU, OUR LADY OF. The principal shrine in Ceylon, situated amid jungle in the diocese of Jaffna. The church was founded in the seventeenth century, and has been a place of pilgrimage since the eighteenth: people come in thousands from all over the island and from southern India, both Christians and non-Christians. It is the local belief that the bite of snakes is harmless within the grounds of the shrine. The chief pilgrimage days are July 2 and August 15.

MADONNA (Ital., my lady). A picture, statue, or other image of the Blessed Virgin. "The Madonna" is sometimes used in English for Mary herself. "Madonna-braided" is hair braided on either side of the face, as in some Italian pictures. "Madonna lily" is the White lily often shown in pictures, especially of the Annunciation, as an emblem of our Lady; also called the Mary lily.—"Madonna" and "La Madonna" are terms very commonly used in Italian where the English-speaker would say "our Lady" or "the Blessed Mother."

The word Madonna accompanied by an epithet is frequently used to distinguish a particular work of art, especially Italian ones: for example, the Ansidei Madonna (Raphael), the Madonna of the Burgomaster Mayer (Holbein), the M. of the Councillors (Dalman), the M. of the Girdle (Matteo di Giovanni), the Granduca Madonna (Raphael), the M. del Latte (a carving; Rossellino), the M. of Lucca (Jan van Eyck), the M. of the Magnificat (Botticelli), the M. of Melun (Fouquet), the M. of the Rocks (Leonardo), the M. of the Rosegarden (Schongauer), the Sistine Madonna (Raphael). For non-Italian works "Virgin" is often used similarly, e.g., the Virgin of Melun.

MAGNIFICAL HYMN, The (*Megalynarion*). After the consecration and invocation in the Byzantine Mass the celebrant makes a commemoration of

164

the Mother of God, and in the Liturgy of St. John Chrysostom the choir sings the following hymn, beginning in Greek *Axion estin,* in Slavonic *Dostoino yest:*

"It is indeed proper to bless thee, Mother of God, ever blessed and completely sinless one and the mother of our God. Higher in honor than the kherubim and incomparably more glorious than the seraphim, who inviolate didst bring forth the Word of God—thee do we magnify, Mother of God in truth."

It is called the Magnifical Hymn because at the morning office it is sung with the Magnificat (*q.v.*). In Russian iconography it has produced a special type of picture, our Lady *Dostoino yest,* and among Greek-speakers it is almost a "national anthem"; its recitation has been indulgenced by the Holy See. This hymn is sometimes displaced by another, notably by the following in the Liturgy of St. Basil:

"Full of grace, thou art the joy of all creation, of the company of angels and of mankind; thou art the hallowed temple, spiritual paradise and boast of maidenhood, whence God took flesh when He who was our God before the ages became a child; He made thy womb His throne, making thy bosom broader than the heavens: thou art the joy of all creation, Full of grace—Glory be to thee."

MAGNIFICAT, The. The canticle of the Blessed Virgin, from the first word of the Latin text, *Magnificat anima mea Dominum,* "My soul doth magnify the Lord" (Luke 1:46-55). It

forms part of Vespers in the Roman rite and its variants and in the various Little Offices B.V.M. (*q.v.*); in the Byzantine rite it is sung at Lauds (Orthros). When Vespers is sung solemnly, the altar, ministers, choir, and people are censed during the Magnificat; it is recited or sung standing and with a sign of the cross at the first verse, since the words come from the gospel. In some places on certain occasions the Magnificat is accompanied by special solemnities, such as the ringing of bells (on the feast of the Visitation), the repetition of the antiphon (*q.v.*) after every two verses, or, in processions, the singing of double Alleluias in the same way.

Just as the Lord's Prayer, the Our Father, is the best of all possible Christian prayers, standing in a class by itself, because it is taught us by Jesus Christ himself, so the Magnificat is the best of all hymns, because the words are Mary's own words and they form part of the inspired Holy Scriptures. There are and can be no better words in which to express love and veneration for her, the woman in whom so great, unexampled, wonders have been wrought by the power of God: for Mary it was a hymn of worship and thanksgiving, as it has been ever since for all who revere her. As a good Jewess, Mary was steeped in the Old Testament, the sacred writings of her people, which echo throughout the hymn. The words "lowliness" in the second verse and "lowly" in the sixth of course do not mean that Mary was claiming humility for herself: they refer to her general state of lowlihood and her humble station in life, the wife of an obscure workman, whom God was so marvellously exalting. The following translation is from the Confraternity version of St. Luke's gospel:

"My soul magnifies the Lord,
and my spirit rejoices in God my Savior;
Because he has regarded the lowliness of his handmaid;
for, behold, henceforth all generations shall call me blessed;
Because he who is mighty has done great things for me,
and holy is his name;
And for generation upon generation is his mercy,
to those who fear him.
He has shown might with his arm,
he has scattered the proud in the conceit of their heart.
He has put down the mighty from their thrones,
and has exalted the lowly.
He has filled the hungry with good things,
and the rich he has sent away empty.
He has given help to Israel, his servant,
mindful of his mercy—
Even as he spoke to our fathers—
to Abraham and to his posterity forever."

The anonymous author of *The Mirror of Our Lady* (c. 1440) suggests four reasons why it is specially appropriate that the Magnificat should be sung at Vespers: "One, for at Evensong time of the world our Lady by her singular assent brought health to mankind. Another cause is that we should daily have in mind the incarnation of our Lord Jesu Christ, which was wrought in the eventide of the world, for joy of which this song was made. The third is that our Lady is likened to the evening star that beginneth to appear at eventide. The fourth is that minds that have been laboured and wearied in the day with many thoughts and much business should then be comforted with the song of joy of our Lady, and be helped by her prayers against temptations of the night."

MANGER OF BETHLEHEM, The. "She brought forth a Son, her firstborn, whom she wrapped in his swaddling-clothes, and laid in a manger . . ." (Luke 2:7). A manger ("crib" means the same thing) understood as a wooden receptacle on legs is unknown to Palestine; there a manger was a clay or stone trough on the floor, or in a niche in the wall. St. Jerome, who went to live in Bethlehem in 385, says in a sermon that the original (?) manger in the cave of the Nativity there was of clay, and complains that it had been swept away to make room for one made of silver. He does not blame such devotion, he says, but the clay one was much more precious. (Elsewhere, in a letter, he also complains of a man who puts letters to his sweetheart in the new manger, for her to pick up when she comes to pray.) A "place of the manger" is still shown to pilgrims to the cave, but the silver crib has disappeared long ago. It is well known that for at least nine hundred years the church of St. Mary Major (*q.v.*) at Rome has treasured five pieces of wood as being part of the manger into which Mary put the Babe. But it seems quite clear that a mistake has been made. Apart from the fact that St. Jerome says nothing about any wooden crib, one of these fragments bears a ninth-century inscription relating to a picture of martyrs on horseback, a picture of which this and the other pieces apparently formed part. The Palestinian archeologists Fathers Vincent and Abel, o.p., reject the authenticity of this relic.

MANIFESTATION OF OUR LADY, The. Just as in sixth-century Gaul there was a feast in honor of the Blessed Virgin in the middle of January, so there was a similar observance in parts of the East. The Coptic calendar still mentions our Lady's death on a date equivalent to January 28, when the Ethiopians celebrate the Manifestation of our Lady. The liturgical books of both rites (which are closely related) make reference to a story told in the apocryphal *Passing of Mary* (*q.v.*), which is somewhat reminiscent of the incident of Oza and the Ark of the convenant in I Paralipomenon (13:9-12): A Jew contemptuously pushes our Lady's bier as it is being carried to burial, he loses the use of his hands, and they are restored by St. Peter. (The place of this alleged happening is still pointed out at Jerusalem.)

MARČA, OUR LADY OF, Križevci. During the seventeenth century the monastery at Marča, now in Yugoslavia, was the headquarters of a body of Catholics of the Slav-Byzantine rite. In 1739 the monastery was burnt down by brigands, and eventually a new see was established at Križevci, in the province of Zagreb. Here was enshrined in the cathedral an icon of the Mother of God, brought from Marča, where it had been greatly revered. It is still much venerated. There is another shrine at Križevci, our Lady of Carantania.

MARIA DESOLATA. See DESOLATION OF MARY.

MÁRIABESNYÖ. A Hungarian shrine on the Danube, between Budapest and Gödöllo. It originated in 1759, when a figure of our Lady carved in ivory was found buried in the ground. It has been estimated that 500 villages send pilgrims here every year, and thousands more come from Budapest.

MARIA-EICH. A shrine at Planegg, near Munich. About the year 1700 a little figure of our Lady was carved in an oak-tree (*eichbaum*) at this place. It became so much venerated by the Bavarians that the figure was detached from the tree and enshrined in a chapel at Planegg, to which pilgrimages are still made.

MARIA-LUSCHARI. Our Lady of Luschariberg was formerly the most popular shrine in the Austrian province of Carinthia, but it is now just across the border in Italy. It has been a place of pilgrimage since 1360, when a shepherd is said to have found the wonderworking statue of Mary under a juniper shrub there, 5,000 feet up in the mountains. Another famous shrine once in Austria and now in Italy is the Heiligenberg, Monte Santo (*q.v.*), near Gorizia (Görz).

MÁRIANOSZTRA. The name of this Hungarian shrine is a magyarized form of the Latin *Maria nostra,* "our Mary." Originally it was a monastery of the monks of St. Paul the Hermit (who have care of Czestochowa, *q.v.*), but they were disbanded by the Emperor Joseph II. The buildings eventually became a state penitentiary for women, and the nuns in charge established a shrine of our Lady, which attracted many pilgrims. The nuns have now been turned out. Márianosztra was a favorite resort of the great Ottokar Proházka, bishop of Székes Fehérvar, who did so much for religion in the Danubian countries before his death in 1927.

MARIA-PLAIN. An Austrian shrine near Salzburg. In 1633 fire consumed a church in Regensburg but spared the image of our Lady therein, which was taken to the castle of Fuerstenegg. Later it was set up for veneration on Plain Mountain, and in 1671 a new church was built to enshrine it. The image was crowned in 1751, and this is annually commemorated on the fifth Sunday after Pentecost, the day of the crowning.

MÁRIAPÓCS. This is one of the most important shrines in Hungary, the treasured sanctuary of Hungarians of the Byzantine rite, people of Ruthenian origin who form the eparchy of Hajdudorog. It is in charge of Basilian monks, who have (or had) a monastery there. The Virgin of Máriapócs has been sung by great Hungarian poets, including the Protestant Andrew Ady (d. 1918), and Cardinal Mindszenty once led a national pilgrimage to the shrine. The original of the image, our Lady of Tears, is in St. Stephen's basilica at Vienna.

MÁRIAREMETE. A Hungarian shrine in the Buda hills, six miles from Budapest. It flourished in the middle ages, was destroyed, and revived in the nineteenth century, later becoming a place of national pilgrimage. At one of these, led by Cardinal Mindszenty, 800,000 people are said to have walked from the capital. The shrine was till recently in care of the Servites.

MARIA-STEIN. A Swiss sanctuary near Basel, where an ancient wonderworking image of our Lady is venerated. The shrine is attached to a monastery, founded at Beinwill from Einsiedeln (*q.v.*) about 1085; the community moved to Maria-Stein in 1648, when the shrine had already been in existence for two hundred years. It originated when a child fell down a cliff-face and was unharmed; the pilgrimage chapel is hollowed out of the rock. There is another Maria-Stein pilgrimage in the Austrian Tyrol, near Wörgl, overlooking the valley of the river Inn.

MARIA-TAFERL. An Austrian shrine near Marbach, on the Danube, known as our Dear Lady at the Hill of Taferl. It has been in existence since 1642, and has grown up round a small *pietà* (*q.v.*)

MARIAZELL. The chief shrine of our Lady in Austria, at the village of Mariazell, beautifully situated in the mountains southwest of Vienna. It was established at the Benedictine monastery there about 1157, and the statue is said to be at least of that age. The sanctuary was always a favorite one with the Habsburg monarchs, but under Joseph II the pilgrimage was suppressed for a time. The first renewed pilgrimage, in 1792, was led by the famous Cardinal Migazzi, who induced the emperor again to allow the vesting of "the poor statues of the Mother of God." Pilgrims come from long distances during the summer months, but the shrine festival is on September 12, feast of the Name of Mary. They are said to number over a quarter-million annually, contributed to by the numerous visitors who come to the village for skiing. But, quite apart from that attraction, the shrine has long been noted for the variety of Central European nationalities among its votaries. The statue is a small seated one, of lime wood; our Lady is indicating her Child, and her outward-looking expression is very attractive. But the image is often obscured by robes, to match its surroundings in the great baroque abbey-church.

MARIENLEGENDEN. See LEGENDS OF OUR LADY.

MARIFORM LIFE, The. This expression is used by spiritual writers to designate a conscious living conformably to the good pleasure of Mary, whose union with God is closer and more perfect than that of any other creature. To progress in this life, some concentrate on the manifold virtues with which our Lady was endowed; others, on deepening their love for her. As the spirit of Christ strengthens love of God the Father in the soul, so also it increases love for the Virgin Mary; graces come to us through her, and so union with God in and through her is the more complete. This mode of spiritual life characterized a Carmelite recluse of Malines, Mary Petyt (d. 1677), and was developed by her Carmelite director, Father Michael-of-St.-Augustine; it is possible that the writings of the last named influenced St. Louis Grignion de Montfort, who was so insistent on the part that devotion to Mary has in "the transformation of self in Jesus Christ." He writes in his *True Devotion* (*q.v.*): "St. Augustine calls the Blessed Virgin *forma Dei*, the 'mold of God.' . . . Whoever is poured into this divine mold is quickly formed and molded into Christ and Christ into him": he soon becomes Godlike, for that mold formed the God-man. Those who choose this way are like "molders who, having found the beauteous mold of Mary wherein Jesus was naturally and divinely formed, cast themselves into her that they may become the living likeness of Christ." And remember, says the saint, "that only that which is molten and liquid is poured into a mold, which means that the old Adam in you must be destroyed and dissolved away that you may become the new man in Mary."

MARIOLATRY. In its strict sense, this word signifies giving to the Blessed Virgin Mary that divine worship which must be given to God alone, that is, a sin of idolatry. The classical historical example of Mariolatry is the obscure fourth-century sect in Arabia called Collyridians; they offered sacrifice to Mary in the form of little cakes, and were denounced by St. Epiphanius. The same idolatrous practice was remarked by Leontius of Byzantium in the sixth century. From time to time, through genuine misunderstanding or in the heat of controversy, charges of Mariolatry have been brought by opponents against the Catholic Church, and also against the Orthodox and other dissident Eastern Christians. The charges are, of course, false: *cf.*, Hyperdulia; Prayer; Veneration, etc.— The word Mariolatry is sometimes used colloquially to signify, not an idolatry, but errors and exaggerations, real or supposed, about our Lady and her veneration. *Cf.*, Errors and Excesses; Heresies.

MARIOLOGY. The science which treats of the Blessed Virgin Mary from the viewpoints of history, theology, devotion, and speculation; the content of that science. In its dogmatic aspect Mariology is concerned with Mary as the mother of the God-man Jesus Christ, and the truths about her (technically called her pre-

rogatives, *q.v.*) that are associated with that fact. If what is known about Mariology in the very early days of the Church be compared with the Mariology of today, very great and striking differences are at once apparent. For example, no one supposes that the Apostles and the Fathers of the Church explicitly professed faith in the Immaculate Conception, for in the then state of Christian thought the matter had not arisen. In the sphere of practice they were not acquainted with any complex and widespread system of devotion (*q.v.*) to the Mother of God, for such devotion and devotions (*q.v.*) are to a large extent products of ways of thinking about Mary that were as yet unknown. The same sort of differences, in varying degrees, can be seen by comparing any past age of the Church with our own. Mariology, then, provides one of the two outstanding examples in later times (the other is the theology of the papacy) of the principle of theological development; that is, the progressive unfolding of the content of the Christian revelation, the drawing of latent truths from the "deposit," the faith once and for all delivered to the saints.

The four gospels of God's written word give relatively little explicit information about Mary; but that little includes things that are crucial, and the ultimate foundation of all that is to follow: above all, the Holy Spirit comes upon her and the power of the Most High overshadows her, and she becomes the mother of Jesus, who is called the Son of God. The subsequent development, unfolding, and clarifying of the Church's tradition can be associated with certain outstanding events and movements. Of these by far the most important was when in 431 the Council of Ephesus (*q.v.*) by condemning Nestorianism made it clear that, as Mother of Christ, Mary is Mother of God. In any but an elementary sense Mariology began there. Already there had been hints, gropings, adumbrations. In the second half of the second century St. Justin, St. Irenaeus, and Tertullian had seen Mary as the New or Second Eve (*q.v.*); in the third century St. Hippolytus associates the sinlessness of Christ with her perfection; in the fourth, St. Jerome, St. Ambrose, and Pope St. Siricius stand up for her perpetual virginity. But it was Ephesus that opened the way for confident development.

Two centuries later the Church formally set her seal on belief in the Mother's perpetual virginity (*q.v.*). That she had conceived virginally was known from the beginning; and, at the same time that the doctors just mentioned were teaching, her continuing virginity was emphasized, on the one hand, by the ascetic preoccupations of the monks of the desert (who were sometimes led into extravagance) and, on the other, by such devotional writings as the hymns of St. Ephraem the Syrian. A parallel development was the belief in the Virgin's actual sinlessness (*q.v.*). Already, too, though the Assumption (*q.v.*) would not be formally defined by the Church for another fifteen hundred years, the faithful were beginning to see that the sinless body that carried the Savior had not known the corruption of the grave: the *Passing of Mary* (*q.v.*) is an apocryphal document, but it at least shows what some people were thinking about.

The earlier middle ages in the West saw "the more authoritative acceptance of Marian devotion as an integral part of the Church's life"; and the eleventh century was a veritable "Marian era," the enthusiasm of the monks spreading to the people. At the same time a shift of emphasis began to take place. In the earlier centuries concern with the Blessed Virgin was largely (but not wholly) intellectual and theological, and religious thought received much of its impulse from the East. Now Mariology was becoming primarily affective, Mary was seen as a special object of love and devotion, theological ideas were "humanized." We hear much of her joys and her sorrows, Mary as "the prophetess at the foot of the Cross" gave place to the Mother sharing the sufferings of her Son. It was the epoch of shrines and pilgrimages, of the Christmas crib and the "Legends of our Lady" (*q.v.*), of the Mary-Mass (*q.v.*) and the rosary. Theological activity of course there was: it was the later middle ages that put the Immaculate Conception (*q.v.*) "on the map," but, ironically enough, at first as a stumbling-block and bone of contention.

By its denials the Protestant Reformation was an incentive to the elaboration of the theology of the Mother of God, and the seventeenth century, in spite of widespread Jansenism, has been called the flowering-time of modern Mariology. Much Mariological writing still carries the imprint of a Spanish or French origin at this time, both for good and less good, and it has not always been properly "naturalized" and universalized by the genius of other Christian peoples. Professor Jean Guitton has written that the seventeenth century gave some Marian spirituality "a rather rhetorical tone, a certain unctuous archness which it will take a long time to get rid of" (*The Blessed Virgin Mary*, Kenedy, 1954). But the recall to theology was nothing but good, whatever criticism may be brought against some of the constructions and enthusiasms of that time (*cf.*, Slavery to Mary). Mary's compassionate intercession, Cardinal de Bérulle reminded his era, "owes its existence solely to the mystery of the Incarnation and to her dependence on the Word made flesh."

In later times two elements in Mariology have been preponderant, apart from its foundation in the Incarnation. The definition of the Immaculate Conception in 1854 led to a notable intensifying of popular devotion in terms of that mystery; and in the conclusion to *Ineffabilis Deus* (*q.v.*) Pope Pius IX expresses the Church's confidence in Mary as mediatress and reconciler of mankind. The mediation (*q.v.*) and advocacy of the Blessed Virgin have been a commonplace from early times; and now it is a firmly established doctrine of theology that Mary's continued mediation is an actual condition of the life of grace merited by Christ for men, a concomitant in fact, of the economy of grace. The Mariology of today, by emphasizing the connection between Marian theology and that of the whole mystery of salvation (*cf.*, Redemption, Mary and the), shows that Mariology is not "a branch artificially attached to the rest of theology"; and its constant searching of the Holy Scriptures enables our Lady always to be seen in her proper perspective, "in relation to the Lord Jesus Christ and not for her own sake."

One other feature of contemporary Mariology must be mentioned as posing problems both for the theologian and the historian, and that is the reported visions or appearings of the Mother of God on this earth. Such reports, and the popular enthusiasm aroused by them, are of course nothing new; but in these days there is more will and greater facilities for the examination of them critically, both as to authenticity and significance. To some, ecclesiastical authority has given varying measures of approval; and the rise of Lourdes was the most significant Marian happening between the definition of the Immaculate Conception and that of the Assumption.

MARTYRS, OUR LADY OF THE. The most famous church dedicated under what became this name is the Pantheon at Rome. It was originally built by Marcus Agrippa in 25 B.C. as a temple of Jupiter, Venus, Mars, and all the gods; in 609 or 610 A.D. it was consecrated to God by Pope St. Boniface IV in honor of the Blessed Virgin Mary and All the Martyrs. The day of the dedication, May 13, is noted in the Roman Martyrology. From its round shape, the church is commonly called Santa Maria Rotonda. St. Mary of the Martyrs at the shrine at Ossernenon, near Auriesville, N.Y., refers particularly to St. Isaac Jogues, St. John Lalande, and St. René Goupil and the North American martyrs in general; in 1897 a church was built under the same invocation at Nagasaki, in honor of the Japanese martyrs put to death three centuries before. In 1147 King Alonso I of Portugal built a church at Lisbon in honor of our Lady of Martyrs and in memory of those who had fallen fighting against the Moors; it is a well-known shrine among the Portuguese. It was dedicated on May 13, the same date as the Roman church mentioned above, and is privileged to have a special Mass and Office of our Lady on that day.

MARY, THE BLESSED VIRGIN: HER LEGEND.

The word "legend" (which at root means simply "something to be read") is here used to distinguish a complex of stories, belief in which was widespread among Christians from early times, but for the truth of which the Church does not by any means vouch. Some of these stories or particulars are referred to as matters of accepted knowledge by some of the Fathers (notably St. Gregory of Nyssa and St. John Damascene), and in later ecclesiastical writings of various kinds; but so far as our knowledge goes they can most of them be traced to well-known apocryphal writings (q.v.), and the faithful are by no means bound to accept them: indeed, as will emerge below, there is not a little that is unbelievable, on various grounds.

According to this complex of popular tradition the Virgin Mary was daughter of Joachim, a wealthy man of the royal house of David, and his wife Ann, of the priestly house of Aaron (cf., Parents). They long lived childless, but after prayer and fasting before God a child, Mary, was conceived and born. This was exaggerated into a story that St. Ann conceived without the intervention of her husband—a belief that was later rejected by the Church. When the child was three years old she was presented and offered in the Temple. The high priest, says the *Protevangelium of James* (q.v.), "set her down upon the third step of the altar, and the Lord God sent grace upon her; and she danced with her feet, and all the house of Israel loved her." Thenceforward, we are told, year after year, Mary lived in the company of other maidens in the Temple, "as if she were a dove that dwelt there," receiving food from angels and other wonders. But in fact there seems to be little likelihood that women, even young girls, can ever have lived within the Temple precincts; St. Ambrose (d. 397) is clear that Mary lived with her parents throughout her childhood.

When Mary was twelve (other accounts say fourteen) the high priest Zachary was told by an angel to summon the widowers among the people, and the Lord would show by a sign which of them was to be this maiden's husband. When they were assembled,

Zachary collected their staves and carried them within the Temple and prayed: and behold! from one of the staves a dove came forth and alighted on the owner's head. The man was Joseph, and Zachary said to him, "You have been chosen by lot to take this maiden of the Lord into your keeping." Joseph protested, saying he was an old man, with children, and he feared to be laughed at. The high priest overcame his objections, and Joseph was betrothed with Mary. She, according to some accounts, had already bound herself by vow to life-long virginity, a thing somewhat foreign to Jewish thought and practice, so that the high priest had said, "Mary has found a new way of life: she binds herself to remain a virgin to God."

Some time after, Mary was chosen as one of the maidens to spin thread, "true purple and scarlet," for a veil for the Temple. Going out to fetch water from the village well she heard a voice which said, "Hail, thou who art full of grace; the Lord is with thee; blessed art thou among women!" She looked around and could see nobody, so she hurried back home, trembling; "and taking the purple, she sat down on a seat and drew it out." Then the angel appeared before her and completed his announcement, very much as St. Luke records it. But another version makes this second part happen on the following day. These narratives make a great deal of what followed Joseph's discovery of Mary's pregnancy, and the *Protevangelium of James* puts into her mouth the astonishing statement that she "had forgotten the mysteries

of which the archangel Gabriel had spoken"! We are also told that Joseph and Mary were haled before the priests and elders for marrying by stealth, when God cleared them through the "waters of ordeal." But this Jewish legal test was for women only, not men, as the book of Numbers shows (chap. 5).

The *Protevangelium,* which implies that Mary was nearly seventeen at the time, adds some particulars to the birth of Jesus, such as Joseph's search for a midwife and the evidence furnished of Mary's physical virginity after childbirth. The special contribution of the *Gospel of Pseudo-Matthew* (*q.v.*) is a considerable amplification of the flight into Egypt: the holy Babe talks and does miracles; He comforts His Mother and wild beasts become harmless; when Mary carries the Child into a heathen temple, all the 355 idols fall down and are broken ("thus plainly showing that they were nothing"), and all the people of the place are converted— it will be noticed that the atmosphere is quite different from that of the true gospels.

So far as our Lady is involved, these amplifications of what the gospels tell us are concerned with the earlier and later periods of her life. The belief that she met her Son when He was being led to execution is apparently not recorded very early; on the face of it such a meeting is likely, and the devotion of the way of the cross (fourth station) has now carried the idea all over the world, so that it is familiar to the hearts of the faithful everywhere. The question of Mary at the Resurrection is referred to herein under that word, and under *Passing of Mary* an outline is given of one of the apocryphal accounts of her death and taking-up into Heaven. These accounts vary considerably, being altered, amplified, and embellished by their different authors or editors.

It will be seen, then, that early non-biblical beliefs varied considerably in content and value, and they cannot always be reconciled with one another. Those who wrote them down were prompted by love and veneration for the Mother of God: but this does not guarantee that they never exaggerated or were never mistaken. This is emphasized in such a work as the so-called *Gospel of Thomas* which, in addition to crude and puerile miracles, attributes to the Boy Jesus the bringing of death on a companion who had jostled Him, and the striking blind of those who criticized Him for so doing! In reading these works that profess to fill in the historical gaps of the Church's tradition there come to mind the words of St. Epiphanius (d. 403), with reference to a startling fable about the later years of our Lady: "For my part, I dare not speak; I keep my thoughts to myself and hold my tongue." And of St. Peter Damian six hundred years later, who blamed the curiosity of those who inquire about things concerning which the evangelists chose to keep silent. *Cf.,* Tradition and Legend.

MARY, THE BLESSED VIRGIN: HER LIFE. The only particulars of the life and qualities of the Virgin Mary that are undoubtedly true are found in the written word of God, the Bible, and in the dogmatic teaching of the Church: anything that is not found therein, or unquestionably deducible therefrom, is, at the best, uncertain. Thus, her birthplace (*q.v.*) —Sepphoris, Nazareth, Jerusalem?— is a subject of discussion; her parents (*q.v.*), childhood, and early background are first mentioned only in apocryphal writings (*q.v.*). But the Church teaches that this obscure Hebrew child was chosen from eternity and formed to God's purposes from the first moment of her existence: kept free from the stain of Adam's sin and, throughout her life, guiltless of all fault and transgression; positively, always co-operating perfectly and in all respects with God's will for her own unique destiny.

The first passage of the gospels that speaks of Mary is also the most important, for it announces her divine motherhood. She was a maiden living at Nazareth (*q.v.*), betrothed to a man named Joseph (*q.v.,* and *cf.,* Betrothal). To her comes the angel Gabriel, who addresses her as "full of grace" and "blessed," and delivers God's message: the power of the Holy Spirit is coming upon her, she will bear a son, Jesus, the Holy One, who "shall be called the Son of God." She accepts the humanly unbelievable: "Behold the handmaid of the Lord; be it done to me according to thy word" (see ANNUNCIATION). At that moment of a maiden's acceptance in faith and love the history of mankind is changed; through the New

Eve, God sends salvation to the New Israel, "even as he promised unto our fathers, to Abraham and to his seed for ever." We are not told Mary's age at that great moment: about thirteen would be in accordance with Jewish custom, which in Palestine at that time implies a greater maturity than that age suggests in more northern countries and later ages.

The angel had told her that her kinswoman Elizabeth was with child; and accordingly Mary soon sets out to visit her. At her arrival, Elizabeth's babe, who is to be John the Baptist, stirs in his mother's womb, and she greets Mary with Gabriel's words: "Blessed art thou among women!" And, she adds, "Blessed is the fruit of thy womb! How have I deserved that the mother of my Lord should come to me? For behold, the moment that the sound of thy greeting came to my ears, the babe in my womb leapt for joy. And blessed art thou who hast believed, because the things promised thee by the Lord shall be accomplished." And Mary replies with that great hymn of thanksgiving, the Magnificat (q.v.), praising God who has so exalted her lowliness that "henceforth all generations shall call me blessed"—a prophecy that has been amply fulfilled in the Church of Christ. It is an utterance of the purest exultation, rejoicing in her own motherhood and the deliverance of her people.

The Annunciation message was wholly joyful, but in her acceptance of it Mary welcomed all that God should will or allow in her regard, whatever it might be. And now per-haps the first of her sorrows came to her, for, though St. Matthew does not say so, it is likely that she knew of Joseph's distress about her. When his betrothed proved to be with child, Joseph was deeply disturbed. The use of marriage after betrothal was not prohibited among the Jews, but he had not known his promised bride; and it came into his mind to put her away, but privately, so as not to shame her. Then it was that an angel appeared to him in a dream, and told him not to be afraid to take Mary to himself, "for that which is begotten in her is of the Holy Spirit. And she shall bring forth a son, and thou shalt call his name Jesus; for he shall save his people from their sins." And Joseph, writes St. Matthew, "did as the angel of the Lord had commanded him, and took unto him his wife." That is to say, he completed the existing betrothal by a formal marriage. It was a virginal marriage: the Church taught from the earliest times that the virginity (q.v.) which was Mary's when she conceived the Word remained inviolate throughout her life.

Some months later, in accordance with the requirements of a census of the people, Joseph and Mary journeyed from Nazareth in Galilee south to Bethlehem (q.v.) in Judea, a distance of about sixty miles. The time for Mary's delivery had now come. The place was crowded and there was no room in the inn (St. Luke says nothing to suggest they were turned away roughly); but they found accommodation in a stable, which a very long tradition says was a cave in the rock. Here Mary gave birth to Jesus

Christ; and the God-man was wrapped in swaddling clothes and laid in a manger (*q.v.*). That same night, at the word of an angel, shepherds came down from the hills and found Mary and Joseph and the Babe: which when they had seen, they understood what the angel had said to them; and when they told their story, people wondered. "But Mary kept in mind all these words, pondering them in her heart."

The order of and time between subsequent happenings are not clear from the gospels. Wise men—their number is not specified—were guided from the east to Bethlehem by a star; "they found the Child with Mary his mother, and falling down they worshipped Him," offering their gifts. Afterward, Joseph was warned by an angel in a dream to take the Child and His mother to Egypt, for fear of King Herod. Of this flight into Egypt no details are given, except that it was made by night; it is not known how long it lasted, whether weeks or years, or whereabouts in Egypt the Holy Family went. But when they returned, still under direct guidance from on high, Joseph avoided Judea and they settled in Nazareth. They were in Jerusalem sometime after the fortieth day from the birth of Jesus, for Mary to make her legal offering (*cf.,* Purification, Feast of the) and for the presentation of the Child in the Temple. It was then that Holy Simeon, filled with the Spirit, said to Mary, "Behold, this child is destined for the fall and for the rise of many in Israel, and for a sign that shall be contradicted. And thy own soul a sword shall pierce. . . ." He foresaw the time when she would have to see, and suffer with Him, her Son's rejection by the greater part of His people, culminating in His passion and death on the cross.

The thirty years that Jesus passed in His home at Nazareth are well called His hidden life. As child and boy He grew in physique, wisdom, and grace, under the fostering care of His parents (Luke 2:40, 51-52); He grew up to be known simply as "Mary's son, the carpenter" (Mark 6:3), one who had not studied (John 7:15). For the rest, we are told nothing about Him or His mother, except for one arresting incident involving them both, when He was twelve years old. A day's journey out of Jerusalem on returning from their annual visit for the Passover, young Jesus is missing. On the third day He is found in the Temple, discussing with the learned. "Son," cries Mary, "why hast thou treated us thus? Thy father and I have been looking for thee, griefstricken." And He replies, "How is it that you looked for me? Did you not know that I must be in my Father's house?" St. Luke tells us that Mary and Joseph had been astonished at Simeon's words about Jesus as a baby, they were astonished to find him among the teachers, and now "they did not understand the word that he spoke to them." It seems they had not yet reached a full understanding of His nature and mission. But again Mary "kept all these things carefully in her heart," doubtless that through contemplation there should come increase of knowledge (q.v.).

The evangelists refer to Mary on but few occasions during our Lord's public ministry. The first of them is the wedding feast to which He and His mother were invited, at Cana, not far from Nazareth. The details of the text of St. John's account of what happened there have been much discussed by commentators. What is clear is that Mary's faith urged trust in Jesus—"Do whatever he tells you"; and His first miracle that followed, when water was turned into wine, was the beginning of faith in His disciples (John 2:11). At two moments in His preaching, Jesus uses references to His mother as occasions for emphasizing that first things must be put first. Once while He was speaking He was told that His mother and His brethren (i.e., kinsfolk) were outside, looking for Him. "Who is my mother and who are my brethren?" He asked; and He indicated His disciples—"Behold my mother and my brethren! For whoever does the will of my Father in Heaven, he is my brother and sister and mother." Another time, a woman in the crowd exclaimed, "Blessed is the womb that bore thee, and the breasts that nursed thee." And He replied, "Rather, blessed are they who hear the word of God and keep it." In both cases our Lord stresses that faith and obedience to God come before all else, and carries the gaze on from Mary's physical motherhood to her spiritual sublimeness.

Mary was the wife of an artisan in a provincial town, and the greater part of her outward life was no doubt spent accordingly, in household work, looking after her husband and Son. Is it fanciful to add, with a short holiday once a year, when they went up to Jerusalem for the Passover? (Luke 2:41). It seems that she sometimes accompanied Jesus when He was preaching in Galilee, which suggests that by then St. Joseph was dead; and this appears to be borne out by St. Mark (6:3) and perhaps St. Matthew (13:55), where Joseph's name is not mentioned. He was certainly dead by the time of the Passion (cf., John 19:26-27), and Mary had to bear the agony of that time without his support. The gospels say nothing of Mary's meeting Jesus as He was led to Calvary for execution; indeed, they are silent about all those sorrows and sufferings (q.v.) of hers at this time which have meant so much to later ages. But they are all contained in a single line of St. John: "Now there stood by the cross of Jesus, his mother. . . ." And he adds that precious passage: "When, then, Jesus saw his mother and the disciple whom he loved standing by, he said to his mother, 'Woman, behold thy son.' Then he said to the disciple, 'Behold thy mother.' And from that hour the disciple took her into his home."

In the Acts of the Apostles, St. Luke writes that, after our Lord's resurrection (q.v.) and ascension, the Apostles retired to an upper room, and there "continued steadfastly in prayer with the women and Mary, the mother of

Jesus, and with his brethren"; and they were all together when, at Pentecost, "they were all filled with the Holy Spirit." This is the last happening in Mary's life that the New Testament records, and nothing whatever is known of her closing years (cf., Ephesus). She was still under sixty years old at the time of our Lord's ascension, and a considerable time could have elapsed before her death (q.v.); but "the fitness of things" suggests that the period was in fact short. There is likewise complete lack of reliable information about the circumstances of that final destiny, preserved by the Church's tradition, that we call her Assumption (q.v): when, "unblemished in her conception, a virgin inviolate in her divine motherhood, the noble companion of the Divine Redeemer who won complete victory over sin and its consequences, she finally obtained, as the crowning glory of her privileges, preservation from the grave's corruption. Like her Son before her, she overcame death and was raised body and soul to the glory of Heaven, where as queen she shines gloriously at the right hand of her Son, the deathless King of ages" (Pope Pius XII, in *Munificentissimus Deus*). *Cf.*, Mary, The Blessed Virgin: Her Legend.

MARY, THE BLESSED VIRGIN: IN THEOLOGY AND PRACTICE. The teaching and practice of the Catholic Church in respect of the Blessed Virgin Mary is referred to herein mainly under the following heads, which see: her Assumption; Definitions of Marian Dogma; Devotion to Mary; her Holiness; her Immaculate Conception; her Intercession; our Lady in the Liturgy; Mariology; Mediation; Mother of God; Mother of Mankind; the New Eve; Prayer to Mary; the Redemption and Mary; her Sinlessness; Type of the Church; Veneration of Mary; her Virginity. Summary accounts of this sort can provide no more than, as it were, a rudimentary skeleton of what the Blessed Virgin means in traditional Christianity: for these particulars to have body and life, our Lady must be seen in the widest setting, in relation to the Church and to the whole mystery of man's salvation. *Cf.*, e.g., Type of the Church.

MARY MAJOR, ST., Feast of the Dedication of. A number of festivals in the calendar have their origin in the commemoration of the dedication of a church. This one, on August 5, celebrates the dedication of the third of the Roman patriarchal basilicas, to which at first the name of Liberian Basilica was given, because it was founded in the time of Pope Liberius (d. 366). It was restored and consecrated under the name of the Virgin Mary by Sixtus III about 435, and is now generally known as St. Mary Major (Santa Maria Maggiore; Great St. Mary's), because in both age and dignity it is the chief church in Rome among those dedicated to God in honor of our Lady, and so is the head of Mary's churches in western Christendom. In the liturgical books it is called St. Mary *ad Nives*, "of the Snow," from a story that the Mother of God chose this place for a church under her invocation by a miraculous fall of snow upon the spot in midsummer; and that she appeared to a patrician named John, who founded this church during the pontificate of Liberius at the site thus indicated on the Esquiline Hill. No mention is found of this miracle until some hundreds of years later, and it is now everywhere recognized as a myth. There can be no doubt that when the general calendar is revised the old name of Dedication of St. Mary will be restored to this feast, as was done in the Benedictine calendar in 1915.

This church has sometimes also been known by the name of St. Mary *ad Praesepe*, "of the Crib," from the reputed relics of the wooden manger (*q.v.*) in which Jesus was laid at Bethlehem, which are kept in a crystal reliquary beneath the high altar. The church as it is today was restored in 1743. One of its chief glories is the fifth-century mosaics: those on the triumphal arch were put up after the Council of Ephesus (*q.v.*) in honor of the Mother of God, and those in the apse were in 1295 altered to include her glory in Heaven. Other churches elsewhere, mostly in Italy, are also called St. Mary Major or equivalent names, e.g., at Bologna and Vercelli; and other calendars besides the Roman celebrate the dedication of Mary's churches (See DEDICATION, FEASTS OF).

In the Borghese chapel of the basilica is the most venerated image of our Lady in Rome, an ancient Byzantine painting known as "St. Mary, Help of the Roman People": Pope Pius XII refers to it by this title in *Fulgens Corona* (*q.v.*). It is one of the best known of the icons attributed to St. Luke (see LIKENESSES), but it was painted centuries after his time. It is of the Hodegetria (*q.v.*) type, our Lady holding the Child in her left arm: her "far-looking" expression is of very great beauty. This picture was carried in procession through the streets of Rome to the Lateran basilica at the fifteenth centenary of the Council of Ephesus in 1931, to St. Peter's in 1950 on the eve of the definition of the Assumption, and again to St. Peter's in 1954, to be crowned by Pope Pius XII at the institution of the feast of Mary the Queen. The image has been twice crowned before, by Clement VIII in 1597 and by Gregory XVI in 1838. This second occasion was in thanksgiving for the deliverance of Rome from a cholera epidemic.

MARY OF AGREDA, REVELATIONS OF. Mary of Agreda (b. 1602; d. 1665) was abbess of a Franciscan convent in her native town of Agreda in Spain: she seems to have been the first person to attempt to supplement in detail the very little that is known about the life of the Blessed Virgin Mary. Her famous book on this subject was published only after her death, being printed at Madrid in 1670, under the title *La mistica ciudad de Dios . . . , historia divina y vida de la virgen madre de Dios . . .* : "The Mystical City of God . . . , the Divine History and Life of the Virgin Mother of God. . . ." Abbess Mary claimed to have received her material by revelation from God, in circumstances that were as unconvincing as they were remarkable: and she gave a detailed account of our Lady's life from her conception to her death. The book stirred up a controversy that lasted for many years. In 1681 the Roman Inquisition condemned the work, and Pope Innocent XI forbade it to be read (but was induced to allow it in Spain, only); his successor, Alexander VIII, confirmed the forbiddance. It was also condemned by the doctors of the Sorbonne and Bossuet in France, and by Dom Eusebius Amort in Germany; the Spanish Inquisition and several universities and learned men defended it. Among the charges brought against "The Mystical City" were that it obscured the Incarnation, that its attitude to the Blessed Virgin was very exaggerated, that matter from apocryphal writings (*q.v.*) was presented as revelation, and that in places the writer had expressed herself with considerable impropriety and made assertions calculated to bring the Catholic religion into contempt. Later editions of the book seem to have been more favorably received. All agree, however, that whatever the mistakes she made in her writing, Mary of Agreda was personally a woman of holy life, though the cause of her beatification did not reach a successful conclusion. *Cf.,* Revelations and Communications.

MARY-MASS. See DE BEATA.

MARYKNOLL, OUR LADY OF. The Catholic Foreign Mission Society of America was founded in 1911 by Father (later Bishop) James A. Walsh and Father Thomas F. Price; its headquarters is at Maryknoll, near Ossining on the Hudson River, some thirty miles north of New York City. From the first the great work of these missionaries was dedicated in our Lady's honor. In the courtyard of their buildings at Maryknoll, whose architectural details suggest their far-flung activities, is a shrine of our Lady of Maryknoll: the life-size figure of Mother and Child stands in an open-sided temple suggestive of the Far East.

MASS, OUR LADY IN THE. See LITURGY, OUR LADY IN THE.

MASS, VOTIVE. A private votive Mass is one which a priest is at liberty to celebrate at his own choice on certain days instead of that of the day. Votive Masses of our Lady may be selected from those of her Saturday office (*q.v.*), according to the season, as well as from her usual Masses. There is no votive Divine Office, except that of our Lady on certain Saturdays.

MASS OF OUR LADY. The Church has the custom of offering Mass in honor of Mary and of other saints, in thankfulness for their victory, due to Christ's sacrifice, and to ask their intercession in Heaven; and so for convenience we speak of a Mass of our Lady, of St. Andrew, etc. But every Mass is in fact Jesus Christ's sacrifice and is, and can be, addressed and offered to God alone. The Council of Trent declared (sess. xxii, can. 5): "If anyone shall say that to celebrate Mass in honor of the saints and to obtain their intercession with God, as the Church intends, is an imposture, let him be anathema." The proper (*q.v.*) parts of a Mass of our Lady (or other saint) makes reference to the person and occasion celebrated. In the Byzantine rite no feast of our Lady or other saint, however important, ever replaces the (Resurrection) Mass and Office of a Sunday; the feast's liturgical texts are combined with those of the Sunday. See also FEASTS; OFFICE OF OUR LADY (COMMON; SATURDAY); MASS, VOTIVE.

MATERNITY. See MOTHER; MOTHERHOOD.

MAY DEVOTIONS. See MONTH OF MARY.

MEDAL. A small flat metal disk, usually round, bearing an image, engraved, stamped, or otherwise produced, on one or both sides. Religious medals have a great variety of subjects: Christ, His Mother or other saints, a mystery of religion, shrines, commemorations, etc. The use of such medals has grown enormously since the sixteenth century, and especially since the introduction of mass-production: but even before this there had been many hundreds of medals associated with shrines of our Lady alone. To investigate and list all the Mary medals, past and present, of various kinds, would be a virtually impossible task.

To regard a medal as a mascot or an amulet, something bringing "good luck," is of course superstitious. A medal is a reminder of that holy person or thing whom it represents: and its efficacy consists in the Church's blessing of it, whereby she asks for God's grace upon the wearer, sometimes in indulgences attached to it and in the wearer's devotion. This is expressed in the prayer of blessing of the Miraculous Medal (see below) in the following words: "Almighty and merciful God, who has been pleased often to effect marvels for the good of souls through many appearances of the Immaculate Virgin Mary upon earth, generously pour out thy blessing upon this representational medal: so that those who look upon it religiously and wear it devoutly may both experience her protection and obtain thy mercy." In the case of some medals, there is an additional efficacy coming from a private revelation (*q.v.*) promise.

MEDAL, MIRACULOUS, The. "The Sacred Medal of the Blessed and Immaculate Virgin Mary, popularly called the Miraculous Medal," as the Roman Ritual says, is one of the best-known medals of our Lady at the present day. It is oval in shape, bearing on one side an image of Mary standing on a half-globe, with rays of light coming from her fingers, surrounded by the words, "Mary, conceived free from sin, pray for us who have recourse to thee"; on the reverse, a cross, the initial M, the heart of Jesus garlanded with thorns and that of His Mother pierced by a sword, all set about with twelve stars. This design was revealed in 1830 to a Sister of Charity of St. Vincent de Paul, St.

Catherine Labouré, in her convent chapel in the Rue du Bac at Paris. On November 27 in that year took place the principal of several visions. According to her own account, written down in 1841, and to what she told her director, Sister Catherine saw our Lady as described above, followed by a sight of the second design; and she heard an inward voice telling her to have a medal struck representing these things, and promising that all who wore it with devotion should receive great graces through the intercession of the Mother of God. This or a similar vision was repeated in the following month and on other occasions up to September, 1831.

Sister Catherine confided in her confessor, M. Aladel, and after investigation the Archbishop of Paris allowed the medal to be struck. The first 1,500 were issued in June, 1832, and a book on the subject by M. Aladel had a huge sale in several languages, including Chinese. In 1836 the archbishop instituted an official inquiry into the visions, but Sister Catherine could not be induced to give evidence before it. Nevertheless the tribunal, taking into consideration the circumstances, the character of the nun concerned, and the prudence and level-headedness of her director, presented a favorable though informal report. Two years later a confraternity with the medal as its badge was founded at the church of our Lady of Victories (q.v.) in Paris. Perhaps the most famous event in connection with this medal is the conversion of Alphonse Ratisbonne in 1842. He was an Alsatian Jew who, having reluctantly agreed to wear the medal, received a vision of Mary in that form in the church of Sant' Andrea delle Frate in Rome, whereupon he became a Christian and a priest, and founded a religious congregation, the Fathers and Sisters of Zion.

In 1894, after a careful examination of the case by the Congregation of Sacred Rites, Pope Leo XIII instituted a *feast* of our Lady Immaculate of the Sacred Medal, for November 27, the date of the event and the day before St. Catherine's own feast (she was canonized in 1947). It is kept by the Congregation of the Mission, the Sisters of Charity of St. Vincent de Paul, and some other congregations and dioceses. The epithet "miraculous" seems to be due to the circumstances of the medal's origin rather than, as is commonly supposed, to miracles connected with its devout use. But the proper of the Mass has several references to God's miracles, while its introit is a very appropriate text from Exodus 13:9 as a reminder of the lesson of the miracles and the medal: "Like a mark branded in the hand, to be kept in view like a badge worn on the forehead, so the law of the Lord shall be continually on thy lips." The wonders of grace and goodness associated with this medal are exceedingly numerous, and it has gone all over the world; it has given rise to the Association of the Children of Mary Immaculate and the Association of the Miraculous Medal, and the Legion of Mary has incorporated the design in its standard. See MEDAL; REVELATIONS AND COMMUNICATIONS; VISIONS.

There is a National Shrine of the Miraculous Medal at Germantown, Pa., founded in 1915 by the priests of the Congregation of the Mission (Vincentians), and it is a great center of pilgrimages both by individuals and parties. There is another at the old-established church of the Assumption at Perryville, Mo., where the Vincentians have a seminary. This shrine was given its present imposing form in 1930, the first centenary year of St. Catherine Labouré's visions.

MEDIATION, MARY'S. To mediate is to intervene between two persons or parties who are at variance, in order to reconcile them. In the redemption of mankind there is one sole mediator between God and man, Jesus Christ, who as God-man died to reconcile men to His Father: "For there is one God, and one mediator between God and men, himself man, Christ Jesus . . ." (I Tim. 2:5). In a secondary and derived sense, the blessed in Heaven mediate for us by their prayers; and the faithful on earth can mediate for one another, by mutual prayer and the offering of good works, sufferings, and joys to God, through His Son Jesus Christ our Lord, who alone is our redeemer and savior (cf., James 5:16).

In the lesser mediation of the blessed in Heaven, the intercession (q.v.) of the Blessed Virgin has a preeminent and special place, her prayer has a preeminent and special weight, as a direct consequence of her special relation to our Lord, her Lord and Son, with whom she, the first-fruits of the Redemption, was so closely associ-

ated from Nazareth to Calvary (cf., Redemption, Mary and the). Her mediation is universal: "By bringing Him forth," says St. Thomas Aquinas, "she in a way dispensed grace to all"; in Heaven, under Christ, she intercedes for all graces for all men. She has not, of course, the power of producing grace: all supernatural grace is God's grace, given through Christ; Mary intercedes for it on our behalf "according to Christ's will, and when He wills to save, Mary at once prays. He wills according to her prayer, but then she prays according to His will" (Cardinal Newman). Nor is the intercession of the other saints made superfluous by Mary's: it is simply subordinate.

Since her assumption into Heaven, every single grace, merited through Christ's redeeming act and granted to mankind, is bestowed through Mary's intercession. Theologians argue that, as by her consent to God's will she co-operated in the divine action that brought about *all* graces, so her prevailing prayer has a corresponding part in the bestowing of each and every one of those graces. This belief has the support of such doctors as St. Bernard, St. Robert Bellarmine, and St. Alphonsus Liguori, and of all modern theologians; recent popes have spoken in the same sense when exercising their ordinary teaching authority in encyclical letters (e.g., St. Pius X in *Ad diem illum*). Furthermore, in 1921, at the request of Cardinal Mercier, Pope Benedict XV conceded to Belgium a feast of our Lady, Mediatress of All Graces; it has since been extended to other countries, orders, and dioceses: e.g., China, Wales, the Franciscans and Dominicans, Clifton, Hexham, and Leeds in England.

The collect of the Mass for this feast addressed to our Lord as "our mediator with the Father," asks that we may obtain all we ask, through His and our Mother whom He has made "mediatress between thyself and us." In this Mass, the references of the proper (*q.v.*) to Mary as mother serves as a reminder that her mediation is but an aspect of her divine and spiritual motherhood. Her work is specifically maternal; and as her Son is universal Head, so she, in and through Him, is universal Mother. *Cf.*, Intercession; Prayer to Mary; Redemption, Mary and the.

MEDIATRESS, MEDIATRIX, OF ALL GRACES. See MEDIATION, MARY'S.

MEMENTO RERUM CONDITOR. The hymn at the little hours and Compline in the Little Office B.V.M. (*q.v.*). The following is a translation by Father C. C. Martindale:

Remember, Maker of us all,
Into our world thou once didst come
Made manifest in human flesh,
The child of Mary's stainless womb.

O Mary, Mother of God's grace,
Protect us from the foe's alarms;
Dear Mother, kind and pitiful;
Hold us when dying in thine arms.

Jesus, to thee be glory paid
Whom once the maiden Mother bore:
And to the Father praise be given
And Holy Ghost for ever more. Amen.

MEMORARE, The. A prayer, named from its first word in Latin, of which there are many English translations, none of them very graceful. The following is a well-known one:

"Remember, O most loving Virgin Mary, that never was it known that any one who fled to thy protection, implored thy help, and sought thy intercession, was left forsaken. Filled, therefore, with confidence in thy goodness, I fly to thee, O Mother, Virgin of virgins; to thee I come, before thee I stand a sorrowing sinner. Despise not my words, O Mother of the Word, but graciously hear and grant my prayer."

Although this prayer is now very well known among English-speaking Catholics it began to be used among them only relatively lately; it may have been brought to England by French *emigrés* at the Revolution, and to America by French clergy, since it was in France and during the seventeenth century that it seems first to have been popularized. In many prayerbooks it is still headed "Prayer of St. Bernard"; there seems no doubt at all that this is a mistake, a misunderstanding due to the fact that the prayer became very closely associated with the name of Claud Bernard (the "poor priest"; d. 1641), of the clergy of Paris, who popularized it in France. But this priest did not write it, for it was in existence in the previous generation to his: it remains anonymous. Claud Bernard's enthusiasm for the Memorare was due to his sudden recovery from an illness after reciting it, a recovery he was moved to attribute to a miraculous interposition of the Blessed Virgin.

MERCY, OUR LADY OF. A feast under this title is kept on March 18 and other dates in a number of places, particularly in Italy, where there is a celebrated sanctuary of the name at Savona. Here, it is said, our Lady appeared to a working-man in 1536, urging that the people of Savona should do penance for their offenses against her Son, promising "mercy, not justice." A church was built, with a marble statue of Mary, which was crowned by Pope Pius VII in 1815. There is another statue, also reputed miraculous, in the church of St. John of the Florentines at Rome. Other shrines are a fishermen's sanctuary at Bonaria in Sardinia (crowned in 1870), the very old shrine at Mézières, near Rheims, and at York (*q.v.*). The dedication of churches under this name is not uncommon in North America. The representation, popular in the West at one time, of our Lady of Mercy stretching out her cloak to cover and protect her children, seems to have originated in Cistercian monasteries in the thirteenth century (*cf.* also, Protecting Veil). The alternative title Mother of Mercy is, of course, also found. The feast of our Lady of Mercy kept by the Dominicans on September 24 is the same as that of our Lady of Ransom (*q.v.*), which is called by that name elsewhere as well. There is a Confraternity of our Lady, Mother of Mercy, originating at Pellevoisin (*q.v.*).

MIASENA, OUR LADY OF. A feast observed in the Greek and Melkite calendars on September 1, commemorating the miraculous recovery from a lake of an icon of Mary at the monastery of Miasena in Armenia. This event is reputed to have taken place about the year 850. September 1 is the beginning of the ecclesiastical year in the Byzantine rite, and this hymn is among those sung on this day: "Creator of the universe, who by thine own power didst appoint times and seasons, bless the round of this year with thy goodness, Lord. Keep thy rulers and people in safety and save us all, by the intercession of the Mother of God."

MIRACLES, OUR LADY OF, Brescia. This north Italian shrine originated with a painting of the Blessed Virgin on the outside of a house; during an epidemic in 1478 it became the occasion of miracles of healing. There are several other shrines of this name in Italy and elsewhere (e.g., Aubervilliers and Mauriac in France), sometimes called "of Portents" (*Prodigiorum*), which name particularly commemorates a series of miracles recorded in several parts of Italy in 1796-97. The observance of a feast of our Lady of Miracles is a very widespread custom, on a great variety of dates.

MIRACLES AND OUR LADY. A miracle is an effect wrought by God in nature and above the powers of all nature. It does not imply any violation of the laws of nature but only a suspension of those laws. The laws of nature do not hold with absolute necessity like the laws of mathematics, but depend in their operation on the co-operation of God, who can withhold this if He pleases. Only the power of God can bring about a miracle; what are called the miracles of our Lady are marvels done by God at her intercession. Such "miracles of our Lady" fall roughly into three categories: those wrought in favor of an individual or individuals after prayer to Mary in general; the same, but in connection with a particular shrine or image; and general manifestations, such as a "weeping Madonna" (*q.v.*).

Many happenings pass as miracles simply because they are piously believed to be such; but for a miracle to be known it must be proved. First, it has to be proved that the event alleged actually took place, that the report of it is not a mistake, an exaggeration, or even a fraud. Secondly, it has to be proved that the event was miraculous, that no natural explanation of it is forthcoming, and that it was not simply due to the ordinary providence of God. (It is often very difficult to distinguish between a miracle and an ordinary effect of divine providence in response to prayer.) A decision on an alleged miracle can be given only by ecclesiastical authority, generally the local bishop, speaking after the happening has been investigated by expert advisers. The decision when given, whether for or against, is a human decision, resting neither on divine revelation nor infallible authority: it is, then, possible for it to be wrong. The verdict must be listened to with respect; but an individual is not forbidden to investigate the matter for himself and prudently to entertain a personal opinion. What he must not do is to uphold his opinion in a way that is presumptuous and lacking in respect toward authority; nor must he seek to impose any opinion on other people by appealing to their "faith"—it is a matter of evidence, not of faith.

The greater number of seeming or reputed miracles never come under the official scrutiny of the ecclesiastical authorities at all (*cf.*, Lourdes). When it is a question of bygone ages, it has to be borne in mind that a great deal more is known today about natural causes and factors than in times past, and standards of what is and what is not good evidence are much higher. The medieval books of "Legends of our Lady" (*q.v.*) and many old biographies of saints show clearly how little attempt was made to discriminate fact from error, or even from narratives that at first were meant to be nothing more than edifying fiction; and in admiring the simple faith of our forefathers it is desirable not to overlook the element of simple credulity.

Popular belief in doubtful miracles, exploded legends, and the like is sometimes defended on the ground that they encourage and feed people's devotion and do no harm. Another view is that God's cause is not really served by the diffusion of falsehood or things doubtful, however harmless in themselves; and that the proven glories of Mary and the other saints are more than sufficient for our homage without the addition of anything tainted with uncertainty. Our own times are not free from credulousness, and these things can be harmful in their effects. In an article in the *Osservatore Ro-*

mano in 1951 Msgr. (now Cardinal) Alfred Ottaviani warned Catholics against "unchecked statements about supernatural happenings that are supposed to have taken place, such as are somewhat widespread at the present time, statements which raise a danger of throwing discredit on true miracles."

As well as the kinds of miracles referred to above, Mary's solicitude and loving intercession are manifested no less through what are termed miracles of grace, such as amendment of life or recoveries of faith; these, however, belong wholly to the supernatural order and are not miracles in a strict sense. But "ordinary miracles," such as instantaneous recovery from an incurable disease or preservation in circumstances of inescapable danger, do not stop there: every miracle has a further significance, it is a sign pointing beyond itself—often, no doubt, a sign that only the recipient himself can read. And it is the sign that matters more than the miracle, as our Lord shows. To those who sought Him after He had fed the five thousand He said, "Amen, amen, I say to you, you seek me, not because you have seen signs, but because you have eaten of the loaves and have been filled. Do not labor for the food that perishes, but for that which endures unto life everlasting, which the Son of man will give you . . . ," and what follows (John 6:22-36). But in the specific topic of our Lady and miracles, the first and last thing that strikes the imagination is her close association with her Son's first miracle, at the wedding feast at Cana, when she said to those who stood by, "Do whatever he tells you." *Cf.*, Visions; Wonderworking Images.

MIRROR OF JUSTICE. Latin, *Speculum justitiae,* an invocation in the Litany of Loreto. "Justice" here does not have the familiar sense of equity between persons but means goodness, righteousness, the virtues of Mary. The Society of Mary (Marists) observes a feast under this name on March 9, and the Annonciade nuns, founded by St. Joan of Valois, have a similar one on July 12, the Ten Virtues of Mary. Mary, writes Cardinal Newman, reflects our Lord, as the surface of still water or a looking-glass reflects. So far as creature could, she reflected His divine holiness, and therefore she is the Mirror of Holiness or, as the litany says, of Justice. "Do we ask how she came to reflect His sanctity?—it was by living with Him. We see every day how like people get to each other who live with those they love. . . . Now, consider that Mary loved Her divine Son with an unutterable love; and consider too she had Him all to herself for thirty years . . . as she was full of grace before she conceived Him in her womb, she must have had a vast incomprehensible sanctity when she had lived close to God for thirty years— a sanctity of an angelical order, reflecting back the attributes of God with a fullness and exactness of which no saint upon earth, or hermit, or holy virgin, can even remind us. Truly then she is the *Speculum justitiate,* the *Mirror* of Divine *Perfection.*"

MIRROR OF OUR LADY, THE.
See OFFICE, BRIDGETTINE.

MOHAMMEDANS. See ISLAM.

MOKAMEH, OUR LADY OF.
Mokameh is on the river Ganges, fifty miles from Patna, capital of the province of Bihar, and is recent among Indian shrines. The large church was dedicated in honor of the Mother of Divine Grace in 1947; it is built not in a European but in an Indian style, and our Lady's image shows her clothed in a *sari*. Many pilgrimages to this shrine are organized by the Jesuit missionaries who minister in the diocese of Patna; the chief day is November 3.

MOLEBEN. See ENTREATY OF THE MOTHER OF GOD.

MONDOVÌ, OUR LADY QUEEN OF. The image at this Piedmontese shrine is said to have been originally depicted on a pillar by a charcoal-burner of Vicoforte, about the year 1540. It became famous for miracles, and in due course the present great sanctuary was built. The chief feast is on Mary's birthday (September 8).

MONTAIGU, OUR LADY OF. A
Belgian shrine at Sichem, near Louvain, going back to the setting up of a small statue of Mary in an oak-tree during the fourteenth century. The statue disappeared in 1579, but was soon replaced by another, which became reputed an occasion of miracles of healing. The oak having died, it was cut down and the wood used for making reproductions of the image. For the original, a church, seven-sided in shape, was built, surrounded by a fortified enclosure (Montaigu was a hill of military importance). The statue, very small and simple, but decked out in clothes, is above the high altar, which stands at the spot where formerly the oak grew. Montaigu is still one of the most popular shrines in Belgium; there is another of the same name in France. *Cf.,* Lanherne.

MONTALLEGRO, OUR LADY OF.
This sanctuary, beautifully situated above Rapallo in Italy, overlooking the Tyrrhenian Sea, dates from 1557, when a small painting on wood, an icon representing the Falling Asleep of our Lady, was found by a peasant, who said it had been pointed out to him by the Mother of God herself. It may have come originally from Ragusa (Dubrovnik) in Dalmatia. Among the pilgrims to the shrine have been St. Bridget from Sweden and St. Francis de Sales, and it has become rather popular among English people during the past quarter-century. The icon was crowned in 1767, and lately a new hospice for pilgrims and retreat-house have been built. Feast: July 2.

MONTE NERO, OUR LADY OF.
The story of the origin of this Italian shrine on a hill behind Leghorn is that, in 1345, a crippled shepherd found there a picture of the Mother and Child, and was straightway cured of his lameness. The sanctuary has had a checkered history, but it is still a center of devotion and is now cared

for by Benedictine monks of Vallombrosa; they are here allowed to sing a Mary-Mass every Saturday. The picture has been attributed to more than one Italian master of the fourteenth century; a feature of it is the bird perched on Mary's wrist, held by the Child with a golden thread. This image was crowned in 1690 and there is a feast, of our Lady of Grace, on August 24, with a proper (*q.v.*) Mass.

MONTE OLIVETO. Monte Oliveto Maggiore, a sanctuary in Tuscany, is the cradle of the Benedictine congregation of St. Mary of Mount Olivet, founded in 1319 by Bl. Bernard Tolomei. He and his companions chose the Rule of St. Benedict on the advice of Bishop Guy of Arezzo; it is said that the bishop had had a dream in which our Lady had told him to give the Benedictine rule and a white habit to some persons who at that time were unknown to him.

MONTE SANTO, Camporosso and Gorizia. The first is the oldest Marian sanctuary of the Italian region of Venezia Giulia, founded in 1360. It was destroyed in World War I, and rebuilt. It stands nearly 2,000 feet above the sea, and before World War II attracted 100,000 Italian, Slovene, and Austrian pilgrims every year. It is distinguished from the Monte Santo shrine near Gorizia as *Il Chiarore,* the Shining. This last, formerly in Austria, dates from 1539, when Mary appeared to a young girl on the mountainside. The image was crowned in 1717. This sanctuary, which used to attract 200,-000 pilgrims a year, also was destroyed

in World War I, and built up again. It is in charge of the Franciscans. Feast: June 6.

MONTE SENARIO. The cradle of the order of Servants of Mary, begun here by a group of hermits, the Seven Holy Founders. In consequence of a vision of the Blessed Virgin they withdrew from Florence to this deserted hillside. Uncertain what way of life to follow, they again turned to our Lady; she appeared to them and told them they were to be her servants, what habit they were to wear, and what rule to adopt. From that day in April, 1240, they were known as the Servants of Mary, or Servites. Their church on Monte Senario, rebuilt in 1700, is a favorite resort of pilgrims from Florence and further afield.

MONTE VERGINE. A very famous Benedictine sanctuary in the Campanian region of Italy; its religious history goes back to pre-Christian times, when there was a temple of Cybele there. A chapel of the Blessed Virgin was built in the seventh century, and in 1119 St. William of Vercelli founded the monastery that still exists, high up on the mountain. In the church is a large icon of the Mother and Child, "of Constantinople," said to have been brought to Italy by King Baldwin of Jerusalem, which came into the possession of the monastery in 1310. The dark figures stand out strikingly from the gold background; the present lower part of the picture is a later addition. There are some 200,000 pilgrims yearly to Monte Vergine, notably at Whitsuntide and on September 1. There is a church at Seattle, Ore., dedicated in honor of our Lady of Monte Vergine, and other at New Brunswick, N.J.

MONTH OF MARY. As a personal name, May is now used as a familiar form of Mary, but as the name of the fifth month of the year it is derived from the Roman goddess Maia. From early times this season of the year was marked by merry-making and various customs having reference to the spring. Some of these customs persisted through the middle ages, and even down to our own time, but with no particular religious significance (e.g., the maypole, and the "queen of the May"). The Benedictine monk John Lydgate (d. *c.* 1450) began a May-day poem with an invocation of "Mighty Flora! goddess of fresh flowers. . . ." Individuals here and there adapted one or other of these observances to religious ends: for example, Bl. Henry Suso (d. 1365) sometimes set up a May-garland in honor of our Lady. But the custom of dedicating the month to her, putting up temporary shrines, having processions and other special services in her honor, is quite a late development. Something of the sort was done at the Franciscan church of St. Clare in Naples by the beginning of the eighteenth century, and soon after in northern Italy; at Grezzana, near Verona, the combating of superstitious observances was particularly in view. From about this time the custom spread with some rapidity; it was introduced into Ireland, for instance, in 1818, at the Ursuline convent, Waterford. The observance appears to have been much fostered by the Society of Jesus. The first certain book of May devotions was published by an Italian Jesuit, Father Annibale Dionisi, about 1726; in it he says; "When we make an offering we ought to give of our best, so that among all the months of the year we choose the most beautiful, May, the season of flowers, which invites us to crown [Mary] with the blossoms of good deeds." He then suggests the putting up of a little shrine in the home, and saying the rosary or the Loreto litany before it, and other devotions. But, he says, be careful not to say too many prayers, so that they have to be hurried or the people taking part get tired, "especially children and busy people." May devotions were first introduced into England about 1840, by Father Aloysius Gentili, of the Institute of Charity.

It will be seen, then, that the name of the month, crowning a girl as the May-queen, dancing round the maypole, and so on, have nothing to do with the Queen of Heaven historically and traditionally. Until the institution in 1954 of Mary the Queen, for May 31, there was no Marian feast during the month that was observed everywhere. On the other hand, Cardinal Newman points out that May "belongs to the Easter season, which lasts fifty days, and in that season the whole of May commonly falls, and the first half always. The great feast of the Ascension of our Lord into Heaven is always in May, except once or twice in forty years. Pentecost, called also Whitsunday, the feast of the Holy Ghost, is commonly in May, and the feasts of the Holy Trinity and Corpus Christi are in May not unfrequently. May, therefore, is the time in which there are such frequent Alleluias, because Christ has risen from the grave, Christ has ascended on high, and God the Holy Ghost has come down to take His place. Here then we have a reason why May is dedicated to the Blessed Mary. She is the first of creatures, the most acceptable child of God, the dearest and nearest to Him. It is fitting then that this month should be hers, in which we especially glory and rejoice in His great providence to us, in our redemption and sanctification in God the Father, God the Son and God the Holy Ghost." Further, the cardinal remarks the important saints' days that occur this month: three of our Lord's apostles, St. John, St. Philip, and St. James; two great doctors, St. Athanasius and St. Gregory Nazianzen, and several popes; St. Monica and St. Philip Neri; a feast of the Cross and of an archangel, Michael. Had he been writing today he would have been able to add two more doctors, St. Bede and St. Robert Bellarmine.

In lists of devotions for the months (which do not always agree with one another) May is not the only one during which Mary is specially honored: there is August, her Immaculate Heart; September, her Seven Sorrows; October, the rosary. Special observances in May and October have been given official recognition, and are (with other popular devotions) specially referred to by Pope Pius XII in *Mediator Dei* when he says: "These practices encourage the faithful to receive the sacrament of penance more often, to take their part devoutly in the eucharistic Sacrifice and to receive holy communion; to meditate, too, on the mysteries of our redemption and to follow the example of the saints: they therefore cause us to take part in the liturgy with greater spiritual profit."—In the Eastern Church the special dedication of months is unknown, though December is in an informal way Mary's month—and very appropriately, in view of Christmas. But some Eastern Catholics have adopted the Western practice in a measure; the Ukrainians, for example, deck the icon of the Mother of God with flowers during May, and every evening sing a *Moleben* in her honor (see ENTREATY).—See the poem by Gerard Manley Hopkins called "The May Magnificat."

MONTSERRAT. The Benedictine abbey of Montserrat in Catalonia stands high on a terrace of a mountain of astonishing structure and coloring, twenty-two miles from Barcelona —one of the most magnificently situated monasteries in the world. It was founded in the ninth century, it is said in consequence of the finding of an image of our Lady there, but it does not seem to have been a pilgrimage center before the thirteenth century. The small black statue of our Lady of Montserrat, the "Morenata," of the same type as our Lady Underground (*q.v.*), is enshrined above the altar of the great abbey-church. During the Spanish civil war of 1936-39 the monastery was closed, and twenty-three of its monks were shot, simply because they were men of God. That was not the first disaster in Montserrat's history, yet it still lives on, with its great pilgrim establishment, as the chief Marian sanctuary in Spain. As a Russian has written, "Montserrat is like a great allegory. Down below are the gloom of industrial Monistrol, human passions, worries, anxieties. If one wants to go to God, one must . . . climb up a long and weary journey . . . through dark tunnels of self-denial, into the unknown."—The feast of our Lady of Montserrat is kept on April 27, with proper Mass and Office (including several places in Latin America). It is a Catalan custom for engaged and newly married couples to make a pilgrimage to the shrine of our Lady of Montserrat, the patroness of Catalonia.

MORNING STAR. Latin, *Stella matutina,* an invocation of our Lady in the Litany of Loreto, first used by St. Peter Damian (d. 1072); by her merits, said Pope Urban IV in 1476, she, like the morning star, outshines all other constellations. "It is Mary's prerogative to be the Morning Star, which heralds in the sun. She does not shine for herself, or from herself, but she is the reflection of her and our Redeemer, and she glorifies *Him.* When she appears in the darkness, we know that He is close at hand" (Cardinal Newman). There is a church of this name at Pittsfield, Ill.; and the Carmelites have an anthem beginning *Ave, Stella matutina,* "Hail, Morning Star": its authorship is attributed to St. Simon Stock (d. 1265), but it has also been claimed for Peter the Venerable (d. 1156).

MOTHER OF GOD. "The Blessed Virgin Mary is really the Mother of God, because she conceived and bore in His human nature Jesus Christ, who is true God and true man" (Gasparri's Catechism). The central and fundamental truth of Christianity is the fact that "the Word was made flesh and dwelt among us." That Word is the Son of the Father, the Second Person of the Blessed Trinity. The Word-made-flesh is Jesus Christ, the God-man, one undivided person in whom are two natures, divine and human. The Virgin Mary gave birth to that God-man: she became the mother of Christ, the Savior, and therefore mother of God. This does not mean the absurd idea that Mary generated the Godhead, any more than a mother generates her child's soul. It means simply that she is mother of a divine person, an eternal Person, God born as man. Her divine motherhood is real, not merely verbal, because "the mystery fulfilled in her womb was that, through a singular, unique oneness of person, the man is God in God, just as the Word is flesh in flesh" (St. Vincent of Lérins). That truth, that the Blessed Virgin is Mother of God, the Church finally made clear at the Council of Ephesus (*q.v.*) in the year 431: it is Mary's fundamental dignity and the source of all her other prerogatives (*q.v.*) and endowments; it is the origin and the justification of all the honor and veneration that are given to her.

At the moment of the Annunciation (*q.v.*), when the mystery of Mary's divine motherhood came to pass, the angel greeted her on that account as "full of grace" (*q.v.*) and "blessed," because "he who is mighty hath wrought great things for me." She was called from eternity to be the Mother of God, and it was in view of that destiny that from her first moment of existence she was filled, by anticipation, with Christ's redeeming grace. And by grace—freely given, freely accepted—she devoted her life to her Son, from first to last co-operating in the divine purpose for the redemption of fallen mankind. Before the mystery of God born of a woman, and all that flows therefrom, man can but wonder and worship. And he sees, dimly, as in a mirror, what St. Albert the Great tried to put into words: "The Son draws out the Mother's excellence to infinity; the boundless excellence of the Fruit shows something of a boundless excellence in the tree that bore the Fruit." Mary is but a human creature: the dignity of her divine motherhood is beyond measure. *Cf.,* Virginity, Our Lady's.

In a homily, read at Matins on the feast of the Motherhood of our Lady, St. Bernard says: "Happy Mary, who lacked neither humility nor virginity! And in truth an extraordinary virginity, which was not impaired but honored by fruitfulness. A no less remarkable humility, which was glorified rather than lessened by her fruitful virginity. Virginity and humility that accompanied a fruitfulness that is beyond compare. Each of these is a marvel. Each is beyond anything known. Each is wholly unexampled. . . . Yet since we see and read that God is wonderful in His saints, what cause for astonishment is there that He shows Himself still more wonderful in His mother? And so, you who are married, give reverence to this integrity of the body found in human flesh; you holy maidens, give reverence to the Virgin's fruitfulness. All of you, men and women, find your pattern in the humility of the Mother of God."

MOTHER OF MANKIND. "The Blessed Virgin Mary, Mother of God, is also our mother by that adoption which makes us brothers of her Son. Jesus Christ himself confirmed this at His death on the cross, when He gave all men, in the person of St. John, to the Blessed Virgin to be her children, saying 'Woman, behold thy son,' and at the same time He gave His mother to all men to be their mother, 'Behold thy mother'" (Gasparri's Catechism). Mary, then, is the mother not only of the Redeemer but also of the redeemed; as St. Augustine says, she is spiritually the mother of the members of that Head whose mother she is physically. When she brought forth Jesus Christ, she brought forth the New Adam, the head of restored mankind; in accepting her destiny as mother of the Savior she co-operated in bringing to birth the faithful members of the Church whose head He is, who together form His body in a mystical sense. Mary is mother of the whole Christ, of His natural body and of His mystical body. Those, too, who by baptism are made brothers of Christ are made sons of His Father by adoption; and as His Father becomes theirs, so does His mother become theirs also. "Mary is the mother of those who live by grace as Eve is the mother of those who die according to nature," as St. Peter Chrysologus puts it in one sentence, echoing St. Ephraem: "Through Eve man was brought to his grave; through Mary, he was recalled to Heaven." For many centuries now religious writers have seen in the crucified Lord's words to John and Mary a most solemn confirmation of the truth of the Blessed Virgin's spiritual motherhood of all men. Pope Pius XII writes in the encyclical letter *Mystici Corporis:* "Thus she, who was the mother of our Head according to the flesh, became by a new title of grief and glory [at the Passion] the spiritual mother of all His members. . . . And upon the mystical Body of Christ, born of the Savior's pierced heart, she bestowed the same motherly care and fervent love with which she fostered and nurtured the suckling child Jesus."

The fact that that universal motherhood is spiritual or mystical does not make it any the less real. Mary is men's mother, and she acts toward them accordingly. Throughout the ages Christians have experienced that she cares for the welfare of the souls and bodies of her spiritual children with the same solicitude that she cared for her divine Son; and they in turn seek to be subject to her as He was subject to His earthly parents (Luke 2:51), to do what she would have them do. What that always is, she herself has said: "Do whatever He tells you" (John 2:5). Trust in the power and goodness of Mary was summed up, eight hundred years ago, by St. Anselm, called the Doctor of Mary: "If you, Mary, are silent, there are none

who will pray, none who will help; when you pray, all will pray and help. A hundred thousand voices cry out to you a thousand times, to the Queen who is so good to men, and all of them are saved. I, too, will cry to you, and shall I not be helped?" *Cf.,* Mediation, Mary's; New Eve.

MOTHER-TITLES in the Litany of Loreto. Our Lady is invoked under twelve mother-titles in the Litany of Loreto. Some of the current English translations are not altogether satisfactory. *Admirabilis* is not in the superlative, nor does it mean "admirable" as now used, but "wonderful," as Cardinal Newman translates it. Again, *amabilis* does not convey our "amiable" (agreeable, friendly) but something much stronger, "dear" or "lovable." Mother Undefiled is displeasing: Newman has "sinless." The titles then are: Holy Mother of God, Mother of Christ, Mother of Divine Grace (*q.v.*), Most Pure Mother, Most Chaste Mother, Inviolate Mother, Sinless Mother, Lovable Mother, Wonderful Mother, Mother of Good Counsel, Mother of the Creator, Mother of the Savior. The meaning of these is clear, except perhaps Mother of the Creator, which at first sight might seem startling. But in fact it is nothing more than the familiar truth, affirmed in the first invocation, that our Lady is the Mother of God, on which Cardinal Newman reflects: "Is this title as given to Mary more wonderful than the doctrine that God, without ceasing to be God, should become man? Is it more mysterious that Mary should be Mother of God, than that *God* should be *man?* Yet the latter . . . is the elementary truth of revelation, witnessed by prophets, evangelists, and apostles all through Scripture. And what can be more consoling and joyful than the wonderful promises which follow from this truth, that Mary is the Mother of God?—the great wonder, namely, that we become the brethren of our God . . ." (*Meditations and Devotions*).

MOTHERHOOD OF OUR LADY, Feast of the. This feast, observed throughout the Western Church on October 11, celebrates Mary as mother of God, and bears the same sort of relation to the Annunciation and to Christmas as does the Synaxis (*q.v.*) of our Lady in the Byzantine rite. It was long known in Portugal and elsewhere, but was finally instituted in 1931 by Pope Pius XI in view of the fifteenth centenary of the Council of Ephesus (*q.v.*). At the same time the Pope ordered at his own cost the restoration of the Marian mosaics in St. Mary Major (*q.v.*), much decayed through age, and issued an encyclical letter, *Lux veritatis.* In this, among the objects of the new festival, is named one that was particularly close to the heart of Pius XI, ". . . that Mary, who is loved and revered so warmly by the separated Christians of the East, would not suffer them to wander and be unhappily led further away from the unity of the Church, and therefore from her Son, whose vicar on earth we are."

MOUNT CARMEL, OUR LADY OF. This title derives from Mount Carmel on the coast of Palestine also called the Hill of Holy Elias (III Kings 18): it is the cradle of the Carmelite Order. The friars still have a monastery there (the present building dates from 1827), and here Jews and Mohammedans join with Christians to honor the prophet Elias and the maiden Mary. The church is in the form of an equal-armed cross, and a statue of our Lady of the Scapular stands above the altar. The patronal feast-day of the Carmelites was originally the Assumption; but between 1376 and 1386 the custom arose of observing a special feast of our Lady on July 16, which is the reputed date of the Brown scapular (*q.v.*) vision. This custom appears to have originated among the Carmelites in England. At the beginning of the seventeenth century this became definitely the "Scapular feast," and began to be observed outside the order; in 1726 Pope Benedict XIII extended it to the whole Western Church, under the title Commemoration of Our Lady of Mount Carmel. In the proper Mass for the day no mention is made of the scapular or St. Simon's vision, but they are referred to in the lessons of the second nocturn at Matins. In 1672 four special invocations were allowed to the Carmelites in the litany, viz., Beautiful Mother of Carmel, Virgin Flower of Carmel, Patroness of Carmelites, and Hope of all Carmelites (see also SEQUENCE). The feast of our Lady of Mount Carmel is specially popular among the Italian people, and it is the titular feast of a number of pilgrim shrines, e.g., our Lady of Avioth (*q.v.*) in France; she has a sanctuary at Aylesford (*q.v.*) in England. The Mass of the day is one of those that has the introit *Gaudeamus*, with its peculiarly lovely melody: "Rejoice we all in the Lord as we keep holiday in honor of Mary, that blessed maiden whose festival makes angels glad and sets them praising the Son of God."

MOUNT SAINT ANN, Silesia. This sanctuary is the greatest pilgrimage resort of Silesia. It originated with a fifteenth-century statuary group of St. Ann, with Mary and the Child Jesus, but it has become a definitely Marian shrine. Pilgrims come from great distances, young people particularly during May, older ones in August. The shrine is in the care of the Franciscans, whose friary was built in the sixteenth century.

MUCKROSS, OUR LADY OF. Muckross abbey, near Killarney, was refounded as a Franciscan friary in 1440, and it survived the dissolution until 1652. There are considerable ruins, some of the most interesting and beautiful in Ireland, and in the cloister garth stands a great yew. Under this tree the wonderworking medieval statue of our Lady is said to have been buried; and then, we are told, the tree took on a new lease of life, putting forth shoots and foliage to conceal the hiding-place.

MUKAČEVO. The icon of the Mother of God at the Basilian monastery of Rosvigovo, near Mukačevo, was a principal object of pilgrimage of the Ruthenian Catholics of Byzantine rite in the Podkarpatska Rus. After this territory passed from Czechoslovakia to the U.S.S.R. in 1946, the monks were dispersed.

MUNIFICENTISSIMUS DEUS. The opening words and title, "The God of all generosity," of the apostolic constitution wherein, on November 1, 1950, Pope Pius XII defined the Assumption (*q.v.*) as a dogma of faith. The Pope describes how, when requests for the definition of this doctrine had reached him in large numbers from all parts of the world, he consulted with the bishops of the Church, and with almost unanimous voice they agreed that it could and should be defined: "This common consent is of itself an absolutely certain proof, which admits of no error, that the privilege in question is a truth revealed by God." The history of the doctrine and its development by the Fathers and later theologians, and other testimonies, are then set forth at some length. "Therefore, since the universal Church, which the Spirit of truth actively and infallibly directs in perfecting knowledge of revealed truths, has manifested her belief in various ways down through the centuries; and since the bishops of the whole world almost unanimously petition that the truth of the bodily assumption of the Blessed Virgin Mary into Heaven be defined as a dogma of divine and Catholic faith—which truth is founded on Sacred Scripture, is deeply embedded in the minds of the faithful, has received the approval of liturgical worship from the earliest times, is perfectly in keeping with the rest of revealed truth, and has been lucidly developed and explained by the studies of learned and wise theologians—we deem that the moment preordained in the plan of divine Providence has now arrived for us solemnly to proclaim this extraordinary privilege of the Virgin Mary." The dogma is solemnly defined in these terms: "By the authority of Jesus Christ our Lord, and of the blessed Apostles Peter and Paul, and by our own, We proclaim, declare and define it to be a dogma revealed by God that the Immaculate Mother of God, the Ever-virgin Mary, when the course of her earthly life was finished, was taken up body and soul into the glory of Heaven."

MYANS, OUR LADY OF. Myans in Savoy, near the Mont Cenis tunnel, has been a pilgrimage center since at least the thirteenth century, and its small "black virgin" was an object of the devotion of St. Francis de Sales. The church was half destroyed at the French Revolution, but the statue was saved and later enshrined again in the restored building, where it was crowned in 1905. The sanctuary is particularly resorted to by pilgrimages of men, and the image was taken to Rome by a Savoyard pilgrimage for the definition of the dogma of the Assumption in 1950.

MYSTERY. The word mystery has several specifically Christian connotations, but we are concerned here only with what are called the "mysteries of the rosary." These are certain events in the life of Jesus Christ and His mother Mary, upon which meditation is made when saying the rosary (q.v.). They are fifteen in number, divided into three groups, the meditation on each mystery being accompanied by a decade (q.v.) of vocal prayers. The first group belongs to Mondays and Thursdays ("white roses"), the second to Tuesdays and Fridays ("red roses"), the third to Wednesdays, Saturdays, and Sundays ("golden roses").

The Joyful Mysteries are: (1) The Annunciation: Mary is greeted by the Angel. (2) The Visitation: Mary visits her cousin Elizabeth. (3) The Nativity: Christ is born in Bethlehem. (4) The Child Jesus is presented in the Temple. (5) The Boy Jesus is found among the teachers in the Temple.

The Sorrowful Mysteries are: (1) Christ's agony in the garden. (2) Christ is scourged. (3) Christ is crowned with thorns. (4) Christ carries the cross to Calvary. (5) The Crucifixion: Christ dies on the cross.

The Glorious Mysteries are: (1) The Resurrection: Christ rises from the dead. (2) The Ascension: Christ returns to the Father. (3) Pentecost: the Holy Spirit comes down upon the Church. (4) The Assumption: Mary goes up, body and soul, into Heaven. (5) The Coronation of our Lady and the Glory of the Angels and Saints.

The coronation has been added to the last mystery only relatively lately, but it now generally supplants it. In his *Catholic Catechism* (Eng. trans., 1934) Cardinal Gasparri gives the whole, as above. The first edition of the *Garden of the Soul* (1740) has:

"The Blessed Virgin's eternal felicity, and that of all the blessed in the kingdom of Heaven."—The enumeration of these mysteries shows how mistaken are those who think of the rosary in terms of "vain repetition." It is concerned with the whole work of our redemption through Christ, and the anticipated first-fruits of that work, His own Mother; and of the accompanying prayers it has been well said that they form a sort of ground-bass "which we may liken to the 'Holy, Holy, Holy' of the heavenly choirs."

MYSTICAL ROSE. Latin, *Rosa mystica,* an invocation of our Lady in the Litany of Loreto: "I grew to my full stature as . . . a rose-bush in Jericho . . ."—". . . yours to burgeon like a rose-bush that is planted by running water" (Ecclus. 24:18; 39:17. *Cf.* the quotation from St. Bernard under ROSARY). The rose is esteemed the queen of flowers, and Mary is the queen of spiritual flowers. "Mystical" means, in a sense, "hidden," and Cardinal Newman suggests that the epithet can here be taken as referring to the fact that Mary's body is "hidden" in Heaven, instead of being, like the bodies of so many other great saints, enshrined on earth for all men to behold. The term can also refer to Mary as the greatest contemplative or mystic. *Cf.,* Flower Names.

N

NAME OF MARY, The. *Mary* is the English form of the Hebrew *Miryam* or *Miriam,* which was the name of the sister of Moses and of several women in the New Testament as well as of our Lady. About the year 400, St. Jerome interpreted the name as meaning "star of the sea" (*stella maris*), and this interpretation has been popular ever since; it was adopted by St. Isidore of Seville (d. 636), and St. Bernard (d. 1153) gave it further currency. But others, including St. Peter Chrysologus (d. *c.* 450) and St. John Damascene (three centuries later), said the name means "lady." The learned are still discussing the matter. It is claimed that at any rate the name Mary has nothing to do with "star," "sea," or "bitterness." Other interpretations that have been favored are "beloved of God," "beautiful one," "perfect one"; strangely enough from the point of view of suitability, a case has been made for "rebellion." A view that can be supported is that it means "wished-for child"; this is the interpretation favored as probable by the Oxford *Dictionary of English Names* (2nd ed., 1950), with "rebellion" as less probable. An interesting point is that while in the case of the other Marys who appear in the New Testament we find in the Greek text simply the form *Maria,* the best manuscripts almost uniformly spell our Lady's name *Mariam.* This seems at least to mark a sense of her dignity: for her alone the Old Testament form of the name is preferred (*cf.,* Muire and Moira in Ireland). See NAMES, MARIAN.

A *feast* of the Holy Name of Mary was granted to Cuenca in Spain in 1513 and extended to the whole country and southern Italy in 1671. Twelve years later Pope Innocent XI decreed it to the whole Western Church in thanksgiving for the driving back of the Turks from Vienna by the king of Poland, John Sobieski; it is now kept on September 12, the date of the victory and only four days after our Lady's birthday, and has been adopted by the Maronite rite in the East. There is a confraternity of the Name of Mary, with headquarters in Rome.—Devotion to the Holy Name of Jesus, especially associated with the preaching of St. Bernardine of Siena and St. John of Capistrano in the fifteenth century, will have prepared the way for a similar commemoration of Mary. In either case honor is given to the name as a symbol representing its bearer, and of course the name Mary was revered long before there was a feast. "In time of danger, of difficulty, of uncertainty, think upon Mary, call upon Mary. Do not let her name depart out of your mouth or out of your heart"; thus St. Bernard in a sermon wherein, as he said, he spoke "for a little about this name." And the last prayer of the Little Office B.V.M. (*q.v.*) in St. Bernard's own order, the Cistercians, is the praise, "May the lovely name of our Lord Jesus Christ and of His most blessed Mother be blessed for ever and ever. Amen."

NAMES, MARIAN CHRISTENING. For long the name Mary and its equivalents were not in very common use among Christians; it began to spread in western Europe from the twelfth century, and rapidly increased in popularity. It was then fairly common in England, but became rarer for a time after the Protestant Reformation; but it soon came back, and by the middle of the eighteenth century nearly one in every five English girl babies was christened Mary: at this time Maria (to rhyme with "fire") was also popular. Mary is still one of the most popular names in English-speaking countries. In Ireland it was hardly used before the seventeenth century, but now a quarter of the girls receive it. In Irish Gaelic, the form *Muire* is reserved for the Mother of God, *Maire* or *Moire* being the font forms. Among other forms of the name are: in French, *Marie;* in Dutch, German, Italian, Latin, Hungarian, Portuguese, and Spanish, *Maria;* in Greek, *Mariam, Maria;* in Polish, *Marja;* in Rumanian, *Marie;* in Russian, *Marya* (pet-form, *Masha*); in Scots Gaelic, *Maire;* in Hebrew, *Miryam;* in Syriac and Arabic, *Maryam;* in Welsh, *Mair.*—In some countries, notably France, Mary has been popular as a secondary name for boys, but this custom has never taken root in English-speaking lands.

In a few religious congregations of men and many of women it is taken as a second name "in religion" of all the members.

There are of course many pet-forms and diminutives of Mary in English, such as *Molly, Polly, May, Mamie, Mariot* (now obsolete). *Marion* or *Marian* is not Mary-Ann but a diminutive, as is *Maureen* (of Maire) and perhaps *Marilyn*. Marlene seems to be a form of Magdalen, and Marina and Rosemary have nothing to do with Mary. Marietta is said to derive from Marie-Antoinette, through the place called Marietta in the state of Ohio. The French diminutives *Mariette, Marianne,* and *Manon* are occasionally met among English-speaking people, and even the Bavarian *Mariel.* In Spanish-speaking lands Maria seems less popular than the names of her feasts, such as *Dolores* (Sorrows), *Mercedes* (Ransom or Mercies), *Asunción,* and the like; the same sort of name appears among Italians (*Assunta, Concetta, Carmela,* etc). From time to time fruitless attempts have been made by the ecclesiastical authorities to discourage such names. *Stella* (star) is not Marian in origin but, like certain flower names (Lily, Rose), is sometimes accommodated to our Lady. *Cf.*, Name of Mary; Ethiopia.

NAMES, PLACE, MARY IN. In the Old World places acquired the name of our Lady or other saint through the dedication of the local church, the presence of a tomb or shrine, and similar reasons. In the New World European explorers, colonists, and immigrants deliberately chose religious names for their settlements, and not only those of sacred persons but other names of religious significance as well (e.g., Vera Cruz, meaning True Cross): Columbus, sailing in the "Santa Maria," called Watling's Island San Salvador (Holy Savior), and among the West Indies are found the Virgin Islands. Mary's part in this can be illustrated from some of the names of cities that today designate the dioceses of various countries. In the Argentine there are Mercedes (Ransom) and Rosario (Rosary); Santa Maria in Brazil; Concepción in Chile; Socorro (Help) in Colombia; Asunción and Concepción in Paraguay. In Canada there is the see of Sault-Sainte-Marie, and the Latin name of Montreal is Marianopolis, recalling the original French designation of Ville-Marie; the province of Quebec is peppered with Notre-Dames of this and that, and other Marian names. Among the old Indian centers are Sainte-Marie-aux-Hurons (*q.v.*) and Notre-Dame de la Jeune Lorette.

The United States has no see with a Marian designation, though the diocese of Marquette was at first called after another Sault-Sainte-Marie. There is a number of Marian place names throughout the country. Virginia and Maryland, however, are not among them, both being named for earthly queens: the first for the unmarried Elizabeth I of England, the second for Henrietta Maria, the Catholic wife of King Charles I. Among the places called St. Mary or St. Mary's are St. Mary's in Georgia and in West Virginia, capital of a county; there are several Marysvilles

and other combinations, some doubtless not of religious origin. There are three Assumptions in the Middle West; Carmels in New York and California, and several Mount Carmels elsewhere; Conceptions in Minnesota and Missouri; a Guadalupe in California and an Immaculata in Pennsylvania; several Loreto or Lorettos, notably the one in Pennsylvania; a Lourdes in Illinois and another in Iowa; a Maria Stein in Ohio; a Marienthal in Kansas; a Merced (Ransom) in California; a Mercedes in Texas; a Rosaryville in Louisiana; and a Socorro (Help) in Texas and in New Mexico, the last giving its name to a county. Many of the above and other American settlements have grown up around Catholic institutions of one sort or another. There is an immense number of Marian place names in Latin America.

With a few exceptions, such as St. Marychurch and Marystow in Devon, and Marylebone (St. Mary's on the Brook) in London, Mary names in England take the form of such combinations as Chadwell St. Mary (Essex), Ottery St. Mary (Devon), Stratford St. Mary (Suffolk), Week St. Mary (Cornwall), St. Mary Cray (Kent). This form sometimes distinguishes between places of the same name. But English Marian names are not very numerous (Virginstow, in Devon, refers to St. Brigid of Kildare), nor are they in Wales, where the places called Llanfair (Marychurch) were given the name late, and under foreign influence. There is a considerable number in Ireland (Kilmurry, Tobbermurry, etc.), and such places of pilgrimage as Lady's Island (*q.v.*);

and some in Scotland, e.g., Mary-burgh, Marykirk, Ladykirk.

NATIVITY. See BIRTHDAY.

NATIVITY OF MARY, THE. An apocryphal writing (*q.v.*) in Latin, based on the *Gospel of Pseudo-Matthew* (*q.v.*), and improperly attributed to St. Jerome; it ends with the birth of Jesus. Its matter, or that of *Pseudo-Matthew,* furnished material for whole cycles of medieval miracle-plays (e.g., those of Chester and Coventry in England), which did much to spread and popularize the stories concerned.

NAZARETH. As the place of the Annunciation, and the home of the Holy Family until the public ministry of Jesus Christ began, Nazareth is specially associated with our Lady in the minds of Christians. It was not, as is often supposed, an out-of-the-way place in a remote corner of northern Palestine, but lay in a frontier district of some importance. It stands in the hills, facing south over the plain of Jezreel, its neat white houses looking down into the Valley of Gardens, with olive and fig trees and hedges of cactus—surely the most attractive little town in Palestine. Something is said about its principal sanctuary under the entry herein: ANNUNCIATION, FEAST OF THE. Other sacred sites, to which the name of Mary's Son or St. Joseph are attached, are no less remindful of her: notably the Melkite church, which may well stand on the site of the Synagogue wherein the Holy Family worshiped; it is called in Arabic the Teaching-

place of the Messiah. This recalls Luke 4:16-30. Local tradition points out the brow of the hill whence His neighbors would have cast Jesus (verse 29); and on the Haifa road is the chapel of our Lady of Fear, where Mary is supposed to have watched what was happening: "But He, passing through their midst, went His way."—Cana of Galilee, so much associated with Mary's name, is generally identified with the village of Kafr Kanna, about seven miles northeast of Nazareth; but some argue for Khirbet Kana, farther away across the plain of Battof.—There are churches dedicated in honor of our Lady of Nazareth in Portugal and Brazil, at Roanoake in Virginia, and in Quebec province; and a *feast* under that title in the diocese of Belèm do Pará (Brazil), where there is a pilgrim-shrine. There is also a diocese of Nazareth in Brazil.

NESTORIANISM. See EPHESUS.

NEW CALEDONIA, OUR LADY OF. Within a year of the definition of the Immaculate Conception in 1854, the missionaries of the Society of Mary dedicated a mission station in New Caledonia (Oceania) to Mary under this title. After a time "The Conception" ceased to be a mission station, but it has continued to this day as a pilgrimage place for the whole of New Caledonia. The sanctuary is about ten miles from the capital, Noumea.

NEW EVE, The. At a very early stage in Christian thought, beginning with St. Justin (d. *c.* 165), it is found that, with Christ as the New Adam (*cf.*, e.g., Rom. 15:12 ff.), there is associated the idea of the Blessed Virgin as the New Eve. As man's first disobedience, The Fall, was brought about through a woman—"The woman . . . gave me of the tree, and I did eat"—so the coming of the Redeemer was likewise through a woman —"Behold the handmaid of the Lord. . . ." Between about the year 155 and about 210 there are three classical passages from the Fathers, who between them represented the Christians of Palestine, of Asia Minor and Gaul, of Africa and Rome. These three writers, St. Justin, St. Irenaeus, and Tertullian, in effect all say the same thing. In the words of Irenaeus: "Eve was led away by an angel's word to flee God after transgressing His word. Mary had good tidings brought by an angel that she should bear God within herself after obeying His word. The first disobeyed God; but the second was drawn to obey Him, and thus the virgin Mary became advocate of the virgin Eve. As the human race was sentenced to death through a virgin, so it was saved through a virgin: the scales are balanced—a virgin's disobedience by a virgin's obedience. While the first man's sin was amended by the First-born, the serpent's guile was overcome by the dove's [Mary's] simplicity; and we were freed from those chains of death by which we had been bound."

Those words were written by one who had sat at the feet of St. Polycarp, who in turn had been a personal disciple of St. John, the beloved apostle. And on through the centuries that followed there is a long series of similar allusions by the Fathers of both East and West. Coming down to our own era, in the bull *Ineffabilis Deus*, defining the Immaculate Conception, Pope Pius IX uses the Eve-Mary antithesis, as does Pope Pius XII in the encyclical letters *Mystici Corporis* and *Ad caeli Reginam;* while in the apostolic constitution defining the Assumption, *Munificentissimus Deus*, particular emphasis is laid on it: "Especially must it be remembered that from the second century onward the Fathers thought of the Virgin Mary as the New Eve, who, subject indeed to the New Adam, was nevertheless most closely associated with Him in that conflict with the Enemy from the depths . . . which was to lead to complete victory over sin and death. . . ." The idea of Mary as the New Eve occurs in Eastern liturgies, and it is familiar— though perhaps not always appreciated—from the second stanza of the hymn *Ave, maris stella:* Gabriel's *Ave* reversing the name of *Eva*.

The doctrine of the New, the "reversed," Eve at once suggests our Lady's surpassing holiness, and ultimately leads on to the truth of her freedom even from original sin; and both of these doctrines have a bearing on that of the taking up of her sinless body into Heaven. Again Pope Pius XII, in *Mystici Corporis*, points to its significance for Mary's part in the Redemption (*q.v.*): "She it was who, free from all sin, whether personal or inherited, and ever most closely united with her Son, offered Him on Golgotha to the Eternal Father together with a whole offering of her mother's rights and love, like a New Eve, for all Adam's children, contaminated through his unhappy fall." And the Pope at once goes on to refer to our Lady as the spiritual mother of all Christ's members. The first Eve was the mother of all mankind (Gen. 3:20) according to the flesh; the second Eve, according to the spirit, is the mother of the new mankind that was born of the pouring out of her Son's blood upon the cross. Cf., Mother of Mankind.

"Let us all rejoice today at the Lord's triumph," says St. John Chrysostom in an Easter homily, "He has turned against Satan the very arms with which the Evil One was once victorious. How? I will tell you. A maiden, a tree and death represented our defeat: and it is these three that have become our principles of victory. In place of Eve, we have Mary. In place of the tree of knowledge of good and evil, there is the wood of the Cross. In place of Adam's death, the death of the Savior." Adam, head of the human race according to the flesh, was the ultimate source of all our woe; Christ, head of the new mankind according to the spirit, is the sole source of all our bliss; as Eve contributed to the fall of mankind in Adam, so Mary co-operated in the redemption (q.v.) of mankind in the New Adam.

NEW FRANKEN. See HELP, OUR LADY OF.

NEW ZEALAND, SHRINES OF. See under AUSTRALIA.

NICULA. A Rumanian Basilian monastery and sanctuary of the Mother of God in Transylvania. It is specially noted for its icons painted on glass: one of these shows our Lady with bowed head and clasped hands; at the side at the top is God the Father, then Christ on the cross, and at the foot St. George, Constantine, and St. Helen, and the archangel Michael. Some icons at Nicula show saints with six fingers to the hand, a curiosity that has not been satisfactorily explained. Thousands of pilgrims came to Nicula before 1948, but in that year the communist government dispersed the Catholic monks and installed Orthodox religious there.

NORWAY, SHRINES OF. In medieval Norway the chief sanctuary of the Blessed Virgin was her church at Bergen. Other notable Marian churches were at Borg, Gran, Mjösa, Oslo, Tromsö, and Trondheim. The tiny body of Norwegian Catholics today equal their predecessors in devotion to the Mother of God, but they have not yet got a pilgrimage shrine.

NOT MADE BY HANDS, IMAGES. Just as pagan antiquity had its images "come from heaven" (diïpetes), so there are Christian representative images of which it is popularly said they were not made by human hands (Greek akheiropoietos; Russian nerukotvorny). Some of them are of the Mother of God; for instance, our Lady of Rossano, an icon in the cathedral of that city in southern Italy. As an expression of admiration at human skill the phrase is admissible, but it cannot be taken literally: the works in question have nothing about them to suggest that they have anything but a natural origin.

NOTRE-DAME. A French term of reference for a church dedicated in honor of our Lady, often with the name of the place added, e.g., Notre-Dame de Paris, de Montréal (cf., the term Frauenkirche in Germany). This and cognate usages have been introduced into other countries by French missionaries and religious, so that, for example, Convents of Notre-Dame are found, rather anomalously, in England. The best-known instance of this name in America is doubtless the University of Notre Dame in Indiana, in full, Notre Dame du Lac, "our Lady of the Lake."

NOVENA (from Lat. *novem*, nine). A prayer, or formula of prayers and praises, for some particular object or occasion extended over a period of nine consecutive days. The origin of the idea of Christian novenas is doubtless the nine days that elapsed between our Lord's ascension and the coming of the Holy Spirit at Pentecost, during which the Apostles "continued steadfastly in prayer with the women and Mary . . ." (Acts 1:14). Novenas as known today are comparatively recent; a development was to make the prayer, not on successive days, but on one day a week for nine weeks; thence the custom arose in some churches of repeating the same novena indefinitely, the so-called perpetual novena. A novena can, of course, be made privately, as well as publicly in church.

The oldest novena in honor of Mary seems to be that in preparation for the feast of her Immaculate Conception, inaugurated by the Franciscans, which was first indulgenced by the Holy See in 1764. Since then novenas for all her chief feasts have been indulgenced. One of the best-known novenas is that of the Miraculous Medal; other very popular ones are those to our Lady under the invocations of Perpetual Help, of Lourdes, and of Mount Carmel. In the United States novenas have been more intensively developed and attained greater popularity than in any other country in the world: an example, at the sanctuary of our Sorrowful Mother at Chicago, is referred to herein under that title.

NOVGOROD, OUR LADY OF. A miraculous icon at the cathedral of Novgorod in Russia, painted in the twelfth or fourteenth century. It is of the early type of our Lady of Blakhernae (q.v.), known as "of the Sign" (Znamenie): Mary stands with hands raised (orans), the Child being represented conventionally on her breast, often within a circle, or on a shield which the Mother holds. As with the Garment (q.v.) at Blakhernae, this image was associated with the defense of the city. Feast: November 27.—This type of image has considerable extension: it is found in our Lady of Sharfeh at the Catholic seminary of the Syrian rite in the Lebanon. Among the Greeks it is called Platitera (platos, breadth), with reference to the liturgical text, "Thy bosom has God made a throne, and thy womb vaster than the heavens."

O

O, OUR LADY OF THE. See EX-
PECTATION OF OUR LADY.

O GLORIOSA VIRGINUM. The
second part of the hymn *Quem terra,
pontus, sidera* (*q.v.*), used at Lauds
in the Common and Little Offices
(*qq.v.*) of our Lady. Father Caswall's
translation begins "O Queen of all
the virgin choir" and is found in
many hymn-books; Monsignor R. A.
Knox made a new one for the *Westminster Hymnal*, no. 104; and there
are many others.

**OAK, OUR LADY OF THE, Vi-
terbo.** In 1417 a vine-grower outside
Viterbo, in Italy, affixed to an oak-
tree a tile on which was painted an
image of Mary. Half a century later
people began to resort to this Madonna della Quercia, "at the oak,"
and a church was built around it.
Most of the tree having been carried
off as souvenirs, what was left of it,
with the image in place, was enclosed
in a highly decorated marble shrine.
This sanctuary has been visited by a
remarkable number of people who
were afterward canonized or beatified;
in the adjoining friary, Father Lacor-
daire prepared to revive the Order of
Preachers in France, and a copy of
our Lady of the Oak was set up in
their first church at Nancy. A feast
of Mary under this name, which is
found in other places as well, is kept
throughout the diocese of Viterbo
(September 25).

OCEANIA, SHRINES OF. Among
the multitudinous islands of the Pacific two groups are unique, in that
they form respectively a diocese
(Honolulu) and a vicariate apostolic
(Guam) within the ecclesiastical province of San Francisco on the mainland of the United States. These territories are ministered to mainly by
Fathers of the Sacred Hearts of Jesus
and Mary (Picpus) and Capuchin
Franciscans, respectively. The cathedral of Honolulu is dedicated in
honor of our Lady of Peace and another well-known Marian church on
Oahu is our Lady of the Mount;
there is a Lourdes shrine at Honokaa
on Hawaii, as at a number of other
places in the Pacific islands. On
Guam, the episcopal church at Agaña
is dedicated under the title of the
Name of Mary, and at the academy
of the Belmont (N.C.) Sisters of Mercy
she is venerated as our Lady of Guam.

The older and more important
Melanesian sanctuaries are on New
Caledonia and at Lomary (*qq.v.*).
North of the Coral Sea, a statue of
our Lady at Visale, in the South
Solomons, was the only thing in the
mission left standing after the bom-
bardments of World War II; it is
now a center of special devotion. In
the North Solomons, at Hahela on

207

Buka, a Lourdes shrine built by the native people attracts pilgrims from the whole vicariate. Another center due to the missionaries of the Society of Mary is the statue of our Lady of Sorrows at Port Vila in the New Hebrides. There is a number of small local shrines in the Polynesian islands, especially of our Lady of Lourdes. Farther away, and in very different cultural conditions, the Indonesian archipelago provides such local shrines as our Lady of Jakarta, with its striking indigenous statue of Mother and Child. See also AUSTRALIA AND NEW ZEALAND; PHILIPPINE ISLANDS.

OCTAVE (Lat. *octava* [*dies*], eighth [day]). The commemoration of a feast in varying degrees over a period of eight days, counting the feast itself; the last day of such a commemoration. Since the virtual abolition of octaves in the Roman rite in 1955, no feast of our Lady is so honored. Analogous customs continue in the Eastern rites: the Byzantine Melkites, for instance, commemorate the Assumption of the Mother of God over nine days, the Birthday and Presentation over five.

OFFICE, BRIDGETTINE. The daily choir-office proper to the nuns of the Order of the Most Holy Savior (Bridgettines) is of Marian interest because, though not a Little Office B.V.M. (see below) in the ordinary sense, it is nevertheless specifically an office of our Lady. It is composed on the model of the Roman Divine Office, but there the resemblance may be said to end. There are fixed psalms, hymns, antiphons, etc. for each day

of the week, and these daily offices are subject to alteration only on a few great feasts; and the hymns, antiphons, etc. are all directly related to the Blessed Virgin. In the same way the daily conventual Mass is always a "Mary-Mass," with Credo and Gloria, except on the greater feasts. The three long lessons, different each day, at Matins are those contained in the *Sermo angelicus,* which figures among the Revelations of St. Bridget (*q.v.*), of which she heard in angelic vision the words, "Behold I have now cut the cloth to make a tunic for the Mother of God, the Queen of Heaven; do thou now sew it together as best thou canst."

In connection with this office mention must be made of the book called the *Mirror of Our Lady,* sometimes wrongly described as a commentary on the Little Office B.V.M. It is in fact a detailed commentary on the Bridgettine office, written for the nuns of Syon abbey in England (still in existence) by an unknown author, probably about 1440. It is a work of quite unusual interest and charm; no doubt its length, and the fact that it is geared to so little-known an office, explains why no modernized edition has ever been published. This is how the author expounds the verse *Rorate caeli,* "You heavens, send dew from above . . .": "By 'heavens' are understood angels, that dewed from above when Gabriel came down with salutation to our Lady. By 'clouds' are understood prophets, that rained with busy prophecy of the coming of our Lord Jesu Christ. By 'the earth' is understood our Lady that was opened by consent to Gabriel's greeting, and so bare our Saviour Jesu Christ, from whom sprang righteousness, that is to say, grace that maketh a man rightful. By 'the Lord' is understood the Father of Heaven, that made our Lord Jesu in His manhood. Read now again the chapter, and you will find it plain and easy to understand." Elsewhere the writer warns the nuns in homely fashion against following their own private devotions during public service: "As wine and ale are good drinks by themselves, but if they were mixed together men would not drink them, right so our Lord wishes His service to be said whole, each hour by itself, without mixing any other thing in it. Therefore He forbade in His law that any man should sow his field with divers seeds at once. For the seed of these holy hours ought to be sowed in the field of your souls in their own time by themselves."

OFFICE OF OUR LADY, COMMON. The proper parts of the Mass and Divine Office used wholly or in part on certain feasts of the Blessed Virgin. The introit of the Mass is the famous verse from Sedulius (*q.v.*), *Salve, sancta parens*, the epistle is from Ecclesiasticus (24:14-16), and the gospel that passage from St. Luke containing the words, "Blessed is the womb that bore thee . . ." (11:27-28). The three office hymns have all become well known in English: *Ave, maris stella, Quem terra, pontus, sidera*, and *O gloriosa virginum* (*qq.v.*); and in the ninth lesson at Matins the Venerable Bede comments on the gospel thus: " 'Rather, blessed are they who hear the word of God

and keep it.' The Savior gives gracious approval to the woman's testimony; and He says that not she alone was blessed who was found worthy to give birth to the Word of God according to the flesh: but also all those who, by hearing that Word and conceiving in faith according to the spirit, strive to bring it forth by good works, and as it were to nourish it in their own hearts and those of their neighbours. For verily was the Mother of God blessed in that she gave flesh to the Word of God in time; but still more blessed in that she ever keeps that same Word in her love throughout eternity."

OFFICE OF OUR LADY, LITTLE. A daily form of prayer, modeled on the eight hours of the Divine Office, but with only a few small variations, for the days of the week and in Advent; the hymns, antiphons, etc. have special reference to the Blessed Virgin. It was of monastic origin, as a supplement to the Divine Office sung in choir, and was probably at first used only privately; but with other lesser offices it became part of the monks' communal worship. From the monasteries the use of the Little Office spread to the diocesan clergy and to the more educated lay people, and by the twelfth century it was firmly established as a popular form of prayer. Today, some monastic orders (e.g., the Cistercians) still recite it in choir every day or on some days, and it is obligatory on the Carthusians in private; it is the usual daily office of some lay-brothers and lay-sisters, and of the nuns of numerous active congregations. But the Little Office is *par excellence* the daily set prayer of lay people, especially those who are members of one or other of the third orders, of all of which it is the normal office. In the past there have been many forms, "uses," of the Little Office, and in a lesser degree that is still so.

Roman Use. The Angelical Salutation is said at the beginning of each hour. *Matins* consists of the invitatory psalm 94; the hymn *Quem terra, pontus, sidera* (*q.v.*); three psalms with their antiphons (Ps. 8, 18, 23 on Sunday, Monday, and Thursday; 44, 45, 86 on Tuesday and Friday; 95, 96, 97 on Wednesday and Saturday); the Lord's Prayer; three lessons from Ecclesiasticus 24, each with a blessing beforehand and responsory after (in these passages the divine Wisdom relates how she came forth from God and reached her full stature in Holy Zion: these words have been accommodated to our Lord and then in due measure to Mary; in Advent the lessons are from Luke 1:26-38); the *Te Deum.* *Lauds:* three psalms with their antiphons, 92, 99, 62; the Song of the Three Children (Dan. 3:57-88); Psalm 148; little chapter; hymn, *O gloriosa virginum* (*q.v.*); the Benedictus (Luke 1:68-79), with its antiphon, followed by Kyrie, a collect, commemoration of the saints, and the anthem B.V.M. (*q.v.*) according to the season. The *Little Hours* (Prime, Terce, Sext, None) have each the same hymn, *Memento rerum Conditor* (*q.v.*), with three different psalms, little chapter, Kyrie, and collect. *Vespers:* five psalms, 109, 112, 121, 126, 147, with antiphons mostly taken from the

Song of Songs, a poem whose numerous love symbolisms include that of God for Mary; little chapter; hymn, *Ave, maris stella* (*q.v.*); the Magnificat (*q.v.*), with its antiphon, ending with Kyrie, a collect, and a commemoration of the saints. *Compline* has three psalms, 128, 129, 130; hymn, *Memento* (above); little chapter; the *Nunc Dimittis* (Luke 2:29-32) with its antiphon; Kyrie, collect, blessing, and anthem B.V.M.

Other Uses. Other Little Offices in use are those of the Portuguese diocese of Braga, of the Premonstratensian canons regular, of the Carthusian and Cistercian monks, and of the (Calced) Carmelite and Dominican friars. Of these, Braga is very like the Roman, and the Carthusian is quite different. But for lay people the Carmelite and Dominican offices are most important, as they are used by the tertiaries of those orders: a few particulars of Dominican usage will give an idea of the differences. At Matins the psalms, 8, 18, 23, are the same every day, and the three lessons are Marian compositions in rhyming verse. The hymns at Matins, Lauds, and the little hours are in the old versions: *Quem terra, pontus, aethera, O gloriosa Domina,* and *Memento salutis Auctor.* At the little hours and Compline there is a short responsory after the little chapter, but no Kyrie. After the collect at Lauds and Vespers there are commemorations of the day, of St. Dominic, of all saints of his order, and for peace. The Compline psalms are 131, 132, 133, and the hymn is the last three verses of *Ave, maris stella.* The Hail Mary with which each hour begins and ends is the medieval form, finishing at the words "thy womb, Jesus"; after Compline, the *Salve Regina* (*q.v.*) may be said instead. See also OFFICE, BRIDGETTINE.

It will be seen that the Little Office B.V.M. is not only a summary of the Western form of that Divine Office with which the Universal Church praises the Lord seven times a day (Ps. 118:164), but is in itself a wonderful treasury of prayer, drawn in the main from that unsurpassed source of all prayer, the written word of God. Busy people are sometimes discouraged from using the Little Office because of its relative length. But if really necessary it can be spread over several days, or certain hours only, e.g., Lauds and Vespers, may be said every day; and there is no need to say it in Latin. Its real drawback is its lack of variety and of direct connection with the Church's festivals. This has been remedied in a measure in a new edition published by Father Augustine Bea, s.j., in 1953. This includes special lessons, responsories, little chapters, antiphons, and collects for six seasons of the year; and 28 feasts are marked by proper antiphons for the Benedictus or the Magnificat or both, and sometimes by a proper collect. This new version has received the approval of the Holy See, and all religious communities using the Little Office are at liberty to adopt it.

OFFICE OF OUR LADY, SATURDAY. Except in Advent and Lent there are certain Saturdays throughout the year when Mass and Office of the Blessed Virgin may be celebrated instead of those of the day.

There are five Mass propers provided, according to the season; and there is a special third lesson at Matins for each of the months of the year, all taken from the Western Fathers, except November, which is from St. Basil.—In the Portuguese rite of Braga this Saturday office has a special importance and is called the *Cantica canticorum,* "Song of Songs."

OFFICE OF THE IMMACULATE CONCEPTION, LITTLE. A miniature office of prayer said by many of the faithful, notably by Children of Mary (*q.v.*), both privately and at their meetings. It is divided into seven "hours," with the usual names. Each hour consists principally of four stanzas of a hymn and a prayer in collect form addressed to our Lady; Compline ends with a commendation that includes the collect of the Mass of the Immaculate Conception. These elements are interspersed with verses and responses, of which some are adapted to Mary from their usual forms. The collect prayer is the same throughout, but the hymn stanzas vary from hour to hour: those at Matins begin *Salve, mundi Domina:*

> Hail, Mistress of earth,
>   Queen of the heavens!
> Hail, Virgin of virgins,
>   Star of the dawn!

The Jesuit lay-brother, St. Alphonsus Rodriguez (d. 1617) said the Little Office of the Immaculate Conception daily for forty years and greatly helped to popularize it: so much so, that its composition was attributed to him and it was printed under his name. This is now known to be a mistake: such offices existed before his time, and he learned it from a printed copy. —At one time it appears to have been the custom in some parts of Ireland for groups of women to say this office together, in the Irish language, while they were spinning.

OLOVO, OUR LADY OF. When in the fifteenth century the Turks occupied Zvornik in Bosnia (Yugoslavia), they turned the church into a mosque. Its image of Mary, hidden in a tree, was found by a Turkish soldier, who threw it into the river Drina. Thence it was taken, miraculously, as was said, to a hill near Olovo, where a chapel was built to shelter it. It became so famous for miracles that pilgrims came from all over the Balkans. In 1704 the Turks burnt the chapel and the image; but two hundred and fifty years later, in the Marian year 1954, both were restored. The discovery of two old books, containing engravings showing their original appearance, enabled this to be reproduced.

OOSTACKER. The Lourdes shrine at Oostacker, close to Ghent in Belgium, is a sanctuary in its own right. It was first built, in 1872, by a woman of title as an annex to her aquarium of rare fish! Local people began to visit it, and some cures took place; and then in 1875 there occurred there one of the most famous of all miracles attributed to the intercession of our Lady of Lourdes: that of Peter de Rudder, who had been almost helpless for eight years owing to his leg

having been smashed by a falling tree. His injuries were healed instantaneously. Oostacker continues to be a quiet unassuming Flemish country shrine, but from that day to this pilgrims have flocked thither; a large church was built and put in charge of the Society of Jesus, and hundreds of *ex-voto* tablets in it testify to the health of soul and body found there.

OROPA, OUR LADY OF. The sanctuary of the Black Virgin of Oropa, high in the Alps north of Biella, is traditionally associated with St. Eusebius of Vercelli, who died in 371; but the circumstances of the story are anachronistic. Yet the shrine is certainly an old one, and throughout the middle ages was associated with a community of canons regular. The vast range of buildings there today was begun by the dukes of Savoy, early in the seventeenth century, and forms one of the most complete pilgrimage centers in the world (there is even a cinema theater); it is recorded that here in 1895, contemplating the space and beauty of the mountains, Marconi heard the first call to his life's work. The black, painted cedar-wood statue has been crowned four times, the last in 1920; the three superimposed diadems (the fourth is represented by a halo of twelve stars) can hardly be said to add to the beauty of the image. Feast: August 26.

ORPHANS, MOTHER OF. In some early Irish praises of Mary she is called Mother of Orphans; and a feast under this title is kept by the congregation of clerks regular called

Somaschi, on September 27. It was on this date in 1508 that St. Jerome Emiliani, a prisoner-of-war, escaped from captivity under our Lady's protection, and renounced the world. Later he founded his congregation at Somascha, in northern Italy, to look after orphans and abandoned children.

ORTHODOX CHURCH. See EASTERN CHURCHES.

OSTRABRAMA, OUR LADY OF. See VILNA, OUR LADY OF.

OTOME TOGE, OUR LADY OF. In 1951 a chapel was dedicated at Tsuwano in Japan, commemorating the martyrs there of 1868-73 and having particular reference to the visions of our Lady accorded to one of them, John Baptist Yasutaro. These martyrs were exiles from among the old Urakami Christians (cf., Ura); Mary is said to have appeared to Yasutaro every evening of the fortnight during which he was enclosed in a cell 3 ft. by 3. This shrine was established by the Jesuit missionary Father Paul Nebel, and a special feast and procession of our Lady of Otome Toge is observed on the second Sunday in May. The shrine prayer is: "Sorrowful Lady of Otome Toge, make us think of God while doing each moment's duty."

OUR LADY. The most usual expression in English for the Blessed Virgin Mary, when speaking or writing informally. In other European languages that use it, it is generally confined to the names of churches, shrines, etc., or to more formal usage (French, *Notre-Dame;* Spanish, *Nuestra Señora;* Portuguese, *Nossa Senhora*). It is not used much in German or Italian, and is unknown in the East, though the lovely *Despoina hemon* occurs in Greek prayers (*cf.,* Titles). The usage spread in western Europe from the twelfth century, perhaps being popularized by the Cistercians, following the example of St. Bernard, who speaks of *Domina nostra;* and the conventions of courtly love were not without their influence.

But in England "our Lady" is much older, the first surviving use being by the poet Cynewulf toward the end of the eighth century. "Our Lady Saint Mary" became the classical English expression; and the abbreviation, "our Lady," is not so much a title as a familiar term of relationship and affection, as we speak of "my sister" or "our mother." For a thousand years this use of "our Lady" has been characteristic of the English, and sometimes a puzzle to other people. At the inquiry into the life of St. Thomas of Hereford, who was canonized in 1320, a woman witness spoke of invoking the "kind Lady." The Italian commissioner did not understand the phrase, and asked what lady she meant. The Englishwoman replied that "it was the Lady of Heaven, for in her country that was the usual way of asking for blessed Mary's help."

OUR LADY'S BANDS (i.e., bonds). An obsolete English expression for the state of pregnancy.

P

PALESTINE, SHRINES OF. See ANNUNCIATION (feast); BETHLEHEM; JERUSALEM; MOUNT CARMEL; NAZARETH; VISITATION (feast).

PANAGIA. *He Panagia,* "The All-Holy," is the ordinary colloquial term used in Greek when referring to the Mother of God in speech.—The oval medallion of our Lady worn by Byzantine bishops together with, sometimes instead of, the pectoral cross, is called a *panagia* (or *enkolpion*).—The "Raising of the Panagia" is an observance after dinner on feast-days in Orthodox monasteries, and elsewhere as an intercession for travelers. The deacon raises a triangular-shaped piece of bread, saying, "Great is the name of the Holy Trinity. All-holy God-bearer, help us"; Psalm 120 is sung, with other chants, and each person present partakes of bread and wine after passing them through the smoke of incense. According to the *Horologion,* this observance recalls the Assumption; it is said to derive from a tradition that, on the third day after Mary's death, the Apostles were at table, having put aside a portion of bread in memory of the risen Lord; and Mary appeared to them in glory, and said "I shall be with you till the end of time."

PARAKLESIS. See ENTREATY OF THE MOTHER OF GOD.

PARENTS OF OUR LADY, The. Of the parents of Mary nothing is known with certainty; all that we are told about them, even their names, Joachim and Ann, comes ultimately from apocryphal writings (*q.v.*). But Catholics are at liberty to retain as pious beliefs anything in an uncanonical book that does not conflict with the teaching of the Church, and it is a widely held tradition that our Lady was a child of promise, as related in the *Protevangelium of James* (*q.v.*). The story there told is that there was a man, "exceeding rich," whose childlessness was made a public reproach to him, and he went into the wilderness to fast and pray to God. At the same time his wife, Ann, "mourned in two mournings, and lamented in two lamentations," and as she sat praying beneath a laurel-bush an angel appeared and said to her: "Ann, the Lord has heard your prayer, and you shall conceive and bear, and your seed shall be spoken of in all the world." And Ann replied: "As the Lord my God liveth, if I beget either male or female I will bring it as a gift to the Lord my God; and it shall minister to Him in holy things all the days of its life." An angel likewise appeared to her husband, and in due time was born of them Mary, who was to be the mother of God.

It will be noticed that this story

bears a startling resemblance to that of the conception and birth of Samuel, whose mother also was called Ann (I Kings 1); it may be it is only a parallel, but it is one that suggests confusion or imitation in a way that the obvious parallel between the parents of Samuel and those of St. John the Baptist does not. Nevertheless, that our Lady should have been a child of prayer is certainly in accord with the fitness of things and the ways of God. It is interesting to notice that a doctor of the Church, St. Peter Damian (d. 1072) gives it as his opinion that it is blameworthy curiosity to inquire about things that the evangelists did not think it necessary to tell us, and specifically mentions the parents of our Lady.

In the East St. Joachim and St. Ann were venerated from an early date, but the whole Western Church has had a feast of Ann only since 1584 and of Joachim since 1621, now on July 26 and August 16, respectively. Some calendars celebrate the two together on the same day. Sainte-Ann-de-Beaupré in Canada is one of St. Ann's greatest pilgrimage shrines. The name Ann, Anne, or Anna is the Hebrew *Hannah,* which signifies "grace." "Joachim" has never been in general use in English-speaking countries. St. Epiphanius, preaching in the fourth century, said: "From the root of Jesse sprang King David, and from the tribe of David the holy Virgin. Holy, I say, and the daughter of holy folk. Her parents, Joachim and Ann, indeed pleased God in their lives, and in their blessedness brought a child to birth, the holy maiden

Mary, who was both mother of God and God's temple. Furthermore, these three, Joachim and Ann and Mary, offered a sacrifice of praise to the Trinity. For Joachim means 'the Lord prepares,' and out of him was prepared the temple of the Lord, that is, the Virgin. And Ann means 'grace,' and she was given a grace when, in answer to their prayers, such a fruit was born to them and they were given this holy Virgin."

PASSING OF MARY, THE (*Transitus Mariae;* also called "The Falling Asleep of Mary). An apocryphal writing (*q.v.*) found in Greek, Latin, Syriac, Coptic, and other languages, dating from the fourth century, but in the Greek version claiming to be written by St. John the Evangelist. The various versions differ a good deal, but their general tenor is as follows: Mary, praying at the empty tomb of her Son in Jerusalem, asks Him to return to her, and He, through the archangel Gabriel, tells her that she shall be taken to Him. Mary goes to Bethlehem with three maidens, where she prays that John and the other apostles may be sent to her, and this prayer also is granted. John from Ephesus and the other apostles from the different countries where they are scattered are miraculously transported to Bethlehem, and those of them who are dead are brought from beyond the grave. At Mary's request each of them tells how and where he received his summons: John was about to celebrate the Holy Mysteries, when the Spirit spoke to him and a cloud of light snatched him up; Peter in Rome heard a voice at dawn; Matthew was at sea in a storm, and so on. The wonders attending Mary's last hours, the miracles of healing wrought by her, and the miraculous transportation of herself and the apostles back to Jerusalem to escape the anger of the Bethlehem Jews, are then described. On the Lord's Day, Christ Himself appears in glory, and there is a touching account of His reunion with His mother. He tells Peter to begin a hymn, and while they are singing Mary blesses each of them. "And the Lord stretched forth His undefiled hands and received her holy and blameless soul." The apostles bury the body in a tomb at Gethsemane, where angelic voices are heard glorifying the Son who had been born of her. "And when the third day was ended, the voices were no longer heard; and from that time forth all knew that her stainless and precious body had been transferred to Paradise." Another account says that, the apostle St. Thomas having arrived late, the tomb was opened that he might see Mary's body, and it was no longer there.

It is possible that this narrative did a lot to spread belief in Mary's assumption, but it has no value as direct testimony to the truth of that doctrine or the circumstances of the event, some of which are exceedingly extravagant and suggest an atmosphere quite different from that of the New Testament: indeed, an official document of the sixth century, formerly attributed to Pope St. Gelasius I, condemned, among other apocryphal works, a book on this very subject, *Transitus Mariae;* whether it was one of the extant versions of the *Passing of Mary* that was thus reprobated is not known. In so doing the doctrine of the Assumption (*q.v.*) was not of course being condemned, but a particular presentation of it. In his apostolic constitution *Munificentissimus Deus* (*q.v.*), defining the dogma of the Assumption, Pope Pius XII, in referring to early testimonies to the doctrine, does not mention the *Passing of Mary*. Nevertheless the work has some value as evidence for the existence of some conscious belief in Mary's assumption at the time it was written.

PATRON SAINT, OUR LADY AS. Where nations, places, dioceses, trades, etc. are concerned, the Blessed Virgin does not have the numerical leadership as patron saint that she has in the dedications of churches. Historical and other local considerations come strongly into play, and so it is found, for example, that St. Patrick is the patron of Ireland, as her evangelist, St. James of Spain and of the diocese of Compostela, because of his shrine there, and so on. Some countries appear to have no definite patron saint at all, and our Lady appears more often in "new" countries than in others: for instance, Mary, Queen of Angels, is patroness of Costa Rica; our Lady of Guadalupe, of Mexico; our Lady, Help of Christians, of Australia and New Zealand; our Lady of the Immaculate Conception, of the United States. This last is particularly interesting, because the sixth Provincial Council of Baltimore proposed it, and Pope Pius IX confirmed the choice in 1847, eight years before the definition of the dogma of Mary's freedom from original sin. In Europe, on the other hand, our Lady as formal principal patron saint of a country is less common, and sometimes recent, e.g., of France only since 1922.

The same rough distinction between new and old can be found among diocesan patrons. The eighteen dioceses of England and Wales, established in 1850 or later, all have our Lady as principal patron, with only one exception; whereas every one of the ancient Irish dioceses has a local saint as patron, thus emphasizing the traditional force of local history in this matter of patronages and dedications. Analogous, but more domestic, factors have been at work in the choice of patrons of trades, professions, and undertakings, and of saints invoked against various ills and in emergencies. There is a very great variety of these, often differing from place to place, and Mary rarely figures among them. Choice by allusion to an event in a saint's life plays a big part, e.g., St. Matthew as patron of customs-officers (*cf.*, Matt. 9:9), St. Paul invoked against snake-bite (*cf.*, Acts 28:3-5); and Pope Benedict XV recognized this (no doubt with a smile) when he declared our Lady of Loreto (*q.v.*) to be the heavenly patroness of airmen. At the other extreme of locomotion, St. Mary of the Angels is looked on as patroness of the cab-drivers of the city of Rome.

Cf., Dedications of Churches; Names, Place.

PATRONAGE OF OUR LADY, Feast of the.

Like a number of other Marian feasts, this of our Lady's patronage or protection is first found in Spain, where it was granted in 1656 in thanksgiving for all the victories over the Moors. It spread to many other parts of the world, on various dates, but has since been dropped from a number of calendars. Among the Cistercians it has particular reference to St. Alberic's vision of our Lady, in which she assured him she would always watch over and protect that order of monks. The feast is specially observed with reference to the sanctuary of Chartres and of our Lady of Miracles at Lucca. The word "patronage" is sometimes added to the name of a patronal feast, e.g., the Patronage of the Blessed Virgin Mary of Help at Santiago de Guatemala. *Cf.*, Protecting Veil; Mercy, Our Lady of.

PEACE, OUR LADY OF.

See QUEEN OF PEACE.

PELLEVOISIN.

A country village in the diocese of Bourges in France. Here in 1876 Estelle Faguette, a domestic servant, who was dying of consumption, made a remarkable recovery, and lived another half-century, till 1929. Estelle associated her recovery with five visions of our Lady which she claimed, followed by ten others in the same year. She stated that Mary said to her, "If you want to serve me, be simple, and let your words and deeds agree"; and that, among other communications, she said she was very distressed by people's neglect of her Son in prayer and the Blessed Sacrament. She also showed Estelle a white scapular with an image of the Sacred Heart upon it, and told her to ask her bishop to encourage its use in reparation to Jesus. The scapular was in due course approved and a confraternity of Mary, Mother of Mercy, instituted to spread its use; but no mention was made of Pellevoisin in connection with its approval (though St. Margaret Mary was referred to), and it was forbidden to make statues or pictures of our Lady wearing it. The archbishops of Bourges have never pronounced on Estelle Faguette's reputed visions, and the Roman authorities have shown themselves very reserved on the subject. Pilgrims however come to the commemorative chapel at Pellevoisin. There is a shrine of our Lady of Pellevoisin in New York, in St. Paul's church on 117th Street, between Park and Lexington Avenues; and at McIntosh, Ont., there is a church of our Lady under that name. *Cf.*, Revelations and Communications; Visions.

PENRHYS, OUR LADY OF. Penrhys, at a grange of the Cistercian abbey of Llantarnam, was the principal medieval Marian shrine of Wales. It is not improbable that it originated in the "baptism" of a pre-Christian sacred tree and well. Welsh poets of the middle ages sing of the crowds of pilgrims, the beauty of its image, "nursing Jesus with a kiss," the intercession of the maiden Mary,

y Forwyn Fair, and the miracles of healing. One of them wrote: "A goodly place is the hill-top and its wooded slope, and a virgin sanctuary beside the high wood. There is her image enthroned, there the soul's pardon may be gained, in the glade of Mary's five joys." At the dissolution of the monasteries the statue was taken to London and burnt, at the same time as such famous images as our Lady of Walsingham (*q.v.*) and of Ipswich. Just four hundred years later, in 1939, what remains of the sanctuary was presented to the archdiocese of Cardiff, and organized pilgrimages and individual pilgrims again make their way thither. It lies on a mountain-side, just below the summit of Mynydd Penrhys in the Rhondda valley, near the coal-mining town of Pontypridd. Mary's Well, in Welsh *Ffynnon Fair,* is covered by a simple building, and near by a stone statue of the Mother of God has been set up in the open air. The church at Ferndale is dedicated in honor of our Lady of Penrhys, and has a statue of her.

PERPETUAL HELP, OUR LADY OF. This title is generally given in Great Britain as "of Perpetual Succour," but perhaps Constant or Unfailing Help would be better than either. The name derives from one of the most famous of all pictures of Mary, an icon (*q.v.*) of the fourteenth century, painted (on walnut wood) perhaps in Crete. But the story that it was stolen from a Cretan church by an Italian merchant, and given up in consequence of a girl's vision of our Lady, has little historical support. It was venerated, famous for miracles, in the Roman church of St. Matthew *in Merulana* (in charge of the Irish Augustinians for a century) from 1499 till 1798, when the church was destroyed in war; the picture was saved, however, and in 1866 it was set up in the Redemptorist church of St. Alphonsus, on the site of St. Matthew's. In the following year it was crowned. Since then numberless copies and reproductions of the icon have gone all over the world, some of them themselves wonderworking: but many unofficial reproductions have been made from copies in which unwarrantable liberties have been taken with the original design. Faithful copies may be seen in Redemptorist churches (e.g., at Clapham in London, and at Bishop Eton, Liverpool, which has the first copy of the icon to be sent out of Rome); there is a specially good one in the Bishop's chapel at the Ukrainian seminary in Stamford, Conn., the gift of Pope Pius XI. But the foremost shrine of our Lady of Perpetual Help in the New World is in the Redemptorist church at Roxbury, Mass. The picture, one of several copies sent from Rome, was set up over the altar in 1871; later it was given a special shrine, and it has been the occasion of a number of striking cures. Another important shrine is at the Ruthenian convent of Basilian nuns at Mount St. Macrina, Uniontown, Pa.

There are other paintings of a similar type at Bari in Italy, Almeria in Spain, in Greece, Russia, Crete, and elsewhere. The two angels in the picture are Michael and Gabriel; they are showing the instruments of the Passion to the Child, who clings to the Mother's hand, shaking loose a sandal. Hence this type of icon is called "of the Passion" in Russia and "of the Frightening Vision" in Greece. But this interpretation, of fear, does not, on religious grounds, commend itself to all lovers of the picture.

Pope Pius IX, who was very fond of this picture, inaugurated a *feast* of our Lady of Perpetual Help (June 27). As well as by the Redemptorists (with proper Mass and Office, on the Sunday before June 24), it is observed in many places, including the dioceses of Savannah and Oklahoma City, and of Leeds and Middlesbrough in England. The collect of the Mass refers to the "glorious image that we revere" of her who is at all times ready to help us, the Mother of our Lord Jesus Christ.—There is a confraternity of Mary under this name, the first member of which was Pope Pius IX; it is under the direction of the Redemptorist Congregation.

PHILIPPINE ISLANDS, SHRINES OF THE. The two chief shrines of the Philippines are our Lady of Antipolo and our Lady of the Turumba (*qq.v.*). Other important ones are at Zamboanga on Mindanao, and our Lady at the French Rock (*Peña de Francia*) at Nueva Caceres. This last has a feast proper to the sanctuary on the third Sunday of September. At Santa Rosa there is an annual festival of flowers in May, when the statue of Mary is carried in procession, as is done elsewhere in the islands.

PICTURES. See ICONS; IMAGES; SHRINES.

PIETÀ. This Italian word designates an image, carved in stone, cast in metal, or sometimes painted, of Mary mourning over the body of her dead Son: she is represented seated, with the body lying across her knees. Such images began to be common at the end of the middle ages, as a result of popular devotion to the compassion and sorrows (*qq.v.*) of our Lady. They were at first especially a product of Germany, so much so that Michelangelo's *pietà*, now in St. Peter's at Rome, was criticized by some as a "Lutheran innovation." Even if it had been of Lutheran origin, the *pietà* would not have therefore been any the less a legitimate form of Christian image. Most of these images are very realistic, characteristic products of the high Renaissance, and some are the works of very famous artists: but the appeal of many of them is aesthetic and emotional rather than religious. Among the well-known *pietàs* in the United States are replicas of Michelangelo's at the Sanctuary of the Sorrowful Mother (*q.v.*) at Portland, Ore., and in the Servite church at Chicago, and one in the church of St. Francis at 135 West 31st Street, New York City. The *pietà* in the church of the Cistercian nuns at Stapehill abbey in England was a gift of Queen Amélie, wife of King Louis Philippe, in 1842.

PILGRIMAGES. A pilgrimage is a journey to a sacred place undertaken as an act of religious devotion. This may be done simply out of piety toward some hallowed spot or devotion to a particular person; or it may be to ask the fulfilment of some need or as an act of thanksgiving or penance, or it may be something of all these. Formerly a pilgrimage was often imposed as an act of penance, for in times past there was a strong penitential element in every pilgrimage owing to the difficulties, dangers, and hardships of travel; today the penitential element usually depends on the disposition of the individual pilgrim. But the Church's blessing on pilgrims does not fail to ask that God may be to them "help in the business in hand, comfort on the journey, shade in heat, shelter in rain and cold, lift in weariness, refuge in misfortune, support in slippery places, harbor in storms," thus detailing the "toil and tribulation" of a similar prayer of medieval times.

Pilgrimages by individuals, and then of organized parties, to the holy places of Palestine are heard of soon after the Peace of the Church in 313; it seems likely that the first distinctively Marian shrine was her church at Ephesus (*q.v.*), wherein the council of 431 acclaimed her as Mother of God. St. Willibald, who was in Palestine around 727 and was the first English pilgrim to leave an account of his travels, speaks of going into Galilee, "to the place where Gabriel first came to our Lady and said 'Hail Mary.'" In Jerusalem he saw the place where the Virgin's funeral procession was stopped (*cf.*, Manifestation of our Lady); and he visited the church of Mary in the valley of Josaphat "and in the church is her tomb —not that her body lies at rest there, but as a memorial to her." Most of the shrines of our Lady whose names are still known are of later medieval or subsequent origin. Among those which, either in the past or the present, have had a widespread reputation and attracted pilgrims from outside their own country are the following: Mariazell in Austria, Walsingham in England, Lourdes in France, Altötting in Germany, Trim in Ireland, Loreto in Italy, Czestochowa in Poland, Fatima in Portugal, our Lady of Vladimir at Moscow, Montserrat in Spain, Einsiedeln in Switzerland; Cap-de-la-Madeleine in Canada; Holy Hill at Hubertus, Wis., in the United States; our Lady of Guadalupe in Mexico. Other pilgrimage shrines may be found listed herein under the names of the various countries, with some cross-references for further particulars. *Cf.* also, Shrine, in general.

The Roman Ritual contains forms for the blessing of pilgrims (especially to the Holy Land) both when they set out and when they return. The prayers refer to God leading Abraham out of Ur toward Canaan, the safe passage of the children of Israel through the sea, and the journey of the three Wise Men, led by a star; and ask that the faithful may follow in the footsteps of St. John the Forerunner and attain to Him who was foretold by John, Jesus Christ our Lord.

PILLAR, OUR LADY OF THE. There are several pilgrim-shrines of this name, of which two are famous. The *Vierge du Pilier* is in the upper church at Chartres cathedral. It is a "Black Virgin," carved in wood, dating from the fifteenth century. The Mother is seated, robed, and her hair gilt, with the Child on her left knee. The statue formerly stood under an arcade of the rood-loft, but in 1806 was moved to its present place on a pillar in the choir-aisle. This image was crowned in 1855.

The *Virgen del Pilar* is at Saragossa in Spain, and is celebrated among all Spanish-speaking people. The statue stands on a marble pillar in St. Mary's church, and it is popularly associated with the apostle St. James the Elder, who is supposed to have established the sanctuary in consequence of a vision of Mary. There is no serious evidence of the shrine older than the twelfth century. It is difficult to see the statue itself because of its stiff robes, but it is a small standing figure of Mother and Child, carved in wood. It was crowned with a diadem of very great value in 1905. Military insignia are found near the statue in recognition of the Blessed Virgin being patroness of the armed forces of Spain, under the title Immaculate for the army, Mount Carmel for the navy, and Loreto for the air arm. The feast of our Lady of the Pillar is kept throughout Spain (and in some other places) on October 12. There is a church dedicated under this title at Clayton, Mo., and there are others elsewhere in the Americas.

PITY, OUR LADY OF. This name must not be confused with that of our Lady of Mercy: it refers to Mary's compassion or grief on Calvary, and was very common in medieval England. The pertinent image ultimately became the *pietà* as we now know it: "our blessed Lady having the afflicted body of her dear Son, as He was taken down off the cross, lying along in her lap . . . named the image of our Lady of Pity." See COMPASSION OF OUR LADY; PIETÀ.

POCHAEV, OUR LADY OF. This wonderworking icon was brought from Constantinople into Volhynia in 1559 and given to a woman named Anna Goyska, in whose care it was the occasion of her nephew recovering his sight. She gave it to the monks of Pochaev in 1597; it became very widely known and venerated, and in 1773 was solemnly crowned. After the Polish revolt of 1830 the tsarist government aggregated the Pochaev monastery to the Russian Orthodox Church; it continued to be a popular shrine till after World War II, when the territory in which it is reverted from Poland to the U.S.S.R.

POLAND, SHRINES OF. Such is the fame of our Lady of Czestochowa (*q.v.*) that it has eclipsed all other Polish sanctuaries in the minds of foreigners; but the number of shrines of Mary in Poland is very large, many of the images are said to be miraculous, and many of them have been crowned at one time or another. Among these Polish shrines there may

be mentioned the following: our Lady of Berdycrow (crowned in 1756); O.L. of Bogucice; O.L. of Borek; O.L. of Cracow (shrine founded in 1220); O.L. of Glatz; O.L. of Górka Duchowna; O.L. of Gostyn (*q.v.*); O.L. of Grysów; O.L. of Jazlowice; O.L. of Koden; O.L. of Kozle; O.L. of Kalwarja Zebrzydowska; O.L. of Lesnia; O.L. of Lerajsk (crowned in 1752); O.L. of Mikulczice; Mount St. Ann (*q.v.*); O.L. of Myszowice; O.L. of Pacláw (crowned in 1882); O.L. of Pszów; O.L. of Rokitten (*q.v.*); O.L. of Springborn; O.L. of Victory in the Polish Dominican church at Lwów; O.L. of Vilna (*q.v.*), O.L. of Walbrzych (crowned statue); O.L. of Warta (crowned statue); O.L. of Wielkie Piekari (*q.v.*); O.L. of Zakrzewo; O.L. of Zbaraz; O.L. of Zyrovitse (*q.v.*). A feast of St. Mary, Queen of Poland, is observed on May 3.

POMPEII, OUR LADY OF. The shrine near the ruins of Pompeii is known all over the world, but its origin is recent. The picture, of our Lady of the Rosary, with St. Dominic and St. Catherine of Siena, a painting of no artistic merit whatever, was found in a very dilapidated condition in a Naples junk-shop; it was bought for a dollar by Bartolo Longo and his wife in 1875. They required it for the local Rosary confraternity, which Longo had been moved by Heaven to establish, in circumstances of considerable difficulty. Miracles were reported in connection with the picture, pilgrims came, and a church was begun in 1876. Today, as well as a hospice for pilgrims, there are in connection with the sanctuary a huge orphanage for girls and a trade-school for boys whose fathers have failed them. The whole great establishment has been taken under papal protection. The image was crowned in 1887, and it is visited by hundreds of thousands of people every year. Feast: May 8. Several churches in the United States are dedicated in honor of our Lady of Pompeii.

PONTMAIN. On January 17, 1871, during the Franco-Prussian War, German troops were advancing on the town of Laval, near the border of Mayenne and Brittany. That evening at Pontmain, a country village in the same diocese, four children, in the presence of other people, claimed to see our Lady: they were Eugène and Joseph Barbadette, Jeanne-Marie Lebossé, and Françoise Richer, aged from ten to twelve. The vision of a "tall, beautiful lady" appeared in the sky, and stars had a part in its details. While the people, who had gathered with their priest, were singing the Magnificat, the children read in the heavens the words, "My children, pray!" Then "God will soon answer your prayers." Then "My Son is moved with pity." A crimson crucifix appeared in the Lady's hands, she smiled, and slowly ceased to be seen. With comings and goings, praying and singing, and some other modifications in the apparition, the whole thing lasted from about 6 P.M. till nearly 9.

Three days later the German troops withdrew to the Loire and Sarthe, and on January 28 the war came to an end. The Catholics of France were not slow to connect these events, and after the Bishop of Laval's commission of inquiry had reported favorably, Pontmain was chosen as the site of a national votive church. It was consecrated in 1900, and the shrine was taken charge of by the Oblates of Mary Immaculate, a congregation which Joseph Barbadette eventually joined. Many pilgrims resort to Pontmain, whose sanctuary is extensive but still not over-grown. A feast of our Lady of Pontmain, "of Hope," was allowed in 1877, for which a proper Mass and Office were accorded more recently; the statue was crowned in 1934. There is a township and church of Notre-Dame-de-Pontmain in Labelle county, province of Quebec. *Cf.*, Revelations and Communications; Visions.

PORT, NOTRE-DAME DU. The meaning of Port in this name is uncertain. It designates a shrine in the crypt, "the Underground," of the church of the same name at Clermont-Ferrand in France; as at Chartres, the crypt contains a well (*cf.*, Underground, Our Lady), and the venerated image is somewhat similar in design. The present statue is an eighteenth-century copy of one that disappeared at the Revolution. The age of the original is uncertain, but it was said to be a rough amateurish work; the present one, whose face and hands have been painted black, was crowned in 1875. The oldest shrine in Auvergne is our Lady of

Orcival, but this other was brought into prominence by what was regarded as a miraculous end to a long drought in 1614, and it is still a place of pilgrimage.

PORTAÏTISSA (Gr., "door-keeper"). See IVIRON, OUR LADY OF.

PORTICU, OUR LADY IN. A feast of this name is kept at her church in Rome, and also in the Welsh dioceses of Cardiff and Menevia, on July 17. James Stewart, the "Old Pretender" (*de jure* King James III and VIII), established perpetual intercession for the reconciliation of England with the Holy See in this church, and the prayers are still said. His second son, Cardinal Henry of York, received the cardinalatial title of this church, as did Cardinal Aidan Gasquet in 1924. See also ROMAN CHURCHES.

PORTIUNCULA. The cradle of the great Franciscan order of Friars Minor was a tiny chapel dedicated in honor of St. Mary of the Angels (*q.v.*), standing on a little piece (*porziuncola*) of ground near Assisi; it is now enclosed within the basilica that is similarly dedicated. It gave its name to the Portiuncula indulgence; for the "Rosary Portiuncula" indulgence, see ROSARY, FEAST OF THE.

PORTUGAL, SHRINES OF. When he had established the independence of his country, against both Léon and the Moors, King Alfonso Henriques (d. 1185) put Portugal under the protection of the Blessed Virgin. He founded the great Cistercian monas-tery of St. Mary at Alcobaça and built a sanctuary for her to commemorate his triumphs. A like devotion to our Lady has always characterized the Portuguese, and from them it passed to their territories in South America. Nevertheless, before about 1940, most Catholics outside Portugal would have been hard put to it to name a Marian shrine in that country: now all the Christian world has heard of Fatima (*q.v.*). Other Portuguese shrines are our Lady of Arrabida; O.L. in Exile, Lisbon; O.L. of Light, Pedragao; O.L. of Martyrs (*q.v.*), Lisbon; O.L. of Mercy, Santarem; O.L. of Nazareth, Pederneira; O.L. of Sameira; O.L. of the Valley, Lisbon.

PRAISERS OF OUR LADY. Groups of people in medieval Italy who met together to sing the praises (*laude*) of Mary, who accordingly were known in Italian as *laudesi*. The seven young men, the Seven Holy Founders, who joined together to found the Servite Order near Florence in 1233, were members of a brotherhood of *laudesi* in Florence. *Cf.,* Benediction.

PRAISES OF OUR LADY. Another name for the festival of Akathistos Saturday in the Byzantine rite (see AKATHISTOS HYMN); and a feast of our Lady in the Syrian and Maronite rites. *Cf.,* Synaxis.

PRAYER to Mary. Invocation of the saints is the corollary of their power of intercession (*q.v.*). After affirming that power, the Council of Trent went on to say that "it is a good and useful thing suppliantly to invoke [the saints], and to ask them for their prayers, help and assistance, in order to obtain benefits from God. . . ." The earliest extant evidence for the practice of invoking the angels and saints is contemporary with, generally the same as, that for belief in their intercessory power, from the early third century. Direct invocation of our Lady was a later development, but how much later is uncertain: it was not improbably practiced among the faithful for some time before surviving records certainly refer to it, e.g., St. Ephraem (d. c. 373).

"All prayer is directed to God, who alone can give us what we ask. But, that they may intercede for us with Him, we pray also to the blessed in Heaven, especially the Blessed Virgin, and even to the souls in Purgatory" (Gasparri's Catechism). It follows, as the Catechism of the Council of Trent points out, that "We use two forms of prayer, differing in the manner of address: for to God we properly say, 'Have mercy on us, hear us'; to the saints, 'Pray for us.' . . . Everyone must take the greatest care not to attribute that which belongs to God to anyone else." When a prayer to our Lady asks her to grant this or that actual gift, and uses similar expressions, it is understood that she is being asked to obtain it by her intercession with God.

Invocation of the Blessed Virgin Mary of course does not take the place of prayer to God; prayer addressed to Mary is in fact prayer *to* God *through* her. In the Roman liturgy the Church sometimes directly asks her and other saints for their prayers, and this is much more marked in Eastern rites. But there is, and there can be, no question of "putting the Blessed Virgin between man and God": in a famous passage of his *Apologia,* Cardinal Newman declares his own long experience: "The Catholic Church allows no image of any sort, material or immaterial, no dogmatic symbol, no rite, no sacrament, no saint, not even the Blessed Virgin herself, to come between the soul and its Creator."

Petition by way of invocation is not the only form of prayer to Mary. The Mother of God is "higher in honor than the cherubim and incomparably more glorious than the seraphim," and prayer of honor and reverence is offered to her accordingly. When they are given set forms, these praises display a great variety, and many of them are used congregationally as well as in private prayer; often they are hymns or anthems; there are forms of prayer ("devotions") having reference to our Lady's prerogatives or to the events of her life; and there are all the Marian propers (*q.v.*) of the public liturgy. In the West these last are mainly scriptural adaptations; in the East they include many remarkable ecclesiastical compositions, such as the Magnifical Hymn (*q.v.*), quoted from above. See also DEVOTION TO MARY; DEVOTIONS, MARIAN; LITURGY, OUR LADY IN THE; VENERATION.

PREFACE OF OUR LADY. At certain seasons and occasions the preface of the Mass has a special pertinent text. There is such a proper preface for use on feasts and in other Masses of the Blessed Virgin, a reference to the particular feast or occasion being inserted as required. It runs as follows:

"Right indeed it is and fitting, proper and for our welfare, that we should always and everywhere give thanks to thee, holy Lord, almighty Father, eternal God, and that we should together praise, bless and extol thee on this festival of the . . . of blessed Mary, ever-virgin. She it was who by the overshadowing of the Holy Spirit conceived thine only-begotten Son and, without losing the glory of her maidenhood, brought forth our Lord Jesus Christ to be the light of the world for ever. It is through him that thy majesty is praised by Angels, worshipped by Dominations, feared by Powers; through him that the heavens and the celestial Virtues join with the blessed Seraphim in one glad hymn of praise. We pray thee let our voices blend with theirs, as we humbly praise thee, singing: Holy, holy, holy. . . ."

There are a few prefaces of our Lady of local or restricted use; e.g., the Carmelites have one for our Lady of Mount Carmel.

PREROGATIVES, OUR LADY'S.

"Prerogatives" is the technical term used by theologians to express those fundamental endowments of our Lady that distinguish her from all other human beings. Her first and principal prerogative is that she is Mother of God (*q.v.*), and this is the source of all the others, which can be divided into negative and positive. Her negative prerogatives are that she was un-

touched by original sin (her Immaculate Conception, *q.v.*); she was untouched by actual sin (her sinlessness, *q.v.*); though a mother, her sexual integrity was unimpaired (her virginity, *q.v.*); she was exempt from the corruption of the grave and the delay of her bodily resurrection (her Assumption, *q.v.*). Her positive prerogatives are her secondary mediatorship (see MEDIATION) and her right to veneration (*q.v.*) by the Church and its members.

PRESENTATION OF OUR LADY, Feast of the.

This feast, on November 21, is one of the five universal feasts (*q.v.*) of Mary, but it made a late appearance in the West. It was considerably earlier in the East, where it bears the title of the Entrance of the Mother of God into the Temple. Our Lady's presentation there and its circumstances are narrated in the apocryphal *Protevangelium of James* (*q.v.*). But the real origin of the feast was probably the dedication of a church of the Mother of God, New St. Mary's, at Jerusalem in 543. In the West the feast is first heard of in England, at Canterbury and Winchester, in the eleventh century. Later it went out of use in those places and won only gradual acceptance elsewhere, not being finally admitted to the general Roman calendar until 1585. The proper of the Mass is the common of our Lady, "Salve," with a special collect asking that, as Mary, dwelling-place of the Holy Spirit, was presented in the Temple, so may the faithful through her intercession be found worthy to be presented in the temple of God's glory.—In Eastern liturgy the story of the presentation in the Temple is understood as an illustration of the fact that, throughout her life, Mary was totally dedicated to Christ and that this dedication was rooted in a contemplative faith. Hence the feast is regarded as of special relevance to monastic life.—Confusion is sometimes caused by the fact that in the East, and in the past sometimes in the West, the name Presentation, referring to the Child Jesus, is given to the feast that the Roman calendar calls the Purification of our Lady.

PRIESTHOOD, MARY'S. "The whole race of Christians, rightly called by the chief of the Apostles 'a chosen race, a kingly priesthood,' must offer sacrifice for sins, both for themselves and for the whole of human kind" (Pope Pius XI, *Miserentissimus Redemptor,* 1928). This analogous sharing in Christ's priesthood is given to every Christian in the sacrament of baptism, and more fully in confirmation; and every member of the Church offers a true sacrifice, but only through a priest properly so called, who has received the "character" and power of holy orders; and who, because he represents Jesus Christ, the head, offers the Holy Sacrifice in the name of the people. The more the faithful Christian is identified with the will of Him who is both High Priest and Victim, the more he shares by this spiritual priesthood of holiness in the common analogous priesthood. This our Lady does in a far higher degree than anybody else; and indeed, some theologians maintain that she shares in

Christ's priesthood in a way special to herself. St. Pius X wrote in *Ad diem illum:* "Not only because she consented to become the mother of the only Son of God so as to make the sacrifice for the salvation of men possible, but also in the fact that she accepted the mission of protecting and nourishing the Lamb of sacrifice, and when the time came led Him to the altar of immolation—in this also we must find Mary's glory. Mary's community of life and suffering with her Son was never broken off . . ." But just as the lay faithful are not called priests, although they share in Christ's priesthood, so it is better not to refer to Mary as a priest.

In recent times Mary's priesthood has been discussed with renewed vigor, partly under the influence of devotional enthusiasms and the spirituality of "victim souls." There have, however, been exaggerations and misunderstandings, and ecclesiastical authority has had to step in. In 1927, Cardinal Merry del Val in the name of the Holy Office wrote to an Italian bishop, informing him that devotion to the "Virgin Priestess" is not approved because of the grave mistakes to which it can give rise; an image of Mary apparently garbed in priestly vestments had already been prohibited in 1916. Father Garrigou-Lagrange writes in *Mother of the Saviour* (Dublin edn., pp. 223-224): "Though Mary may be termed co-redemptrix in the sense we have explained, there can be no question of calling her a priest in the strict sense of the word since she has not received the priestly character and cannot offer holy Mass nor give sacramental absolution. But . . . her divine maternity is a greater dignity than the priesthood of the ordained priest in the sense that it is more to give our Saviour His human nature than to make His body present in the Blessed Eucharist. . . . We must affirm, too, as has recently a careful theologian who has devoted years to the study of these questions (E. Dublanchy, s.m., in *Dict. de Théol. cath.*, art. Marie) that 'it is a certain theological conclusion that Mary co-operated in some way in the principal act of Jesus' priesthood, by giving, as the divine plan required, her consent to the sacrifice of the Cross as it was accomplished by the Saviour.' . . . But even if Mary cannot, for the reasons given, be spoken of as a priest in the strict sense of the term, it remains true, as M. Olier has said, that she received the fullness of the *spirit* of the priesthood, which is the spirit of Christ the Redeemer." It would appear that possible further developments of the subject of Mary's priesthood depend in the first place on a deeper study of the nature of Christian priesthood in general. *Cf.,* Redemption, Mary and the.

PRIMA-PRIMARIA. See SODALITY OF THE BLESSED VIRGIN.

PROCESSIONS. The fundamental reason for a procession in Christian worship is the necessity for getting a number of persons, few or many, from one place to another with decency and good order. Such, for example, is the procession of clergy and ministers from sacristy to altar before solemn Mass in the Roman rite; or the pro-cession to the altar with the bread and wine at the "great entrance" of the Byzantine rite. Then arose the custom of processions, singing the Litany of the Saints, through the streets or fields, in a spirit of penitence to avert calamities. Later still there arose purely devotional processions, such as those of our Lady during May or at other times. In these it is usual to carry a statue or picture, or at least a banner, of Mary, and appropriate hymns are sung. Such a procession is simply a ceremonious action in honor of the Mother of God. The Roman Ritual reminds those taking part in a procession that they should carry themselves with dignity, modesty, and recollection, without laughter, chattering, or looking about (this does not mean that they should assume a miserable expression). The only liturgical procession associated with our Lady is that on the feast of the Purification; but this is always observed on February 2, even if the Mass is of Sunday and not of the Purification. *Cf.,* Candlemas; Salve Procession.

PROMPT SUCCOR, OUR LADY OF, New Orleans. The statue of our Lady of Prompt Succor or Help, patroness of Louisiana, was brought to New Orleans in 1810 by Mother Saint-Michel Gensoul, an Ursuline nun and victim of the French Revolution. The statue, housed in a chapel in the grounds of the Ursuline convent on State Street, is much resorted to by the faithful. It is a dignified, very French image, the Mother standing erect, supporting the Child in her left arm; the figures were crowned in 1894. Not only that: a special feast of our Lady of Prompt Succor was approved for the archdiocese of New Orleans by Pope Pius IX in 1851; it is observed on January 15. On the day on which in 1815 the Americans beat off the British troops from New Orleans, Mother Saint-Michel inaugurated a solemn thanksgiving, and it is still observed. A confraternity was established at the convent to spread devotion to Mary under this invocation, which originated with Mother Saint-Michel, who asked our Lady for a quick and favorable reply to her letter to Pope Pius VII, asking permission to go to America. She received it.

PROPER (Lat. *proprium,* one's own). The proper of the Mass consists of those parts which are variable according to the day or feast: viz., the introit, collects, epistle, gradual, gospel, offertory-verse, secret prayer, communion-verse, after-communion prayers, with sometimes the preface, and occasionally a sequence added. In Masses of our Lady (*q.v.*) all or some of these parts make reference to her and to the mystery that is being commemorated. But not every one of Mary's numerous titles, invocations, and names has a special feast day and specifically proper office: for example, our Lady *della Salute* at Venice is kept on the Presentation, our Lady of Rocamadour in France on the Assumption, but our Lady of Genazzano (Good Counsel) has a special feast and proper Mass on April 26, and so on. In English- and German-speaking lands in particular special minor feasts of Mary

are rare: they are observed on her greater festivals.

PROPHECY, OUR LADY IN. See BIBLE.

PROSE. See SEQUENCE.

PROTECTING VEIL OF OUR LADY, Feast of the. The Russians, Ukrainians, and other Slavs of the Byzantine rite observe this feast on October 1. Its origin is this: one Andrew was at Matins in the church of Blakhernae (*q.v.*) at Constantinople, at a time when the city was being ravaged by an epidemic, toward the end of the tenth century. As he prayed, he saw a vision of the Mother of God, with St. John the Baptist and St. John Chrysostom: she appeared above the sanctuary, taking her veil from her head and spreading it out as if to protect her children. It is said that from that moment the plague ceased, and the commemoration was inaugurated in recognition of our Lady's care. In 1952 the Orthodox Church of Greece adopted this feast for October 28, the day of the Greek national festival. The Protecting Veil has given rise to a special type of icon (*Pokrov*) representing the above thought, and a similar idea is to be found in Western iconography. Here perhaps it arose from the antiphon *Sub tuum praesidium* (*q.v.*); but the Italian painter from Siena, Duccio di Buoninsegna (1260?-1339?) who used the theme, was completely under Byzantine influence. The same idea was extended to representations of St. Barbara, St. Ursula, and other saints, and in modern times it has been adopted by the Apostleship of the Sea. Both icon and feast are sometimes called the Patronage or Protection of the Mother of God, a name also given to a commemoration of our Lady's protection celebrated in Spain and elsewhere (see PATRONAGE, FEAST OF THE). The Byzantine observance has of course a certain similarity to the "Scapular feast" in the West. *Cf.*, Mercy, Our Lady of.

PROTESTANTS AND THE VIRGIN MARY. It is well known that those people who withdrew from the communion of the Catholic Church to form new religious bodies at and after the Protestant Reformation repudiated, among many other things, important Catholic beliefs and most or all Catholic practice in relation to the Blessed Virgin. Her power of intercession, for example, was denied and prayer to her abandoned, pilgrimages were condemned as superstitious, and her shrines destroyed. Neither the theological and historical reasons advanced by Protestants in support of their views, nor the excesses to which those views often gave rise, need be gone into here. But it must be emphasized that these things, so shocking in the eyes of Catholics, were not prompted by any contempt for Mary inherent in Protestantism, which recognized her as the maiden whom God's angel had declared to be full of grace, the virgin who had given birth to Jesus Christ, the Redeemer of mankind; she was therefore worthy of all love and respect. To such a Protestant and Puritan as John Milton she was still "the Virgin blest." On the other hand, the general tendencies of Protestantism and the effects of religious controversy were such that, in practice, the attitude of most Protestants to Mary for long appeared to be one of neglect and indifference, if not worse.

Much of this has changed with the passage of time. Today there can be found at one extreme of Protestantism a whittling away of the significance of Mary that would have shocked some early reformers; at the other extreme there is belief and practice in her regard hardly, if at all, distinguishable from those of the Catholic Church. If we look at something in between, at what may be called "Prayer-Book Anglicanism" (Protestant Episcopalian), it is found that our Lady is far from ignored. In the calendar of the Book of Common Prayer are marked the feasts of the Purification, the Annunciation, the Visitation, her Nativity, and her Conception (not *Immaculate* Conception, of course); and the Magnificat (*q.v.*) is sung every day at Evensong. In *Hymns Ancient and Modern* are found such things as "Shall we not love thee, Mother dear" and a translation of the Matins hymn from the common office B.V.M. in the Roman Breviary. The first public statue of our Lady in England after the Reformation was put above the door of the university church of St. Mary at Oxford, in 1637, by an Anglican clergyman. The good man got into trouble—but the statue is still there; and now there are many others in Anglican churches throughout Great Britain, and in America and elsewhere. What is perhaps the most famous line about our Lady in English literature was written by a thorough-going Protestant, William Wordsworth: "Our tainted nature's solitary boast."

The Oxford Movement that began in 1833, and gave Episcopalians such hymns as John Keble's "Ave Maria! Blessed Maid!" began a "return to Mary" whose influence was far-reaching and whose impetus is not spent. In America Henry Adams (though he wrote some curious things about her) impressed on his fellow-Protestants that "force for force, the Virgin was as intelligible as the dynamo and as powerful." In our own day Lutherans such as the theologian Hans Asmussen write books on Mary, the Mother of God; a Congregational minister of very high standing, Dr. Nathaniel Micklem, can suspect "a serious failure in [Protestant] thought and imagination" about our Lady; a French Calvinist, Pastor Max Thurian, can write in the same sense; fifty years ago a prominent Welsh minister, Emrys ap Iwan, was preaching the dignity of Mary: by pondering the evidence of the Bible, many Protestants see her in a clearer light. Plenty of the old prejudice and misunderstanding still remain, and doubtless will long remain: but in general the atmosphere is far more sympathetic than it was. There can be no doubt that Protestants are often distressed and "put off" by the way in which Catholic teaching about and veneration for Mary are sometimes expressed, ways which seem to them exaggerated and uncontrolled: and in looking at these accidentals, they fail to see the solid content clearly. Mary, the Maiden-Mother, appeals to the heart of mankind; and the hearts of Protestants, who love her Son so dearly and faithfully, are not closed to that appeal.

PROTEVANGELIUM OF JAMES, or Gospel of the Infancy. An apocryphal writing (*q.v.*) which in its present form perhaps belongs to the third century, but its basis goes back to the second. Many of its elements are worthless, even puerile and fantastic, but it is valuable as a witness to the veneration for the Mother of Jesus in those early times. The first part is devoted to her life until the Annunciation. It is this work which first professes to tell us about Mary's parents (*q.v.*) and the circumstances of her birth, her presentation and residence in the Temple, and the miraculous choice of Joseph (*q.v.*) as her husband. Her virginity and bodily integrity after the birth of Jesus are strongly emphasized. The name of St. James the Less was attached to this pseudo-gospel.—The term *protevangelium* is applied to an important passage of the canonical scriptures, viz., Gen. 3:15: *cf.,* Bible, Mary in the.

PSALTER, OUR LADY'S. This name is sometimes given to the rosary (*q.v.*) because in its full form it has 150 Hail Marys, which corresponds to the Psalter with its 150 psalms. Before the rosary received its present form there was a custom of reciting 50, 100, or 150 *Aves,* often accompanied by a deep bow or prostration at each one. There was a story told in the twelfth century of a nun in England, Eulalia of Shaftesbury, who used to say a "psalter" of 150 Hail Marys every day, until our Lady appeared to her and told her to say only 50—and to say them more slowly. There were also series of 150 verses, addressed to Mary and each beginning *Ave,* each of which had some reference to the corresponding psalm, the first verse to Psalm 1, and so on. In modern times these collections of verses have been given the name "Ave-Psalm-Psalters." The holy woman Bl. Mary of Oignies (d. 1213) emphasized this association of Marian devotion with the Psalter by reading the whole of the latter every day and saying the Hail Mary once after each psalm.—The custom of saying Hail Marys on beads was preceded by saying the Lord's Prayer in the same way, so that the makers of rosaries were called "paternosterers" in English and other languages; in London they worked in Paternoster Row, near to Ave Maria Lane, Creed Lane, and Amen Corner, a section ravaged by bombs in World War II.

PSEUDO-MATTHEW, GOSPEL OF. An apocryphal writing (*q.v.*) of the fifth century or later, pretending to be a translation into Latin by St. Jerome of a Hebrew text by St. Matthew. It contains much of the matter of the *Protevangelium of James* (*q.v.*) but differs in details, generally in the direction of the more marvellous. It contains an early reference to the idea that Mary had made a formal vow of virginity. The story of the ox and the ass worshiping at the manger in Bethlehem derives from this writing; but its main original part is the amplification of and miraculous embroideries on the flight into Egypt. An incident of a palm-tree bending over at the word of the Child Jesus to enable His Mother to pick some dates is the ultimate source of the curious old English "Cherry-Tree Carol."

PUIG, OUR LADY OF. This shrine of our Lady of Ransom near Valencia, in Spain, is associated with the early days of the Mercedarian Order, about whose origins there is some uncertainty. The place attained celebrity through the great victory of the Christians over the Moors in 1238, and some very remarkable wonders are related about the finding of our Lady's image and the building of the sanctuary. King James I of Aragon, "el Conquistador," proclaimed our Lady of Puig patroness of the old kingdom of Valencia. There is a different shrine of the same name at Barbastro, in Aragon; both have proper feasts.

PURIFICATION OF OUR LADY, Feast of the. In the East this is treated as a feast of our Lord, His meeting with Simeon or Presentation in the Temple. In the West it is included among the feasts (*q.v.*) of Mary, though the text of its Mass and Office are more concerned with her Son: indeed, in the proper of the Mass our Lady is mentioned only in the gospel passage. Already at the end of the fourth century the fortieth day after the celebration of Christ's birth was observed with special solemnity in Jerusalem, and from there no doubt it spread throughout the Eastern Church. In due course the festival spread to the West, being one of those that Pope St. Sergius I ordered to be solemnized in Rome, *c.* 700. On the same day, February 2, a procession with candles is made before Mass (see CANDLEMAS).

The law of God given by Moses to the Jews ordained that, forty days after the birth of a boy (eighty after a girl), the mother should present herself at the Temple and make an offering, whereupon she would be cleansed from legal uncleanness. The Blessed Virgin Mary clearly did not come within the intent of this law: but she chose to observe it, both out of respect for God's law and because her neighbors would expect it of her. And, being poor, she made the offering appointed for the poor (Lev. 12:8; Luke 2:24). Her visit to the Temple for this purpose is also commemorated in the Church in the Blessing of a Woman after Childbirth (commonly called "churching"). No idea of purification of any kind is contained in this Christian rite, for the honorable begetting and bearing of a child incurs no sort of taint. But, as indicated above, this is rather a feast wherein the inseparable association of Mary with Jesus is emphasized; and its real object is made clear in the antiphon to the Magnificat at second Vespers: "This day the blessed Virgin Mary presented the child Jesus in the Temple, and Simeon, filled with the Holy Spirit, received Him into his arms, and blessed God for ever."

PURITY OF OUR LADY, Feast of the. This feast is kept, on October 16 and other dates, by the hermit-friars of St. Augustine, the Theatine clerks regular, throughout Portugal, and elsewhere. The collect of the Mass prays that we who celebrate Mary's unsullied maidenhood may be pure in mind and body through her intercession.

Q

QUEEN, MARY AS. "Queen" and its equivalents (*despoina, basilissa, domina, regina*) is an epithet applied to the Blessed Virgin from ancient times, beginning at least with the Syrian St. Ephraem in the fourth century; other early writers who use it are St. Gregory Nazianzen, the poet Prudentius, St. Jerome, St. Peter Chrysologus, St. Andrew of Crete, and St. John Damascene. Later it appeared in the liturgies of both East and West, becoming familiar to the Christians of the Latin rite especially through the anthems *Ave Regina caelorum, Salve Regina,* and *Regina caeli* (*qq.v.*). In the Litany of Loreto, Mary is addressed by no less than twelve queen-titles, namely: Queen of Angels (*q.v.*), of Patriarchs, of Prophets (these two look back to the Old Covenant with Israel, under whose law Mary was brought up as a child), of Apostles (*q.v.*), of Martyrs (*q.v.*), of Confessors (i.e., witnesses to Christ), of Virgins, of All Saints (*q.v.*), Queen conceived free from original sin, Queen taken up into Heaven, Queen of the Holy Rosary, Queen of Peace (*q.v.*). In the Marian year of 1954 Pope Pius XII instituted a new feast, of Mary the Queen, to be observed throughout the Western Church on May 31.

In the encyclical letter *Ad caeli Reginam,* inaugurating this feast, Pope Pius expounds the twofold basis of Mary's queenship: her divine motherhood and her close association with Christ in the work of the Redemption (*q.v.*). He refers to Gabriel's words about Mary's Son, "of His kingdom there shall be no end," and Elizabeth's greeting to "the mother of my Lord," and observes that from early times writers regarded these as likewise heralding her own queenship. And he quotes St. John Damascene: "She indeed became mistress of all creation when she became mother of the Creator." The Pope goes on to say that as Christ, the New Adam, is king not simply because He is the Son of God, but also because He is our Savior, so, by a sort of analogy, the Blessed Virgin is queen, not only as Mother of God, but also as the New Eve who was associated with the New Adam. "It is true that, in the full, proper and absolute sense, the God-man Jesus Christ alone is king [sovereign lord]. Nevertheless, as mother of Christ our God and associate in the divine Savior's work in His conflict with the Enemy, and in His triumph over all adversaries, Mary shares in the kingly dignity, though in a limited and analagous way." *Cf.,* Redemption, Mary and the.

QUEEN OF ALL SAINTS. A Mass, among those in the Missal for certain places only, joins Mary under this invocation with her as Mother of Fair Love (*q.v.*). The first place to have

234

had a separate feast of our Lady, Queen of All Saints, seems to have been Ancona in Italy, where there is a much-revered miraculous image of this name, crowned in 1814.

QUEEN OF ANGELS. See ANGELS, OUR LADY OF THE.

QUEEN OF APOSTLES. A feast of Mary under this title is observed in Pallottine, Redemptorist, and other churches on the Saturday after Ascension day. It has a proper Mass; the collect refers to the coming of the Holy Spirit upon our Lady and the apostles, and asks Almighty God that, under Mary's protection, "we may be enabled faithfully to serve thy majesty, and by word and example to spread abroad the glory of thy name." *Cf.,* Cenacle, Our Lady of the.

QUEEN OF MARTYRS. See MARTYRS, OUR LADY OF THE.

QUEEN OF PEACE. A feast of our Lady, Queen of Peace, is celebrated on July 9 and other dates by the Congregation of the Sacred Hearts of Jesus and Mary (Picpus Fathers) and others. It was first granted in 1658, with reference to a wonderworking statue then in the Capuchin church in Paris, later in that of the Sacred Heart sisters in the Rue Picpus. The years 1914-18 gave a renewed and very actual significance to the invocation Queen of Peace, and after World War I it was added to the Litany of Loreto. The Lady chapel of the great cathedral being built at Liverpool in England is to be a thank-offering to our Lady, Queen of Peace. The title is not uncommon in church dedications, and there is a pilgrimage shrine of Notre-Dame de la Paix at Johnville, P.Q.—A celebrated shrine of our Lady of Peace is that at Toledo in Spain. The image was given this name because a truce was concluded with the Moors after it was set up in the cathedral in 1085. The local feast, on January 24, is also associated with a famous vision of our Lady said to have been accorded to St. Ildephonsus (d. 667), who was archbishop of Toledo.

QUEM TERRA, PONTUS, SIDERA. The hymn appointed for Matins in the Common and Little Offices (*qq.v.*) of our Lady; its second part, beginning *O gloriosa virginum,* is used at Lauds in the same offices. It is a revision of a medieval office-hymn, *Quem terra, pontus, aethera,* and is ascribed to St. Venantius Fortunatus, but seemingly with little authority. There are many translations into English, of which Father Caswall's is one of the best known, beginning "The Lord whom earth and air and sea." The equally well-known version of J. M. Neale, "The God whom earth and sea and sky," is given in the *Westminster Hymnal,* no. 103.

QUINCHE, OUR LADY OF. Unlike many Latin American images of Mary, the cedar-wood statue of our Lady of Quinche, in Ecuador, is of an informal type, and its devotees refer to it informally as *La Pequeñita,* "the Little One." It is said to have been carved, by a Spaniard, so long ago as 1586. The Quinche shrine is very remotely situated on the edge of the Andes, and is a distinctively Indian sanctuary; its statue is sometimes taken on visits to other places.

QUITO, OUR LADY OF. This image in the capital of Ecuador is said to date from the first Spanish settlement in 1534; it has certainly been venerated there for a long time, and is popularly called our Lady of the Earthquake. It represents the Sorrowful Mother, and in the early years of the twentieth century devotion to Mary under the title of Quito was introduced into England by the Servite friars in London. Pope St. Pius X accorded them an indulgence for those who should pray before her picture, and the devotion was greatly promoted in England by the Sisters of the Holy Child Jesus, Mother Cornelia Connelly's congregation. The original image at Quito was crowned in 1918. Feast: April 28.

R

RAMA, OUR LADY OF. Rama has had perhaps the most unhappy history of any shrine in Yugoslavia. It was first the home of our Lady of Sinj (*q.v.*), and during this time, in 1557, six of the Franciscan custodians were murdered by the Turks. Their friary was burnt down, but later a new church was built, in which was enshrined an image, which might well be called Queen of Martyrs. For in 1942 the sanctuary was destroyed by the partisans of Joseph Broz (Tito), and the Franciscans all massacred, with the exception of one old man.

RAMABANTA. Since 1945 the Church has found many new adherents among the people of Basutoland, South Africa, and in 1949 a shrine of our Lady of Fatima was inaugurated at Ramabanta. Under the care of the Oblates of Mary Immaculate it is now the scene of considerable pilgrimages. Here, as elsewhere in Africa, torchlight processions are specially popular, and people come to the shrine from long distances.

RANSOM, Feast of our Lady of (Latin *B.M.V. de Mercede;* Spanish *N.S. de la Merced;* French *N.-D. de la Merci*). This feast originated with the Order of Blessed Mary of Ransom (Mercedarians), founded in the thirteenth century in Spain for the redeeming of captives from among the Moors. It was extended first to all Spain and then, in 1696, to the whole Western Church, to be kept on September 24, having in view the ransoming of the faithful from the bondage of sin and Hell (see the collect at Mass). It is not altogether clear why this feast should have been chosen for this distinction; it is associated with a vision of Mary to St. Peter Nolasco (d. 1258), the actuality of which has been seriously contested. Cardinal Prosper Lambertini defended the authenticity of the vision; but on becoming pope, as Benedict XIV, it was his intention to have suppressed the feast so far as the general calendar was concerned. (It was in fact removed from the Benedictine calendar in 1915.) This historical uncertainty detracts not at all from the dignity of our Lady invoked as "of Ransom" or "of Mercy" (*q.v.*), who is specially venerated in Spain. She is the patroness of Barcelona, where a famous statue of her is the resort of pilgrims, and there is another well-known shrine at Puig (*q.v.*), near Valencia. There is a confraternity, scapular, and novena (*qq.v.*) of our Lady of Ransom.—The invocation of Mary under this title for the return of the English people to Catholic unity has nothing to do with the historical and liturgical aspects of her feast. Our Lady of Pity was an old name for her in England, expressing

237

a cognate idea to "ransom," and she may be regarded as interceding for that country's release from the bonds of religious error.

RECONCILIATION, OUR LADY OF. See LA SALETTE.

REDEMPTION, MARY AND THE.
There is only one redeemer of mankind, Jesus Christ; He alone, the Son of God, could and did pay the price of human salvation, He alone was capable of the infinite love that was necessary to wipe out the world's sin (cf., I Tim. 2:5; Acts 4:12). At the same time, man was raised by the Redemption from his nothingness and enabled himself to co-operate, through grace, in that very work (cf., John 15:15). Reborn in the waters of baptism, men can earn grace whereby they may work out their own salvation in fear and trembling (Phil. 2:12), and by prayer and good works on their behalf contribute toward the salvation of others. Every Christian may be a fellow-worker with Christ, sharing in His work for His Body, the Church, and in this sense can co-operate with Him in His redemptive work. The truth that creatures share in the supreme work of Christ is seen at its clearest and highest in the Blessed Virgin Mary.

As one of the redeemed, a member of Christ's mystical body, Mary's part in this matter is in the first place like theirs: a bringing about of the application of the fruits of His redemptive act. But Mary co-operates in a far deeper, closer, more effective sense than anyone else can do, be-cause of her intimate union with Jesus and His work for mankind. For she is Mother of the Redeemer, herself by anticipation the first-fruits of the Redemption, not cleansed but uniquely preserved from original sin. She it was, it has been observed, "who prepared, fashioned, nourished and bore the Redeemer, the Priest, the Victim, *the Altar* of the one infinite sacrifice. Hence all her ministrations as mother, from the first instant of the Incarnation, were *sacrificial* and *redemptive*" (Father L. E. Bellanti, s.J.). So Christ-like is she, so attuned to God's will, so full of grace, that no limit can be put to the grace she wins for others; in the sense that the redeemed are able to merit for others besides themselves, Mary's merits plead to God for every grace for every other human being—her co-operation in her Son's redemptive work is universal, it stands alone in degree and extent.

The payment of the price of our salvation through the merits and satisfactions of Christ, culminating in the sacrifice of Calvary, by which a boundless treasury of forgiveness and grace was set up, to which treasury nothing was to be added in future ages, is called by theologians the objective Redemption; and they all agree that Mary co-operated remotely in the objective Redemption by being the mother of Christ. The application of the fruits of the objective Redemption is called the subjective Redemption, and in this Mary co-operates through her mediation (*q.v.*). But the great majority of theologians also teach that Mary shared proximately or immediately in the objective Redemption with, through, and subordinately to Christ, in paying the once-for-all price of redemption on Calvary itself: proximately, because her mother's consent was given while the sacrifice of Calvary was being actually accomplished.

Mary's manifold sufferings were expiatory: not of her own sins, for she was sinless, but by the offering of those sufferings to God in union with the sufferings of Christ for the sins of all the world. Pope St. Pius X declared: "Because of this fellowship of suffering and purpose between Mary and Christ [on Calvary], she 'merited most worthily to become the restorer [reparatrix] of a lost world,' and therefore the almoner of all the gifts that Jesus earned for us by His blood-shedding and death" (Ad diem illum). And Benedict XV: "The Blessed Virgin suffered with her suffering Son, and nearly died with Him when He died; she gave up her mother's rights in her Son for man's salvation and, so far as she was able to do so, she immolated that Son to conciliate divine justice: so that she may rightly be said to have redeemed the human race with Christ" (Inter sodalicia, 1918). In the encyclical letter Miserentissimus Redemptor Pius XI refers to Mary as actually offering her Son on Calvary, and the same idea is repeated by Pius XII in Mystici Corporis. But "although Mary associated herself with the offering of her Son, this affective oblation formed no part of that great liturgical offering on Calvary in which Christ alone was priest and victim. Thus, it is only Christ who paid by way of sacrifice the actual price of our redemption. It is only Christ who merited our justification in the strict sense of the term (de condigno). Mary, to quote Benedict XV, immolated her Son 'in so far as it was hers to do' (see above). In the words of Pius X, Mary 'merits for us congruously (de congruo) . . . what Christ merited for us condignly.'" (Father Paul F. Palmer, s.j., Mary in the Documents of the Church, p. 97.)

Theologians therefore regard it as justifiable to speak of our Lady as "co-redemptress," a term that has come into increasing use of late years. Father E. Dublanchy writes: "Since the word 'co-redemptress' signifies of itself simple co-operation in the work of the redemption, and since it has received in the theological usage of centuries the very precise meaning of secondary and dependent co-operation . . . there can be no serious objection to its use, on condition that it be accompanied by some expression indicating that Mary's role in this co-operation is secondary and dependent" (Dict. de Théol. cath., art. Marie). Pope Pius XI used the term of her in a public address in 1934, and the Holy Office indulgenced a prayer in 1914 in which Mary is addressed as co-redemptress of the human race. Nevertheless, there are some who hold that the popular use of this term, unexceptionable though it be in its theological sense, is undesirable, on the ground that it could be misunderstood by those not properly informed. For it does not in itself convey (at any rate in English:

cf., *Shorter Oxford Dictionary*, s.v. Co-) that Mary's preeminent and unique association with Jesus in the redemption of mankind is itself redemptive only by analogy, since the Redemption was completely the work of Christ and of no one else. But the question of an expedient popular terminology and the full extent and nature of our Lady's unquestionably unique human part in the Redemption are different matters; both are still much discussed. *Cf.*, Mediation, Mary's; New Eve; Priesthood, Mary's.

REFUGE OF SINNERS. A feast of our Lady under this title, on August 13 and other dates, is widely spread. There is a shrine of Mary, Refuge of Sinners, at Puebla in Mexico. Its image is a copy of one that Bl. Antony Baldinucci (d. 1717) used to carry on his missionary journeys in Italy. The statue was brought to Mexico by Father John de Guica, s.j., and the devotion spread all over the country. The Puebla feast is on July 4. There is a shrine of the same name at Caleras in Mexico, and another at Lucca in Italy; and after the founding in Paris of the Confraternity of the Immaculate Heart of Mary for the conversion of sinners, a feast of the Immaculate Heart B.V.M. under the title Refuge of Sinners was granted to Paris, and taken up by several other French dioceses.—"Almighty and merciful God," says the collect of the Mass of our Lady, Refuge of Sinners, "who didst appoint the blessed and ever-maiden Mary to be the refuge and help of sinners, grant that under her protection we

may be kept from all guilt and obtain the happiness that waits on thy mercy." *Cf.*, Stone, Our Lady of.

REGINA CAELI. The first words and title of the anthem of our Lady (see ANTIPHONS) said or sung after the Divine Office throughout paschal-time; during the same time it is said instead of the Angelus (*q.v.*), and in the Carmelite rite before the last gospel at Mass instead of *Salve Regina* (*q.v.*). It is also used for other purposes, such as an antiphon to the Magnificat. This anthem is a greeting of joy at the Resurrection, and its simple plainsong melody is of peculiar loveliness. The words are:

Regina caeli, laetare! Alleluia!
Quia quem meruisti portare—Alleluia!
Resurrexit sicut dixit. Alleluia!
Ora pro nobis Deum. Alleluia!

℣. Gaude et laetare, Virgo Maria—Alleluia!
℞. Quia surrexit Dominus vere. Alleluia!

Oremus. Deus qui per resurrectionem Filii tui Domini nostri Jesus Christi mundum laetificare dignatus es: praesta, quaesumus, ut per ejus Genitricem Virginem Mariam perpetuae capiamus gaudia vitae. Per eumdem Christum Dominum nostrum. Amen.

Rejoice, thou Queen of Heaven! Alleluia!
For he whom thou wast found worthy to bear—Alleluia!

Has arisen as he said. Alleluia!
Pray for us to God. Alleluia!

℣. Rejoice and be glad, O Virgin
Mary—Alleluia!
℟. For the Lord hath risen indeed.
Alleluia!

Let us pray. O God, who by the
resurrection of thy Son Jesus Christ
our Lord hast vouchsafed to gladden
the world: grant, we beseech thee,
that through his Mother the Virgin
Mary we may obtain the joys of everlasting life. Through the same Christ
our Lord. Amen.

It was long believed that this was
the oldest of the Marian anthems, for
from the thirteenth century it was
commonly said that it dated from the
days of St. Gregory the Great, in these
circumstances: Rome being devastated
by a pestilence, Gregory ordered a
penitential procession; while it was
passing over the bridge by Sant' An-
gelo, a picture of the Mother of God
being carried, angelic voices were
heard around the image, singing the
first three lines of *Regina caeli*.
Whereupon St. Gregory spontaneously
added the last line. This epidemic
and procession are known to have
taken place, early in the year 590. But
the rest of the story is unheard of
before about 1275, and so far from
being the oldest, *Regina caeli* seems
rather to be the latest of the Marian
antiphons. The earliest known text
of it dates from about 1200, and it
was an adaptation of an existing
Christmas hymn to Mary. Its subsequent popularity and eventual adoption in the Roman Office were due

to the influence of the Franciscan
Friars Minor. The Church's direction
that *Regina caeli* shall be sung or
said standing is one of several reminders that in earlier ages Christians never knelt for prayer (a penitential posture) on Sundays and during the Easter season.

RELICS OF OUR LADY. Nothing
whatever is known about the early
history of those things that purport,
or have purported, to be relics of the
Blessed Virgin. Many of them are first
heard of at the time of the Crusades,
when there was a big transference of
relics of all kinds from the Near East
to western Europe. Moreover, there
is an exceedingly strong intrinsic un-
likelihood that any of the things said
to have been associated with Mary
should have survived from apostolic
times. With regard to the veneration
that is, or has been, accorded to some
of these relics, it must be borne in
mind that the authentication given
them by ecclesiastical authority is not
a guarantee of genuineness. It is rather
a certificate that, at the time it is
given, the certifying authority judges
that the relic concerned is not clearly
spurious, and that he knows no com-
pelling reason why it should not be
venerated.—Much confusion has resulted from the existence of "relics
by association," that is, models or
copies of relics, or things that have
touched relics. Thus, for example, a
piece of fabric that had touched a
supposed relic of our Lady's robe
would come in time to be regarded
as, and called, part of the robe itself.
Nor was this the only kind of oppor-

tunity for mistakes and misunderstandings to arise.

Several churches in East and West claim, or have claimed, relics of Mary's clothing (see GARMENT and GIRDLE, FEASTS OF). The Constantinople girdle was kept in a reliquary which seems to have been identified with our Lady's coffin; it is said that this "coffin" was sent, with the shroud, to the Emperor Marcian and his wife St. Pulcheria by Juvenal, Bishop of Jerusalem, in 452. But the records of these Constantinople relics are very confused, and the relics themselves disappeared at the fall of the city to the Turks in 1453. Part of the alleged girdle is said to be now at the monastery of Vatopedi on Mount Athos. Unspecified Marian relics were enshrined at Evron and Lens in France, and what is regarded as Mary's wedding-ring is to be found in the cathedral of Perugia in Italy. What was believed to be some of her hair was brought to Piazza in Sicily in crusading times and later given to Messina cathedral. Hair relics are, or were, claimed also by several churches in Rome and at a dozen other places in Europe, including the cathedral of Salisbury. Among the relics at the church of St. Amatus at Douay was one of "the Virgin's milk," which is explained herein under BETHLEHEM. The letter said to have been sent by our Lady to the first Christians of Messina in Sicily was probably invented toward the end of the fifteenth century, by a Greek refugee named Constantine Laskaris. The text that he professed to render in Latin appears to have been composed by him-

self; and in any case it was certainly not composed in the first century. A long line of scholars have rejected the authenticity of this "letter," beginning with Cardinal Baronius in 1588. A letter of St. Ignatius of Antioch (d. c. 107) to the Blessed Virgin and her reply, of which the texts are extant, are forgeries, probably of the twelfth century.—It need hardly be pointed out that in view of the belief in Mary's bodily assumption into Heaven it is to be expected that no church would claim to have physical relics of her (except such things as hair). See also LIKENESSES; LORETO, HOLY HOUSE OF; MANGER; SACRED LETTER, OUR LADY OF THE.

RELIGIOUS ORDERS AND CONGREGATIONS and our Lady. It would be difficult to write of religious orders and congregations in relation to the Blessed Virgin without appearing to make invidious comparisons; but attention may not improperly be directed to a few of many special associations and observances, referring first, among the older orders, to the Servites, because of their name, the Servants of Mary. This order was founded by seven young Florentines, members of a confraternity of Praisers (q.v.), who on the feast of the Assumption in 1233 were vouchsafed a vision of Mary; this inspired them to withdraw from the world, to the solitude of Monte Senario (q.v.). Seven years later, we are told, their black habit and distinguishing name were revealed to them in another vision of our Lady. The outstanding Marian devotion of the Servites is to the Sorrowful Mother, in connection with which they have a confraternity, whose badge is the scapular (*q.v.*) of the Seven Sorrows; they have also a special rosary (*q.v.*) of the same name.

Brothers (Friars) of the Order of the Blessed and Ever-Virgin Mary of Mount Carmel designates the two branches of the Carmelites, often known as the Calced or Shod and the Discalced or Barefooted (i.e., sandalled). Mount Carmel in Palestine was the cradle of the order, and its name sufficiently shows its relationship to Mary under that title (*q.v.*). To the Carmelites was granted the privilege of the Brown scapular (*q.v.*). Another order of friars, the Augustinians, is particularly associated with our Lady under the titles "of Good Counsel," with a special scapular (*q.v.*), and "of Consolation," with a confraternity, girdle or cord, and rosary (*qq.v.*). It is thanks to the three branches of the Friars Minor (Franciscans) that devotion to the Joys (*q.v.*) of Mary still flourishes; they also have special associations with our Lady of the Angels (*q.v.*), and there is a feast of Mary, Queen of the Order of Friars Minor, on December 15. The Franciscans were very zealous upholders of the doctrine of the Immaculate Conception (*q.v.*) when it was in dispute. The very close connection between the Order of Preachers (Dominicans) and the rosary (*q.v.*) is well known, and their daily *Salve* procession (*q.v.*) is a characteristic observance. According to the tradition of the Order of our Lady of Ransom (Mercedarians), the name

and establishment of the order were due to visions of the Mother of Mercy granted to St. Peter Nolasco, St. Raymond of Peñafort, and King James of Aragon. The Mercedarians have a confraternity and scapular of our Lady of Ransom (*q.v.*).

Among the monks, Cistercian devotion to our Lady is particularly noticeable, no doubt largely because of the teaching and example of St. Bernard of Clairvaux. Mary is the principal titular of every Cistercian church, with its patronal festival on the Assumption. The white habit worn by these monks is said to be due to a vision experienced by St. Alberic in 1101, when our Lady promised ever to protect the order. Every monastery ("charterhouse") of Carthusian monks has Mary as its principal patron. The Benedictine congregation of St. Mary of Monte Oliveto (*q.v.*) at its foundation in 1319 adopted a white habit in accordance, we are told, with an instruction given by our Lady in vision to Bishop Guy of Arezzo. The same reason is given for the white dress worn by the Canons Regular of Prémontré: Mary appeared to their founder, St. Norbert, in 1120 and indicated this habit to him and the place where his monastery was to be built. It was to another order of canons regular, of the Lateran, that organization and care of associations of Children of Mary (*q.v.*) for girls is due.

The Theatine clerks regular have a confraternity and rosary of Mary Immaculate; and the most famous of all clerks regular, the Society of Jesus, are the originators and directors of the Sodality (q.v.) of the Blessed Virgin. The Servants of the Sick (Camillans) direct the confraternity of our Lady, Health of the Sick, with its own scapular. But of these more recent orders and congregations, many show their special devotion to our Lady by their very names. Thus we have, among others, the Clerks Regular of the Mother of God (founded in 1574), the Augustinians of the Assumption (1845), the Canons Regular of the Immaculate Conception (1866), the Congregation of the Immaculate Heart of Mary (Scheut Fathers; 1863), the Missionary Sons of the Immaculate Heart (Claretians; 1849), the Society of the Immaculate Heart (1842; amalgamated with the Congregation of the Holy Ghost, 1848), the Missionaries of La Salette (1852), the Marian Clerks Regular of the Immaculate Conception (1673; 1909), the Society of Mary (Marists; 1816), the Society of Brothers of Mary (Marianists; 1817), the Little Brothers of Mary (Marist Brothers; 1817), the Company of Mary of Montfort (Montfort Fathers; 1705), the Oblates of Mary Immaculate (1816), the Sons of Mary Immaculate (three congregations), the Brothers of our Lady of Mercy (1839), the Brothers of the Presentation (1802), the Priests of our Lady of Zion (1855).

Among the very numerous congregations of women bearing Mary's name there may be mentioned the nuns of the Annunciation (Annonciade; q.v.), the Canonesses Regular of our Lady (1597), the Sisters of the Assumption (1839), the Little Sisters of the Assumption (1864), the Oblate Sisters of the Assumption (1865), the Cenacle (q.v.) nuns, the Daughters of the Faithful Virgin (1831), the Franciscan Missionaries of Mary (1877), the Sisters of the Immaculate Conception (many congregations), the Sisters of the Immaculate Heart (several congregations), the Sisters of Loreto (founded in Dublin, 1822), the Sisters of Loreto at the Foot of the Cross (founded in the U.S. in 1812), the Society of Marie Auxiliatrice (1854), the Institute of Marie Réparatrice (1854), the Sisters of the Holy Name of Mary (Marist Sisters; 1823), the Missionary Sisters of the Society of Mary (1845), the Daughters of Mary (several congregations), the Institute of the Blessed Virgin Mary (founded by Mary Ward in 1609), the Little Company of Mary (1877), the Sisters of St. Mary (two congregations), the Daughters of Mary Immaculate (1876), the Ladies of Mary (called Daughters of Mary and Joseph in America; 1817), several congregations of Sisters of Notre Dame, the Poor Servants of the Mother of God (1868). There are congregations bearing the name of our Lady of Africa, of the Apostles, of Charity, of Compassion, of Consolation, Help of Christians, of Lourdes, Mother of Mercy, of the Missions, of Peace, of Perpetual Help, of Pity, of the Rosary, of the Sacred Heart, of Victory, of Zion, etc.; and of her Nativity, Presentation, Visitation, etc. Eastern churches and distant lands provide some less familiar names, such as Bannabikira (Daughters of Mary; Central Africa), Maryamat ("The Marys"; Syria), and the Sisters of the Theotokos Pammakaristos (All-blessed God-bearer; Greece).

REMEDIOS, NUESTRA SEÑORA DE LOS. This familiar title is simply a Spanish version of our Lady of Help (q.v.), of whom there are several shrines in Spain, at Valencia, Cordova, Roda, and elsewhere. This popularity was due to the friars of the Order of the Holy Trinity, who had a wonderworking image called N.S. de los Remedios in their house at Madrid. According to them, this image was given by Pope St. Gregory I to St. Augustine of Canterbury when he came to England in 597; at the Reformation it was carried away into Holland, where it came into the possession of a Spanish soldier, who took it home and gave it to the Trinitarians. But no credence can be given to this account. There is a well-known sanctuary of N.S. de los Remedios in Mexico, where in 1576 a church was built on Totoltepec (Montezuma's Hill), near Mexico City, to enshrine her image. It is particularly resorted to by women who pray that their barrenness be taken away. Feast: September 1. There is a similar shrine in the same country on the hill called the Bufa, near Zacatecas. The church of this title at Cholula, in the state of Tlaxcala, stands on top of a huge pyramid that was built by the Mexicans long before ever a Spaniard had been seen in the land.

REMETE, OUR LADY OF. This is one of the oldest Croatian shrines in Yugoslavia: the statue was brought to Remete in 1272, by the Paulite monk Iskvirin, and its church was completed in 1342. The sanctuary was several times devastated by the Turks; but our Lady is still venerated there as Protectress of Croatia, the Faithful Mother and Blessed Virgin of Remete.

REPARATION, OUR LADY OF. The ideas of reparation through and reparation to Mary are now perhaps commonly associated with Fatima (q.v.), but they are older than that. To go back no further, already in 1854 the Sisters of Marie Réparatrice had been founded to make, through Mary, reparation for the sins of mankind, and this congregation was granted a feast under the title B.M.V. Reparatricis (for May 2). Churches were dedicated in honor of our Lady of Reparation; in England, for instance, that of the Preacheresses at Carisbrooke and the parish church at West Croydon. More lately, in his encyclical letter on the Sacred Heart of Jesus in 1928, Pope Pius XI offered a prayer of reparation to that heart in which occur the following words: ". . . we offer it in union with the atoning acts of thy Virgin Mother, of all the saints, and of the religious faithful on earth. . . . Loving Jesus, be pleased to accept this our act of expiation as a voluntary offering, through the intercession of the Blessed Virgin, our model in reparation."

Pope St. Pius X granted a plenary indulgence for first-Saturday devotions in honor of Mary made in a spirit of reparation for impieties against her. The originator of these was Dolores Inglese (d. 1928), who became a nun at Rovigo in Italy.

Prompted by our Lady, she began the observance of communion of reparation, and later composed special prayers. Pope Benedict XV accorded a plenary indulgence at the hour of death to those who have carried out these Marian reparatory observances for eight consecutive first Saturdays.

RESURRECTION, MARY AND THE.

The biblical records of Christ's rising from the dead say nothing about our Lady in connection with it, and in St. Mark's gospel (16:9) it is stated that the risen Lord appeared first to Mary Magdalen. The early Fathers are similarly silent, though St. Ambrose has a reference to the matter, which is often quoted but seems somewhat ambiguous (*De virginitate,* iii, 14). Later, a belief gained currency that after the resurrection Jesus showed Himself to His Mother before anyone else, and the view has been supported on the ground that that is what might be expected: it is argued that, our Lady's faith being preeminent, she would almost necessarily have had a corresponding vision. Many solid theologians and exegetes are of the opinion that Mark 16:9 need not be taken literally. On the other hand, it is also in accord with Christian ideas that the Lord should appear to one out of whom He had cast seven devils, even before appearing to her whom the malice of the Evil One had never touched. And if the tradition be correct that identifies Mary Magdalen with the "woman who was a sinner" (Luke 7:37 ff.), there is a strong fittingness for the life of Him who came to save sinners that it was to the abused flesh of the penitent that the radiant and glorified body of the Son of God was first made manifest. However, there is no certainty either way.

In the Byzantine liturgy reference is made to a popular idea that, as an angel came to announce the Incarnation to Mary, the Resurrection was made known to her in like manner. In the ninth ode of Matins at Easter there is sung: "The angel spoke to her who is full of grace, saying, Rejoice, pure Virgin; again I say, Rejoice; for thy Son has risen from the grave on the third day, He who has raised up the dead. Ye people, rejoice! Shine, new Jerusalem, shine, for the glory of the Lord has dawned upon you. Exult, Zion, and be glad! And thou, pure Mother of God, be joyful at thy Son's rising from the dead." This is also sung at Mass at Easter, in place of the Magnifical Hymn (*q.v.*).

REVELATIONS AND COMMUNICATIONS through our Lady.

The revelations and communications of which there is question here are called *private,* as being given by Almighty God, through the Blessed Virgin, to a person or persons for their own benefit, and for the benefit of others who may come to hear of them. They are therefore quite distinct from the *universal* or *public* revelation for all men delivered once and for all to Israel and to the Apostles of Jesus Christ. There have been many such private revelations and reputed revelations through or about Mary during the course of Christian history, and the character of their content has varied considerably. For example, the communications attributed to Ann C. Emmerich and those claimed by Mary of Agreda (*qq.v.*) contained much matter that purported to be historical; those of St. Bridget (*q.v.*) included much that was devotional and expository, partly for the benefit of her nuns; to St. Catherine Labouré's visions is due the Miraculous Medal (*q.v.*); while the showings to Dame Julian (*q.v.*) were purely personal experiences for the encouragement of her faith and love.

Revelations as understood here do not necessarily involve the communication of any information that is new. The "messages" claimed for the half-dozen outstanding appearings of Mary since 1846 disclose nothing new or startling. (It is interesting to note that their recipients were all children, eleven girls, five boys, between the ages of fifteen and seven.) The Immaculate Conception (Lourdes, Beauraing) was already an article of faith; consecration to the Immaculate Heart (Fatima) had been advocated for years; the rosary (Fatima) had been in popular use for centuries; reparation to and reconciliation with God through amendment of life (La Salette, Fatima), and the merciful love of Jesus and His Mother (Banneux, Pontmain), are truths as old as Christianity; attention was drawn to unknown waters at Lourdes and Banneux, but divine healing of bodily ills is no new thing. The total effect of the messages and lessons of these occasions is of Almighty God emphasizing, through the Blessed Virgin, the fundamental things of Christian living: prayer, repentance and penance for sin, self-sacrifice, personal goodness, the ever-present mercy of Christ, and the compassion of His Mother.

From time to time the Church officially approves a particular private revelation by declaring that it contains nothing contrary to faith or morals and that it is believable upon a historical probability, and she permits its publication for the use and benefit of the faithful. In a classical passage of his work on Beatification and Canonization, Cardinal Prosper Lambertini (afterward Pope Benedict XIV), declares that a revelation so approved cannot be believed with divine faith, but only with human faith. As the Provincial Council of Malines put it in 1937: "The verdict of the Church does not at all offer these matters as having to be believed; it simply declares that they are not contrary to faith or morals, and that there is evidence providing grounds for a pious and prudent assent of human belief." These things have to be repeated, because some people are inclined to be over-credulous where alleged private revelations are concerned, and the Church does not encourage credulousness about such things. A given example may be prudently doubted or rejected, in the same way as certain visions and miracles; but to reject them all systematically, "on principle," as it were, would be highly rash and presumptuous.

The Church looks principally at the doctrinal content of a private revelation, rather than at the words in which it is expressed or the alleged circumstances. And it is not always easy to get at the exact truth, for there are numerous possibilities and opportunities for misunderstanding, misreporting, and misinterpretation. For instance, as Dom Ernest Graf has pointed out, "When reading private revelations we should be careful to take into account the period in which the seer lived and his or her mental outlook, for all these things have a great deal to do with the account the favored soul is able to give of the heavenly manifestations granted to her" (Introduction to *Revelations and Prayers of St. Bridget*). And the historian of Catholic spirituality, Father Pierre Pourrat, has remarked several times on the tendency of mystics "to regard all their inspirations as revelations properly so called. Their declarations must not be taken too literally" (*Christian Spirituality*, ii, 94). In any case, too much importance can be given to apparently supernatural communications. Writing in the *Osservatore Romano* in 1951, Cardinal (then Monsignor) Alfred Ottaviani gave a word of warning about this: "True religion rests in the true faith, in that revelation which ended with the death of the last of the Twelve Apostles, which has been entrusted to the Church as its interpreter and custodian. Nothing else necessary to our salvation can be revealed to us. . . . Even the best accredited visions cannot furnish us with new elements of life or doctrine, but only with new motives for fervor. . . . Love of God consists in doing the will of God and obeying His commandments. This is true religion." See also MIRACLES; VISIONS.

ROBE. See GARMENT.

ROCAMADOUR. The legend that accounts for this name, Rock of Amadour, in the diocese of Cahors, says that Amadour was a servant of the Blessed Virgin (later, even more surprising identifications were made); he came to Gaul and in this remote part of Quercy built the first chapel of Mary on French soil. No credence whatever can be given to these stories. The shrine of our Lady of Rocamadour has been traced back historically at least to the twelfth century: its roll of famous pilgrims includes St. Dominic and St. Louis IX, and it was the occasion of much devotion to Mary from numerous pilgrims in the middle ages, and again in recent times. The situation of the sanctuary is extraordinary, amid medieval fortifications, giddily perched on a precipice, surrounded by a waste of barren spectacular country. The venerated statue is equally remarkable: our Lady appears to be resting her weight on her hands, which are supported on the arms of her chair; the Child is balanced on her left knee. Those people to whom "modern" church art seems an innovation, should take a look at this very ancient image. Feast: August 15.

ROCK, OUR LADY OF THE. There are several shrines of this or a similar name, one of the best known being the Madonna del Sasso at Locarno in Switzerland. The Franciscans established a house there in the thirteenth century. One of the friars had a vision of our Lady, and the pilgrimage church of the Annunciation was accordingly built there in 1616. In the same country there is a pilgrimage chapel of St. Mary at the High Rocks (Marienkapelle zu hohen Flüen) in the Valais canton. Here the statue of our Lady of Sorrows is said to have been found floating in the river Rhône. The shrine of our Lady at the Rocks at Castel Sant' Elia in the Italian region of Lazio is approached up 144 steps. These were cut from the living rock by an eighteenth-century hermit, Joseph Rodio, and it took him fourteen years. At the top is an image of Mary, in a little chapel, that was crowned in 1896. The place is in charge of the Franciscans.

ROERMOND, OUR LADY OF. The statue called our Lady in the Sand, at Roermond in the Netherlands, is said to have been found in a well in 1453; the well still forms part of the sanctuary, for its water has been the occasion of many cures. The shrine has a disturbed history, like other Lowland shrines since the middle ages, its latest troubles being during World War II, from which it has made a happy recovery. The statue was crowned in 1877, and for the past century nearly the sanctuary has been looked after by the Redemptorists.

ROKITTEN, OUR LADY OF. After belonging to the Obolensky family and others, this image in the seventeenth century was enshrined in the Cistercian church at Rokitten in the diocese of Gniezno in Poland. It became famous for miracles, and a special feast of the translation to Rokitten was instituted. The picture shows our Lady, without the Child, crowned by angels.

ROMAN CHURCHES AND SHRINES. The principal church and sanctuary of the Mother of God in Rome is *St. Mary Major* (*q.v.*). Other popular shrines are as follows: *St. Mary in Cosmedin,* one of Rome's loveliest churches, which has a painting of the Mother and Child brought from the East during the iconoclast troubles of the eighth-ninth centuries; it was crowned in 1673, after a miraculous occurrence which is commemorated every year on June 5, the Manifestation. *St. Mary at the Hills (dei Monti),* built at the foot of the Viminal and Esquiline hills over a wall-painting, formerly part of a Poor Clare convent, that was rediscovered in 1580: this event is celebrated yearly on April 26. (It was in this church that St. Benedict Labre was seized with his death sickness.) *St. Mary of the People (del Populo),* where the twelfth-century image above the high altar is specially dear to the Romans; the church was rebuilt in 1472. *St. Mary in Porticu (q.v.) in Campitelli,* where there is venerated an ancient image, formerly in the Portico of Octavia. It is said to have been miraculously revealed to St. Galla (d. *c.* 550), and is greatly revered by the Romans; it was crowned in 1650, and translated to the present church, built in thanksgiving for deliverance from plague, in 1667 (feast: July 17). *St. Mary of the Street (della Strada),* a famous shrine at the Gesù church of the Society of Jesus, with a feast on May 24; it was crowned in 1638 and, the crown having been stolen, again in 1885. The *Madonna of Motherhood,* in St. Augustine's church, a much venerated group (naturalistic in character) of the Mother and Child and St. Ann, crowned in 1851. *Our Lady of Perpetual Help* (*q.v.*) in the church of St. Alphonsus. The *Mother of Divine Providence,* crowned in 1888, in the Barnabite church of San Carlo ai Catinari. *Our Lady of Victory,* an image in the Carmelite church of that name, brought from Bohemia in 1622. The *Madonna of Divine Love,* a fourteenth-century wall-painting in a church on the Via Ardeatina; it was much resorted to when Rome was threatened during World War II.

Among the other important and interesting churches of our Lady in Rome are: St. Mary of the Angels, built by Michelangelo; S.M. dell' Anima; S.M. in Aquiro; S.M. across the Bridge (*in Traspontina*); S.M. in Broad Street (*in Via Lata*); S.M. in the Chapel; S.M. in Domnica; S.M. of the Heavenly Altar (*in Ara Caeli, q.v.*); S.M. and the Martyrs, also called S.M. the Round, that is, the Pantheon; S.M. above [the Temple of] Minerva (*sopra Minerva*), the only real gothic church in Rome; Old St. Mary's (Santa Maria Antiqua), with a wonderful range of early wall-paintings; S.M. of Peace; S.M. of the Priory, of the Knights of Malta; S.M. of the Staircase (*della Scala*), has its name from an image found under some stairs; S.M. across the Tiber (*in Trastevere*), with its specially lovely sanctuary, and image of our Lady of Clemency; S.M. in Vallicella, the *chiesa nuova* of St. Philip Neri; S.M. in the Way (*in Via*).

In the past, at certain times (notably Lent) the clergy and people of Rome went in procession with the pope to a particular church, where he sang Mass: the days and churches are still noted in the Missal. The following of these stational churches were our Lady's: St. Mary Major, S.M. across the Tiber, S.M. in Broad Street, S.M. in Porticu, S.M. in Domnica. Fifteen cardinals take their titles from Mary's churches in Rome, namely: *Cardinal priests:* St. Mary of the Heavenly Altar, S.M. of Peace, S.M. of the People, S.M. of Victory, S.M. in the Way, S.M. the New, S.M. above Minerva, S.M. across the Bridge, S.M. across the Tiber; *Cardinal deacons:* Saint Mary in Aquiro, S.M. in Cosmedin, S.M. in Domnica, S.M. in Porticu, S.M. in Broad Street, S.M. of the Staircase.

ROOT OF JESSE. See GENEALOGY OF MARY.

ROSARY. A set form of prayers and meditations said with the help of a string of beads whereon to keep count of the prayers; these beads are also called a rosary. "The Rosary," without qualification, invariably means our Lady's, or the Dominican rosary. This consists of a string of beads divided into five sets (decades), each of ten small and one larger bead (a crucifix with two large and three small beads is always added but is not necessary). Each decade is associated with one of fifteen mysteries of the faith, so that a full rosary has fifteen decades and corresponding prayers; such full rosaries are cumbersome and therefore uncommon. The method of saying the rosary is to recite the Lord's Prayer (large bead), the Hail Mary ten times (small beads), and Glory be to the Father (large bead), meditating the while on the pertinent mystery (*q.v.*), which belongs to one of three groups, called joyful, sorrowful, and glorious. These meditations on events in the life of Jesus Christ and His Mother are of the essence of the devotion; it is accordingly not a mechanical repetition of the vocal prayers but a loving dwelling on God's mercies, to which those prayers are a sort of accompaniment.—On the extra beads referred to above the Apostles' Creed and Lord's Prayer are said, once each, and Hail Mary thrice. "Hail, holy Queen" (*q.v.*) is frequently added.

There is one considerable variation in the saying of the rosary, found in two forms. Some Catholics of Byzantine rite give the Hail Mary, in its old shorter form, a different and appropriate ending in each decade, for example: "Hail, Mary . . . thy womb Jesus, who suffered for us upon the cross. Amen." This custom also exists in parts of Germany and German-speaking Switzerland, but there the variable interpolation is followed by the usual last clause, "Holy Mary . . ." etc. This adding of appropriate words to Hail Marys after "thy womb, Jesus" was the practice of a Carthusian monk, Dominic of Prussia (d.

1461), and it is believed by some to be the origin of the meditations in the rosary and so to be a most important influence in its development.

The origin of the rosary is extremely obscure. According to the tradition of the Order of Preachers, accepted by a number of popes since 1495 and referred to in the Roman Breviary, the rosary, much as we know it, was devised by St. Dominic himself, and used by him in his missionary work among the Albigensian heretics, in consequence of a vision in which our Lady revealed it to him. No tradition of the kind has been more passionately supported and few have been more damagingly attacked. The controversy on this matter of history has been carried on at intervals for two hundred years, sometimes rather bitterly. The use of beads or similar objects as a device for aiding the memory and keeping count is not only pre-Dominican but pre-Christian; and the custom of saying a number of *Paters* or *Aves* and keeping count of them on a string of beads was widespread in the West before the thirteenth century. (The famous Lady Godiva, of Coventry in England, had a string of precious stones for that purpose *circa* 1075.) On the other hand, there was no uniform way of saying the rosary till a considerable time after St. Dominic's death, and his earliest biographers do not mention the prayer. But whatever the truth of the matter may be, the rosary is very properly distinguished as Dominican; the friars of that order gave it the form it now has and for centuries have zealously spread its use throughout the world, bringing thereby unnumbered blessings to countless souls and sending up a ceaseless chorus of worship before God.

No Christian is too simple or unlettered to make use of the rosary; it may be the vehicle of high states of prayer as well as of the simplest aspiration or petition; as a form of private prayer it comes only after the biblical psalms and those prayers with which the Church as church praises almighty God and His Christ and gives honor to the Blessed Virgin. No form of prayer is so widely and frequently used among Catholics of all sorts and conditions (and by some non-Catholics), or so warmly and often recommended to the faithful by their pastors, from the popes downward, and its use is continually increasing. Indeed, the popularity of the rosary is so great that there is sometimes a tendency to forget that there are other forms of everyday prayer, and accordingly both church services and private prayer may be narrowed in scope; nor does it make the same strong appeal to everybody. Young children, for instance, sometimes find it too long and monotonous; meditation comes no more easily to children than to grown-ups, and there are some spiritual directors who advise even adults not to attempt to say more than one decade at one time, since loving and intelligent attention is much more important than "doing it all." But no human activity is free from difficulty or the hazards of its own virtues; "Let us then," says the Roman Breviary, "honor the most holy Mother of God by this devotion which is so acceptable to her; so that she, who has so often been moved by the rosary prayers of Christ's faithful to bring their earthly adversaries to naught, may likewise grant that they may overcome the powers of Hell." There follows a passage from a sermon of St. Bernard in which he says: "Eve was a thorn, wounding, bringing death to all; in Mary we see a rose, soothing everybody's hurts, giving the destiny of salvation back to all. Mary was a rose, white for maidenhood, red for love; white in body, red in soul; white in her seeking after virtue, red in treading down vice; white in cleansing her affections, red in mortifying her flesh; white in her love of God, red in compassion for her neighbor."

Seeing that eleven of the fifteen mysteries of the rosary are concerned primarily with the incarnate Son of God it may seem curious to some that it should be called our Lady's rosary: the explanation is doubtless at first due to its connection with her "psalter" (*q.v.*) and the numerous Hail Marys recited, and to the account of its allegedly miraculous origin, which for a long time was unquestioned. The word itself is derived from Latin *rosarium,* a rose-garden, whence a wreath or garland, and it is also sometimes called "chaplet" or "crown" (*qq.v.*), which mean the same thing. Other devotions in which beads are used are also called by these names, and are listed below, all under "rosary." The Eastern rosary (*kombologion, chotky, mătanie*) is quite different from the Western (100 or 107 beads) and is almost purely monastic; it does not necessarily make reference to our Lady.—A rosary does not lose its blessing or indulgences if it is lent, given away, or bequeathed, or if only four or five beads are missing; but if it is damaged beyond use they are lost, and also if it is sold, unless the sale was agreed to *before* it was blessed. The so-called Crosier beads is simply an ordinary rosary specially indulgenced, 500 days for each bead, by a canon regular of the Holy Cross or other priest having the necessary faculty. For the *feast*, see below. See also BEADS; HAIL MARY; MYSTERY.

ROSARY, BRIDGETTINE. This chaplet, in commemoration of the life of the Blessed Virgin, is proper to the nuns of the Order of the Most Holy Saviour, but can of course be used by other people too. It has six decades of the Lord's Prayer once, Hail Mary ten times, and the Apostles' Creed once, with a final addition of Our Father once and Hail Mary thrice. The sixty-three Hail Marys total the years of our Lady's life according to the computation of St. Bridget, the Swedish foundress of the order. The seven Our Fathers may be considered as commemorating the seven joys and sorrows of which our Lord's life was the occasion to His mother.

ROSARY, Feast of the. It was through a series of victories in battle that a feast of our Lady under the name of her rosary was inaugurated and extended in the Western Church. (It is unknown in Eastern rites, except among the Italo-Greeks and Maronites and in Malabar.) Pope St. Pius V in 1572 ordered an annual commemoration in Rome of our Lady of Victory to ask God's protection and to thank Him for having delivered western Christendom from the arms of the Turks by the sea victory of Lepanto in the previous year: a victory which seemed a direct answer to the prayers and penitential processions of the rosary confraternities in Rome made while the battle was actually being fought. A year later Gregory XIII changed the name of the observance to that of the Rosary, fixing it for the first Sunday in October (the day of Lepanto); this commemoration was allowed in any church that had an altar dedicated in honor of the rosary. A century later it was allowed to the whole of Spain. In 1716, on August 5, feast of the dedication of St. Mary Major, another victory was gained over the Turks, at Peterwardein (now Petrovaradin in Yugoslavia), again while Marian processions were taking place in Rome, and the siege of Corfu was raised shortly after. In thanksgiving for this Clement XI decreed that the feast of the Rosary should be observed throughout the Western Church. It is now kept on the date of the battle of Lepanto, October 7, except by the Dominicans, who observe the original first Sunday of the month. On this feast a plenary indulgence *toties quoties* may be gained in every church wherein the Rosary Confraternity (*q.v.*) is established, by those who visit the rosary altar or the image of our Lady and fulfil the conditions; this is the so-called "Rosary Portiuncula" indulgence.

ROSARY, THE LIVING. This association is independent of the Rosary Confraternity (see below). Each member binds himself to say one decade daily over a given period. The mysteries are distributed amongst each group of fifteen members so that the whole rosary is recited by the group each day.—There is a not uncommon practice in the United States of having a large group in a public celebration arranged in formation as a rosary; each element says aloud the first half of each Our Father or Hail Mary or Glory, and the rest respond. This also is called a Living Rosary.

ROSARY, THE PERPETUAL. See ROSARY CONFRATERNITY.

ROSARY CONFRATERNITY. The first specifically Rosary confraternity of which there is record seems to be that established at Douay in Flanders in 1470. Four years later one was established at Cologne that was especially well known; it already had members in England in 1486. Since those days the Rosary Confraternity has spread all over the world and contributed incalculably to the diffusion of this prayer. The organization of these confraternities and permission to establish them in parishes is and always has been a prerogative of the Dominican Order. To become a member it is absolutely necessary to have one's name entered in the register of any church where the confraternity is established; and one's beads must be specially blessed by a priest having the special faculties. The member's obligation is to say the fifteen mysteries once a week (one decade may be said at a time), meditating on each mystery while the prayers are said. Among the numerous special indulgences is one of 2,025 days for each Hail Mary, provided the name Jesus be pronounced devoutly.

The Association of the Perpetual Rosary (sometimes called "Our Lady's Guard of Honor") is formed of groups of members of the Rosary Confraternity who, in addition to their weekly obligation, spend one hour (by day or night) once a month saying the fifteen mysteries and other prayers. These hours are so arranged that the recitation of the rosary is kept up continuously, to the praise of Jesus and His Mother and with special regard to those who are at "the hour of their death."

ROSARY HYMNS. The rosary has produced no outstanding hymns in either Latin or English. The proper office for the feast, given by Pope Leo XIII in 1888, contains four hymns taken from the Dominican office, and English rosary hymns are translations of these. That for first Vespers celebrates the joyful mysteries, *Caelestis aulae nuntius:*

The heavenly messenger reveals
  A mystery divine;
A virgin Mother full of grace
  He hails with reverent sign.

For Matins, the sorrowful mysteries, *In monte Olivis consito:*

Deserted, prostrate on the ground,
  Our Saviour prays on Olivet,
O'erwhelmed with dread and bitter
    woe,
  And crimsoned with His bloody
    sweat.

For Lauds, the glorious mysteries, *Jam morte victor obruta:*

Now Christ, the conqueror of death,
  Breaks sin's enslaving chain,
And rising from the tomb returns
  And opens Heaven again.

For second Vespers, comprehending all the mysteries and calling on mankind to weave a garland of roses for the Mother of fair love, *Te gestientem gaudiis:*

Exulting with exceeding joy
  Or pierced with sorrow's wound,
O virgin Mother, thee we sing,
  In glory clothed around.

The last verse, in the meter of the Latin:

We lay our homage at thy feet,
  Lord Jesus, thou the Virgin's Son,
With Father and with Paraclete
  Reigning while endless ages run.
    Amen.

These translations of the first verses are by the Stanbrook nuns (*The Roman Breviary,* in English, 1936); the last is from the Marquis of Bute's Breviary. Other translations of the hymns have been made by Bishop E. G. Bagshawe, of Nottingham, Monsignor H. T. Henry, of Philadelphia, Mr. W. H. Shewring (the Vespers hymns), and there are adaptations by Father J. P. Conway, O.P.

ROSARY SUNDAY. In Dominican churches, the first Sunday of October, feast-day of the rosary in the Order of Preachers; the blessing of roses (*q.v.*) takes place on this day.

ROSARY OF OUR LADY OF CONSOLATION, or of the Girdle. This is a rosary blessed and given at the enrollment of a member of the Augustinian confraternity of the Girdle B.V.M. (*q.v.*). The prayers are the Our Father and Hail Mary twelve times each, in honor of the twelve Apostles, with meditation on the articles of the Apostles' Creed; followed by the same prayers once in honor of Jesus Christ, King of Apostles, and "Hail, holy Queen" in honor of our Lady of Consolation.

ROSARY OF THE IMMACULATE CONCEPTION. This consists of three groups of one large and four small beads, with a medal of the mystery attached. On each large bead Our Father is said and on the small ones Hail Mary; each series begins with the acclamation "Blessed be the holy and immaculate conception of the Blessed Virgin Mary," and ends with "Glory be to the Father. . . ."

ROSARY OF THE IMMACULATE HEART. This chaplet consists of five groups, each of Our Father once and Hail Mary seven times, in honor of the Immaculate Heart of Mary. Other prayers are prescribed between the groups.

ROSARY OF THE SEVEN JOYS.

This is also known as the Franciscan Crown or Seraphic Rosary, and consists of seven decades of Our Father once and Hail Mary ten times, in honor of the seven joys (q.v.) of Mary. There are several ways of saying it; usually the joy to be meditated on is named after the name Jesus in the first Hail Mary of each decade, thus "Hail Mary . . . Jesus, whom you did conceive with joy. Holy Mary . . . etc." At the end Hail Mary is added twice more, to complete the seventy-two years of Mary's life (according to this tradition). It is the tradition of the Franciscans that in the year 1422 a young novice was about to leave the order because he no longer had opportunity to crown our Lady's statue with flowers as he had been wont to do "in the world"; whereupon Mary appeared and taught him how to plait a spiritual garland of prayers in honor of her joys.

ROSARY OF THE SEVEN SOR-ROWS.

This chaplet is proper to the order of Servants of Mary and consists of seven series, each of Our Father once and Hail Mary seven times, with meditation on her sorrows (q.v.). It is concluded by Hail Mary three times more in memory of the Mother's tears and asking for true sorrow for sin.

ROSES, BLESSING OF.

On the feast of the Rosary (q.v.) roses are blessed and distributed in honor of our Lady in Dominican churches, and sometimes in other churches wherein the Rosary Confraternity is established. The prayer of blessing in the Roman Ritual asks that through the power of the Cross the roses may be a healing and protecting perfume for souls and bodies, especially of the sick.

RUMANIA, SHRINES OF.

The Rumanians are predominantly Orthodox; indeed, they form the second largest unit of the Eastern Orthodox Church. There is a sizeable minority of Catholics of Byzantine rite, and a rather smaller one of Latins, many of them Hungarian. Before the communists came to power, the principal Byzantine sanctuaries of the Mother of God were Nicula (q.v.), Prislop, and Bicsad, all at Basilian monasteries, and the great cathedral of her Presentation at Cluj. There were important Latin-rite shrines at Sumuleu (Csiksomlyó, q.v.) and Máriáradna (both Franciscan) and Kolozsvár (Cluj; Jesuit). There are many well-known Orthodox Marian churches, such as that of her Falling Asleep at Cernica (Wallachia), the Annunciation at Vad, the Falling Asleep at Neamtu, and the icon of Golea at Jassy (all in Moldavia), the Varadia church and the Poor Monastery of the Presentation at Semlacul Mic (both in Banat), and Appasul de Jos and Hodos Bodrog in Transylvania (Ardeal); the last named was built in 1498 and has three famous icons. The oldest image of our Lady in Rumania is a sixth-century carving found in Dobruja in 1915.

RUSSIA, SHRINES OF. In the days of old Russia (whose passing there is no need to regret, without for a moment condoning the horrors that followed) the Russian people were deeply devoted to making pilgrimages: before 1914, particularly did more ordinary peasant people from Russia make their way to the holy places of Palestine than from any other country. The shrines of their own land were of course involved in the disasters that followed the revolution. Sanctuaries were destroyed, and with them many holy icons; others, including some of the most revered, were carefully preserved, but are now displayed in art galleries and museums—and some people feel that it is almost better that a religious image should be destroyed than that it should be made an exhibit in a museum. But the religious memory of them lives on, in the hearts of many people and in the liturgical commemorations made of them. Monsignor F. G. Holweck (*Calendarium liturgicum*, 1925) found the names of 245 venerated and wonderworking icons of Mary in Russian menologies. The following are among the principal Marian images, shrines, and feasts; they of course pertain to the now separated Russian Orthodox Church, but are equally venerated by the few Russian Catholics and by others who know them: Our Lady of the Don (*q.v.*); O.L. of Iviron (*q.v.*); O.L. of Kazan (*q.v.*); O.L. of the Caves at Kiev; O.L. of Korsun (sometimes called "of Ephesus"); O.L. of Kostroma; O.L. of Kursk (*q.v.*); O.L. of Novgorod (*q.v.*); O.L. of the Passion (*cf.*, Perpetual Help, Our Lady of); O.L. of Smolensk; O.L. of Tikhvin; O.L. of Vladimir (*q.v.*); O.L. of Yaroslavl.

S

SABBATINE PRIVILEGE, The. The Church sanctions the pious belief that the souls of those who die in charity and have worn the Brown scapular (*q.v.*), observed chastity according to their state, and daily recited the Little Office B.V.M., or abstained from flesh meat on every Wednesday and Saturday, or faithfully observed some other such work, will receive help "through Mary's unceasing intercession, her devoted pleadings, her merits and her special protection; and this especially on Saturdays [*Sabbata*], the day dedicated by the Church to the Blessed Virgin."

This is the form approved by the Holy Office in 1613 of a privilege recorded in 1421, when it purported to derive from a bull of Pope John XXII in 1322, issued in consequence of a vision of our Lady on behalf of the Carmelite Order. The conditions of the privilege vary somewhat in different interpretations, in some of which Mary is represented as promising that those who observed them would be freed from Purgatory on the first Saturday after death. On this last point the Holy See has been very reserved, as also somewhat about the authenticity of John XXII's bull. In commending the Brown scapular in 1950 Pope Pius XII simply said: "Indeed this most gentle Mother, by her intercession with God, will not be slow in opening the gates of Heaven as soon as possible to her children who are expiating their faults in Purgatory, a trust which is based on the promise known as the Sabbatine Privilege."

SACRO MONTE, The, Varese. This sanctuary of the Sacred Hill at Varese in Lombardy is said to have had its origin in a chapel built to commemorate our Lady's appearing to St. Ambrose there, during the later fourth century. The sanctuary grew in popularity, especially after a convent of Augustinian nuns was established in the fifteenth century. The principal shrine is the church of the Immaculate Conception, with chapels of the mysteries of the rosary.

SAGUENAY, OUR LADY OF THE. See LOURDES SHRINES.

SAIDNAIA, OUR LADY OF. Outside of Palestine, the most famous sanctuary of the Mother of God in the Levant is at a convent of Orthodox nuns, Dair as-Sagura, within the walls of an ancient fortress on a hill near Damascus. The origins of this shrine are no longer known, but it goes back to before the separation of the Orthodox Church from Old Rome. The tradition that associates the convent with the Emperor Justinian I (d. 565) is mistaken, as is the attribution of its miraculous icon to St. Luke (see LIKENESSES). This icon of our Lady of

Saidnaia is said to have been brought to its present home in 870, from Constantinople or Jerusalem. The shrine was formerly well known in the West, where from about 1200 it was popularized by the stories of strange miracles that were related of the image; today it is much resorted to by Mohammedans as well as Christians. Feast: March 24.

SAINT GEORGE'S, OUR LADY OF, Southwark. In 1790 a small staute of the Blessed Virgin and her Child was set up in a public chapel in London Road, south of the Thames; it was perhaps the first image of the kind to be thus publicly venerated in England after the Reformation. In 1848 it was moved to the new church of St. George near-by, which became the cathedral of the diocese of Southwark. This church was destroyed by enemy-action during World War II; but the statue was saved, and in 1954 it was crowned, in anticipation of being enshrined above the Lady altar when St. George's shall have been rebuilt.

SAINT LUKE, MADONNA OF, Bologna. An image that has made its church at Bologna one of the most famous shrines of Italy. It came originally from Constantinople and belonged to some hermitesses, who in 1193 built a chapel for it. The icon was attributed to St. Luke, quite mistakenly. At Rogation-tide every year it is carried in procession to the cathedral of Bologna, and there displayed for the veneration of the faithful. This, or one like it, was one of the two or three representations of Mary that St. Bernadette did not find disappointing, or worse. Feast: 5th Sunday after Easter. For the attribution of this and other pictures to St. Luke, see LIKENESSES.

SALMESTONE, OUR LADY OF. The ancient buildings of Salmestone, at Margate in Thanet, were a cell or grange of the abbey of St. Augustine at Canterbury, and the chapel (now restored) was consecrated in 1326. In 1936 the buildings were given to the Benedictine monks of St. Augustine's, Ramsgate. An outdoor shrine was established in 1947, with an excellent modern statue: our Lady is seated, and the Child, standing in her lap, is casting ears of wheat upon the earth, emblematic of the sacrament of His Body and Blood.

SALUTATION OF OUR LADY. An old English name for the Annunciation; it is of interest because it survives as an inn name, "The Salutation." As late as the eighteenth century a few of these inns still carried a sign-board on which Gabriel was depicted appearing to Mary. The inn name "The Angel," still common, has the same origin: on the sign he was shown carrying a scroll on which the opening words of his message were written. "The Virgin" also was formerly used as a sign, of which there were still examples at Worcester and elsewhere a century ago. John Stow in his *Survey of London* (1603) says that the Inn of Court at which the young Thomas More was first entered as a law student had formerly been a public hostelry called "Our Lady's" inn, from its sign. Another inn sign was the Bleeding Heart (there was still a Bleeding Heart Yard in London in the days of Dickens): this certainly did not refer to the Sacred Heart of Jesus, popular *cultus* of which was unknown in those days, but it is said to have reference to Mary's heart pierced by the sword of her sorrows.

SALUTE, SANTA MARIA DELLA, Venice. This famous baroque church was built as a thank-offering to our Lady of Protection, for deliverance from the plague of 1630; for a short time it sheltered the icon of Mary the Victory-bringer, seized from Constantinople during the Fourth Crusade (now in St. Mark's). Its place was taken by another image, rescued from Crete when the Turks overran the island in 1645. It is famed for miracles all over Veneto. Feast: November 25.

SALVE PROCESSION. About the year 1230 Bl. Jordan of Saxony established in the Dominican friary at Bologna the custom of singing *Salve Regina* (see below) every day after Compline. This was the origin of the custom in the Order of Preachers whereby, after Compline, the friars go in procession to the image of our Lady singing that anthem. They kneel from the words *Eja, ergo* to *exsilium ostende,* and the superior sprinkles community and people with holy water. While returning to the choir an anthem in honor of St. Dominic is sung. "A most trustworthy religious," wrote Bl. Jordan, "assures me that often in spirit he has beheld the Mother of God fall at her Son's feet to pray for the welfare of the order, while the brethren sing the words, 'Turn then, our advocate. . . .' " Cistercian monks and other religious also sing the final *Salve* of the day with special solemnity: a medieval Benedictine chapter declared that, "We think it necessary that before sleep we should call upon the help of her who crushed the Serpent's head, so that the crafty Serpent may not beguile at night those whom he is unable to overcome in their waking hours." The Carmelites have a *Salve* procession on Saturdays and the eve of feasts of our Lady.

SALVE REGINA. The first words and title of the fourth of the anthems of our Lady (see ANTIPHONS), said or sung from Trinity Sunday till Advent.

Salve Regina, mater misericordiae;
Vita, dulcedo, et spes nostra, salve!
Ad te clamamus exsules filii Hevae.
Ad te suspiramus gementes et flentes
    in hac lacrimarum valle.
Eja ergo, advocata nostra,
Illos tuos misericordes oculos ad nos
    converte.
Et Jesum benedictum fructum ventris
    tui
Nobis post hoc exsilium ostende.
O clemens, O pia, O dulcis Virgo
    Maria!

℣. Ora pro nobis sancta Dei genetrix.
℟. Ut digni efficiamur promissionibus
    Christi.

Oremus. Omnipotens et sempiterne Deus, qui gloriosae Virginis Matris Mariae corpus et animam, ut dignum Filii tui habitaculum effici mereretur, Spiritu Sancto cooperante, praeparasti: da ut cujus commemoratione laetamur, ejus pia intercessione ab instantibus malis et a morte perpetua liberemur. Per eundem Christum Dominum nostrum. Amen.

This is so well known as to be the most popular prayer to Mary after the Angelical Salutation. There are several English translations, that in commonest use being the rather pedestrian prose one beginning "Hail, holy Queen!" The following is the version printed in the first edition (1740) of Challoner's *Garden of the Soul:*

Hail to the Queen who reigns
     above,
Mother of clemency and love:
Hail thou our hope, life, sweetness;
     we,
Eve's banished children, cry to thee.

We from this wretched vale of tears
Send sighs and groans unto thine ears;
Oh! then, sweet advocate, bestow
A pitying look on us below.

After this exile, let us see
Our blessed Jesus, born of thee:
O merciful, O pious maid,
O gracious Mary, lend thine aid.

℣. Pray for us, O holy Mother of
     God.
℟. That we may be made worthy of
     the promises of Christ.

Let us pray. O almighty and eternal God, who didst prepare the body and soul of the glorious Mary, mother and virgin, that by the co-operation of the Holy Ghost she might become a worthy dwelling for thy Son: grant that, as we rejoice in her commemoration, so by her pious intercession we may be delivered both from present evils and from everlasting death. Thro' the same Jesus Christ our Lord. Amen.

Who wrote *Salve Regina* has been much discussed. Like several other Marian pieces, it has been attributed to St. Bernard; but the most likely candidate seems to be Bl. Hermann the Cripple, who probably wrote *Alma Redemptoris mater (q.v.).* It was widely used in church services during the middle ages, the Cistercian monks being specially active in popularizing it, and its lovely plainsong melody seems to have helped to spread it. Apart from its use as an anthem B.V.M., it is now said by a Carmelite celebrant between the blessing at Mass and the last gospel, by the Servites after Mass, and in the Mozarabic rite after the dismissal; it also forms part of the prayers said for Russia after low Mass in all churches of Latin rite. The singing of *Salve Regina* after Compline is done with special solemnity in certain religious orders (see SALVE PROCESSION, above), and an evening *Salve* was common in parish churches in the middle ages: guilds and confraternities were founded and endowed to keep up this observance, which seems to have been—curiously enough—the origin of Benediction (*q.v.*) of the Blessed Sacrament, and also—no less curiously—of the daily anthem in Anglican (Episcopalian) cathedral and collegiate churches.

It appears that in the past *Salve Regina* was particularly favored by sailors, who would sing it every evening aboard ship. On Thursday, October 11, 1492, Christopher Columbus noted in his journal: "When they had said the Salve, which all sailors are in the habit of saying and singing on their way, and they were all assembled, the admiral urged and warned the men to guard the stern forecastle well and to keep a good look out for land." The New World was first sighted the next day. From the same source it is learned that the sailors taught the native people of the newly discovered islands to say "the Salve and the Ave Maria with their hands raised to Heaven, making the sign of the cross."

SALVE, SANCTA PARENS. See SEDULIUS.

SANCTA MARIA, SUCCURRE MISERIS. A well-known invocation, used as an antiphon in the Common and Little Offices B.V.M. (*q.v.*): "Holy Mary, give aid to the unfortunate, encourage the faint-hearted, help the unhappy, pray for the people, speak for the clergy, intercede for dedicated women." In another form it is a responsory at Matins in the same offices: "Happy indeed art thou, holy Virgin Mary, and worthy of all praises, for from thee arose the Sun of righteousness, Christ our Lord. Pray for the people, speak for the

clergy, intercede for dedicated women; let all those who are keeping thy sacred festival experience thy help."— *Devotus femineus sexus* does not mean "devout female sex," as it is often translated; *devotus* here means "bound by vow," i.e., principally, nuns, hence "dedicated women" as given above. In the earliest known form of the invocation, as used at Arles in the mid-sixth century, monks are mentioned as well as nuns.

SATURDAY and Mary. In sanctioning the preaching of the Sabbatine Privilege (*q.v.*) in 1613, the Holy Office referred to Saturday as "the day dedicated by the Church to the Blessed Virgin," and some devotional writers have exercised no little ingenuity in explaining at length why this should be so. There is in fact no fundamental reason for choosing Saturday in particular for "Mary's day," unless it be for her unshaken faith during the Saturday when her Son lay dead in the tomb; the observance in fact grew up only gradually and under various influences. There is an analogy with May as the Month of Mary (*q.v.*); but the Saturday dedication is much older, and has been more formally adopted in the Western Church through the institution of the Saturday Office (*q.v.*) of our Lady. By the eleventh century there was a custom in some churches of celebrating a Mass of our Lady on free Saturdays, and this was much encouraged by a doctor of the Church, St. Peter Damian (d. 1072); later, the "Legends of our Lady" (*q.v.*), with their stories of graces and helps given on Saturdays, did a lot to encourage the devotion. Once the idea of the Saturday dedication had "caught on," it was natural that the existing fast (*q.v.*) on that day should be popularly associated with Mary, though it had nothing to do with her.—It is said that in England in the thirteenth century there was an unofficial custom of resting from servile work on Saturday afternoons in Mary's honor. It would certainly be fanciful to see in this the origin of the "English week-end." *Cf.,* Reparation, Our Lady of.

SCAPULAR (from Lat. *scapula,* shoulder). A scapular is primarily part of the habit among the older religious orders, worn over the tunic. It is a strip of woolen material with a hole in the middle for the head, so that it rests on the shoulders, half of it falling in front and half behind. It it usually the width of the shoulders and reaches to the ankles. It originated in the working overall of monks, but later took on the meaning of the yoke of Christ and became the most significant part of the religious dress of those who wear it. Among members of the lay third orders of the friars (and Benedictine oblates and *confratres*) the custom grew up of wearing miniature scapulars *under* the clothing, to represent the habit which as tertiaries they are entitled to wear in private. Similar miniature but even smaller scapulars were also adopted by members of certain confraternities and then by unattached individuals, with various specific devotional significances. A small scapular is made of two rectangles of woven wool of the designated color and size, joined by two cords sewn on so that it may be put on over the head. It may be worn next the skin or between garments. The wearing of any scapular constantly is indulgenced in varying measures.

The meaning of the scapular and the spirit in which it is to be worn is expressed in the following prayer with which the Church blesses the Brown scapular: "Lord Jesus Christ, Savior of mankind, stretch forth thy hand and bless this garment which thy servant is to wear with devotion for love of thee and of thy mother, the virgin Mary of Mount Carmel; so that, she pleading for him, he may be defended from the Evil One and abide in thy grace until death."

SCAPULAR, BLUE. See SCAPULAR OF MARY IMMACULATE.

SCAPULAR, BROWN. Properly called the Scapular of the Blessed Virgin Mary of Mount Carmel, but often referred to simply as The Scapular. This is the oldest and best known of Marian scapulars (see below). According to the tradition of the Carmelite Order the Mother of God appeared to St. Simon Stock in England on July 16, 1251, showed him a big scapular, and said: "Dear son, take this scapular of your order as a badge of my brotherhood and a special sign of grace for you and all Carmelites. Whoever dies in this garment will not suffer everlasting fire. It is a token of salvation, a safeguard in danger, a pledge of peace and of the covenant." The authenticity of this event has been seriously criticized by some; but the lessons at Matins on the feast of our Lady of Mount Carmel still recount St. Simon Stock's vision and (though they do not refer to the promise "Whoever dies in this garment will not suffer everlasting fire") say: "It is religiously believed that those of [Mary's] children who are enrolled in the scapular confraternity, keep the slight abstinence and say the few prayers prescribed, and observe chastity according to their state of life will certainly be comforted by her motherly affection while they are being purified in the fire of Purgatory, and through her intercession will be the sooner called thence to the heavenly home." (For the details of this passage, see SABBATINE PRIVILEGE.)

Every Catholic understands that the wearing of a scapular must be accompanied by true faith and unwearied effort toward godly living. Pope Pius XII, writing on the Brown scapular in 1950, said: "The sacred scapular, which may be called the habit or dress of Mary, is a sign and pledge of the protection of the Mother of God. But this does not mean that they who wear it are free to think that they can gain eternal salvation while yet being slothful and negligent of spirit, for the Apostle warns us to 'Work out your salvation with fear and trembling'" (Phil. 2:12). The Pope commends the use of the scapular to the faithful and emphasizes it as a sign of consecration to the Mother of God; it is certainly one of the most widely spread of all Marian devotions, which the Carmelite friars are unwearied in promoting to the honor of Mary and

the good of souls. *Cf.,* Scapular Confraternity.

SCAPULAR, FIVEFOLD. Five scapulars, those of the Holy Trinity, the Passion, the Immaculate Conception, the Seven Sorrows, and Mount Carmel (Brown), worn as one upon a single pair of bands. To gain the indulgences it must be blessed with the form in the Roman Ritual.

SCAPULAR, GREEN. The name given to a single piece of green cloth, attached to a green cord, bearing on one side an image of our Lady and on the other an image of her heart, with the inscription, "Immaculate Heart of Mary, pray for us now and at the hour of our death." It originates in visions of the Blessed Virgin vouchsafed to Sister Justine Bisqueyburu, of the Daughters of Charity of St. Vincent de Paul, in France between 1840 and 1846; she understood that its religious use would particularly contribute to the conversion of those who have no faith. It is blessed by a priest, and worn on the person or simply retained, without the usual formalities required for a scapular; the above prayer should be said daily. The Green scapular was twice approved by Pope Pius IX.

SCAPULAR CONFRATERNITY. There are several confraternities whose members wear a particular scapular, but The Scapular Confraternity, without qualification, always means the confraternity of the Brown scapular of the Order of our Lady of Mount Carmel. This confraternity arose probably in the sixteenth century, deriving from previous Carmelite societies (one at Florence wore scapulars in the year 1280), and it is today one of the largest of all Marian associations. The enrollment of members is a prerogative of the Carmelite friars, but faculties are given by the order to other priests. Those who have been enrolled and wear the Brown scapular can profit from the Scapular Promise (see SCAPULAR, BROWN) and, by fulfilling additional conditions, from the Sabbatine Privilege (*q.v.*); they can also gain a very large number of indulgences on fulfilling the required conditions, and they share in all the spiritual goods of the Carmelite Order. From its beginning the Carmelite habit has been a medium of consecration to God and our Lady; and in 1950 Pope Pius XII referred to the scapular as a sign of consecration to Mary's heart, which consecration "we have recently so strongly recommended."

SCAPULAR FEAST. See MOUNT CARMEL, OUR LADY OF.

SCAPULAR MEDAL. A medal which may be substituted for one or more devotional scapulars with which the wearer has been invested; it must receive the corresponding blessings and then carries all the pertinent indulgences and privileges. It may be worn round the neck or in any other suitable way. This medal bears an image of Jesus Christ, showing His heart, on one side and of the Mother of God on the other. The faithful are urged not to substitute the medal for a cloth scapular without good reason.

SCAPULAR OF THE IMMACULATE HEART OF MARY. This was instituted by the Missionary Sons of the Immaculate Heart in 1877. It is white, and bears an image of Mary's loving and pure heart. The prayers of blessing ask that whoever wears it with thanksgiving, calling upon God's holy name, may persevere in godliness and be safe in body and soul.

SCAPULAR OF MARY IMMACULATE. This, the Blue scapular, originated in a vision of Jesus Christ which we are told was granted to Mother Ursula Benincasa, foundress of the Theatine nuns in 1617. It is worn by those who are enrolled in the Confraternity of the Immaculate Conception of the Theatine clerks regular, whose headquarters is at the church of Sant' Andrea della Valle at Rome. The members share in all the spiritual good works of the Theatine Order.

SCAPULAR OF OUR LADY OF GOOD COUNSEL. This scapular is associated with the Augustinian friars. It is white, having on the front the words "Mother of Good Counsel," with a representation of her, and on the back the papal tiara and keys, with the words "Son, follow her counsel" (Leo XIII). The prayer of blessing asks our Lord, man's angel of great counsel and peerless counsellor, to hallow this scapular of His Mother of Good Counsel, that those who wear it may by His grace follow wise advice and earn everlasting happiness.

SCAPULAR OF OUR LADY, HEALTH OF THE SICK.

The scapular of the Confraternity of the Ministers of the Sick (Camillans), whose headquarters is at the church of the Magdalen in Rome. It is black and bears an image of Mary from the picture in that church. The prayer of blessing asks that whoever wears it in honor of the Mother of God, Health of the Sick, may enjoy wholeness of mind and body and attain everlasting life. A small red cross on the back part of the scapular is blessed separately to the same end.

SCAPULAR OF OUR LADY OF RANSOM.

The scapular of the confraternity of the Mercedarian Order, which was originally founded to ransom Christian captives among the Moors and elsewhere. It is white, with an image of Mary of Ransom on the front. In the rite of blessing this scapular the idea of ransom is given a spiritual interpretation.

SCAPULAR OF THE SEVEN SORROWS.

This scapular is black, and usually has an image of Mary of Sorrows on the front. It originated in the late middle ages with the order of Servants of Mary (Servites), whose confraternity it still distinguishes. The wearer is invested with the words: "Dear brother, receive this garment of the Blessed Virgin Mary, a special sign of her servants, in remembrance of the seven sorrows she experienced during the life and death of her only Son; that thus clothed you may always live under her protection."

SCHÖNSTATT, OUR LADY OF.

This German shrine of the Wonderful Mother (*Mater admirabilis*) is of modern origin, having been established in 1914. It is near Coblenz, and is cared for by the Pallottine fathers. It is a center of Marian devotion and Catholic Action for the whole of Germany.

SCOTLAND, SHRINES OF.

The principal medieval shrines of the Blessed Virgin in Scotland were: the Lady kirk of Kyle at Monkton in Ayrshire; the Lady chapel at Newhaven, near Edinburgh; our Lady of Grace, Fochabers, with its holy well, and another pilgrim-well not far off at Ordiquhill; the Douglas Virgin in Glasgow cathedral; our Lady of Elgin; our Lady of the Shield (*q.v.*); one at Whitekirk in East Lothian, to which Aeneas Silvius Piccolomini (later Pope Pius II) made a pilgrimage in wet weather and thus contracted rheumatism; and several shrines in Aberdeen, Perth, and Edinburgh, including one in the High Kirk of St. Giles. The Loreto chapel at Musselburgh, built for a relic of the Holy House (*q.v.*) in 1533, attained a quick fame but soon came to an end at the Reformation; and the same applies to the Franciscan shrine of our Lady of Ayr. Other pilgrimage shrines were at Dundee, Melrose, Paisley, and Scone. Our Lady of Aberdeen (*q.v.*) is still venerated; so is one of the Edinburgh images, our Lady of Holyrood (*q.v.*). But the most popular Scottish shrine today is Carfin (*q.v.*). On South Uist in the Hebrides the people marked the Marian year of

1954 by building wayside shrines around their island, and setting up a statue of our Lady, Queen of the Isles, looking out over the Atlantic.—It is curious that in Scotland, where Protestantism took on a specially dour aspect, several burghs still display the image of our Lady on their municipal coats of arms. The Capuchin church at Uddingston in Lanark is dedicated under the name of our Lady of Scotland.

SEAT OF WISDOM. Latin *Sedes sapientiae,* an invocation of our Lady in the Litany of Loreto. "Mary has this title in her litany because the Son of God, who is also called in Scripture the Word and Wisdom of God, once dwelt in her, and then, after His birth of her, was carried in her arms and seated on her lap in His first years. Thus, being, as it were, the human throne of Him who reigns in Heaven, she is called the Seat of Wisdom. . . . Mary for thirty continuous years saw and heard Him . . . , able to ask Him any questions which she wished explained, and knowing that the answers she received were from the Eternal God, who neither deceives nor can be deceived" (Cardinal Newman). There is a feast under this title in two or three places.

SECRET OF LA SALETTE, The. In 1879, when she was forty years old, Mélanie Calvat, one of the two children concerned in the vision of La Salette in 1846, published a book which included what purported to be the full content of the secret she said was communicated to her on that oc-

casion. In letters to two bishops, the Congregation of the Holy Office at Rome expressed the wish that the book should be withdrawn from circulation, but it continued to be widely read and discussed. In 1915 the Holy Office forbade under penalties any further discussion of the "so-called Secret of La Salette"; but, it added, "this decree is not directed against devotion to the Blessed Virgin invoked and known by the title of Reconciler of La Salette." Nevertheless the book was reissued in 1922, and in the following year it was put on the Index of Forbidden Books. See LA SALETTE.

SEDULIUS. The Latin form of the name (Siadhal) of a fifth-century Irish poet from whose works is taken the introit, *Salve, sancta parens,* said or sung in many Masses of our Lady: "Hail, holy Mother, in thy womb there lay a king who bears o'er earth and Heaven endless sway." This is the only introit verse that bears the name of a non-biblical writer: generally it is taken from a psalm, in recognition of the fact that it was formerly a whole psalm sung at the entrance (*introitus*) of the celebrant and ministers. Sedulius also wrote two hymns used in the Christmas and Epiphany offices.

SEED-TIME, Feast of our Lady in, and of Sheaves. Feasts kept in the Syrian rite on January 15 and May 15 respectively. The second is also kept in the Maronite and Chaldean rites. The names sufficiently explain their occasion and purpose. The Syrian doctor St. Ephraem sings in his seventh hymn on our Lady: "Come, ye wise, learned heralds of the Spirit, prophets who truly saw hidden things in your visions, husbandmen who sowed and went hopefully to your rest, rejoice at the fruitful harvest! Behold the Full Ear of life lying in my arms, who gives food to the hungry and satisfies the needy! Rejoice with me, for I have reaped in joy!"

SEQUENCE. Early in the middle ages a practice was begun of singing a sort of hymn, called a "sequence" or "prose," after the gradual at Mass on certain feasts. These sequences became very numerous and many of them were very inferior compositions; so in 1570 Pope St. Pius V abolished all of them in the Roman rite except four: those for Easter, Pentecost, Corpus Christi, and the Dead. When in 1727 the feast of the Seven Sorrows B.V.M. was extended to the whole Western Church, the famous *Stabat Mater dolorosa* (*q.v.*) was included in the proper Mass. This allowing of a sequence on a lesser festival was no doubt due to the hymn's great popularity. Among the Marian sequences authorized for particular orders or places are the Carmelite *Flos Carmeli* (*q.v.*), and *Gaude Virgo, Mater Christi* (Seven Joys B.V.M.) and *Laetabunda canant pie* (Immaculate Conception), both for the Friars Minor of St. Francis.

SERMO ANGELICUS. See BRIDGET, REVELATIONS OF ST.

SHIELD, OUR LADY OF THE. There are many examples in history of images of our Lady being brought to fields of battle, or of a Marian device being displayed on military standards, and of subsequent victory being attributed to her intercession. In his famous *Atlas Marianus* (1672), William Gumpenberg refers to an image of the Wonderworking Queen of Mount Badon or of the Shield. Henry of Huntingdon (d. 1155) and later writers narrate that when he overcame the Saxon invaders at the great battle of Mount Badon (*c.* 500), "King" Arthur bore an image of the Blessed Virgin on his shield. The origin of the story was, no doubt, the statement of Nennius, early in the ninth century, that Arthur "carried the image of the ever-virgin St. Mary on his shoulders, and the heathen were put to flight," at the battle of Castell Guinnion; and this was confused with a very similar later reference to Mount Badon. Heraldic devices were unknown till centuries after these battles. Before the Reformation the church of St. Mary at Wedale (now Stow) in Scotland claimed to possess the remains of the Arthurian "image"; this relic was held in great veneration, and a spring nearby was known as the Lady's Well.

SHONGWENI, OUR LADY OF. On the top of a 2,000-foot hill in a lonely place between Durban and Pietermaritzburg in South Africa there stands a statue of Mary, Mediatress of All Graces. Of recent years this hill of Shongweni has become a place of pilgrimage, to which on May 31 numbers of Africans come from all over Natal, and even farther afield. The sick are blessed, and there is a torchlight procession, with much singing of Zulu hymns; the pilgrimages are to a consderable degree spontaneous and unorganized.

SHRINE. This word is derived from Latin *scrinium,* which designated a box to contain books or papers, and so it came to be applied to a box or casket which enclosed sacred relics. This use of "shrine" has been almost entirely replaced by "reliquary," and a shrine is now a place which for some particular reason is regarded as specially holy. Apart from places which are sacred shrines in their totality (e.g., Jerusalem, Rome), a shrine is usually a church, chapel, or other particular spot hallowed by some event that happened there, or by the presence of the tomb or relics of some holy person, or by the presence of a much-venerated image, or the like. Such shrines may be of local, national, or international fame, and visits of devotion or pilgrimages are made to them accordingly. The word shrine is also applied to any image, in a church, in a home, or in the open air, to which special devotion is accorded and marked outwardly by the presence of flowers, candles, and perhaps a lamp burning before it. A shrine in this last sense may be permanent or temporary, e.g., a special shrine of our Lady during May.

The first pilgrimage shrines were the tombs of the martyrs, but as time went by shrines of other saints (usually at their burial-places) became very numerous. Those of our Lady mostly grew up around a greatly venerated statue or picture, generally one famous as a vehicle of wonders in the spiritual and temporal orders; some, notably Lourdes and Fatima (*qq.v.*) in our own day, originated in Mary's manifesting herself to people. The number of Marian pilgrim-shrines in the world today is exceedingly large; many of them are survivals from the past, others are of recent growth; to estimate their number is virtually impossible, for so many of them are of purely local interest and unknown outside their own localities. It is, too, difficult to define "shrine" and "pilgrimage" satisfactorily for purely statistical purposes. In this book some of the more important of Mary's shrines are listed under names of countries, with cross-references to further particulars of many of them. According to Monsignor F. G. Holweck (*Calendarium liturgicum,* 1925), Marian shrines that have their own liturgical commemorations are most numerous in the Roman, Apulian, and Sicilian provinces of Italy, and at Moscow; then come France, Spain, and Portugal, with the countries that speak their languages; and finally German- and English-speaking lands. *Cf.* also, Pilgrimages.

The value of shrines and pilgrimages is as focal-points of devotion and as incentives to piety and godly living. Not everyone is able to avail himself of these helps and opportunities: ill-health, old age, poverty, duties may stand in the way. That need be no matter for repining: pilgrimages are but one among many good works, and in an ultimate analysis all their graces may be found in our parish church. As Father Joseph A. Jungmann, s.j., writes in *The Mass of the Roman Rite* (vol. I, p. 253): "One of the most revolutionary innovations which Christianity produced was the departure from a cultus of place-worship connected with certain localities—holy mountains, mystic groves, even the sacred Temple in Jerusalem. Worship can take place wherever a holy people are gathered before God, for this people is the true temple of the Lord (2 Cor. 6:16; 1 Cor. 3:16). . . . The true sanctuary is to be found neither in Garizim nor in Jerusalem, but in every place where true adorers worship God in spirit and in truth (John 4:21 ff)."

SICILIAN HYMN, The.

The hymn *O sanctissima, O piissima,* popular among Sicilian sailors, no doubt partly because of its very catchy tune: it begins:

> O sanctissima,
> O piissima,
> Dulcis virgo Maria!
> Mater amata,
> Intemerata,
> Ora, ora pro nobis.

"Most holy one, most godly one, kind maiden Mary! Mother beloved, mother inviolate, pray for us." See *Pius X Hymnal* (McLaughlin & Reilly Co.), No. 103.

SIGN, OUR LADY OF THE.

See NOVGOROD, OUR LADY OF.

SINJ, OUR LADY OF.

Sinj is near the Dalmatian coast of Yugoslavia. In a Turkish attack during the wars of the fifteenth century, some of the defenders saw the figure of a woman, surrounded with light, on one of the bastions. It was taken to be our Lady, whose image in the Franciscan church was greatly revered. The friars removed the image to Rama (*q.v.*), where it remained for two hundred years. Then it was brought back to Sinj, and enshrined in a new church.

SINLESSNESS OF OUR LADY.

It is an article of faith that the Blessed Virgin Mary was free from all stain of original sin, and that she was also free of all actual sin, even venial. This last truth was stated by the Council of Trent in 1547, in its canon 23 on Justification: "If any one shall say that once a man is justified . . . he can throughout his life avoid all sins, even venial (except by a special privilege of God, such as the Church holds the Blessed Virgin enjoyed), let him be anathema." This doctrine, unlike that of the Immaculate Conception, has been held explicitly and without dispute in the Church from early times. It is true that certain great doctors, St. Basil, St. John Chrysostom, St. Cyril of Alexandria, thought there was reason to believe that Mary fell into some small faults, e.g., of pushing herself forward (Matt. 12:46; John 2:3); but the general tradition of the East was expressed by the Syrian doctor St. Ephraem in one of his fourth-century hymns: "Of a truth, it is thou and thy Mother alone who are wholly beautiful in every way; for in thee, Lord, there is no spot, and in thy Mother no stain." Later, St. John Damascene, St. Andrew of Crete, and many others spoke in the same sense, and some of their tributes have been incorporated into the Eastern liturgies. As for the West, a well-known passage of St. Augustine can speak for all: "With the exception of the holy Virgin Mary, whom I cannot, out of respect for the Lord, allow to come into the question at all when we are treating of sin—for how can we know of any greater degree of grace that could have been bestowed on her for complete victory over sin, when she merited to conceive and bring forth Him who, as we all know, was without sin? With the sole exception, then, of the Blessed Virgin, if we could bring together all holy men and women, and ask them whether when they lived on earth they were without sin, what are we to suppose that they would reply? Would they say what this man [the heretic Pelagius] says? Or what the apostle John says? I put it to you that, no matter how great their holiness when in the body, they would answer such a question in a single loud voice: 'If we say that we have no sin, we deceive ourselves, and the truth is not in us' " (I John 1:8). In that first sentence, Augustine gives the reason for our Lady's sinlessness —the honor and respect of her divine Son required it.

SIOUX, OUR LADY OF THE. Crowds of people do not go on pilgrimage to the mission of the Jesuit fathers at Porcupine, hidden away in the Sioux country of South Dakota. But the Lourdes grotto there, beloved of the people of the mission, may well be taken as representative of the many unassuming little shrines scattered over the United States— and other countries as well. The name, our Lady of the Sioux, is given to a picture at the mission; it was painted by a Sioux Indian, William Bergin, and Mary has the face of one of his own people. (For information about this shrine the editor is indebted to Zsolt Aradi's *Shrines to Our Lady Around the World,* New York, 1954.)

SLAVERY TO MARY. An attitude or relation to the Mother of God expressed in terms of "slavery" or "servitude" is particularly associated with three holy men, Cardinal Peter de Bérulle (d. 1629), Henry Boudon, Archdeacon of Évreux (d. 1702), and St. Louis Grignion de Montfort (d. 1716). Archdeacon Boudon explained it as a "sacred transaction made with the Queen of Heaven and earth whereby a person dedicates his freedom to become her slave, recognizing her as absolute mistress of his heart, giving up to her the rights arising from good actions, devoting himself entirely to the service of her majesty, which he will ever uphold." Cardinal de Bérulle put it this way: "I accept and recognize you [Mary] as my sovereign, in honor of the dependence that the Son of God, my Redeemer and my God, was willing to have upon you as His mother"; and the cardinal formulated this in a vow of dedication to Jesus Christ "in the state of perpetual slavery to His most holy Mother." This idea became popular in many parts of western Europe, and popularity brought exaggeration and deformation, so that, without criticizing Bérulle's teaching, "slavery to Mary" was discouraged by Rome because of the abuses to which it was giving rise. It was rehabilitated by St. Louis de Montfort. He taught in his *True Devotion* (*q.v.*) that this "holy slavery to Mary" is simply loving "slavery to God" through her: "One may call and make oneself Mary's slave in order thereby to become more perfectly Christ's slave. The Holy Virgin is the means through whom our Lord came to us; she is also the means through whom we can go to Him." Confraternities of Mary, Queen of our Hearts, were established in 1899 at the church of our Lady of Lourdes at Ottawa, and in 1913 at Rome, which propagate Montfort's teaching; these confraternities have been approved by the Holy See, which marks their difference from those confraternities of "Holy Slavery" which Rome dissolved in the past, and all recent popes have recommended the devotion. See CONSECRATION TO MARY.

Already in 1623 exception was taken to the word "slavery," and much of the difficulty that some people feel about the devotion is simply due to the use of this word as its name. No doubt the usage is justified in the abstract; but in our use of words and metaphors their psychological effect has to be taken into consideration. To many, "slavery" is a bad-sounding word that is difficult to fit happily into the Christian vocabulary nowadays: our Lord himself calls us His brethren and His friends. It may well be thought that the fetters of a chain can hardly be regarded as a good symbol of Christian love.

SNOW, OUR LADY OF THE. This name is sometimes given to churches in snowy places; and for a special explanation see MARY MAJOR, ST., FEAST OF THE DEDICATION OF. The defeat of the Turks by Prince Eugene of Savoy at the battle of Petrovaradin on the feast of this dedication, August 5, in 1716 (*cf.*, Rosary, Feast of the), accounts for two neighboring sanctuaries of this name. Our Lady of the Snow at Tekije (Yugoslavia) is a church built by the Jesuits, on the site of a Turkish mosque, in 1701; ever since the victory it has been regarded as a shrine of deliverance. The Franciscan church of our Lady of the Snow at Szeged (Hungary) was named for the same occasion. Popular enthusiasm adapted the Roman legend to the battle, and Prince Eugene's victory was attributed to the blinding of the enemy by a miraculous fall of snow. There are a number of other shrines of this title elsewhere, such as Maria-Schnee in the Pensterthall, Austria.

SODALITY OF THE BLESSED VIRGIN MARY (sometimes called simply The Sodality: from Lat. *sodalis,* comrade). The first of this world-wide group of Marian societies was founded in 1563 at the Roman College of the Society of Jesus, by Father John Leunis or Léon. It was a gathering of his pupils, under the protection of our Lady of the Annunciation, to seek perfection of life and perseverance in study and good works. It was so successful that in 1584 Pope Gregory XIII recognized it as a *Prima-Primaria,* First and Leading Sodality, empowering it to aggregate similar societies to itself, imparting to them its own privileges. The movement spread rapidly to Jesuit colleges in other countries, and by 1751 there were already 1,400 affiliated groups, of schoolboys, students, and grown men, and some of clergy. In that year Pope Benedict XIV authorized similar societies to be established for women and girls in Jesuit churches and affiliated to the *Prima-Primaria;* later on, this privilege was extended to Marian sodalities organized in other churches.

These sodalities have continued to grow in numbers and in effectiveness in their twin aims, sanctification of self and apostleship toward others; a remarkable number of saints and other famous men and women have belonged to them. Their direction is characterized by careful supervision of the members and a maximum opportunity for them to develop their personal abilities and potentialities. In a letter to the father general of the Jesuits in 1950, Pope Pius XII made it clear that the sodalities of our Lady with apostolic aims directed by the Society of Jesus are part of organized Catholic Action.

When the Society of Jesus was suppressed in 1773, the Jesuit sodalities were taken over by the local clergy. At the restoration of the Society in 1814, the Jesuits did not take back these numerous sodalities, but organized others of their own. This accounts for the existence today of many diocesan societies of Children of Mary, affiliated to the *Prima-Primaria,* over which the Society of Jesus has no authority and no responsibility. See also CHILDREN OF MARY.

SOLEDAD, NUESTRA SEÑORA DE LA. See SORROWS, SEVEN, FEASTS OF THE.

SORROWFUL MOTHER, SANCTUARY OF OUR. This is the chief shrine of our Lady of Sorrows in the United States, and one of the outstanding sanctuaries in the Americas. It is at Portland in Oregon, and was inaugurated by the Servants of Mary (Servites) in 1926. The ground covered is on two levels, the greater part being at the top of a 150-foot cliff, in most striking surroundings. There are a number of different shrines among the lawns, trees, and flowers, a great bronze statue of our Lady of Sorrows overtopping all; seven groups in limewood represent those seven sorrows. In the cliff-face on the lower level a large space has been hallowed out to shelter an altar, and above it is a marble replica of Michelangelo's *pietà* (*q.v.*).

The Servite church in Chicago, Ill., has a shrine of our Lady of Sorrows that is perhaps even more widely known, for it was there in 1937 that a novena was inaugurated to Mary under that title. Within a year there were thirty-eight novena services each Friday, for over 70,000 people. Since then numberless other people in many parts of the world have participated in it, far more than have ever been able actually to visit either of these sanctuaries.—The Sorrowful Mother shrine at Marywood, near Bellevue, Ohio, was established by Father De Sales Brunner over a hundred years ago. Unhappily the original image of Mary was destroyed in a fire in 1912; but the shrine has been rebuilt and attracts more pilgrims than ever.

SORROWS, SEVEN, Confraternity of the. The first Servite confraternity of Mary's sorrows was established at Bologna in Italy in 1598, and nine years later Pope Paul V put all similar confraternities (including a famous old Flemish one) under the same order of Servants of Mary. The members wear a black scapular (see SCAPULAR OF THE SEVEN SORROWS), and among their recommended prayers is the rosary of the seven sorrows (q.v.).

SORROWS, SEVEN, Feasts of the. There are two feasts of the Seven Sorrows B.V.M. observed throughout the Western Church, on the Friday in Passion week and on September 15, of which the first especially commemorates her "Compassion" (q.v.) and is so called in some calendars. They were added to the general calendar so late as 1727 and 1814, respectively, the feast of September 15 being of Servite origin. The proper of the Mass is the same for both days, except the collect, and both include the sequence Stabat Mater dolorosa (q.v.). In the course of history these feasts have been known by various names, some of which survive locally (e.g., our Lady of Pity in Portugal and Brazil), and have given rise to related observances, such as devotion to our Lady de la Soledad, "alone and grief-stricken," in Spanish-speaking lands. Braga in Portugal has two special votive Masses of Mary, her Lamentations and of Pity.

SORROWS, SEVEN, STATIONS OF THE, or Via Matris. The stations of Mary's Sorrows (q.v.) is a devotion proper to the order of Servants of Mary. It is analogous to the stations of the Cross, and probably originated soon after, at the end of the middle ages. As well as in Servite churches, the seven stations are sometimes found in others, by permission of the prior general of the order. The devotion has been richly indulgenced by the Holy See. The Via Matris provides the principal prayers of the novena that originated at the shrine of the Sorrowful Mother (q.v.) in Chicago.—Other Servite devotions in honor of the Seven Sorrows consist in recalling them with prayers on seven consecutive Fridays, and similar prayer every day of the month of September.

SORROWS OF OUR LADY. There are two aspects of this subject in the history of Christian devotion: Mary's "Compassion" (q.v.) at the foot of the cross, and the sorrows of her whole life, now generally enumerated as seven. This second development began as a popular movement, firstly in Flanders, during the fifteenth cen-

tury, and for long the sorrows en-
visaged varied in number and subject. They were eventually resolved
into Simeon's prophecy (Luke 2:35),
the flight into Egypt, the loss of the
boy Jesus at Jerusalem, Mary's meeting with Jesus on the road to Calvary, the crucifixion, the taking down
of His dead body, and its burial in
the tomb. Of these, the second was
formerly very commonly replaced by
the massacre of the Innocents, whose
poignancy is intensified by comparison with the divine Child's safety.
Devotion to the Sorrowing Mother
is distinctive of the Servite Order,
which has popularized her sorrows
as a subject for meditation throughout the centuries. In images of our
Lady of Sorrows she is represented
with her heart pierced by seven
swords (q.v.), a well-known example
being the bust between the two altars
in the Calvary chapel at Jerusalem,
which has been justly described as
"amazing." There is a Servite confraternity, a novena, a rosary, and
a scapular (qq.v.) of the Seven Sorrows. See also SUFFERINGS.

In the sermon read at Matins on
the feasts of the Seven Sorrows St.
Bernard says: "The Virgin's martyrdom is set before us both in the
prophecy of Simeon and in the story
of the Lord's passion. The holy old
man said of the child Jesus, 'Behold,
this child is set for a sign which shall
be contradicted'; and to Mary he said,
'Your own soul a sword shall pierce.'
Truly, blessed Mother, did it pierce
your soul, for only by passing through
your soul could it penetrate the body
of your Son. And when this Jesus of
yours had given up the ghost, and
the cruel spear which opened His
side could not touch His soul any
more, it pierced through yours. His
soul was indeed no longer there, but
yours could not be torn thence."
There is an English version of the
Vespers hymn for the September feast,
Jam toto subitus vesper eat polo, that
is surely an improvement on the
Latin original (second stanza):

Under the world-redeeming rood
The most-afflicted Mother stood;
Her Son, upon its altar laid,
Th' eternal expiation made.

SOUTHWARK, OUR LADY OF.
See SAINT GEORGE'S, OUR LADY OF.

SPAIN, SHRINES OF. Although
the early liturgy of Spain may have
had only one feast (q.v.) of our Lady
before the tenth century (the Annunciation, on December 18), a
church is said to have been dedicated
in her honor at Toledo so early as
the year 587; and there is evidence
for an important Marian sanctuary
near the same place at the end of the
following century. Spaniards have
long been distinguished by a very
strong devotion to Mary, which they
carried overseas to South America. It
was a Castilian king, Alfonso X (d.
1284), who was the first, so far as
records go, to associate her with the
month of May, in his Songs (*cantigas*)
of Mary. Her sanctuaries in Spain are
very numerous: in a book of pastoral
theology by a dean of Tarragona cathedral, Dr. D. Salvador Rial, a list
of local Marian invocations runs to

fourteen pages. Montserrat and our Lady of the Pillar (qq.v.) at Saragossa are outstanding. Others that must be mentioned are: our Lady of Aránzazu (q.v.); O.L. of Almudena, Madrid; O.L. of Ransom (q.v.), Barcelona; O.L. of Begoña, Bilbao; O.L. of the Chapel, Jaén; O.L. of Covadonga (q.v.); O.L. of Europe (q.v.); the Mother of the Forsaken (q.v.); O.L. of Fuencisla, Segovia; O.L. of Fuensanta, Córdova; O.L. of the Girdle (q.v.), Tortosa; O.L. of Guadalupe (q.v.); Our Lady of the Kings, Seville; O.L. of Light, Majorca; La Macarena, a very remarkable statue of the weeping Mother, much resorted to by bullfighters; O.L. of Miracles, Madrid; O.L. of Peace (q.v.) at Toledo and of Inward Peace at Madrid; O.L. of El Pueyo, Barbastro; O.L. of Puig (q.v.); O.L. of Semon and of Serra, Tarragona; O.L. of Sorrows, Granada; O.L. of Tenerife (q.v.); O.L. of Valvanera, Calahorra; O.L. of San Lorenzo and the Vulnerata (q.v.) at Valladolid; O.L. of Veruela (q.v.); O.L. of Villa Viciosa, Córdova; O.L. of the Waters, Carcagente; the White Virgin of Pamplona; the Virgin de la Concha, Zamora. Some of these shrines have a proper local feast; others of them keep their patronal festival on September 8, our Lady's birthday.

SPOUSE. This term, which has a rather artificial sound in modern English, is often applied to St. Joseph, "spouse of the Blessed Virgin." In Latin, sponsus means one who is betrothed; but in English "spouse" now means husband or wife. The gospels tell us that Joseph was betrothed or "espoused" to Mary (cf., Betrothal), and later he "took unto him his wife" (Matt. 1:24); although the union was not consummated, this was a true marriage, and Joseph and Mary became husband and wife (in Latin, conjux). The most generally useful English translation of sponsa is "bride."

STABAT MATER DOLOROSA. A hymn of Mary's sorrows which has become very familiar and well loved through its use at the service of stations of the cross. Its authorship has been much discussed; it is most commonly attributed to a Friar Minor, Bl. Jacopone of Todi (d. 1306). There are very many English translations, including versions by Dominic Aylward, Aubrey de Vere, John Bannister Tabb, and Edward Caswall. The following is Monsignor R. A. Knox's rendering of the opening stanza (Westminster Hymnal, no. 37):

By the cross her vigil keeping
Stands the Queen of sorrows weeping,
    While her Son in torment hangs;
Now she feels—O heart afflicted
By the sword of old predicted!—
    More than all a mother's pangs.

This hymn is sung as a sequence (q.v.) at Mass on the two feasts of the Seven Sorrows B.V.M., and, divided into three, is the hymn for Matins, Lauds, and Vespers at the Lenten commemoration. It found its way into the liturgical books of some dioceses and religious orders during the late middle ages, but was not admitted to the general Roman service books till 1727. The *Stabat Mater* is a very moving expression of highly personal devotion; but for that very reason it is somewhat out of accord with the traditional spirit of the Roman liturgy. It has, writes Father J. A. Jungmann, "an accent that is emotionally lyrical rather than hymnic, and in its immersion in Christ's sufferings it shows traces of individualistic piety . . . hardly consonant with the objective spirit of common prayer" (*The Mass of the Roman Rite,* i, 3,2,5). The hymn has been given settings by many musicians from Josquin des Prés to Dvorak, including, of course, Rossini and Listz.

STABAT MATER SPECIOSA. This is a less well-known companion hymn, or as some stern critics say a parody, of *Stabat Mater dolorosa,* celebrating Mary's joy at Christmas. It was rescued from oblivion by Frederick Ozanam, founder of the Society of St. Vincent de Paul, who printed it in his *Poètes franciscains en Italie au xiiie siècle* in 1852. It has been translated into English by, among others, J. M. Neale and Monsignor H. T. Henry. Its author is not known, but it was not necessarily written by the same hand as the *Dolorosa.*

STAR OF THE SEA. This is probably the most popular interpretation of *Miryam,* the Hebrew original of the name Mary. It appears to be due to St. Jerome, writing about the year 400, and the expression, *stella maris* in Latin, passed into the Western Christian vocabulary and maintains to this day its popularity as an epithet of our Lady.

The English scholar Alcuin (d. 804), in an inscription for an altar, refers to her as *lux et stella maris,* light and star of the sea. St. Bernard (d. 1153) expatiates on "this name, which is said to mean star of the sea, so well and aptly applied to the Virgin Mother. . . . Whoever you are, if you find yourself being tossed about in the gales and storms of this world's waters . . . , fix your eyes on the brightness of this star. . . . If the winds of temptation rise, if you are running on the rocks of tribulation, look to the star, call to Mary." St. Bonaventure (d. 1274) writes: "This name is most fitting for Mary, who is to us as a star above the sea. . . . She guides to a landfall in Heaven those who navigate the sea of this world in the ship of innocence or penance. . . . Well do we compare Mary to a star of the sea, because of her shining purity, her brightness, all that she does for us." The anonymous author of *The Mirror of Our Lady* (*c.* 1440) writes that it is appropriate to praise Mary early in the morning because "Some say that at Matins time there appeareth a star in the firmament whereby shipmen are guided on the sea and bring themselves safely to port, and it is our Lady that succoureth mankind in the troublous sea of this world and bringeth her lovers to the haven of salvation." The expression is familiar in hymnody, from *Ave, maris Stella* and the second line of *Alma Redemptoris Mater*—"Star of the deep and gateway of the sky"—to Dr. Lingard's

"Hail, Queen of Heav'n, the ocean star."

In the Litany of Loreto, Mary is invoked as Morning Star (*q.v.*) but not as Star of the Sea. The latter title is a common church dedication in the United States and elsewhere; a variation, our Lady of the Waves, is found at Dunbar in Scotland and Vatersay in the Hebrides, there is a Notre-Dame des Flots near Havre in France, and doubtless similar names in other places. The shrine of our Lady of Bonaria at Cagliari, in the island of Sardinia, is a sanctuary of Mary under this aspect; the proper office of the local feast (April 24) is full of pertinent allusions. There is a well-known church of our Lady of the Star in Naples.—In Mediterranean sailing-directions as early as the thirteenth century the compass rose or card, as well as the pole star, was referred to as the *stella maris*. See also NAME OF MARY.

STARKENBURG, OUR LADY OF, Missouri. One of the most attractive images of the Mother and Child in America is at Starkenburg, Rhineland, Mo. It was first set up here in a log chapel in 1852, and was called the White Lady, from the color of her long veil. Then the log chapel became a stone church, and the White Lady was put away in the attic as being not grand enough for her new surroundings. She was rescued by a sacristan, who built her a little chapel under the trees, to which pilgrims began to come. So she was again turned out, to make way for a more imposing image. Now the White Lady of Starkenburg stands above the altar of a new church built in 1910; the second statue that supplanted her, the Mother of Sorrows, is in a side chapel of the same building; and the whole forms a delightful shrine which attracts many pilgrims.

STATUES. See IMAGES; SHRINES.

STONE, OUR LADY OF. This shrine is at the convent of the Dominican sisters (third order) at Stone, Stafford county, in England. The wooden statue of Mother and Child was given to Mother Margaret Hallahan, foundress of the convent, by the Reverend Dr. James Spencer Northcote in 1862; it was enshrined in the open air in 1953 and at once began to attract pilgrims. There is also at this sanctuary a much venerated statue of Mary, Refuge of Sinners, given to Margaret Hallahan by a Belgian priest some time before she started teaching in Coventry. On three evenings in 1845 it was carried in procession round the church there, the first recorded processions of our Lady in England since the Reformation; and May devotions celebrated before it are said to have been the first in England. It is a charming small wooden image, painted and gilt, and is vested in the continental manner. Pope Pius IX granted an indulgence to prayer before this statue.

STONE GATE, OUR LADY OF THE, Zagreb. This image of Mary with her Child, in a street of Zagreb in Yugoslavia, was specially venerated by the people after it had survived, miraculously it seemed, a great fire in 1733. In 1933 it was solemnly crowned by Archbishop Antony Bauer (the predecessor of Cardinal Stepinać in the see of Zagreb), in the presence of the King and Queen of Yugoslavia, members of the Orthodox Church, who had presented one of the crowns. On that occasion Mass of the Roman rite was sung in the Slavonic language.

SUB TUUM PRAESIDIUM. The antiphon to the Song of Simeon at Compline in the Little Office B.V.M. (q.v.). In many places it is sung or said after the rosary or the Litany of Loreto or at the end of night prayers. "We take refuge beneath thy protection, holy Mother of God: do not turn thine eyes from our prayers in our need, but for ever set us free from all evil, thou glorious and blessed Virgin." A variation is: "We take refuge beneath thy protection, where the weak find strength: therefore do we sing thy praises, maiden Mother of God." There are equivalent anthems in the East: the Russians have one beginning "Steadfast protectress of Christians, do not disregard the beseeching voice of sinners . . ."; and the Syrians, "Protect us under thy wings from all dangers, Mother of God. . . ." This is probably the most ancient formal prayer to our Lady; it has been found in a Greek papyrus said to be of the third century.

SUFFERINGS, OUR LADY'S. From the time that Simeon foretold her heart would be pierced as by a sword (Luke 2:35), Mary's life as related in the Gospel was full of suffering. It had already been foreshadowed when Joseph was so deeply disturbed on her account (Matt. 1:18-20), and the glory of Bethlehem was preceded by the fatigues of the journey from Nazareth and the search for lodgings (Luke 2:1-7). Soon after, there was the flight into Egypt, with its fears for the Child's life and grief for those other mothers so suddenly bereaved. The next thing we are told is the disappearance of the boy Jesus, and long hours of prolonged searching (Luke 2:42-48). At some unknown date after that, mourning and grief will have been brought to Mary by the death of her husband Joseph.

From the beginning of her Son's public ministry Mary saw Him hated and reviled: even His fellow townsmen tried to kill Him (Luke 4:29), and His own relatives wanted to restrain Him because, they said, "He has gone mad" (Mark 3:21). Some have maintained that, throughout all the years from the Annunciation, Mary lived with the knowledge of her Son's final sufferings in her mind, and herself suffered accordingly. The gospel does not support such a view, and it is not in fact known when Mary first learned the mystery of Christ's redeeming death (cf., Knowledge). The Annunciation itself was a message of joy, at which Mary welcomed God's will, whatever it might be; her own words in the Magnificat (q.v.) have no hint of sadness; even Simeon's prophecy about the sword is part of a moment of exultation. When the time of the Passion came, we are left to infer the depth and height of Mary's suffering and in what manner she bore it. There have been those who attributed to her a sort of exaggerated stoicism; and there has been exaggeration in the other direction (*cf.,* Swoon of our Lady). Mary's suffering was commensurate with her boundless love for Jesus; she suffered as only a mother, and a perfect mother, could suffer, sharing so deeply the agony of the perfect Son; but she was mistress of herself (St. John tells us she *stood* at the foot of the cross), and saw beyond the moment to its end and meaning, of which Jesus must have talked with her (*cf.,* Matt. 16:21). As so often, the voice of the faithful opens the heart of a mystery, in this case in the words of a German folk carol, wherein St. Peter says to our Lady at the Passion:

Nay, Mary, cease your weeping, dear:
Those wounds, they are but small,
For they win Heaven, for all!

With the glorious Resurrection the work of redemption, in which Mary had been chosen to co-operate in joy and in sorrow, was complete. But in the years that followed she must still have experienced the sorrows of this world; hatred still pursued the memory of her Son, hatred that brought some of His dearest followers to violent death, starting with the stoning of the deacon Stephen (Acts 7:54-60). Hers was the human lot: earthly suffering can end only with earthly life. *Cf.,* Sorrows of our Lady.

It has ever been believed in the Church that the sentence pronounced on Eve, "In sorrow shalt thou bring forth children" (Gen. 3:16), passed over the New Eve, and that she underwent none of the pains of childbirth. "There were two childbearings of Mary," wrote St. Antoninus (d. 1459), "The first, whereby the Savior came to us, was painless; nay rather, it was piercingly delightful. But of the spiritual childbearing, whereby she engenders us to God, she could say, 'Look and see if there be any sorrow like to my sorrow.' " This belief in the painlessness of the birth of Jesus is particularly marked in the Byzantine liturgy. At Matins on Holy Saturday, for example, the following words are put into Mary's mouth: "My eternal Son, at thy wondrous birth all suffering passed me by, I was filled with a joy outside of nature. But now, O my Son, I see thee dead, all life gone, and I am pierced through with a sword of grief. Rise then from the grave, that I may be magnified by thee."

SUFFRAGE, OUR LADY OF. *Suffragium* is a Latin word rather difficult to render into English in this connection: it refers to Mary's prayers on our behalf, so perhaps "of Intercession" or "of Support" would do. In some churches a feast of this name is observed soon after All Souls' day with reference to our Lady as interceding for the souls in Purgatory. "Grant, we beseech thee, almighty God," says the collect of the Mass, "that through the prayers of the blessed and ever-maiden Mary we may obtain clemency for the souls of the faithful and for ourselves the gifts of thy grace unto life everlasting."

SWEDEN, SHRINES OF.

The principal churches of our Lady in Sweden before the Protestant Reformation were at Dragsmark, Helsingborg, Lund, Mariefred, Örebro, Sigtuna, Skænninge, Visby, and Ystad, and there was a celebrated statue of Mother and Child at St. Bridget's abbey of Vadstena. The Swedish Catholic body to-day, however, is very small and scattered, and at present seems to have no pilgrimage shrine.

SWITZERLAND, SHRINES OF.

Some of the Swiss shrines of Mary date from the early sixteenth century or before; others are associated with events during the Reformation period, such as Maria-Rickenbach in the Bernese Oberland and Bourgillon in the Fribourg canton, where the images were saved from destruction by the iconoclasts. The fame of the sanctuary of Einsiedeln (q.v.) is world-wide. Others are: our Lady of Geneva, a statue of Mary Immaculate given by Pope Pius IX in 1859; O.L. of the Churchyard, at Glis in Valais, a shrine for a thousand years; O.L. of Sorrows, at Gormund, near Neudorf, Lucerne; O.L. of Help, on a mountain at Gubel, in the canton of Zug; O.L. of the Rock (q.v.) at Locarno; Maria-Bildstein, in the canton of Sankt-Gallen; Maria-Riederthal, at Bürglen, near Altdorf, Uri; Maria-Stein (q.v.); O.L. of Compassion at Werthenstein; O.L. of Zitail (q.v.).

SWOON OF OUR LADY, The.

This curious name—sometimes made more curious in English by being called the "Spasm" (Lat. spasmus)—developed at Jerusalem in the middle ages. An apocryphal writing (q.v.) called the Gospel of Nicodemus makes much of Mary's agony during her Son's passage to Calvary, and the idea grew up that when she met Him on the way she fainted; this idea perhaps contributed to the development of devotion to Mary's sorrows. This alleged happening was naturally associated with the traditional site of the fourth station in Jerusalem, and at least since the twelfth century there has been a church there called St. Mary of the Swoon: the present building is modern, built for the Catholics of Armenian rite. (Cf., our Lady of Fear, under NAZARETH herein. The word spasmus is sometimes used of Mary's sufferings at the Passion in general, not always without a suggestion of her being completely overcome by them.)—That Mary should have been so far carried away by personal sorrow at a moment when the redemption of mankind was about to be finally achieved would certainly seem to be an exaggeration; and Pope Benedict XIV was following Julius II when he rebuked preachers and artists for representing the Mother of God as swooning away (see SUFFERINGS). Very different from such excess of emotion was Cardinal Newman's tone when meditating on the fourth station: "Mary would rather have had all His sufferings herself, could that have been, than not to have known what they were by ceasing to be near Him.

. . . He was now carrying the load of the world's sins, and, all holy though He was, He carried the image of them on His very face. . . . What a meeting of Mother and Son! Yet there was a mutual comfort, for there was a mutual sympathy. . . ."

SWORDS, SEVEN. "And Simeon . . . said to Mary his mother, '. . . thy own soul a sword shall pierce.' " These words spoken by Holy Simeon when Jesus as a baby was presented in the Temple led naturally to Mary's sorrows (*q.v.*) being represented pictorially as so many swords piercing her heart, Simeon's prophecy being the first. But it must not be overlooked that Simeon's words as a whole were primarily triumphant and thankful: "My eyes have seen thy salvation . . . a light of revelation to the Gentiles and a glory for thy people Israel" (Luke 2:30-32).

SYNAXIS OF OUR LADY. In the Byzantine rite a synaxis (Gr., assembly) is the gathering of the faithful to celebrate saints associated with a feast on the previous day. On the day after Christmas there is a synaxis of the Mother of God, a commemoration of her divine motherhood. Other Eastern Christians have a similar observance on the same day: in the Syrian and Maronite rites it is called our Lady's Praises, and in the Chaldean rite her Congratulations, "the day of lullabies." There is a synaxis of St. Joachim and St. Ann on the day after Mary's birthday and of Gabriel the Archangel after the Annunciation. *Cf.,* Circumcision.

SYRIA AND LEBANON, SHRINES OF. The combined population of these two states is in great majority Mohammedan, though in the Lebanese republic there is a bare majority of Christians. In both states they form a remarkable mixture of rites and allegiances: the Catholics are nearly all of various Eastern rites, Maronites being the most numerous. The chief sanctuaries of the latter are our Lady of the Almond Trees at Luwayzeh, our Lady of Bikfaya, and our Lady of Kannubin, which has been the summer residence of the Maronite patriarch since the fifteenth century. Our Lady of the Look-Out, near Sidon, is in charge of Catholic Melkite monks; the Armenian Catholics have a pilgrimage shrine at Bzommar (*q.v.*), and those of West Syrian rite one at Sharfeh. In the Christian quarter of Tripoli there is a sanctuary of our Lady of the Ward (Saidyat al-Harat); a new shrine was inaugurated at Harissa (*q.v.*) in 1954. The principal Orthodox shrine of the Mother of God is at Saidnaia (*q.v.*), near Damascus.

T

TABLES, NOTRE-DAME DES,
Montpellier. This French sanctuary
appears to have got its name from the
ex-voto tablets hung around it. It was
resorted to from early times, its black
wooden statue, enclosed within a large
silver one, being so famed for miracles
that a special feast was already established in 1189. After suffering at the
hands of Huguenots, when the statue
disappeared, the church was utterly
destroyed at the Revolution; but the
cultus of Notre-Dame des Tables was
kept alive and carried on in the
church of the Jesuits at Montpellier.
Feast: August 31.

TAMANURA, OUR LADY OF.
The best-known shrine of our Lady of
Lourdes in Japan, and the one that
comes closest to being a place of national pilgrimage, is at the church of
Imochi at Tamanura in the Goto Islands. It was built by the people between 1895 and 1899, and many cures
have been recorded there: it has a well
into which Lourdes water is poured
every year on February 11. This sanctuary was founded by the Marianist
Father Pelu.

TE DEUM MARIALE. An adaptation or interpolation of the thanks-
giving-hymn *Te Deum laudamus*
with reference to the Blessed Virgin.
There were a number of these written
in the middle ages and later, of which
the best-known begins:

Te Matrem Dei laudamus, te omnis
terra veneratur, aeterni Patris
sponsam. . . .
We praise thee, Mother of God, all
the earth reveres thee, bride of
the eternal Father. . . .

At least two such were composed in
England, one of them, by Thomas of
Elmham, a Benedictine monk, including a prayer to Mary on behalf of
England. The following two verses of
this are interesting on account of
their reference to our Lady's Dowry
(*q.v.*):

Te ergo quaesumus Angligenis sub-
veni, quos pro Dote propria de-
fendisti. . . .
We therefore pray thee help the English people, whom thou hast defended as thine own Dowry. . . .
Salvum fac populum tuum, Domina,
et a mortis peste Dotem tuam
libera.
Save, Lady, thy people, and deliver
thy Dowry from the curse of
death.

While recognizing the love of Mary
that prompted outpourings of this
kind, it can hardly be a matter for regret that they were but a passing fashion, though they persisted into the
eighteenth century, getting ever farther away from their original. And
even today something of the sort may

still be heard occasionally at some pilgrim shrines, it is said. *Cf., Gloria, Farced.*

TENERIFE, OUR LADY OF. According to tradition, the Guanches of Tenerife in the Canary Islands were venerating an image of the Mother and Child before the Spaniards finally took possession and converted them to Christianity. This statue became the center of a popular shrine, and veneration of our Lady of Tenerife (under the name of "Candelaria") had already spread to parts of Latin America by the mid-sixteenth century.

TENDERNESS, OUR LADY OF. See VLADIMIR, OUR LADY OF.

THEOTOKION. One of the class of rhythmical hymns, of varying length, of the Byzantine rite called *troparia.* Except on feasts of our Lord, every group of these hymns is followed by one in honor of the Mother of God, accordingly called a *theotokion.* There is a large number of these *theotokia,* whose presence underlines the unity of Mary with Christ through her motherhood, and His unity with her through His sonship. The following is a *theotokion* for Saturday Vespers: "Your mysteries are glorious beyond the power of thought, O Forth-bringer of God; for being sealed in holiness and confirmed in maidenhood, you were seen in very truth to be the Mother who did give birth to the true God. So then, entreat Him to save our souls." When one of these hymns commemorates our Lady at the foot of the cross, as on Wednesday and Friday, it is called a *stavrotheotokion.*

THEOTOKOS. The first anathema of St. Cyril, Archbishop of Alexandria, who presided at the oecumenical council held at Ephesus (*q.v.*) in the year 431, runs: "If anyone should not confess that Emmanuel is truly God and that in consequence the Holy Virgin is *theotokos* —for she brought forth according to the flesh the Word of God made flesh—let him be anathema." From that time on, the Greek word *Theotokos* has been the key-word of Mariology. In English it is commonly translated Mother of God, but it is more literally rendered God-bearer, or God's forth-bringer. The Latin equivalents are *Deipara* and *Dei Genitrix,* both of which are much used. Cardinal Newman wrote of the word Theotokos that it "carries with it no admixture of rhetoric, no taint of extravagant affection—it has nothing else but a well-weighed, grave, dogmatic sense, which corresponds and is adequate to its sound. It intends to express that God is her Son, as truly as any one of us is the son of his own mother."—In the East, the expression Theotokos, and its equivalents in other tongues, is very commonly used when referring to our Lady, especially in the liturgy of worship and in writing. See MOTHER OF GOD.

THORN-BUSH, OUR LADY OF THE. The name of this shrine near Chalôns-sur-Marne in France is due to a legend that had its origin in the devotion of the Augustinian canons of

Saint-Victor to the sinless Mother of God, unscathed among the world's flames, like the Burning Bush (*q.v.*): during the middle ages these canons had charge of the church at this place. The sanctuary decayed during the Wars of Religion and the Revolution, but it was restored during the nineteenth century, and the small medieval statue of our Lady repaired and replaced. It is now once more a place of local pilgrimage.

THREE HAIL MARYS, The. A series of seven prayers to our Lady, one for each day of the week, written by St. Alphonsus Liguori (d. 1787). Each prayer is followed by the Hail Mary, said three times in reparation for impieties spoken against her. This devotion, indulgenced by the Holy See, has been widely popularized by two French Capuchins. An archconfraternity of the Three "Hail Marys" has its centre at Blois in France, where there is a pilgrimage church inaugurated in 1932.—There is an indulgenced prayer, "Most holy Virgin, Mother of the Word made flesh . . . ," and a threefold invocation of her in her virginity, each followed by Hail Mary thrice.—There is also a devotion of three Hail Marys daily in honor of the power, wisdom and loving mercy of the Blessed Virgin, with the invocation, "Mary, my Mother, preserve me from mortal sin." This is said to have been revealed to St. Mechtildis (d. 1298).

TITLES OF MARY. The official title (if the expression may be allowed) of Mary in the Western Church is simply the Blessed Virgin Mary (*Beata Maria Virgo*). But in ordinary speech and writing she is of course referred to in a variety of ways, by titles of dignity and honor or more familiar expressions of love and reverence, and these vary from country to country. In English-speaking lands "our Lady" (*q.v.*) is easily the most usual mode of reference, though in North America "the Blessed Mother" has become very popular in recent years (there is at least one church called by this name, at Owensboro, Ky.). Among Protestants, "the Virgin Mary" is usual, but "the Blessed Virgin" or simply "the Virgin" may sometimes be heard. The French speak of "the Holy Virgin" (*la Sainte Vierge*) or "the Most Holy Virgin" (*la Très-Sainte Vierge*), or just *la Vierge* or Marie. In German, "the Mother of God" (*Die Muttergottes*) is common; "our dear Lady" (*Unsere liebe Frau*) is also used; *Gottesgebärerin* is theological (meaning Theotokos, *q.v.*). Italians speak of *la Santa Vergine, Maria santissima*, and, very commonly, *la Madonna* (*q.v.*); while Spaniards say *la Virgen* and Poles *Najswietsza Panienka*, "the Blessed Virgin." And so on. The classical expression for Mary in the East is *Theotokos* (*q.v.*) and its equivalents, e.g., in Slavonic, *Bogorodytse;* but the colloquial Greek expression is *Panagia* (*q.v.*). Russians and other Slavs commonly speak of "the Holy Virgin," "the Mother of God," and "the Ever-Virgin Mary."

In addition to these familiar and colloquial names there is a great variety of epithetical expressions used in litanies, sermons, and devotional and theological writings; of these, some figure in the Litany of Loreto (*q.v.*), and a number of others are listed by Father Paul F. Palmer, s.j., in his *Mary in the Documents of the Church* (1952). But apart from all these there is an almost endless series of Marian titles properly so called, designating particular feasts, images, shrines, and dedications of churches. Many of these are mentioned in their proper places in this book; there here follows a list of some other such titles that are unusual and not mentioned elsewhere herein. They are grouped under countries, but some of them are found in more than one land; place-name titles are excluded.

Belgium: our Lady of the Burning Candle, O.L. of the New Plantation, O.L. of the Passers-by, O.L. of the Singing Birds. *Canada:* O.L. of the Atonement (Alberta), Notre-Dame de Jacques Cartier (Quebec), O.L. of the Fields, N.-D. du Foyer (Montreal), N.-D. de l'Île Maligne, N.-D. du Lac des Habitants (P.Q.), O.L. of the Portage (Ontario), N.-D., Porte de l'Aurore (Montreal), O.L. of the Prairies, O.L., Queen of our Hearts (Saskatchewan), O.L. of the Smile. *Cyprus:* the Panagia of Aphrodite, O.L. the Cave-dweller. *England:* St. Mary le Bow, St. Mary Matfellon, St. Mary Abchurch, St. Mary Axe, all in London (the last is a name widely familiar through John Wellington Wells's song in Gilbert and Sullivan's *The Sorcerer!*), St. Mary on the Quay (Bristol), O.L. of the Garden Gate (Somers Town), O.L. of the Bower (Wiltshire), O.L. of Good Winds (Apostleship of the Sea). *Egypt:*

Mother of Light. *Ethiopia:* Covenant of Mercy. *France:* O.L. of the Globe, O.L. of Life, O.L. of the Marsh, O.L. of the Silver Foot, O.L. of the Three Stones, O.L. of the Vale of Love, O.L. Well-Met. *Greece:* the Panagia who-sees-all. *Holland:* O.L. of the Inkpot. *Ireland:* Queen of the Poor. *Italy:* O.L. of the Bakery, O.L. of the Bed, O.L. of the Blackbirds, O.L. of the Boat, O.L. of the Corner, Mother of Confidence, O.L. of Eternity, O.L. of the Fence, O.L. of the Foundry, O.L. Halfway-Up (a hill), O.L. of the Lamp, O.L. of the Moving Eyes, O.L. of Perseverance, O.L. under the Organ, O.L. of Sweet Waters, O.L. of Tears, O.L. of Tillage, O.L. of the Wilderness, O.L. of the Window, O.L. at World's End. There are a number of names in Italy, and elsewhere, referring to trees: "of the Larches," "of the Plum Tree," etc. *Portugal:* O.L. in Exile (in Egypt). *Russia:* O.L., Provider for the Poor, O.L. of Sweet-Smelling Flowers, O.L. of Unexpected Joy. *Sicily:* O.L. of Paradise, O.L. of the Water-Bringer. *Spain:* O.L. of Good News, the Virgin Suckling, O.L. of the Kine. *United States:* O.L. of the Airways (Mass.), O.L. of the Bright Mount (Calif.), O.L. of the Cataract (Niagara Falls, N.Y.), O.L. of the Cedars of Lebanon (Mass.), St. Mary of the Eternal (Pa.), O.L. of the Gardens (Ill.), O.L. of the Gulf (Miss.), O.L. of the Knobs (Ind.), O.L. of the Missions (Fla.), O.L. of the Railways (Mass.), St. Mary of the Woods (Ind.). Topographical titles, such as "of the Lake" and "of the Snows," are fairly common in North America. See also MADONNA; SHRINES.

TITULAR OF CHURCHES, St. Mary as. See DEDICATIONS.

TOMB OF OUR LADY. See ASSUMPTION, PLACE OF THE.

TONGLU, OUR LADY OF. Tonglu is in the diocese of Paotingfu in north China, a mission founded by the Vincentians. After the town had been preserved from the Boxers during the insurrection of 1900, a Chinese priest, Father Wu, built a church there dedicated in honor of our Lady of China. He had a picture made of the Mother and Child to be set above the altar; and in it our Lady was shown wearing robes copied from a portrait of the last Manchu empress, Tzu-hsi. But the image appears to be more European than Chinese in form and feeling. The Mother is enthroned in imperial robes, and the Child stands with outstretched hands in her left arm. The Tonglu sanctuary was finally established by Father J. Trémorin, C.M., in 1929, but in 1942 church and shrine were completely destroyed by communists. The original picture was, however, saved intact. This shrine of our Lady of China was particularly visited at Easter, Christmas, the Assumption, and All Souls.

TOUTE GRÂCE, NOTRE-DAME DE, Nicolet. This shrine at Nicolet in the province of Quebec is the sanctuary of the Centre Marial Canadien. It was built in 1952, and already draws numerous pilgrims from all parts. The center with which it is associated is well known for its Marian publications, library, and art gallery.

TOWER OF DAVID. Latin *Turris Davidica*, an invocation of our Lady in the Litany of Loreto, accommodated from the Song of Songs (4:4), "Thy neck rising proudly, nobly adorned, like David's embattled tower . . .": first used of her by Honorius of Autun (d. *c.* 1135). In its simplest meaning a tower is a building for defense, a "strong-point," and Mary is the Tower of David, "the high and strong defense of the King of the true Israel."

TOWER OF IVORY. Latin *Turris eburnea*, an invocation of our Lady in the Litany of Loreto, accommodated from the Song of Songs (7:4), "Thy neck rising proudly like a tower, but all of ivory . . .": first used of her by Honorius of Autun (d. *c.* 1135). "A tower is a fabric which rises higher and more conspicuous than other objects in its neighbourhood. . . . It is expressly noted of [Mary] that she *stood* by the Cross. She did not grovel in the dust, but *stood upright* to receive the blows, the stabs, which the long passion of her Son inflicted upon her every moment." And so, in her strength and generosity, as compared with the weakness of Peter and the other apostles at the Passion, Mary is "fitly imaged as a Tower. . . . She is called the Tower of Ivory to suggest to us, by the brightness, purity and exquisiteness of that material, how transcendent is the loveliness and the gentleness of the Mother of God" (Cardinal Newman).

TRADITION AND LEGEND. In its strict sense in a Catholic context the word *Tradition* designates the body of divinely revealed truths appertaining to faith and morals, not contained in the Sacred Scriptures, but transmitted orally to the Church by Christ and the Apostles. But "tradition" or "traditional" is also very commonly used of a large variety of beliefs (and practices) simply as having been accepted by many people for a long time, and perhaps approved, even encouraged, by authorities in the Church. This second meaning of the word and its derivatives is sharply distinguished from the first meaning. That something is traditional in this second sense does not prove that it is true; a tradition of this sort can be mistaken or undesirable: it is a matter of evidence and judgment, not of faith. Thus, the Assumption is part of the Church's Tradition, proposed by her for the belief of all the faithful; but the tradition of, say, the miraculous transfer of the image of our Lady of Notown is not part of the Church's Tradition, and she does not propose it for our belief.

Sometimes, through careless and harmful use, the word tradition is given a general connotation of necessary truth that, in fact, it has only in relation to the Tradition of the Church. On the other hand, the word *legend* is nearly always given a connotation of falsity that it does not necessarily bear. Etymologically, a legend is simply something to be read (Lat. *legere,* to read), and originally designated a composition about the life of a saint to be read in church. But in course of time the present unfavorable meaning became attached

to the word, a development for which good reasons were not lacking. Strictly speaking, then, a legend may be true or false or a mixture; but it is not always possible to ascertain with certainty which it is. It has to be borne in mind that legends, in the bad sense, can gain regrettably easy currency. Three hundred years ago a Scottish priest wrote about the image of our Lady of Abereen (*q.v*): "The common belief of the vulgar people there [Brussels] is that this statue was thrown into the sea at Aberdeen, and carried on the waves of the sea miraculously to Ostend. So easy a thing it is for fables to find good harbor, where verities would be beaten out with cudgels." *Cf.,* Mary: her Legend; Legends of our Lady; Miracles, etc.

TRANSITUS MARIAE. See PASSING OF MARY, THE.

TRIM, OUR LADY OF. The abbey of Augustinian canons regular at Trim in Meath was perhaps the most celebrated Marian sanctuary of medieval Ireland. "The image of the Blessed Mary of Trim" is referred to before the end of the fourteenth century; but the following century was the time of its greatest fame, when the English king Henry VI protected pilgrims to it and many miracles were reported. The shrine was destroyed in 1539, but the statue was saved and kept for veneration at the mansion of the Hammonds in Trim until 1642. In that year Sir Charles Coote occupied the town, and his son had the statue chopped up for firewood to warm his father on a cold day.

TRSKI VRH, OUR LADY OF. The little statue of our Lady of Jerusalem at Trski Vrh (Krapina) in Yugoslavia is said to have been brought thither from Palestine by a Franciscan friar. It soon was in repute as wonderworking. When in 1750 the cattle of the place were unscathed in an outbreak of disease, the people in thanksgiving built a new church; there the statue has been enshrined ever since.

TRUE DEVOTION TO THE BLESSED VIRGIN. The book called *A Treatise on True Devotion to the Blessed Virgin* was written by St. Louis Mary Grignion de Montfort, a French priest who died in 1716 and was canonized in 1947. His famous work, however, disappeared from view and was not published till 1843. But during the century that followed it attained a great influence, and was widely popularized, especially by the Company of Mary, Montfort Fathers, whose founder St. Louis Grignion was. The book was translated into English in 1862 by Father F. W. Faber, who said of its author that "those who take him for their master will hardly be able to name a saint or ascetical writer to whose grace and spirit their mind will be more subject than to his."

St. Louis Grignion characterizes true devotion to Mary by five qualities: as being inward, from the spirit and heart; tender, with a childlike confidence; holy, in emulating Mary's virtues; unwavering in perseverance; and disinterested, loving her because she is so worthy of love. The particular practice of this devotion with which he is principally concerned is consecration to Jesus Christ by a total consecration of oneself to the Blessed Virgin; for perfection in this, all actions should be done "*by* Mary, *with* Mary, *in* Mary and *for* Mary, so that we may do them all the more perfectly *by* Jesus, *with* Jesus, *in* Jesus and *for* Jesus." St. Louis Grignion uses the phrase "slavery to Jesus in Mary" to express the close unity between them, "a union so close that one is all in the other, Jesus in Mary and Mary in Jesus: or rather, she no longer is, but Jesus only in her—it is easier to separate its light from the sun than Mary from Jesus."

The way in which the book is written does not appeal to all readers, but its teaching (which is again referred to herein under CONSECRATION TO MARY and SLAVERY TO MARY) has been recommended by every pope since the work was published. St. Pius X re-read *True Devotion* before writing his encyclical letter *Ad diem illum* for the fiftieth anniversary of the definition of the Immaculate Conception.

TURUMBA, OUR LADY OF THE. This image is venerated at Pakil on the Laguna de Baie in the Philippine Islands. Like a number of other images in various parts of the world, it is said to have been found in the water, by men fishing in the lake. It was carried to the church by people singing a song in praise of Mary called *turumba,* and that name was given to the statue. It represents our Lady of the Seven Swords (*q.v.*); the face and hands are of ivory, and it is clothed in a silken robe, with gold bracelets on the arms. The shrine of our Lady of the Turumba has now been in existence for over a hundred years. Its principal festival day is the anniversary of the finding of the image on the Wednesday after Easter, and processions of dancers are a feature of the celebrations, the dances accompanied by shouts and hand-clapping. A stream behind the church has been dammed up to form a pool for pilgrims to bathe in.

TWELVE STARS. See CROWN OF TWELVE STARS.

TYPE OF THE CHURCH, MARY AS. The early Fathers often looked on the Church in a "personalized" way which is nowadays less familiar. For St. Augustine or St. John Chrysostom, for instance, the Church is the New Eve, the bride of Christ brought forth from the side of the New Adam, herself the new mother of all mankind: at one and the same time the Church is mystically Christ's body and His bride. (This figure of marriage often recurs in the New Testament: e.g., Luke 5:34-35; John 3:29; Ephesians 5:25-27; Apocalypse 21:2, 9.) Moreover, the Fathers saw her as a virgin bride. Whereas Israel had been unfaithful with strange gods, the Church of the new covenant keeps the integrity of the faith and life delivered to her (St. Paul speaks of presenting the Church at Corinth as a chaste virgin to Christ; St. Augustine defines virginity of heart as a faith that is wholly pure). And not simply a virgin, but a virgin who is also a mother: "Nobody can have God for father un-less he has the Church for mother," says St. Cyprian (d. 258). She brings forth her children in the waters of baptism; she feeds them with the milk of her teaching and her sacraments; she, the maiden-bride, forms Christ in her members, as Christ was formed in the womb of the maiden-bride Mary.

It is, then, clear what is meant by Mary as type, as figure, of the Church. Mary, too, is the New Eve (*q.v.*); she, too, is the bride, the bride who remains virgin yet becomes a mother: the mother of Christ and spiritually the mother of His members, the faithful. The virgin Church and the virgin Mary both watch over the integrity of the faith (*cf.*, Destroyer of Heresies), and both are divinely preserved from the errors and corruptions of the world. Both represent the feminine and maternal element in the daily carrying on of the work of the redemption achieved once for all in the death and resurrection of Jesus Christ. Each is the Bride and Wisdom of the Old Testament, and the Woman of the New (*cf.*, Bible, Mary in the). Each is totally dependent on Christ as His handmaid; yet each enjoys the closest intimacy with Him and shines with an unearthly beauty, reflected from the beauty of the Only-begotten of the Father, full of grace and truth.

"Head and body, one single whole, Christ: of one God in Heaven and one mother on earth. Sons both many and one: for as the head and members are one son, as well as more than one, so Mary and the Church are one mother and more than one, one virgin and more than one. Each of the two is mother, each virgin. Each conceives by the same Spirit without bodily attraction, each sinless one brings forth an offspring to God the Father. Sinless Mary provides the Head for the body; the Church by the remission of all sin provides the body for the Head. Each is the mother of Christ, but neither gives birth to the whole without the other. Therefore, what in the God-inspired Scriptures is said universally of the Church, virgin and mother, is also said individually of Mary; and what is said in a special way of Mary, virgin and mother, is rightly understood, but in a general way, of the Church, virgin and mother: so that when Scripture is understood to be speaking of either, it can be applied to one or the other almost indifferently and in a mixed way. Again, each faithful soul also is the bride of the Word of God, mother, daughter and sister of Christ. Each faithful soul is understood in its own sense to be virgin and fruitful. The same thing therefore is said universally for the Church, in a special way for Mary, individually for the faithful soul: and it is the Wisdom of God who speaks, the Word of the Father. . . . Christ dwelt for nine months in the tabernacle of Mary's womb. He dwells till the end of the world in the tabernacle of the Church's faith. He will dwell for ever and ever in the knowledge and love of the faithful soul" (Isaac of Stella, Sermon lxi, on the Assumption).

U

UKRAINE, WESTERN, SHRINES OF. The Catholics of Slav-Byzantine rite in Western Ukraine and neighboring lands have had a number of pilgrimage shrines of the Mother of God. Some were lost when the imperial Russian government dissolved the Catholic Ruthenian church in its territories during the century following the partition of Poland (1791-1875): among them, those of Kholm (crowned in 1765) and Pochaev (*q.v.*). Others continued to flourish till the Soviet government annexed the Western Ukraine during World War II: such as Dobromyl, Hosiv (*q.v.*), Kalvarya, Pasliv, Sambir, Zovkva, and the shrines in St. George's cathedral at Lviv (Lvov) and of the Zarvanytsia icon (crowned in 1867). There was also an ancient and much revered miraculous icon in the Polish Dominican church at Lviv. It was of Greek origin, our Lady of Victory, and was brought from Kiev to Halych about 1113. A seventeenth-century icon of Mary, Comfort of the Suffering, was found in the Ukranian church of St. Barbara in Vienna in 1934; it is now enshrined in that church. See also CZECHOSLOVAKIA.

UNDERGROUND, OUR LADY. The first recorded reference to a statue of our Lady in a cave beneath the cathedral at Chartres is in 1389, the story being that it was carved before the birth of Jesus Christ to give honor to a virgin who should bear a child; later on this work was attributed to the Druids of Gaul, of whom Julius Caesar wrote. The statue was destroyed at the Revolution, but its nature is known from a copy and pictures that still exist, and it seems to have been not older than the twelfth century. The cave has been filled in, but there is a chapel near by in the cathedral crypt which enshrines an image, the Child-bearing Virgin, on the lines of the destroyed statue—the Mother crowned and enthroned with the Child on her lap, right hand raised in blessing (*cf.*, Notre-Dame-du-Port). The famous well close by, Le puits des Saints-Lieux-Forts, seems to have nothing to do with our Lady Underground.

UNITED STATES OF AMERICA, SHRINES OF THE. It is well known that the sixth Provincial Council of Baltimore dedicated the United States of America to Mary Immaculate in 1846. After the *Te Deum* at the end of their deliberations the conciliar fathers solemnly sang, "Eternal honor to the most blessed Virgin Mary, patroness of these provinces!", and in their pastoral letter they wrote: "We take this occasion, brethren, to communicate to you the determination, unanimously adopted by us, to place ourselves and all entrusted to our care throughout the United States under the special patronage of the Mother of God, whose immaculate conception is venerated by the piety of the faithful throughout the Catholic Church. . . . To her then we commend you, in confidence that through the one mediator of God and men, the man Jesus Christ, who gave Himself a redemption for all, she will obtain for us grace and salvation. The grace of our Lord Jesus Christ be with you all. Amen." It is a matter of history that since that moment the growth of devotion to and of shrines of the Blessed Virgin in the United States has been very marked.

In North America as a whole the older sanctuaries of Mary that became in varying degrees pilgrim-shrines were naturally mostly in the French northern and in the Spanish southern sections. But during the past 150 years many others have arisen, due to the enterprise of religious orders, the action or spiritual experience of individuals, or brought about in other ways. The following are among the principal ones in the United States. *Washington, D.C.:* The National Shrine of the Immaculate Conception (*q.v.*). *California:* La Purísima Concepción, near Lompoc. *Florida:* our Lady of La Leche (*q.v.*), St. Augustine. *Illinois:* church of the Annunciation, Aurora; church of the Sorrowful Mother (*q.v.*), Chicago. *Indiana:* Lourdes shrine at Notre Dame University. *Kentucky:* Lourdes shrine at the church of St. Aloysius, Covington; Mother of Good Counsel (*q.v.*) mis-

sion, Hazard. *Louisiana:* Our Lady of Prompt Succor (*q.v.*), New Orleans. *Massachusetts:* O.L. of Perpetual Help (*q.v.*), Roxbury. *Minnesota:* chapel of the Assumption, Cold Spring. *Missouri:* shrine of the Miraculous Medal (*q.v.*), Perryville; O.L. of Starkenburg (*q.v.*), Rhineland. *New Hampshire:* O.L. of Grace (*q.v.*), Colebrook; O.L. of La Salette (*q.v.*), Enfield. *New Jersey:* O.L. of the Rosary, Summit. *New Mexico:* "La Conquistadora" (*q.v.*); O.L. of Guadalupe, Mesilla Park; Lourdes shrine (*q.v.*) at Seboyeta, and another at San Juan Pueblo; O.L. of the Assumption, Zia Pueblo (*q.v.*). *New York:* church of Notre Dame, New York; O.L. of Pellevoisin (*q.v.*), New York; O.L. of Lourdes (*q.v.*), Brooklyn; O.L. of Victory (*q.v.*), Lackawanna; O.L. of Maryknoll (*q.v.*); Lourdes shrine, New Lebanon. *Ohio:* O.L. of Consolation (*q.v.*), Carey; Lourdes shrines (*q.v.*) at Cincinnati and Euclid; O.L. of the Rosary, Parma Heights; the Sorrowful Mother (*q.v.*), Marywood. *Oregon:* Sanctuary of the Sorrowful Mother (*q.v.*), Portland. *Pennsylvania:* Shrine of the Miraculous Medal (*q.v.*), Germantown. *South Dakota:* O.L. of the Sioux (*q.v.*). *Wisconsin:* O.L. of Good Help (*q.v.*), New Franken; O.L. of the Holy Hill (*q.v.*), Hubertus.

W. H. Auden has written: "There are millions of devout Catholics in the States, but I doubt if any of them anticipate a day when there will be pilgrimages to the shrine of, say, our Lady of Kalamazoo." Mr. Auden was not questioning the devotion of American Catholics: he was writing about something quite different. But in any case his doubt is mistaken: a pilgrimage shrine to Mary is liable to arise at any time at any place in the Union.

Among the outstanding Marian institutions of the United States are: The Mariological Society of America, with headquarters at the Holy Name College, Washington, D.C.; the Marian Library at the University of Dayton, Ohio; Our Lady's Library at the Marian College, Poughkeepsie, N.Y. The following organizations may also be mentioned: the Central Association of the Miraculous Medal, Germantown, Pa.; the Scapular Bureau and Marian center, New York, N.Y.; the Central Office of the Sodality of Our Lady, St. Louis, Mo.; the Blue Army, Ave Maria Institute, Washington, N.J.; the Consecration Center of the Montfort Fathers, Bay Shore, N.Y.; and Marytown, Militia of Mary Immaculate, Kenosha, Wis.

URA: OUR LADY OF JAPAN. In 1864 Father Bernard Petitjean, of the Paris Foreign Missions, built a church in honor of the Japanese martyrs of 1597 in the Ura district of Nagasaki. It was here, in the following year, that a number of Japanese Christians made themselves known to him: they were descendants of the survivors of the massacres of 1638, from when until 1832 the Church had been apparently dead in Japan. In 1867 Father Petitjean (then bishop) set up a statue of our Lady at the church in memory of the event, and named it our Lady of Japan. It is visited by numerous pilgrims every year, especially on March 17, when a feast of St. Mary of the Finding of the Christians is kept throughout Japan. In the suburb of Urakami, where many of the hidden Christians lived, a commemorative chapel of our Lady was destroyed by the atom bomb in 1945, but the Ura cathedral was spared.

V

VEIL. See GARMENT; PROTECTING VEIL OF OUR LADY.

VELEHRAD. A principal pilgrimage place of Czechoslovakia, as here in 884 died St. Methodius who, with his brother St. Cyril, was the evangelizer of the Southern Slavs. Velehrad has been the scene of congresses of Catholics and Orthodox in the interests of Christian unity; and the icon of the Mother of God in the Jesuit church was venerated by Christians of all rites and obediences.

VENERATION of our Lady. Veneration is the word most commonly used in English to express that *cultus* of *hyperdulia* (*qq.v.*), and the love, trust, and gratitude, with which the Church honors the Blessed Virgin; for convenience it is here distinguished from the personal devotion (*q.v.*) of individual Christians, which depends on and is nourished by the Church's veneration. As has been explained under FEASTS, veneration of Mary in the Church's public worship was delayed, and its development at first slow. Theology was quicker to give her her proper place. Already in the second century the idea of Mary as the New Eve was established; every catechumen learned to reverence her as mother of the Lord Jesus, conceived of the Holy Spirit; and when in 431 the Council of Ephesus (*q.v.*) vindi-

cated her also to be the Mother of God, the way was open to all the subsequent developments of Mariology (*q.v.*) and *cultus*.

This veneration of our Lady in the East was already reaching full stature in the sixth century, and it gradually attained a degree of intensity from which it has never gone back. In the West its progress was for long not consistent and unbroken, but was subject to ups and downs. But there was a great revival in the eleventh century, and its impulsion lasted through the ages that followed, liturgy (*q.v.*) and private devotion interacting on one another. Another period of development began with the mystics and spiritual writers of the seventeenth century, which in turn had deep effect on the notable intensification of Marian veneration in modern times. A testimony to this is the fact that, of eleven lesser Marian feasts today celebrated throughout the West, ten have been extended to the whole Western Church since 1683.

In the Church's *cultus* of Mary is found the answer to a vital problem presented by Christianity: the relation between man and God, between nature and grace, in the work of salvation. Mary, a creature, is venerated as mother of the divine Redeemer; thus she, a human woman, is enabled to co-operate in the work of redemption; by faith she accepts God's gift, by grace she co-operates with grace to save the world. In her the Church sees the fine flower, the synthesis, of redeemed mankind: the Creator of all has taken human manhood, and in return, as it were, made us in some sense sharers in the divine nature (*cf.* first antiphon at Lauds on the Circumcision). In honoring Mary, the Church is not looking at her own worth, but at the wonders of grace with which Almighty God has, in Christ Jesus, filled her and the human community of which she is queen. Veneration of tthe Blessed Virgin is firmly grounded in sound doctrine and receives its inspiration from the written word of God, notably from those four passages in the gospels that are like pillars and signposts in this matter: The angel's greeting, "Hail, full of grace, the Lord is with thee: blessed art thou among women"; and Mary's answer, "Behold the handmaid of the Lord; be it done to me according to thy word." Her words at Cana in Galilee: "Do whatever He tells you." The woman's exclamation, "Blessed is the womb that bore thee, and the breasts that nursed thee"; and our Lord's reply, "Rather, blessed are they who hear the word of God and keep it." And finally, those words from the cross: "Woman, behold thy son. . . . Behold thy mother." From that hour the disciple took her into his own home; so also has Mary been taken into the house of the Church. *Cf.*, Devotion to Mary; Liturgy, Our Lady in the; Prayer to Mary.

VERUELA, OUR LADY OF. A Cistercian monastery was founded at Veruela, near Borja in Spain, in 1146 by Pedro de Atarés, lord of Borja; in the church was enshrined a small statue of our Lady, which Pedro declared he had found at the direction of the Blessed Virgin herself. There the statue has been venerated ever since. In 1877 the monastic buildings were occupied by the Jesuits, who locally observe a feast of the Appearing of our Lady of Veruela on November 15. The image was crowned in 1881.

VESSEL. In the Acts of the Apostles (9:15) it is written that the Lord said of St. Paul, "This man is a vessel chosen by me, to bear my name before nations and kings and the children of Israel." In the Litany of Loreto this term "vessel" is three times applied to our Lady in this sense of carrying something precious. (1) *Vas spirituale*, "Spiritual Vessel." Friar Bernardine dei Busti (d. 1500) called her the Vessel of the Holy Spirit, but here the meaning seems rather to be that she passed her life in the realm of spirit no less than in the world of men, living by faith and not by sight: as St. Paul says of our true home, it is in Heaven (Phil. 3:20). (2) *Vas honorabile*, "Vessel of Honor," is the equivalent of an expression used of Mary by St. Epiphanius of Salamis over fifteen hundred years ago; but before him St. Paul had called all the righteous vessels of honor, as chosen by God (Rom. 9:21). (3) *Vas insigne devotionis*. This expression has suffered at the hands of translators. *Insignis* is not at all happily rendered by the ambiguous word "singular": Glorious

Vessel of Devotion is nearer to it. Nor can devotion be taken here simply in the sense of devoutness. It refers, as Cardinal Newman suggests, to Mary's devotedness, dedication, to her Son. A devoted wife follows her husband about with her eyes; "she is ever seeking some means of serving him; and, if her services are very small in their character, that only shows how intimate they are, and how incessant." And how much more so with our Lady, "because she was His mother, and because she had Him and all His sufferings actually before her eyes, and because she had the long intimacy of thirty years with Him, and because she was from her special sanctity so ineffably near to Him in spirit"; above all, when she stood and suffered with Him on Calvary.

VIA MATRIS. See SORROWS, SEVEN, STATIONS OF THE.

VICTORIES, OUR LADY OF. The title "of Victory" seems to have originated in Constantinople, where there was a very famous image of the Mother of God of that name (*Nikopoeia*): it is said to be the one now in St. Mark's at Venice. Our Lady of Victories in Paris is the best-known church of the Blessed Virgin in that city after Notre-Dame, largely on account of its association with the Miraculous Medal (*q.v.*). There in 1838 was organized the Confraternity of the Immaculate Heart of Mary, Refuge of Sinners, of which that medal is the badge and which did so much to carry it across the world. The statue, dating from 1630, was crowned in 1856: a "celebrated but ungraceful image," as Edmund Waterton calls it. A *feast* under the title our Lady of Victory (the plural is an English and French form) is kept in a number of places on various dates, e.g., October 26 in the archdiocese of St. Louis, Mo. The well-known church of our Lady of Victories in London, once the pro-cathedral of the archdiocese of Westminster, was destroyed by bombing in World War II; whereas that of the same name in Quebec, built after the English had been beaten off in 1690, still stands.—The Paris church was the inspiration of Father Nelson H. Baker in forming the Association of our Lady of Victory to help the orphanages of which he had charge at Lackawanna, N.Y. The great church, dedicated there in 1926 as the National Shrine of our Lady of Victory, represents America's gratitude for all the good that God did through the instrumentality of that devoted priest, whose work for orphans lives on after him.

VIETNAM, SHRINES OF. See INDO-CHINA.

VIGIL, or Eve (Lat. *vigilia*, a watching). After 1955 the only feast of our Lady in the Roman calendar having a vigil, that is, a liturgical preparation for the feast on the day before, is that of the Assumption. Eastern custom in the matter varies: the Byzantine Melkites, for example, include the Immaculate Conception, Birthday, Presentation, Annunciation, and Assumption among their vigils.—In the Servite Order there is an observance called the Vigil daily before Vespers: it consists of the recitation of Psalms 8, 18, and 23 from the Little Office B.V.M. (*q.v.*), followed by the three lessons and responsories.

VILNA, OUR LADY OF. A celebrated Polono-Lithuanian image, also called "of Ostrabrama," as being displayed at one of the city gates. It was painted in the middle of the seventeenth century, and shows the Blessed Virgin without the Child, her head bowed as in prayer. The calendar of the Cistercian nuns of Vilna has a feast of the Mother of Mercy, referring to this image, on November 16; it is revered by Orthodox as well as Catholics. There are churches dedicated in honor of our Lady of Vilna in New York, Chicago, and Worcester, Mass., and of our Lady of Ostrabrama in Boston, and elsewhere.

VIRGIN-TITLES in the Litany of Loreto. Our Lady is invoked under seven virgin-titles in the Litany of Loreto. As elsewhere, one or two of the current English translations might be improved: "venerable," for example, as commonly used, has a distinct suggestion of old age. The titles are: Holy Virgin of virgins, Most Prudent Virgin, Virgin to be Honored, Virgin to be Proclaimed, Powerful Virgin, Compassionate Virgin, Faithful Virgin. *Praedicanda* is, literally, "to be preached," but translated "proclaimed." Of *Virgo prudentissima* Cardinal Newman said: "It must be

recollected that she is not only the great instance of the contemplative life, but also of the practical: and the practical life is at once a life of penance and of prudence, if it is to be well discharged. Now Mary was as full of external work as any Sister of Charity at this day. . . . Now, always to be awake, guarded, fervent, so as to be able to act not only without sin, but in the best possible way in the varying circumstances of each day, denotes a life of untiring mindfulness. But of such a life, prudence is the presiding virtue. It is, then, through the pains and sorrows of her earthly pilgrimage that we are able to invoke her as the *Virgo prudentissima.*"

VIRGIN OF THE POOR. See BANNEUX.

VIRGINITY, OUR LADY'S. That Jesus Christ, the God-man, was born of a virgin, is declared by the gospels themselves, in Matthew 1:18 and in Luke 1:34-35 and 3:23; and this was the explicit belief of the Church from the beginning. Already by about the year 100 the doctrine was being denied by opponents of the Church; a few years later St. Ignatius of Antioch refers to it as a mystery of God; St. Justin (d. *c.* 165) meets the objections of a Jew; the earliest records of a formulated creed speak of Jesus as "born of the Virgin Mary" (e.g., Tertullian's quotations, *c.* 200). The Fathers (*q.v.*) are unanimous in their teaching, and Mary's virginity is an outstanding element in the earliest records of Christian devotion to her.

"In order," says St. Thomas Aquinas (*Summa theol.*, III, xxviii, a.2), "that Christ's body might be shown to be a real body, He was born of a woman; in order that His Godhead might be made clear He was born of a virgin."

But the Church does not stop short at affirming the virgin-birth. The Lateran Council of 649, confirmed by the sixth General Council, at Constantinople in 681, declared that Mary "brought forth Jesus without loss of integrity, and after His birth preserved her virginity inviolate," that is, she remained a virgin in and after childbirth, throughout her life. Mary's virginity in childbirth is attested by the tradition of the Church; the Fathers illustrate it by such analogies as light passing through glass, and the Lord's risen body coming out of the closed tomb and passing through locked doors (John 20:19): "Mary is a good gate," wrote St. Ambrose, "that was closed and was not opened. Christ passed through it, but He opened it not." That our Lady thenceforth remained virgin all her life has been questioned chiefly on the ground of the scriptural references to the "brethren of Jesus." Of several proffered explanations, the right one seems to be that "brethren" here means simply relatives, kinsmen, "fellow-clansmen," an interpretation which the Greek and Aramaic words for "brother" readily allow. *Cf.*, Genealogy of Mary.

"Thou didst bear God and the Word according to the flesh, thou didst keep thy virginity before His birth, thou didst remain a virgin after His birth, and we have been reconciled to God through Christ thy Son" (St. Ephraem). "Mary, mistress of maidenhood, did not fail; it could not be that she who had borne God could think of bearing a man. And Joseph, a godly man, did not so lose his mind as to seek bodily relationship with the mother of the Lord" (St. Ambrose). "Because we read it, we believe that God was born of a virgin; because we do not read it, we do not believe that Mary wedded after the birth of her child. And we do not say this because we would condemn marriage; surely virginity itself is the fruit of marriage" (St. Jerome). Thus do three fourth-century doctors of the Church bear witness to the Church's teaching and express the mind of the faithful throughout the ages. Mary's personal maidenhood has made virginity one of the most popular and characteristic of Christian ideas, whose influence on the theory and practice of sexual chastity has been incalculable.

But, as Abbot Vonier wrote in *The Divine Motherhood* (chap. v), "Mary's virginity as the Mother of God is more than a mere preservation of her personal virginity." It is of a higher kind, a divine mystery, a supernatural gift such as is found in no other maiden. "She is the virgin she is, not in spite of her motherhood, but because of her motherhood. . . . Her virginity is a positive, divine quality, not simply a preservation of the natural maiden state." And, while not ignoring the personal aspect, it is to this aspect, the maidenhood of the Mother, that the Church's public prayer keeps on drawing attention: "A virgin has borne God in the flesh"; "A virgin has brought forth the Savior." At Matins of Christmas day in the Byzantine rite is sung: "Virgin God-bearer, who has given birth to the Savior, thou hast turned back the age-long curse of Eve . . . carrying in thy bosom God the Word made flesh. . . . Come, let us praise the Mother of the Savior, who was yet a maiden even after bearing child. . . ."

VIRTUES, OUR LADY OF. Another name, found in several languages, for our Lady of Miracles (*q.v.*). "Virtues" has here the significance of "powers."

VISIONS of our Lady. Visions, supernatural perceptions, are commonly divided into three classes: (1) *Bodily* or sensible, when (a) something which is naturally invisible is seen with the human eye (St. Bernadette's visions were almost certainly of this kind); or when (b) Almighty God directly modifies man's eye so that it seems to see something (the "dancing sun" at Fatima could have been of this kind); (2) *Imaginative,* produced by God in a person's imagination, sometimes in a dream during sleep (e.g., the angel that appeared to Joseph [Matt. 1:20, and elsewhere]); (3) *Intellectual,* when the mind is able to perceive a spiritual truth, without any sense image (e.g., as experienced by St. Teresa of Avila). Dame Julian (*q.v.*), for example, experienced all these forms: "All this was shewed by three ways," she says, "that is to say, by bodily sight, and by words formed in my understanding, and by ghostly sight." When appearings of the Blessed Virgin are in question, it is generally a matter of (1), bodily or sensible vision.

Already in the fourth century St. Gregory of Nyssa relates that St. Gregory the Wonderworker (d. *c.* 270) had been vouchsafed a vision of John the Evangelist and the Mother of the Lord; and at Mary's bidding John had disclosed "the mystery of godliness" to him. Since then there has been a long succession of reported appearings of Mary in different parts of the world, many of which have received varying degrees of recognition from the authorities of the Church. In the past 150 years the most celebrated examples have been the visions of St. Catherine Labouré (see MEDAL, MIRACULOUS) and of St. Bernadette at Lourdes (*q.v.*), with those at Faima and La Salette (*qq.v.*); there have been others at Banneux, Beauraing, and Pontmain (*qq.v.*). More recently, the bishops concerned have not yet pronounced on alleged happenings at Heede and Pfaffenhofen, in Germany: in the first case four school children, sisters, said that first our Lady and then our Lord appeared to them many times from 1937 to 1940; in the second, a young woman of twenty-two claims that Mary appeared to her in 1946. Among several other cases still undecided are Pellevoisin (*q.v.*) and the reports from Trefontane in Rome, which were much publicized in 1947. In over a dozen other cases of recent years, the local bishops have totally rejected what were claimed to be supernatural events involving our Lady, and forbidden any *cultus* (*q.v.*) in respect thereof: for example, at Ezkioga in Spain in 1931, at Bergamo in Italy in 1944, at Espis in France in 1947, at Lipa in the Philippines and at Aspang in Austria in 1948, at Necedah in Wisconsin in 1951, and at Asseiceira in Portugal in 1954.

The general principles governing the authenticity of supernatural visions, the recognition of them by ecclesiastical authority, and the duty of the faithful in their regard are the same as those set out herein under MIRACLES: it is a matter of evidence, not of faith. In referring to these things the popes, and those speaking in their name, often do not positively affirm, but instead use such expressions as *ut pie creditur, ut asserunt, ut fama est*—"as is piously believed," "as people say," "as the report goes." For the Church is less concerned with the facts about visions and miracles than with the propriety of the devotions to which they give rise and the orthodoxy of the teaching which is associated with them; on this, see REVELATIONS AND COMMUNICATIONS. It may be added here that when, as sometimes happens, the researches of scholars disprove some vision, miracle, relic, or the like, which has been long and widely credited, it is not to be expected that the Church should hurry to impose, as it were, discontinuance of the cherished belief: for she has never put it forward as part of, or necessary to the integrity of, the deposit of revealed truth.

VISITATION BY OUR LADY, Feast of the. This festival commemorates Mary's visit to her cousin Elizabeth who, herself with child with John the Baptist, recognized "the mother of my Lord," and Mary praised God with the Magnificat (Luke 1:39-56). The feast was given to the whole Western Church, for July 2, in 1389, and its rhythmical office was composed by an Englishman, Cardinal Adam Easton. Pope St. Pius V abolished this office, together with the vigil and octave that had been observed. The feast is practically unknown in the East, though the Greeks have the commemoration of the enshrining of our Lady's robe at Blakhernae (*q.v.*) on the same day; for this reason the Catholic Melkites, when they adopted the Visitation, fixed it for the Friday after Easter, when the Orthodox Greeks keep our Lady of the Fountain (*q.v.*). The Visitation is now also kept in the Maronite and Chaldean rites.

There has been much discussion about where our Lady stayed with St. Elizabeth. Hebron, Bethlehem, and Jutta have been suggested; but an old tradition puts it at Ain Karim, a village about four miles west of Jerusalem. This was adopted by the crusaders, who called the place St. John *in Montana,* with reference to the birth of John the Baptist. The present sanctuary of the Visitation there, beautifully situated on a rocky plateau against the mountainside, incorporates parts of a church considerably anterior to the Crusades.

In the lessons for the second nocturn of Matins on this feast St. John Chrysostom concentrates on John leaping in his mother's womb, and does it with superb rhetoric: "Tell us, John, how you could see and hear when you were still enclosed in the darkness of your mother's womb? How did you behold these divine things? How did you leap and exult? 'Herein is a great mystery accomplished,' he replies, 'something far beyond human understanding. It is but right that I should do something new in nature, because of Him who will do new things above nature. Even though I am yet in the womb, I see . . . I perceive with my ears . . . I cry aloud . . . I exult . . . I leap . . . I run before the Savior's coming, and by my witness go before Him to you.' "

VLADIMIR, OUR LADY OF. One of the most famous and most beautiful of all icons of the Mother of God: she is depicted cheek to cheek with the Child, whose arms caress her, yet it is a strong and noble work, completely free from "sweetness" and sentimentality. It is the great example of a type of icon that the Russians call *Umilenie* and the Greeks *Eleousa*, "Tenderness." It was probably painted in Constantinople in the twelfth century, but is first heard of at Kiev, whence it was taken in 1155 to the city of Vladimir. It became famous for wonders and was reverenced as Russia's most sacred image, so that it was in 1395 enshrined in the cathedral of the Assumption in the Kremlin at Moscow. Several times the Tartars were beaten back under

its inspiration, and it was carried to critical places at times of stress: the last time was when it was taken to the battle-front during World War I. All the tsars were crowned and patriarchs installed in the presence of this image up to the revolution; in 1919 it was removed to the Tretiakov Gallery in Moscow, where it still is. It has been reproduced many times in copies and book-illustrations. Our Lady of Vladimir is commemorated in Russian calendars on May 21, June 23, and August 26.

VULNERATA, The, Valladolid. In 1596 the English, under Essex and Raleigh, raided Cadiz in Spain. The sailors dragged a statue of the Mother and Child out of a church, and shamefully mutilated it, leaving it lying in the market place. The superiors and students of the English College (seminary), founded seven years previously at Valladolid, petitioned the governor of Castille that they might have the statue in order to make reparation for their countrymen's crime, and in 1600 it was solemnly translated from the chapel of the Countess of Santa Gadea. It is still enshrined above the altar of the chapel of the English College at Valladolid, just as it was left by the raiders: the face of the seated figure of our Lady hacked about, her forearms cut off, and only a part of one foot remaining of the Child. A proper feast of the Mutilated (*Vulnerata*) Virgin is observed at the college on the Sunday after the Immaculate Conception, and a Mass and litany of reparation are sung every Saturday.

the world more than others, statues or pictures of Mary have been reported to shed tears or display similar phenomena. Such alleged happenings are not easily submitted to adequate examination, and possible natural explanations are usually forthcoming: the interest aroused generally dies down as quickly as it arises. Among cases that have received some ecclesiastical recognition are those at Treviglio in 1522, Rho in 1583, and San Severino in 1519, liturgical commemoration of the event being allowed in each case. These three were all in Italy. A contemporary case was at Syracuse in Sicily (1953). An official inquiry was instituted, and eventually the bishops of the island declared that the fact of weeping was beyond doubt. Cardinal Ruffini, Archbishop of Palermo, had already warned his people that assent to the findings of the commission (whatever they might be) could only be based on the trustworthiness or otherwise of the human witnesses: it could not be a matter of faith. *Cf.*, Miracles.

WELLS AND SPRINGS. The association of wells and other springs of water with religious observances is one of the most ancient, widespread, and persistent of manifestations of popular religious devotion. It goes back to long before the days of Christianity; and even down to recent times ecclesiastical authorities have been faced with the task of abolishing the custom or turning it into Christian channels. There was the same difficulty with regard to sacred trees (the oak St. Boniface cut down

at Geismar is not forgotten). One way of dealing with it appears to have been to set up a crucifix or an image of our Lady or other saint at the spring or tree; in this and other ways holy wells came to be associated with Christian shrines, and miraculous cures were often claimed for their waters. This custom doubtless also accounts in part for the number of images of our Lady of which local tradition says "It was found in a tree." Many fountains of water were associated with the Mother of God, and nowadays the most famous of them is one unknown to our ancestors and quite free from heathen associations—the spring at Lourdes to which our Lady herself drew St. Bernadette's attention.

Holy wells are specially common in Celtic countries. Specifically Mary wells are numerous in Scotland and Ireland, where the one at Rosserkin, Co. Mayo, has a chapel built in 1684; the most famous of the Welsh ones, at Penrhys (*q.v.*), is now again a resort of pilgrims. There were several in England before the Reformation (two at Walsingham), and the well at Fernyhalgh (*q.v.*) is part of a shrine to this day. It was with reference to a cure claimed for our Lady of Muswell ("mossy well"), near London, that the Protestant John Norden wrote, about 1593: "Absolutely to deny the cure I dare not, for that the High God hath given vertue to waters to heal infirmities is evident by the Holy Scriptures, as by the cure of Naaman the leper, by washing seven times in Jordan, and by the Pool of Bethesda, which heal'd the next that stepp'd thereinto after the water was mov'd by the angel."

WERL, OUR LADY OF. A popular shrine in Westphalia. The statue of the Blessed Virgin was removed from its shrine at the Reformation, and was forgotten for one hundred thirty years. It was then set up once more in the church at Werl, which became a place of pilgrimage. The image was crowned in 1911.

WEST GRINSTEAD, OUR LADY OF. West Grinstead in Sussex is one of the places in England where the Catholic faith has been practiced unbrokenly since before the Reformation, for long under the protection of the Caryll family. The present church was built in 1876, and in 1882 the rector, Monsignor J. M. Denis, enshrined in it a copy of the picture of our Lady of Consolation of which the original is at the Consolata (*q.v.*) at Turin. It was crowned in 1893. The shrine has become a place of pilgrimage, the principal day being the Tuesday after the second Sunday in July; the Priest's House, built in 1640, with its relics and memories of penal times, is an important part of the sanctuary. There is a branch of the Consolata confraternity at West Grinstead, and the shrine has received papal and diocesan indulgences.

WIELKIE PIEKARI. The most popular sanctuary of the Upper Silesian industrial area in Poland. The image venerated there is an icon of our Lady, which has been crowned.

Among the more recent pilgrims was Cardinal Ratti, afterward Pope Pius XI, when he was nuncio at Warsaw.

WILLESDEN, OUR LADY OF. During the middle ages Willesden was a country village northwest of London; in its parish church was a "Black Virgin," whose reputation for miracles attracted many pilgrims. The statue was taken away and burnt at the Reformation. By the later nineteenth century Willesden had become an industrial suburb of London. In 1886 a small Catholic church was opened there; and in due course a new image of our Lady of Willesden was set up in it, which in 1931 was translated to the Lady chapel of a large new church. The statue was crowned in 1954; annually on the last Sunday in May it is carried in procession through the streets of the parish. It was carved from the wood of an oak that grew near the ancient shrine. This sanctuary has received papal and diocesan indulgences, and owing to its metropolitan location it is likely to grow yet more in popularity. Above the shrine are inscribed the words:

Imago per nefas abducta
Amore filiorum reducta.

"Wickedness took the image away; loving children have brought it back."

WINTON, OUR LADY OF. Winton is the abbreviated form of the name Winchester (Lat. *Wintonia*), and St. Peter's church in that city has a notable statue over the Lady

altar: it is of fifteenth-century date and probably Flemish in origin. It was found in an antique-shop at Canterbury in 1927, but how it came to England is not known. The statue of our Lady in the nave of Winchester cathedral was celebrated in the middle ages.

WOMANHOOD, MARY AND THE IDEAL OF.

It is a commonplace that Christianity has had a profound influence in the formation of womanly ideals and the determination of women's status and activities in human society. Slowly over centuries, in many parts of the world and in differing degrees and ways, the position of women has been ameliorated and raised, ideas about the relations of the sexes have been modified and humanized; in these changes, the teaching of Christianity has had a preponderant (but not exclusive) part. Some, indeed, of its detailed effects in the far past are often overlooked: for instance, the administrative and disciplinary rule of some women superiors over male religious in medieval times, such as at St. Hilda's monastery at Whitby in England, Fontevrault in France, and in the Bridgettine Order.

It is likewise a commonplace that in this process the significance of a particular woman, the Blessed Virgin Mary, has been a most important element. It is summarized (and a little oversimplified perhaps) in people's minds by the words of Bl. Henry Suso (d. 1365): "For the sake of the gentle Mother of God, I am accustomed to pay deference to all women." Such a historian of civilization as W. E. H. Lecky has fully recognized the remarkable social influence of the ideal of our Lady, while less careful writers have sometimes exaggerated its effect. Not even at those times and places when Mary was most widely revered and appealed to was the effectiveness of the ideal allowed to be wholly operative by weak and sinful human nature.

Two things are fundamental in the social influence of Mary, the ideal of virginity and the ideal of motherhood. Nothing is more remarkable than the respect for virginity in either sex, undertaken or accepted for God's sake, observable in Christianity from the beginning. This was no inheritance from the Jews, among whom any childlessness was a reproach. It was no outstanding part of our Lord's recorded teaching: His one allusion to the matter is in rather cryptic terms (Matt. 19:11-12). It would seem that Mary's example was decisive, and teachers such as St. Gregory Nazianzen and St. Ambrose relate Christian virginity directly to her as model and pattern. It is therefore not a merely negative thing, much less an irreligious decrying of the God-created flesh; but a reaching-out to an ever closer union with the Creator, an ever greater appreciation of all that is spiritual on this earth as well as in the Jerusalem that is above.

But our Lady's virginity (q.v.) is essentially bound up with her motherhood, the supreme and unique example of maidenhood that is fruitful; and so with the ideal of the one, there goes the ideal of the other.

Christian regard for motherhood is no mere exaltation of vital, "creative," human power; it is no mere pleasing sentiment, which can be aroused as readily by a kitten as by a baby. Rather is it an ideal of love, rooted in that love of God who gave His only-begotten Son to be born of a woman that all men might be re-born to everlasting life. That Mother of that Son could not but become the pattern of all mothers, commanding for them a respect and consideration that the first Eve had done so much to weaken and spoil among human kind. In the New Eve (*q.v.*) the divine idea of womanhood was restored to the world; and when Christ was born on this earth not only the love of mothers but all human love was involved. St. Paul, for example, calls on husbands to love their wives as Christ loves the Church; and the first-fruits and pattern of His hallowing love is seen in His own Mother, "without spot or wrinkle or any such thing . . . holy and without blemish."

WONDERWORKING IMAGES. There have been, and are, in various parts of the world but especially in Italy and the East, a large number of images of our Lady reputed to be wonderworking or miraculous. The expression is, of course, a figure of speech: only the power of Almighty God can bring miracles to pass. But He can, and there is much evidence that He does, make use of images (and other things) as occasions for these manifestations of His power and love; and when the image represents our Lady, no doubt it is done at her intercession. It would be tedious and repetitive to attempt to list these miraculous and grace-bringing pictures and statues; but the following are notable examples, one from each country named: *Albania,* a copy of the picture of our Lady of Good Counsel at Skodra; *Austria,* O.L. of Zell; *Belgium:* O.L. of La Sarte; *Byelorussia,* O.L. of Pochaev; *Czechoslovakia,* O.L. of Tyn, Prague; *England,* statue at the Franciscan convent, Goodings, Berkshire; *France,* O.L. of Aubervilliers; *Germany,* O.L. of Ettal; *Greece,* O.L. of Cassiope; *Holland,* O.L. of 's Hertogenbosch; *Hungary,* O.L. of Györ; *Ireland,* O.L. of Benada; *Latvia,* O.L. of Aglona; *Poland,* O.L. of Czestochowa; *Portugal,* O.L. of Sameira; *Rome,* O.L. of Perpetual Help; elsewhere in *Italy,* O.L. of Good Counsel at Genazzano; *Rumania,* O.L. of Csiksomlyo; *Russia,* O.L. of Vladimir; *Spain,* O.L. of Montserrat; *Switzerland,* O.L. of Einsiedeln; *Western Ukraine,* O.L. of Hosiv; *Yugoslavia,* O.L. of Jerusalem at Trski Vrh; *India,* O.L. of Bandel; *Syria,* O.L. of Saidnaia, Damascus; *Canada,* O.L. of the Cape; *United States,* O.L. of Prompt Succor at New Orleans; *Mexico,* O.L. of Guadalupe; *The Argentine,* O.L. of Lujan; *Brazil,* O.L. *Aparecida,* near São Paulo; *The Philippines,* O.L. of the Turumba. Most of the above images are referred to herein under their names. *Cf.,* Not Made by Hands, Images; Miracles; Weeping Madonnas.

WORSHIP OF THE VIRGIN. See HYPERDULIA; MARIOLATRY.

Y

YORK, OUR LADY OF. The statue of our Lady, Mother of Mercy, at St. Wilfrid's church at York in England formed part of a wayside shrine at Moorseele in Belgium during the seventeenth century; in 1688 it was moved to a new shrine at Menin, where it was cared for by Dominican nuns. After the Revolution it eventually came into the hands of a private family, one of whose members, the Abbé Richard Van de Pitte, brought it to England in 1869. It was this priest who enshrined it at York, in 1884, in a building separate from the church, where it is now an object of pilgrimage. The image of Mother and Child is carved from two pieces of oak, of different ages: one piece bears the date 1627, but the earliest history of the statue is a matter of speculation. A prayer invoking our Lady of York has been indulgenced by the Bishop of Middlesbrough, and Mass is offered at the shrine every Wednesday for those who pray to her.

YOUGHAL, OUR LADY OF. The image called our Lady of Graces of Youghal is in fact enshrined in the Dominican church at Cork. It is an ivory carving in relief of the Mother and Child, only $4\frac{1}{2}$ by 2 inches over all, and very much worn. It was made probably about the year 1300, in northern France. Its earlier history has been the object of a good deal of research; its first owner, Archbishop Maurice O'Carroll of Cashel, wore it round his neck, and in 1316 it was buried with him in the Dominican church at Youghal. The public history of the image began about 1480 when, having been recovered from the tomb, it was set up in the Youghal church and became an object of pilgrimage. It was cherished in the same neighborhood throughout penal times, but by 1823 was in the custody of the Friars Preachers at Cork. The ivory today stands above the Rosary altar in their church, in a silver-gilt reliquary given in 1617 by Onoria, daughter of James Fitzmaurice Fitzgerald of Desmond. In its new home the image has attracted the same popular devotion as at Youghal, and graces are multiplied as of old.

YUGOSLAVIA, SHRINES OF. The inhabitants of this country are principally composed of Orthodox Serbs and Catholic Croats and Slovenes, among whom shrines of Mary are very numerous. A number of them are associated with the struggle against the Turks from the fourteenth century on. Among the chief *Croatian* shrines may be named: Our Lady of Aljmas; O.L. Radovanska at Bela; O.L. of Biskupeć (*q.v.*); O.L. of Bistrica (*q.v.*); O.L. of the Snow, Dezevice; O.L. of Pity, Dubrovnik (Ragusa); O.L. of the Sea, Rijeka

(Fiume); O.L. of Gorica; O.L. of Peace, Hrvatski Karlovci; O.L. of Ilaca (the Bosnian Lourdes); O.L. of the Cloister, Kobas; O.L. of Kondzila, near Teslić; O.L. of Marča (*q.v.*), Križevci; O.L. of Kutjevo, near Pozega; O.L. of Mount Carmel, Milna; O.L. of Olovo (*q.v.*); O.L. of Volavska at Petrovina; O.L. of Sutinska at Pregrada; O.L. of Rama (*q.v.*); O.L. of Remete (*q.v.*); O.L. of Sinj (*q.v.*); O.L. of Poisan and others at Split (Spalato); the Black Virgin at Subotica; Tekije (see SNOW, OUR LADY OF THE); O.L. of Trski Vrh (*q.v.*); O.L. of the Visitation, Vukovina; O.L. of the Stone Gate (*q.v.*), Zagreb; O.L. of Zadar (Zara); and O.L. of Loreto (*q.v.*) at Trsat (Tersato).

The oldest *Slovene* shrine is actually over the frontier in Austria, Gospa Sveta at Klagenfurt. It goes back to at least the twelfth century, and is visited by Austrians as well. Another important Slovene sanctuary is our Lady of the Birch Trees, near Ljubljana. Others are at Brezje; Čatež, near Zaplazu; a stone statue in the church of the Conventual Franciscans at Črna Gora; a fourteenth-century icon at Dobrova; the Franciscan churches at Maribor and Nova Štifta; the Salesian shrine at Rakovnik, inaugurated in 1920; an icon in the Franciscan church at Svata Gora; our Lady of Višarje (5,000 feet up in the Carnic Alps); Žalostna Gora, near Borovnica, and the same near Novo Mesto.

Among the shrines in *Serbia*, of the Orthodox Church, are those at the churches of the Rose and of the Veil, and at the Presentation monastery, all three in Belgrade; at a monastery of the same dedication at Mount Čeblar; the Hodegetria (*q.v.*) at Peć; the Leviška at Prizren; at the Miljcov monastery, on the Morava river; at the Rayinovats monastery, near Belgrade; at the Toplica monastery; and at the Voyssilovica monastery, near Gracanica.

Z

ZIA PUEBLO. Forty miles north of Albuquerque in New Mexico is Zia Pueblo, scene of an Indian pilgrimage, *fiesta,* and procession every August 15. The mission was founded early in the seventeenth century; and the present adobe church of Nuestra Señora de la Asunción was built in 1692, from the ruins of the original one, damaged during the Pueblo revolt of 1680. The statue of the Mother of God is a small figure, clothed in bright robes, and there is also a picture of the Assumption, given to the church by the Sandoval family in 1798.

ZION, ST. MARY OF. A feast of the Ethiopic rite, kept on November 30. Among the ideas involved are those of Mary as the temple of the incarnate God, with reference to the Temple at Jerusalem, and of Mary as a city of refuge from the enemies of the soul. In the West there is an ancient pilgrim-shrine of our Lady of Zion near Nancy in Lorraine, where her feast is observed on September 10. The Priests and Sisters of our Lady of Zion were founded by Theodore and Alphonse Ratisbonne, converted Jews, in the mid-nineteenth century.

ZITAIL, OUR LADY OF. A shrine 8,000 feet up in the Swiss Grisons. Here a shepherd is said to have had a vision of Mary, in which she said to him, "Tell the people that plague, famine and war are awaiting them if they do not repent of their misdeeds." There is no road, railway, or shelter at this shrine, of which the Bishop of Chur has said that "People go there to pray: there is nothing else to go there for." The sanctuary is several hours' hard walk from the nearest village.

ZOSEH, OUR LADY OF. This, the most celebrated Marian shrine of China, is situated on a wooded hill about twenty miles from Shanghai, adjoining the Jesuit astronomical observatory which was occupied by the communists in 1950. At this present writing (1954) the shrine seems to be unmolested. The site was first noticed as suitable for a shrine by Father Gonnet, s.j., in 1844, and twenty years later a chapel was built by another Jesuit, Father della Corte. It soon attracted pilgrims, and when persecution threatened the Christians of central China in 1870 they made a vow, in consequence of which a large church was built. On the tower stands a statue of our Lady with outstretched arms, offering her Child to China and the world, and here in 1923 the country was dedicated to our Lady under the title "of Zoseh." In 1948 the statue in the church was crowned, "Queen of China," by the papal nuncio, the first ceremony of the kind to take place in China. Although so near to Shanghai, Zoseh is not an easy place to get at; yet on this occasion 50,000 people were present. This is representative of the large numbers of pilgrims who come to Zoseh: not only from the neighborhood, but from far away, such as the flotillas of fishermen from the lakes in the dioceses of Nanking and Soochow. The hill of Zoseh was occupied in times past by two Buddhist monasteries.

ZYROVITSE, OUR LADY OF. A Ruthenian sanctuary near Novogrudok, Lithuania-Poland, where in the seventeenth century there was a monastery of the Eastern monastic order; it was resorted to by both Catholics and Orthodox. The icon was much revered by the martyred bishop St. Josaphat Kuntsevich (d. 1623). In 1719 a copy of it was found in the monastery of the Ruthenian monks in Rome, who enshrined it in their church of SS. Sergius and Bacchus. Miracles were reported here, and it became so well known that the Romans referred to the church as Santa Maria del Pascolo (*Zyr* = pasture). The Basilian monks of St. Josaphat still guard the image in that church. The original was set up about 1475, and was mentioned in Russian menologies on May 7.

FILMMAKERS SERIES

edited by
ANTHONY SLIDE

In Preparation

STARS of the SILENTS

by
EDWARD
WAGENKNECHT

Filmmakers, No. 19

The Scarecrow Press, Inc.
Metuchen, N.J., & London
1987

Library of Congress Cataloging-in-Publication Data

Wagenknecht, Edward, 1900–
   Stars of the silents.

   (Filmmakers ; no. 19)
   Bibliography: p.
   Includes indexes.
   1. Moving-picture actors and actresses--United States--
Biography. 2. Silent films--History and criticism.
I. Title. II. Series: Filmmakers series ; no. 19.
PN1998.A2W237 1987   791.43'028'0922 [B] 87-4508
ISBN 0-8108-1992-9

It would have been more logical if silent
pictures had grown out of the talkie instead
of the other way around.

Mary Pickford

CONTENTS

EDITOR'S FOREWORD

In 1962, Edward Wagenknecht published The Movies in the Age of Innocence, which I, personally, consider to be the best book ever written on the American silent film. It is not the definitive volume--no one has or ever will write a definitive book on the subject--but The Movies in the Age of Innocence captures the essence of the subject so perfectly and with such perception. Above all, it illustrates what it was like to grow up during the era of silent films. With profundity, it documents what appealed to a filmgoer and what did not. The silent cinema is lucky in that it had such an energetic supporter as Edward Wagenknecht, who has the intelligence and knowledge to write of it with scholarship and enthusiasm. No other period of film history has had the benefit of such a firsthand account as given in The Movies in the Age of Innocence.

I remember after my first book, Early American Cinema, was published in 1970, how thrilled I was to receive a letter from Edward Wagenknecht. Since then, Edward and I have become good friends; I have visited with him and his wife, Dorothy, on many occasions at their home in West Newton, Massachusetts; I have had the honor to co-author two books with him, The Films of D.W. Griffith and Fifty Great American Silent Films: 1912-1920; graciously, he contributed a foreword to my 1978 Scarecrow Press publication, Aspects of American Film History prior to 1920.

As the number of volumes in the Filmmakers series has grown, I thought to ask Edward to prepare a book collecting together some of his essays and articles on various silent film personalities. The Movies in the Age of Innocence is currently unavailable, and it occurred to me that some of the chapters from that book might well be revised and expanded for inclusion here. Through the years I have seen, or at

vii

least heard mention of, a number of pieces which Edward had written, but which had long been out of print or available only from esoteric sources. These also deserve a wider circulation, which this book will provide.

I am pleased that Edward Wagenknecht was agreeable to the publication of this book of essays. They vary considerably in length and often reflect a particular moment in screen history. Some of the essays have a documentary quality, whereas others analyze a subject's career with affection. All are major contributions to the study of the silent actor or actress in American film history.

Anthony Slide

IN THE BEGINNING ...

In the beginning there were no stars in the silent sky. It was "the pictures" we went to see, pictures that <u>moved</u>. Nobody had ever seen a picture move before, but we could see <u>people</u> on the street every day. Sometimes, as with "Hale's Tours," which were travel pictures, photographed from a moving train, and better cinema, being better adapted to the medium, than many more pretentious productions afterwards, there were no people at all. When the films were foreign, as they often were in the days when Pathé dominated the world film trade, the people were there all right, but they were too remote from us in America to register as individuals, and in the comparatively long shots that then prevailed, they all looked pretty much alike anyway. I have myself recorded elsewhere how startled I was when watching Maurice Costello, one day as a small boy, I suddenly became aware that I had seen that face before, and I first encountered the (abbreviated) name of a film player in a hand-lettered sign before a nickelodeon which, having first given the name of the film, added, as an afterthought, in smaller type, "Miss Lawrence in the Leading Role."

Anybody who has ever seen any of the now valuable posters that have survived from the early days must have been impressed by the realization that the effort of the producers was concentrated not upon the players, hardly even upon the individual film, but rather upon the firm name. This was what dominated the poster, often spread across the top in type considerably larger than any employed elsewhere. The trade-mark too was ubiquitous--Biograph's circled AB, Vitagraph's eagle, clutching or supporting a shield decorated with a big V, Essanay's Indian head, Kalem's sunburst, Pathé's beautiful red rooster and all the rest--not only on the posters but on the titles and captions and sometimes even on the sets.[1] I think G. M. Anderson was the real pioneer when he put his

1

name on the posters for his "Broncho Billy" films. He was
the "A" of Essanay, as George K. Spoor was the "S"; he was
therefore running his own show, and his vanity as an actor
must have got the better of his caution as a producer. We
had all seen him on the screen in The Great Train Robbery
in 1903, but nobody knew who he was then, and all he had
a chance to do was to get himself shot trying to run away
from the bandits. Now, however, he could put a little circled halftone photograph of himself in the corner of the poster
with his name under it.

It cannot have been long after this that Vitagraph sometimes put "Bunny" into the titles of some of the comedies John
Bunny made for them. In the early days Vitagraph cannily
differentiated their posters from those of all their competitors.
Instead of the lithographed one-sheet, with one picture in
glaring color, that everybody else was using, they employed
a variety of often beautiful art nouveau colored backgrounds,
with several scenes from the film inset in the form of black-
and-white halftones; a little later they took a leaf from Anderson's book and added small circled portraits of some of their
leading players.

The motivation behind the de-emphasis upon the actors
seems to have been the fear that if they became aware of
their value they would demand more money, a fear which later
turned out to have been well founded. They were "employees";
they "worked" for the "company"; they were paid "wages"
comparable to those received by other "employees" in other
lines of work at the time. In 1911 Claire McDowell was taking
home fifty dollars, presumably for a week's work, from Biograph; her husband, Charles Hill Mailes, got only forty, as
did that fine actor Alfred Paget, and poor old W. Chrystie
Miller had to get along with thirty-five. Biograph was the
longest holdout on the anonymity of players; in the early days,
the "Answer Man" of the Motion Picture Story Magazine was
telling his correspondents with wearisome iteration that he
could not answer questions about Biograph players. At the
same time, his publication, the first fan magazine, which began in February 1911, was exercising an incalculable influence
upon establishing the importance of the player and along with
it the star system. Biograph did not surrender until 1913,
and I well remember the day I came across the elegant sheet
they then issued, posted before my favorite nickelodeon. It
carried the portraits of twenty-six players and would strike

you today as an astonishing mixture of actors still famous
and actors long since forgotten. I never expected to see it
again, but Kemp R. Niver has now accommodated me with a
reproduction of it in the end-papers of one of his very valuable books about early American films.[2] The independents
of course had given in long before; there would not have
been much point in Carl Laemmle's advertising that "The Biograph Girl is Now an IMP," after luring Florence Lawrence
away from Griffith, if he had planned to keep her under
wraps.

The personality cult was flourishing in those days in
all branches of the theater business, except perhaps the
circus. At the Metropolitan Opera House, only Enrico Caruso
and Geraldine Farrar could be sure that they would always
sing to sold-out houses; one Saturday night when Farrar was
a last-minute replacement for the ailing Emmy Destinn in Madama Butterfly, the theater was half empty. Charles Frohman
supplied his stars with a new play every autumn, and Maxine
Elliott casually remarked that a good actress was more important than any play. As late as the early 1920s, I can remember, Powers' Theater, the sanctum sanctorum of the legitimate
drama in Chicago, did not bother to put the name of the play
on the electric sign. The name of the star was enough; the
"vehicle" was immaterial.

Quite as interesting as all this however is the fact that
even well-informed film historians may well encounter some
surprises in running over the successes and failures of the
early days. In 1912 the Motion Picture Story Magazine issued "twelve beautiful portraits of motion picture players" in
color, to be supplied to subscribers only, and they were beautiful portraits (I wish I still had my set). This is the list as
it appeared in the announcement:

1. Alice Joyce
2. Maurice Costello
3. Arthur Johnson
4. Mary Fuller
5. Carlyle Blackwell
6. G. M. Anderson
7. Mildred Bracken
8. Francis X. Bushman
9. Florence Lawrence
10. Marion Leonard

11.   Gwendolen Pates
12.   Florence Turner

It is reasonable to suppose that the editors considered all
of these very prominent, popular players. The following
still appear in The Film Encyclopedia, by Emphraim Katz
(Perigree-Putnam, 1979): 1, 2, 3, 5, 6, 8, 9, 12; David
Ragan's Who's Who in Hollywood (Arlington House, 1976) also
includes 10. But none appear in the much more select and
less actor-oriented Biographical Dictionary of Film by David
Thomson (Morrow, 1976).

Reflections on the vagaries of fame may also reasonably
be inspired by the popularity contests conducted by the
same magazine. In the October issue 1913 the winners of
a contest in which more than seven million votes were cast
was announced. Nine persons polled more than 200,000 votes
each. They were in order:

1.   Romaine Fielding
2.   Earle Williams
3.   J. Warren Kerrigan
4.   Alice Joyce
5.   Carlyle Blackwell
6.   Francis X. Bushman
7.   G. M. Anderson
8.   Muriel Ostriche
9.   Arthur Johnson

Fielding, now completely forgotten, was an easy win-
ner--1,311,018 votes, as compared to 739,893 for Williams,
his closest runner-up. No other woman came within hailing
distance of Alice Joyce with 462,380. Muriel Ostriche, the
only other woman among the big winners, polled only 212,276,
and Mary Pickford, way down in fifteenth place, had 108,641.

Just one year later the results of the "Great Artist
Contest" were announced. The big winners were now Earle
Williams (487,295) and Clara Kimball Young (442,340), yet
Williams had polled far fewer votes than in 1913, when he
had finished second, and Romaine Fielding, the big winner
in 1912, had dropped down into Mary Pickford's old place,
the fifteenth. Mary, meanwhile, had moved up to third place,
obviously the result of her triumphs in Hearts Adrift and
Tess of the Storm Country. She was followed in order by

J. Warren Kerrigan, Mary Fuller, Marguerite Clayton (who remembers her?), Arthur Johnson, Alice Joyce, Carlyle Blackwell, and Francis X. Bushman.

It is interesting to ask how much of this cult of personality survives today. There are still big "names" in filmdom, and financially they are far more handsomely rewarded than anybody was in the old days. But there seems to be an increasing tendency for each film to stand or fall on its own, and my own impression is that the stars awaken less personal and less intense reactions now than they did then. In this connection, I recall myself, about eleven or twelve years old, asking a classmate whether he "liked" Florence Lawrence. Being an odd little boy, he asked carefully, "Do you mean like her acting or do I have an affection for her?" to which, being very austere in those days, I replied very properly, "Her acting, of course." Whereupon my friend, suddenly throwing away the careful distinction he had painfully set up, came back with "Yes, I do, but I have an affection for her too."

I suppose it is possible that somewhere in America two small boys may today be asking each other such questions about Meryl Streep or Jessica Lange, but I am inclined to doubt it.

In any case, this book is dedicated to the cult of personality and to the film past. It remains only to add by way of prolegomenon that it owes its existence to the editor of the Filmmakers series, Anthony Slide, my collaborator in The Films of D. W. Griffith (Crown Publishers, 1975) and Fifty Great American Silent Films, 1912-1920 (Dover Publications, 1980), who wanted me to collect the pieces that, at one time or another, I had written about various silent stars. The amount, if any, of commentary and revision to which these materials have been subjected is indicated, where relevant, hereinafter.

NOTES

1. See the excellent reproductions of early trade-marks on the endpapers of Fred J. Balshofer and Arthur C. Miller, One Reel a Week (University of California Press, 1967).

2. Biograph Bulletins, 1896–1908, compiled with an introduction and notes by Kemp R. Niver, edited by Bebe Beng-
   sten (Los Angeles, Locare Research Group, 1971). The
   figures I have quoted relating to Biograph salaries are
   taken from the checks reproduced in the endpapers of
   another of the Niver-Bengsten books, Mary Pickford,
   Comedienne (1967). The latest, very ambitious publication of this team is Early Motion Pictures: The Paper
   Print Collection in the Library of Congress (Library of
   Congress, Motion Picture, Broadcasting, and Recorded
   Sound Division, 1985).

MARY PICKFORD

I cannot remember when I first saw Mary Pickford on the screen, though I could tell you when and where I first encountered such late Biographs as A Beast at Bay, Friends, Lena and the Geese, and The Informer, which latter was part of my Thanksgiving Day in 1912. I never saw The New York Hat until the Museum of Modern Art began reviving it after I was grown up. At one time, heaven only knows how, I even got it into my head that Lena and the Geese was Mary's first film.

Of her Imps I remember best Science and In the Sultan's Garden. I own an 8mm print of Artful Kate as reissued by Blackhawk, and when I was about twenty, I saw a revival of Going Straight, in which I remember Mary as behaving with taste and restraint while everybody around her was "acting" his head off. I have sometimes wondered whether I may be the only person left alive who remembers seeing her in the Majestic Little Red Riding Hood, in which she dreamed the whole adventure, just as Dorothy dreamed her trip to Oz in the M-G-M version of L. Frank Baum's masterpiece, to my displeasure in both instances.

Science, in which King Baggott also appeared, was an unacknowledged steal from "A Dog's Tale" by Mark Twain, and, as I remember it, was on the same reel with something called Hector, in which a dog appeared along with the feet of a number of human beings. I assume this was based on a contemporary short-lived comic strip of the same name which was similarly designed, but since no such title is indexed in Maurice Horn's definitive World Encyclopedia of Comics (Chelsea House, 1976), I cannot find out anything about it. Mary spoke of all her Imps with extreme contempt, and certainly the few stills I have of various Imp productions look pretty amateurish. I have no reason to believe that In the

Sultan's Garden was notably better than the others, but one
can never tell what will stimulate a child's imagination, and
for me it had all the wonder of The Arabian Nights. I long
thought of it affectionately, and it came back to my mind
when, in 1917, I delighted in the Ali Baba insert in The
Little Princess. The real distinction of In the Sultan's Garden however is that it nearly finished off Mary. In her
autobiography she relates how she was sewed into a sack and
cast into the Hudson River, masquerading as the Bosphorus,
with a knife to cut her way out and how an uninvited motor
boat cut its own way into the fantasy world and came close
to cutting her to pieces. This must have indicated a high
water mark of directorial folly even in the reckless history of
motion picture production.

What surprises me most however in view of what Mary
Pickford later meant to me is that though I was perfectly
familiar with her in my early movie-going days, she did not
then stand out from many others; at this time I am sure I
was more interested in Florence Turner or Florence LaBadie
or Gwendolen Pates. There was a curious hiatus in my movie-
going around the beginning of World War I, and I did not see
Mary in any of her Famous Players features until after we
moved from Chicago to Oak Park in the spring of 1915.
Then I went one night to the Oak Park Theater to see
Fanchon the Cricket, not so much because she was in it as
because I had seen the play at the People's Theater as a very
small child. This was my first visit to one of the four Oak
Park institutions that were most important to me during my
ten years residence there, the others being Oak Park High
School, the Oak Park Public Library, and the First Congregational Church. And this too was the night I capitulated
completely to Mary Pickford. Thereafter I missed none of
her pictures, though it took me a while to catch up on all
the Famous Players items I had missed (except for A Good
Little Devil, which I have never seen), for I had to wait for
some of them to be reissued by Paramount in 1918 or 1919,
and from 1917 on I went to see all her films as often as I got
the chance.

The earliest letter from her in my files is dated 1918,
and in 1919 she sent me the handsome sepia print, personally
inscribed, which I reproduced in The Movies in the Age of
Innocence. We first met when she stopped off in Chicago on
her way to the East and Europe on her honeymoon trip with

Douglas Fairbanks. Thirteen years later, when I myself was
honeymooning, my bride and I visited her at the United Artists studio, and before we left, she took the girl aside,
while New York waited on the long distance telephone, to
tell her that if we should have a child, she wished very much
to be his godmother. I remember all this made Douglas Fairbanks very nervous; in 1932, it seems, transcontinental telephone calls were still exciting even to movie stars.

I always wanted to write about her, but for many years I
resisted the impulse to do so at any length; I cannot account
for this block except by the assumption that I must have
feared my ability to do the subject justice. Finally, however,
I turned out the following, which I here reprint without substantial alteration from The Movies in the Age of Innocence,
copyright © 1962 by the University of Oklahoma Press.

"AMERICA'S SWEETHEART"

When Mary Pickford published her autobiography, Sunshine and Shadow, through Doubleday in 1955, I reviewed it
by writing her an open letter on the front page of the Chicago Sunday Tribune Magazine of Books:[1]

Dear Mary Pickford:
When I reviewed Mary Garden's autobiography for
the Tribune, Fanny Butcher accused me of writing a
love letter to Miss Garden. I didn't, really; I was
saving that for you.
Much of my writing career has been devoted to
trying to capture in words the people and the ideas
by which my youth was molded. But I have always
found great difficulty in writing about you. Partly
this may be because you have not given me a chance
to see you on the screen for twenty years. I have
never quite forgiven you for that, and, as I have
told you, I much regret that my children have had
to grow up without seeing you every week or every
month as I did when we were both much younger.
As Mr. DeMille says in his introduction to your
book, there has been no other career like yours.
Alistair Cooke has called Garbo "every man's harmless

fantasy mistress." Well, she was never mine. And
neither were you, though for a very different reason.
I should have felt it blasphemous to think of you
thus. You speak of your appreciation of your title
"America's Sweetheart," but I am sure you know we
always read it with a difference.

We who loved you were, in general, much simpler
people than the sophisticates who go to the movies
nowadays, and you meant more to us than anybody
can mean to them. We accepted you without question
or analysis; we adored you in the honest simplicity
of our hearts. And, paradoxically, your appeal was
the more complicated on that account. Your own personality cast a Madonna-like exaltation about you,
and the roles you often played made you our mischievous child. Neither Garbo nor any other actress
in these latter days has commanded your range.

In giving us this book, Mary, you give us a chance
to renew our youth. I know much more of you than
most of your fans, but even I have learned much. Do
you remember when you told me that you couldn't
write your autobiography yet because you could not
yet tell the truth about some of the people whose
lives had touched yours? Though you did not say
so, we both knew that you were thinking of Owen
Moore and Douglas Fairbanks. I think you have done
it in this book, with perfect charity and perfect can-
dor.

It seems odd that you should have been so little a
part of your own public. Did we, perhaps, interpret
you to yourself, and is "Our Mary" our creation as
well as yours? I agree with you that Less Than the
Dust (or, as the lady misremembered the title,
"Cheaper Than the Dirt") was a terrible film, but The
Pride of the Clan was much better than you thought
it. (Thirty years after it was made at Marblehead,
Mass., I found production shots of it still on exhibition there.) I cannot understand why you thought
Pollyanna goody-goody as you played it, nor how not
only you but all your advisers thought A Poor Little
Rich Girl unsuccessful until your public had informed
you otherwise. Of all your films, this is the one I
should most like to see again.

Good luck with your book, Mary, and all God's
best to you.

Yours sincerely, as ever,
Edward Wagenknecht

Doubleday followed up on this review with a "Dear
Mary Pickford" display advertisement in the book-review
journals--"We got the idea of sending you a love letter from
the unabashed mash note the man wrote on the front page of
the Chicago Tribune Magazine of Books"--and Miss Pickford
herself wrote me that she had read my article "at least ten
times."

By the time this book is published, babies born after
Mary Pickford made her last film will have reached the age
of thirty. Now that motion pictures are no longer very important to American young people, it must be very difficult
for any such person to realize what she meant to America
when she really was "America's sweetheart"--not only the undisputed queen of the movies but, by all odds, the most
famous woman in America. For though the "America's Sweetheart" tag, invented by "Pop" Grauman, was sedulously
cultivated by her press agents, and though her career was
intelligently geared and self-directed toward the success
which she had deliberately set for herself as a goal (when
she went to Belasco in 1907, she told him that she was the
father of her family and that she must achieve a substantial
success before she was twenty), none of this would have suf-
ficed without an enthusiastic public response, and nobody
who lived through the years of her fame can doubt that that
response was spontaneous, enthusiastic, and impassioned--the
kind that cannot be manufactured or bought.

The Pickford career was not built overnight, and Mary
herself never had any real confidence that it would last. In
her eyes it was "a temporary and freakish phenomenon," and
just as some singers live in perpetual fear of losing their
voices, so she braced herself with the thought "that every
year might be my last in pictures." When she was told, on
one occasion, that she had drawn a larger crowd than the
President, she could not help thinking "that a white elephant
taking a morning stroll ... would draw a much larger and
more curious throng than either of us."

As early as 1909 a trade-journal review of To Save Her Soul remarked that "the young woman of the Biograph stock who takes the leading character plays it with fine expression and charming innocence." In 1912 a reviewer of Friends found "exquisite grace and charm ... displayed by the little woman who essays the heroine of this truly interesting episode of the West during the period of the seventies." Yet Mary won none of the popularity contests which the fan magazines conducted in the early days, and though even then I knew people who loved her and regarded her as a being apart, it was not until after she had gone with Famous Players and made Hearts Adrift and Tess of the Storm Country that it really became clear that she who had hitherto been one among many charming actresses was destined to soar in public favor until she occupied a crag all her own. In March, 1917, she polled 1,147,550 votes in a popularity contest conducted by The Ladies' World, outdistancing her closest competitor, Alice Joyce, by a cool half-million. Vachel Lindsay reviewed A Romance of the Redwoods in The New Republic under the caption "Queen of My People." "To reject this girl in haste," he wrote, "is high treason to the national heart."[2] Photoplay once published her picture without a name-tag; if any reader did not recognize her, he was invited to write in. When she had recovered from a serious bout with influenza in the spring of 1919, the Chicago Tribune printed her photograph with this caption:

> The most beloved face in the world--Mary Pickford's thousands of ardent admirers followed the news of her illness as devotedly and sympathetically as if it were a personal sorrow.

The Tribune knew: their film critic, Mae Tinée, had done nothing but answer the telephone all day, assuring Mary's devotees that she was getting better. In 1926, Dorothy Gish came back from England with the shocking news that a London schoolgirl, asked what "M.P." stood for, had replied "Mary Pickford." More shocking--and more touching--still was the story of the congressman's daughter who came home from Sunday school one day with "Mamma, they asked us today who we wanted to be like." "And?" queried her mother. "Oh," sighed the child, "I told them the Lord, but I meant Mary Pickford."

We all idealized Mary in those days, much as that girl

did. Reading Schiller's Die Jungfrau von Orleans in school,
I came across Dunois' great tribute to Joan of Arc:

> Wenn die Wahrheit
> Verkörpern will in sichtbarer Gestalt,
> So muss sie ihre Züge an sich tragen!
> Wenn Unschuld, Treue, Herzensreinigkeit,
> Auf Erden irgend wohnt--auf ihren Lippen,
> In ihren klaren Augen muss sie wohnen!

I am willing to give the reader three guesses whom I was immediately reminded of! Nor was this a wholly idiosyncratic
reaction. "There is a radiance about her," wrote Gerald D.
McDonald of Miss Pickford in his review of Sunshine and
Shadow," and audiences never doubted that even without the
make-believe she was kind, noble and true."[3] And James
Card added that "there is something heavenly about Mary
Pickford. It is a quality, we must admit, most uncommon in
motion pictures."

    This of course is why she caused such agonizing
throughout the length and breadth of America when, in March,
1920, she divorced Owen Moore and married Douglas Fairbanks. We knew that she had lived miserably with--and apart
from--Moore for many years; we knew, too, that Fairbanks'
former wife had already remarried after their divorce. No
matter! We could not bear the thought that "Our Mary"
could, in any way, have even put herself in the way of being
suspected of doing wrong. And the Reverend J. Whitcomb
Brougher, pastor of the Temple Baptist Church in Los Angeles, had to come out with a long statement, which was
solemnly syndicated throughout America, and in which he assured us that the Pickford-Fairbanks marriage was "Scriptural," and that he had agreed to perform the ceremony only
after he had investigated all the circumstances and satisfied
himself that there was no Christian or Biblical impediment.

    For all this, Miss Pickford has been much neglected,
both by film historians and by modern film aficionados. Her
films were, for the most part, long unavailable for rescreen-
ing, and for some time most of those which had survived
could be seen only at the George Eastman House in Rochester.
But I think the basic reason is that, more than any other
great star, Mary Pickford really did belong to the Age of Innocence. Her films encourage, and submit to, little analysis.

Thus while it is quite as easy to be enthralled by Mary's antics in, say, Rebecca of Sunnybrook Farm as by Griffith's heroics in, say, The Birth of a Nation, it is more difficult to write about them.

Mary Pickford was born Gladys Smith in Toronto, on April 8, 1893. Her family was Irish Catholic on her mother's side, English and Methodist on her father's--a situation which led, absurdly, to her being baptized twice, once by a Catholic priest and once by a Protestant minister. Pickford was her Irish great-grandmother's maiden name. Her Grandmother Faely was an excellent storyteller and mimic. Her childhood was poverty-stricken and filled with hardship. As a small child she used to worry about God and the devil and sin--and how she had got here--and how she could get back to the place she had come from, which was much nicer. She was also greatly interested in money--so that on one occasion she was narrowly restrained from breaking the keys of the piano to retrieve a five-cent piece that had been dropped between them--and in beauty, since she not only bought rosebuds from the florist but also begged wilted roses of him, which she carefully ate to possess herself of their desirable properties.

She made her stage debut as a small child in a stock company production of The Silver King, from which she went on to Uncle Tom's Cabin, East Lynne, The Little Red Schoolhouse, and The Fatal Wedding. ("Baby Gladys Is a Wonder," said the playbills.) It was a great day when she, her mother, her sister Lottie, and her brother Jack all got jobs with Chauncey Olcott in Edmund Burke; not only were they now all together but they got out of the fleabitten theaters in which they generally played. She assumed the name Mary Pickford at David Belasco's suggestion in 1907, when she played for him in The Warrens of Virginia.

The first motion pictures she ever saw were "Hale's Tours" in Chicago, while she was playing there in The Warrens. She was violently carsick. In the spring of 1909, at her mother's suggestion, and against her own better judgment, she made a second, and this time successful, try to get work with Biograph. (She had also flirted vainly with both Kalem and Essanay.) Her first impression of D. W. Griffith was that he was "a pompous and insufferable creature," and the word "studio" frightened her and made her

think of Stanford White and Evelyn Nesbit. The first film
in which she worked was What Drink Did, but her scene was
cut out. She appeared briefly in Her First Biscuits; but her
earliest real part was in The Violin Maker of Cremona. She
was a member of the first Biograph company which went to
California, producing Ramona and other films. In 1911,
Laemmle lured her from Biograph to Imp by offering her
$175 per week, but she found the Imp standards of produc-
tion distressingly low, was unhappy, and left after nine
months. Much briefer was her stay, that same year, with
Majestic. In 1912, Miss Pickford returned to Griffith and
Biograph and stayed there until Belasco offered her the leading role in his production of Madame Rostand's play A Good
Little Devil in 1913, when she left the screen, as she believed, forever.

Zukor brought her back by making a screen version of
A Good Little Devil while the play was still running. Edwin
S. Porter directed, and Belasco supervised, but the actors
were required to go through their lines just as if they had
been on stage. Apparently Zukor at once realized both that
A Good Little Devil was a very bad picture and that Mary
Pickford was a star who gave much richer promise of establishing his new Famous Players Film Company on a firm foundation than any of the cinematically inexperienced great
personages whom he was bringing in from the stage. Although it was made in May, 1913, the picture was not released
until March, 1914, after three other Pickford Famous Players
features had been shown. The first was Porter's and J.
Searle Dawley's production of Miriam Nicholson's novel In the
Bishop's Carriage, released in September, 1913. In November, Dawley followed with Caprice, the play in which Mrs.
Fiske made one of her early successes, and in which the
song "In the Gloaming" was first sung. If these pictures
left any questions in anybody's mind about Mary's success,
all doubts were removed when Porter's Hearts Adrift, from
Cyrus Townsend Brady's story, "As the Sparks Fly Upward,"
was released in February, 1914. In this innocent but touching little romance, Mary played a Spanish girl shipwrecked on
a deserted island, and later joined by a man (Harold Lock-
wood), also the survivor of a wreck. They marry each other
and have a child, after which, of course, the man's family
arrives with a rescue party, and Nina throws herself and her
baby into a volcano.[4]

Encouraged by the success of Hearts Adrift, Famous
Players ventured unloading A Good Little Devil; hard on its
heels (March, 1914), they released Porter's production of
Grace Miller White's story Tess of the Storm Country.[5] If
any one film can be said to have "made" Mary Pickford, it
was Tess--I can still remember how stock companies used to
advertise their stage productions of it as "Mary Pickford's
Great Success"--and this may now seem a little hard to explain, for though Mary works hard in Tess, she gets little
help from anybody, and none whatever from Porter, whose
direction quite lacks emphasis or definition of any kind.
Moreover, there is not a single close-up in the film. But it
did present her as a violent, warm-hearted squatter girl in
a variety of appealing situations. When she gets religion
from her high-toned, Divinity School-student lover, she
"cribs" a Bible from the mission and devotes herself industriously to learning--and practicing--its teachings, and when
her lover's sister bears a child out of wedlock to his best
friend, she not only takes both mother and child into her
shack but protects the girl by telling her brother that she
herself is the child's mother. When she is punished for
stealing milk for the child from its own grandfather's icebox,
she says, "I have been beaten. Now am I to have the milk?"
When the baby is dying, she marches into the church with it
and herself baptizes it before the congregation after the
clergyman has refused to do so. And when, at last, all confusions are ironed out, and she gets her proposal of marriage, she replies, "I air Daddy's brat, but [after the proper
interval] I air your squatter." The materials were there all
right, and if Porter would not sort them out for us, we were
quite intelligent enough to do it ourselves. I remembered
Tess affectionately for years, and it was not until I saw it
again for this book that I realized how much superior the 1922
remake, directed by John S. Robertson, was. (Tess, of
course, was the only film Miss Pickford ever remade.)

The year 1914 was filled out with four lesser films:
The Eagle's Mate, a Southern mountain story, from the novel
by Anna Alice Chapin (July); Such a Little Queen, from the
play by Channing Pollock in which Elsie Ferguson had starred
(September); Behind the Scenes, which opposed a career to
domesticity and in which domesticity won (October); and finally Cinderella (December), which I remember most fondly
as a radiant, springlike thing, but of which unfortunately I
cannot renew my impressions.

In 1915 there was a heavy reliance on screen adaptations of stage successes: Mistress Nell in February (the most innocent of all conceptions of Nell Gwyn, from the George C. Hazelton play which had been acted by Henrietta Crosman); Fanchon the Cricket in May (which goes back ultimately to George Sand, and which as acted for so many years by Maggie Mitchell had been one of the great successes of the American theater); two Frances Hodgson Burnett pieces--The Dawn of a Tomorrow in June and Esmeralda in September, and, in November, a Madame Butterfly, directed by Sidney Olcott, but announced as having been adapted from the John Luther Long story rather than from either the Puccini opera or the Long-Belasco play. I loved both Mistress Nell and Fanchon, and The Dawn of a Tomorrow gave Mary Pickford an excellent opportunity to express the religious feeling of which at her best she was capable. Since Geraldine Farrar was now a Lasky star, it seems odd that Butterfly should have been assigned to Mary. When it was released the Dramatic Mirror found it a triumph "photographically and technically" but thought that the tragedy had been "so softened that it is practically eliminated" and Cio-Cio-San's emotions "so rigorously suppressed that it was hard to realize that they existed." With this Miss Pickford must have agreed, since Samuel Goldwyn quotes her as having complained that the picture had no action whatever and ought to have been called "Madame Snail." It seems to me much better, however, than what I remember of Little Pal (July), an original story for the screen, in which she played a half-blood Alaska Indian girl who seldom had even an opportunity to smile. A Girl of Yesterday (October), directed by Allan Dwan, was a very light comedy about an old-fashioned girl brought up to date, from a story by Miss Pickford herself.[6] But probably the most successful Pickford film of 1915 was a lively and entertaining waif story called Rags (August), from the pen of Edith Barnard Delano.

At the beginning of 1916 it was announced that Miss Pickford would receive half a million dollars during 1916 and that she would also have a larger voice in the selection and production of her films. The first four pictures released in 1916 were still under the Famous Players trade-mark: The Foundling (January); Poor Little Peppina, a Kate Jordan story (March); The Eternal Grind (April); and Hulda from Holland (July). Peppina was directed by Sidney Olcott, the others by John B. O'Brien. The first two are both waif

stories, though the child is not an orphan but merely one
who has become separated from her parents. Reviewing
Peppina in 1961, I did not think it nearly as good a picture
as I had considered it in 1916, and it may be that if I could
review Hulda, I should have the same experience with it; on
the other hand, since it was another Edith Barnard Delano
story, it might very well hold up as successfully as Rags
does. The Eternal Grind was a somewhat depressing sweat-
shop yarn, with Mary as the high-minded girl, contrasted
to her sister, who goes astray. There is (literally) a shot-
gun wedding for the sister, with Mary holding the gun behind a curtain. The Chicago censor board "pink-slipped"
The Eternal Grind, which meant that it could be shown only
to adults. The Oak Park Theater did not run it, and I had
to go in to Austin to see it at the Plaisance.

There was no Pickford film between July and November;
then came the first Artcraft, Less Than the Dust, a story of
India, directed by John Emerson, in which Miss Pickford
played a girl of the bazaars. The trade journals had announced with great fanfare that from now on Miss Pickford
would produce her own pictures; Artcraft exchanges were
opened in various cities to handle them; and the general public did not know until later that Zukor was behind the whole
enterprise. Miss Pickford was promised a larger measure of
control than ever materialized--this was the basic reason
why she finally left Zukor for First National in 1918--and
when, after the production of A Poor Little Rich Girl, the
imagined failure was used to discipline her and bring her
into line. In May, 1917, it was announced that the Famous
Players-Lasky Corporation, as it had now become, had
"acquired" Artcraft, and afterward for a few years this
organization used both the Paramount and Artcraft trade-
marks and even issued "A Paramount-Artcraft Special" at
quite regular intervals.

The year 1917 was possibly the greatest in Mary's
career; if we stretch it to include January, 1918, when
Stella Maris (which was, of course, produced during 1917)
came out, I think there can be no doubt of this. She
worked all the year with top-notch directors. First came
The Pride of the Clan (January) and A Poor Little Rich
Girl (March), both directed by Maurice Tourneur. There
followed two Cecil B. DeMille films: A Romance of the Redwoods (May) and The Little American (July). A Poor Little

Rich Girl was the last film Miss Pickford was ever to make in the East; with A Romance of the Redwoods she transferred her producing activities permanently to California. In September, with Rebecca of Sunnybrook Farm, she found one of her best directors in Marshall Neilan, who directed all her pictures from Rebecca through M'liss in 1918, and returned to her for Daddy Long Legs in 1919 and Dorothy Vernon of Haddon Hall in 1924. They closed the year together with The Little Princess (November), and, as I have already said, they opened 1918 with William J. Locke's Stella Maris. There is not a poor picture in the series.

When in the summer of 1961 I was re-examining all the Pickfords I could find at Eastman House, I purposely avoided Mary's "patriotic" wartime picture, The Little American, having no desire to relive wartime hysteria. It is the story of an American girl with a German lover who is maneuvered into the war zone (after being torpedoed on the way), only to find her lover transformed into a "Hun," who first comes close to raping her, and then, upon discovering her identity, is so quickly redeemed that he defies the whole German high command for her sake. Since then I have seen The Little American again, and though I have not changed my feelings about it, I must admit that it is still a well-made and absorbing film.[7]

For the others, no reservations need be taken. A Poor Little Rich Girl, made from the Eleanor Gates novel and play, has always been one of my favorite films: a rich, yet somehow not inharmonious, combination of Mary's gift for mischief with Tourneur's fine pictorial sense, which is seen at its best in the dream sequences in which the delirious child relives all the joys and sorrows of her life in fresh nightmare patterns. I have been told that Kate Douglas Wiggin did not care much for Mary's Rebecca, and I can understand why this might be the case, for the book is a minor masterpiece, unsurpassed in its kind in American literature, and the film makes changes in the story and adds many irrelevant pranks; yet, for all that, I think its spirit has been miraculously preserved. Certainly Mary never made a happier picture, nor one that sparkles more brightly or offers a faster succession of entertaining situations. The Little Princess was more somber and wistful, and therefore less popular, but audiences of imagination did not love it less.

Stella Maris is often called Miss Pickford's greatest
film. I should hate to have to choose between it and two or
three others, but there can be no doubt that it is the most
unusual thing she ever did. She was very lovely as the
crippled rich girl Stella Maris, protected from all the evil and
sorrow of the world by her enforced isolation and painfully
shocked into awareness by the contacts which follow her recovery after an operation; and she was more than startling as
the twisted slavey Unity Blake, who adored Stella and the man
who adored her, and finally committed murder and suicide that
they might be happy together. Stella Maris had, too, a quite
extraordinary performance by Marcia Manon as the sadistic,
drunken wife of John Risca, whom Unity finally liquidated.

It was her last really first-rate Artcraft. There followed Amarilly of Clothes-Line Alley (March, 1918), a Belle
K. Maniates story about a girl of the lower class who learns
that "you can't mix pickles and ice cream"; Bret Harte's
M'liss (May, 1918); and then three quite trifling comedies--
How Could You, Jean? (June, 1918); Johanna Enlists (September, 1918), and Captain Kidd, Jr. (April, 1919), all ex-
pertly directed by the ill-starred William Desmond Taylor.

During 1919, First National released three Pickford
films. The first, Jean Webster's Daddy Long Legs (May), is
one of her most famous and successful pictures. Both of the
others were directed by Sidney Franklin. The Hoodlum (September) is a somewhat inconsequential slum comedy. Heart
o' the Hills (December) is a John Fox, Jr., story, very good
of its kind. In the spring of 1919, Miss Pickford joined
with D. W. Griffith, Charles Chaplin, and Douglas Fairbanks
to form the United Artists Corporation, through which all the
rest of her films were released. [8]

Her United Artist offerings began auspiciously in Janu-
ary, 1920, with Eleanor H. Porter's Pollyanna, directed by
Paul Powell. Her only other 1920 film was Suds (June),
directed by Jack Dillon, a screen version of the play 'Op o'
Me Thumb, by Frederick Fenn and Richard Pryce, in which
Maude Adams had starred. For this startling departure Miss
Pickford was perhaps fortified by the success of Stella Maris;
but Suds was more daring, not only because it lacked the
carrying emotional force of the earlier story, but because
Stella Maris had permitted Mary to play the ugly little drudge
and at the same time give the audience a chance to enjoy

"America's Sweetheart" with her golden curls in a more conventional kind of role. Here the little slavey who worked in
a London laundry had to carry the whole picture, and we
never saw the golden curls at all except in the brief interlude
in which she told of her life not as it was but as it ought to
be, an excellent burlesque of popular chivalric literature.
(They used Gothic type for the subtitles of this portion of
the film, but the fine ladies and gentlemen all talked cockney
dialect. They also had Pickford curls on Lavender, the
broken-down horse!) Why have the people who cherish
Chaplin, Keaton, and the Sennett films overlooked Suds?
Perhaps the only adequate answer is Dr. Johnson's to the
lady who asked him why he had defined "pastern" as "the
knee of a horse." "Ignorance, Madame," said the doctor,
"pure ignorance."

        The year 1921 saw three films; it was the last in which
she was to give us so much. The Love Light (January) and
Through the Back Door (May) were comparatively unimportant,
though The Love Light, in which Mary played an Italian girl
who is married, unknowingly, to a German spy, was an interesting attempt to experiment with grown-up roles. The
year ended on one of the high points of her career with her
final return to Mrs. Burnett for one of her most elaborate
films, Little Lord Fauntleroy (September), in which she played
both the boy and Dearest, his mother. Frances Marion, who
had done so many of Miss Pickford's scenarios, directed The
Love Light, in which her husband Fred Thomson was the
leading man. This is the only time Mary was ever directed by
a woman. The other two films were credited jointly to Jack
Pickford and Alfred E. Green, but it has been generally
agreed that Jack Pickford's contribution was nominal.

        In 1922 came the remake of Tess of the Storm Country,
already mentioned. In 1923 and 1924, with Rosita, directed
by Ernst Lubitsch, and Dorothy Vernon of Haddon Hall,
Miss Pickford made two more attempts to break away, in different directions, from the child roles with which she had so
long been associated. Rosita was one of a number of screen
versions which have been made of the old play Don Caesar
de Bazan, and Dorothy Vernon, of course, was a Tudor costume picture, gorgeously mounted, of another novel by
Charles Major, who wrote When Knighthood Was in Flower.

        Both these films had their merits, Dorothy Vernon

being, for my taste, the better of the two; but her own, or
her public's, lack of enthusiasm for them, or a combination
of both, left Miss Pickford with the feeling that she should
return to child roles. She did so with Little Annie Rooney
(1925), directed by William Beaudine, a good deal of which
was given over to kid gang-fighting and the solution of a
murder mystery. To my way of thinking, it was the poorest
film she had made in some time, but it proved popular.
Beaudine also directed its successor Sparrows (1926), a
somewhat Dickensian piece about greed and loyalty on a baby
farm in the swamps. Sparrows is Dickensian in its preoccu-
pation with children, in its background of crime and mystery,
and above all in the Squeers-like creature of murderous instincts (Gustav von Seyffertitz) who runs the farm. It was
beautifully photographed--some of the scenes looked almost
like paintings--but I do not see how anyone could speak of
it as a great story of intense dramatic vitality. About half
of it was devoted to tracing Mary's escape through the swamps
with her ten little protégés, sometimes in close proximity to
huge, vicious crocodiles, who would have liked nothing better
than to devour them all.

    Sparrows was followed in November, 1927, by an enter-
taining love story, My Best Girl, in which she played with
Charles B. ("Buddy") Rogers, and which turned out to be
her last silent film.[9] With it, too, Miss Pickford acquired
Sam Taylor, who directed all the rest of her pictures except
the last, Secrets, which was directed by Frank Borzage.
She received an Oscar for Coquette (March, 1929), the play
by Ann Bridges and George Abbott in which Helen Hayes had
been so successful on the stage. It was her first talking
picture and the first (except for Kiki it was also the last)
in which she was to capitalize on the screen on her newly
bobbed hair. Her Katherine in The Taming of the Shrew
(October, 1929), the only film she ever made with Douglas
Fairbanks (she says he was so difficult during its production
that he permanently destroyed her faith in her ability to make
pictures), lacked the physical stamina traditionally associated
with the role; it assumed (non-Shakespeareanly), as Sothern
and Marlowe used to do, that Katherine "caught on" to what
Petruchio was doing and "played along" with him. (In the
film this was conveyed by having Petruchio speak the "Thus
have I politely begun my reign" soliloquy to his dog, and be
overheard by Katherine from a balcony.) If the Pickford-
Fairbanks Taming of the Shrew was a less successful screen

adaptation of Shakespeare than those which Laurence Olivier
was later to achieve, it was still probably the best that had
been accomplished up to its time. The picture which followed,
the French farce Kiki, which David Belasco had adapted for
Lenore Ulric, and in which she had given such a blockbuster
of a performance,[10] was not a bad picture, but Mary seemed
out of place in it. I regretted her decision to retire from
the screen with Secrets (1933), but she could hardly have
ended her career with a finer film. Her scenes with Leslie
Howard, when their baby dies without his being aware of
what is happening, while he is defending their cabin against
an Indian attack, were surely among the finest sequences she
ever played.

     Nobody has ever questioned Miss Pickford's great skill
and knowledge in all matters relating to motion-picture technique, but there is a tendency among those who do not know
her films well to identify her exclusively with the portrayal
of children and young girls

               Standing with reluctant feet,
               Where the brook and river meet.

If this were true, I should not think it necessary to apolo-
gize for it in any terms of abjectness. Most actors specialize
in one thing or another, and if you are going to specialize,
it seems to me that children and young girls afford a very
good field. I can think of highly regarded actresses who
have specialized in prostitutes, and I do not believe that
prostitutes are more important than young girls or that they
are more varied in their motivations or more difficult to
portray. "A woman of moral depravity," said Julia Marlowe,
"offers the modern playwright greater scope than a good
woman because her life is full of incidents that are dramatic."
But, she added, rightly, that "it takes a greater artist to
make a good woman interesting than to make a base woman
sympathetic and thrilling."

     As a matter of fact, however, it was not until after
the beginning of the feature era that Miss Pickford became
definitely associated with ingénue roles, and it was not until
A Poor Little Rich Girl that she appeared all through a feature film as a child. As we have already seen, the public
preference for seeing her in youthful roles became an ever-
increasing problem to her as she grew older, and she made

a number of attempts to break away. "Through my professional creations," she says, "I became, in a sense, my own
baby," and I think there can be no doubt that her cutting
her curls (an act which she later questioned her right to
have performed) was an attempt to destroy the persona
standing in the way of her future development.[11] Nevertheless, Mary's children and girls were not undifferentiated;
of course there was a family relationship between them, but
is not this also true of the types favored by certain other
actresses? Gwen in A Poor Little Rich Girl, for example, is
a very different girl from either Rebecca or Pollyanna--more
helpless and less resourceful and considerably more wistful.
She also gives the impression of being considerably younger.
Her movements, her reactions are all those of a small child;
so too is her fright when she is told by a lazy servant that
she cannot be taken to her father's office because the place
is full of bears. When she asks another girl, "Are you
scared of BEARS?" she reads the line like a small child, and
it is no exaggeration to speak of her "reading" such lines,
though the film is silent, and we cannot hear what she says
except in the mind's ear. Her tantrums are a small child's
tantrums too, entirely lacking the elements of calculation and
self-satisfaction of which Rebecca is capable or the sense of
compulsion which sometimes possesses Polyanna.

What I am saying of course is that the composite Pickford character was considerably less simple than she is generally supposed to have been. As I have already said, if
she was "America's Sweetheart," she was also America's--and
the world's--darling child, sometimes even problem child.
But she was also the Madonna in The Foundling and again,
briefly, in Douglas Fairbanks' production of The Gaucho in
1927.

She was, to be sure, in general, "good," and if you do
not like good women in art--or if you subscribe to the juvenile
and idiotic nonsense that bad women are more "interesting"--
then she is not for you; but if you reject her on this ground,
I fear you will have to reject most of Shakespeare's heroines
with her. What you will have to learn, however, before you
can approach her intelligently, is that "good" and "saccharine"
are not synonymous terms.[12] I have already spoken of Mary's
high jinks. Her repertoire in this kind was as rich and
varied as that of the slapstick artists who did nothing else,
and sometimes, as when, in Through the Back Door, she tied

scrubbing brushes on her feet and turned the kitchen into
a skating rink, she achieved a ballet-like ecstasy.

In Rags, Tess of the Storm Country, and several other
films, she was a captivating and innocent young virago, with
what you would have called outrageous conduct in anybody
else accepted as endearing in her because of the disarming
air of innocence that went along with it; and in Daddy Long
Legs she was a devil toward all who were in authority over
her at the orphan asylum but a tower of strength to every
abused younger child. In Rags she made her first appearance riding on a goat. Overalls-clad, she charged head-on
into a gang of boys who were abusing a dog, disciplined her
drunken father in a saloon, and compelled him to return the
money he had stolen; then she went into a temper tantrum,
culminating in free-swinging a chair about her head after one
of the habitués of the place had ventured to rumple her hair.
In The Pride of the Clan she used equally violent methods to
get the fishermen into church. In The Foundling she fed
Mrs. Grimes's birthday cakes to the puppies, and when the
dogcatcher tried to seize her own dog, she not only resisted
him but unlocked the back of his wagon and set every animal
imprisoned in it loose in the streets. She also made a
statuette of the cruel Mrs. Grimes and then punished it;
probably she did not know that she was practicing witchcraft,
but the impulse was there. In Poor Little Peppina she and
her brother Beppo (Jack Pickford) attacked a servant and
kicked him in the shin in order to get in to see the duchess
when Peppina needed her help to avoid an unwelcome marriage,
and from there went on to more violence, culminating in an
escape for Peppina in Beppo's clothes. But perhaps she was
more vigorous in Tess than anywhere else. She jumped on
Dan Jordan's back when he tried to put out the squatters'
fire, made impudent faces at Elias Graves and did a mocking
dance step to tease him, and rushed into a tug of war when
the warden was taking a net from a fisherwoman so that she
got pulled along the ground on her bottom.

In Rags, again, Mary prepares to entertain an admirer
(Marshall Neilan) at a miserable little lunch in her poor hut.
She gets everything arranged to her satisfaction, but when
she steps out for a moment, her drunken father and his
companions come in and wolf the food. Mary, returning, ar-
ranges the few remaining scraps on Neilan's plate and greets
him with a disarming "I was so hungry I jes' couldn't wait

for you." James Card has rightly compared this with the
famous scene in The Gold Rush in which Chaplin waits for
the girl who never comes, and Iris Barry long ago pointed
out the Chaplinesque elements in her arrangement of her hat
and gloves before she sets out for church in The New York
Hat. These are no isolated instances, and since Mary was
doing this kind of thing before Chaplin came to the movies,
there can be no question of indebtedness on her part.
Unity Blake's pantomime with John Risca's coat in Stella
Maris, which culminates when she makes him put his arm
about her--perhaps the best thing about Mary's characterization of Unity is that she holds our sympathy for the girl
even when she quite fails to keep her "place"--is Chaplin to
the life. And Rebecca is full of this kind of thing: consider the dance-step movement Rebecca performs backward
during her embarrassment while selling soap to Mr. Aladdin,
or her recitations at school; consider her battle with the
divided door when she arrives at the brick house (so like
Keaton's never-ending war with gadgets). In closing the
upper half she knocks the bottom half open again, and when
she stoops back under to remedy this, the upper half knocks
her hat off. Finally, consider the wonderful running and
jumping from one piece of oilcloth to another, trying not to
step on Aunt Miranda's carpets, culminating in a run down
the final strip close to the camera, ending in a dead stop and
jerk which brings her hat down over her eyes and inspires
her to remark that she is sure she is going to like it here.
In Hulda from Holland she falls through a skylight onto a
young man's bed. In the way of gadgetry again, she has
regular Rube Goldberg contraptions on her bed curtains and
fishing tackle in Tess, and when she arrives in England in
Less Than the Dust, she makes a floral offering to a suit of
armor.

It must not be supposed that even in her feature pictures, made when she had become such a valuable theatrical
property that she could do virtually nothing without consider-
ing its probable effect upon millions of admirers, did she ever
give the impression of having wrapped herself in cotton wool
or of not understanding the world she lived in. In Madame
Butterfly she killed herself for love (not by the traditional
hara-kiri method, to be sure, but more genteelly by wading
out into the water). In Hearts Adrift she cast herself and
her child into a volcano. In Stella Maris she committed both
murder and suicide. She was a girl thief in both Less Than

the Dust and In the Bishop's Carriage. As a messenger boy
in Poor Little Peppina she choked on a cigar; in M'liss she
picked up a five-foot snake. In A Romance of the Redwoods
she saved Elliott Dexter, as a reformed road agent to whom
she was not married, by pretending that she was pregnant
by him, using doll clothes as garments which she had prepared for the expected baby. The sheriff married them on
the spot, and not until after they had got away did he understand that she had tricked him. The Moving Picture World
thought this situation very daring and speculated on how the
public would take it, though stipulating that "it is hardly
necessary to add that the acting and personality of Mary
Pickford make the situation without actual offence."

If the reviewer had remembered his Biographs, he might
have been less shocked. Miss Pickford has denied that she
got good parts at Biograph from the beginning. "I got what
no one else wanted, and I took anything that came my way
because I early decided that if I could get into as many pictures as possible, I'd become known and there would be a
demand for my work." It is certainly true that in many of
the Biographs I have seen she is shown briefly and ineffec-
tively. Nevertheless, Griffith gave her a wider range of
roles at Biograph than she was ever to have again, and if
she could have continued on this basis, the misunderstandings
concerning her which I have been opposing here would never
have arisen. Look at the scene in which she "vamps" the
British sentry in the otherwise comparatively ineffective 1776;
or, The Hessian Renegades (1909) if you want to see how early the fetching manners so eagerly exploited in her later
films were beginning to develop. On the other hand, there
is hardly a trace of them in the many pictures in which she
was cast as an Indian, and, as she says, she played mother
to people who were only a few years younger than herself.
When she acted Glory Quayle in To Save Her Soul, Griffith's
one-reel adaptation of Hall Caine's The Christian, she could
not give Griffith what he wanted from her because she was
too young to understand the emotions she was supposed to
express.

In Fate's Interception (1912), with Mary as a Mexican
Indian girl, we have the Madame Butterfly situation without
a mock marriage and without any imputation of innocence to
the woman in the case. Not only has she been living with
her American lover without benefit of clergy, but after she

has been jilted, she sends her Mexican admirer to kill him; through a fluke, the Mexican is killed instead, and she goes back to the American! "Who shall blame?" asks a subtitle. One might expect there would be a good many takers.

A much better--and better known--picture of the same year, Friends, goes in for more ambivalence, ending with the question "Which shall she choose?"--Walthall or Lionel Barrymore. But the amazing thing is that the girl, elegantly dressed in an 1890's gown with balloon sleeves (it had belonged to Mrs. Pickford), lives alone and receives her admirers in a room over the village tavern, where much of the action takes place. How much we are intended to read into this is doubtful, but it is safe to say that if the director and the players were conscious of all the implications, many of their 1912 customers must have missed them (I am very well acquainted with one who did).

Finally, what shall be said of yet another 1912 film, The Female of the Species? Oddly enough, Griffith called it "A Psychological Tragedy," yet it has a happy ending. Claire McDowell, her husband Charles West, her sister Mary, and a lone girl played by Dorothy Bernard wander through a wind-swept desert as the sole survivors of a massacre. The husband makes up to Bernard and shortly thereafter dies. Although the girl is entirely innocent, the wife suspects her and treats her cruelly, and the climax comes when, for what seemed in 1912 an interminable time, she stands over her sleeping form with a hatchet, "half mad with brooding," trying to make up her mind whether to kill her or not. The girl is saved when the woman is distracted by the cry of an abandoned Indian baby nearby, and reconciliation ensues. The psychological motivation here is none too clear; otherwise The Female of the Species is a stark and powerful film, with a grim natural background much like that Sjöström was later to use in The Wind. But the interesting thing is that Griffith did not cast Miss Pickford as the wronged girl and proceed to exploit a sentimental, Little Nell kind of helplessness, as almost any later director would have done. Instead he gave this role to Dorothy Bernard, who did not play it in anything approaching a sentimental manner, and he made Mary the wife's bitter and abetting sister, who went through the whole film with a frown between her eyes and a sneer on her lips, encouraging Claire McDowell's murderous desires and exuding venom toward her potential victim.

The Female of the Species was an interesting film, and
I am glad to have seen Mary in this aspect, yet I doubt very
much that anybody would really have preferred to have her
career develop along The Female of the Species lines rather
than Tess of the Storm Country lines. I well remember myself, aged twelve, coming home from The Female of the
Species at the Victoria and announcing that I had seen a
perfectly horrible picture! I even told the manager so afterward, and he agreed with me, or said he did, despite his
general enthusiasm for Biograph films. All our naïveté notwithstanding, I cannot help believing that in the larger view
the Age of Innocence did pretty well by Mary Pickford--and
by us.

Benjamin Hampton[13] points out that Mary "is the only
member of her sex who ever became the focal point of an
entire industry." Her rivalry with Chaplin changed the salary pattern for the whole film business, so that Zukor actually tried to keep her from going to his competitors by offering to pay her a large salary every week for a number of
years not to make motion pictures--there is devotion to the
film medium for you, and to Mary, too. Make whatever qual-
ifications and reservations you like, for us Mary was sweetness and light, and this was more important to us than any
possible characterization. If we made her up, this was all
the more credit to ourselves. If there are no girls in the
world like those she portrayed, then, since life imitates art
quite as much as art imitates life, it was all the more important that such girls should appear on the screen, where
their influence would extend farther and among more susceptible people than in any other medium. Whatever history
makes of her, and whichever of her films may survive, no
other generation will ever have her as we had her. If you
say that you do not understand how we were able to read
such ineffable meanings into her, I can only remind you of
the painter and the lady who could not see the effects of
which he had spoken in the great painting. ("Don't you
wish you could, Madame?" he asked her. "Don't you wish
you could?") But none of that is very important. The important thing is that we did it. And because we did it, we
shall cherish her in our hearts as long as we live, along with
the memories of our own youth, and be grateful in troubled
times for the joy she brought us.

NOTES

1. May 29, 1955 (reprinted by permission). Miss Pickford's
   autobiography is, of course, the most important single
   source of information concerning her, but among the
   many articles signed with her by-line, see also "My Own
   Story," Ladies Home Journal (July, Aug., Sept., 1923);
   "The Greatest Business in the World," Collier's (June
   10, 1922); "Ambassadors," Saturday Evening Post (Aug.
   23, 1930). Her religious views were expressed in two
   little books published by H. C. Kinsey & Company (New
   York): Why Not Try God? (1934) and My Rendezvous
   with Life (1935). Julian Johnson deserves credit for the
   pioneer attempt to tell Miss Pickford's story in "Mary
   Pickford: Herself and Her Career," Photoplay (Nov.
   1915, Jan. and Feb., 1916), supplemented in the same
   magazine by David Belasco, "When Mary Pickford Came
   to Me" (Dec., 1915). Margaret Case Hariman had a
   "profile," "Sweetheart," in The New Yorker (Apr. 7,
   1934). James Card, "The Films of Mary Pickford," with
   "An Index to the Films of Mary Pickford," Image, Vol.
   VIII (1959), 172-91, is very important.

2. Vol. XI (1917), 280-81.

3. Films in Review, Vol. VI (1955), 295-97.

4. Hearts Adrift was the first Pickford feature film ever
   made in California. In his book, written with Dale
   Kramer, The Public Is Never Wrong (Putnam, 1953),
   Adolph Zukor reports, amazingly, that it "flopped,"
   thus proving that, as historians, producers may be
   quite unreliable.

5. All of Miss Pickford's films between The Eagle's Mate and
   Esmeralda (both inclusive) were directed by James Kirk-
   wood, except Such a Little Queen, which was directed
   by Hugh Ford.

6. Although Miss Pickford turned out many scenarios in
   the Biograph days, this was apparently the only feature
   film for which she ever wrote the story. According to
   her cameraman Charles Rosher, she had a very important share in the direction of all the films on which he
   worked with her except Rosita, which was wholly in

charge of Ernst Lubitsch. She calls Rosita "the worst
picture I ever made, bar none," thus usurping a distinction which, I think, clearly belongs to Less Than
the Dust.

7. Compare the tribute Harvey O'Higgins pays Mary's acting
in this film in his article "To What Green Altar?" New
Republic, Vol. XVIII (1919), 80–81. He is speaking of
the scene in which a wounded French soldier, carried
past her, salutes. "There came over her face the look
of a mother who sees a dying child reach for a toy from
her hands. Pitiful and apologetic, with a halting, awkward, painful gesture, she returned his salute ... and
her face was all purely human maternal tenderness; and
she tried even to smile encouragingly, but with a certain
heart-broken blindness as if she could not quite see him
for the mist of tears in her eyes; and then the struggling
smile achieved complete expression in a conflict of emotion
that mirrored the most subtle aspects of reality as only a
great imagination could conceive them.

"There was nothing theatrical about it. There was
nothing stereotyped.... But you might go a long way
and see a great deal of famous acting without meeting the
expression of an emotion so true, so poignant, and so
beautiful."

8. See Arthur L. Mayer, "The Origins of United Artists,"
Films in Review, Vol. X (1959), 390–99.

9. The last years of Miss Pickford's once happy marriage to
Douglas Fairbanks were clouded by his infidelity. She
received her final decree of divorce from him on January
10, 1935. On June 26, 1937, she made her third, very
fortunate and happy, marriage to "Buddy" Rogers.

10. It seems odd that Norma Talmadge had anticipated Miss
Pickford's production of both of her last films--Kiki and
Secrets. As a matter of fact, Miss Pickford filmed
Secrets twice but disliked the first production and de-
cided not to release it.

11. In her autobiography she writes of being overwhelmed
by the avalanche of public criticism which followed her
act. "You would have thought I had murdered someone,
and perhaps I had, but only to give her successor a

chance to live." In 1929 bobbed hair was still a moral
issue in America; it marked the difference between the
old-fashioned "womanly" woman and her "emancipated"
successor, between the Victorian maiden and the "flapper." When Mary Pickford, who had been the symbol
par excellence of all the cherished old values, cut her
hair, it seemed to many as though the citadel had been
betrayed from within. When, as late as 1925, Miss Pickford had appealed through Photoplay for letters telling
her what she should play, the 25,000 people who responded were overwhelmingly in favor of the youthful
roles, the gist of the argument being that other actresses could portray emotional maturity but that what
Mary was doing could be done by her alone. The stories
most frequently asked for were "Cinderella" (which she
had already done), Anne of Green Gables (which Mary
Miles Minter had done), Alice in Wonderland, The Little
Colonel, and Sara Crewe (which she had done as The
Little Princess). Disney is said once to have considered
a production of Alice with Mary as the human child and
cartoons for the fairyland characters.

12. Miss Pickford was not one of her own fans. In her auto-
     biography she declares that she never made a film which
     she liked in its entirety, and in her 1923 articles in the
     Ladies' Home Journal she went even further: "Of all the
     films that I have made I do not believe that there is one
     that is even half-way right or one that I would care to
     have brought out twenty years from now except as a
     curiosity, as a family album might be brought out."
     Once--horrible thought!--she even planned to buy up
     her films and destroy them. I am sure, therefore, that
     she would not mind my saying that while it never troubled
     me greatly, I do know what people mean when they object
     to a certain stock "cuteness" at times in her characteriza-
     tions of children and young people, though I should pre-
     fer to describe this as a tendency to apply, at times, just
     a shade too much pressure. This seems to me her only
     fault as an actress within her range (I speak here of
     faults, not limitations), and I must take care not to over-
     stress it, for she was, in general, an extremely restrained
     actress.

13. A History of the Movies (Covici-Friede, 1931).

LILLIAN GISH

I first met Lillian Gish at the Blackstone Hotel in December 1920, when she came to Chicago for the local opening of Way Down East at the Woods Theater. I did not meet Dorothy until January 1922, when both she and Lillian came for the opening of Orphans of the Storm and occupied the box just behind mine at the Great Northern Theater. After I moved to New England we met more frequently, and my friendship with both sisters, which was extended to embrace my family as soon as I had acquired one has been a blessing for which I shall always be thankful. It chanced that when I came to New York in 1961 to work on The Movies in the Age of Innocence at the Museum of Modern Art Film Library, Dorothy was out of town, and she graciously placed her rooms in the Elysée Hotel at the disposal of my wife and myself.

The essay that follows first appeared in 1927 as Number Seven in the series of University of Washington Chapbooks edited by my late, lamented friend Glenn Hughes, who thereby became my first publisher. It was revised very slightly for its reappearance in The Movies in the Age of Innocence, and this version was reprinted in 1980 in the very handsome booklet which the Museum of Modern Art brought out to commemorate its Gish retrospective, on which occasion Charles Silver generously described it as "the classic critical appreciation of Miss Gish's early work." However this may be, it reappears here without further change.

The meeting in Chicago referred to at the end of my discussion occurred, again at the Blackstone and later at the railroad station, when Lillian and her mother stopped off between trains when she was on her way to the Coast to take up her M-G-M contract. It is interesting to reflect that of the roles I mention in my penultimate paragraph as being

naturals for her, Ophelia is the only one she ever had a
chance to play. This was in the famous 1936 New York stage
production, directed by Guthrie McClintic, in which John
Gielgud was the Hamlet and Judith Anderson the Queen. As
early as 1936 however, Edward Steichen had taken a marvelous
portrait of her as Ophelia, which is handsomely reproduced
as #116 in his autobiography, A Life in Photography (Doubleday, 1963), where it is strangely mislabeled "Romola." The
news about the film of that title, to which I refer at some
length, is better however. Long considered a lost film, it
has now been recovered and is currently (1986) available in
casette form for the VCR from Danny Burk, 2316 Mishawaka
Avenue, South Bend, Indiana, 46615.

LILLIAN GISH: AN INTERPRETATION*

        Just what it is that makes a fine artist in the theater
is a subject on which probably no final decision will ever be
reached, but at least it is now clear that the popular impression of the great actor as a chameleon-like creature who
wholly sinks his own individuality in the role that he plays,
who nightly reduces himself to putty and then proceeds to
construct a new and alien character from its foundations, is
an excellent definition of what such an artist is not. Without great personality, great art simply cannot exist, and
this truth has long been recognized in connection with the
other arts. The individuality of the great painter is evident
in all his canvases: a Corot cannot be mistaken for a Millet
or a Van Dyck for a Frans Hals. In literature too it is only
the second- and third-rate stuff that might have been written
by anybody: Chaucer and Fielding and Conrad are "there,"
visibly and incontrovertibly "there," in every line that they
wrote. It is so also in the theater, for the creative process
is essentially one in all the arts. An actor may, according
as his experience of life has been wide or narrow, according
as he himself is simple or complex, single- or many-sided,
work in a wide field or he may specialize within a comparatively narrow range. What is worth remembering, however,
of a really versatile player like David Garrick, as against the

*Copyright © 1927 by Edward Wagenknecht, copyright re-
newed by Edward Wagenknecht, 1955.

limited portrayer of a type, is not that Garrick has sub-merged his personality, but rather that, through sympa-thetic comprehension and intelligence, he has enlarged it to embrace a much wider segment of life. Zola conceived of art as a corner of nature seen through a personality. If acting is in any sense among the arts, why should we not grant to the actor this same privilege--to re-character his material in terms of his own personality--which we impose upon the poet as a duty? We may grant it or not as we choose; we may even justify our obtuseness by the cant that acting is not "creative" but merely "interpretative." Still the actor will continue to do it, as he has always done it, because it creates the only condition under which acting can exist at all.

I admit that this is dangerous doctrine, but I do not happen to know any true doctrine that is not dangerous. I am not trying to absolve the actor from "faithfulness" to the author whose plays he presents; I am simply suggesting that in acting itself there is a larger creative element than is commonly supposed. The plain truth of the matter is that unless a play is purely a "closet-drama"--and therefore de-void of all essential dramatic quality--it is not finished at the time it is printed: it does not really come alive until some man or woman of genius makes it live upon the stage. The very great plays--Hamlet, for example--are never completed. Hamlet is no longer Shakespeare's exclusively but the world's, and it will not be really finished until the last great actor has presented his conception of it.

In short, I believe that the actor, like the poet, cannot possibly create anything greater than his own soul. It is precisely this experiential quality that marks the difference between mere vulgar impersonation--which is of no signifi-cance--and genuine portrayal of character--which is of value because it assists in the understanding of life. That which the actor does not understand, and which has not been passed through his own alembic, may indeed startle for the moment through technical brilliance; but in the long run it is ineffective, like the famous legendary sermon which the devil once delivered with great energy against all the hosts of darkness, and which won no converts, simply because the preacher himself did not believe in it.

The bearing of all this upon my subject is, I trust,

fairly obvious. Miss Gish is not, in the usual sense, a versatile actress. Her temperament is not naturally and obviously "dramatic," and she always claims the right to make her roles over to suit Lillian Gish. Yet she has come to be accepted as the outstanding serious artist of the screen, the authentic, incomparable interpreter of the drama of the shadows. As far back as 1920, John Barrymore called her an American artist worthy to rank with Duse and Bernhardt, an American girl who had equaled if not surpassed the finest traditions of the theater.

I hope I may not be misunderstood. I am not saying what the unenlightened so often say: that "Lillian Gish is always the same." Each of her portraits is an individual achievement: he who feels or who pretends to feel that her Mimi and her Hester Prynne are the same person, or that her Angela Chiaromonte is not an essentially different girl from her Henriette Girard, is surely completely blind to other than very elementary and wholly obvious distinctions: fine shadings in art are not for him. Versatility, in the usual sense, is comparatively easy for the character actor: he presents, one after another, wholly different types, and he has all the resources of makeup to sustain the illusion. But Miss Gish is not a character actress. She has played only sensitive young women, most of them about the same age, many of them facing not wholly dissimilar problems. The business of differentiation for such a player is ten thousand times more difficult than it is for the character actor; I think hardly any careful student of acting will deny that she has triumphantly met the test.

But what is more to the point for my argument is that in and through all her carefully differentiated characterizations, she has expressed also her own point of view, a distinctive something which is Lillian Gish and nobody else on earth. Her Hester Prynne is not precisely Hawthorne's Hester: she is Lillian's Hester. This point has sometimes been cited against her; as a matter of fact, it is the highest praise that could be given. Hawthorne's Hester Prynne exists in Hawthorne's pages: why should Lillian Gish seek to create her over again? Is it not better to begin under Hawthorne's spell but to go on from there independently to work out her own conception as he did his?--a conception which, precisely because it does represent the reaction of another individuality, will help us better to understand not

only Hawthorne but the life experience which both artists,
and which all artists, seek to interpret?

This, I believe, is the essentially "poetic" note in the
work of Lillian Gish--a thing to which so many have referred
but which hardly anybody has understood. The girl's work
seems "poetic" because she is a poet, that is because she is
a creator. She is like the poets in that there is something
distinctive in the way she apprehends life, and she uses her
roles as the poet uses words and the musician tones--not to
reproduce what somebody else has done but to express directly her own authentic impression. Hence also the marvelous sense of completeness, of perfection that she gives
you. The part and the actress are one: there is nothing
extraneous. In a very deep and very true sense, she is
the profoundest kind of actress: that is to say she does
not "act" at all; she is.

This is not of course what most people mean when they
refer to Lillian as "poetic." Usually, I am afraid, they mean
that she is pretty. Sometimes--God forgive them!--they are
even trying to say that she is weak. The novelist Joseph
Hergesheimer was one of Lillian's most ardent admirerers, yet
he would seem to have been blind to some of her most important qualities. Hergesheimer objected strenuously to The
White Sister, for example, which he claimed he never went to
see. "I had no wish to see Lillian's pale charm against the
rigid whiteness of a nun's headdress." But it was precisely
the qualities which repelled Hergesheimer in The White Sister
that attracted Lillian: she wanted to do the story, as she
once told me, most of all for the privilege of filming the assumption of the veil, a ritual which she considered one of
the most beautiful things in modern civilization.

I do not, however, wish to convey the impression that
I am in any sense unmoved by Lillian's beauty. She is completely a being of lyric loveliness, even to her very name.
The affinity between her given name and her spirit is a
commonplace; if there were only one thing in the world by
which to symbolize her, one would instinctively choose the
lily. To most persons I suppose her surname means nothing,
but this is their misfortune. It should mean romance, the
pathos of distance and of faraway perfect things; it should
carry them back to buried Babylon, to the Gilgamesh epic
and the marvelous adventures of Gish.

Lillian's physical frailness--her Dresden china quality--
connects here, and it is this which is commonly regarded as
her most serious limitation. Actually it is nothing of the
kind. It is true that it bars her from playing coarse types--
which make up the most of life--and that it limits her capacity for heroic expression. It is hardly conceivable that any
other producer than D. W. Griffith could have discerned her
gifts at the time she entered pictures: to anyone else, the
pale child she was then must have seemed, as a dramatic
actress, the world's worst bet. Griffith, with his passion
for delicacy and his uncanny knowledge of his craft, per-
ceived at once that what might have handicapped her on the
stage was precisely what would make her on the screen. In
a large auditorium, physical coarseness of feature is no hand-
icap; it may even be an advantage. But the merciless
camera, with its magnified features and its enormous close-
ups, brings the actor almost on top of his audience, register-
ing every movement, showing up inevitably the most trifling
defect. Except Mary Pickford, there is nobody whose con-
tour quite suits the camera, quite stands the test, as does
Lillian's. And it would be difficult to find two actresses who
appear in more radically different lights. Mary photographs
always with cameolike precision: she stands out against her
backgrounds with crystal clarity, like Lucrezia Bori at the
opera. Lillian's outlines, on the other hand, are dreamlike,
subdued; she seems to float on the screen like a remembered
vision of Botticelli's women.

This lyrical coloring in Lillian seems immensely precious:
doubly so because she lives in an age when most girls have
definitely outlawed overtones, when everything must be frank
and open, everything ruthlessly displayed, no matter how
ugly it may be. Something of the lyrical goes into whatever
she does, glorifies it with the interpenetrating quality of the
imagination, makes it impossible for her to be drably realistic,
no matter what her role. Frequently she plays what are
called in the movies "cotton stocking" parts. But what she
gives you of poverty in these instances is never its drabness
and hardness but only its singleness and sweet humility.
The star example is the scene in Way Down East in which
Anna Moore, her mind oppressed by the dread dogma of infant damnation, herself baptized her dying child. Miss Gish
played the scene with utter realism--her walk, her expressions, the very arrangement of her clothes all suggesting the
strain of recent childbirth. Many an actress could have done

that, but I do not know who could have followed her in the
next step she took, who could have lifted the whole scene,
as she did, away from squalor, beyond the physical, who
could so beautifully have suggested the age-old miracle of
the girl become mother.

But Lillian's lyricism could never have served to win
her present place for her had it not been coupled with a
dramatic intensity all the more striking because the body
through which she expresses it seems so frail.   The effect is
virtually to blot out the flesh: when she really lets herself
go, she is like nothing so much as a pure white flame.
Though she has done finer things since, her closet scene in
Broken Blossoms, the helpless child's pitiful terror of the
brutal father who was hammering against the door, trying to
get in and kill her, will remain in the memory of all her
audiences as the best single expression of her wonderful
capacity for utter surrender to emotion.   It was hysterics
photographed, yet it was fine art; hysterics are not naturally
beautiful.

I have already touched on the exaltation, the profound
mysticism of Miss Gish's playing.   Even her beauty is not a
thing in itself: you never think of her as a "beauty" in the
sense in which you think thus of many women of the theater.
She is essentially the Puritan in art: there are many phases
of experience that she does not care to touch.   It is indeed
because of her own sensitiveness, because through all these
years in the theater she has, in a sense, kept herself in a
world apart, that she has become so incomparable an interpreter of the experience of sensitive women.   In the ordinary,
vulgar sense of the term, there is no more sex in her screen
manifestations than there was for Dante in the Beatrice of the
Commedia.

Miss Gish's work on the screen is pure emotion: there
is no suggestion of mind in it, and here, as always, she is
profoundly right, for the visible presence of intellect in acting can only rob it of spontaneity, make it labored and self-
conscious.   But all who have watched Lillian's development
know that the mind is there notwithstanding: nothing could
be farther from the truth than to imagine that the lovely
things she has created came into being spontaneously, as
mere emanations of herself.   And she is still growing, for
each appearance marks, in some respect, an advance.   Twelve

years ago, in <u>The Birth of a Nation</u>, I did not indeed find her
extraordinarily effective; of all her more important characterizations, this of Elsie Stoneman seems to me the least. But as
Annie Lee in <u>Enoch Arden</u>, released that same year, she did
immensely fine work, running the whole gamut from youth to
age, and doing it with splendid sincerity and with poignant,
touching sweetness. As the French girl Marie in <u>Hearts of
the World</u> she went even deeper, and after I saw her in
<u>Broken Blossoms</u> in 1919, I told her, out of my ignorance,
that I did not see how she could ever equal the performance
she had given here. Yet Lillian has gone far, far beyond
what then seemed unutterable perfection.

In four of her recent pictures, Miss Gish has been engaged in a profound and beautiful study--the study of woman's attitude toward her love. In <u>La Bohème</u> it was the love
which gives blindly, eagerly, in answer to desire. In <u>Romola</u>
it was the austere love which, precisely because it loves, will
accept nothing from the beloved except the best. In <u>The
White Sister</u> love and God were in conflict, and God won.
And in <u>The Scarlet Letter</u> the love was tainted with sin and
worked its way out, through suffering, to salvation.

Of these four characterizations, it is difficult to make
a choice, but I think the one which moved me most was precisely the one which has been the least popular--<u>Romola</u>.
This film surely did not earn very much money for its sponsors, for it was enormously expensive, and it wholly lacked
the melodramatic appeal which a great costume film must have
if it is to capture the movie public. Lillian's own role, too,
was not essentially dramatic, there was no furniture broken,
and the general public could not do other than remain comparatively indifferent to her quiet, gently incisive baring of
a woman's soul. Lillian herself--the artist's divine dissatis-
faction upon her--did not quite share my enthusiasm for this
picture. "I hope you will like <u>Romola</u> when you see it," she
had written me. "It caused me so much trouble and there
are so many things in it that I would have different from
what they are that I can never think of it now without a
great feeling of sadness for what we might have done with
that beautiful story." Nevertheless, it is here that she has
given us a characterization worthy, in its perfections, to
rank with Mary Garden's portrait of Mélisande in Debussy's
ultimate opera. For the first time, as I watched <u>Romola</u>, I
felt that I was really beginning to understand what supreme

devotion, what never-failing effort it must have cost Lillian
Gish to develop her art to the point to which she had brought
it here. The old-time violence, the occasionally hysteric
quality that was the hangover from her Griffith days, was
gone, but the dramatic intenseness that had accompanied it
and saved it and made it beautiful remained--repressed,
quivering with life. A twitch of her expressive mouth, a
shift of expression in her eyes, and she had accomplished
what in the old days it took all the resources of her body to
achieve less perfectly. The finest example of all this in
Romola comes at that moment in the house of Tessa when
Romola first realizes that Tito has been unfaithful to her.
Actually Lillian did nothing in that moment save look at Tito
and then back at Tessa's baby which she was holding in her
arms. Slowly the realization dawned that her husband was
the father of this child, and the tears welled up in her eyes,
but they did not overflow. Amazement, incredulous wonder,
wounded pride, and the pure woman's instinctive recoil from
an unchaste man--they were all there in that look; yet beneath and above them all were love and pity--for Tito, and
for Tessa, and for the child.

In Romola, Lillian appeared to be turning inward--more
self-contained than she used to be--an entity complete. In
a measure this may have been due to the accident of material.
But in a deeper sense I do not believe it was, for Lillian is
growing daily, broadening, developing, shifting the stream
of her life to deeper channels. If this tendency continues
she will in the future be less of an "actress" than now; she
will be rather a symbolist, an "essentialist"--if there is such
a word--and her screen images will be not so much characterizations as projections, pictures, embodiments (I know not
how to name them) of the varied aspects of the spiritual life.
One shudders to think what effect such a process might have
upon Lillian's box-office popularity, but what a sense of
wonder she could bring to our souls, what deepening and
beautifying of this amazing mystery we call life. And Lillian
could do it if her managers would give her the chance, could
leave behind her "pictures of the floating world" which might
well live as long in the imaginations of men as Homer's portrait of Nausicaä.

Indeed, I believe Miss Gish to be capable of much
greater roles than any she has yet played. She has etched
a precious number of lyrical and dramatic moments, but

frequently the stuff from which she has wrought has been
the veriest melodrama. Imagine what she might be in <u>Lancelot
and Elaine</u> or as Mélisande or Francesca da Rimini. Imagine
what she might do with Ophelia or with any of the later
spiritualized heroines of Shakespeare--with Miranda or Per-
dita, for example. She is not easy to fit with roles that shall
be at once adaptable to the screen and suited to her genius:
for the mere clash of earthly passion--the quality most frequently and most picturesquely exploited by "emotional" ac-
tresses--is simply not for her.

Sometimes I am inclined to be a little impatient about
these things: I suppose everybody, now and then, feels that
the careers of his favorite artists are being less intelligently
managed than he himself could manage them. Yet the last
time I saw Lillian, one night in Chicago, when she and her
delightful mother left for California, it came over me suddenly
that all such fretting was futile. What difference does it make
what Lillian plays so long as she is Lillian? That at least no
casting director can ever take away from us. Here is the
source of the impression she makes, for she herself is among
the poets. She may bring us art and literature from the
treasure houses of Europe, or she may float on an ice cake
down some river of her native land. Whatever she does, she
will always be beauty--emotionalized beauty, through which
one catches sudden, radiant glimmerings of the wonder of
life.

CLARINE SEYMOUR

Before Clarine Seymour passed into D. W. Griffith's employ, she had been briefly involved with the Thanhouser company, whose studio was in New Rochelle, New York, where she lived with her family, and with Pathé in nearby New Jersey and had spent two unhappy years in California, whither she had been sent to work for a Pathé subsidiary.

She appeared in four Griffith films: The Girl Who Stayed at Home (released March 23, 1919), with Robert Harron, Richard Barthelmess, and Carol Dempsten; True Heart Susie (June 1, 1919), with Harron, Miss Dempster, and Lillian Gish; Scarlet Days (November 10, 1919), with Barthelmess, Ralph Graves, Miss Dempster, and Eugenie Besserer; and The Idol Dancer (March 22, 1920), with Barthelmess and Creighton Hale. She was still alive when The Idol Dancer, which afforded her much the best showcase for her gifts and charms that she had yet had, was released, but it was still in general circulation when she died, at the age of twenty-one, in New Rochelle, on Sunday evening, April 25, after an emergency operation for strangulation of the intestines. At the time of her death, on the verge of signing a lucrative new contract, she was working as Kate Brewster, the role afterwards assigned to Mary Hay, in Griffith's Way Down East, and, according to Lillian Gish, who loved and admired her, she may still be glimpsed at a distance in some of the long shots of that famous film.

Her death seemed to me a particularly poignant example of the tragedy of unfulfillment and frustrated hopes by which human beings have been tortured from time out of mind and of which agony Tennyson's In Memoriam remains one of the great monuments. It chanced that on August 8, 1920, I was asked to speak at the Sunday evening service of the Frances E. Willard Methodist Episcopal Church, in Oak Park, Illinois,

where I then lived, and knowing, as I did, that the Seymours
were Methodists, it seemed to me not inappropriate to include
some of the thoughts that had come to me in connection with
this matter in a discourse not otherwise concerned with
Clarine. (I remember that one neighbor woman, not otherwise
distinguished for piety, was deeply shocked that I should
have dared to mention a motion picture actress in church.)
I sent a transcript of my remarks to the Seymours, and this
brought me from Clarine's father what was probably the most
moving as it was certainly the saddest as well as one of the
longest letters I have ever received. Not long afterwards,
when his business brought him to Chicago, we met and dined
together, when I heard much more about Clarine.

        Albert V. Seymour worshipped his daughter, and he
was as much crushed by her death as a man can be if he is
to go on living. Nevertheless he declared that both he and
his wife had been helped and strengthened by what I had
written to a far greater extent than, as I read my poor words
over now, nearer seventy than sixty years after having ut-
tered them, seems easily credible. "What you did for us,
you will never know." Nobody else, among all the hundreds
they had heard from, he declared, had helped anything like
so much. A friend had had my remarks set up in type and,
as I remember it, Mr. Seymour told me that some ten copies
had been struck off, of which half had been elegantly bound
in tooled leather and the others enclosed in plain gray wrap-
pers. I have one of these latter, which must be by all odds
the rarest of my sixty-odd productions, antedating by a cool
seven years my first true publication, Lillian Gish, An Interpretation.

        Though I had something to say of Clarine Seymour in
The Films of D. W. Griffith, what follows hereinafter has
never before been reprinted. I have made one cut at the
end and minutely retouched the style throughout, for, like
Henry James and Walter de la Mare, I seem to be constitution-
ally incapable of reprinting anything without tinkering with
it; this is probably the only quality I share with these great
writers. Of at least all the earlier pieces included in this
volume I should probably have to say that if I were writing
them today I should put some things rather differently.
Nevertheless, in view of the comfort my words gave the
Seymours I have always been both glad and grateful that I
said what I did in 1920.

*   *   *

For life is a profoundly wonderful thing, and death,
which sometimes cuts it off so cruelly, has no power to
change its character. The Grim Reaper can call a halt to
our bodily functions, but his power ends there. A few
months ago a young girl died, her feet on the very threshold
of what promised to be a brilliant career in motion pictures.
She was beautiful; she was talented; she was good. She was
an adherent of your own Methodist Church, the kind of girl
whose labors in the theater have already done much to remove the traditional hostility between the pulpit and the
stage and to make it increasingly possible for both to work
together for the common welfare. Her work was not finished;
it was just begun. Only recently the foremost director of
motion pictures in the world had rescued her from obscurity
and given her an important place in his company. She lived
only long enough to justify his faith in her, and then, suddenly and without warning, just when it seemed that the
hour was at hand for which all the rest of Clarine Seymour's
life had been lived, the golden thread was snapped.

There is something particularly baffling about such a
death that compels us to revise many of our easy-going
theories of optimism. Not even Pollyanna could find anything
to be glad about in this. There is a sense of incompleteness,
of unfairness about it that tempts us to doubt the very
foundations of justice. Somehow or other we feel that this
girl has been cheated, that life was not quite fair to her.
One could hardly blame those who loved and who knew her
intimately if in her death their faith and their philosophy
should desert them. Indeed, I myself, who never knew her
in life, felt something of this when I came out from my first
view of The Idol Dancer, in which Clarine Seymour's potential
first shone forth in its full suggestiveness.

Our attitude toward such an event must, I suspect, be
largely determined by whether we regard death as an enemy
or a friend. Surely it is not only the life-weary who have
learned to regard him in the latter aspect. It was that
radiant spirit Saint Francis of Assisi who said that because
he had loved life, he must also love life's sister, death. Only
the view of the centuries can be adequate if we are to achieve
any sane view of the great things of the spirit; we can never
hope to understand them unless we are able to rise above the

small concerns of this little hour. And in the light of the
centuries it does not matter very much whether we live
nineteen years or ninety; what does count finally and ever-
lastingly is the kind of life we live while we are here. Did
not the Greeks comprehend something of this when they
framed their fine saying that "whom the gods love die young"?
Those sweet and delicate flowers whose blooming delights our
precious gardens for a brief space, and who all too soon for
our happiness are transplanted to the gardens of God, there
to bloom forever in ineffable beauty and splendor, leaving
behind them only the sweet, poignant fragrance that will
linger with us forever--these have no small nor contemptible
part to play in the economy of God. These who were born
not for a lifetime of labor but for the radiant glory of an
hour, who shall say that they give us less than the millions
of their toiling and striving fellows? Joan of Arc died at
nineteen, Stevenson at forty-four. Jesus, in thirty-three
years, did more for mankind than all the rest of us in un-
totalled millions of years. Shakespeare represented Romeo
and Juliet as perishing miserably after a few harried, glorious hours of love, but the memory of that love, preserved in
his imperishable verse, has made the love of all high-minded
men and women a better and grander thing for all time. It
is a heart-breaking thing to lay the young away, and we
have a right to spurn those who, with hearts untouched by
grief, would persuade us that what has happened is not so
bad after all, but there are worse things in the world than
the death of the young. The spirit that goes back to the
Father pure and strong, the glorious idealism of youth still
a full-blown and glorious blossom, the vital powers of life
undepleted and life's integrity untarnished--such a spirit is
not the least fortunate among the sons and daughters of men.
There are parents of living children who might well find it
in their hearts to envy those who have lost this girl. Somewhere along the path of life, death lies in wait for all of us,
and none of us shall escape him. The real tragedy is not
that people die but that millions of them never really live.

What right, after all, have we who are still upon this
earth to speak of those who have left it as "dead"? Doubtless if the unborn child could be given a glimpse of the
larger world upon which he is soon to enter, he would shrink
from the experience as we, the "living," shrink from the experience that we call death. But we are all in the womb of
time, and life is a succession of births. Suppose that what

we call death is simply one of them, an entrance into a larger
world. Certainly this world in which we live does not belong
to us. The sceptre of power is held in the hands of dead
men. The lives we live were conditioned long ago by those
who have gone before us. The ideals, the principles, the
habits by which we live are not our own but were established
by those who died ages ago. Surely it is impossible for anyone who has ever felt anything of the glory and splendor of
human life to think of Shakespeare or to think of Lincoln as
dead. Is anyone dead who was ever fit to be alive?

Finally, let no man seek to undercut our comfort by
pointing out that we do not <u>know</u> we are immortal. In the
last analysis we cannot <u>prove</u> anything that really matters to
us. As Browning says, "you must mix some uncertainty with
faith if you would have faith be"; demonstration belongs to
the realm of mathematics and never gets very far outside it.
But unless the girl whose life and death has inspired these
remarks receives somewhere, somehow, the chance for life
that was denied her here, there is something wrong with the
universe. It would be impertinent to pity her; it is more
reasonable to believe that her eyes see much that is hidden
from us, that for her death was what Peter Pan expected it
to be, "an awfully big adventure." And for those who loved
her here the mantle of life as we know it will always be invested with a sweeter, finer sanctity because for a little
while it clothed her.

GERALDINE FARRAR

Geraldine Farrar has the distinction of having been the only prima donna who ever built herself a secondary career as a silent film star. She was the first great singer I ever heard, and I have heard none since that I liked quite so well. How I came to know her and to write about her and the relationship between what is printed here and my other writing and living are sufficiently indicated in the piece itself as to call for no further commentary here. The following article first appeared in Films in Review in January 1977 (Vol. XXVII, pp. 23-39), where it was accompanied by a filmography by Anthony Slide and was copyrighted © by the National Board of Review of Motion Pictures, Inc. Except for such mechanical alterations as were necessary to make the FIR style conform to that employed in this book, it is reprinted without alteration.

GERALDINE FARRAR'S FILM CAREER*

Geraldine Farrar was one of the famous women of the century (in the 1920s The New York Times included her name in a list of the ten greatest women in America), and motion pictures were only an interlude in her spectacular international career. All fourteen of her films were made between 1915 and 1920 and then only as a means of furnishing her with summer employment, when she was not occupied in the opera house and concert hall. She was the first celebrated diva to condescend to grace the still fairly lowly screen, and her condescension was considered almost as important from the point of view of enhancing its prestige as had been Sarah Bernhardt's appearance in the first Famous Players film, Queen Elizabeth, in 1912. Moreover she so quickly acclimated

---

*Reprinted by permission of Films In Review. New York.

herself to the new medium that she was soon under no need to rely on a carry-over from her operatic glamour. When in 1919 the Strand booked Shadows, one of her least significant films, the line extended for a block down Broadway.

Miss Farrar was born in Melrose, Massachusetts, on February 28, 1882, the adored only child of Sidney Farrar, store-keeper and baseball player and his wife, Henrietta Barnes Farrar. Her ancestry was English (not, as has often been stated, Irish); her surname is accented on the first syllable, not the second; the well-known Victorian cleric F. W. Farrar belonged to the same family.

Both her parents sang in the local Unitarian church. The child manifested unusual musical sensitiveness almost from babyhood, and there was never any question in her mind about what she wished to do. She studied first in Boston and New York; then, in 1899, she and her parents went to Europe on borrowed funds to fit her for an operatic career. She found an ideal teacher in Lilli Lehmann, and on October 15, 1901, made her debut as Marguerite in Faust at the Royal Opera in Berlin, where she soon became the idol of both the public and the Royal Family. After almost equally successful appearances in other European musical centers, she came to the Metropolitan Opera House in New York as Juliette on November 26, 1906, and here she remained until her retirement from opera, her final appearance being in Leoncavallo's Zaza on the afternoon of April 22, 1922. She left the opera when she did because she had long ago made up her mind that her operatic career would end when she was forty and not, as the gossips of the time would have it, because she was offended over Maria Jeritza's being permitted to sing Tosca. She was always a lady who knew her own mind, and once she had made it up, nobody could change it. As the director of the Metropolitan, Gatti-Casazza, was himself to observe, he found some difficulty in learning "that with you 'no' means 'no.'" Though she had firmly rejected any arranged tribute at her farewell performance, the spontaneous demonstration which was set off was something that the opera house had never witnessed before nor was ever to see again. Incidentally one of the "Gerry-flappers," as she herself told me many years later, was a young lady not herself wholly unknown to fame, named Dorothy Gish.

Following her retirement from the opera, Miss Farrar
made an extensive tour in a condensed version of Carmen.
In the fall of 1925 she was preparing to appear in New York
in Lehár's Frasquita when she was taken sick; recovering,
she wrote me that she regarded her illness as providential
since the Broadway sponsors of her vehicle had so altered
its opéra comique character that she would have felt hopelessly out of place in what they managed to evolve. She
rested until 1927, then reemerged, white-haired, as a lieder
singer to warm appreciation among the cognoscenti and
continued in this aspect until she gave up singing altogether
in 1932. Thereafter the public heard her only in a lecture
tour and as radio commentator at the Saturday afternoon
Metropolitan Opera broadcasts. She died of a heart ailment,
on March 11, 1967, at her home in Ridgefield, Connecticut;
New York radio programs were interrupted to note her
passing.

Miss Farrar's motion picture debut came about through
Morris Gest. Knowing of the singer's interest in the medium,
Gest took Jesse L. Lasky to a performance of Madama Butterfly, and when Lasky expressed the proper enthusiasm, he
asked him what he would say if he were to be told that he
might secure Miss Farrar to appear in Lasky films. Lasky is
said to have replied, "I should say that you were crazy,"
but once he was convinced that Gest was in earnest and
knew what he was talking about, a firm offer was soon made
and accepted.

Because the war was now making it impossible for her
to spend her summers in Europe, the offer reached the singer
at an opportune time. In her autobiography, Such Sweet
Compulsion (Greystone Press, 1938), she says that she welcomed it also because she was having trouble with her voice,
but it is hard to see how this factor can have been importantly involved, for the 1915 contract called for three pictures to
be made during eight summer weeks when she would not have
been singing anyway, and though she did not make the first
of her ten appearances at the Metropolitan during the 1915-16
season until February 15, 1916 (it was by far the shortest of
her sixteen seasons there), she did start out on a concert
tour in October 1915, and also sang in opera in Chicago from
November to January.

The amount of money she received for her eight weeks

work has been variously stated, but there can be no doubt
that, by the standards of the time, it was large. Moreover
there were numerous "fringe benefits"--transportation to
and from the coast in her private car, a house and a studio
bungalow dressing room in Hollywood, music on the set, etc.
When she arrived, the mayor of Los Angeles turned out to
greet her in the company of cowboys and schoolchildren,
and there was a great dinner the next night at the Hollywood
Hotel. She was the first star to receive what was afterwards
known as the "full treatment."

        Interesting people are often victimized by the malicious
tongues of smaller persons who endeavor to cut them down to
a size they can comfortably comprehend. This had first happened to Miss Farrar in Berlin, where it involved no less a
personage than the Crown Prince, "whereupon my father ...
retaliated by a physical reminder to one editor that such
slanders are not circulated with impunity about young American women." It seems a pity that Sidney Farrar was not
still around to take care of the author of a recent very bad
book about one of Miss Farrar's Hollywood associates who saw
fit to regale his readers with stories about how Miss Farrar
traveled to Hollywood with a gigolo and entertained herself
by dancing wildly to jazz music on board the train. After
she arrived, moreover, she is said to have got on very badly
with both DeMille and the lady whom she herself refers to as
"the amiable Jeanie Macpherson" so that Carmen's battle in
the cigarette factory became a knock-down fight in good
earnest.

        The truth of the matter is that Miss Farrar traveled
to California in the company of her parents, Mr. and Mrs.
Morris Gest, and her personal entourage; as for her dancing
en route, she did amuse herself and the company by putting
on a burlesque of the Russian ballet to music by Rimsky-
Korsakoff. Jazz in 1915 had hardly emerged far enough from
the brothels in which it was born to find employment in such
a connection. Miss Farrar always detested it; in fact she
disliked even more respectable popular music. Almost alone
among the great singers of her time, she refused to end her
concerts with the ballads which were then almost the rule in
this connection, though I have known her to finish with
"Annie Laurie," sung to her own accompaniment. Once John
McCormack, whose art she admired and respected highly, remarked that, through a long singing career, he had learned

that "it's the last group that gets them," to which she replied tartly that that might well be true but if you were
going to put it upon that basis you could hardly call yourself an artist. She also disappointed the Victor Company by
recording far fewer such numbers than any other Red Seal
artist with her sales potential, and in spite of her great
admiration for Fritz Kreisler, she told me that she disliked
her charming record of "Star of Love" from his Apple Blossoms.

     Her relations with DeMille, who directed all her Lasky
pictures, were nearly ideal. Both persons spoke of each
other with the highest respect, for the only thing they ever
disagreed about was the merits of Lou Tellegen, and about
that, as Miss Farrar lived to learn, in the most painful possible way, DeMille was right. The book to which I refer
could have exposed its author and publishers to a suit for
libel if she had still been alive when it appeared, but she
would not have brought it, for she believed that to be
capable of such things was in itself sufficient punishment,
and she would have felt degraded if she had dignified them
by paying attention to them. Once indeed she told her distressed mother that if it made people happy to think her a
prostitute, she would let them think it. "What difference
can it make so long as I don't have to be one?"

     The three films made at Lasky in the summer of 1915
were Maria Rosa, Carmen, and Temptation, in that order.
It had been understood from the beginning that Carmen was
to be the pièce de résistance, but DeMille insisted on doing
Maria Rosa first to give the star a chance to become accustomed to the cinematic style, so far removed from the operatic type of acting to which she was accustomed. Oddly
enough, Tellegen, whom she was not to marry until February
8, 1916, had recently appeared in Maria Rosa with Dorothy
Donnelly on the New York stage.

     DeMille's decision was a sensible one, though as it
turned out, his caution was unnecessary, for Miss Farrar
adapted herself to both the camera technique and to studio
conditions with perfect ease, and at once found herself
adored by the prop boys as she had always been by the
stage hands at the opera house. The only problem at the
outset was that her eyes were such a light grey that, under
the harsh lights of 1915, her first closeups showed her

with the sightless orbs of a statue; she says she nearly
fainted when she saw them. This was overcome by hanging
black velvet before her and having her gaze steadily at it
to enlarge her pupils. Nevertheless Maria Rosa was a useful
rehearsal for Carmen. A love story of old Spain, it appealed
to some of the same emotions, but the prominence of the
revenge-motif in it would probably have made it less palatable
to the general public than the more familiar story had it been
released first.

        In his autobiography, Hollywood Saga (Dutton, 1939),
William C. deMille, who did the scenarios for both Carmen and
Maria Rosa, declared that Carmen, which they had all considered a great film in 1915, looked completely outmoded now.
I am afraid that when deMille made this statement he was
rather too firmly committed to the thesis that "movies are
better than ever," for when, in 1974, I saw again the beautifully tinted Eastman House original exhibition print of Carmen,
it did not seem to me to have lost much. My only real surprise was that Miss Farrar's Carmen was considerably tougher
than I had remembered it, and much more so than her operatic
Carmen, which, as Francis Robinson has remarked, remained
firmly in the French operatic tradition. This interested me
especially in view of Miss Farrar's having made her first appearance in Bizet's opera in 1908, singing Micaela to the
Carmen of Maria Gay and Caruso's Don Jose (her record of
Micaela's air, recorded at that time, is still one of the most
touching souvenirs we have of the lovely purity of her early
voice), and when I asked her whether Gay's Carmen was
good, she replied, "Yes, it was good, but you wouldn't have
liked it because it was a very coarse Carmen." Certainly
there can be no question as to the success of the film at the
time, the critics and the public being equally ecstatic, though
Julian Johnson complained that deMille's scenario gave Carmen
a chance to be sincere "at no point." The scenario, it
should be remembered, followed Prosper Mérrimée's story, not
the opera libretto, to avoid the payment of ruinous copyright
fees.

        Carmen had all the exploitation that 1915 could devise
for it. It was first exhibited, at Miss Farrar's suggestion,
in Boston's Symphony Hall on October 1, and Lasky took a
four-page advertisement in the Moving Picture World for October 30, elegantly set up in script, with quotations from the
reviewers. I have a book in my library, published as a part

of the film's exploitation, which is a bibliographical curiosi-
ty. Both the cover and the spine are lettered: "GERALDINE
FARRAR Photo-Drama Edition of CARMEN," with a past-on
picture on the cover of Carmen dancing on the table between
Escamillo and Don Jose. The title-page reads "CARMEN/
Based/on Prosper Mérimée's story, illustrated/from the Jesse
L. Lasky Photoplay released/through the Paramount Picture
Corporation/Produced under the direction of/Cecil B. DeMille
and/acted by/GERALDINE FARRAR/By arrangement with/
Morris Gest/A. L. Burt Company, Publishers/114-120 East
Twenty-third Street/New York." But turn the page, and
you will read: "Copyright, 1915, by Houghton Mifflin Com-
pany/All Rights Reserved/Published November 1915," and at
the end of the volume, as was customary in Houghton Mifflin
books of the period, one reads: "The Riverside Press/Cam-
bridge Massachusetts/U.S.A." At first I supposed this was
simply a reprint edition of what had been originally a Houghton Mifflin book, but the publishers assure me that this was
not the case; though prepared and copyrighted by Houghton
Mifflin Company and printed at The Riverside Press, the
volume was never published except by Burt. Note that no
author is anywhere named.

Temptation was a "quickie" of which neither the star
nor the director thought highly; perhaps the most interesting
thing in it was the shots it contained showing Miss Farrar in
various operatic costumes. She herself has described it as
the type of story "that has since served anybody who can lay
claim to a vocal chirp--how the little home-town girl makes
good in grand opera, upon merit and virtue." But The New
York Times proclaimed it "as good [as] if not better than
Carmen," and the New York Dramatic Mirror thought it
brought out the star's "wonderful personality," "magnetism,"
and "inimitable histrionic power" more strongly. If Miss
Farrar had not been herself, she might well have left Hollywood at the end of her first sojourn there feeling that in the
eyes of the movie moguls, critics, and public, she could do
no wrong. Fortunately for her, and for us, she had been
spoiled by experts, and it had affected her not at all.

In the phenomenally hot summer of 1916, she returned
to the coast, this time to make only one film. DeMille's first
super-spectacle, Joan the Woman, which was of course the
story of Joan of Arc. A lifelong Joan idolater, Miss Farrar
welcomed the assignment with enthusiasm, in spite of her fear

of horses, the uncomfortable armor she was obliged to wear,
and the danger to which she was exposed in the battle scenes
and in Rouen marketplace. She had to stand in water up to
her waist; DeMille was desperately afraid she would come down
with laryngitis; she didn't, but he did! She did not mind
doing the scene in prison in which rats ran over her, for
they were really "charming little white mice" disguised and
following trails of sugar, but she had to have her skin, hair,
and clothing treated to prevent scorching in the scene at the
stake and hold saturated cotton in her nostrils and mouth.
One particularly unbearable day, when everybody else was
wilting while she bloomed, a minor actress asked her, "Won't
you tell me how you do it, Miss Farrar? Don't you ever
mind anything; the heat or the long waits or anything?" She
threw back her head and laughed. "Not a bit of it," she
replied. "I'm too much interested all the time to know what's
happening on the outside of me."

There was never any question in Miss Farrar's mind
that Joan the Woman was her best film; I think it was the
only screen characterization that she valued on a level with
her work in the opera house. "I spent as much thought and
energy in making her live again--if only on the shadow
stage--the blessed Maid of Orleans, as upon any of my opera
creations." I was still in high school when this film appeared,
and I remember how one of my classmates and I tried to persuade one of our teachers to go to see it and how she refused "because I cannot imagine Geraldine Farrar in a spiritual role." She would not have needed much imagination, but
a little more knowledge of Miss Farrar's achievements might
have been in order. If it was the Carmen-Zaza side of her
art which attracted the widest public, this showed more about
them than it did about her. She cared much more for her
Elisabeth in Tannhäuser and for the Goose Girl in Humper-
dinck's lovely fairy opera, Koenigskinder, which she created
at the Metropolitan on December 28, 1910. She even calls
Gatti-Casazza "stupid" because he would not permit her to
revive this cherished work toward the end of her operatic
career.

Though both Vachel Lindsay and Alexander Woollcott
were comparatively unimpressed by Miss Farrar's Joan (Woollcott would have preferred Mae Marsh, and Julian Johnson
talked about Edith Storey), actually the only real fault that
can be found with her performance is that, at thirty-four,

she was a bit mature for the part; if she could have come to
it a decade earlier, she would have been perfect. According
to DeMille, the film was called Joan the Woman because Miss
Macpherson wished "to emphasize the humanity of Joan of Arc
rather than project the conventional, and so frequently false,
image of a saint. We portrayed Joan as a strong peasant
girl, with a sense of humor and human sympathy, ever faithful to her Voices, but tempted and fearful too--a woman of
flesh and blood, whose heroism was as much in her victory
over herself as in her victory over the English. That is
what real saints are like, I think."

There was some pioneering color work in the film as
well as some marvelous lighting and photographic effects,
though some of the sets now seem overcrowded. Though it
was less popular than Carmen, it was at once regarded as
one of the "big" pictures of its time. Its most serious weakness, as DeMille himself later believed, was the attempt made
to link it all up with World War I through introducing Eric
Trent (Wallace Reid) as the reincarnation of an English soldier who had (unhistorically) loved Joan and been involved
in her downfall and who must atone for his fault by dying
for France in World War I. Joan the Woman was long unavailable and at one time believed to have been lost, but Eastman
House now has a print. I can think of no picture which
might better be made available to collectors.

The summer of 1917 was Miss Farrar's last on the Lasky
lot; this time she made two pictures--The Woman God Forgot
and The Devil Stone. The first of these, a highly theatrical
piece involving Cortez, Montezuma, and the Aztecs, and partly filmed at Yellowstone Park, shows DeMille carrying on the
super-spectacle tradition which he had begun to establish in
Joan, and though it can hardly be necessary to say that it
lacked the authenticity of Joan, it was extremely picturesque,
gorgeously mounted and photographed, and made very good
entertainment; I remember going to see it at the Oak Park
Theater two nights handrunning when it appeared. The Devil
Stone was more modern, but its Breton background, making
good use of the California coastline, its overtones of superstition and the supernatural, and the interlude in which Miss
Farrar appeared as a Viking queen with vicious wolf-hounds
at her feet made it a much headier mixture than Temptation
had been in 1915 as well as a more imaginative work.

Miss Farrar's break with Lasky and her hearkening to the siren song of Samuel Goldwyn, who had been part of the Paramount organization but had now established Goldwyn Pictures, was unfortunate, for Goldwyn had not yet found the secret which was to make his later productions so outstanding, and the material he gave her, as well as most of his other stars (notably Mary Garden) was inferior to what she had had under DeMille. Sadly enough, the break was occasioned by the one serious mistake she ever made during her lifetime, her marriage to the handsome, charming (on occasion), but petulant, selfish, and amoral Lou Tellegen, who had been brought to this country as Sarah Bernhardt's leading man, for the quarrel was over the inability of the Lasky organization to view Tellegen's abilities through Miss Farrar's eyes. Her divorce from Tellegen, which was preceded by much misery and long-drawn-out, expensive litigation, was not handed down until 1923, but DeMille thought he had begun to take his toll of her even while she was making Joan the Woman. During the preliminaries, Tellegen talked big and foolishly about the revelations he was going to make concerning Miss Farrar, but when finally it was all over and a reporter called his bluff, the mountain labored and failed to produce even a mouse. "You may say," he replied, "that Miss Farrar still has my warmest admiration, as an artist and as a woman. She is a great artist, a great woman, a pure woman."

When, in the early 1930s, having run through two more marriages and heaven only knows how many "affairs," sick and poor and down on his luck, Tellegen committed a horrible, messy suicide in Los Angeles, a reporter roused Miss Farrar one night to ask her for a comment. She was reported to have replied, "Why should that interest me?" but this has no significance save as a rebuke to the bad manners of the reporter. What she wrote me in a letter soon afterwards was very different in tone, and in her autobiography she dismissed the tragedy with "May those tormented ashes rest in peace" and "I would not wish any human soul the task of working out such a Karma."

All seven of Miss Farrar's Goldwyn pictures except The World and Its Woman (Frank Lloyd) were directed by Reginald Barker, The Turn of the Wheel, The Hell Cat, Shadows, and The Stronger Vow in 1918 (The Hell Cat at Cody, Wyoming, the others at Fort Lee, New Jersey), The

World and Its Woman, Flame of the Desert, and The Woman
and the Puppet at Goldwyn's new Culver City studio in 1919.
With both her directors and with her fellow-actors Miss Farrar
continued to enjoy a smooth working relationship, but the
films themselves brought her little satisfaction. The Turn of
the Wheel she describes as "a tale of Monte Carlo that allowed
me to walk through many scenes in priceless jewels, furs and
Bird of Paradise hats." The Hell Cat and Shadows were both
Willard Mack stories (Mack being the current husband of
Pauline Frederick, then also a Goldwyn star). Shadows ("my
first role picturing mother-love") was built around the agonies suffered by a respectable society woman when a black-
mailer turns up from her past as an Alaskan dance-hall girl.
The plot was very similar to what Griffith had used in the
one-reel Confidence in which Florence Lawrence and Arthur
Johnson had appeared in 1909, but I can still see Miss Farrar,
with a long train on her dress, sweeping confidently through
the halls of her palatial home to receive the telephone call
which is to shatter her world. As Mack first conceived The
Hell Cat, she thought it a Perils of Pauline "brainstorm"; as
filmed it made her the half-Irish half-Spanish daughter of a
sheep-herder, plunged into a war with the cattlemen, and
wearing a costume which, it seems safe to say, was unknown
to the frontier. She thought the film well named, but the
comfortless conditions under which it was made, in sizzling
heat and with the near proximity of rattlesnakes constituted
the real ordeal. If The Stronger Vow, which had a Spanish
background, was no masterpiece either, its materials were
more congenial to her, and she liked it better, as did I.

The World and Its Woman, a senselessly titled opus,
which brought an opera singer into the Russian revolution,
was something of a mishmash, but it had its moments, of
which Frank Lloyd, as always, made the best that could have
been made, and it remains Goldwyn's most ambitious attempt
to match the "big" pictures of the Lasky years. Flame of
the Desert, filmed partly in the desert at Oxnard, involved
an Egyptian uprising and a love affair between a sheik and
an English noblewoman, thus bringing Miss Farrar within
hailing distance of the emergent Valentino. The Woman and
the Puppet, about a Spanish dance hall girl, the sexiest
film in which Miss Farrar ever appeared, had a solid literary
foundation in the novel of the same name by Pierre Louÿs.
It was to be filmed again, less discreetly, by both Marlene

Dietrich (The Devil Is a Woman) and Brigitte Bardot (A Woman Like Satan).

An interesting incident occurred during the filming of The World and Its Woman. Clarence Bull, at the beginning of his career, was photographing a processional court scene, when his camera bounced off its tripod and fell smack into the middle of Farrar's long train, pulling her up so sharply that she might have had a bad fall if her husband had not caught her. The youngster thought his job was gone, but before anybody else had a chance to move, Miss Farrar came over to him to assure him that everything was all right. This action was completely in character. A good many people are ready to do the kind and considerate thing when they think of it, but Miss Farrar always thought of it in time to activate the impulse effectively. She once cued Charles Hackett through a whole performance of La Bohème (he knew the music but had never sung the role on the stage), and one night, when Martinelli's suspenders broke in Zaza, so that he could not budge from the couch where he was sitting, she improvised new business for the whole scene on the spur of the moment, and nobody in the audience ever found out that anything had been wrong.

In his autobiography, Behind the Screen (George H. Doran, 1923), Samuel Goldwyn complains rather wistfully that Miss Farrar seemed less satisfied when she was working for him than she had been in her Lasky days, but he neglects to mention that Lasky had given her much better material. Even so their only acrimonious difference was over Tellegen, who played with her, and often against her, in her last three Goldwyn pictures, upstaging her at every turn, and demanding more prominent billing than his stature at the time warranted, a demand foolishly seconded by his wife. But if Miss Farrar gave Goldwyn some bad moments over this, she atoned for it handsomely, as he himself acknowledged, when he came to her in New York with the news that her last pictures were not yielding the return that had been expected and the suggestion that she take a vacation from the screen. She at once offered to relieve him of all further obligations to her and suggested that they then and there tear up the contract which still had two years to run. This gallant gesture, which cost her a quarter of a million dollars, was unique in Sam Goldwyn's experience, but she could never understand why he had been so much impressed by it. Years

later, after her singing days were long behind her, he ran
into her in Boston and suggested that, now that sound was
available, she return to Hollywood and do Carmen over again.
He thought it would be "a great show." It would indeed,
she replied, if she were fool enough to do it; only she was
not.

Before that, however, there was one more, unimportant picture. It was The Riddle: Woman, from the play by
Carl Jacoby, in which Bertha Kalich had starred, and it was
made for Pathé, who had offered her "a staggering sum" for
two films, but after she saw the first, she refused to make
another. Though I saw The Riddle: Woman, I remember only
one sensitively played scene with Madge Bellamy.

Thus Lou Tellegen, who was the curse of Miss Farrar's
private life, came close to jinxing her motion picture career
as well. It was indeed a bitter piece of irony that a woman
of her almost fantastic fidelity should have had to suffer a
broken marriage. She was the most faithful of daughters,
and her mother's sudden death, at the beginning of 1923, in
the midst of the divorce squabbles and while Geraldine was
away on a concert tour, was the great sorrow of her life.
"She was like a member of my body and she worshipped me.
I was everything that she had conceived. She lived to see
everything for which she had existed borne out in most
beautiful fashion. But with her went half my interest in
singing." Sidney Farrar lived on until 1935, with his daughter's loving care and thought never far from him, and then
died at the same time as my mother. "We must be worthy of
our parents," she wrote me, "and of ourselves."

Miss Farrar's word was as good as her bond, and once
she had admitted you to her friendship, you could count on
her forever. During World War I she was sometimes under
fire because, though she sold Liberty Bonds, she remained
aloof from the current campaign of hate and refused to think
of her friend Kaiser Wilhelm II as "the Beast of Berlin,"
which was the currently favored appellation. Noting a signed
photograph of him on her piano at Fairhaven in 1946, I remarked, "I see you have restored the Kaiser." "'Restored'!"
she replied indignantly. "He has never been away. He stood
there all through World War I." During Miss Farrar's later
years, her admirers showered her every February 28 with
birthday greetings. As she grew older, I began to wonder

whether we were not killing her with kindness, for her sense
of the fitness of things required that all these greetings must
be acknowledged with a letter, and the labor thus imposed
upon her was great.

In such a matter as this, one can perhaps best speak
for oneself. In 1924, while I was still a graduate student at
The University of Chicago, I wrote an article about Miss
Farrar, "Singer of Singers," which was published in The
Circle, a campus magazine. Of course I sent her a copy. It
reached her in Buffalo, where she was touring her abbreviated
Carmen; she telegraphed her thanks, following her telegram
with a long letter, and our correspondence remained unbroken
to her death. In later years I sent her my books as they
were published, and she read and commented on them. The
last I was able to send her, Merely Players (1966), arrived
during her final illness, but even this had to be acknowledged,
and she had her housekeeper-companion, Miss Sylvia Blein,
write to thank me for it.

In 1929, meanwhile, I had published through the University of Washington Book Store my Geraldine Farrar: An
Authorized Record of Her Career, in a limited edition which
she signed. During the writing of this book, I was often
obliged to appeal to her for odds and ends of information
which I could not find elsewhere. Though she was on tour
at the time, all such letters were answered upon receipt. I
was greatly amused when one day I received a letter in which
she said she was too much pressed to give me what I needed
at once but that I should hear from her very shortly. When
I woke up next morning, there was a special delivery letter
in my mailbox. In July 1957 I had an article about her
records in High Fidelity, which pleased her, though, like me,
she was annoyed by the silly title which the editor had
clapped upon it, "Geraldine the Great." What I had to say
about her in my semiautobiography, As Far As Yesterday
(1968), was, however, written just after her death, so that
she never saw it.

In conclusion I cannot help raising the question whether
Miss Farrar's movie career, considered as a whole, deserves
to be rated as a credit or a debit in her record. The answer
must be qualified. From the standpoint of strictly aesthetic
judgment, I should unhesitatingly place both Carmen and
Joan the Woman on the credit side; the other items are more

doubtful. Her films did of course notably swell her pocketbook, and they brought her before hundreds of thousands
of people who never heard her in opera or concert. It
seems safe to say that some of these were drawn into both
the opera house and, to a larger extent, because opportunities were available over a much wider area, the concert hall,
and I should think too that many of these must have gone
on to buy her records, to their lasting enrichment as well
as hers. As a matter of fact, I myself was interested in Miss
Farrar long before I became seriously interested in music, and
I feel deeply indebted to her, among other things, for what
became one of the lasting joys and comforts of my life.

On the other hand, I should have to say that though
Miss Farrar never did anything on the screen that was unworthy of her morally (The Woman and the Puppet came
closest), she did do much that was unworthy of her artistic
endowment. Such films as Maria Rosa, The Stronger Vow,
and The Woman and the Puppet accented the Carmen-Zaza
side of her art, at the expense of the Elisabeth-Goose Girl
side, which, as I have already indicated, both she and those
who cared most for her, valued more, and I think encouraged
misconceptions about her among those who did not know her
well. (Personally I would say that, even among the ladies
of questionable morality in her repertoire, Manon was, if not
more congenial to her temperament, at least better qualified
to bring out the more delicate shadings in her art than the
broader, perhaps stronger roles; as Carl Van Vechten anticipated me by observing, she was, especially during her early
years, generally charming in what are called ingenue roles.)
Perhaps it is not possible here to strike a balance that will
satisfy everybody; hence I must content myself by saying
that I am glad Miss Farrar had her fling in the movies if only
because it gave me a chance to see more of her, and she was
one of those artists rare in any generation of whom one does
not wish to miss anything they may have to give.

Miss Farrar was no cheerful idiot, and there was little
about how the world has wagged during these latter days that
was to her liking, but boredom, whining, cynicism, and cheap
disillusionment were as impossible to her temperament as to
that of her great contemporary, Mary Garden. We have her
word for it that "the realized dreams of my young girlhood"
seemed "every bit as desirable" in her maturity "as they were
in the dream-days." But she was not so foolish as to suppose

that anything worth having in this world can be had without a price. In Geraldine Farrar: The Story of an American Singer, the brief account of her career which she published through Houghton Mifflin Company in 1916, long before writing her longer autobiography, she said:

> I have been asked, in summing up these experiences of my artistic career, so far, if it has all been worth while? From my point of view, yes.   That is, what you believe to be the most complete fulfillment of yourself and the gratification of your ambitions is always worth while....
>
> It is, however, distinctly not worth while, to my mind, unless Fortune smiles upon you in abundance, for art is not the medium stratum of life, but its flowered inspiration and emotional poetry; it demands and obtains its sacrifices and sorrows which modify and chasten its glory, and your own soul best knows the toll you pay.

MAY McAVOY

The best account of May McAvoy's career is in DeWitt
Bodeen's article in Films in Review for December 1968 (Vol.
XIX, pp. 482-96). She was born in New York City on September 18, 1901, to a Scottish father, who died while she
was very young, and an Irish mother. The family business
was a large livery stable for the carriage trade which stood
on the site later occupied by the Waldorf-Astoria Hotel.
The film that made her famous and in which she was first
noticed by most of her later admirers (including this one),
John S. Robertson's production of Barrie's Sentimental Tommy (1921), was not her first; in fact I was shocked to observe that it is no less than the fifteenth entry in Mr. Bodeen's filmography. The first was something inauspiciously
entitled Hate (1917), but the second, To Hell with the
Kaiser (1918), has real value as providing materials for a
still much needed day of national humiliation, for it illustrates
the stupidity, vulgarity, and banality to which patriotics can
descend in wartime. Surely every civilized American must
find it both painful and salutary to remember that the con-
temporaneous German idea of war propaganda was embodied in
such films as Madame Du Barry and Anna Boleyn; when they
were released over here after the war, we called them Passion and Deception.

The only film in which Miss McAvoy appeared for Paramount before Sentimental Tommy was the version of Mrs.
Wiggs of the Cabbage Patch (1919) which starred Marguerite
Clark, whom she admired, as Lovey Mary, with Mary Carr,
of Over the Hill fame, as Mrs. Wiggs, directed by Hugh
Ford. May played "Australy," one of the Wiggs brood, and
apparently neither Ford nor Paramount was greatly impressed
by her, for she was not signed up for anything else. What
now surprises me more is that evidently she did not greatly
impress me either, for I cannot remember her in this film,

which stands in sharp contrast to the impact with which she
struck me, as a then to me quite unknown actress, in Sentimental Tommy. Carl Sandburg, at that time motion picture
critic for the Chicago Daily News, once described her as "a
star-eyed goddess," and the tribute was richly deserved,
but beautiful though she was, her beauty always took second
place compared to the moral and spiritual sensitivity in which
she seemed to me to outrank nearly all her cinematic contemporaries.

The Paramount contract followed all right after Sentimental Tommy, for though the film was not a box office
success, it had every critic in the land singing her praises.
She became a star in a series of films for Realart, a Paramount subsidiary (the first, believe it or not, was called A
Private Scandal), and when the anti-trust laws put Realart
out of business, she appeared under the Paramount banner,
where she might have continued longer if, in an encounter
described in Mr. Bodeen's article, which both parties seem
to have managed badly, she had not mortally offended Cecil
B. DeMille. And at this point we had better turn to the
article about her which I published in Vanity Fair in December 1924. Except for three pieces which I had done in my
teens for the now forgotten Photo-Play Journal, this was my
first contribution to a magazine of national circulation, and
it set me up accordingly.

THE NEGLECTED GENIUS OF THE MOVIES*

Sometimes a good thing does come out of Nazareth--or
even out of Hollywood. I am quite aware that it is dangerous
to use the word "genius" in connection with the movies; like
all superlative and absolute expressions, it has been enormously misapplied. Yet sometimes, I am persuaded, the
miracle will occur, and, in such a contingency, it is highly
important that it shall not perish for lack of appreciation.

It seems to be the rule, in this craft, that picturesque
charlatans shall have immediate recognition, while the few sin-

*Courtesy VANITY FAIR. Copyright © 1924 (renewed) 1952,
1980 by The Condé Nast Publications Inc.

cere and earnest artists struggle long with public neglect.
The case of Lillian Gish is perfectly in point. Thanks to the
popular success of such films as Way Down East and The
White Sister, she is just now beginning to enter into her own.
Yet she was a great actress in Enoch Arden ten years ago.
Mae Marsh, Henry Walthall, Emily Fitzroy--it would be easy
to multiply examples. Even Mr. Griffith has, in general,
been most successful with his least significant pictures. The
Birth of a Nation is only an apparent exception, for it owed
its tremendous vogue to its bad melodrama, its appeal to
prejudice and passion, rather than to some of the really superb things it contained. And it is undeniable that the first
adequate appreciation of Charlie Chaplin came from the outside. To the producers he was, at the outset, simply a
great clown, a happy accident, whose enormous popularity
was to be joyfully--not thankfully--accepted, but need not,
for any reason, be analyzed. So far as I recall, it was
Mrs. Fiske who, in an article in The Independent, first dared
suggest that Chaplin was an artist.

Seen by this light, our neglect of May McAvoy remains
regrettable but ceases to be surprising. Over three years
have gone by since she appeared on the screen as Grizel in
John Robertson's production of Sentimental Tommy. Since
then we have made Gloria Swanson rich, put Barbara LaMarr
on the front page, vastly overestimated such good actresses
as Leatrice Joy, and made utter fools of ourselves over such
utter catastrophes as Rudolph Valentino. But what about
May?

It is useless to try to tell anybody who did not see her
as Grizel how good she was. What can I say here save that
she presented a beautifully-shaded, finely sensitive, utterly
finished characterization? And what can that mean to those
who have no memories? Beauty and pity were the great elements in it, and all welled up, as it were spontaneously,
from the depths of a seemingly incalculable sensibility. You
could not analyze her appeal, but you could say definitely
that it was the appeal of art. It is possible, of course, to
be a great actress without being a great artist or, indeed,
without being an artist at all. Power, passion, sensibility--
every other quality which makes for a striking performance--
may well exist in one who is quite innocent of the nice adaptation of means to end, the wholly conscious creation of
beauty, the ability to isolate a case or a fragment of life and

build it up into a perfect unit, which qualities are the very
essence of art.   But May was, from the outset, not a happy
windfall; she was visibly marked by the passion for perfection.   You knew at once that she would not "register," that
she would not "act," that she was one of the gifted few who
could put soul, the impress of personality, upon the screen.
Grizel was her first important part--(I did not even remember
her in Mrs. Wiggs of the Cabbage Patch)--and that, naturally,
did not diminish the marvel of her dexterity.   Most really
good players must actually grow up with the camera, gradually learning its technique, slowly and by dint of much bungling
coming to adapt themselves to it.   But May was a star born
full-orbed.   No need for her to learn the tricks of the camera:
she seemed to have been born with them in her blood.
Rather, perhaps, so great was her sincerity, that mere tricks
were things to be dispensed with.

Sentimental Tommy was an utter failure at the box office.   At the Randolph Theatre in Chicago, where it had its
local première, it was quietly taken off after two or three
days to make room for the late Mr. Arbuckle.   Yet, despite
the fact that the film had nothing like the circulation it deserved, there were a few of us who had seen it.   They were
still making stars in those days, and for the time May's name
was in electric lights under the banner of the Realart (God
save the mark!) Film Company.   For them she made several
pictures, some of which were worse than others, but no one
of which was suited to Grizel.

For it was Barrie who, at the outset, had struck exactly the right note for her, a fact of which the producers, in-
sensible of overtones, were, of course, serenely unconscious.
What she needed was a rôle which called for deep sensibility,
a delicate, fragile thing which nobody else could play, a
thing touched with fantasy, brooded over, perhaps, by a
sense of that Mystery into which everything that is human
shades off.   The producers failed when, with customary obtuseness, they tried to make a genius into an ordinary pretty
girl star.   In the first part of Morals, she inhabited a
Turkish harem; once she was A Homespun Vamp.   She was
not extraordinary in either manifestation, for there was nothing to challenge her endowments.   To this day, indeed, she
depends, to a degree, upon imaginative stimulus.   If, for
instance, somebody unfamiliar with her work were to saunter
out, after reading my article, to see her in William deMille's

mystery melodrama, The Bedroom Window, he would surely
conclude that I was either mad or infatuated: he would see
a charming presence but little more.   Similarly, in her latest
manifestation, in Lubitsch's exceedingly bad melodrama,
Three Women, she plays her tasteless role no better and no
worse than any young woman of intelligence might play it.

Three times, since Sentimental Tommy, she has met
the challenge, and twice at least--in Clarence and in Only
38--she revealed herself in a delightfully new phase of comedy.   In the latter, as an infant puritan, firmly bent on com-
pelling her mother to conform to the standards of the Massachusetts Bay Colony, she was excellent; she revealed a
sense of humour, the existence of which I, for one, should
not have suspected.   Her work was uncontaminated by the
spirit of farce; it was marked by the exalted earnestness
which is so eminently characteristic of her, and it was, therefore, excruciatingly funny.   But the real opportunities of
which I am thinking were furnished by Kick In, West of the
Water Tower, and The Enchanted Cottage.

It was Kick In which probably saved her artistic life:
it came a long, long time after Sentimental Tommy, but it
gave her the first opportunity she had had to demonstrate
to the sceptics that her success on that earlier occasion had
not been fortuitous.   Here she was the girl-wife of a young
thief, a lovely flower blooming in the midst of corruption, and
she carried out the idea by setting three lovely bits, fine as
cameos, in the midst of a film otherwise wholly vile.   One was
that moment of unutterable tenderness in which, entirely
without the use of sub-titles, she told Gareth Hughes, here
playing opposite her just as splendidly as he did in Sentimental Tommy, that she was going to have a baby.   I don't
know what to say about that moment, but it contained the
pure gold of the cinema, a bit of pantomime as great as anything Chaplin ever did.   (The thing was repeated, much less
effectively, in West of the Water Tower.)   In another scene
of Kick In, she came down a rickety stairs from an upper
chamber in which she had looked upon the dead face of her
husband, laughing and chatting gaily to throw the police off
the scent, and the look in her eyes as she did it was unfor-
gettable.   Finally, in another flash, she threw herself into
the night of the river.   As I watched her, it came over me
suddenly that Dickens, so perfectly suited to the screen, so

wretchedly neglected or distorted by the screen, would offer an incomparable field for her.

The other two instances are recent, and need not be discussed at length. I do not forget, as I name West of the Water Tower, that the motion picture version of that strong and honest story was an emasculated thing; but for me at least May and Glenn Hunter put it over triumphantly, in spite of every obstacle in their way. It was beautiful acting, absolutely perfect team-work: their love scenes were of the very essence of youthful ardour. In the end they made strange and moving use of that most hackneyed of all melodramatic devices--reconciliation through the child.

The Enchanted Cottage, again a fantastic thing be it noted, and again a John Robertson production, brought an even greater opportunity. The idea--the transformation of ugliness into beauty through the power of love--is not new: it occurs both in The Tale of the Wyf of Bath and Ricky of the Tuft, and it has roots which run deep in world-literature. For Miss McAvoy it brought the opportunity to enter the field of character-acting, but that was not its prime significance. More wonderful than the make-up--wholly strange, yet wholly natural, and never approaching caricature--was the magnificent way in which the lyric note was consistently sustained through agony and ugliness; more wonderful still was the inerrant projection, with Richard Barthelmess, of the profound poetry of the parable. Of all screen characterizations, only Mary Pickford's in Stella Maris was comparable with Miss McAvoy's here, and the note of fantasy was lacking in Stella Maris.

So today May is quietly awaiting further opportunities. She is ready for a spectacular career if only the producers may be given wit enough to see it. I am completely willing to admit that she has her own limitations: I don't think she will ever have the power to wring, almost to break, the heart, which is Lillian Gish's greatest gift. But in her field she is incomparable, and I have already shown that the complaint sometimes made--that she is suited only to one type of part--is wholly unjust. Even if it were true, it would hardly constitute a criticism. The artist is rare who can do more than one thing perfectly, and the deliberate attempt to be versatile at any cost probably does more than anything else to foster insincerity in American acting.

It was odd that May should have made one of her earliest appearances in a Marguerite Clark picture, for the fortuity united momentarily the only two screen exponents of the fairy spirit. Miss Clark was not perhaps a wholly exceptional artist, but this she did have, and it is precisely here, on a higher plane, that Miss McAvoy's greatest gift lies. I think hardly any close student of her work can deny that she is perfectly capable, if her career is properly managed, of introducing a renascence of fantasy upon the screen. Nobody now living could play the heroines of Perrault as she could play them. Here she is quite alone: Lillian Gish is too emotional for this work, and the sense of humanity is too pervasive in Mary Pickford. But May's temperament is exactly right: she has the crisp coolness, the sensitiveness, the childlike earnestness. Fantasy is, of course, the one field in which the screen is incomparable, the field in which no other medium can touch it, and I believe that May has come to the Kingdom for just such a time as this. Maurice Tourneur should direct, for he is as good with fairy tales as he is bad with melodrama.

In calling Miss McAvoy the neglected genius of the movies, I do not mean that she is without her followers. They exist; they are fairly numerous. But aesthetically, as a factor in her development, they mean almost nothing. I have heard plenty of talk about her "starry eyes," but of true appreciation of what she really is, of genuine understanding of her elusive genius, I have seen very little. Of course, she has grown in America in defiance of everything we could do. We do not deserve such a gift as hers; we do not know how to foster it, how to appreciate it. And so, at a time when she should be in the hands of some great teacher of acting, this divine girl drifts from director to director, and most of them are idiots who will do all in their power to stifle her art.

Yet, as I said at the outset, miracles do occur. Genius has a strange way of thriving to bless us, despite everything we do to kill it. May has already, on several occasions, shown herself something of a miracle woman. Let us hope that someday she will feed the five thousand starving moving picture enthusiasts and more.

*   *   *

Thus it was in 1924, and if all this now sounds rather high-and-mighty, not to say "snippy," for a youngster of twenty-four, the explanation may be that he was showing the influence of Carl Van Vechten and other "advanced" critics whom he admired at the time. Perhaps even he thought that Vanity Fair rather favored a "sophisticated" and authoritative tone. But it may be also that it is characteristic of twenty-four-year-old writers to attempt to be as high-and-mighty as possible.

What seems more to the point however is to inquire what if anything needs to be modified in my article in the light of Miss McAvoy's later career. The last entry in Mr. Bodeen's filmography is dated 1929, and most, though by no means all, of her later pictures were made for Warner Bros. In the 1940s and 1950s she worked as an unbilled contract player for M-G-M. I never saw her without pleasure, and I often found fine, sensitive acting in unexpected places, for example in the scene in Tarnish (1924), where, heartbroken just after having discovered the infidelity of her lover, she is surrounded in the street by a crowd of New Year's revelers who will not let her go until she has said "Happy New Year." But I am sadly obliged to add that I do not believe she ever found another opportunity to match those that had come her way in Sentimental Tommy and The Enchanted Cottage.

When I arrived in Boston in the summer of 1926 for my first visit to that city, four downtown theaters were playing McAvoy films. The best by all means was Laurence Trimble's My Old Dutch at the Columbia, a remake of a play he had previously filmed in 1915 when he and Florence Turner were working together in England. The Exeter Street had a farce called The Savage, in which May was teamed with Ben Lyon, and I do not even remember what the other two were.

Two brief digressions seem in order here. Laurence Trimble, who married J. Stuart Blackton's daughter Marion, was a remarkable man who seems to have had an almost Saint Francis of Assisi-like way with animals. He came into pictures in 1910 because Vitagraph wanted his remarkable collie, who became "Jean, the Vitagraph Dog," the first canine star. Jean is still remembered lovingly by old-time movie fans, and I have her in an 8mm print of a little thing called A Tin-Type Romance with Florence Turner and Leo Delaney. Trimble

later owned an even more famous movie dog, Strongheart, and
became a gifted trainer of Seeing Eye dogs.

The Exeter Street Theater was at one time the oldest
motion picture theater in Boston in continuous operation. The
building it inhabited, the First Spiritual Temple, which William Dean Howells thought one of the most beautiful in the
city, dated back to the days when Boston was a great center
of the American interest in spiritualism. I believe they began
showing pictures about 1915, and the theater was operated
by the church for its benefit. It was in its glory when I
came to Boston to live in 1947. This was when the J. Arthur
Rank Organization was turning out one fine English film after
another; most of them played the Exeter Street, which drew
upon the whole Boston area for its clientele. I became acquainted with its manager, the late Miss A. Viola Berlin, and
two of my three sons worked for her while in college. The
building, handsomely renovated, now houses a department
store. But there has been nothing new in Boston to take the
place of the old Exeter Street Theater.

By all means the best known of Miss McAvoy's later
films were Lady Windermere's Fan (Warner Bros., 1925),
which was Ernst Lubitsch's production of the Oscar Wilde
play; the M-G-M 1926 Ben Hur; and The Jazz Singer (Warner
Bros., 1927), which has the bad distinction of having murdered the silents. Lady Windermere's Fan, which really fea-
tured Irene Rich, a then popular Warners star, rather than
May, was a good film of its kind, and May was good in it,
but her role was too suave, too sophisticated, too conventional to afford scope for her special quality; in her later
years she was inclined to regret that people who did not know
her other work had seen her in this. Ben Hur of course was
one of the great achievements of the dying silents, but May
herself said about everything that needed to be said as to her
part in it: save for one or two bits any competent young actress could have done everything she was called upon to do.
And in The Jazz Singer, which was silent so far as she was
concerned, even the bits were lacking, though she remained
as always lovely to look upon.

Before leaving the subject of Miss McAvoy's career
however, something must be said of a great role she desperately wanted and never had a chance to play: I mean of
course Peter Pan. When the 1924 Paramount production was

in contemplation, more actresses coveted this role than were
probably ever again to compete for another with the single
exception of that of Scarlett O'Hara in Gone With the Wind,
including a number who would have been quite dreadful in it
and who ought to have thanked God devoutly that they were
disappointed. At that time the motion picture editor of the
Chicago Tribune, whose not precisely subtle nom de plume,
inherited by her successors, was Mae Tinée, had a gift for
stimulating her readers to write letters, and I was not too
obscurely involved in this correspondence on behalf of May
McAvoy, who had already proved her skill as an interpreter
of Barrie and who seemed to me more likely to capture the
fairy spirit than any other possible contender. Along with
a good many others, she had hoped that Peter Pan would be
directed by John S. Robertson, who had guided her through
Sentimental Tommy, but it went instead to Herbert Brenon.
I do not know what authority if any she had in later life for
thinking Brenon responsible for choosing the seventeen-year-
old, then unknown Betty Bronson for Peter, but the truth
seems to be that Barrie had the final choice and that he
chose Miss Bronson from the tests submitted to him.

Barrie himself seems to have been disappointed in the
film both because its producers used hardly any of the suggestions he had carefully drawn up for them and because he
thought they had merely filmed the play instead of using the
resources of the camera to create something the stage could
not achieve.[1] This latter criticism is at least partially sound;
there are certainly too many scenes in the Darling nursery,
just as, two years later, when Brenon and Bronson turned
out another Barrie play, A Kiss for Cinderella, the scenes
between Cinderella and her policeman were allowed to run too
long. I must confess, however, that since everybody knew
the film version of Peter Pan would be shown in many places
to many people who would never have a chance to see the
play, a pretty good argument could be made for keeping as
close to the latter as possible, and personally I could forgive
Brenon for much more than the shortcomings I have suggested
here for the wonderful scene in A Kiss for Cinderella showing
the transformation of household articles into Cinderella's coach
and attendants, a moment of cinema magic that has never been
surpassed. And surely no valid criticism of any importance
can be entered concerning Betty Bronson's own performance
as Peter. It must go without saying that she did not play
the role quite as May McAvoy would have played it, nor

would it have been wise for her to try. And obviously her
performance lacked something that May's would have had.
But upon its own terms it was exquisite, amazingly so for so
young and inexperienced a performer; there was no suggestion of amateurishness about it. Her youth was enchanting,
and she was probably more successful than May could have
been in suggesting a certain boyish--or girl-boyish--insou-
ciance. She played the role with her feet and legs bare, and
her grace of movement never faltered. It was evident at
once that there was a new personality on the screen, quite
different from May's, but like hers as definitely out of the
usual mold, and something with which Hollywood would have
to reckon.

Hollywood met that challenge in the same way it had
met May's, which is to say that it did not face up to it at
all. There are indeed interesting resemblances between the
McAvoy and Bronson careers. Both arrived in Barrie vehicles. Both supported Al Jolson, May in The Jazz Singer,
Betty in The Singing Fool (Warner Bros., 1928), during
whose filming she said he treated her very badly. Both
lived lives completely untouched by any whisper of scandal
or indiscretion. Each married only once and bore one child,
in each case a son. There was also, to be sure, one contrast. Betty died on October 21, 1971, nearly a month short
of her sixty-fifth birthday, and May lived until April 26,
1984; she would have been eighty-three in September. But,
alas, both careers petered out. We have already seen what
happened to May McAvoy. Paramount followed Betty's Peter
Pan with a modern comedy, Are Parents People? and then
turned to more picturesque material in Not So Long Ago and
The Golden Princess; all three films were released in 1925.
She was lent to M-G-M to appear as the Madonna in Ben Hur,
where she did the little she had to do perfectly. I thought
The Cat's Pajamas and Everybody's Acting, both 1926 and the
latter a Marshall Neilan production, charming trifles; then
at Christmas time came A Kiss for Cinderella. But of what
I saw after that I should have to say what I said of the later
McAvoy films: the star was always charming and as good an
actress as the material she was supplied with allowed her to
be. (With her later work on the stage, mostly in southern
California, including a Viola in Twelfth Night at the Pasadena
Playhouse, and her television appearances we naturally have
nothing to do here.) In short, both these young ladies (and
how many others?) went through the paces of the familiar

Hollywood story: the movies were always good at recognizing unusual talent but much less successful in nourishing and developing it.

NOTE

1. See Roger Lancelyn Green, <u>Fifty Years of Peter Pan</u> (London: Peter Davies, 1954), and cf. DeWitt Bodeen, "Betty Bronson," <u>Films in Review</u>, Vol. XXV, pp. 577-89, December 1974.

THE DUNCAN SISTERS

Since Topsy and Eva (United Artists, 1927), which had been freely derived from their musical comedy success of the same title, was the only silent film in which the Duncan Sisters ever appeared, their place in this book must necessarily be marginal. The film's direction was officially credited to Del Lord, but its production was obviously not all clear sailing, for at one point no less a person than D. W. Griffith was called in to straighten things out, and Vivian Duncan told me she thought his contribution to what finally emerged an important one.

It seems reasonable nevertheless that the girls should be here, for their presence indicates an important point about early screen history. Though pictures would then hardly yet seem to have been in existence long enough to have grown stale, as a matter of fact producers were forever reaching out for novelties in every direction, and any human being who became either famous or notorious in any line of activity might fairly safely expect to be dragged in. Essanay even tagged the young woman whom H. L. Mencken called "the Butte Bashkirtseff," who, quite without Marie Bashkirtseff's talent, had tastelessly exploited her own idiosyncrasies in I, Mary MacLane, and would die forlornly at last in a Chicago slum, and put her in something called Men Who Have Made Love to Me. But a better example would be Evelyn Nesbit, who, though she had authentic experience in show business, was thought of as having primarily interested the public through her demented husband's murder of the great architect Stanford White, and whom, around World War I, William Fox attempted to make into a star by some of the same methods he had used on Theda Bara. This enterprise might well have been more successful than it was (Willie Hammerstein did develop Miss Nesbit into a vaudeville headliner) if it had been managed with some taste and judgment.

It must be remembered that if Fox created Theda Bara, he
also destroyed her; as D. W. Griffith once observed, not
even Sarah Bernhardt could have long survived in the kind
of junk Fox dealt out to her.

Vivian Duncan died in Los Angeles on September 19,
1986.

In its original form, what I had to say about the Duncan Sisters was written some time in the 1920s. As related
hereinafter, the sisters read it and liked it when I met them
in Seattle in 1928, but it was never published until I made
it a chapter in my semi-autobiography, As Far as Yesterday.
It is here reprinted, with no changes whatever from that
publication, which was copyrighted in 1968 by the University
of Oklahoma Press.

*   *   *

For some reason or other, my tastes have always
tended to be rather more "highbrow" in music than in some
other areas where I might be supposed to be better informed.
Consequently I have never cared much for that form of entertainment which, for want of a better term, is called "musical
comedy." As a child I was taken to such shows of the
period as The Time, The Place, and the Girl; The Girl Question; and A Knight for a Day, which starred the then-popular
Mabel Hite. Later I saw the Dolly Sisters in Oh, Look! after
which one of my parlor tricks was a pretty good imitation of
Harry Fox singing "I'm Always Chasing Rainbows." When the
old-fashioned musical comedy began to transform itself into
whatever takes its place now, I got in on the ground floor
by seeing Blossom Time and The Student Prince, but I did
not very industriously pursue my explorations. The dominant tendencies in modern serious drama do not greatly charm
me, and I have sometimes suspected that if the true spirit of
the theater lingers anywhere in our world, it is in the musicals that it must be looked for (George Jean Nathan once
pointed out that when people stopped building theaters that
looked like theaters and began to build theaters that looked
like undertaking parlors instead, what was presented on the
stage also began to alter itself to correspond), but I am now
inclined to leave the documentation of this impression to the
investigations of others.

Of course I was taken to see Montgomery and Stone in
The Wizard of Oz, and I fancy this was my first musical.
Naturally I was charmed, though I recall being vaguely
troubled by the show's departures from the book I knew by
heart. (If I had been a child when the M-G-M film was
made, in which the whole Oz adventure became a dream of
Dorothy's in delirium, I am sure I should have stalked out
of the theater in indignation.) But I think more magic clings
for me, though only with the vaguest pegs to hang it on, to
two other musicals of the early 1900's which seem largely to
have disappeared from theatrical history.

The first was an extravaganza called The Top of the
World, whose scene was laid at the North Pole and in which
I believe Santa Claus was one of the characters. That is
nearly all I remember about it except a general atmosphere of
white glitter and one buxom lady in white tights whom I did
not think at all pretty, yet the very vagueness contributes
to the atmosphere of wonder which lingers with me to remind
me of an occasion when I escaped from the world of actuality
into a better world of the mind. As a matter of fact, the
transition was gracefully prepared for. The Top of the World
was presented at the lovely Studebaker Theater, which is on
Michigan Avenue, always for me the most enchanted part of
Chicago, and before the show began my mother and I stopped
off to see a relative by marriage who kept a floral shop in
Van Buren Street, between Michigan and Wabash, where the
atmosphere seemed almost as romantic to me as on the stage
itself, and where the kind lady gave me a flower so that I
might carry the flavor of her establishment away with me.

My other early memory is even vaguer, for I cannot
even remember the name of the show. All I know is that I
saw it at the Great Northern, that it had a Chinese or Japanese setting, and that in the last act a good part of the stage
was occupied by an enormous grinning Billiken. Now Billiken
was a benevolent-looking Oriental idol, a kind of good-luck
symbol, of whom miniature reproductions soon flooded the
novelty shops of America, so that he became as omnipresent
as whatever people fastened to the radiator caps of motor
cars at a later period, and if, as I assume, he originated
in this show (I cannot recall ever having seen him before,
and he endured for years afterwards), then it must have
exercised considerable influence, yet I have never been able
to identify it. I once asked the late Charles Collins of the

Chicago Tribune, whom I had reason to believe well-nigh
omniscient in such matters, about it, but he did not know
any more than I did.   There are fairy tales in which children
go to a land where they find all the toys they have ever
lost; perhaps there is also a land where we can refurbish our
lost memories.   Or perhaps not, for if I could see this show
again, I might not enjoy it nearly as much as I did then unless I could also be the boy who saw it, and that, I fear, I
can never be.

Once, however, during my adult years, I was enthralled
by a musical comedy, and this was Topsy and Eva, with the
Duncan Sisters.   The book was by Catherine Chisholm Cush-
ing, and the music was credited to the girls themselves, who
had previously done "kid" acts in a number of big musicals,
including Fred Stone's Tip Top.   Topsy and Eva, which put
Rosetta into the blackface she never got off again, opened in
1923 in Los Angeles, but its greatest success was in Chicago,
where it played for over a year at the Selwyn Theater.   I
do not know how many times I saw it, but I was present on
the last night, when, in imitation of the "Tom-shows" of days
gone by, all the characters were doubled.

I expected the Duncan Sisters to go on to other big
musicals (my pet project for them was an Alice in Wonderland
with Vivian as Alice and Rosetta as the White Rabbit), but
this did not happen.   Though the success of Topsy and Eva
in New York did not match its acclaim in Chicago, they found
themselves "stuck" with the name characters much as Joe Jef-
ferson was "stuck" with Rip Van Winkle or Rose Melville with
Sis Hopkins, and they went on playing them in vaudeville
and, later, nightclub engagements across the world until
Rosetta was killed in an automobile accident late in 1959.

I had met Vivian once, very briefly, in Chicago, but I
became better acquainted with the sisters when they came to
Seattle, where I was then living, in 1928, to play the Pantages
circuit.   Or perhaps I should say I became better acquainted
with Vivian, for although Rosetta was never other than
charming to me, she had the habit of disappearing into her
dressing room between the grueling four-a-day schedule they
were playing and leaving her sister to entertain their visitors.
It was obvious that Rosetta was a temperamental young lady
whose spirits alternated between the heights and the depths,
but this is no wonder, for her energy on the stage (and I

suspect off it, when she was really interested) was tremendous, and no girl's physique could have endured the strain,
which must have been even more psychic than physical,
without cooling-off periods in between.

Vivian, on the other hand, was a gorgeous peaches-
and-cream kind of girl, right off the candy box, and with
a disposition to match. She was pretty enough so that not
even her heavy stage make-up (it was about the heaviest I
have ever seen on anybody and it would have been quite
out of the question to take it off between shows) could make
her other than very well worth looking at. One night we
dined together at a neighboring cafeteria (she still in make-
up), and I cannot honestly say that we did not attract attention. I often suspected that she was considerably bored
with us all, but she never ceased to be the gracious hostess,
and the atmosphere backstage was as decorous as in church.

Structurally Topsy and Eva was an old-fashioned musical comedy, in which no excuse was too flimsy to stop the
story for a song-and-dance number. For all that, the story-
line was important. "Tom-shows" had been a part of the
American theatrical picture since the 1850's, and their fascina-
tion was in the American blood. The Duncan Sisters gathered
the last great Uncle Tom harvest because they had the wit to
see that theatrical taste had not changed so much as "smart"
people supposed, and that all that was needed to give Topsy
and Eva a new lease on life was to apply a modern veneer.

None of the countless Little Evas of the past can possibly have been prettier than Vivian Duncan, and none can
have undertaken the character more determined to project
the last essence of its sweetness. What made her acceptable
in a day when most of them would have been rejected out of
hand was that whenever her role was in danger of turning
uncomfortably saccharine, she would turn about and "kid"
it. Either she would wickedly sham fainting in order to get
something she wanted, or offer plain aid and encouragement
to the enemy of all things sentimental, present on the scene
in the person of Miss Topsy, or else she would break out
with spirit, doing funny, jazzy things with her voice. Thus
she was at once romantic and realist, a fairy child and a
hard-headed little girl of earth.

Topsy was a rather more complicated matter, for Topsy

was an outrageous person even in Mrs. Stowe's novel, and
she certainly did not grow more demure in Rosetta Duncan's
tender hands. As Eva inherited the stage tradition of the
angel child, so the mantle of the long inexhaustible blackface comedian fell on Topsy's shoulders, and her remark that
Al Jolson was her "mammy" was no idle jest. Now blackface
comedians are traditionally men. To give the role instead to
a young and attractive girl and then have her beat her
predecessors at their own game, marshalling six or seven
times as much exuberance as any of them were ever able to
command--all this may not seem like a very long step to take.
But it is the kind of step that makes history in the theater.

Outrageousness was by no means all Topsy had however,
nor could it alone have accounted for her reception. She
added charm to incongruity, and the combination proved irresistible. Whether or not one liked all the things she said
and did--she adlibbed freely, and, like all such players,
she was not always the same--it was impossible not to like
her. The tiny, half-naked little figure of the first act, so
inadequately enclosed in somber rags, so essentially helpless
for all her impudence, made an immediate appeal, and the effect thus gained was never forfeited.

Many spectators, of course, were under the impression
that she was the dominant figure. In a way this was true,
but it was only half true. The Duncan stage partnership
was not a rivalry; both sisters were necessary to the effect
that was created, and neither could have done without the
other. Vivian had no such prolonged "scene" as fell to her
sister with "Topsy's Prayer," or, later, in vaudeville, with
the remarkable "Curbstone Blues," and she always did much
less, but what she was, was tremendously important. Even
very great actors sometimes do their best work when they
seem to be doing nothing, for it is cruelly difficult to do
nothing on the stage, and it is even more difficult to make
nothing into something. Certainly Rosetta's dynamism gained
much from having Vivian's lovely restfulness as a background.
Repose is as necessary in life as action, and as necessary in
art as in life, and two Topsies would have destroyed each
other and the audience with them. When Vivian was called
upon to take the center of the stage she never had any difficulty in doing so, and when she stretched out her arms in
the calcium glare and cried, "O Topsy, don't go!" she
awakened more emotion than it was altogether reasonable to

expect the situation to generate. Often, however, she
seemed to be merely observing what Rosetta was doing, with
sympathy, yet with a certain detachment too, much as she
viewed her visitors backstage.

The Duncan Sisters suggested a fresh wholesomeness
which was not the quality most frequently encountered in
the musical-comedy stars of their time, but they also had a
good deal of tart commentary on hypocrisy and pretension,
much of which was no less effective for being implicit rather
than explicit. One does not often associate this with attractive
girls, and at one time I thought Rosetta might develop along
the lines later laid down by Elaine May. Their mockery of
our musical aspirations in "Vocalizing" was delightful; so too
was their burlesque of our sentimentality in "In Sweet Onion
Time." I have never heard anybody sing the Negro spiritual
"Heav'n, Heav'n" better than they did, and they brought art
worthy of much better music to such numbers as "Baby Feet
Go Pitter Patter Cross My Floor." I am not sure whether they
could have sung Hänsel und Gretel or not, but I should have
liked to see them try. Their career was a record of splendid
generosity; they always gave freely of their means and of
themselves, and I am sure many theatergoers must remember
them, as I do, with great affection.

CLARA BOW

According to Rudy Behlmer, who did the career article on Clara Bow for Films in Review, she was born in Brooklyn on July 29, 1907. Lois W. Banner's piece in Notable American Women puts the date exactly two years earlier. Both the Katz and Thomson film encyclopedias also opt for the 1905 date, but according to Katz the event occurred on August 25.[1]

She made her first contact with films by winning a "Fame and Fortune" contest sponsored by the Eugene V. Brewster publications, but her role in the film in which she appeared, Beyond the Rainbow (Robertson-Cole, 1926), ended up on the cutting-room floor, leaving her to be rediscovered by one of Griffith's old henchmen, Elmer Clifton (Phil Stoneman in The Birth of a Nation and the Rhapsode in Intolerance), who gave her a tomboyish role in Down to the Sea in Ships (W. W. Hodkinson, 1923), which I saw and liked. But I did not see her again before Victor Fleming's Mantrap (1926), based upon the Sinclair Lewis novel, and there had been thirty-two others in between! I later caught up on her first Paramount, Herbert Brenon's Dancing Mothers, and thereafter I saw everything she did.

Her career took a nosedive after the bad publicity that attended her difficulties with a secretary at the end of the twenties (the secretary went to jail), and her Paramount contract was cancelled at her own request after a sound version of Kick In (1931). She liked only a very few of her films. "It wasn't like I thought it was going to be," she later said of her career. "It was always a disappointment." And again, more reflectively, "A sex symbol is always a heavy load to carry, especially when one is very tired, hurt and bewildered." Between 1923 and 1931 she had appeared in fifty-three films, fourteen in 1925 alone, eight each in 1924 and

1926, six in 1927, and four each in 1928 and 1930. Of all
her films my own favorite is the circus picture Dangerous
Curves (1929), directed by Luther Mendes, in which she
was supported by Richard Arlen, Kay Francis, and Joyce
Compton, a charming actress who never received the recognition she deserved. Though it was one of her sound films,
I have chosen one of my stills from Dangerous Curves because the photograph catches so well the wistful sadness that
underlay all Clara Bow's high spirits.

After leaving Paramount, Clara made two pictures for
Fox--Call Her Savage and Hoopla (1932-33), of which the
former was much the more successful, though Hoopla had an
outstanding director in Frank Lloyd. In 1931 she married
Rex Bell, one of the few people who had stood by her during
her ordeal, to whom she bore two sons. They moved to his
ranch in Nevada, where Bell became lieutenant governor in
1954, but in later years the mental illness which plagued her,
as it had plagued her mother before her, made it necessary
for them to live apart. She wanted much to play Cleopatra
and Scarlett O'Hara, but the closest she came to a comeback
was to become the mystery voice, Mrs. Hush, on 1947 radio
programs. Bell died in 1962, and she followed him, of a
heart ailment, on September 27, 1965.

The piece which follows was written during her later
Paramount days and sent out by Arch Reeve, then Paramount's
publicity chief, as a press release to American newspapers.
In Seattle, where I was then living, and where the newspapers avidly seized upon anything that had to do with anyone
connected with the university, especially if they could read
sensationalism into it, it rated feature stories; what happened
to it in other cities I never inquired. As I stated in the
article itself, it was less a defense of Clara Bow than an attack upon the vultures who, as I saw it, were sweeping down
upon her. I never met her, either before or after the event,
but she wrote me a touching letter, in which she declared
that what I did had importantly helped her not to lose her
courage at a very difficult time and that she only hoped that
some time she might be able to do something similar for some
other human being. She could not have been more charming
about it, nor did she ever forget. I heard from her again in
1947, and her tone was still the same. As for the article,
though slightly shortened here, it has been subjected to no
important alterations.

THE CASE FOR CLARA BOW

I rise to a point of order.

We have a new indoor sport among us. Many enjoy it
more than miniature golf. It is a very easy game to play
because there are no rules connected with it. The only re-
quirement is that the player shall lack a certain sense of
fairness and decency.

The game is played around a girl. She is a girl who
has never done any of the players any harm, who has indeed given many of them a good deal of innocent pleasure.
The object of the game is to discredit her, to humiliate her,
and ultimately to deprive her of her employment. To this
end any tactics may be used. One may circulate gossip and
slander about her. One may repeat stories one has heard
others tell, even though one may have no evidence that they
are true. One may watch her comings and goings, day in
and day out, and every time she makes a false step employ
newspaper headlines to make the whole world know about it.
One may use even her illnesses and misfortunes, to say nothing of the wrongs she suffers at the hands of others, and
twist them into weapons to be employed against her. One
may make a matter of public discussion out of intimately personal matters that could not, by any stretch of the imagination concern anybody except the girl herself. One may
write open letters to her, reading her moral lectures in public, discourses in which one professes to have only her own
best interests at heart, but which, at the same time, one
takes pains to fill with sly, covert, underhanded insinuations
concerning her private life. One may make her a whipping
post for the sins of a whole community. One may tacitly assume that she is a person of no consideration whatever, that
everything she thinks and says and does must necessarily be
wrong, that nothing about her could possibly be right.

The game goes off rather expeditiously if the girl has
red hair. And there is one other little thing: her name
should be Clara Bow.

Now it is not necessary to like Clara Bow. De gustibus
non disputandem est. It would be stupid to pretend that she
has made no mistakes. Nobody--least of all Clara Bow her-

self--would claim that she has never done anything that it
would not have been better to leave undone. This is no time
to idealize her or to get romantic over her. But it is time--
and it is high time, to insist that she be treated with common
decency, that she receive the ordinary courtesy to which
every human being is entitled.

She has not had that. She has never had it. In the
spring of 1926 she created a sensation as Alice Joyce's flapper
daughter in Herbert Brenon's film production of Edgar Selwyn's play, Dancing Mothers. Her vividness, her pert ways,
her seemingly inexhaustible vitality, her warm human friend-
liness seemed to bring a new vitality to the screen, and
thousands of picture-goers at once took her to their hearts.
But simply because she was such a vivid personality she also
inspired violent partisanships. It was evident at once that it
was going to be difficult for people to be neutral about her.
In itself this was all to the good, for it is only insignificant,
namby-pamby people who never inspire partisanship. Dante's
Limbo was occupied by those who were pleasing neither to
God nor to His enemies. For nearly five years now Miss Bow
has held her place as one of the most sensational figures on
the screen, and for nearly that same length of time those who
did not care for her have been as narrow- and as mean-
minded toward her as they could possibly manage. Long before there was any gossip about her, they proclaimed that
she was common, that she was coarse and vulgar, and that
no intelligent human being could possibly take an interest in
her. But it does not always seem to work out that way.
Emil Jannings, Walter Huston, Ludwig Berger, Frank Tuttle,
and Ruth Chatterton are, none of them, exactly illiterates in
the field of dramatic art. All have expressed admiration for
Clara Bow's work on the screen, and Victor Fleming called
her death scene in Children of Divorce (1927) the finest he
had ever seen.

But why were so many people shocked by Clara Bow in
the first place? The answer, I believe, is simple. People
were not shocked by Clara Bow so much as they were shocked
by the "flapper." Miss Bow made her first great success in
a flapper role; she was typed; she was identified in the public mind with that kind of personality; she became the Great
American Flapper par excellence; people felt that in rejecting
her they were rejecting everything that was cheapening and
degrading young girls. Nobody, to be sure, knew just what

a flapper was, but that only made things that much easier.
For it is undeniable that for the bulk of the movie public an
actress is just what she plays.

Yet, so far as my observation has extended, Clara Bow
never appeared in an unworthy picture. She appeared in
poor pictures and stupid pictures, but she never appeared in
a film that could reasonably have been called immoral. That
is more than you can say for some of the cultivated ladies
and gentlemen who invaded the screen with the advent of
sound and whom Clara's enemies welcomed with open arms as
ministers of culture to the lowly movie! Dancing Mothers
contained unpleasant sequences, but it was as moral a drama
in its outlook as any that has ever appeared. Nor was there
anything among Clara's succeeding vehicles that was not innocence itself compared to what the screen offered after the
sophisticates got hold of it. Generally she played good,
though undeniably lively, girls, and when she did not she
was generally reformed in the course of the action. It was
once said of O. Henry that though quick to don the guise of
modernity he was impervious to its spirit, and the same might
well be said of her. Poor though they have been in many
ways, her films have consistently glorified the old-fashioned
virtues of romantic love, honesty, and fidelity.

Came 1927. Flappers somehow were not quite so shocking as they had been. Clara Bow now began her career as
a star in a picture called It. The film swept the nation.
Nobody was sure what "it" was, any more than anybody had
quite known how to define the flapper. But what else could
it be than what you thought it was? Again the stigma of vulgarity was fastened upon her.

Yet obviously no human being ever became the idol of
thousands upon the basis of sex appeal alone. Sex appeal is
far too omnipresent for that; nobody has a monopoly of it.
Frankie Bailey's legs in another generation, Ann Pennington's
"dimpled knees" were famous. But why these particular legs
or these knees? Obviously there must have been something
else there. Nobody has ever denied that Clara Bow has sex
appeal. She is not the Witch of Endor. She is chock full of
sex appeal. It is honest and healthy and unashamed. It is
splendidly normal; there is not the slightest suggestion of
decadence about it. But if you seek to explain her vogue on

the basis of this quality alone, you have adopted one of those over-simplistic explanations that explain nothing.

The attitude of the motion picture public toward its favorites is a curious and complicated thing. In many cases genuine affection enters into it. But there is a tremendous amount of jealousy also. The large salaries film stars receive (Clara Bow has never received much by motion picture standards), the notoriety they receive, the adoration that is showered upon them--all this has its effect. All that is needed to start a scandal is one liar, one envious, evil mind. Once the story is in circulation, the public half fears, half hopes to find it true, and on this basis ends by believing it, and revenges itself by trampling upon what it has loved.

Not of course in every case. If so, we should have few players left. But every few years we have to have a great movie scandal. Somebody must be thrown to the wolves. Then that somebody is forced into oblivion, and the public settles down again and licks its virtuous jaws.[2]

It is sometimes assumed that such things are necessary to maintain moral standards. Let us not call vile things by fine names. In the first place, it is highly doubtful that the fear of exposure--especially brutal exposure--ever restrained a sinner. A sense of being treated unfairly does not make people better; it makes them worse. Those who are determined to go to the devil in this world generally manage to get there, and of all the methods that have been devised to restrain them, the only one that has ever worked is the method of faith and love. Can anyone seriously believe that it is the really fine people, the genuinely pure people who take part in the kind of pastimes that I have been describing? My own feeling is that it is far more likely to be the sadists and the hypocrites, and I firmly believe that when they get to hell, they are going to have to look up, not down, upon the most culpable of their victims and this regardless of whether what they have said about them has been literally true or false.

For the moment then Miss Clara Bow seems to be the public's latest goat. She has served in this capacity for many weary months, and during this time she has been subjected in the public prints to almost every conceivable form of humiliation. A man with a scar on his face visited the Paramount

studio one day, and in a few hours the newspapers were proclaiming that she had entertained a notorious racketeer.
Whether or not such things are unfair to Clara Bow is not
the question. They are a disgrace to every American.

Let the reader of this article understand the writer
clearly. He neither possesses nor pretends to possess any
information about Clara Bow's personal affairs. If he had it,
I hope he would have sufficient taste and judgment to keep it
to himself. This article is not primarily a <u>defense</u> of Clara
Bow but an <u>attack</u> upon cruelty and irresponsibility. But
even if the worst that has been said about her should turn
out to be true, I should not care to be the first to cast a
stone at her. Everybody who is at all familiar with her history knows that fate pretty consistently stacked the cards
against her. Life did not even begin to give her, as a child,
the things to which every child is entitled. It says much for
the native goodness of her endowment that, in spite of such
handicaps, she should have been able to preserve a native
sweetness and kindness of disposition as well as she has.
Then, suddenly, she won a "Fame and Fortune" contest, got
a chance in pictures, and sometime later, after intervening
disappointments, found herself a triumphant success on the
screen, had money, admirers, adulation--everything she had
always wanted and had never had--all this in one of the
hardest, most fiercely competitive businesses on the face of
the earth. What wonder if she made mistakes, even serious
mistakes?

It was a beautiful thing to see, Clara Bow's enthusiasm
in those first early days of her success. She was so gloriously happy, so wonderfully alive. Happy and yet wistful--
as if she were wondering what might be waiting for her
around the corner. Nothing she has ever said of herself
was more revealing than her remark that now that she was a
motion picture star perhaps it would not be necessary for her
to cry when she got a run in her stocking. She thought that
perhaps life had got through playing tricks on her.

But life had only begun. The Clara Bow of today has
traveled far from the breath-taking girl of those early films.
She has been hurt--not once but many times. Of all the
things that have been said about her, the most absurd is
that she is hard. She lacks many things. There are many
graces that she has never attained. Indeed part of her dif-

ficulty is that she is something of an anachronism, lacking
the glittering, sleek, well-groomed sophistication upon which
the present generation prides itself. She is a throw-back to
an earlier, franker, more honest age, but she is not hard.
Life would be much easier for her if she were. Her natural
tendency is to take people at their own evaluation. So she
walks into one trap after another; the spotlight is turned full
upon her, and the others walk off scot-free.

It is a mistake to suppose that society is ever seriously
concerned about evil. Society punishes not evil but indiscretion; it bears down heavily upon those who do not play the
game according to the rules. Clara Bow will never do that
because she does not know how. She will never pretend to
be anything except exactly what she is. Yet I feel there is
much capacity for development in her, both as an artist and
as a woman. It would be presumptuous in the extreme to
send her a telegram reading: "Dear Prodigal Daughter:
Come home. All is forgiven." She is the one who will have
to forgive us.

NOTES

1.   Films in Review, Vol. XIV, pp. 451-65, October 1963;
     Barbara Sicherman et al., eds., Notable American Women:
     The Modern Period (The Belknap Press of Harvard Uni-
     versity Press, 1980); Ephraim Katz, The Film Encyclope-
     dia (Perigree-Putnam, 1970); David Thomson, A Bio-
     graphical Dictionary of Film (Morrow, 1976). Alexander
     Walker's discussion in The Celluloid Sacrifice (Hawthorn
     Books, 1967) has value. There are fairly long chapters
     on Clara Bow in Norman Zierold, Sex Goddesses of the
     Silent Screen (Henry Regnery Company, 1973) and
     Robert Parish, The Paramount Pretties (Arlington House,
     1972). The only book-length biography, The "It" Girl,
     by Joe Morella and Edward W. Epstein (Delacorte Press,
     1976) is just about what one would expect from the title.

2.   I intrude at this point to observe from the vantage
     ground of a later day that standards in these matters
     shift from time to time. Lillian Gish once told me that
     no less a person than Irving Thalberg came to her during
     her M-G-M period to ask permission to invent a scandal
     for her on the ground that this might stimulate more

interest in her films. She replied that if she could not
interest the public except upon this basis, she thought
she might as well find some other line of work.

CHARLES CHAPLIN*

The man who, after a career of unexampled adulation and execration, finally came to be known as Sir Charles Spencer Chaplin was born in London on April 16, 1889 and died at Vevey, Switzerland on Christmas Day, 1977. He was the star of stars in the silent sky; it is refreshing to be able to make at least one statement that cannot be challenged. "Praising one of Mr. Chaplin's pictures," wrote the critic of the New York Herald-Tribune when The Gold Rush appeared in 1925, "is like saying that Shakespeare was a good writer." It is true that much nonsense has been written about him. But it is also true that responsible people have called him the greatest actor in the world, the Dickens of the twentieth century, and the one universal man of our time.

His entry into films, by way of Mack Sennett's Keystone studio, at the very end of 1913, was late compared to that of the Biograph people who went back to 1908 or 1909, to say nothing of George Méliès and Max Linder in France and Edwin S. Porter in this country, who began still earlier, and even at Keystone Fred Mace, Ford Sterling, and Mabel Normand had established themselves before him. But he began to invent the persona we later came to call inaccurately the Little Tramp with his second film, Kid Auto Races at Venice, released on February 7, 1914, and public acceptance came very quickly. "Even then," he said later, "looking back upon his early days, "I realized I would have to spend the rest of my life finding out more about the creature. For me he was fixed, complete, the moment I looked in the mirror and saw him for the first time, yet even now I don't know all the things there are to be known about him."

---

*Some passages in the first part of this chapter make use of materials which appeared in a different form in the author's book The Movies in the Age of Innocence. Copyright © 1962 by the University of Oklahoma Press.

Mary Pickford in <u>Rebecca of Sunnybrook Farm</u> (1917).

Mary Pickford as Dearest in <u>Little Lord Fauntleroy</u> (1925).

Mary Pickford, with Frank Losee and Gertrude Norman, in
Fanchon the Cricket (1915).

Lillian and Dorothy Gish as the Two Orphans in D. W. Griffith's Orphans of the Storm (1922).

Lillian Gish as Romola in Henry King's production of George
Eliot's novel (1924).

Clarine Seymour.

Lillian Gish, with Lars Hanson, in one of the films she likes best, Victor Sjöström's production, The Wind (1928).

Clarine Seymour, with Robert Harron, in her first film for Griffith, The Girl Who Stayed at Home (1919).

Clarine Seymour, with Richard Barthelmess, in The Idol
Dancer (1920).

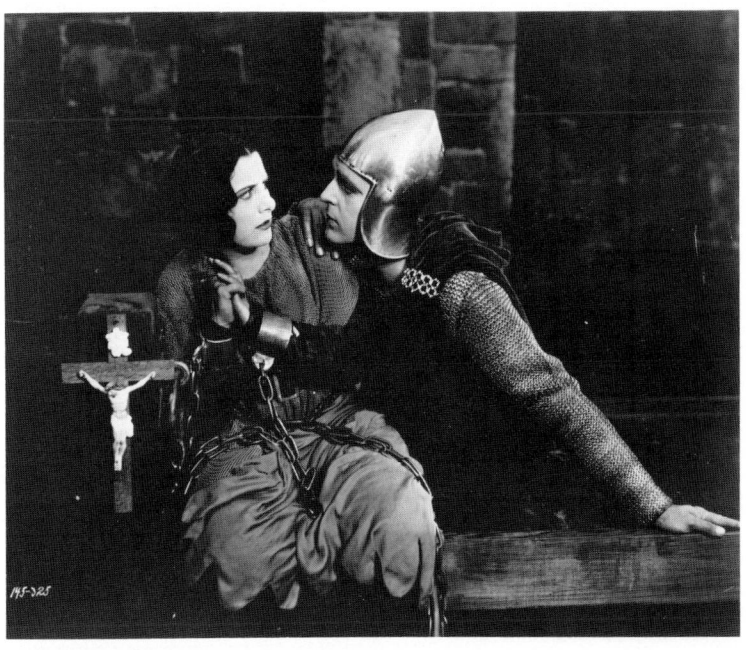

Geraldine Farrar, with Wallace Reid, in Joan the Woman (1917).

Geraldine Farrar as Carmen, after the fight in the tobacco factory, in Cecil B. DeMille's production (1915).

Geraldine Farrar as Joan of Arc in Cecil B. DeMille's Joan the Woman (1917).

May McAvoy, in John S. Robertson's production of J. M. Barrie's <u>Sentimental Tommy</u> (1921).

May McAvoy and Richard Barthelmess as the lovers as the world sees them in Robertson's production of Pinero's play, <u>The Enchanted Cottage</u> (1924). Their friend is Holmes Herbert.

May McAvoy and Richard Barthelmess as the lovers in The Enchanted Cottage as they appear in the eyes of love.

Rosetta Duncan as Topsy and Vivian Duncan as Eva, with Nils Asther and Myrtle Ferguson in the screen version of their musical comedy success, Topsy and Eva (1927).

Clara Bow.

Clara Bow presents Clara Bow.

Clara Bow, with Richard Arlen, in <u>Dangerous Curves</u> (1929).

Charles Chaplin, with Mack Swain, in <u>The Gold Rush</u> (1925).

Charles Chaplin, with Jackie Coogan, in <u>The Kid</u> (1921).

Charles Chaplin, with Paulette Goddard, in their dream house, in Modern Times (1936).

There had been nothing like this before, and there
would be nothing like it again; Chaplin swept first America
and then the world. This had not been prepared for by
either him or the film industry; both were nearly overwhelmed
by surprise. He was shamelessly imitated by other so-called
comedians without either taste or talent, none of them surely
more unnecessary or objectionable than the gentleman who is
currently (1986) engaged in doing IBM commercials on television. A comic strip known as "Charlie Chaplin's Comic
Capers" ran for two years (1915-1917) in American newspapers, and the actor entered folklore while still a young man
when children took him up into their counting games and soldiers into marching songs in World War I. There were cartoons on the screen also, and after they had lost him, his
second employers, the Essanay Company, were greedy and
unscrupulous enough to gather up his scraps and discards
and issue them in various forms, as when they expanded his
two-reel burlesque of Carmen into four reels and turned it
into a weariness to the flesh.

    Chaplin stayed with Keystone only a year, but during
that year he appeared in thirty-five films (one-reelers, two-
reelers, and split reels, plus the six-reel Tillie's Punctured
Romance, which starred not him but Marie Dressler and was
directed by Mack Sennett). Compared not only to the great
features of his later years but even to the Essanays and
still more emphatically to the Mutuals that followed, the Keystones were crude casual stuff, yet they were very important
for Chaplin's career. In his great days he was more, vastly
more, than a Keystone slapstick comic, yet he never ceased
to be that too. On the foundations laid at Keystone he
erected such an impressive edifice that there were times when
the foundations were hidden, but they were there all the
same, and they were indispensable. Technically Chaplin remained an old-fashioned film-maker to the end of his days;
it was no accident that he continued his single-handed
heroic fight for the true cinema of the silents long after
everybody else had given them up for some mishmash or
amalgam of disparate qualities that neither God nor man could
describe and that only Divine mercy could tolerate.

    Keystone, to be sure, was not the only influence upon
these tendencies. There was the English music hall world
into which Chaplin was born. There was the Karno troupe
where Mack Sennett found him when they were touring

America. And there was D. W. Griffith; according to Theodore Huff, Chaplin saw The Birth of a Nation nearly every
week during its long first run in Los Angeles, a fact all the
more suggestive in view of the strong influence which Dickens
exerted upon both men.[1] In his latter days, the conditions
governing film production were such that Chaplin was obliged
to use a pre-prepared scenario instead of working everything
out in his head while in action, which was what both he and
Griffith had initially preferred, and he also had to tolerate
and pay for much technical equipment that he did not need or
use or even in some cases understand. But he did not love
these things. "We used to go into the park with a step-
ladder, a bucket of whitewash, and Mabel Normand," he once
remarked wistfully, "and make a picture."

It is astonishing how far the groundswell ran ahead of
critical opinion and intelligent understanding. In October
1914 the Motion Picture Magazine (it had by this time dropped
the word "Story" from its title, as if to indicate that what
went on behind the screen was now quite as important in its
table of contents as the pictures themselves) listed the top
hundred players in its recently concluded "Great Artist"
contest; Chaplin's name was not among them. During that
same year he had had no write-up of any kind in the outstanding trade journal, the Moving Picture World, and up to
October 24, when his picture appeared in a display advertisement for Dough and Dynamite, he had rated only passing
mention there in reviews of Keystone films. Moreover, though
both Dough and Dynamite and His Trysting Place got display
reviews, on November 7 Sydney Chaplin was identified as
"brother of Charlie Chaplin (the funny drunk) of Keystone
fame."

When Chaplin signed with Essanay, the World, beginning to stir in its sleep, declared that "Mr. Chaplin in a re-
markably short time has created for himself a unique position
in the film world." It was no thanks to them that he had,
and they still knew so little about him that they speculated
about "the name of the director under whom he will work" at
Essanay, yet Sennett had learned as early as May 1914 that
Chaplin could not function effectively unless he was left virtually in control of his films.[2] On January 23, 1915, Essanay
boasted in a display advertisement that they were "now offer-
ering exhibitors the greatest stars the photoplay world has
ever seen--the 'A.B.C..' of drama and comedy--Mr. G. M.

Anderson, Mr. Francis X. Bushman, and Mr. Charles Chaplin." But this announcement was arranged so that Anderson
("Broncho Billy"), co-owner of Essanay, though now nearing
the end of his stellar career, got the top of the page and
Chaplin the bottom, even though he was called "the most
wonderful comedian ever seen on the screen ... in himself a
guarantee of ESSANAY QUALITY." And even on August 7,
with Bushman lost to Metro, Henry B. Walthall rated the top
half of a page advertisement with The Woman Hater, directed
by Charles Brabin, while Chaplin and The Bank must make
do with the lower half.

    The New York Dramatic Mirror made an even worse
showing at a later date. Reviewing Mary Pickford's first
Artcraft, Less Than the Dust, on November 11, 1916, the
reviewer found that there were "comedy moments, bordering
on the Chaplinesque, which might better have been eliminated." When Chaplin's marriage to Mildred Harris was reported
on November 23, 1918, it was thought necessary to identify
him as "Charles S. Chaplin, reputed to be the funniest of all
film comedians," and as late as 1919, the Mirror gave Sunnyside a bad review, indulging in asinine conjecture that Chaplin might be slipping because he no longer had his brother
Sydney on hand to guide him. But the booby prize must go
to the distinguished Theatre magazine, where, in October
1919, one Harcourt Farmer pulled out all the stops in an article entitled, "Is the Charlie Chaplin Vogue Passing?" According to this super-refined commentator, Chaplin's appeal
"was an exceedingly unintellectual one," directed toward "the
lowest of human instincts."

    Such accusations were not peculiar to Mr. Farmer how-
ever. In 1915 the Chicago Tribune's respected drama critic,
Percy Hammond, reported having seen Chaplin "blithely performing functions ... that even I would decline to report,"
and the generally sensible Julian Johnson, reviewing
Shanghaied for Photoplay, found him "as usual ... funny
with a funnyness [sic] which transcends his art and his vulgarity." And in Variety of all media, Sime Silverman, reviewing Work, went out of his way to declare that "never
anything dirtier was placed upon the screen than Chaplin's
'Tramp,' and while this may have been objected to by the
censors, it merely taught Chaplin what to avoid and how far
to go." Since The Tramp and The Bank are the real gems
among Chaplin's Essanays and the most striking demonstra-

tions we had had yet of his capacity for pathos and tenderness, one is left rubbing his eyes and wondering what in
the world the writer thought he was talking about.

Even stupid misapprehensions however are seldom manufactured quite out of whole cloth. The Keystone world was
a rough, coarse, in many respects even brutal world whose
joyful, exuberant sadism was only redeemed by the apparent
immunity of its denizens to all the violence that would have
destroyed even a robot in the actual world that we inhabit.
It was a world of park benches, beaches, saloons, dance
halls, flop-houses, flirtatious girls and jealous husbands, in
which drunkenness and a kick in the pants were supposed
to be funny in themselves (not until City Lights would Chaplin learn how to use drunkenness as an end beyond itself).
Like much in the contemporary comic strip, to say nothing
of vaudeville and burlesque, the Keystones were undeniably
an assault upon the then still officially respected gentility.
What the writers I have quoted overlooked however is that
while Chaplin used all these things, he balanced them neatly
by placing a pathetic helplessness and an incongruous fastidiousness over against them. This began with the Little
Tramp's costume itself, especially the rattan cane, long antedating the touches of tenderness which toward the end sometimes threatened to take over. At the beginning of The Kid
his cigarette case was a sardine can filled with butts he had
picked up in the alley, but he handled it with all the elegance
of an affected clubman. Sleeping out of doors beside a
rickety fence in A Dog's Life, he thoughtfully stopped up a
tiny hole to protect himself from a draft. In Pay Day he arrived at work late, carrying a lily in his hand as a propitia-
tory offering. And in The Champion his own fastidiousness
was extended even to his bulldog. They are both hungry
when the Tramp thoughtfully offers the dog the first bite of
his lone frankfurter, but the latter will not touch it until it
has first been seasoned to his taste.

Buster Keaton widens the scope of our present inquiry
when he remarks that Chaplin's Tramp was "a bum with a
bum's philosophy. Lovable as he was he would steal if he got
the chance. My little fellow was a workingman and honest."
Actually the unfastidious Mack Sennett had said the same
thing in a more exaggerated form when he observed that it
was a long time before Chaplin "abandoned cruelty, venality,
treachery, larceny, and bribery as the main characteristics

of the tramp." Later critics have often echoed such senti-
ments. Thus Griffith and Mayer found the young Chaplin's
"smile of ... angelic innocence ... coupled with a surprising
streak of meanness, violence, and a certain deliberate vulgarity,"[3] while Robert Payne wildly declared that "Charlie
had never been a sentimental figure. He was the murderer
[where, I wonder before Monsieur Verdoux, in which he did
not play the Tramp], the pimp, the panderer, the seducer,
the criminal, the artist, and l'homme moyen sensuel from the
beginning, just as we have been all these things ourselves."

This is a curious list. But even when such charges
are made in an exaggerated form, is the presence of such
elements in Chaplin's persona really "surprising"? My answer
is no, and the reasons lie deeper in the nature of comedy
and of human life itself than can well be elaborately expounded
here. When one of Sir Walter Scott's daughters objected to
something as "vulgar," her father gave her a lesson in ety-
mology, telling her that "vulgar" was derived from the Latin
"vulgus" and that it merely indicated that the thing under
consideration belonged to humanity as a whole, to which it
would be very unseemly for her to hold herself superior or
from which she could expect to keep herself apart. So far
as Chaplin is concerned, the distinguished American actress
Mrs. Fiske met the issue head-on when, in an article published in the very last number of Harper's Weekly, she flut-
tered the dovecotes by hailing him as "a great comic artist,
possessing inspirational powers and a technique as unfaltering
as Réjane's." His vulgarity she admitted but pointed out that
he shared it with other comic geniuses from Aristophanes to
Swift. "Vulgarity and distinguished art can exist together."[4]
What all this means of course is that nobility's natural affinity
is with tragedy and even more with the epic. It is the function of comedy to cut man down to size, and the painful contrast between human aspiration and human achievement has
always been a very important part of its stock in trade. Man
is an animal who has developed or who has been given a soul,
but so long as he retains any vestiges of his animal heritage,
he must expect from time to time to be humiliated by it. On
the whole, it seems safer to accept this fact than to hold oneself austerely above it. If the Little Tramp has seemed at
times a half satiric image of humanity itself, as he surely has,
he could hardly have achieved this had all the elements in his
make-up to which some critics have taken so much exception
been left out. I would admit freely however that in the days

when he emerged upon the screen as the idol of American children, there was some justice in the fear expressed by many parents that the example some of his aspects presented to their offspring was undesirable.

With certain comparatively insignificant exceptions, the Little Tramp was the only persona in whose aspect Chaplin presented himself to his public up to and including Modern Times (1936). This character bears certain resemblances to some of the early heroes of the American comic strip, notably to Carl Emil Schultze's Foxy Grandpa and Frederick Burr Opper's Happy Hooligan. Both strips began in 1900, but "Foxy Grandpa" folded in 1918 while "Happy Hooligan" went on until 1938. Foxy Grandpa resembled Chaplin in the astonishing variety of his skills. Whatever trick or art he needed to prove himself a master of in order to outwit his mischievous grandsons he was ready to produce at the drop of a hat. He was the eternal trickster, the immemorial clever man of folklore. Hooligan, on the other hand, was the everlasting fall guy. All heart, he rushed to the assistance of anybody who needed him ("I'll help youse"), but something nearly always went wrong. Even the one he had tried to help often turned against him, and he would be carted off to jail by his irreconcilable enemy, the stupid Policeman, who could never get it out of his head that Hooligan was "a desperate character." Perhaps Chaplin resembled Hooligan most closely in Modern Times, where his rides in the patrol wagon occur with such rhythmical regularity that they virtually become an element of structure in the film.

Yet not altogether, and this is the point from which I may seem to have been wandering. For both Foxy Grandpa and Happy Hooligan were comparatively simple characters, Foxy all cleverness and Happy all heart, the fall guy with some overtones from the great tradition of the Fool in Christ. Before Krazy Kat no other character in the comic strip radiated such goodness; even the long suffering Mrs. Katzenjammer was capable of losing her temper. Foxy Grandpa's goodness was taken for granted of course, but it was never stressed or thrust into the foreground; we simply assumed that though he would always foil the boys, he would never hurt them. Charlie, like all really great comic characters, was much more complicated. We called him the Little Tramp because we had to call him something, but he spilled over the label; no label could have embraced him. He was no more

a tramp than Happy Hooligan was a hooligan; both characters
worked when work was available. In one aspect he was the
Terrible Meek that shall inherit the earth, but he would steal
even from a baby when he was hungry enough, as he did in
The Circus, and when circumstances were such that he and
his generally much more powerful antagonists exchanged roles
so as to give him a momentary advantage, he rarely failed to
avail himself of it.

It is no accident surely that, in dealing with a character of such complexity, one must in the end forsake not only
the comic strip but the popular theater too and turn instead
to the great world figures of literature and tradition. Gerald
D. McDonald underlined this element as well as anybody:

> Before Chaplin became the universal "little man," he
> was the Trickster. In the Keystone comedies and at
> certain times in all his later pictures, he was the
> simpleton who was also a clever rogue, with talents
> near to genius in useless endeavors but inept and
> bungling in what he was supposed to do. Charlie
> was the mischief-maker, Till Eulenspiegel of the
> merry pranks. He was the fool, sometimes gullible
> and stupid, sometimes impudent and cunning, dis-
> playing a high degree of effrontery and chicanery.
> His misadventures echoed stories known all over the
> world, the trickster tales, which have been among
> the best-liked.[5]

In one aspect Chaplin was as much a determinist as Theodore
Dreiser, showing humanity as the sport of circumstances, yet
at the end of City Lights, where he is recognized at last by
the flower girl who owes the restoration of her sight to the
heroically comic efforts he has made to raise the money to pay
for her operation, he becomes for a moment something holy.
He was too wise now to reward the little man by uniting him
with the girl, as he had been united with Edna Purviance at
the end of both The Vagabond and The Kid or with Georgia
Hale in The Gold Rush. He asks for no reward and receives
none save that of remaining his own outcast self, a heart-
breaking but not a cynical conclusion, since virtue must be
its own reward or submit to corruption. Many centuries ago,
an unknown woman walked the streets of Alexandria with a
torch in one hand and a pitcher of water in the other, saying, "With this torch I will burn the heavens and with this

water quench the fires of hell, that men may love God for Himself alone." The Little Tramp we see at the end of City Lights would have understood what she meant.

As a performer Chaplin's greatest gift was probably his ability to combine brilliant, apparently spontaneous improvisation with a mathematical exactitude in timing. I have compared his repertoire of skills with Foxy Grandpa's; he could skate, dance (he once declared, "I think in terms of dance"), walk the tightrope, even if necessary with monkeys swarming over him, and descend or even mount the pole in the fire station. Whatever the performance in question called for he could do, and, what is even more difficult, if at the same time it was necessary for him to pretend that he was unable to do it, he could do that too. Moreover, to achieve these ends there were no difficulties he could not face and no indignities and discomforts he would not submit to. The dog Scraps scratched dirt into his face while digging up the pocketbook in A Dog's Life. A diabolical child pummeled him mercilessly in The Pilgrim. In City Lights a blind girl emptied a cup of water in his face while he sat watching her in silent adoration. In The Circus he allowed himself to be shut up in a lion's cage, though he admitted he was afraid. In his last Keystone, His Prehistoric Past, he let himself down over a cliff by using a snake as a rope,[6] and in A Night in the Show he fell asleep in a stage box and woke up with the snake charmer's pets draped all over him. And in Modern Times he submitted to terrific punishment when the mechanical feeder that was being tested in the factory where he worked (naturally he was the victim chosen for the experiment) went wild. We have always known that in achieving his effects he must have possessed an incredible patience, but this was never really demonstrated to us until we saw his discards and his rehearsals in the 1986 television series, "Unknown Chaplin."

To discuss Chaplin as a pantomimist it would be necessary to review his whole oeuvre; that is what he essentially was. Such scenes as the David and Goliath sermon in The Pilgrim and the Oceana roll and shoe-eating scenes in The Gold Rush are famous, but I think no one of these surpasses the examination of the alarm clock in The Pawn Shop, which, incidentally, contains another brilliant bit, where, pleading against being discharged from the shop, he invents a whole army of dependent children, indicating the height of each with reference to himself. The alarm clock itself he examines, with the appropriate tools, as a physician, a jeweler, a dentist, a plumber, and others, including perhaps a housewife. He cuts it open with a can opener and smells the contents, finding them very unpleasant, pulls out the springs and measures them as if he were a clerk in a dry goods store, and when they squirm on the counter, squirts something on them to make them quiet, as if he were an exterminator. This treatment of an object as if it were something alive but not only that but something alive which is perpetually changing into something else, as in the fairy tales, is of course very Dickensian. In One A.M. the stuffed animals by which Charlie is frightened are no more alive than the folding bed with which he has so Buster Keaton-like an encounter, which recalls Dickens's remark that he was not sure whether it was his gift or his infirmity to be conscious of resemblances between wholly unrelated things which nobody else had ever been able to see.

All this of course passes much more quickly on the screen than it can be described, for there is a bewildering abundance of action in the Chaplin films. "He does things," said one of his early admirers, the great painter John Singer Sargent, who used to go to see his pictures in Boston nickelodeons with his friend Isabella Stewart Gardner, the creator of Fenway Court; "he does things, and you're lucky if you see them."[7] It was a sapient observation. We are lucky to have been alive in the only time thus far in which they could be seen; only probably nobody ever has seen them all. Everybody has been amused by the scene in The Kid in which Chaplin tries to teach Jackie Coogan table manners, but how many have noticed with Walter Kerr[8] that it is not the Kid's eating with his knife that he objects to but rather to his holding it so that he is in danger of cutting himself with its sharp edge? Kerr and Theodore Huff each tried to write down everything Chaplin did in the Pawnshop scene, and each missed some things that the other observed.

This amazing fertility being what it was, Chaplin's fondness for what, if he were a writer, we should have to call quoting himself is both interesting and curious. The dead end slum street of Easy Street reappears essentially in both A Dog's Life and The Kid, in the latter even in the heaven scene! The fight sequence in City Lights recalls The Champion. A dog atached to Chaplin's waist wreaks havoc on the dance floor in both A Dog's Life and The Gold Rush.

Modern Times recalls both the monkeyshines with the escalator
in The Floorwalker and the roller-skating in The Rink, and it
is Modern Times too that presents the most masterly example
of quotation with variation or development that we find in all
Chaplin. In The Tramp he starts off sadly but jauntily at
the end down the lonesome road. This is also the final fade-
out of Modern Times. Dispassionately considered, the future
does not look much brighter now than it did in The Tramp,
but this time he has a girl by his side, and with her he
walks down that road for the last time and out of silent films
forever. In life, though he did not know it yet, he was on
his way to find and to found the home of his own he had
said he always wanted, though it was not Paulette Goddard
but Oona O'Neill who was destined to give it to him.

     None of these considerations, I think, could cause much
disagreement. The situation is altered however when we come
to social criticism. It has been customary to find the most
striking early example of Chaplin's later tendencies in this
direction in a powerful scene near the beginning of The Immigrant. The immigrants sail past the Statue of Liberty in
New York harbor ("Give me your tired, your poor," etc.),
only to be roped in like cattle until they can be dragged out
to be examined by the impersonally brutal immigration inspec-
tors. Walter Kerr plays this down as social criticism in favor
of developing the case for Chaplin's philosophical detachment
(the man who can be everybody must also inevitably be nobody). Kerr cites his undeniably ambivalent treatment of
labor difficulties in Modern Times, where the workers have
no sooner returned after the reopening of the factory before
they idiotically vote a strike. For all this, I still find it difficult to believe that Chaplin can have used the scene in The
Immigrant or many others in his films without realizing their
implications. Paulette Goddard has been quoted as having
said that Charlie "sometimes thinks he thinks." Acute as
this is, it is not really devastating. It is hardly the business
of the artist as artist to do more, for he is always likely to
function far more effectively by his perceptions than his
formulations, and we must not forget that perceptions too can
be both penetrating and illuminating; if this were not so,
there would not be much point in reading Emerson. During
his later years, Mark Twain devoted much of his energy to
propaganda writing in various fields, but when the adherents
of the various causes he had seemed to support attempted to
bring him into line, expecting him to take out his membership

card and play the game according to the rules, they were
generally disappointed. "My instincts and interests are
merely literary," he wrote on one such occasion, "they rise
no higher, & I scatter from one interest to another, linger-
ing nowhere. I am not a bee. I am a lightning bug."
Chaplin, we may be sure, might have said much the same.
He was no joiner or party man. The Communists would have
been as unhappy with him as the Republicans.

Chaplin made fourteen films for Essanay, mostly two-
reelers, released between February 1, 1915 (His New Job)
and May 27, 1916 (Police).[9] As I have already observed,
The Tramp and The Bank seem to me the best of these. Not
only is the former memorable for its striking emergence of
human feeling, but the farm where the tramp finds employment
is a place and the people he encounters there, though characterized upon an elementary level, are unmistakably alive.
If the slapbang, knockabout gymnastics involved are not
superior in kind to what we had already seen in the Keystones, they are still executed with greater skill. The bid
for sympathy carries over into The Bank, where the fact
that the cashier, to whom Edna the stenographer is attracted,
and the hapless janitor, who is enamored of her, have the
same given name leads to false hopes on the part of the latter
which are satisfied only in one of Chaplin's most successful
employments of the dream as a vehicle of wish-fulfilment.
The immediate predecessor of this film, A Woman, is most
memorable for Chaplin's amusing female impersonation, but
the implacable Sime Silverman still understood him so little
as to declare that unless he could find a good scenario writer
he was through, and when A Night in the Show appeared in
November 1915 Julian Johnson echoed him to the extent of
sighing "Oh, for a Chaplin author!" That jewel Chaplin
would find all right. But his name was Charles Chaplin, who
was the only person who could possibly have served successfully in this capacity.

In 1916 Chaplin went to Mutual, and it was announced
that he would make twelve two-reel comedies in a year for
$670,000 (it would actually take him a year and a half). The
first, The Floorwalker, was released on May 15, 1916, and
the last, The Adventurer, on October 22, 1917. In between
came The Fireman, The Vagabond, One A.M., The Count,
The Pawnshop, Behind the Screen, The Rink, Easy Street,
The Cure, and The Immigrant.

Several of these have already been referred to in various connections. They were not all equally good; I doubt that anybody would put either The Floorwalker or The Fireman at the head of the list. Taken as a group however they were certainly the best series of two-reelers ever made or to be made, and probably Easy Street would poll more votes as the finest of all such films than any other possible contender for that title. Chaplin was to make immensely greater single films later on, but never again would he accomplish anything like so much in a comparable period.

With The Floorwalker Chaplin added an important new comedian to his company, the immense, on the screen ogreish looking Scot, Eric Campbell, who off screen was reputed one of the gentlest of men. Campbell appeared in every one of the Mutuals except One A.M. and then managed to get himself killed in an auto crash before he could move over into the feature period. He got his best chance as the bully of Easy Street, who tangled with Chaplin after the latter, this time a genuine bum had got religion at the Hope Mission, under the gentle mourner's bench ministrations of Edna Purviance and Albert Austin, and joined the police force. Ironically it was Campbell's most spectacular feat in his battle with Officer Charlie that proved his undoing. When he bent down the lamp post, he simply gave Charlie the chance to get the bully's head rammed into the lamp, where he could turn on the gas and asphyxiate him. Everybody else had been frightened away by the battle, and when they returned to find the bully lying on the pavement, Charlie naturally received credit for a conquest. Easy Street then became a model community, and in the last scene we found all its denizens flocking dutifully to the mission for Sunday morning service, including the gigantic Campbell, in a suit several sizes too small for him, with the wife he had hitherto used mainly as a punching bag thoughtfully and ostentatiously placed on the wall side of the sidewalk.

Campbell got his next best opportunity in the most thoughtful film of the Mutual series, The Immigrant, where he played the frightening waiter who goes through an elaborate cat-and-mouse game with Charlie, who believes himself to have lost the only money he had to pay for the food he had ordered for Edna and himself. I must not however leave the impression that Chaplin's Mutuals depended for their effect on Campbell any more than they did, for several of them

were worthy of far more comment and analysis than I have
space for here. The Vagabond has much of the charm of
The Tramp and is executed with far more finesse, and The
Count, The Rink, and The Cure are all vintage Chaplin.
Some have felt that the last film of the series, The Adventurer, which in some respects looked forward to The Pilgrim,
had less depth and more slapstick than its immediate predecessors. This may well be true, but it was certainly funny
enough richly to merit the popularity it enjoyed.

Chaplin went next to First National, under whose banner eight films were released, of which the first was A Dog's
Life (April 14, 1918) and the last The Pilgrim (February 26,
1923). Unless we wish to count Tillie's Punctured Romance,
which as already observed was not really a Chaplin film, and
the aborted "Life," which was begun at Essanay but of which
only fragments have been seen in other films, The Kid (February 6, 1921) was his first feature-length film, but his First
National output included three significant films of intermediate
length: A Dog's Life and Shoulder Arms (both 1918, each
in three reels) and The Pilgrim (four reels). The First
National two-reelers were Sunnyside and A Day's Pleasure,
in which latter Jackie Coogan made his generally unobserved
screen debut before The Kid (both 1919), The Idle Class
(1921), and Pay Day (1922).

The hopelessly inept working title of A Dog's Life was
"I Should Worry"; it is said to have been inadvertently but
very happily renamed by Sir Harry Lauder, when he visited
the studio during the agonies attending its creation and told
Chaplin he was leading a dog's life. The name has a double
meaning, referring to both the life the dog leads and that
which the man shares with him; the two are neatly paralleled and interwoven. The way man and beast work together
at the lunch wagon, where Scraps wolfs the frankfurters out
of the frying pan while his master steals one muffin after
another off the plate and crams them into his mouth, without
either apparently chewing or swallowing them, while the pro-
prietor is turned the other way, is only one example of what
occurs throughout. The gulf between two different levels
of creation has been bridged with ease.

Chaplin himself wrote that when he began this film he
was "beginning to think of comedy in a structural sense, and
to become conscious of its architectural form. Each sequence

implied the next sequence, all of them relating to the whole."[10]
Walter Kerr has described these sequences as "six balletis-
tically conceived and executed 'turns.'" and Chaplin's fault-
less timing was never better exemplified than here. In the
first he eludes the policeman who is trying to apprehend
him for stealing a frankfurter from a wandering vendor by
always managing to roll to the other side of the broken fence
beside which the action is staged; in the second somebody
always crowds in to the window at the employment office a
split second ahead of him. Whatever social criticism may appear in this film is much less explicit than it afterwards became with Chaplin, but David Robinson is fully justified
when, in his definitive biography of the actor,[11] he speaks
of the "core of reality" the picture contains.

The backgrounds are grubby, often depressing, sometimes even disgusting, except at the very end, where, in
glaring yet somehow effective contrast to the rest of the
film, we find Charlie and Edna in the completely unrealistic
fairy-tale cottage their unexpected windfall has enabled them
to set up. Finally they bend lovingly over the cradle where
the spectator expects them to find a baby but which is occupied only by Scraps with a litter of puppies. I believe, by
the way, that Kerr forces the note when he writes that this
is intended to suggest "that this is all we are to expect of
this family." The contrast between expectation and discovery
is all we are entitled to at this point; one must not be too
subtle in interpreting even Chaplin.

By the box office standard, Shoulder Arms was one of
the most fantastically successful of all the Chaplin films; if
it seems at all less funny now than it did in 1918, the
reason is simply that, being by all means the most topical
thing he ever did, it has inevitably dated somewhat. He
made it against all advices (Hollywood thought it dangerously
unsafe to "kid" the war), and it was originally planned as
a five-reeler. Part I was to deal with Charlie's miserable
home life with four children and a virago of a wife, who was
not to appear but make her presence manifest by flying
missiles and other tokens of affection. From this the summons from the draft board would come as a relief, and considerable footage was to be devoted to the difficulties incident to his physical examination, during which he would
find himself considerably embarrassed by being obliged to
run about before stenographers and others with inadequate

covering. Part II was to be substantially what we now have,
and Part III was to depict a banquet where Charlie, having
captured thirteen Germans by, as he says, surrounding them
and topped this off by bagging the whole high command, was
to be honored by the Allied heads of state. Part III was
never made, but Chaplin spent a month on Part I before de-
ciding to junk it (a bit was used in 1986 in "Unknown Chaplin"). As the picture now opens, we find Charlie the most
inept recruit in the training camp, and the whole overseas
portion, which is practically the entire film, is first a nightmare and then a wish-fulfillment dream; this was the most
elaborate use Chaplin ever made of a time-honored device
which runs back almost to the dawn of narrative itself. At
one point filming was briefly interrupted to make Chaplin's
little propaganda picture, The Bond, but this was not the
only difficulty encountered. At one point he was so discouraged that he afterwards claimed he might have junked
the whole picture if Douglas Fairbanks had not roared over
it uncontrollably when it was screened for him.

It is true that many of the scenes in Shoulder Arms
burlesque if not the war itself at least the popular serious
war pictures of the time, which is no doubt the reason why
Shoulder Arms is still enjoyed while To Hell with the Kaiser
and The Kaiser, the Beast of Berlin are left to enjoy the
oblivion they have richly deserved. This caused none of
the trouble that had been feared; probably neither the pa-
triots nor the patrioteers became aware of it. For that matter, the film was still close enough to the mood of the moment so that it ought to have been reasonably safe. Chaplin
hated war, but he was certainly not a consistent pacifist,
nor, as I have already suggested, a consistent ideologist in
any aspect. In World War I The Bond was supplemented by
his own Liberty Loan tours, and in World War II he was to
agitate earnestly for the opening of a second front.

Probably the most hilarious sequence in Shoulder Arms
is that made up of the scenes in which Charlie wanders
about (it was filmed in 100 degree heat) disguised as a tree
and stands in imminent danger of being chopped down for
firewood; the weakest, I think, are those in which both he
and his brother Sydney go to bed in a flooded dugout (surely Chaplin does force the note when he tries to fluff up his
submerged pillow). The most touching moment in the
trenches is the scene, quite justly praised by the great

English actor Squire Bancroft, in which, having received no
mail of his own, Charlie reads another doughboy's letter over
the latter's shoulder, his face reflecting sympathetically every
shade of anxiety and relief the other experiences. But there
is tenderness too as well as humor in his scenes with Edna
as a French girl living in a ruined house, most of which has
been shot away, and there was never a better illustration of
Chaplin's penchant for going through all the correct forms exactly, even when they have become perfectly meaningless,
than the way he locks the door and pulls down the shade
after entering this ruin. It is a tribute to both players that,
even today, it is difficult not, in some degree, to share their
anxiety when the Germans arrive.

       The basic idea in The Pilgrim is that an escaped con-
vict should steal a clergyman's clothes while the latter is taking a swim, after which, arriving at the town where the
minister is expected to conduct his first service, he is obliged to undertake functions for which, to put it mildly, he
has not been trained. His sermon, which is the story of
David and Goliath in pantomime, is mainly relished by a small
boy, whose appreciation inspires the "minister" to acknowledge
the applause in terms which would have been more appropriate
to a vaudeville headliner than a preacher. The original idea
for this film, as described by David Robinson, was much
more mordant and sophisticated than anything that reached
the screen; indeed Robinson hardly exaggerates when he says
that it looks forward to Monsieur Verdoux. As it stands, the
worst one can say of The Pilgrim is that it is hardly respect-
ful to churchgoing people or to organized religion. The
Deacon (Mack Swain) has a whiskey bottle sticking out of
his back pocket and seems to be engaged in an intrigue with
a woman, but since all the church people except Mrs. Brown,
her daughter (Edna Purviance), and the humane and understanding Sheriff are presented in terms of such broad caricature that they could not possibly be taken seriously, little
of the offense that had been feared seems to have material-
ized. In The Pilgrim Chaplin "throws away" more fine
touches than any other comedian would have had on hand to
stress. When he buys his railroad ticket he grasps the bars
of the ticket window as if they were the bars of his cell.
He runs off in fear from the elopers who want him to marry
them, tries to ride under a railway coach even when he has
a ticket in his pocket, bolts from Henry Bergman sitting next
to him in the train when he notices that he has a star on his

vest, sees twelve choir singers as twelve jurors, and holds
out his wrists for handcuffs upon encountering the Sheriff.

Essentially The Pilgrim is situation comedy; there is
more story-interest than in either of the other films, and the
Brown home is a real place, where the audience, like Chaplin, is glad to linger. There is also a diabolical child with
a passion for hitting people, who has a non-stop talker for
a mother and an understandably morose father, excellently
played by Sydney Chaplin. But the real complication is
provided by the appearance of our hero's old "college chum"
(less euphemistically, cell-mate), who tries to rob the Deacon
of his wallet and Mrs. Brown of her mortgage money, leading
to heroic and ultimately successful opposing efforts on
Charlie's part and brilliant, faultlessly timed teamwork between Chaplin and Charles Riesner as the crook, all of it
skillfully managed to give the convict-minister a chance to
redeem himself.

What this all leads up to is one of the most brilliant
and satisfactory conclusions of any Chaplin film. Having
identified the convict, the Sheriff performs his duty by taking him into custody, but instead of carrying him to jail, he
rides with him to the Mexican border, where he asks him to
pick some flowers for him. Charlie must cross the border to
achieve this, but he obediently brings them back to his cap-
tor, and it is not until he is literally kicked over the line
that he succeeds in reading the Sheriff's mind. For a moment he is sure that he has found peace and freedom at
last, but Mexican revolutionaries shooting at each other soon
disabuse him of this idea, and we last glimpse him running
away from the camera as fast as he can, with one foot in
Mexico and the other in the States.

The Kid, "a picture with a smile--perhaps a tear," was
released on February 6, 1921 and greeted with international
acclaim. Chaplin's undisputed masterwork to date, it still
remains one of his finest achievements. It also signalized the
emancipation of screen comedy from the old two-reel format
and a too constricting reliance upon slapstick formulas.

The triumph was not Chaplin's alone. Part of it belonged to six-year-old Jackie Coogan in the title role. Chaplin had glimpsed the child doing a bit at the end of his
father's vaudeville act at the Orpheum Theater, but Jackie's

film possibilities did not occur to him until he heard a fortunately false report that Arbuckle had signed him up. The
star's generosity in sharing his spotlight with a child, the
tenderness he manifested toward him on screen and the patience nobody could avoid knowing he must have exercised
behind it in order to get such a performance out of an in-
fant--all this added up to the fullest and most winning revelation of Chaplin's own humanity that his public had yet been
vouchsafed.

        Not that the old slapstick was all gone, nor the old
caricature either. The latter survived mainly in the Bully
with whom the Tramp was compelled to tangle through the attack the Bully's little brother makes upon the Kid (the Bully
even demonstrates his prowess by bending down the lamppost,
like Eric Campbell in Easy Street) and, to a lesser extent, in
the comic "country doctor" who comes to attend the Kid when
he is taken sick (why a "country doctor," incidentally, in
the city?). Such criticism as the film has inspired has not
been directed at these things however but rather at its alleged sentimentality and especially at the heaven scene in the
Tramp's dream at the end, where he, the Kid, the Policeman,
and even a dog cavort with wings in a slum court; when
Chaplin visited him, even J. M. Barrie went out of his way
to criticize all this as unnecessary.

        The line between sentiment and sentimentality is thin
and wavering, and it would not be reasonable to expect everybody to agree as to just where it lies. For me Charlie's awkward if ingenious attempts to care for the child's needs are a
daringly successful combination of comedy and tenderness,
and his rescue of the Kid from the truck in which he is being
carted out to the orphan asylum as exciting as any rescue
performed in the movies by cowboys or cavalrymen. But the
dismissal of Edna Purviance, "whose only sin was motherhood,"
with her illegitimate baby, from the county institution at the
beginning of the picture is sentimental, and her implied equa-
tion, pictorially conveyed, with Christ carrying his cross up
Calvary is considerably worse than that. Later her transformation between scenes from a lone girl, too poor to care
for her child, to a successful prima donna is the very stuff
of cheap romantic fiction. When Chaplin in later years re-
edited the film, he cut the scenes, heavily loaded with pretty
obvious symbolism, showing a sadfaced young bride marrying
an old man, obviously not for love, and he spared us the

sight of Edna with a kind of halo around her head, formed
by light shining through a stained-glass window, but he let
the cross symbolism stand. Was he also responsible, I wonder, for the disappearance from prints of the film now being
circulated of the amusing scene in which the Tramp makes
an embarrassed examination of the baby to determine whether
he has a boy or a girl on his hands? If so, he was here
making more of a concession to his Miss Nancy critics than I
should have expected from him.

As for the heaven scenes specifically, I am not prepared to go to the barricades for either defense or attack.
The best thing about them is that they contain nothing that
would not fall comfortably within the range of the Tramp's
experience and imagination, but they do not seem to me to
reflect either Chaplin's comic genius or his inventiveness at
the height of their creativity. The best touch comes at the
very end--the shooting of the Tramp-angel, just before the
Policeman wakes him up to take him to the Kid, now happily
reunited with his mother. Indeed the pretty obvious deriva-
tion of this incident from the shooting of the Wendy-bird
when she flies to the Never-Never Land in Peter Pan even
makes Barrie's criticism seem a little awkward.[12]

The sentimentalities too, one must admit, are nicely
flavored with aspic. Jackie's first appearance, now aged five,
sitting on the curb-stone manicuring his nails, is a prime
example of the familiar Chaplin trade mark, elegance in
squalor. More important is the Tramp's quite understandable reluctance to assume the responsibilities of fatherhood.
When Edna puts her baby into a parked automobile with a
note begging the finder to love and care for him, the car is
stolen by two thieves who are unaware of his presence in it.
When they find him, they dump him summarily in the alley
where the Tramp stumbles upon him. He tries first to dispose of him by putting him into a baby carriage which already has one occupant, and when this does not work, he
passes him off on an old man who attempts to play the same
trick on the same woman, with rather terrifying results.
The baby back on his hands, Charlie sits down on the curb
beside a sewer opening, lifts the cover, and gazes into it,
obviously tempted for a moment to find the solution of his
problem here, but I doubt that any audience has ever been
really afraid he may accept this.

Nevertheless there is an underlying anarchistic, anti-
authoritarian note in The Kid that makes it a characteristic
product of Chaplin's mind and art. You get this not only in
what is said about the baby's illegitimacy at the beginning
but much more clearly in the violently unfriendly, Intolerance-
like portrayal of the authorities who later on try to take the
Kid away from the Tramp. In a sense nobody could have
made a better or more tender father than Charlie, but he can
hardly be said to be bringing up the Kid as a law-abiding
citizen. The very first idea that occurred to Chaplin when
he decided to try to make a picture with Jackie was that of
the scenes in which they should go out together, the Kid
breaking windows by throwing stones through them and the
Tramp as glazier just happening along then to mend them for
a consideration. The Polizei are as much the enemies here
as in any Keystone, and when the officer appears just as the
Kid is preparing his arm for a good swing, the latter instant-
ly turns himself into something like a juggler, precisely as
Chaplin himself would have done. When that same functionary
shows again just as one of his victims is paying Charlie for
her mended window, the latter promptly returns her dollar,
and when the Kid stays close enough to him to awaken sus-
picion, he kicks him away as if he were a strange stray dog.

There is one interesting exception to all this in The
Kid however. Religion is not generally very prominent in
Chaplin films. But the Tramp and the Kid carefully say grace
before meat, and after the latter has been smuggled through
a window into Charlie's bed in the flophouse, he rouses the
suspicions of the person in charge by the necessity that lies
upon him not to go to the toilet, as the audience might have
expected, but to kneel down to say his prayers, thus obliging
the Tramp to dig up another dime. When all is said and done
however, The Kid owes the affection in which it has always
been held not to any ideas which may or may not be involved
or expressed in it nor yet to any technical perfections but to
the warm human feeling by which it is irradiated and the
charm of an adorable child.

Though Chaplin had joined with Mary Pickford, Douglas
Fairbanks, and D. W. Griffith to form United Artists Corporation in the spring of 1919, his First National contract was
still hanging around his neck like an albatross, and United
Artists did not get a picture out of him until 1923 nor one in
which he starred until 1925. His partners were not happy

about this nor pleased that he should insist upon beginning
with A Woman of Paris (October 1, 1923), with which he
hoped to make an independent star of Edna Purviance.   This
was a serious, sophisticated "Continental" drama, very much
out of tune with the then dominant trends in American film-
making.   Chaplin's direction was praised (he made a brief,
unbilled, unrecognized appearance in one scene), but the
film did very little for the United Artists exchequer nor did
it prevent Miss Purviance's career from grinding to a halt.

Production on The Gold Rush began in December 1923
and ended on May 21, 1925.   The official release date is
August 16, 1925, the date of the New York première, but
Hollywood had seen the picture at Grauman's Egyptian
Theater on June 26.

The ultimate source was a stereoscopic picture of hope-
ful miners climbing the long slope leading to the Chilkoot
Pass which Chaplin saw at Pickfair one Sunday morning, but
the scene in which Charlie's partner, Big Jim McKay (Mack
Swain), in his hunger-induced delirium, sees him as a
chicken and takes after him with a knife was suggested by
the Donner Party tragedy of 1846-47.   Eighty-seven people
were trapped by snow without food in the Sierra Nevada
mountains, with the result that about half starved to death
and the rest were said to have kept themselves alive by can-
nibalism.   Theodore Huff conjectured that Harold Lloyd's
Safety Last might have influenced the closing cabin scenes
and F. W. Murnau's The Last Laugh the happy ending.
Still working without a scenario, Chaplin began developing
his film in "a series of comedy sequences" and discarded
some of them, including one which involved love passages
with an Eskimo girl.   The epical opening shots of the unend-
ing snake-line line of miners approaching the pass was filmed
in Nevada, but most of the work on location was done, under
painfully primitive conditions, at Truckee, beside Lake Tahoe,
not far from the actual Donner Pass, and some of the snow
scenes were shot in southern California with artificial snow.

Chaplin had said that his next film must be an epic,
and he is on record as having later referred to The Gold
Rush as "the picture I want to be remembered by."   There
has never, I think, been any serious question that it is one
of his finest achievements, though photographically it is
less rewarding to watch than some of the others, as the

predominance of snowscapes becomes monotonous. Personally too I find Chaplin's introduction as a "long prospector" teetering along the edge of a precipice, with a bear coming out of a cave behind him and then lumbering off unseen into another, infelicitous and glaringly movie-like in the bad sense, especially coming as it does after the stark reality of the great opening shots. To a certain extent I would say the same also of the climactic teetering of the cabin at the end until it goes over into the abyss a split second after Charlie has got out, though what goes on inside during his and Big Jim's attempts to get out is all out of the top drawer. At the beginning however, the note of reality, daringly but triumphantly blended with the best Chaplin high jinks, is soon regained in the cabin of the killer Wolf Larsen, where the Tramp is unable to obey Larsen's orders to get out because the wind keeps blowing him back in. Big Jim finally proves too strong for Larsen himself and gets his gun away from him, after it has strangely persisted in pointing itself at Charlie, much like the shell from the Big Bertha in The Great Dictator. It must have been a tricky business to divide so much of the action in The Gold Rush between the two cabins, but the structural problems involved here seem to me to have been successfully solved.

As we have seen, Chaplin wanted The Gold Rush to be an epic. Epic or not, much of it is straight comedy drama rather than what his audiences had been accustomed to in other Chaplin films. Lita Grey, who had appeared briefly as the Flirtatious Angel in the heaven scene of The Kid, was originally cast as the dance hall girl with whom the Tramp falls in love, but after she became the second Mrs. Chaplin, the role went instead to Georgia Hale, who had made a good impression in Josef von Sternberg's The Salvation Hunters and who turned in a vividly pert performance which stood in sharp contrast to the more restful placidity to which we had become accustomed with Edna Purviance. The most famous comedy routines in the film are the Oceana roll dance which Chaplin does in imagination at the table, entertaining Georgia and her friends at the New Year's Eve dinner to which they never came, the boot-cooking and eating to which he and Mack Swain are reduced when facing starvation, and the scenes in which we see Chaplin as a chicken through his companion's delirium-crazed eyes. There were eleven takes of the roll dance, and if there is a single grace or a single affectation of the ballet dancer that Chaplin did not take off to

the life I do not know what it is.   There were sixty-three
takes of the boot-eating scene, to which three shooting days
were devoted, and we are told that the after effects of the
licorice the two men consumed were not pleasant.   But the
wonderful thing about this scene is not that starving men
are eating leather but rather that Chaplin was able to open
up a shoe as if it were a roast fowl, handle shoe laces like
succulent spaghetti, and suck off the nails by which the
sole was fastened with such connoisseur-like relish.   By the
same token, what makes the chicken scene so hilarious is
not that Chaplin wears a very funny chicken costume but
rather the amazing resemblances between his human movements
and those of a barnyard fowl.

If these are the highlights, there is much more besides.
Though only a few examples can be given here, mention must
surely be made of the elegance of his cooking, even though
he is only cooking a dirty old shoe (this too, then, must be
added to the skills whose mastery he could conjure up when
a picture required it.) What gourmet cook could be more
fastidious than he about wiping a speck off a platter before
setting the boot down upon it, or, for that matter, what
could be more exquisitely inappropriate than his rushing to
set the table neatly the moment he has shot the bear that
will deliver him and Big Jim from starvation or each other?
His old time craft appears when he piles up the snow he has
removed from before a building in front of the place next
door, whose owner had churlishly refused to hire him, thus
necessitating his employment there also, and his virtually
reducing Henry Bergman to the status of a servant when the
latter has taken him in out of the cold to feed him and thaw
him out.   The same kind of luck he enjoyed in Easy Street
when, having asphyxiated Eric Campbell, he gained the un-
deserved reputation of having bested him by brute force,
attends him here when his opponent in the dance hall is
knocked out by a heavy clock falling upon him.   On the
other hand, the spectator who is not forced to recall any experience of his own by the embarrassment Charlie suffers
when Georgia seems mistakenly to be making advances to him
or responding to his own timid interest in her must have had
a very fortunate life, and nothing could be at once funnier
and more pitiful than her mock-acceptance of his invitation to
dinner and then returning to pick up her forgotten gloves
just in time to catch him going through the seemingly insane
antics that register his exaltation.

Finally one may ask of The Gold Rush whether it contains any of the social criticism one has come to look for in
Chaplin films. Is it too fanciful, I wonder, to find a touch
of it at the close, in the contrast between the way our Lone
Prospector and his partner have been regarded all through
the picture and the respect they enjoy now, after Big Jim
has found his "mountain of gold"? It is the difference between night and day, yet, except that they are better
dressed, nothing has changed about them except that they
are now rich. Not even Georgia seems unaffected by this.
True, she tries to protect Charlie even when she believes
him to be a stowaway on the boat in which they are both returning to the States. But would she have gone along with
his introduction of her as his prospective wife if he had
been as she had first seen him in the dance hall?

Chaplin's next film, The Circus (January 6, 1928), requires much less discussion than The Gold Rush, and since
it has sometimes been downgraded with reference to his other
features, I hasten to add that I do not say this disparaging-
ly. The only thing that can reasonably be said against The
Circus is that it marks no fresh development in Chaplin's
work, being essentially a series of amusing comedy routines
or gags, with the Little Tramp's affection for and attempt to
protect the helpless young equestrienne who is being abused
by her brutal stepfather, the owner of the circus, providing
the by now indispensable element of tenderness. Of course
he supposes her to return his affection, and of course she
gives her heart to the high-wire artist Rex instead, and after
Charlie has risked his life trying to become a high-wire artist himself, in order to impress her, he magnanimously re-
linquishes her to her lover and turns away from her and the
circus alike down the same lonesome road he had negotiated
as far back as The Tramp. Georgia Hale being unavailable
at the time of production, the feminine lead went instead to
Merna Kennedy, who turned in an acceptable though not
memorable performance (the poor girl was to die of heart
failure in 1944 at the age of thirty-five).

The circus which provides the background for the action of this film is a small affair, traveling in "the sticks,"
and the Tramp becomes a successful performer by accident
when his naturally awkward actions, upon chance forcing him
into the ring, rouse the mirth of an audience, bored by the
tired regular performers. The complication that develops is

that the Little Tramp is only funny by nature, not art, and his greedy employer keeps him from realizing that he is the hit of the show so that he can keep him on at a property man's salary. Chaplin was forced to retain and maintain a circus for a whole year, since though he was making a rather simple film, production, which began on January 11, 1926, was anything but that. About everything that could have happened to upset schedules did happen, including a studio fire and, even worse, the agony and scandal attending Lita Grey's divorce proceedings, which turned Chaplin's hair white and reduced him and his company to idleness for some time.

The basic idea with which the film began was Chaplin's vision of himself as "on a high place troubled by something else, monkeys or things that come to me and I can't get away from them." It was thus that he described it to Henry Bergman.[13] At this time he was thinking of the situation in terms of a vaudeville act; it was Bergman who persuaded him he must have a circus and taught him tightrope walking besides. This man, who lived from 1868 to 1946, was by all means the most versatile actor (he also functioned as an assistant director) in Chaplin's regular company; he apparently could handle any sort of role, male or female; it seems the only assignment he ever refused was when Chaplin wanted him to play the owner of the circus in this picture. Because Bergman did not believe he could bring himself to abuse a girl he accepted the less important role of an old clown instead.

Filming began, out of sequence, with the tightrope scenes, of which more than 700 takes were made, the last not until the end of February, and Chaplin even went back to the tightrope for four more days after the preview of The Circus at Glendale, California, on October 28, 1927. The Little Tramp was supposed to have a pulley attached to his back, but it came off by accident, which did not make it easier to cope with the monkeys who stripped off his pants and got their hands and tails into his ears and eyes and mouth. This was the most spectacular scene, but it was not necessarily funnier than a number of others nor more dangerous to make than the scenes showing Chaplin in the lion's cage, of which 200 takes were made. At the beginning of the film however, the fun house provides opportunities for quite as much entertainment as these more dangerous sequences. Chaplin alone in the labyrinthine confusions of the hall of mirrors is quite funny enough, but when he is joined by the policeman and

the crook, confusion is worse confounded. There is more fun
when he horns in on the vanishing lady and reduces the ma-
gician's act to nonsense, but perhaps the best of all is when,
to escape the policeman who is pursuing him, he turns himself into a mechanized dummy on the exterior of the fun
house.

Like The Gold Rush, City Lights, "A Comedy Romance
in Pantomime," has always been regarded as one of the high
peaks in the Chaplin range. It began with the idea of a circus clown who has lost his sight and must go through various comic-pathetic maneuvers to conceal his misfortune from
a sick daughter, and it was only after this had been discarded as "too icky" that the blindness was transferred to a
flower girl. The manic-depressive drunken millionaire whom
Charlie saves from drowning himself (and nearly drowning
him too in the process) and who only recognizes him and
makes him free of his mansion, his purse, and his Rolls-
Royce when he is generously drunk but throws him out when
he is meanly and curmudgeonly sober was originally conceived
as one of two rich men who should "conduct the experiment
of giving a wretched tramp a night of luxury and pleasure
and then dumping him back on the Embankment where they
found him."[14] This was soon combined with the germ of what
became the basic idea in Charlie's relationship with the girl,
that is to say, setting one helpless person over against another to whom he should seem something splendid. The famous ending which has already been discussed in these pages,
where the Tramp, after his release from the jail term he has
served because he had been unjustly suspected of stealing
the money he had given the girl to cover the expenses incur-
red in recovering her sight, re-encounters her who had never
seen him before, was in mind almost from the beginning,
though not in quite the form in which we have it now.

Shooting began on December 27, 1928, after nearly two
years work on the story. Huff says that 800,000 feet of film
were exposed and that the cost of production was $1,500,000.
After a sneak preview at the Tower Theater, the official West
Coast première was held at the new Los Angeles Theater, on
January 30, 1931, when both Chaplin and the audience were
infuriated by the incredible stupidity of the management in
interrupting the film so that the audience might have time to
admire the building! Chaplin, already nervous about the
reception of a silent film in 1931, and further incensed by

what he considered lukewarmness on the part of United
Artists and the difficulties he experienced in getting the
bookings he wanted, rented the George M. Cohan Theater
for the New York première, which occurred on February 6.
The picture ran there for twelve weeks and, according to
Chaplin's autobiography, showed a profit of $400,000.

Production however was far from being roses all the
way. One delay was caused by the remodeling of the studio
necessitated by the widening of La Brea Avenue. The prize-
fight sequence, which was made last, with Hank Mann, whose
association with Chaplin went back to Essanay days, went
expeditiously—four days of rehearsal and six of shooting.
But Chaplin fired Henry Clive, who played the eccentric millionaire until Harry Myers replaced him, after six weeks of
filming, because he refused to do the attempted drunken
suicide scene in cold water, and he dismissed Harry Crocker
as a kind of assistant director for some reason neither man
ever spelled out.

The great problem however was the flower girl. The
difficulty here was to find somebody who could seem blind
without turning up the whites of her eyes. Chaplin thought
he had found her in Virginia Cherrill, a Chicago society
girl with no theatrical experience and with one of her di-
vorces already behind her, but the two never achieved real
rapport. Miss Cherrill lacked not only professional experience
but in Chaplin's opinion a professional attitude also. At one
time he kept her on the payroll for six months without ever
using her, during which time he tested both Georgia Hale,
his associate in The Gold Rush, and the then unknown girl
who afterwards enjoyed a brief, pleasant career as Marian
Marsh. (Miss Hale desperately wanted the role; how she
would have played it, I have no idea, but Edna Purviance
would have been just right for it in her younger days.)
Chaplin took five days to rehearse one scene with Miss
Cherrill that ran seventy seconds, but in his autobiography
he generously admits that this was partly his own fault for
having worked himself up "into a neurotic state of wanting
perfection." The final close-ups, among the few really classical moments in screen history, required seventeen retakes.

Walter Kerr has described the beautiful structure Chaplin achieved in City Lights so well as to leave nothing for
subsequent writers to do but quote him:

The comedy and the love story depend utterly on
each other; neither can move until the other requires
it to do so. If there is a prize-fighting sequence,
hilarious in itself, or a street-sweeping sequence or
a soap-and-sandwich sequence, it is only because
Chaplin must attempt these things in order to find
money for the blind girl he loves. No gag is gratuitous; it grows directly out of the need of a helpless
girl and her knight unvaliant.[15]

Yet the gags are funny enough in themselves so that nobody
would have the heart to dispense with them even if they
were gratuitous. Chaplin and Albert Austin are both well
accommodated in the scene in which the sandwich of Charlie's
white wing associate gets mixed up with the bar of soap with
which Charlie is washing himself, but the white wing episode
as a whole is more subtly underplayed. Like Charlie's other
enterprises, his work here has been undertaken to raise
money for the girl, but the procession of horses at the corner
of the street where he is working, climaxed by the sudden unexpected appearance of a circus elephant is enough to threaten
even his devotion. When a loose thread from his clothing
manages to get itself involved with the ball of wool the girl
is winding up, he is too much the gentleman to tell her what
has happened but contents himself by squirming until she has
finished. The humor is broader in the early sequence where
he puts on a pretty good imitation of an art connoisseur in
order to indulge himself admiring the statue of a nude girl in
an art store window while standing on a sidewalk which opens
and closes from one minute to the next to accommodate an as-
cending and descending elevator.

Sound effects are used when Charlie at a party half
swallows a whistle which makes its presence known to the dis-
ruption of a singer's performance and in the very first scene,
where he is found asleep when the tarpaulin covering a civic
monument is withdrawn for a dedication ceremony at which
both the mayor and an unidentified female dignitary are making noises which burlesque not only the gabble generally
emitted on such occasions but the then comparatively new
sound pictures themselves. Since the monument is dedicated
to "Peace and Prosperity," perhaps the crowning touch comes
when the hapless Tramp, trying desperately to extricate himself from his predicament, is impaled through his pants by the
sword held by one of the figures on the monument and im-

mobilized in mid-air, with his derby pressed reverently against his breast until the band finishes playing that other aesthetic monument of peaceful sentiment, the National Anthem.

Modern Times, released February 5, 1936, nearly nine years after The Jazz Singer, was not only the last of Chaplin's silent films, but the last true silent film ever made by anybody,[16] and surely it is one of the richest of all his pictures in its social criticism.[17]

According to Chaplin's own account in his autobiography, Modern Times began with his perception of Paulette Goddard "as being somewhat of a gamine. This would be a wonderful quality for me to get on the screen. I could imagine us meeting in a crowded patrol wagon, the tramp and this gamine, and the tramp being very gallant and offering her his seat." Then he remembered what a reporter had told him of the factory belt system in Detroit and how it reduced healthy young farm boys who had been lured into the city into nervous wrecks.[18] The producers of René Clair's A Nous la Liberté at one time considered Chaplin guilty of unauthorized borrowings from that film, but Clair himself, who admired Chaplin greatly and considered himself indebted to him, seems to have been unmoved.

Work began on October 11, 1934, and the last retakes were made on August 30, 1935, the café scenes, which took twelve days and employed 250 extras, being shot last. Five weeks had been spent on the department store scenes, with the roller skating, in which, thanks to trick photography, Chaplin seems to be skating blindfolded on the edge of an open space, using up eight days. The factory set cost $50,000, and the slum cityscape set covered five acres. The total cost of the production was $1,500,000, and 215,000 feet were exposed. After previews in San Francisco and Glendale, the picture opened at the Rivoli in New York on February 5, 1936.

The opening shots are as masterly in their way as the beginning of The Gold Rush: animals are being driven to the slaughter while human beings are herded in very much the same fashion into factories and subway stations. The viewer must draw the parallel between the successive shots himself, but the materials are there. The first sequence is

in the assembly line factory (we never learn nor does it matter what is being made), where Chaplin is seen tightening
bolts on a rapidly moving conveyor belt, under constantly
increasing pressure, until he breaks down under a compulsion to tighten everything that even remotely resembles a
bolt, even if it is only an ornamental button on a woman's
dress. It is during this sequence of course that he is
punished by the feeding machine which is being demonstrated
as a means of speeding up efficiency by eliminating the lunch
period but which goes haywire and on which only the auto-
matic napkin always seems to work perfectly. Obviously
Chaplin is not saying that this is a realistically documented
picture of conditions in factories, but he is saying that the
logical tendency of modern mechanization lies in this direction. It is all a perfect commentary on Emerson's "Things
are in the saddle and ride mankind."

Always polite and helpful in his Happy Hooligan aspect,
the Tramp gets into jail when he picks up the red "Danger"
flag that falls off the back of a truck and runs after the
driver to return it, for a protest parade comes up behind
him, and he is mistaken by the police for the leader of a
Communist demonstration. During his stay behind bars he
becomes a hero when, having sided with authority in pre-
venting a jailbreak, he is thereafter treated so well that he
is reluctant to leave when his pardon comes through and,
once free, does his best to get back in, where he can be
comfortable and sure of sustenance.

He meets "the Gamin," as the captions call her, not in
a patrol wagon, as he had first conceived their meeting, but
after what she had done to get there, stealing a loaf of
bread out of a baker's supply wagon. His attempt to save
her by presenting himself as the thief is not wholly disinterested therefore, gallant as he is about it. Neither does it
work, for the well-dressed informer persists in her identifi-
cation of the true culprit, and the film is nowhere more anti-
authoritarian than at this point. The girl is the eldest
daughter of an unemployed workman, and she and her little
sisters have nothing to eat.

The Tramp must make his own plans therefore, which
he does by ordering an enormous meal at a cafeteria and then
unconcernedly telling the cashier he has no money. On his
way to the register, he thoughtfully taps on the window to

summon a passing policeman, and while the two are waiting
together for the patrol wagon, he stops at the cigar stand
next door, where he carefully selects an expensive cigar for
himself and then picks up some candy bars to present to
the little children who are staring at him open-eyed. When
the patrol wagon arrives, the Gamin is in it, and they break
out together, which they are thereafter to remain, on her
initiative, for it would never have occurred to Charlie that
she could wish to attach herself to the likes of him. Every
time he gets out of jail--and it is made abundantly clear
that, under our system of justice, nothing has been accomplished by these incarcerations either for him or for society--
she is there waiting for him.

    For one night he is employed as a watchman in a de-
partment store. He smuggles her in and installs her luxuri-
ously in an elegant bed, but that short-lived break is the
only one either gets until the Gamin, who, by this time, has
established herself as a dancer in a waterfront café, gets him
a job as a singing waiter. Whereupon, now that she is supporting herself, the authorities manifest their usual intelligence by picking her up on an old warrant for vagrancy, and
she and the Tramp, having engineered their escape in an exciting scene, must take to the road again in the final fade-
out.

    There are only two scenes in this film that for me do
not quite come off. The first is the scene in jail, where
Charlie, the pampered prisoner, drinks tea with the minister's
stuffy wife, and they both suffer regurgitations with sound
effects. Not only is this not very funny in itself, but something like it had already been done better in both The Circus
and City Lights. The other is in the café scene, where the
difficulties involved in getting his roast duck to the table of
the irate Lloyd Ingraham are too long drawn out.

    The Gamin (Paulette Goddard) is more important in
Modern Times than any girl had ever been in a Chaplin film
before; as we have seen, his idea for the film began with
her and not with himself. She has a kind of home when we
first see her, but her unemployed father is soon killed and
her little sisters taken to the orphan asylum, after which we
never hear of them again, and she, like Charlie, must live
everywhere or anywhere and nowhere. Until she gets her
job in the café, we have never seen her except in an unat-

tractive, ragged old black dress, with her feet and lower
legs bare; once she has established herself, her changed
status is conveyed pictorially by her appearance in a picturesque costume which is the pink of propriety.

Her dance costume is alluring, but the relationship
between her and the Tramp remains sexless, whether in the
ramshackle hut on the waterfront they share for a time or
in the completely unrealistic dream house of the Tramp's
imagination, where he picks an orrange off the tree at the
door but wipes his hands on the portières. He never so
much as kisses her; indeed the only suggestion of sex in [19]
the entire film comes in the café song that Chaplin sings.
Of Miss Goddard as an actress I will say only that while her
performance seems to me excellent from every point of view,
probably her greatest gift was the extraordinary grace and
fluidity of movement which she shared with such diverse
performers as Douglas Fairbanks, Rudolph Valentino, and
Betty Bronson, as well as, outstandingly, Chaplin himself.
It was very important in silent films.

Though Modern Times was a box office success, Chaplin knew he could not continue production indefinitely without
embracing sound. He made the change with extreme reluctance, both because he considered himself primarily a pantomimist ("and in that medium I was unique and, without false
modesty, a master") and because in this aspect he appealed
to a world audience, much of which must be lost once he began to talk in English.

All three of the sound films he made in America were
daring departures for him, and each in a different way. The
first, The Great Dictator, was not the least daring, yet paradoxically it provided him with an ideal transitional vehicle.

According to Chaplin's autobiography, Alexander Korda
suggested to him "a Hitler story based on mistaken identity"
as early as 1937. Chaplin and Hitler were born within a few
days of each other. Both became world figures, and Hitler
wore in life the same toothbrush mustache that the Tramp
sported on the screen. In every other respect they were
antithetical personalities. [20]

Hollywood was still timid about handling political issues
on September 9, 1939, when shooting on this film began, and

many felt that Hitler was now far too dangerous to be made the object of ridicule. Chaplin understood this point of view, for he himself said afterwards that if he had known about the death camps at the time, he would not have made The Great Dictator.[21]

So much for the daring of the film. What made it such a good transitional vehicle for Chaplin was that since he played two parts in it, it was possible for him to take on Adenoid Hynkel, the dictator of Tomania, without quite giving up his traditional character in the person of the little Jewish barber, still the underdog, who, at the end, speaks for the conscience of the world in the famous six-minute address which his striking physical resemblance to Hynkel gives him the opportunity, indeed forces him, to deliver. The barber, to be sure, is not a tramp, but, as has already been pointed out, "Tramp" is a very partial and inadequate label for the character Chaplin had been projecting all along. It is also true that, in becoming Jewish, the barber had lost a certain universality, but to make too much of this is to miss the essential point that such a crime as Hitler perpetrated in Germany was an assault not merely upon one race but upon humanity itself. As Lowell had put it long ago, "In the gain or loss of one race, all the rest have equal share."[22]

According to David Robinson, The Great Dictator was the first Chaplin film for which a complete shooting script was prepared in advance, and except for the final speech, there were only 168 shooting days, ending in March 1940. The speech was Chaplin's own testament, direct from his heart, and he labored over it until June, while shooting, retaking, and redubbing continued almost to the première. Theodore Huff reported that the picture cost over $2,000,000, and Chaplin himself said that the building of miniature models and props was very expensive and that half a million dollars had been spent before a camera turned.

Until the end of October 1939 Chaplin worked only as the barber in the ghetto scenes, not beginning with Hynkel until December. The gibberish combined with a word of actual German here and there in Hynkel's hysterical orations was brilliantly improvised, but the action in the wonderful ballestistic sequence where Hynkel sports with the balloon-like globe of the world until it finally bursts in his hands, was all worked out in the script and shot in three late December days with retakes in February. At one time consideration was given to supplying Hynkel with a Jewish wife, to be played by Fanny Brice.

After a series of sneak previews, The Great Dictator was shown to a company of invited guests on October 3, 1940. The world première was held in New York on October 15 at the Astor and the Capitol theaters.

Passionately serious as The Great Dictator is in its opposition to tyranny and cruelty, it is only in the final speech that Chaplin finds no room for the Chaplinisms upon which he had built his career. Structurally the opening scenes in which the barber as a soldier in World War I saves the life of the flyer Schultz merely prepares for the role the latter will play in the main action, where, first as a reluctant, then as an oppenly rebellious Nazi, he generously repays his debt, but by way of lagniappe they are loaded with irresistible fooling--the shell from the Big Bertha which, ludicrously missing its target, chases the barber all over the field and the flying upside down with the sun seeming to shine upwards and the barber's watch and water apparently defying the law of gravity.

Hynkel's hysteria, his temper tantrums, his awkward collapses whenever he tries to be particularly dignified--all this is as funny as anything Chaplin ever did or would be if we could forget how close it comes to the original and what that cost the world. What could be more amusing than his stripping Herring (Goering, as played by Billy Gilbert) of the medals with which he is practically covered and almost of his clothing when he is angered in the course of decorating him further? Again, where could you find a more devastating example of black humor than in his conduct when the inventors of a bullet-proof uniform and an infallible parachute have demonstrated with their lives that their claims were greatly exaggerated? ("Herring," says Hynkel, in a tone of mild annoyance, "why do you waste my time like this?") The lengths to which both Hynkel and Napaloni, the dictator of Bacteria (Jack Oakie as Mussolini), go to try to outstage each other when the latter comes to negotiate an agreement and the refusal of Napaloni's train to stay in one place long enough to get to the red carpet placed in time

for Napaloni to dismount are more light-hearted but equally
amusing.

   In view of what the people in the ghetto have to go
through, it may seem surprising that Chaplin should not only
have been able to get so much fun as he did into these
scenes but also that he should have been able to infuse them
with a homely, gemütlich charm that makes it easy to understand Hannah's (Paulette Goddard's) feeling that she loves
her home in spite of all. Paulette's own personality contributes to the effect here of course, as does Hannah's
courage and prowess, even when they can only express themselves by vigorously wielding a frying pan over the heads of
the storm troopers. Chaplin was wise as well as generous in
ending the film as he did with a close-up of her, clinging
starry-eyed with fresh hope, in her Österreichisch (Austrian)
exile, while she listens to the broadcast of the barber's address. The distinguished Yiddish actor Maurice Moscovitch
contributes a fine characterization as a kind of father in
Israel, and the barber's shaving a customer to the rhythm of
"Hungarian Dance, #5" is as delightful as the troop of cats
and kittens pouring out the door when he comes to open his
shop and as successfully executed as the chase over the roof
tops when he is at one point captured. There is no denying
that Chaplin attempted a cruelly difficult feat when he made
The Great Dictator, but he has left us one of the few pleasant documents we have that relate to one of the darkest hours
in human history.

   When Chaplin called Monsieur Verdoux (released April
11, 1947) the cleverest and most brilliant film he had made,
he was in effect turning his back upon his cinematic past,
and his march down the corridor to the guillotine awaiting
him in the final shot must have seemed to many of his admirers an almost blasphemous parody of his long exploration
of the lonely road. For this "Comedy of Murders," the
story of a French Bluebeard, suggested by the career of
Landru, who supported himself and his unsuspecting family
by going through a series of mock marriages with one woman
of property after another, getting control of her money and
then murdering the woman, represented far more of a break
with the old Chaplin than even The Great Dictator, for not
only was there no little Jewish barber here to help bridge
the gap, but the Verdoux character and his adventures offered far fewer opportunities for the old brand of pranks

than had been afforded by even Hitler-Hynkel, the dictator of Tomania.

The original title for Monsieur Verdoux was "Lady Killer," and Chaplin is known to have had the idea in mind as early as 1942. Production from a prepared script did not begin until April 1946, and shooting was completed by early September. The text for his sermon was derived from the German military strategist Karl von Clausewitz, who had said that war was "the logical extension of diplomacy. M. Verdoux," added Chaplin, "feels that murder is the logical extension of business." For thirty-five years Verdoux had earned an honest living, but when the Great Depression wiped him out he adopted his present line.

By the time the film came out, Chaplin was in grave disfavor with both the patrioteers and the professional moralists. Opening at the Broadway Theater, the picture did good business for the first six weeks, then fell off seriously. It was banned in Ohio, and the Loew's theater chain dropped it. Both the American Legion and the Catholic War Veterans attacked it. When it had grossed only $325,000 in the United States during its first two years, Chaplin ordered United Artists to withdraw it.

There had been strong suggestions of determinism in Chaplin's films before this, but he had never gone so far in this direction as he did here. Verdoux sees himself as a product of his time, a small scale, amateurish practitioner of the slaughter which the world lauds and reveres when practiced on a wholesale scale by government itself. "Has it not blown unsuspecting women and children to pieces, and done it very scientifically?" and again, "You wallow in murder ... you legalize it ... you adorn it with gold braid! ... Killing is the enterprise upon which your system prospers ... upon which your industry thrives." Verdoux has no personal ill will toward the women he murders. He is even willing to make away with the street girl[23] he takes to his apartment to feed when she is cold and wet and hungry because (until he has been moved by her story) he wishes to test out a new poison on her. But let us not forget that during World War I a very distinguished American clergyman assured us that it was moral to kill Germans, provided we killed them in love, since it was the motive, not the act, that God regarded, and only recently an American Secretary of State, not generally regarded as a monster, declared that the United States must attack terrorists by military means even if this meant that innocent people would be killed.

For the confusions that developed over Monsieur Verdoux Chaplin himself was responsible to the extent but only to the extent that his thesis was not adumbrated until the close of the film, when it was too late for the audience to apply it to what they had been looking at for two hours, and that even then its exposition was commingled with what must have seemed to many like wholly impractical, amoral, and consequently dangerous theorizing concerning the ambiguous nature of right and wrong. This was not the only difficulty however. Works of art built around a villain-hero are always tricky; even when the audience can easily be brought to withhold moral sympathy from such a creature, psychological sympathy is quite another matter. Shakespeare succeeded gloriously with Macbeth, but Macbeth never succeeded in destroying his conscience, and even Shakespeare's success with Richard III, who did, is more questionable. Galsworthy built a whole play, Escape, around the difficulties decent people must experience in making themselves responsible for returning an escaped criminal to justice, regardless of all consideration of his deserts. The trouble with M. Verdoux is not merely that he kills but that he appears throughout as a cynical, highly polished boulevardier who always knows what is wrong with society but never seems aware of any deficiency in himself. The only suggestions to the contrary are his unsuspecting wife's awareness that he is laboring under a terrible strain and his own references to the desperate times in which he lives. For all that, it is difficult not to respond to his finesse and his politesse, and one can hardly avoid being confused by this. It has often been suggested that Chaplin must have been influenced by Max Linder, the first great film comedian to enjoy an international vogue; whether or not this is true, he nowhere more resembles Linder than here.

In making Verdoux sincerely devoted to his legal wife and child Chaplin was probably thinking of a number of captains of industry, ruthless in business, who were amiable in their private lives. He reproves his son for pulling the cat's tail--"You have a cruel streak in you. I don't know where you get it"--and even carefully avoids stepping on a caterpillar in the garden where he is currently incinerating one of his victims, but he will crush without remorse anybody who

gets in the way of his achieving any of the goals he has set
for himself.

Nevertheless, when due allowances have been made for
all possible imperfect perceptions and communications in
Monsieur Verdoux, it still remains an absorbing piece of film-
making and one of the most thoughtful of films. Except for
Thelma Couvais, who has been made away with when the picture begins, the ladies are clearly and vividly differentiated.
Lydia Floray (Margaret Hoffman), the first whose process of
destruction we see M. Verdoux negotiating, is surprisingly
vivid concerning the brevity of her appearance and the slight-
ness of the material she has to work with, while the raucous
and indestructible Annabella (Martha Raye) not only escapes
him but, unsuspectingly, helps to save him when he falls out
of the boat from which he had planned to drown her. Later,
still unwittingly, she revenges herself by turning up unexpectedly as a guest at his marriage to the wealthy Madame
Grosnay, elegantly played by Isobel Elsom, whom he has long
wooed at considerable expense, and from whom he is now obliged to flee. The absence of struggle at the end, when
Verdoux, facing arrest, so readily throws in the sponge, is
well motivated. The crash of his stocks has ruined him, and
the loss by death of his real wife and child has left him
nothing to live for; there is no more fight left in him.

Chaplin's third talking picture, Limelight (at first called
"Footlights"), the story of a ballerina and a clown, was the
last he was ever to make in the United States. It begins in
London in the summer of 1914, and its theme is "the glamour
of limelight, from which age must fade as youth enters."
Beyond any other of Chaplin's films, it draws upon his earliest memories and makes use of the music hall background
into which he was born. Yet it was for him almost as startling a departure as its predecessor had been. This time it
was not because there was any moral shock, for Limelight
is an old-fashioned, sweet, sad, sentimental love story which
Claire Bloom rightly describes as "the most openly Dickensian
of all his works." But its theme is sombre, and it ends with
death; except in its recreation of a few music hall "turns,"
there is very little comedy.

The clown is the once great Calvero, who through sorrow, loss of confidence, and consequently drink has become
a has-been living in a cheap lodging house. The ballerina

Thereza (Terry), lodging two floors below and hitherto unseen by him, has been brought to the verge of suicide due
to rheumatic fever, the shock of discovering that her beloved sister has become a streetwalker, and psychosomatic
delusion (she comes to believe that her legs are paralyzed
and that she can never walk, much less dance, again). Calvero, returning home drunk, at the beginning of the film,
smells gas coming out of her room and, after making sure
that the odor does not come from his cigar or the soles of
his shoes, breaks in and carries her upstairs. Despite the
objections of the amorous landlady, who is also fond of the
bottle, he nurses her back to health and at last she recovers
both her courage and the use of her legs.

    The healing process is doubly operative. Terry having
given Calvero something to live for, he finds that for the
time being he no longer needs alcohol, but he has inflicted a
different kind of wound on her. Her gratitude passes into
adoration; she avows her love for him and begs him to marry
her.

    Opportunity comes her way through a new ballet at the
Empire, but Calvero fails desperately in an anonymous attempt
at a comeback in a third-rate music hall. He will not consent
to her sacrificing her youth to his age, especially since he
knows she is loved by the young composer (Sydney Chaplin
II) in whose ballet she is appearing and whom he is sure in
his own mind that she loves without quite realizing it or
would do so if Calvero were out of the way.

    He removes himself from her life and is reduced at last
to the status of a street and tavern singer. Terry redis-
covers him and persuades her manager to give him a benefit
at which all the great performers in the field appear to honor
him and where he himself wins a triumph. But the calculated
fall into a drum at the end of his turn is too much for his
spine and his weakened heart, and he dies while Terry is
doing her turn.

    The story was first suggested to Chaplin by the shock-
ing change he observed in the comedian Frank Tinney over a
few years and required eighteen months of preparation. During this period he wrote it all out in the form of a novel running to some 100,000 words and including background biographies of both Calvero and Terry, into which elements of his

own experiences and those of his parents entered feely. The
music for the ballet in which Terry triumphs was also composed, "imagining the dancing," before the ballet itself had
been choreographed. 24

   The first shot was made on November 19, 1951, the last
(save for some retakes the following May, with Oona O'Neill
Chaplin doubling for Claire Bloom, who had returned to England, in some long shots) on January 25, 1952. Chaplin's
scenes with Buster Keaton, whom he brought back to the
screen for his last triumph after a long absence and agonies
of his own, were all shot between December 22, 1951 and
January 12, 1952. But some of Chaplin's own scenes were
done over fifteen times, and he spent three days on one
highly emotional scene with Terry which runs only three minutes on the screen. Once he reduced Miss Bloom to tears
with angry or mock-angry criticisms until he got just the effect he wanted from her.

   In his autobiography Chaplin wrote that when Limelight
was finished he had "fewer qualms" about it than he had had
about any other film. But he is not quite consistent when he
adds that he was uneasy about its reception in London, where
it had its world première at a benefit attended by royalty at
the Odeon, "as it was not the usual Chaplin comedy." It
was previewed on August 2 at the Paramount studio and
opened in New York on October 23, 1952, at both the Astor
and the Trans-Lux theaters.

   The main title of Limelight reads "Charles Chaplin and
Claire Bloom in Limelight." This was the only time Chaplin
ever bestowed quite this honor upon another player, and
Miss Bloom, at twenty, in the full flush of her young beauty,
and with the loveliest voice and most impeccable diction of
any young actress of her generation, proved herself worthy
of it. How important she afterwards considered her experience with Chaplin to have been in her career was best
shown when she called her autobiography Limelight and After.

   Her own view is that Terry was

      just one in the line of damaged heroines inspired by
      the memory of [Chaplin's] mother, extending from the
      blind flower-seller of City Lights to the penniless
      waif of Modern Times and the young female excon of

Monsieur Verdoux. I think that what particularly ex-
cited Chaplin about the Limelight story was that at
long last the damaged girl was to develop into a
mature woman; strong, independent, completely in
command of her powers. What would make the film
so passionate was just that celebration of a young
woman's triumphal recovery, a celebration tempered
of course by the seemingly sacrificial death of the
music hall comedian.

She added that it was not until she had come to know both
the Chaplins more intimately, long after Limelight had been
made, that she fully realized

how much the example of Oona--of her loving devotion and her quiet strength--was responsible for finally erasing the image of broken womanhood that his
mother's suffering had imprinted on his artistic
conscience. [25]

That, I think, about says it. As to the film itself, it
is like Gounod's or Massenet's music: one must either hate
it or love it. There are those who hate it. For them there
is nothing to do. Of them there is nothing that needs to be
said. As for those that love it, there is nothing for me to
say save that I am one.

After being driven out of America in 1952, Chaplin
closed his picture-making career with two films produced in
England. With the second of these, A Countess from Hong
Kong (1967), in which he directed Sophia Loren and Marlon
Brando, we are not here concerned, for though Sydney,
Geraldine, Josephine, and Victoria Chaplin all appeared in
it, their father made only such a token appearance as in
A Woman of Paris back in 1923. But its predecessor, his
eightieth film, A King in New York, was a very different
story.

Chaplin established Attica-Archway, later called the
Roy Export Company, to produce it. He worked on the
script in 1954-55, and the picture was made at the Shep-
perton studios between May 7 and July 28, 1956. It was released in England on September 12, 1957, but Chaplin barred
the American press from the Paris première at the Gaumont

Palace, and it was not seen in the United States until 1976,
the year before his death.

He called A King in New York both "my best picture"
and "my most rebellious picture." He also denied having
preached in it; "it's not political, not 'anti' anything"; "if
I've preached here I'm wrong." But in later years he also
felt that "perhaps I didn't quite understand it. It started
out to be very good and then it got complicated and a little
heavy handed."

Though it was of course not his "best picture," it is
nevertheless a very good one, and most of the criticism that
has been directed at it is nit-picking. But there can be no
doubt that it does "preach." Some of it is autobiographical,
and much of what it says came direct from the heart. Like
King Shahdov, Chaplin had had the experience of fleeing
from a dangerous pursuer, only to find that the poor man
was merely an autograph hunter; like him too he had been
submitted to the indignity of fingerprinting. His activities
had interested the Committee on Unamerican Activities also,
though, unlike the king, he had not actually been commanded
to appear before it.

The film has been called bitterly satirical, yet it seems
to me that though it presents a fairly complete survey of
what its creator did not like in the United States, it views
these things from an altitude of rather Olympian detachment,
and this was a considerable achievement under the existent
circumstances. Among the targets aimed at are waste, extravagance, noise, the barbarities of "rock-and-roll," films
exploiting violence and sexual aberration, inane television
commercials and the conscienceless exploitation of the public
fostered and practiced by Madison Avenue, plastic surgery
for cosmetic reasons, resulting in the production of what
looks neither young nor old nor human, "progressive"
schools, where the pupils have no obligation to learn anything or anything to do but "express" themselves, even if
this takes the form of blowing peas at the masters and distinguished visitors, and, above all else, the multifarious
operations of a senseless bureaucracy placing troublesome
interferences in the way of personal freedom.

King Shahdov is driven from Estrovia to New York by
greedy corruptionists who oppose his anti-war stand and his

interest in the development of atomic power for peaceful purposes (the film was made before the world learned to its cost
that even this might turn out to be a menace to human life).
In America the Atomic Energy Commission shows little interest
in his plans, and when its members do finally pay attention
to him, they immediately find Communist witch-hunting a more
pressing interest than saving the world from being blown up.
After the king's prime minister has robbed him and left him
stranded in a New York hotel with his faithful ambassador and
less than a thousand dollars in his purse, he falls into the
clutches of Madison Avenue. He is first tricked into appearing on television through the use of hidden cameras but comes
into big money when his choking over the whiskey he is given
to drink on a commercial electrifies the country with its unin-
tended comedy. For the television public, it seems, nothing
can be too bad.

The Communist angle enters through the king's interest
in Rupert Macabee, a ten-year-old whom he first encounters
when he visits the progressive school and whose particular
form of self expression consists of libertarian harangues.
Rupert is not a Communist, but his parents have been, and
when they are brought before a Congressional committee, they
come clean so far as their own activities are concerned but
are cited for contempt because they refuse to implicate others.
Whatever may be said about A King in New York in any other
aspect, there can be no denying that when the authorities
get their hands on the boy and destroy his self-respect by
working upon him until he is dragooned into "saving" his
parents by naming their comrades, though he knows this action to be wrong, the film rises to the dignity of a moral
statement that the world is not yet ready to accept a generation after its production.

Oliver Johnston gives Chaplin excellent support as the
ambassador; so does the beautiful Dawn Addams as the Madison
Avenue girl who begins by tricking King Shahdov and ends as
something a little more to him than a friend and a little less
than a lover. Maxine Audley has only a brief appearance as
Shahdov's queen, but she leaves the viewer wishing he might
see more of her. At the beginning of the picture they seem
estranged, but at the end one feels there is a good chance
they may come togehter. Rupert was played by the ten-year-
old Michael Chaplin, and if there were times when it seemed
clear that he was reciting lines he had learned, he nevertheless

gave a good enough account of himself so that one could understand even if one could not quite share his mother's impression that he was even better than Jackie Coogan in The
Kid. His father's own performance was flawless throughout,
and though there were far fewer gags than he had treated
us to in the past, nobody is likely to forget his attempts to
mime his orders for caviar and turtle soup in the restaurant
where the "musicians" are making so much noise that the
waiter cannot hear him nor the scenes in which, having got
his finger stuck in the fire hose, he cannot get it out again
but must take it with him when he appears before the Unamerican Affairs Committee with very moist results.

Though Chaplin was eighty-eight years old when he
died, he was still saying near the end of his life, "I can't
stop--ideas keep popping into my head" and again "To work
is to live--and I want to live." We know only a little of what
these ideas were, but we may be sure that if he had been
given time and strength, he would have worked some of them
out. His lot, like ours, was cast in troubled times, but now
that he is gone, the least we whom he left behind can say of
him is that he made them easier for many of us.

NOTES

1. Huff's Charlie Chaplin (Henry Schuman, 1951) was the
    best book on the subject that had been published to
    date. Robert Payne's The Great Charlie (Andre Deutsch,
    1952) is very good on the Dickens influence.

2. Chaplin made only one film, One A.M. (1916), in which
    he was the only player who appeared on the screen, yet
    in a sense all his films were solo performances. Once
    he had gained control, he devised his stories, directed,
    and enacted the principal role; in later years he even
    composed music for his films. In her autobiography,
    Limelight and After: The Education of an Actress
    (Harper & Row, 1982), Claire Bloom, who, of all the ac-
    tresses who appeared with Chaplin, has been most suc-
    cessful in building a career of her own, has related how
    he directed her every move and inflection. This must
    have been frustrating to people who felt they had some-
    thing to express themselves, but there is no denying that
    it was responsible for the wonderful sense of unity Chaplin

films achieved; in their expression of their creator's individuality, they were more like what one expects from a work of literature than a film. Moreover, though Ben Turpin resented Chaplin's direction, none of the people who appeared with him down the years in film after film (Henry Bergman, Albert Austin, Leo White, etc.) seem to have shared this feeling. From 1915 (A Night Out) to 1923 (The Pilgrim), Edna Purviance appeared in thirty-four pictures with him, and he kept her on the studio payroll until she died in 1958. R. H. Totheroh too remained his principal camera man through many years.

3. Richard Griffith and Arthur Mayer, The Movies (Simon and Schuster, 1957).

4. Minnie Maddern Fiske, "The Art of Charles Chaplin," Harper's Weekly, Vol. LXII (1916), 494.

5. Gerald D. McDonald, Michael Conway, and Mark Ricci, The Films of Charles Chaplin (Citadel Press, 1965), pp. 12-13.

6. This may have been suggested by an incident in another early comic, C. W. Kahles's "Hairbreadth Harry," in which the hero swung himself over a ravine to escape his pursuers by grasping a large serpent hanging from a tree. His Prehistoric Past as a whole was probably suggested by Griffith's caveman picture, Man's Genesis (1912).

7. Quoted by Gilbert Seldes, The Seven Lively Arts, revised edition (Sagamore Press, 1957), p. 35.

8. The Silent Clowns (Alfred A. Knopf, 1975).

9. If we count Triple Trouble, released August 11, 1918, the correct number is fifteen. Triple Trouble is a thing of shreds and patches for which Chaplin is not responsible in its present form, but it has been well thought of and he seems to acknowledge it in My Autobiography (Simon and Schuster, 1964).

10. My Autobiography, p. 209.

11. Chaplin, His Life and Art (McGraw-Hill Book Company, 1985).

12. The legend that Chaplin himself appeared in the original 1904 London production of Peter Pan is apparently just that; see Roger Lancelyn Green, Fifty Years of Peter Pan (Peter Davies, 1954), pp. 93-94.

13. Robinson, Chaplin, pp. 300-301.

14. Robinson, Chaplin, pp. 389-90; see also the following pages, which describe a number of other ideas that were not used, and compare Chaplin, My Autobiography, pp. 325-326.

15. The Silent Clowns, p. 346.

16. The silence is not completely unbroken. The boss in the factory, who illustrates the heroic labors of capitalists by working jig-saw puzzles in his office, barks his orders over a television set-up, and a phonograph record is used to demonstrate the feeding machine to him. There is singing in the café scene, and Chaplin's own voice is heard from the screen for the first time singing a song in gibberish. See Robinson, Chaplin, pp. 465-466, for the evidence that Chaplin at one time considered making Modern Times with dialogue.

17. Some commentators have denied this; moreover Chaplin himself was quite capable of disclaiming "social significance" in his films: "I leave such subjects for the lecture platform. To entertain is my first consideration." In general however the difficulty with such critics seems to be either that the very words "social criticism" frighten them as much as a red flag or, at the other end of the spectrum, that they cannot conceive of the possibility of its existence without commitment to a consistent, pre-formulated program of reform.

18. My Autobiography, p. 388.

19. See Robinson, Chaplin, pp. 462-463, for the ending at one time contemplated, with the Gamin having become a nun! Did this possibility, consciously or unconsciously, lie in the back of Chaplin's mind throughout and in some

way influence the sexlessness of the film?

20. The only comment I can make on the idea sometimes expressed that Chaplin had the same urge to power in art that Hitler manifested in government is to quote Bernard Shaw's alleged response to a passer-by who greeted him with "Mr. Kipling, I presume." "Well," said Shaw, "if you can presume that, you can presume anything." Hitler is said to have spent two evenings screening The Great Dictator, but there is apparently no record of what, if anything, he said.

21. There has been much discussion, without much knowledge, of whether Chaplin was himself Jewish. The most informed opinion indicates that he was not, and that if he had not been absolutely consistent in his denials, the reasons are, first, that he greatly admired Jews and would have been glad to be one of them and, second, that he did not wish, in any sense, to seem to be standing aloof from them in their darkest hour. For a sensible summary of the relevant evidence, see John McCabe, Charlie Chaplin (Doubleday, 1978), pp. 197-200.

22. Chaplin's "Rhythm: A Story of Men in Macabre Movement," with a Spanish civil war setting, originally published in Rob Wagner's Script, is conveniently reprinted by Peter Cotes and Thelma Nicklaus in The Little Fellow (Citadel Press, 1965), pp. 166-168.

23. "The Girl," played by Marilyn Nash, is otherwise unnamed. There is no question that Chaplin did think of her as a streetwalker and later as the mistress, not wife, of the munitions maker by contact with whom she she has since mended her fortunes. The ambiguities concerning her status that appeared in the finished film were due to the meddling of the Breen Office.

24. See Robinson, Chaplin, pp. 550-559, for an interesting account of these matters.

25. Claire Bloom, Limelight and After, pp. 107-108.

L'ENVOI

In the famous Preface to <u>Man and Superman</u>, Bernard Shaw named Blake, Bunyan, Hogarth, and Turner as the four Englishmen whose sense of life and the world he recognized as being most clearly akin to his own. In some sense, I suppose anybody who attempts to choose his favorite artists in any field makes his choice upon some such basis as Shaw has indicated here. But in art as in life the grounds of such consanguinity are often obscure and not easily susceptible of definition. One of the few things we can be quite sure of is that in the theater they are likely to be more personal than in any of the other arts, for among all artists only the actor and the singer use their own bodies-- and souls--as the instruments upon which they perform.

I have sometimes said that actors were like other people, only more so, and I suppose it is for this reason that to reject actors, as in some periods and some societies they have, heaven knows, been openly or tacitly rejected, becomes equivalent to rejecting humanity or being human. Geraldine Farrar was quite right when she remarked that to do her job a singer must "mercilessly" reveal her own personality. "There is no other way." The once popular English novelist, William J. Locke, author, among much else, of Mary Pickford's <u>Stella Maris</u>, once described an artist as a man who wrapped up pieces of his soul in paper and sold them, but a friend to whom I quoted this saying objected that it would have been more accurate to say that he gives them away, for even those who are widely "successful" become really important, in any truly vital sense, to only a comparatively small percentage even among those to whom their names have become household words. Since most movie fans never saw their favorites face to face but only as shadows on the silversheet, it may seem paradoxical that they should have come to feel closer to them than most people ever did to those whom they saw over the

footlights or heard from the concert platform. Part of the
explanation no doubt was that one could see his favorite
movie stars far more frequently than he encountered any
other theater folk, but more important than that, I believe,
was the overwhelming cosiness of the film medium. The
close-up was intimate and revealing beyond anything else
that had been experienced in the theater before, and many
a fan has been momentarily startled when the film flickered
out to its close and he became freshly aware of how far
away from him the screen actually was.

The consanguinity about which Shaw speaks is an in-
finitely varied as well as a vastly capricious and undefinable
thing, and we certainly do not respond to the same qualities
in all the people we like, whence it comes about, I suppose,
that we are often asked, "How can you like him when you
like her?" or its equivalent. In some sense, I have "liked"
all the people I have written about in this book, but in a
deeper sense I have not chosen them but been chosen by
them, and this for reasons which they could no better have
understood than I do. I admit that I have seen people on
the screen whom, to employ an expression once used by the
habitually gentle William Dean Howells, I could have enjoyed
taking out to step on; for the most part, however, I have
been merely indifferent to those who did not attract me.
Some of my favorites have been top-ranking stars while
others have never received anything like the recognition I
considered their due. I have totally failed to respond to
some of the most "successful" players, and there are others
whom I have liked much during their early careers who have
in my judgment failed to develop or at least failed to hold
my interest. I could name names under both headings, some
of which would, I am sure, surprise some of my readers, but
since there are already enough reviewers (one can hardly
call them critics) whose whole stock in trade is to exploit
their prejudices, I shall not do this, for I have always
agreed with one of the greatest American actors of other
days, Richard Mansfield, that "personal abuse is not criticism" and that unless one can criticize with dignity, he had
better not criticize at all.

Since acting is, as I have said, the most personal of
all the arts, I suppose the likelihood is great that those who
like the artist would also, if they had the opportunity, like
the human being behind him. In my own case, I can testify

that, though I have learned much from the personal contacts
I have had with such artists as I have had the privilege of
knowing, generally speaking they have not disappointed me.
I am aware of course (I am even somewhat puzzled) that all
but one of the persons I have written about in this book
are women, and I do not believe the fact that I am a man
more than partially explains this. When I was a boy, my
first great screen idol was a man, Maurice Costello, who was
to me, I suppose, what it would now be fashionable to call
a "father figure," and outside the movies I do not believe
anybody could have been more enthusiastic than I have been
in his response to such varied figures as E. H. Sothern,
John McCormack, and Dietrich Fischer-Dieskau. But that
mystery I must leave, as Chaucer left others, to "divyne"
and bow out as gracefully as I can manage.

INDEX OF NAMES

143

INDEX OF FILM TITLES